Microeconomics
Principles and Tools
Third Edition

Microeconomics
Principles and Tools
Third Edition

Arthur O'Sullivan
Lewis and Clark College

Steven M. Sheffrin
University of California, Davis

Prentice
Hall

Upper Saddle River, New Jersey

Library of Congress Cataloging-in-Publication Data

O'Sullivan, Arthur.
  Microeconomics : principles and tools / Arthur O'Sullivan, Steven M. Sheffrin.—3rd ed.
    p. cm.
  A variety of multi-media instructional tools, including a Web site, is available to
    supplement the text.
  Includes bibliographical references and index.
  ISBN 0-13-035812-6
  1. Microeconomics. I. Sheffrin, Steven M. II. Title.
HB172.O84 2002
338.5—dc21

2001059338

Executive Editor: Rod Banister
Editor-in-Chief: P.J. Boardman
Managing Editor (Editorial): Gladys Soto
Assistant Editor: Marie McHale
Editorial Assistant: Lisa Amato
Media Project Manager: Victoria Anderson
Executive Marketing Manager: Kathleen McLellan
Marketing Assistant: Christopher Bath
Managing Editor (Production): Cynthia Regan
Production Assistant: Dianne Falcone
Permissions Coordinator: Suzanne Grappi
Associate Director, Manufacturing: Vincent Scelta
Production Manager: Arnold Vila
Design Manager: Patricia Smythe
Designer: Steve Frim
Cover Ilustration: Nancy D'Urso
Multimedia Artists: Sarah Arkin and John Hagopian
Print Production Liaison: Suzanne Duda
Composition/Illustrator (Interior): UG / GGS Information Services, Inc.
Full-Service Project Management: UG / GGS Information Services, Inc.
Printer/Binder: R.R. Donnelley/Willard

Pearson Education LTD.
Pearson Education Australia PTY, Limited
Pearson Education Singapore, Pte. Ltd
Pearson Education North Asia Ltd
Pearson Education, Canada, Ltd
Pearson Educación de Mexico, S.A. de C.V.
Pearson Education–Japan
Pearson Education Malaysia, Pte. Ltd

10 9 8 7 6 5 4 3 2 1
ISBN 0-13-035812-6

To Our Children: Conor, Maura, Meera, and Kiran

About the Authors

Arthur O'Sullivan

Arthur O'Sullivan is a professor of economics at Lewis and Clark College in Portland, Oregon. After receiving his B.S. Degree in economics at the University of Oregon, he spent two years in the Peace Corps, working with city planners in the Philippines. He received his Ph.D. degree in economics from Princeton University in 1981 and has taught at the University of California, Davis and Oregon State University, winning several teaching awards at both schools. He recently accepted an endowed professorship at Lewis and Clark College, where he teaches microeconomics and urban economics. He is the author of the best-selling textbook, *Urban Economics*, currently in its fifth edition.

Professor O'Sullivan's research explores economic issues concerning urban land use, environmental protection, and public policy. His articles appear in many economics journals, including Journal of Urban Economics, Journal of Environmental Economics and Management, National Tax Journal, Journal of Public Economics, and Journal of Law and Economics.

Professor O'Sullivan lives with his family in Lake Oswego, Oregon. He enjoys outdoor activities, including tennis, rafting, and hiking. Indoors, he plays chess, foosball, and ping-pong with his two kids, and is lucky to win one of five games.

Steven M. Sheffrin

Steven M. Sheffrin is dean of the division of social sciences and professor of economics at the University of California, Davis. He has been a visiting professor at Princeton University, Oxford University, and the London School of Economics, and served as a financial economist with the Office of Tax Analysis of the United States Department of Treasury. He has been on the faculty at Davis since 1976 and served as the chairman of the department of economics. He received his B.A. from Wesleyan University and his Ph.D. in economics from the Massachusetts Institute of Technology.

Professor Sheffrin is the author of eight other books and monographs and over 100 articles in the fields of macroeconomics, public finance, and international economics. His most recent books include *Rational Expectations* (Second Edition) and *Property Taxes and Tax Revolts: The Legacy of Proposition 13* (with Arthur O'Sullivan and Terri Sexton), both from Cambridge University Press.

Professor Sheffrin has taught macroeconomics at all levels, from large lectures of principles (classes of 400) to graduate classes for doctoral students. He is the recipient of the Thomas Mayer Distinguished Teaching Award in economics.

He lives with his wife Anjali (also an economist) and his two children in Davis, California. In addition to a passion for current affairs and travel, he plays a tough game of tennis.

Brief Contents

Contents

13 Using Market Power: Price Discrimination and Advertising 277

14 Controlling Market Power: Antitrust Policy and Deregulation 293

19   Economic Challenges: Poverty, Aging, and Health Care   399

20   International Trade and Public Policy   417

A CLOSER LOOK

FEATURES

Preface

Our Story

When we set out to write an economics text, we were driven by the vision of the sleeping student. A few years ago, one of the authors was in the middle of a fascinating lecture on monopoly pricing when he heard snoring. It wasn't the first time a student had fallen asleep in one of his classes, but this was the loudest snoring he had ever heard—it sounded like a sputtering chain saw. The instructor turned to Bill, who was sitting next to the sleeping student and asked, "Could you wake him up?" Bill looked at the sleeping student and then gazed theatrically around the room at the other students. He finally looked back at the instructor and said, "Well professor, I think you should wake him up. After all, you put him to sleep."

That experience changed the way we taught economics. It highlighted for us a basic truth—for many students, economics isn't exactly exciting. We took this as a challenge—to get first-time economics students to see the *relevance* of economics to their *lives*, their *careers*, and their *futures*.

In order to get students to see the relevance of economics we knew that we had to *engage* them. With the first and second editions of *Microeconomics: Principles and Tools*, we helped professors to do that by emphasizing an active learning approach. We engaged students by teaching them how to do something—economic analysis. We kept the book **brief, lively, and to the point,** and used the **five key principles** of economics as an organizing theme. The result was that the first and second editions were a success in classrooms across the country, and we strove in this edition to do even better.

Key Changes

We knew that our text's brevity and student accessibility were key strengths and we worked to enhance and preserve them in the third edition. We also found that professors and students truly appreciated our concerted effort to use economic principles to explain current and topical events. For the third edition, we made a systematic attempt to refine this feature of the book. We made a special effort to enhance our chapter opening stories, Economic Detective exercises, and Closer Look boxes. The result is a text that applies economic reasoning to the most current economic controversies and debates.

We also added new text material on developing policy issues with fresh applications of basic concepts. For example, in the microeconomics area we added a new section on electricity deregulation, focusing on the deregulation plans and experience in California, Pennsylvania, and New York. We also provide a progress report on welfare reform. Among the fresh applications are Ecohotels in Central American rain forests, video piracy in China, wind energy, phone service in small villages in Pakistan, satellite radio, genetic testing by insurance companies, and special immigration for high-technology workers.

The September 11, 2001 terrorist attack impacted the economy in many different ways. In this edition, we have updated our discussion of the recent performance of the U.S. economy. We also discuss the implications of the terrorist attack and its aftermath on the markets for different modes of travel. In terms of policy issues, we explore the issues of airport security, patent policy for drugs designed to deal with bioterrorism, and the rationale for the government's bailout of airlines.

In addition to these changes, we undertook a thorough review of our test bank to ensure accuracy and to provide a more focused range of questions for instructors' use. A totally new test bank was added to the supplement package to give instructors even greater flexibility in creating quizzes and exams. We incorporated the *Active Learning* aspect of the text into the questions in the supplement package—focusing new questions on asking students to create graphs, rather than just interpreting them. The Active Learning CD-ROM also was enhanced in this fashion through the addition of a Graphing Tool and Tutorial. In addition, we added videos to the CD-ROM so that students could see the economic experiments referred to in the text in action.

Teaching Philosophy

We began with the idea that an introductory economics course should be taught as if it is the last economics class a student will ever take. Because this is *true* for most students, we have just one opportunity to teach them how to use economics. The best way to teach economics is to focus on a few key concepts and ideas and apply them repeatedly in different circumstances.

We start the book with the five key principles of economics and then apply them throughout the book. This approach provides students with the big picture—the framework of economic reasoning. We make the key concepts unforgettable by using them repeatedly, illustrating them with intriguing examples, and giving students many opportunities to practice what they've learned.

Our book is designed to be accessible to students. We have kept the writing lean, the examples lively and topical, and the visuals exciting.

Principles and Tools

In keeping with the themes of relevance and student accessibility, we have once again organized our text around the **five key principles** of economics. Throughout the text, every point of theory is tied back to the five key principles and is indicated by the key symbol (see margin).

1. **The Principle of Opportunity Cost.** The opportunity cost of something is what you sacrifice to get it.
2. **The Marginal Principle.** Pick the level of an activity at which the marginal benefit equals the marginal cost.
3. **The Principle of Diminishing Returns.** If we increase one input while holding the other inputs fixed, output will increase, but at a decreasing rate.
4. **The Spillover Principle.** In some circumstances, decision-makers do not bear all the cost or experience all the benefits from their decision.
5. **The Reality Principle.** What matters to people is the real value of money or income—its purchasing power—not the face value of money or income.

We use these principles to explain the logic underpinning the most important tools of economics. By using these five principles repeatedly, we reveal the logic of economic reasoning and demystify the tools of economics. Students see the big picture and also learn how to use the tools of economics properly.

"What I Do, I Understand"—Confucius

Our book is based on **Active Learning,** a teaching approach based on the idea that students learn best by doing. Our book engages students by letting them do activities as they read. We implement **Active Learning** with the following features:

- **Economics Detective** exercises provide a few clues and then ask the student to solve the economic mystery.

- **Using the Tools** questions at the end of each chapter give students opportunities to do their own economic analysis. Complete answers appear at the end of each chapter.

- **Economic Experiments** actively involve the student in role-playing as consumers, producers, and policymakers. All these activities are designed to be fun for students and easy for professors, who decide when and how to use them.

- **Test Your Understanding** questions help students determine whether they understand the preceding material before continuing. These are straightforward questions that ask students to review and synthesize what they have read. Complete answers appear at the end of each chapter.

- **Chapter-Opening Stories** open each chapter and motivate the chapter's subject matter.

- Each chapter starts with a list of **practical questions** that are answered in the chapter.

- **Lively Examples** are integrated throughout the text and help bring economic concepts to life. We have hundreds of fresh, new examples in this edition.

- **A Closer Look** boxes are featured throughout the text and provide brief, interesting examples of the tools and concepts discussed in the text.

The Mystery of the Three-Clock Tower

Economic Detective

Back in the days before the inexpensive wristwatch, most people did not carry their own timepieces. Many towns built clock towers in the center of town so that their citizens could know the time. The towns paid for the clock towers with voluntary contributions from citizens. One town in the northeastern United States built a four-sided tower but put clock faces on only three sides of the tower. To most people, this seems bizarre. If you build a clock tower, why not put clock faces on all four sides?

The key to solving this puzzle is the fre̶_____ ̶t̶ turns out that one of the
t̶_____

Using the **TOOLS**

This chapter introduced several new tools of economics, including four different elasticities and a formula that can be used to predict the change in price resulting from a change in supply or demand. Here are some opportunities to use these tools to do your own economic analysis.

APPLICATIONS
1. Projecting Transit Ridership
As a transit planner, you must predict how many people ride commuter trains and how much money is generated from train fares. According to a recent study,[9] the short-run price elasticity of demand for commuter rail is 0.62 and the long-run elasticity is 1.59. The current ridership is 100,000 people per day. Suppose fares increase by 10%.

a. Predict the changes in train ridership over a one-month period (short run) and a five-year period (long run).

b. Over the one-month period, will total revenue increase or decrease? What will happen in the five-year period?

2. Bumper Crops
Your job is to predict the total revenue generated by the nation's corn crop. Last year's crop was 100 million bushels, and the price was $4.00 per bushel. This year's weather was favorable throughout the country, and this year's crop will b̶_____ ̶ bushels, or ̶̶% larger than last year's. The price elasticity of dem̶_____
̶t the effect ̶_____

TEST Your Understanding

1. Money solves the problem of double coincidence of wants that would regularly occur under a system of _____.

2. Why is money only an imperfect store of value?

3. What is the problem associated with the double coincidence of wants?

4. Because we measure all prices in monetary units, money serves as a unit of account. True or false? Explain.

5. Why are checks included in the defi̶_____ of money?

A CLOSER LOOK | JAPAN'S LOST DECADE

Japan's rapid post–World War II economic growth came to a halt around 1992, and by 1993–1994, the country was suffering from a recession. Inflation started to fall as the economy entered the recession. By 1995, inflation had nearly disappeared from the economy, and wholesale prices had fallen for several years.

Yet the reduction in inflation caused problems for the economy. Real estate prices fell nearly 50% starting in 1990. Large banks that were major investors in real estate lost vast sums of money, and became reluctant to make loans for other investments. Inflation rates were lower than business and household borrowers had anticipated. This raised the burden of debt for both businesses and households and made them more reluctant to purchase goods and services. With fewer loans from banks for new investment and reluctant households and firms, aggregate demand for goods and services was weak.

For a number of years, the United States urged Japan to increase public spending to end its recession. Eventual~~~ ~~~ try this approach, but by 2001 the ec~~~ ~~~mp and go~~~

deficits were very large. Nominal interest rates were also very close to zero, making it difficult to use monetary policy to stimulate the economy. Some observers claimed that Japan was suffering from a Keynesian liquidity trap. Faced with these difficulties, restoring the health of the banking system became a major priority for economic policy.

While t~~~ ~~~ in Tokyo, Japan

Book Organization

A course in microeconomics starts with the first four chapters of the book, which provide a foundation for more detailed study of individual decision-making and markets. Part 2 provides a closer look at supply and demand, discussing elasticity, market efficiency, and consumer choice. In Part 3 we start with a discussion of production and costs, setting the stage for an examination of alternative market structures, including the extremes of perfect competition and monopoly, as well as the middle ground of monopolistic competition and oligopoly. There are two applied chapters, one on advertising and price discrimination, and a second on antitrust policy and deregulation. Part 4 discusses the circumstances under which markets break down, including imperfect information, public goods, and environmental degradation. The final part of the microeconomics section explores the labor market and three policy challenges: poverty, the aging of the population, and health care.

The Active Learning Package

Each component of the teaching and learning package has been carefully reevaluated to ensure that it is consistent with the changes made to this edition and with the needs of our audience.

Print Supplements

New Two-Volume Test Bank

Our team of instructors has striven to write, edit, review, and accuracy check the over 9,000 questions in both of the microeconomics and macroeconomics test banks.

Test Bank #1—The test bank for *Microeconomics: Principles and Tools* prepared by Mary Lesser of Iona College, offers approximately 3,000 multiple-choice, true/false, short answer, and graphing questions. The questions are referenced by topic and are presented in sequential order. Each question is keyed by degree of difficulty as *easy*, *moderate*, or *difficult*. Easy questions involve straightforward recall of information in the text. Moderate questions require some analysis on the student's part. Difficult questions usually entail more complex analysis and may require the student to go one step further than the material presented in the text. Questions are also classified as *fact*, *definition*, *conceptual*, and *analytical*. A question labeled Fact tests student's knowledge of factual information presented in the text. A Definition question asks the student to define an economic concept. Conceptual questions test a student's understanding of a concept. Analytical questions require the student to apply an analytical procedure to answer the question.

The test bank includes tables and a series of questions asking students to solve for numerical values, such as profit or equilibrium output. It also contains numerous questions based on graphs. The test bank includes examples of all of the graphs that students have seen in the textbook. The questions ask the students to interpret the information that is presented in the graph.

There are also many questions in the test bank that are not referenced by a graph, but which require students to sketch out a graph on their own to be able to answer the question. The author worked to create many new questions focused on testing the graphing ability of student and their ability to *actively* answering each question.

Test Bank #2—This new addition to the supplement package, prepared by Linda S. Ghent of Eastern Illinois University, will serve as another important resource for instructors. These new test banks for *Microeconomics: Principles and Tools* contain over 1,500 multiple-choice, true/false, and short answer questions. Each question is also keyed by degree of difficulty (*easy*, *moderate*, or *difficult*), topic reference, and type of question (*definition*, *fact*, *conceptual*, or *analytical*).

Instructor's Manual

The instructor's manual to accompany *Microeconomics: Principles and Tools,* prepared by Leonie Stone of SUNY, Geneseo, follow the textbook's organization, incorporating policy problems in case studies, exercises, extra questions, and useful Internet links. The manual also provides detailed outlines (suitable for use as lecture notes) and solutions to all questions in the textbook. The instructor's manual is also designed to help the instructor incorporate applicable elements of the supplement package.

The instructor's manual contains by chapter: a summary, objectives, an outline, opening questions, examples for class discussion, teaching tips, extended examples, problems and discussion questions, Test Your Understanding questions, Internet exercises, and tips for classroom experiments.

Study Guide

The study guide to accompany *Microeconomics: Principles and Tools,* prepared by Janice Boucher Breuer of University of South Carolina, emphasize the practical application of theory. This study guide is a practicum designed to promote comprehension of economic principles and develop each student's ability to apply them to different problems.

Integrated throughout this study guide are Performance Enhancing Tips (PETs), which are designed to help students understand economics by applying the principles and promoting analytical thinking.

Two practice exams, featuring both multiple-choice and essay questions, are included at the end of each chapter. Both exams require students to apply one or more economic principles to arrive at each correct answer. Full solutions to the multiple-choice questions are included, not only listing each correct answer but also explaining in detail why one answer is correct and the others are not. Detailed answers to the essay questions are also provided.

This study guide contains by chapter: an overview of the corresponding chapter in the textbook, a checklist to provide a quick summary of material covered in the textbook and lectures, a list of key terms and their definitions, practice exams, and the detailed answer keys.

Using Experiments, Cases, and Activities in the Classroom

Prepared by Dirk Yandell of the University of San Diego, this manual contains experiments that illustrate topics such as positive versus normative economics and monopoly. The experiments include tables and charts, in addition to an overview, learning objectives, a list of preparations and materials needed, a detailed what-to-do section, an analysis of the results, and questions that require students to interpret and analyze the material.

Color Transparencies

All figures and tables from the text are reproduced as full-page, four-color acetates.

E-Commerce Guide

Electronic commerce is playing an increasingly important role in how business is conducted. Prentice Hall's *Guide to E-Commerce and E-Businesses* provides readers with background on the history and direction of E-Commerce, the impact it has on the economy, and how to use it as a source of economic information and data. This guide can be shrink-wrapped free with a new copy of the third edition.

Technology Supplements

Active Learning CD-ROM

An interactive learning tool for students, the CD-ROM begins with detailed outlines that guide the student through all the key concepts of each chapter. Over 40 Active Graphs (referenced in the text) allow students to change the value of variables and see the effects in the movement of the graphs. New to this edition are seven videos of selected Economic Experiments from the textbook; a Graphing Tutorial and an electronic Graphing Tool. Graphing questions, concept checks, and end-of-chapter quizzes provide ample opportunity for self-assessment. The Active Learning CD-ROM is free with every new copy of the textbook.

TestGen–EQ Software

New for this edition, the print Test Banks are designed for use with the TestGen-EQ test-generating software. This computerized package allows instructors to custom design, save, and generate classroom tests. The test program permits instructors to edit, add, or delete questions from the test banks; edit existing graphics and create new graphics; analyze test results; and organize a database of tests and student results. This new software allows for greater flexibility and ease of use. It provides many options for organizing and displaying tests, along with a search and sort feature. The software can prepare 25 versions of a single test.

Mastering Economics CD-ROM

This CD-ROM, developed by Active Learning Technologies, is an integrated series of 12 video-enhanced interactive exercises that follow the people and issues of CanGo., an e-business start-up. Students use economic concepts to solve key business decisions, including how to launch the start-up company's initial public offering (IPO), enter new markets for existing products, develop new products, determine prices, attract new employees, and anticipate competition from rivals. The videos illustrate the importance of an economic way of thinking to make real-world business decisions. Every episode includes three separate video segments: The first video clip introduces the episode topics by way of a current problem or issue at CanGo. After viewing the first clip, students read more about the theory or concept and then work through a series of multi-layered exercises. The exercises are composed of multiple-choice, true/false, fill-in, matching, ranking choices, comparisons, and one- or two-sentence answers. After completing the exercises, students watch another video clip. This resolution video illustrates one of the possible resolutions to the problem or decision faced by CanGo's management team. A correlation guide that links the Mastering Economics segments with chapters of the book is included in the *Mastering Economics Instructor's Manual* available at *http://www.prenhall.com/osullivan*.

Instructor's Resource CD-ROM

The Instructor's Resource CD-ROM includes the computerized test banks, instructor's manuals, and PowerPoint Presentation. It is dual platform for both PC and Macintosh.

Companion Web Site
(http://www.prenhall.com/osullivan)

The Companion Web site is a content-rich, multidisciplinary Web site with Internet exercises, activities, and resources related specifically to the third edition of *Microeconomics: Principles and Tools*. It includes the following features:

The Online Study Guide, prepared by Fernando and Yvonn Quijano, offers students another opportunity to sharpen their problem-solving skills and to assess their understanding of the text material. The Online Study Guide for O'Sullivan/Sheffrin now contains three levels of both multiple-choice and essay quizzes. Each level includes 10 to 15 questions per chapter. The new third level of questions is focused on testing the students' ability to draw and interpret graphs. The Online Study Guide grades each question submitted by the student, provides immediate feedback for correct and incorrect answers, and allows students to e-mail results to up to four e-mail addresses.

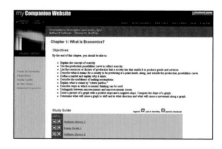

Current Events Articles and Exercises, related to topics in each chapter, are fully supported by group activities, critical-thinking exercises, and discussion questions. These articles, from current news publications to economics-related publications, help show students the relevance of economics in today's world.

Internet Exercises—New Internet resources are added every two weeks by a team of economics professors to provide both the student and the instructor with the most current, up-to-date resources available. The Companion Web site also links the student to the **Take It to the Net** exercises featured in the textbook. These Web-destination exercises are keyed to each chapter and direct the student to an appropriate, updated, economics-related Web site to gather data and analyze a specific economic problem.

Syllabus Manager—For the instructor, the Companion Web site offers resources such as the answers to Current Events and Internet exercises, and a Faculty Lounge area including teaching resources and faculty chat rooms.

Downloadable Supplements—From the Companion Web site, instructors can also download supplements and lecture aids. Instructors should contact their Prentice Hall sales representative to get the necessary username and password to access the faculty resources. The supplements include the following:

- **The PowerPoint Presentation**—This lecture presentation tool, prepared by Fernando Quijano and Yvonn Quijano, offers outlines and summaries of important text material, tables and graphs that build, and additional exercises. The PowerPoint Presentation is included in the instructor's resource CD-ROM and is downloadable from the O'Sullivan/Sheffrin Web site. Many important graphs "build" over a sequencing of slides so that students may see the step-by-step process involved in economic analysis. The package will allow for instructors to make full-color, professional-looking presentations while providing the ability for custom handouts to be provided to the students.

- **The Instructor's Manual**

- **Mastering Economics Instructor's Manual**

Prentice Hall Video Library

A comprehensive video ancillary is available to help bring the major concepts covered in the textbook to life. The Video Library offers a resource for feature and documentary-style videos related to the chapters in the text. The programs have extremely high production quality, present substantial content, and are hosted by well-versed, well-known anchors.

Video Guide

The integrated Video Guide provides a summary of each of the clips in the Video Library. For each video, the guide also supplies running time, teaching notes, and discussion questions, as well as useful tips on how to use the clip in class. Each video is keyed to the appropriate topic in the text.

Online Course Offerings

WebCT

Developed by educators, WebCT provides faculty with easy-to-use Internet tools to create online courses. Prentice Hall provides the content and enhanced features to help instructors create a complete online course. For more information, please visit our Web site located at *http://www.prenhall.com/webct*.

Blackboard

Easy to use, Blackboard's single template and tools make it easy to create, manage, and use online course materials. Instructors can create online courses using the Blackboard tools, which include design, communication, testing, and course management tools. For more information, please visit our Web site located at *http://www.prenhall.com/blackboard*.

CourseCompass

This customizable, interactive, online course-management tool powered by Blackboard provides the most intuitive teaching and learning environment available. Instructors can communicate with students, distribute course material, and access student progress online. For further information, please visit our Web site located at *http://www.prenhall.com/coursecompass*.

CourseCompass with Ebook

This online course provides the features of CourseCompass along with an electronic version of the textbook. The addition of a digital textbook to CourseCompass gives instructors greater choice and flexibility as they design and build their online courses. With this feature, students can remain online and use an eBook for all of their online assignments.

Subscription Options

The Wall Street Journal Print and Interactive Editions Subscription

Prentice Hall has formed a strategic alliance with *The Wall Street Journal*, the most respected and trusted daily source for information on business and economics. For a small additional charge, Prentice Hall offers your students a 10-week subscription to *The Wall Street Journal* print edition and *The Wall Street Journal* Interactive Edition. Adopting professors will receive a free one-year subscription of the print and interactive version as well as weekly subject-specific *Wall Street Journal* educators' lesson plans.

Economist.com Subscription

Through a special arrangement with *Economist.com* for a small additional charge, Prentice Hall offers your students a 12-week subscription to *Economist.com*. Adopting professors will receive a free six-month subscription. Please contact your Prentice Hall representative for further details and ordering information.

The Financial Times Subscription

We are pleased to announce a special partnership with *The Financial Times*. For a small additional charge, Prentice Hall offers your students a 15-week subscription to *The Financial Times*. Adopting professors will receive a free one-year subscription. Please contact your Prentice Hall representative for details and ordering information.

A World of Thanks

There is a long distance between the initial vision of an innovative principles text and the final product. Along the way we participated in a structured process to reach our goal.

We wish to acknowledge the assistance of the many individuals who participated in this process. First we want to thank the participants who took part in the focus groups for the first and second editions; they helped us see the manuscript from a fresh perspective:

Carlos Aquilar, El Paso Community College
Jim Bradley, University of South Carolina
Thomas Collum, Northeastern Illinois University
David Craig, Westark College
Jeff Holt, Tulsa Junior College
Thomas Jeitschko, Texas A & M University
Gary Langer, Roosevelt University

Mark McCleod, Virginia Polytechnic Institute and State University
Tom McKinnon, University of Arkansas
Amy Meyers, Parkland Community College
Hassan Mohammadi, Illinois State University
John Morgan, College of Charleston
Norm Paul, San Jancinto Community College

Nampeang Pingkaratwat, Chicago State University

Scanlan Romer, Delta Community College

Barbara Ross-Pfeiffer, Kapiolani Community College

Virginia Shingleton, Valparaiso University

Zahra Saderion, Houston Community College

Jim Swofford, University of South Alabama

Linda Wilson, University of Texas–Arlington

Janet West, University of Nebraska–Omaha

Michael Youngblood, Rock Valley Community College

A special acknowledgment goes to the instructors who were willing to class-test drafts in different stages of development. They provided us with instant feedback on parts that worked and parts that needed changes:

Sheryl Ball, Virginia Polytechnic Institute and State University

John Constantine, University of California, Davis

James Hartley, Mt. Holyoke College

John Farrell, Oregon State University

Kailash Khandke, Furman College

Peter Lindert, University of California, Davis

Louis Makowski, University of California, Davis

Stephen Perez, California State University, Sacramento

Barbara Ross-Pfeiffer, Kapiolani Community College

Many people read all or parts of the manuscript at various stages. For their helpful criticisms, we thank:

Christine Amsler, Michigan State University

Karijit K. Arora, Le Moyne College

Alex Azarchs, Pace University

Kevin A. Baird, Montgomery County Community College

Donald Balch, University of South Carolina

Collette Barr, Santa Barbara Community College

Mahamudu Bawumia, Baylor University

Charles Scott Benson Jr., Idaho State University

Jay Bhattacharya, Okaloosa–Walton Community College

John Payne Bigelow, Louisiana State University

Scott Bloom, North Dakota State University

Janice Boucher Breuer, University of South Carolina

Kathleen K. Bromley, Monroe Community College

Cindy Cannon, North Harris College

Katie Canty, Cape Fear Community College

David L. Coberly, Southwest Texas State University

John L. Conant, Indiana State University

Ana-Maria Conley, DeVry Institute of Technology

Ed Coulson, Penn State University

Lee Craig, North Carolina State University

Peggy Crane, San Diego State University

Albert B. Culver, California State University, Chico

Norman Cure, Macomb Community College

Irma de Alonso, Florida International University

Sel Dibooglu, Southern Illinois University

Martine Duchatelet, Barry University

Mousumi Duttaray, Indiana University

Ghazi Duwaji, University of Texas, Arlington

David Eaton, Murray State University

Duane Eberhardt, Missouri Southern State College

Carl Enomoto, New Mexico State University

David Figlio, University of Oregon

Dan Georgianna, University of Massachusetts–Dartmouth

Linda Ghent, East Illinois University

Hossein Gholami, Fayetteville Tech Community College

Susan Glanz, St. John's University

Randy R. Grant, Linfield College

Paul C. Harris, Jr., Camden County College

James E. Hartley, Mount Holyoke College

Rowland Harvey, DeVry Institute of Technology

John Henry, California State University, Sacramento

Robert Herman, Nassau Community College

Charles W. Haase, San Francisco State University

Charlotte Denise Hixson, Midlands Technical College

Jeff Holt, Tulsa Community College

Brad Hoppes, Southwest Missouri State University

Calvin Hoy, County College of Morris

Jonathan O. Ikoba, Scott Community College

John A. Jascot, Capital Community Technical College

Thomas Jeitschko, Texas A & M University

George Jensen, California State University, Los Angeles

Taghi T. Kermani, Youngstown State University

Rose Kilburn, Modesto Junior College

Philip King, San Francisco State University
Steven F. Koch, Georgia Southern University
James T. Kyle, Indiana State University
Gary Langer, Roosevelt University
Susan Linz, Michigan State University
Marianne Lowery, Erie Community College
Melanie Marks, Longwood College
Jessica McCraw, University of Texas, Arlington
Bret McMurran, Chaffey College
Thomas J. Meeks, Virginia State University
Jeannette Mitchell, Rochester Institute of
  Technology
Rahmat Mozayan, Heald College
William Neilson, Texas A & M University
Alex Obiya, San Diego City College
Paul Okello, University of Texas, Arlington
Charles M. Oldham, Jr., Fayetteville Technical
  Community College
Jack W. Osman, San Francisco State University
Carl Parker, Fort Hays State University
Randall Parker, East Carolina University
Stephen Perez, California State University,
  Sacramento
Stan Peters, Southeast Community College
Chirinjev Peterson, Greenville Technical
  College
Nampeang Pingkarawat, Chicago State University
L. Wayne Plumly, Jr., Valdosta State University
Fatma Abdel-Raouf, Cleveland State University
Dan Rickman, Oklahoma State University
John Robertson, University of Kentucky
Barbara Ross-Pfeiffer, Kapiolani Community
  College
George Schatz, Maine Maritime Academy

Kurt Schwabe, Ohio University
Mark Siegler, Williams College
Terri Sexton, California State University,
  Sacramento
Dennis Shannon, Belleville Area College
Virginia Shingleton, Valparaiso University
Garvin Smith, Daytona Beach Community
  College
Noel Smith, Palm Beach Community College
Xiaochuan Song, San Diego Mesa College
Ed Sorensen, San Francisco State University
Abdulwahab Sraiheen, Kutztown University
Rodney Swanson, University of California–Los
  Angeles
James Swofford, University of South Alabama
Evan Tanner, Thunderbird, The American
  Graduate School of International
  Management
Robert Tansky, St. Clair County Community
  College
Denise Turnage, Midlands Technical College
Tracy M. Turner, Kansas State University
Fred Tyler, Fordham University
James R. VanBeek, Blinn College
Daniel Villegas, Cal Polytechnic State
  University
Chester Waters, Durham Technical
  Community College, Shaw University
Irvin Weintraub, Towson State University
Donald Wells, University of Arizona
James Wheeler, North Carolina State
  University
Gilbert Wolfe, Middlesex Community College
Virginia York, Gulf Coast Community College

Our greatest appreciation goes out to Carlos Aguilar and his economics students
from El Paso Community College, who gave us their feedback and evaluations with comparable textbooks. The students provided us with positive feedback and constructive
criticism that helped us prepare the third edition:

Erik Acona
Erica Avila
Jaime Bermudez
Israel Castillo
Maribell Castillo
Sarah Davis
Rebekah Dennis
Michele Donohoe
Emmanuel Eck
Patrick Espinoza
Edward Estrada
Kim Gardner
Aleisa Garza

Daniel Heitz
Laura Herebia
Hilda Howard
Melanie Johnson
Brenda Jordan
Eugene Jordan
Vanessa Lara
Harmony Lopez
Stacey Lucas
Maria Lynch
Sindy McElvany
Roger Mitchell
Benny Ontiveros

Louie Ortega

Karen Seitz

Ana Smith

Beverly Stephens

Adrian Terrazas

Chris Wright

From the start, Prentice Hall provided us with first-class support and advice. P.J. Boardman, Marie McHale, Gladys Soto, Lisa Amato, Victoria Anderson, Cynthia Regan, Kathleen McLellan, David Theisen, and Christopher Bath of Prentice Hall contributed in myriad ways to the project. We want to single out two people for special mention. Our Development Editor, Mike Elia, worked patiently with us to make our prose clean and lively, and our presentation utterly clear. Finally, we are deeply indebted to Rod Banister, Executive Editor at Prentice Hall, who used a combination of great organizational skill and a good sense of humor to guide the project from start to finish.

Last but not least, we must thank our families, who have seen us disappear, sometimes physically and other times mentally, to spend hours wrapped up in our own world of principles of economics. A project of this magnitude is very absorbing, and our families have been particularly supportive in this endeavor.

Art O'Sullivan

ARTHUR O'SULLIVAN

Steven Sheffrin

STEVEN SHEFFRIN

Introduction: What Is Economics?

Picture the following scenes:

- Betsy was studying for a midterm when someone invited her to a party. Should she go to the party or stay home and study?
- The Rentz family is tired of paying rent every month to the landlord. Should they buy their own home?
- The young entrepreneurs who started scour.com, an Internet search engine for video and music, have been offered $4 million for a 51% share in their company. Should they accept the offer?
- The California legislature is discussing the governor's proposed budget. Should the legislators accept it or should they give more money to the state's universities?
- The Federal Reserve Board is meeting in Washington, D.C. Should the board cut interest rates?

What do the people in these scenes have in common? Each person or group will make a decision, and each decision will require some economic reasoning.

conomic reasoning involves a careful evaluation of alternative actions. Betsy can have some party fun, but she might get a lower grade on the midterm as a result. The Rentz family can buy a home, but to come up with the down payment, they may sacrifice a family vacation or a new car. The young entrepreneurs can take $4 million now or they can continue to operate on their own and wait for a better offer. The California legislature can give more money to universities, but that means there will be less money for other programs such as prisons. The Federal Reserve Board can cut interest rates and help people who want to borrow money, but the lower interest rates might heat up the economy and cause inflation. Because there are alternative courses of action, people face trade-offs, and economic reasoning helps people think carefully about these trade-offs and then make decisions.

What is Economics?

Economics: The study of the choices made by people who are faced with scarcity.

Scarcity: A situation in which resources are limited and can be used in different ways, so one good or service must be sacrificed for another.

Economics is the study of the choices made by people when there is scarcity, that is, when there are limits to what they can get. **Scarcity** is a situation in which resources—the things we use to produce goods and services—are limited in quantity and can be used in different ways. Because resources are limited, we must sacrifice one good or service for another. Here are some examples of scarcity:

- Like everyone else, you have a limited amount of time today. If you play video games for an hour, you have one less hour to spend on other activities such as studying, exercising, or working.

- A city has a limited amount of land. If the city uses an acre of land to build a park, there is one less acre for apartments, office buildings, or factories.

- A nation has a limited number of people, so if it forms an army, it has fewer people to serve as teachers, scientists, and police officers.

Because of scarcity, people must make choices. You must decide how to spend your time; the city must decide how to use its land; and we as a nation must decide how to divide our people among teaching, science, law enforcement, and the military.

Decisions are made at every level in society. Individuals decide what products to buy, what occupation to pursue, and how much money to save. Firms decide what products to produce and how to produce them. Governments decide what projects and programs to complete and how to pay for them. The choices made by individuals, firms, and governments answer three basic questions:

1. **What products do we produce?** There are trade-offs in the choice among alternative products. For example, if a hospital devotes its resources to producing more heart transplants, it has fewer resources for caring for premature infants.

2. **How do we produce these products?** There are alternative ways to produce the products we desire. For example, utility companies can produce electricity with oil, solar power, or nuclear power. Professors can teach college students in large lectures or in small sections.

3. **Who consumes the products?** We must decide how the products of society are distributed among people. If some people earn more money than others, should they consume more goods? How much money should be taken from the rich and given to the poor?

Scarcity and Production Possibilities

Factors of production: The resources that are used to produce goods and services.

Let's take a closer look at the first question. What products do we produce? The resources that are used to produce products are known as the **factors of production**. Economists have identified five factors of production:

1. **Natural resources** are created by acts of nature. Natural resources—for example, arable land, mineral deposits, oil and gas deposits, and water—are used to produce goods and services. Some economists refer to all types of natural resources as land.

2. **Labor** is the human effort—including both physical and mental effort—used to produce goods and services. Labor is scarce because there are only 24 hours in each day: If we spend time in one activity, such as work, we have less time for other activities, such as recreation.

3. **Physical capital** is made by human beings and is used to produce goods and services; some examples of physical capital are machines, buildings, equipment, roads, pencils, computers, and trucks.

4. **Human capital** is the knowledge and skills a worker acquires through education and experience; human capital, like physical capital, is used to produce goods and services, although not in the same way. Every job requires some human capital: To be a surgeon, you must learn anatomy and acquire surgical skills; to be an accountant, you must learn the rules of accounting and acquire computer skills; to be a taxi driver, you must know the city's streets; to be a musician, you must know how to play an instrument well enough to be paid for playing it. One of the reasons for getting a college degree is to increase your human capital, widening your employment opportunities.

5. **Entrepreneurship** is the effort used to coordinate the production and sale of goods and services. An entrepreneur comes up with an idea for a good or a service and decides how to produce it. The entrepreneur takes risks, committing money and time without any guarantee of profit, hoping of course for success and big profits.

Natural resources: Things created by acts of nature and used to produce goods and services.

Labor: Human effort, including both physical and mental effort, used to produce goods and services.

Physical capital: Objects made by human beings to produce goods and services.

Human capital: The knowledge and skills acquired by a worker through education and experience and used to produce goods and services.

Entrepreneurship: Effort used to coordinate the production and sale of goods and services.

Before we can decide what products to produce, we must determine which combinations of products are possible, given our productive resources and our technological know-how. A production possibilities graph shows an economy's production options, the different combinations of products the economy can produce. The two-dimensional graph can show the production options with two general categories of goods, such as farm goods and factory goods or capital goods and consumer goods. The graph can also show the production options for any pair of specific goods, such as guns and butter, computers and space missions, or houses and automobiles.

Figure 1.1 shows a production possibilities graph for an economy that produces farm goods and factory goods. The possible or feasible combinations of these two types of goods are shown on the curve and in the shaded area. For example, one option is point *b*, with 700 tons of factory goods and 10 tons of farm goods. Another option is point *i*, with 300 tons of factory goods and 20 tons of farm goods. The set of points on the border between the shaded and unshaded area is called the **production possibilities curve** (or production possibilities frontier) because it separates the combinations that are attainable (the shaded area within the curve and the curve itself) from the combinations that are not attainable (the unshaded area outside the curve).

What is the difference between points inside the curve and points on the curve? For any point inside the curve, we can find a point on the curve that generates more of both goods. For example, at point *i* the economy can produce 300 tons of factory goods and 20 tons of farm goods. But we know from point *d* that the economy could produce more of both products: 400 tons of factory goods and 50 tons of farm goods. Producing at point *i* is clearly inferior to producing at point *d*. In general, an economy that is producing at a point inside the production possibilities curve could do better: It could produce more of both goods.

Production possibilities curve: A curve that shows the possible combinations of goods and services available to an economy, given that all productive resources are fully employed and efficiently used.

Figure 1.1

Scarcity and the Production Possibilities Curve

The production possibilities curve (or frontier) illustrates the notion of scarcity: With a given amount of resources, an increase in farm goods comes at the expense of factory goods. The curve is bowed outward because resources are not perfectly adaptable to the production of the two goods.

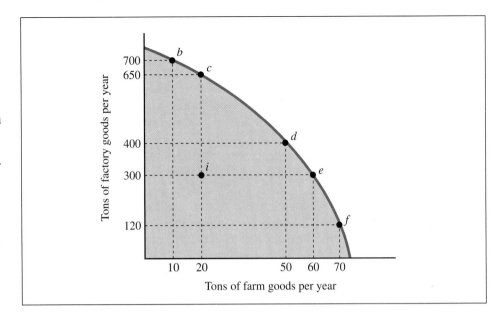

An economy might be at a point below the curve for the following reasons:

- Resources are not fully employed. For example, some workers could be idle, or some production facilities could be idle or underused.

- Resources are used inefficiently. Products can be produced with different mixtures of inputs, and some mixtures produce more output than others. If businesses pick the wrong input mixture, the economy won't produce as much output as it could.

In contrast, when an economy reaches a point on the production possibilities curve, it would be impossible to increase the production of both goods. For every point on the curve, the society's resources are fully employed and used in an efficient manner.

The production possibilities curve illustrates the notion of scarcity. At a given time, an economy has a fixed amount of each factor of production. That means we can produce more of one product only if we produce less of another product. To produce more farm goods, we take resources away from factories. As we move resources out of factory production, the quantity of factory goods will decrease. For example, if we move from point b to point c on the production possibilities curve in Figure 1.1, we sacrifice 50 tons of factory goods (700 tons − 650 tons) to get 10 more tons of farm goods (20 tons − 10 tons).

Compare the move from point b to point c with the move from point e to point f. Starting at point b, a 10-ton increase in farm goods decreases factory goods by 50 tons. Starting at point e, a 10-ton increase in farm goods decreases factory goods by 180 tons. On the lower part of the curve, we sacrifice more factory goods to get the same 10-ton increase in farm goods. Why?

The answer is that resources are not perfectly adaptable for the production of both goods. Some resources are more suitable for factory production, while others are more suitable for farming. Starting at point b, the economy uses its most fertile land to produce farm goods. A 10-ton increase in farm goods reduces the quantity of factory goods by only 50 tons because plenty of fertile land is available for conversion to farming. As the economy moves downward along the production possibilities curve, farmers will be forced to use land that is progressively less fertile. To increase farm output by 10 tons, farmers will need more land and more of the other inputs. As progressively larger quantities of resources are diverted from factory goods, the sacrifice of factory goods becomes

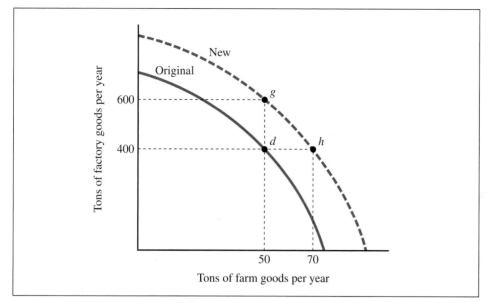

Figure 1.2
Shifting the Production Possibilities Curve
The production possibilities curve will shift outward as a result of an increase in the economy's resources (natural resources, labor, physical capital, human capital, and entrepreneurship) or a technological innovation that increases the output from a given amount of resources.

larger and larger. In the move from point *e* to point *f,* the land converted to farming is so poor that to increase farm output by 10 tons, so much land and other resources are diverted to farms that factory output drops by 180 tons.

What sort of changes would shift the entire production possibilities curve? The curve shows the production options available with a given set of productive resources, so an increase in an economy's resources will shift the entire curve outward. If an economy acquires more resources—natural resources, labor, physical capital, human capital, or entrepreneurial ability—the economy can produce more of both products. As a result, the production possibilities curve will shift outward, as shown in Figure 1.2. For example, if we start at point *d* and the economy's resources increase, we can produce more factory goods (point *g*), more farm goods (point *h*), or more of both goods (points between *g* and *h*). The curve will also shift outward as a result of technological innovations that allow us to produce more output with a given quantity of resources.

The production possibilities frontier could shift inward as well. Suppose a hurricane destroys factories, roads, and train tracks. The economy will have fewer resources available for production, so the production possibilities curve will shift inward. That means the nation will produce fewer factory goods, fewer farm goods, or fewer of both. Similarly, recent wars in Iraq and Afghanistan—which caused widespread destruction of roads, factories, bridges, electricity generation facilities, and housing—shifted the production possibilities frontiers of those economies inward.

Markets and the Invisible Hand

Let's look at how a market-based economy answers the three basic economic questions. A **market** is an arrangement that allows buyers and sellers to exchange things, trading what they have for what they want. For example, the labor market allows workers and firms to exchange time and money. A software firm has money and wants workers to design programs, while the worker has time and wants income to support the family. Similarly, the car market allows consumers and producers to exchange cars and money. A consumer has money and wants a car, while a producer has a car and wants money. By providing opportunities to trade goods and services, markets help society to answer the

Market: An arrangement that allows buyers and sellers to exchange things: A buyer exchanges money for a product; a seller exchanges a product for money.

three basic questions of what to produce, how to produce it, and who gets the products produced.

Markets determine the prices of goods and services, and these prices guide decisions about what and how much to buy and sell. Consider a hurricane in Florida that disrupts the electric power supply and disables refrigerators, so people must use ice to preserve their food. The sudden increase in the demand for ice will increase its price. The higher price will cause consumers to use ice wisely and to switch to foods that don't require refrigeration. At the same time, the higher price will encourage profit-seeking firms to produce more ice to accommodate the greater demand. On both sides of the market, the higher price helps the state to deal with the power disruption caused by the hurricane.

The decisions made in markets result from the interactions of millions of people, each acting in his or her own self-interest. Adam Smith used the metaphor of the invisible hand to explain that people acting in their own self-interest may actually promote the interest of society as a whole.

> *It is not from the benevolence of the butcher, the brewer, or the baker that we expect our dinner, but from their regard to their own interest. We address ourselves, not to their humanity but to their self-love, and never talk to them of our own necessities but of their advantages. [Man is] led by an invisible hand to promote an end which was no part of his intention. . . . By pursuing his own interest he frequently promotes that of the society more effectually than when he really intends to promote it.*

> Adam Smith, *Wealth of Nations* (New York: Modern Library, 1994)

In the last sentence Smith said "frequently," not "always." Smith recognized that individuals pursuing their own self-interest will not necessarily promote the social interest. Later in the book we'll discuss situations in which the pursuit of self-interest will be contrary to the interest of society as a whole. In these cases it is sensible for the government to guide people's decisions to promote the social interest.

In modern economies, most of the decisions about how much to produce, how to produce it, and who gets the products are made in markets. Of course, no economy relies exclusively on markets to make these economic decisions. Later in the book we'll look at how government regulates markets, provides goods and services, imposes taxes to pay for the goods and services it provides, and redistributes income.

TEST Your Understanding

1. List the three basic questions that we can ask about a society's economy.

2. Which of these three questions does the production possibilities curve help to answer?

The Economic Way of Thinking

How do economists think about problems and decision-making? This economic way of thinking is best summarized by noted economist John Maynard Keynes: "The Theory of Economics does not furnish a body of settled conclusions immediately applicable to policy. It is a method rather than a doctrine, an apparatus of the mind, a technique of thinking which helps its possessor to draw correct conclusions." Let's look at some of the elements of the economic way of thinking.

Positive and Normative Economics

The focus of most modern economic reasoning is on positive analysis. **Positive economics** concerns the forces that affect economic activity, and predicts the consequences of alternative actions. Here are some questions answered by positive economics:

Positive economics: Analysis that answers the questions, What is or what will be?

- How will an increase in the price of Internet access affect the number of subscribers?

- How will an increase in the wage for fast-food workers affect the number of workers hired?

- What fraction of an income-tax cut will be spent on consumer goods, and what fraction will be saved?

- How will an increase in interest rates affect investment in factories?

In other words, positive economics answers the questions, What is? or What will be?

A second type of economic reasoning is normative in nature. **Normative economics** answers the question, What ought to be? Here are some examples of normative questions:

Normative economics: Analysis that answers the question, What ought to be?

- Should the government increase the minimum wage?

- Should a commuter who drives to work during the rush hour pay a congestion tax of $5 per day?

- Should the government provide free prescription drugs to senior citizens?

- Should NASA stage a manned mission to Mars?

Although most economists shy away from normative questions and instead focus on positive analysis, economic reasoning is an important part of most policy debates. Economists contribute to the debates by doing positive economic analysis about the consequences of alternative actions. For example, an economist could predict how a $5 congestion tax would affect the number of rush-hour vehicles, and then tell us how much faster traffic would flow. This positive analysis sets the stage for citizens and policymakers to decide whether or not to impose the congestion tax. Similarly, an economist would remind us that a mission to Mars would use resources that could be used for other programs such as college loans, and tell us how a cut in student-loan programs would affect the number of people attending college. After an economist quantifies the trade-offs, citizens and policymakers can make a choice.

To summarize, most modern economic analysis is positive in nature, but is often focused on the question relevant for normative concerns. Nassau Senior, the first professor of political economy at Oxford, summarizes the role of economic analysis in public policy.

> *But the economists' conclusions, whatever be their generality and their truth, do not authorize him in adding a single syllable of advice. That privilege belongs to the writer and statesman who has considered all the causes which may promote or impede the general welfare of those whom he addresses, not to the theorist who has considered only one, though among the most important, of those causes. The business of a Political Economist is neither to recommend nor to dissuade, but to state general principle.*

As you go through this book, you'll find plenty of positive economic analysis relevant to today's policy debates.

Use Assumptions to Simplify

Economists use assumptions to make things simpler and to focus on what really matters. Most people use simplifying assumptions in their everyday thinking and decision-making. For example, suppose you want to travel from Seattle to San Francisco by automobile. If you use a road map to pick a travel route, you are using two assumptions to simplify your decision-making:

- The earth is flat: The flat road map does not show the curvature of the earth.
- The highways are flat: The standard road map does not show hills and mountains.

These two assumptions are abstractions from reality. But they are useful because they simplify your decision-making without affecting your choice of a travel route. You could plan your trip with a globe that shows all the topographical features of the alternative travel routes between Seattle and San Francisco, but you would probably pick the same travel route because the curvature of the earth and the topography of the highways are irrelevant for your trip. In this case, the assumptions underlying the standard road map are harmless.

What if you decide to travel by bicycle instead of by automobile? Now the two assumptions are not harmless unless you want to pedal up mountains. If you use the standard road map and assume that there are no mountains between Seattle and San Francisco, you are likely to pick a mountainous route instead of a flat one. In this case, the simplifying assumption makes a difference. The lesson from this example is that we must think carefully about whether an assumption is truly harmless.

In this book, we use simplifying assumptions to help make it easier to learn a concept or to analyze something. Most of the assumptions will be harmless in the sense that they simplify the analysis by eliminating irrelevant details. Although many of the assumptions are unrealistic, that does not mean that the analysis based on the assumption is incorrect. Just as we can use an unrealistic road map to plan a trip, we can use unrealistic assumptions to do economic analysis. When we use an assumption that actually affects the analysis, we'll alert you to this fact and explore the implications of alternative assumptions.

Most of the economic analysis in this book is based on two assumptions, both of which are realistic in most circumstances:

- **Self-interest.** We'll assume that people act in their own self-interest, without considering the effects of their actions on other people. We assume that a pizza consumer doesn't care about other people who might want to buy the pizza, but only about his or her own well-being. Similarly, we assume that a pizzeria owner doesn't care about how his or her decisions affect other people, but only about the owner's profit. There is solid evidence that most people act in their own self-interest in most situations, so the economic analysis in this book is relevant for a wide range of decisions.

- **Informed decisions.** We'll assume that people make informed decisions. We assume that a consumer deciding what to eat for lunch knows the price of pizza, the prices of alternative foods, and the relevant characteristics of the foods (taste, amount of fat, number of calories). With this information, the consumer can make an informed decision about what to eat. Similarly, the manager of a pizzeria knows the cost of producing pizza, and this information leads to an informed decision about how many pizzas to produce and what price to charge. In most cases, consumers and producers have enough information to make informed decisions. Later in the book, we'll discuss situations in which one side of the market is poorly informed.

Explore the Relationship Between Two Variables

Economic analysis often involves variables and how they affect each other. A **variable** is a measure of something that can have different values. For example, consider a student who has a part-time job and also receives a fixed weekly allowance from her parents. Her weekly income is a variable whose value is determined by the values of the other variables: the number of hours she works, the hourly wage she is paid, and the weekly allowance she gets from her parents.

To explore the relationship between any two variables, such as the hours worked and weekly income, we must assume that the other variables do not change. For example, the student might say, "If I work one more hour this week, my income will increase by $8." In making this statement, the student is exploring the relationship between two variables (work time and income), assuming that the other two variables (wage and allowance) do not change. To be complete, the statement must say, "If I work one more hour this week, my income will increase by $8, assuming that my wage and my allowance do not change."

This book contains many statements about the relationship between two variables. For example, the number of pizzas a person eats depends on the price of pizza, the price of burgers, and that person's income. Suppose we say, "A decrease in the price of pizzas increases the quantity of pizzas consumed." This is a statement about the relationship between two variables—the price of pizzas and the quantity of pizzas—implicitly assuming that the other two variables, the price of burgers and the person's income, do not change in value. Sometimes we will make this assumption explicit by adding a warning label: "A decrease in the price of pizzas increases the quantity of pizzas consumed, **ceteris paribus**." The Latin words mean "other things being equal to what they were before." In the present context, the phrase means "other variables being fixed." From now on, whenever we refer to a relationship between two variables, we assume that the other relevant variables are held fixed.

Variable: A measure of something that can take on different values.

Ceteris paribus: Latin, meaning "other things being equal." In economics, the phrase indicates that all other variables are held fixed.

Think Marginal

Economists often need to consider how a small change in one variable causes a change in another variable. A small change in value is called a **marginal change**. The marginal question is, If we increase one variable by one unit, by how much will the other variable change? The key feature of this marginal question is that one variable increases by a single unit. For the student who is concerned about income, the marginal question is, If I work one more hour per week, by how much will my income increase?

You will encounter marginal thinking throughout this book. Here are some other marginal questions:

- If I spend one more year in school, by how much will my lifetime income increase?
- If I buy one more CD, how many tapes will I sacrifice?
- If a table producer hires one more carpenter, how many more tables will be produced?
- If national income increases by $1 billion, by how much will spending on consumer goods increase?

Answering a marginal question like any of these is the first step in deciding whether or not to pursue a particular activity. You will see more about this as we move along in this book.

Marginal change: A small change in value.

Preview of Coming Attractions: Microeconomics

There are two types of economic analysis: microeconomics and macroeconomics. **Microeconomics** is the study of the choices made by households, firms, and government and of how these choices affect the markets for goods and services. Let's look at three ways we can use microeconomic analysis.

Microeconomics: The study of the choices made by consumers, firms, and government and of how their choices affect the market for a particular good or service.

Understand Markets and Predict Changes

One reason for studying microeconomics is to understand better how markets work. Once you know how markets operate, you can use economic analysis to predict changes in the price of a particular good and changes in the quantity of the good sold. In this book we answer dozens of practical questions about markets and how they operate. Let's look at a practical question that can be answered with some simple economic analysis.

How would a tax on beer affect the number of highway deaths among young adults? A tax on beer will make it more expensive, and young adults, like other beer consumers, will consume less of it. Alcohol consumption contributes to highway accidents, and the number of highway fatalities among young adults is roughly proportional to the total beer consumption by young adults. Therefore, a tax that decreases beer consumption by 10% will decrease highway deaths among young adults by about 10%.

Make Personal and Managerial Decisions

We use economic analysis, on the personal level, to decide how to spend our time, what career to pursue, and how to spend and save the money we earn. As workers, we use economic analysis to decide how to produce goods and services, how much to produce, and how much to charge for them. Let's use some economic analysis to look at a practical question confronting someone considering starting a business.

If the existing music stores in your city are profitable and you have enough money to start your own music store, should you do it? If you enter this market, the competition between the stores for consumers will heat up, leading to lower prices for tapes and CDs. In addition, your costs may be higher than the costs of the stores that are already established. It will be sensible to enter the market only if you expect a small drop in price and a small difference in cost. Of course, there is the risk that the existing stores may try to protect their market shares by cutting prices and increasing their advertising. Indeed, entering what appears to be a lucrative market may turn out to be a financial disaster.

Evaluate Public Policies

Although modern societies use markets to make most of the decisions concerning production and consumption, the government has several important roles in a market-based society. We can use economic analysis to determine how well the government performs its roles in the market economy. We can also explore the trade-offs associated with various public policies. Let's look at a practical question about public policy.

Is it sensible for the government to pay part of the cost of your college education? Think about who benefits from your education. You get many benefits yourself, including higher lifetime income, more career options, and the thrill of learning. But other people also benefit from your education. In the modern workplace, teamwork is important, and the productivity of a team of workers depends in part on the education level of the team members. A college education is likely to make you a better team worker, allowing your fellow workers to be more productive and earn more income. In addition, your college education will make you a more intelligent citizen, which means that you'll

The standard of living has increased dramatically in the last several decades. We eat better food and live in better houses.

make better choices on election day. It is sensible for the government to help pay for your college education because taxpayers (your fellow workers and citizens) benefit from your education.

Preview of Coming Attractions: Macroeconomics

Macroeconomics is the study of the nation's economy as a whole. In macroeconomics we learn about important topics that are regularly discussed in newspapers and on television, including unemployment, inflation, the budget deficit, and the trade deficit. Macroeconomics explains why economies grow and change, and why economic growth is sometimes interrupted.

In the 1930s, over 25% of the workers in the United States could not find jobs. Many banks were closed, thousands of factories were shut down, and the economy nearly ground to a halt. In terms of the production possibilities curve described earlier in the chapter, the U.S. economy was inside the production possibilities curve: Our resources were not fully employed, and we didn't produce as many goods and services as we could. Macroeconomics explains the forces that cause the economy to malfunction in this way and provides insights into how we might fix the economy to allow it to grow.

John Maynard Keynes (pronounced "Canes"), known as the father of "Keynesian" economics, was a renowned economist who taught at Cambridge University in England. During the dismal 1930s, Keynes wrote a book, *The General Theory of Employment, Interest, and Money*. Writing at a time of massive unemployment, Keynes emphasized the short-run benefits of government spending to stimulate the economy and put people back to work. Some examples of government spending that could decrease unemployment are building highways and hiring more public-school teachers.

Modern macroeconomics goes beyond dealing with short-term crises such as high unemployment and considers the issue of growth over the long term. Because of economic growth in the last several decades, people in the United States today enjoy a much higher living standard than that experienced by their grandparents. We drive better cars and live in houses with more amenities, and even many middle-class Americans travel routinely across the country and around the world. We can consume more of all goods and services because the economy has more of the resources needed to produce these goods and services, as indicated by an outward shift of the possibilities frontier. Macroeconomics explains why some of these resources increase over time and how an increase in these resources translates into a higher standard of living.

Macroeconomics: The study of the nation's economy as a whole.

Macroeconomic issues are at the heart of many national political debates. Every candidate for president of the United States must convince voters that he or she understands the concepts of macroeconomics. Once elected, the prospects for reelection depend crucially on how well the economy performs during his or her term as president. If the public believes that the economy has performed well, the president is likely to be reelected. But if the public thinks that the economy has not performed well, they are unlikely to support the incumbent. In recent years, several presidents—including Jimmy Carter and George Bush—were not reelected because the economy performed poorly during their terms as president.

For a preview, let's think about three ways we can use macroeconomic analysis.

Understand How a National Economy Operates

One purpose of studying macroeconomics is to understand how the entire economy works. We can answer the following question with some macroeconomic analysis: Why do some countries grow much faster than others?

In the fastest-growing countries, citizens save a large fraction of the money they earn, and the workforce is well educated. Saving money provides funds that firms can use to purchase machines and equipment. An economy with a well-equipped workforce will grow faster than an economy whose workers are poorly equipped. A country with a well-educated workforce is able to quickly adopt new technologies that increase the productivity of its workforce.

Understand the Grand Debates over Economic Policy

Macroeconomics developed as a separate branch of economics during the 1930s, when the entire world suffered from massive unemployment. With a knowledge of macroeconomics, you can make sense of all sorts of policy debates, including the debate over the wisdom of policies designed to reduce the unemployment rate.

Should Congress and the President do something to reduce the unemployment rate? If unemployment is very high, the Congress and the President may want to reduce it. However, it is important not to reduce the unemployment rate too much, because as we'll see later in the book, a low unemployment rate will cause inflation. Moreover, unemployment can't be reduced overnight. Therefore, it is sensible to take action only if we believe that inaction will lead to persistent unemployment. In macroeconomics, we study the trade-offs associated with policies designed to combat unemployment and inflation.

Make Informed Business Decisions

A third reason for studying macroeconomics is to make informed business decisions. A manager who understands how the national economy operates will make better decisions involving interest rates, exchange rates, the inflation rate, and the unemployment rate. A manager who intends to borrow money for a new production facility could use her knowledge of macroeconomics to predict the effects of current public policies on interest rates and then decide whether to borrow the money now or later. Similarly, a manager must keep an eye on the inflation rate to help decide how much to charge for his firm's products and how much to pay workers. A manager who studies macroeconomics will be better equipped to understand the complexities of unemployment, interest rates, and inflation.

3. Two simplifying assumptions are used extensively in economics. What are they?

4. Suppose your grade on an economics exam is affected by the number of lectures you attend. What is the marginal question you should ask yourself about this relationship?

Summary

This chapter explains what economics is and why it is useful. Economics is about choices made by individuals, organizations, governments, and society as a whole. We can use economic analysis to understand how these choices affect the world around us. We can also use economics to make our own choices as consumers, workers, managers, and voters. Here are the main points of the chapter.

1. The production possibilities curve shows the combinations of goods and services available to an economy and illustrates the notion of scarcity: the production of one product comes at the expense of another. The curve will shift outward as a result of an increase in the economy's productive resources or an improvement in technology.

2. We use microeconomics to understand how markets work, predict changes in prices and quantities, make personal or managerial decisions, and evaluate the merits of public policies.

3. Macroeconomics explains how an economy works and helps us to understand the grand debates over economic policy.

4. To think like an economist, we (a) use assumptions to simplify what we are analyzing; (b) explore the relationship between the values of two variables, holding fixed the values of any other related variables; and (c) think in marginal terms.

5. Two assumptions are used extensively in economics: People act in their own self-interest, and people make informed choices.

Key Terms

ceteris paribus, 9
economics, 2
entrepreneurship, 3
factors of production, 2
human capital, 3
labor, 3

macroeconomics, 11
marginal change, 9
market, 5
microeconomics, 10
natural resources, 3
normative economics, 7

physical capital, 3
positive economics, 7
production possibilities curve, 3
scarcity, 2
variable, 9

Problems and Discussion Questions

1. For some goods and services, the assumption that people have enough information to make informed choices is unrealistic. Provide a brief list of some of these goods and services.

2. For some decisions, you act altruistically rather than acting in your own self-interest. Provide a brief list of such decisions.

3. "If I study one more hour for my economics exam, I expect my grade to increase by 3 points." List the variables that are implicitly assumed to be fixed in that statement.

4. It's your first day on your job in the advertising department of a baseball team. Your boss wants to know whether it is sensible to run one more television advertisement encouraging people to attend an upcoming game. List the relevant marginal questions.

5. Complete the statement: As we switch resources from the production of one good to another, we _____ the production possibilities curve; as we add resources to an economy, we _____ the curve.

6. **Web Exercise.** Visit the Web site for the CIA's World Fact Book *(http://www.odci.gov/cia/publications/factbook/)*. Pick a country and get some data about its factors of production (labor, human capital, natural resources).

7. **Web Exercise.** Visit the Web site of the IndUS Entrepreneurs, a nonprofit organization for entrepreneurs *(http://www.tie.org)*. Access the page describing the organization's programs *(http://www.tie.org/prog.html)*. What does this organization do and how might it be helpful for aspiring entrepreneurs?

Take It to the Net

We invite you to visit the O'Sullivan/Sheffrin page on the Prentice Hall Web site at: **http://www.prenhall.com/osullivan/** for additional World Wide Web exercises for this chapter.

Model Answers for Questions

Test Your Understanding

1. What goods and services do we produce? How do we produce the goods and services we select? Who consumes the goods and services we produce?

2. The production possibilities curve shows the combinations of goods that are available to the economy, so it helps us to answer the first question.

3. People act in their own self-interest; people make informed decisions.

4. "If I attend one more lecture, by how much will my exam grade increase?"

APPENDIX

Using Graphs and Formulas

In this appendix, we review the mechanics of graphing. You'll recognize most of the simple graphs and formulas in this appendix, because they were covered in your high-school mathematics. We'll review them here to prepare you to use them as you begin your own economic analysis.

Using Graphs to Show Relationships

A graph is a visual representation of the relationship between two variables. As we saw earlier in Chapter 1, a variable is a measure of something that can take on different values. For example, suppose that you have a part-time job and you are interested in the relationship between the number of hours you work and your weekly income. The relevant variables are the hours you work per week and your weekly income.

We can use a table of numbers such as Table 1A.1 to show the relationship between time worked and income. Let's assume that your weekly allowance from your parents is $20 and your part-time job pays $4 per hour. For example, if you work 10 hours per week, your weekly income is $60 ($20 from your parents and $40 from your job). The more you work, the higher your weekly income: If you work 22 hours, your weekly income is $108; if you work 30 hours, it is $140.

Table 1A.1 Relationship Between Hours of Work and Income				
Hours worked per week	0	10	22	30
Income per week	$20	$60	$108	$140

Drawing a Graph

A graph makes it easier to see the relationship between time worked and income. To draw a graph, we perform seven simple steps.

1. Draw a horizontal line to represent the first variable. In Figure 1A.1 we measure time worked along the horizontal axis (also known as the *x* axis). As we move to the right along the horizontal axis, the number of hours worked increases, from zero to 30 hours. The numbers along the horizontal axis are spaced equally.

2. Draw a vertical line intersecting the first line to represent the second variable. In Figure 1A.1 we measure income along the vertical axis (also known as the *y* axis). As we move up along the vertical axis, income increases from zero to $140.

3. Pick a combination of time worked and income from the table of numbers. From the second column, for instance, time worked is 10 hours and income is $60.

4. Find the point on the horizontal axis with that number of hours worked—10 hours worked—and draw a dashed line vertically straight up from that point.

5. Find the point on the vertical axis with the income corresponding to those hours worked ($60) and draw a dashed line horizontally straight to the right from that point.

6. The intersection of the dashed lines shows the combination of those hours worked and the income for working those hours. Point *b* shows the combination of 10 hours worked and $60 income.

7. Repeat steps 3 through 6 for different combinations of work time and income from the table of numbers. Once you have a series of points on the graph (*b*, *c*, and *d*), you can connect them to draw a curve that shows the relationship between hours worked and income.

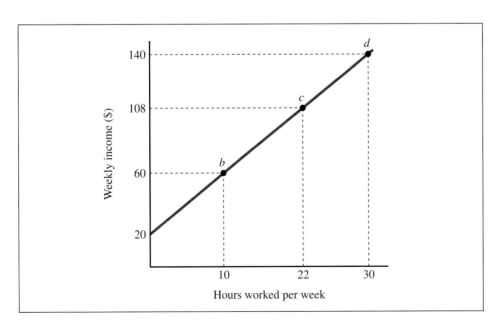

Figure 1A.1

Relationship Between Hours Worked and Total Income

There is a positive relationship between the amount of work time and income. The slope of the curve is $4: Each additional hour of work increases income by $4.

There is a **positive relationship** between two variables if an increase in the value of one variable increases the value of the other variable. An increase in the time you work increases your income, so there is a positive relationship between the two variables. As you increase the time you work, you move upward along the curve shown in Figure 1A.1 to higher income levels.

There is a **negative relationship** between two variables if an increase in the value of one variable decreases the value of the other variable. For example, there is a negative relationship between the amount of time you work and your performance in school. Some people refer to a positive relationship as a direct relationship and to a negative relationship as an inverse relationship.

Computing the Slope

How sensitive is one variable to changes in the other variable? We can use the slope of the curve to measure this sensitivity. The **slope of a curve** is the change in the variable on the vertical axis resulting from a one-unit increase in the variable on the horizontal axis. Once we pick two points on a curve, we can compute the slope as follows:

$$\text{slope} = \frac{\text{vertical difference between two points}}{\text{horizontal difference between two points}}$$

To compute the slope of a curve, we take four steps:

1. Pick two points on the curve: for example, points b and c in Figure 1A.1.
2. Compute the vertical distance between the two points (also known as the rise). For points b and c, the vertical distance between the points is $48 ($108 − $60).
3. Compute the horizontal distance between the same two points (also known as the run). For points b and c, the horizontal distance between the points is 12 hours (22 hours − 10 hours).
4. Divide the vertical distance by the horizontal distance to get the slope. The slope between points b and c is $4 per hour:

$$\text{slope} = \frac{\text{vertical difference}}{\text{horizontal difference}} = \frac{48}{12} = 4$$

In this case, a 12-hour increase in time worked increases income by $48, so the increase in income per hour of work is $4, which makes sense because this is the hourly wage.

Because the curve is a straight line, the slope is the same at all points along the curve. You can check this yourself by using the values between points c and d to calculate the slope.

Moving Along the Curve Versus Shifting the Curve

Up to this point, we've explored the effect of change in variables that cause movement along a given curve. In Figure 1A.1 we see the relationship between a student's hours of work (on the horizontal axis) and her income (on the vertical axis). The student's income also depends on her allowance and her wage, so we can make two observations about the curve in Figure 1A.1.

1. To draw this curve, we must specify the weekly allowance ($20) and the hourly wage ($4).
2. The curve shows that an increase in time worked increases the student's income, assuming that her allowance and her wage are fixed.

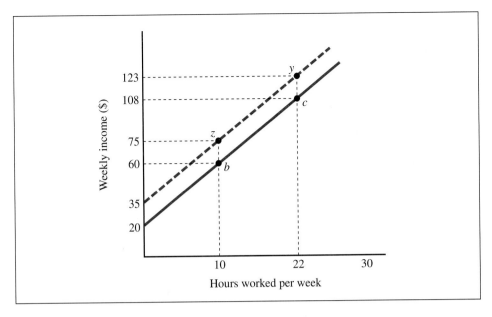

To draw a curve showing the relationship between hours worked and total income, we assume that the weekly allowance ($20) and the wage ($4) are fixed. An increase in the weekly allowance from $20 to $35 shifts the curve upward by $15: For each quantity of work hours, income is $15 higher.

A change in the student's weekly allowance will shift the curve showing the relationship between time worked and income. In Figure 1A.2, when the allowance increases from $20 to $35, the curve shifts upward by $15. For a given time worked, the student's income increases by $15. Now the income associated with 10 hours of work and the higher allowance is $75 (point z), compared to $60 with 10 hours of work and the original allowance (point b). In general, an increase in the allowance shifts the curve upward and leftward: For a given amount of time worked, the student will have more income (an upward shift as a result of the increased allowance). To reach a given amount of income, the student needs fewer hours of work (a leftward shift).

This book uses dozens of two-dimensional curves, each of which shows the relationship between only two variables. That is all a single curve can show. A common error is to forget that a single curve tells only part of the story. In Figure 1A.2 we needed two curves to show what happened when we looked at three variables (work time, allowance, and income). Here are some simple rules that will help to avoid this error:

- A change in one of the variables shown on the graph causes movement along the curve. In Figure 1A.2 an increase in work time causes movement along the curve from point b to point c.

- A change in one of the variables that is not shown on the graph (one of the variables held fixed in drawing the curve) shifts the entire curve. In Figure 1A.2 an increase in the allowance causes the entire curve to shift upward.

Negative and Nonlinear Relationships

We can use a graph to show a negative relationship between two variables. Consider a consumer who has a monthly budget of $150 to spend on CDs (at a price of $10 per CD) and cassette tapes (at a price of $5 per tape). Table 1A.2 shows the relationship between

Table 1A.2   Relationship Between CDs and Tapes

Number of CDs purchased	0	5	10	15
Number of tapes purchased	30	20	10	0

the number of CDs purchased and the number of tapes purchased. If the consumer buys 5 CDs in a certain month, he will spend a total of $50 on CDs, leaving $100 to spend on tapes. With the $100 he can buy 20 tapes at a price of $5 per tape. As the number of CDs increases, the number of tapes decreases, from 20 tapes and 5 CDs, to 10 tapes and 10 CDs, to 0 tapes and 15 CDs.

Using the seven-step process outlined earlier, we can use the numbers in Table 1A.2 to draw a curve showing this negative relationship. In Figure 1A.3 the curve is negatively sloped: The more the consumer spends on CDs, the fewer tapes he can buy. We can use points e and f to compute the slope of the curve. The slope is −2 tapes per CD: A five-unit increase in CDs (the horizontal difference, or the run) decreases the number of tapes by 10 (the vertical difference, or the rise):

$$\text{slope} = \frac{\text{vertical difference}}{\text{horizontal difference}} = \frac{-10}{5} = -2$$

The curve is a straight line with a constant slope of −2 tapes per CD.

We can use a graph to show a nonlinear relationship between two variables. Panel A of Figure 1A.4 shows the relationship between study time and the exam grade that results from study time. Although the exam grade increases as study time increases, the grade increases at a decreasing rate; that means the increase in grade is smaller and smaller for each additional hour of study. For example, the second hour of study increases the grade by 4 points (from 6 points to 10 points), but the ninth hour of study increases the grade by only 1 point (from 24 points to 25 points). This is a nonlinear relationship: The slope of the curve changes as we move along the curve. In Figure 1A.4 the slope decreases as we move to the right along the curve: The slope is 4 between points g and h but only 1 between points i and j.

Another possibility for a nonlinear curve is that the slope increases (the curve becomes steeper) as we move to the right along the curve. This is shown in panel B of Figure 1A.4. The slope of the curve increases as the amount of grain increases, meaning that total production cost increases at an increasing rate. If the producer increases production from 1 ton to 2 tons, the total cost increases by $5 (from $10 to $15). On the upper portion of the curve, if the producer increases production from 10 to 11 tons, the total cost increases by $25 (from $100 to $125).

Figure 1A.3

A Negative Relationship Between CD Purchases and Tape Purchases

There is a negative relationship between the number of CDs purchased and the number of cassette tapes purchased. Because the price of CDs is $10 and the price of tapes is $5, the slope of the curve is −2 tapes per CD: Each additional CD decreases the number of tapes by 2.

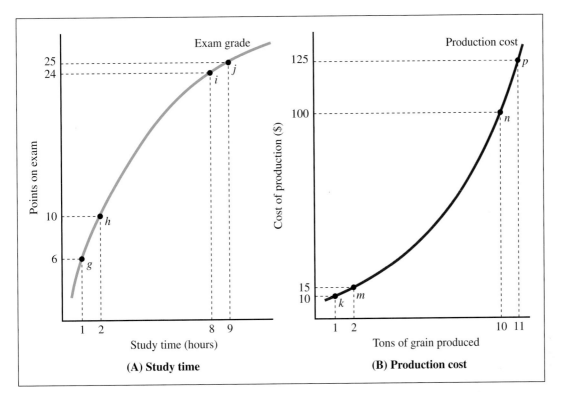

Figure 1A.4

Nonlinear Relationships

(A) Study Time There is a positive and nonlinear relationship between study time and the grade on an exam. As study time increases, the exam grade increases at a decreasing rate. For example, the second hour of study increases the grade by 4 points (from 6 points to 10 points), but the ninth hour of study increases the grade by only 1 point (from 24 points to 25 points).

(B) Production Cost There is a positive and nonlinear relationship between the quantity of grain produced and total production cost. As the quantity increases, total cost increases at an increasing rate. For example, to increase production from 1 ton to 2 tons, production cost increases by $5 (from $10 to $15), but to increase production from 10 to 11 tons, total cost increases by $25 (from $100 to $125).

Using Formulas to Compute Values

Economists often use formulas to compute the values of the relevant variables. Here is a brief review of the mechanics of formulas.

Computing Percentage Changes

In many cases, the formulas that economists use involve percentage changes. In this book we use the simple approach to computing percentage changes: We divide the change in the variable by the initial value of the variable and then multiply by 100. For example, if the price of pizzas increases from $20 to $22, the percentage change is 10%: The change ($2) divided by the initial value ($20) is 0.10; multiplying this number by 100 generates a percentage change of 10%:

$$\text{percentage change} = \frac{\text{absolute change}}{\text{initial value}} = \frac{2}{20} = 0.10 = 10\%$$

Going in the other direction, if the price decreases from $20 to $19, the percentage change is −5%: The change (−$1) divided by the initial value ($20) is −0.05, or −5%.

The alternative to the simple approach is the midpoint approach, under which the percentage change equals the absolute change in the variable divided by the average value or the midpoint of the variable. For example, if the price of pizza increases from $20 to $22, the computed percentage change under the midpoint approach would be 9.52381%:

$$\text{percentage change} = \frac{\text{absolute change}}{\text{average value}} = \frac{2}{(20 + 22)/2}$$

$$= \frac{2}{21} = 0.0952381 = 9.52381\%$$

If the change in the variable is relatively small, the extra precision associated with the midpoint approach is usually not worth the extra effort. The simple approach allows us to spend less time doing tedious arithmetic and more time doing economic analysis. In this book we use the simple approach to compute percentage changes: If the price increases from $20 to $22, the price has increased by 10%.

If we know a percentage change, we can translate it into an absolute change. For example, if a price has increased by 10% and the initial price is $20, then we add 10% of the initial price ($2 is 10% of $20) to the initial price ($20), for a new price of $22. If the price decreases by 5%, we subtract 5% of the initial price ($1 is 5% of $20) from the initial price ($20), for a new price of $19.

Using Formulas to Compute Missing Values

It will often be useful to compute the value of the numerator (the top half of a fraction) of a particular formula. To do so, we must have values for the other two parts of the formula. For example, consider the relationship between time worked and income. Suppose the slope of the curve showing this relationship is $4 per hour. If you decide to work 7 more hours per week, how much more income will you earn? In this case we can compute the change in income by looking at the formula for the slope of the curve:

$$\text{slope} = \frac{\text{difference in income}}{\text{difference in work time}}$$

$$4 = \frac{\text{difference in income}}{7}$$

Because we know two of the three parts of the slope formula (the slope is $4 and the difference in work time is 7 hours), we can figure out the third part (the difference in income) by plugging in different numbers for the numerator until we find the value that satisfies the formula. In this case the answer is $28: Plugging $28 into the numerator, the difference in income is four times the difference in work time, which is consistent with a slope of $4.

There is a more direct approach to computing the value of the numerator or denominator of a formula. We can rearrange the three parts of the formula to put the missing variable on the left side. For example, to compute the difference in income resulting from a change in work time, we can rearrange the slope formula as follows:

$$\text{difference in income} = \text{slope} \times \text{difference in work time}$$

When we plug in the slope (4) and the difference in work time (7 hours), the change in income is $28 = $4 times 7 hours. We can use the same process to compute the value of the denominator, given values for the two other variables.

Key Terms

negative relationship, 16

positive relationship, 16

slope of a curve, 16

Exercises and Discussion Questions

1. Suppose you belong to a tennis club that has a monthly fee of $100 and a charge of $5 per hour for court time to play tennis.
   a. Use a curve to show the relationship between the monthly bill from the club and the hours of tennis played.
   b. What is the slope of the curve?
   c. If you increase your monthly tennis time by 3 hours, by how much will your monthly bill increase?

2. Suppose that to make pizza, Terry uses three ingredients: tomato sauce, dough, and cheese. Terry initially uses 100 gallons of tomato sauce per day, and the cost of other ingredients (dough, cheese) is $500 per day.
   a. Draw a curve to show the relationship between the price of tomato sauce and the daily cost of producing pizza (for prices between $1 and $5).
   b. To draw the curve, what variables are assumed to be fixed?
   c. What sort of changes would cause movement upward along the curve?
   d. What is the slope of the curve?
   e. What sort of changes would cause the entire curve to shift upward?

3. Compute the percentage changes for the following changes:

Initial Value	New Value	Percentage Change
10	11	_____
100	98	_____
50	53	_____

4. The price of jeans decreases by 15%. If the original price was $20, what is the new price?

5. Suppose the slope of a curve showing the relationship between the number of burglaries per month (on the vertical axis) and the number of police officers (on the horizontal axis) is −0.50 burglaries per police officer. Use the slope formula to compute the change in the number of burglaries resulting from hiring eight additional police officers.

6. Complete the statement: A change in one of the variables shown on a graph causes movement _____ a curve, while a change in one of the variables that is not shown on the graph _____ the curve.

Key Principles
of Economics

Your student film society is looking for an auditorium to use for an all-day Hitchcock film program and is willing to pay up to $200 for one. Your college has a new auditorium that would be perfect for your event. According to the campus facility manager, "The daily rent on the auditorium is $450, an amount that includes $300 to help pay for the cost of building the auditorium, $50 to help pay for insurance, and $100 to cover the extra costs of electricity and janitorial services for a one-day event." How should you respond to the facility manager? As we'll see, if you could persuade the facility manager to use the marginal principle—one of the five key principles of economics—you could rent the facility for only $101.

In this chapter, we introduce five key principles that provide a foundation for economic analysis. The dictionary defines a **principle** as a simple, self-evident truth that most people readily understand and accept. For example, most people readily accept the principle of gravity. The five principles of economics provide the underlying logic of economic analysis and also help explain the tools of economic analysis. As you go through the book, you will see these principles again and again as you do your own economic analysis. Here are some practical questions we answer in this chapter:

Principle: A simple truth that most people understand and accept.

1. What is the cost of producing military goods such as bombs and warships?
2. When is it sensible to tighten the emissions standards on cars, reducing the allowable volume of pollution per mile driven?
3. As a firm hires more workers, what happens to the total output of its factory?
4. If a paper producer dumps chemical waste into a river, what is the true cost of paper?
5. Suppose your wage doubles and at the same time the prices of consumer goods double, too. Are you better off, worse off, or equally well off?

The Principle of Opportunity Cost

The principle of opportunity cost incorporates the notion that no matter what we do, there is always a trade-off. We must trade off one thing for another because resources are limited and can be used in different ways: By acquiring something, we use up resources that could have been used to acquire something else. The notion of opportunity cost allows us to measure this trade-off.

PRINCIPLE of Opportunity Cost

The opportunity cost of something is what you sacrifice to get it.

Opportunity cost: What you sacrifice to get something.

Most decisions involve several alternatives. For example, if you spend an hour studying for an economics exam, you have one less hour to pursue other activities. To determine the opportunity cost of something, we look at what you consider the best of these other activities. For example, suppose the alternatives to studying economics are studying for a history exam and playing a video game. If you consider studying for history a better use of your time than video play, then the opportunity cost of studying economics is what you sacrifice by not studying history. We ignore the video game because that is not the best alternative use of your time.

How can we measure the opportunity cost of an hour spent studying for an economics exam? Suppose an hour of studying history—instead of economics—would increase your grade on a history exam by 4 points. In this case the opportunity cost of an hour studying economics is 4 points lost on the history exam. If the best alternative to studying economics were playing video games, then the opportunity cost would be the pleasure you would get from an hour in the video arcade.

The principle of opportunity cost can be applied to decisions about how to spend a fixed money budget. For example, suppose that you have a fixed budget to spend on recorded music and CDs cost twice as much as audio tapes. If you buy a CD, you must sacrifice two tapes: The opportunity cost of one CD is two audio tapes. A hospital with a fixed salary budget can increase the number of doctors only at the expense of nurses or physician's assistants. If a doctor costs five times as much as a nurse, the opportunity cost of a doctor is five nurses.

In some cases, a good that appears to be free actually has a cost. That's why economists are fond of saying, "There's no such thing as a free lunch." Suppose someone offers to buy you lunch if you agree to listen to a sales pitch for a time-share condominium. Although you don't pay any money for the lunch, there is an opportunity cost because you could spend that time in another way. The lunch isn't free because you sacrifice an hour of your time to get it.

Opportunity Cost and Production Possibilities

The production possibilities curve illustrates the principle of opportunity cost for an entire economy. As you saw in Chapter 1, this curve shows all the possible combinations of goods and services available to an economy, assuming that all its productive resources are fully employed. The principle of opportunity cost explains why the production possibilities curve is negatively sloped. At a given time an economy has fixed amounts of productive resources, so the production of one product comes at the expense of another product.

To illustrate the notions of opportunity cost and production possibilities, consider the trade-offs associated with allocating electricity between competing uses. The Pacific Northwest gets about three-fourths of its electric power from hydroelectric dams, and is therefore heavily dependent on rain and snow to fill the rivers to generate power for homes, offices, factories, and farms.

Figure 2.1 shows a production possibilities curve for the production of aluminum and wheat. In drawing this production possibilities curve, one of the resources held fixed is the amount of electric power. The production of aluminum requires enormous amounts of power for the smelting process, and wheat farming in the Pacific Northwest requires irrigation, with water pumps powered by electricity. Given a fixed amount of

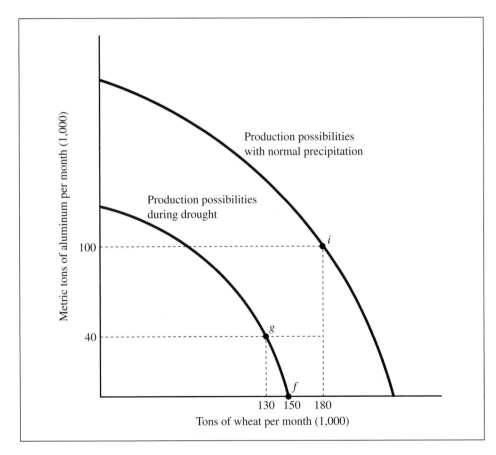

Figure 2.1

Electricity and the Production Possibilities Curve
A drought decreases the amount of electric power available for aluminum smelting and irrigation, shifting the production possibilities curve inward. The region's economy moved from point *i* to point *f*, with aluminum production dropping to zero.

power—and fixed amounts of the other factors of production—there is a trade-off between producing aluminum and wheat. Suppose the region initially chooses point i, with 100,000 metric tons of aluminum and 180,000 tons of wheat.

A prolonged drought in 2000–2001 reduced the flow of water through the region's hydroelectric turbines, reducing the amount of power by about 3,000 megawatts.[1] As shown in Figure 2.1, the drought shifted the production possibilities curve inward, forcing the region to make some difficult choices between aluminum and wheat production. In response to the decrease in hydroelectric power, Bonneville Power Administration (BPA) paid aluminum manufacturers to shut down the region's 10 smelters, so the quantity of aluminum produced dropped to zero. BPA also paid farmers $330 for each acre of land they did not irrigate. Farmers took 90,000 acres out of wheat production, reducing the quantity of wheat produced. In Figure 2.1, the BPA programs moved the region from point i on the production possibilities curve to point f, with zero aluminum and 150,000 tons of wheat.

In this case, the region chose to shut down the aluminum industry, but there were other options. The region could have allocated some of its electric power to aluminum smelting, but given the fixed quantity of hydroelectric power, such a decision would have required a larger reduction in wheat production. In Figure 2.1, the region could have chosen point g, with some aluminum production but less wheat.

Using the Principle: Military Spending, Collectibles

We can use the principle of opportunity cost to explore the cost of military spending. Malaysia bought two warships in 1992, paying a price equal to the cost of providing safe drinking water for the 5 million Malaysians who lacked it.[2] In other words, the opportunity cost of the warships was safe drinking water for 5 million people. In the United States, the opportunity cost of warships could be spending on housing programs for the homeless. When the Soviet Union fell apart and military tensions around the world diminished, citizens in the United States and Western Europe called for massive cuts in defense spending, with the idea of spending the "peace dividend" on social programs. The French cut their annual defense budget by billions of dollars and withdrew 50,000 troops stationed on German soil.[3] In the United States, the number of people employed by the military has decreased, and the Pentagon developed a new program, "Troops to Teachers" to help former soldiers get jobs teaching in local schools.[4] The switch from army duty to teaching reminds us that the opportunity cost of a soldier may be a teacher. For another illustration of opportunity cost, read "A Closer Look: Plowshares, Pruning Hooks, and Ecotels?"

What is the cost of buying a collectible good such as a baseball card, an antique Barbie doll, a Beanie Baby, or a work of art? Suppose you buy an antique Barbie doll for $1,000, intending to resell it for more money a year later. If the price doesn't change and you resell it for $1,000, does that mean that having the doll for a year didn't cost you anything? Applying the principle of opportunity cost, you could have invested the $1,000 in a bank account earning 5% interest, so the cost of having the Barbie doll for the year is the $50 you could have earned in a bank account during the year.

Using the Principle: The Opportunity Cost of a College Degree

What is the opportunity cost of a college degree? Consider a student who spends four years in college, paying $10,000 per year for tuition and books. Part of the opportunity cost of college is the $40,000 worth of other goods the student must sacrifice to pay for tuition and books. Instead of going to college, the student could spend this money on a car, stereo equipment, or ski trips. If instead of going to college, the student could have

PLOWSHARES, PRUNING HOOKS, AND ECOTELS?

The prophet Isaiah predicted, "They will beat their swords into plowshares, and their spears into pruning hooks." All over Central America, old military facilities are being transformed to give eco-tourists a close look at the region's flora and fauna. In the middle of Panama's rain forest, a radar tower used earlier by the U.S. military has been transformed into a seven-room eco-lodge, giving tourists from around the world the opportunity to watch king vultures soar above the forest and view howler monkeys swing from the trees.[5] The Canopy Tower was selected by *Audubon* magazine as one of the world's nine "ultimate outposts" for bird lovers. On the Atlantic side of Panama, the infamous School of the Americas— where the U.S. military educated Latin America military dictators in the arts of war—has been converted into a 310-room hotel. The concrete amphitheater that hosted military briefings will now be used as a vantage point for tourists viewing monkeys and tropical birds.

worked as a bank clerk for $20,000 per year, the other part of the opportunity cost of college is $80,000 that could have been earned during the four years. That makes the total opportunity cost of the student's college degree $120,000:

Tuition and books (4 years at $10,000 per year)	$ 40,000
Opportunity cost of college time (4 years at $20,000 per year)	80,000
Total opportunity cost	$120,000

We haven't included the costs of food or housing in our computations of opportunity cost. That's because a student must eat and live somewhere even if he or she doesn't go to college. But if housing and food are more expensive in college, then we would include the *extra costs* of housing and food in our calculations of opportunity cost.

There are other things to consider in a person's decision to attend college. As we'll see later, a college degree can increase a person's earning power, so there are benefits from a college degree. In addition, there is the thrill of learning and the pleasure of meeting new people. To make an informed decision about whether to attend college, we must compare the benefits to the opportunity costs.

The Marginal Principle

The marginal principle provides a simple decision-making rule that helps individuals, firms, and governments make decisions. Economists think in marginal terms, considering how a one-unit change in one variable affects the value of another variable. When we say marginal, we're considering a small change or an incremental change.

Marginal **PRINCIPLE**

Increase the level of an activity if its marginal benefit exceeds its marginal cost; reduce the level of an activity if its marginal cost exceeds its marginal benefit. If possible, pick the level at which the activity's marginal benefit equals its marginal cost.

Marginal benefit: The extra benefit resulting from a small increase in some activity.

Marginal cost: The additional cost resulting from a small increase in some activity.

The marginal principle enables us to fine-tune our decisions. We can use the principle to determine whether a one-unit increase in a variable would make us better off. For example, a barber could decide whether to keep his or her shop open for one more hour. You could decide whether to study one more hour for a psychology midterm.

The marginal principle is based on a comparison of the marginal benefits and marginal costs of a particular activity. The **marginal benefit** of some activity is the extra benefit resulting from a small increase in the activity, for example, the extra revenue generated by keeping a barbershop open for one more hour. Similarly, the **marginal cost** is the additional cost resulting from a small increase in the activity, for example, the additional costs incurred by keeping a shop open for one more hour. According to the marginal principle, you should continue to increase the activity as long as the marginal benefit is greater than the marginal cost. When you've reached the level where the marginal benefit equals the marginal cost, your fine-tuning is done. It's worth emphasizing that the marginal principle is based on marginal benefits and costs, not total benefits and total costs.

Example: Pedaling for Television Time

To illustrate the marginal principle, consider an experiment conducted by researchers at St. Luke's Roosevelt Hospital in New York City.[6] The researchers addressed the following question, "If a child must pedal a stationary bicycle to run a television set, will he watch less TV, and if so, how much less?"

The researchers randomly assigned sedentary children, age 8 to 12, to two types of TVs. The first had a stationary bicycle in front of the TV, but the TV operated independently of the bicycle: No pedaling was required to operate the TV. In contrast, the second type of TV worked only if the child pedaled a bike facing the TV. The kids in the control group (no pedaling required) watched an average of 20 hours of TV per week, while the kids in the treatment group (pedaling required) watched just a few hours per week.

We can use the marginal principle to explain the results of the experiment. Figure 2.2 shows the marginal benefit of TV time for the control group. The marginal-benefit curve is negatively sloped, reflecting the idea that each hour of TV is worth less than the previous hour: The first hour of TV time is worth more than the second hour; the second hour is worth more than the third; and so on. Specifically, the first hour generates a benefit of $1.30 (shown by point *b*), while the second hour generates a benefit of $1.20 (point *m*). The marginal benefit decreases by $0.05 for each additional hour, reaching $0.35 for 20 hours of TV time (point *n*).

To determine the marginal cost of TV time, we can use the notion of opportunity cost. Suppose that for the typical kid, the value of the next-best alternative use of time is $0.35 per hour. This could be the value of an hour spent playing with friends, reading, studying, or playing videogames. In Figure 2.2, the marginal cost of TV time is constant at $0.35 per hour. Using the marginal principle, we would predict that the typical kid in the control group (no pedaling) would choose point *n*, watching 20 hours of TV per week. It is not sensible to watch the twenty-first hour because the extra benefit exceeds the opportunity cost.

In Figure 2.2, the marginal cost of TV time is higher for the treatment group because pedaling requires effort. To compute the marginal cost of TV for the treatment

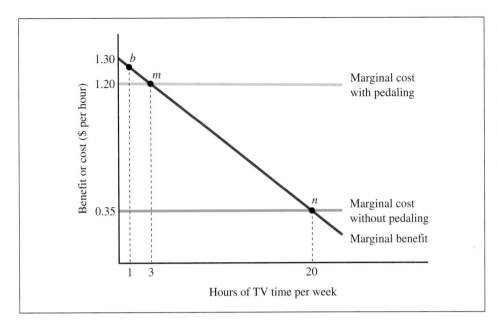

Figure 2.2
**The Marginal
Principle and
TV Time**
If the opportunity cost of TV time is $0.35 per hour and pedaling is not required for TV time, the marginal principle is satisfied at point *n*, and the child will watch 20 hours of TV per week. If pedaling is required and the discomfort of pedaling is $0.85 per hour, the marginal cost of TV time is $1.20 (equal to $0.35 + $0.85), and the marginal principle is satisfied at point *m*, with only 3 hours of TV time per week.

group, we must add the discomfort of pedaling to the opportunity cost of TV time. In Figure 2.2, we assume that the discomfort is measured as $0.85 per hour of pedaling, so the marginal-cost curve is horizontal at $1.20 (equal to $0.35 + $0.85). The marginal principle is satisfied at point *m*, with only 3 hours of TV time. For a pedaling kid, the first hour of TV has a benefit of $1.30 and a cost of $1.20, so it is worthwhile. Similarly, the benefit of the second hour of TV exceeds the marginal cost. For the third hour, the marginal benefit equals the marginal cost, so the marginal principle is satisfied with 3 hours. For the fourth hour of TV time, the marginal benefit is only $1.15, which is less than the marginal cost. Therefore, it would not be sensible to pedal for the fourth hour of TV time.

Using the Marginal Principle: Renting College Facilities, Emissions Standards

Recall the chapter opener about renting a college auditorium to a student film society. If the student group offers to pay $200, should the college accept the offer? The college could use the marginal principle to make the decision.

To decide whether to accept the group's offer, the college should determine the marginal cost of renting out the auditorium. The marginal cost equals the extra costs the college incurs by allowing the student group to use an otherwise vacant auditorium. In our example, the extra cost is $100 for extra electricity and janitorial service. It would be sensible for the college to rent the auditorium because the marginal benefit ($200 from the student group) exceeds the marginal cost ($100). In fact, the college should be willing to rent the facility for any amount greater than $100.

Most colleges do not use this sort of logic. Instead, they use complex formulas to compute the perceived cost of renting out a facility. In most cases, the perceived cost includes some costs that are unaffected by renting out the facility for the day. In our example, the facility manager included $300 worth of construction cost and $50 worth of insurance cost as part of the cost of the auditorium, computing a cost of $450 instead of $100. Because many colleges include costs that aren't affected by the use of a facility, they overestimate the actual cost of renting out their facilities, missing opportunities to serve student groups and make some money at the same time.

We can use the marginal principle to analyze emissions standards for automobiles. The government specifies how much of each pollutant a new car is allowed to emit. For example, the rules specify the maximum volume of carbon monoxide to be emitted per mile of travel. The marginal question is, Should the standard be stricter, with fewer units of carbon monoxide allowed? On the benefit side, a stricter standard reduces the health costs resulting from pollution: If the air is cleaner, people whose respiratory ailments are worsened by air pollution will have fewer visits to doctors and hospitals, lower medication costs, and will lose fewer work days. On the cost side, a stricter standard requires more expensive control equipment on the cars and may also reduce fuel efficiency. Using the marginal principle, the government would make the emissions standard stricter as long as the marginal benefit (savings in health costs) exceeds the marginal cost (the cost of additional equipment and extra fuel).

The marginal principle can be used to think about all sorts of decisions involving how much of an activity to undertake. For an example of decisions involving food and exercise, read "A Closer Look: Why Are We Getting Bigger?"

TEST Your Understanding

1. The cost of a master's degree in engineering equals the tuition plus the cost of books. True or false? Explain.

2. Suppose a nation picks 1,000 young adults at random to serve in the army. What information do you need to determine the cost of using these people in the army?

3. Explain the logic behind the economist's quip, "There is no such thing as a free lunch."

4. If a bus company adds a third daily bus between two cities, the company's total costs will increase from $500 to $600 per day and its total revenue will increase by $150 per day. Should the company add the third bus?

5. Suppose you can save $50 by purchasing your new car in a different city. If the trip requires only $10 in gasoline, is the trip worthwhile?

The Principle of Diminishing Returns

Principle of diminishing returns: As one input increases while the other inputs are held fixed, output increases but at a decreasing rate.

Xena has a small copy shop, with one copying machine and one worker. When the backlog of orders piled up, she decided to hire a second worker, expecting that doubling her workforce would double the output of her copy shop, from 500 pages per hour to 1000. She was surprised when output increased to only 800 pages per hour. If she had known about the **principle of diminishing returns**, she would not have been surprised.

PRINCIPLE of Diminishing Returns

Suppose output is produced with two or more inputs and we increase one input while holding the other input or inputs fixed. Beyond some point—called the point of diminishing returns— output will increase at a decreasing rate.

Xena added a worker (one input) while holding the number of copying machines (the other input) fixed. Because the two workers shared a single copying machine, each worker spent some time waiting for the machine to be available. As a result, although adding the second worker increased the output of the copy shop, output did not double. With a single worker and a single copy machine, Xena has reached the point of dimin-

In the last few decades, the percentage of Americans who are at least 20 pounds overweight has increased steadily, reaching about one-third of the population. In fact, obesity is increasing around the world.[7] We can use the marginal principle to explain the worldwide increase in obesity.

A person gains weight when his or her calorie intake from food exceeds his or her calorie expenditure from physical activity. Over the last hundred years, innovations in agriculture and food processing have reduced the price of food, decreasing the marginal cost of consuming calories. A decrease in the marginal cost of consuming calories will increase food consumption, increasing obesity. Although cheaper food is a factor behind the increase in obesity, the increase in consumption has been relatively small, too small to explain the huge increase in obesity.

What about the expenditure side of the calorie equation? Another factor in the increase in obesity is a widespread decrease in physical activity.[8] Several decades ago, most workers had physically demanding jobs (for example, in factories and farms) and were paid to burn calories: The harder they worked, the more money they earned. In other words, one of the benefits of burning calories was higher income. In recent decades, workers have switched from physically demanding jobs to sedentary jobs in offices. The income from a sedentary job is not related to the worker's physical effort, so one of the benefits of burning calories has disappeared. A decrease in the marginal benefit of burning calories will decrease the number of calories burned, increasing obesity.

What about recreational exercise such as snowboarding, biking, tennis, and basketball? Although we can use recreational exercise to burn those calories that used to be burned on the job, recreational exercise has a cost. In addition to the cost of equipment and club membership, there is the opportunity cost of time spent exercising rather than working, studying, or engaging in other leisure activities.

It appears that changes on the expenditure side of the calorie equation are responsible for the bulk of the recent increase in obesity. Calorie burning has been transformed from a beneficial activity (working harder led to a higher income) into a costly activity (it takes time and money to burn calories off the job). This has naturally led to a decrease in calorie expenditure and increases in obesity.

ishing returns: As she increases the number of workers, output increases but at a decreasing rate. The first worker increases output by 500 pages (from zero to 500), but the second worker increases output by only 300 pages (from 500 to 800).

This principle of diminishing returns is relevant when we try to produce more output in an existing production facility (a factory, a store, an office, or a farm) by increasing the number of workers sharing the facility. When we add a worker to the facility, each worker becomes less productive because he or she works with a smaller piece of the facility: There are more workers to share the machinery, equipment, and factory space.

Table 2.1 Diminishing Returns for Pizza

Number of workers	Total product: pizzas produced	Marginal product
1	12	12
2	18	6
3	21	3
4	22	1

As we pack more and more workers into the factory, total output increases, but at a decreasing rate.

Table 2.1 shows fictitious but convenient data for representing the production of pizza at a particular facility. The production facility is the pizzeria premises, the pizza oven, and all the machines and equipment used to produce pizza. If the pizzeria has a single worker, the single worker assembles 12 uncooked pizzas per hour and pops them into the oven as soon as they are assembled. Suppose he is joined by a second worker, who could also assemble 12 pizzas per hour. Because this second worker shares the pizza oven with the first worker, he will occasionally have to wait before he can pop his assembled pizzas into the oven. Similarly, once the second worker's pizzas are in the oven, the first worker will have to wait to get another batch of his assembled pizzas into that oven. Therefore, we wouldn't expect output to double just because the number of workers has doubled. If total output is only 18 pizzas, adding workers increases output, but at a decreasing rate: Hiring the first worker increased output by 12 pizzas (from zero to 12); hiring the second increased output by only 6 pizzas.

Figure 2.3 shows the pizzeria's **total product curve**, which shows how many pizzas are produced with different quantities of labor. As the pizzeria adds workers, total product increases but at a decreasing rate. Hiring a second worker increases output by 6 pizzas, while hiring a third worker increases output by only 3 pizzas, and hiring a fourth worker increases output by only 1 pizza. It's possible that hiring a fifth worker would not increase output at all or may even reduce output because the workers will get into each others' way.

Total product curve: A curve showing the relationship between the quantity of labor and the quantity of output.

Figure 2.3
Total Product Curve and Diminishing Returns
As the number of workers increases, the number of pizzas produced per hour increases but at a decreasing rate. The second worker increases output by 6 pizzas (from 12 pizzas to 18 pizzas), but the fourth worker increases output by only 1 pizza (from 21 pizzas to 22 pizzas). Diminishing returns occur because workers share a pizza oven.

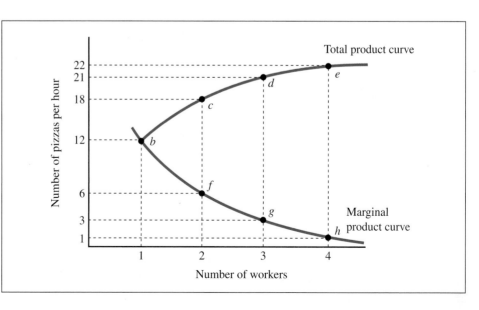

The **marginal product of labor** is defined as the change in output from one additional worker. As shown in the third column in Table 2.1 and Figure 2.3, the marginal product of the first pizza worker is 12 pizzas, and the marginal product of the second worker is 6 pizzas. In a three-worker pizzeria even more time would be spent waiting for an empty oven, and the marginal product of the third worker is only 3 pizzas. When there are diminishing returns, the marginal product of labor decreases as the number of workers increases.

Marginal product of labor: The change in output from one additional worker.

Diminishing Returns in the Short Run

Later in the book, we use the principle of diminishing returns to explore the decisions made by a firm in the short run. The **short run** is a period of time over which one or more factors of production is fixed. In most cases, the short run is defined as a period of time over which a firm cannot modify an existing facility or build a new one. The length of the short run varies across industries, depending on how long it takes to build a production facility. The short run for a hot-dog stand lasts just a few days: That's how long it takes to get another hot-dog cart. In contrast, if it takes a year to build a computer factory, the short run for a computer manufacturer is one year. Diminishing returns occur in the short run because adding workers to an existing facility means that each worker gets a smaller piece of the facility, and each becomes less productive.

Short run: A period of time over which one or more factors of production is fixed; in most cases, a period of time over which a firm cannot modify an existing facility or build a new one.

What About the Long Run?

The principle of diminishing returns is not relevant in the long run. The **long run** is defined as a period of time long enough for a firm to change all its factors of production, meaning that it can modify its existing facility or build a new one. To increase output in the long run, a firm can build an additional production facility and hire workers for the new facility. In the long run, the firm will not suffer from diminishing returns because workers won't have to share a production facility with more and more workers. For example, if the firm builds a second factory that is identical to the first and hires the same number of workers, the firm's output will double. Because firms can duplicate or replicate their production facilities in the long run, the principle of diminishing returns is irrelevant for long-run decisions.

Long run: A period of time long enough that a firm can change all the factors of production, meaning that a firm can modify its existing production facility or build a new one.

The Spillover Principle

In Chapter 1, we discussed the role of markets in determining what goods are produced, how they are produced, and who gets what is produced. The metaphor of the invisible hand suggests that the decisions of millions of consumers and producers, each acting in his or her own self-interest, will frequently promote the interests of society as a whole. Let's consider some circumstances under which we cannot rely on individuals to make choices that are socially desirable.

The **spillover** principle suggests that the costs or benefits of some decisions "spill over" onto people who are not involved in making those decisions. A spillover occurs when people who are external to a decision are affected by the decision. Another word for spillover is *externality*.

Spillover: A cost or benefit experienced by people who are external to the decision about how much of a good to produce or consume.

Spillover **PRINCIPLE**

> **For some goods the costs or benefits associated with producing or consuming those goods are not confined to the person or organization producing or consuming them.**

Let's examine spillover costs first and then turn to spillover benefits. Consider a paper mill that dumps chemical waste into a river, and these wastes make the water unhealthy for drinking. The manager of the paper firm decides how much paper to produce, but some of the costs of producing paper are incurred by people who live in a city downstream from the mill. For example, the city might spend extra money to clean the water before its citizens can safely drink the water. Suppose for each ton of paper produced, the city's water-treatment costs increase by $10. In this case, the spillover cost of paper is $10 per ton. In deciding how much paper to produce, the paper firm will consider the cost of the inputs it buys—for example, it may pay $30 per ton for labor and raw materials—but won't consider the $10 spillover cost incurred by people downstream.

Here are some other examples of spillover costs:

- When Freon leaks from a car air conditioner, it is released into the atmosphere, where it depletes the protective ozone layer and increases the number of cases of skin cancer. A person deciding whether to repair a leaky air conditioner might not consider the effects of releasing freon on the number of cancer cases.

- Your neighbor throws a loud party while you are trying to study. In deciding whether to have the party, the neighbor doesn't consider the consequences for your exam grade.

- Secondhand smoke from cigarettes is bothersome and causes health problems for people who breathe it in.

In each example, the decision-maker incurs some—but not all—of the costs associated with the decision. As we'll see later in the book, the challenge for policymakers is to ensure that everyone who bears the costs of a decision is involved in the decision-making process.

Some goods generate spillover benefits instead of spillover costs. Suppose a farmer is thinking about building a dike or small flood-control dam on a river, at a cost of $100,000. If the farmer's benefit from the dike is only $40,000, he or she won't build it. If three other farmers would experience the same benefit, the total benefit would be $160,000, and it would be sensible for them to get together and build the dike. To make the right decision, we must get all the potential beneficiaries to participate in the decision-making process. If each of the four farmers contributed $25,000 to a dike-building fund, the dike could be built.

There are many goods that generate spillover benefits. Here are some examples:

- If a person contributes money to public television, everyone who watches public television benefits from that contribution. A person deciding whether to contribute doesn't necessarily consider the benefits experienced by others.

- If a scientist discovers a new way to treat a common disease, everyone suffering from the disease will benefit. In deciding what problem to work on, the scientist doesn't necessarily consider the benefits experienced by society as a whole.

- If you get a college degree, you may become a better team worker, so your fellow workers will be more productive and earn more income. In your decision to complete college, you probably didn't consider the benefits to be experienced by your fellow workers.

- If you buy a fire extinguisher, it is less likely that a fire that starts in your apartment will spread to other apartments. In deciding whether to buy an extinguisher, you probably don't consider the benefits to your neighbors.

In each case, some of the benefits spill over onto people who are not involved in the decision-making process, so a decision-maker might decide against taking an action

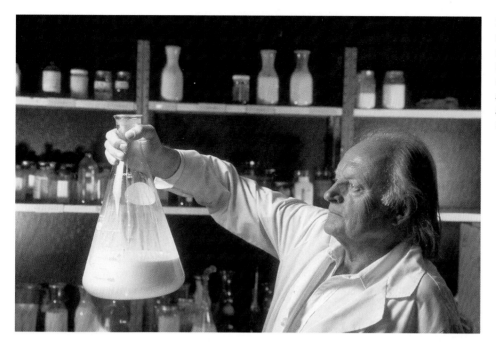

There are spillover benefits from scientific research. In considering what problems to work on, scientists don't necessarily consider the spillover benefits from their research.

that would be beneficial to society. For example, scientists might not spend their time on a project that could reduce disease. Your high-school friends might decide to forgo college because the cost they incur exceeds the benefits they will experience.

If people do not face the full costs and benefits of their actions—including the spillover costs and spillover benefits—we cannot rely on unregulated markets to make decisions that are in the general interests of society. But there are ways for the government to intervene in markets to ensure that decision-makers bear the full costs or experience the full benefits of their actions. Later in the book, we'll discuss some of the ways in which government can solve spillover problems.

TEST Your Understanding

6. When a table producer hired its twentieth worker, the output of its factory increased by five tables per month. If the firm hires two more workers—a twenty-first and a twenty-second worker—would you expect output to increase by ten tables per month?

7. According to the principle of diminishing returns, an additional worker decreases total output. True or False? Explain.

8. For each of the following examples, is there a spillover benefit or a spillover cost?
- Your roommate plays loud, obnoxious music.
- Strip mining causes oil and gas to enter the underground water system, making smoking in your bathtub hazardous to your health.
- A person in a residential neighborhood collects and restores old cars on his front lawn.
- A family contributes $5,000 to an organization that provides holiday meals to the poor.
- A landowner preserves a large stand of ancient trees and thus provides a habitat for the spotted owl (an endangered species).

The Reality Principle

One of the key ideas in economics is that people are interested not just in the amount of money they have, but also in how much their money will buy.

Reality **PRINCIPLE**

> **What matters to people is the real value of money or income—its purchasing power—not the face value of money or income.**

To illustrate this principle, suppose you work in the college bookstore to earn extra money to pay for movies and newspapers. If your take-home pay is $10 per hour, is this a high wage or a low wage? The answer depends on the prices of the goods you buy. If a movie costs $4 and a newspaper costs $1, with one hour of work you could afford to see two movies and buy two papers. The wage may seem high enough for you. But if a movie costs $8 and a newspaper costs $2, an hour of work would buy only one movie and one paper, and the same $10 wage doesn't seem so high. This is the reality principle in action: What matters is not how many dollars you earn but what those dollars will purchase.

The reality principle can explain how people choose the amount of money to carry around with them. Suppose you typically withdraw $40 per week from an ATM to cover your normal expenses. If the prices of all the goods you purchase during the week double, you would have to withdraw $80 per week to make the same purchases. The amount of money people carry around depends on the prices of the goods and services they buy.

Economists use special terms to express the ideas behind the reality principle:

Nominal value: The face value of an amount of money.

- The **nominal value** of an amount of money is simply its face value. For example, the nominal wage paid by the bookstore is $10 per hour.

Real value: The value of an amount of money in terms of the quantity of goods the money can buy.

- The **real value** of an amount of money is measured in terms of the quantity of goods the money can buy. For example, the real value of your bookstore wage would fall as the prices of movies and newspapers increase even though your nominal wage stayed the same.

Using the Reality Principle: Government Programs and Statistics

Government officials use the reality principle when they design public programs. For example, Social Security payments are increased each year to ensure that the checks received by the elderly and other recipients will purchase the same amount of goods and services even if prices have increased.

The government also uses the reality principle when it publishes statistics about the economy. For example, when the government issues reports about changes in "real wages" in the economy over time, these statistics take into account the prices of the goods purchased by workers. Therefore the real wage is stated in terms of its buying power, rather than its face value or nominal value.

TEST Your Understanding

9. Average hourly earnings in the United States increased between 1970 and 1993, but real wages fell. How could this occur?

10. Suppose your wage doubles and so do the prices of all consumer goods. Are you better off, worse off, or just as well off?

11. Suppose your bank pays you 4% per year on your savings account: Each $100 in the bank grows to $104 over a one-year period. If prices increase by 3% per year, how much do you really gain by keeping $100 in the bank for a year?

Using the **TOOLS**

We've explained the five key principles of economics, which provide the foundation of economic analysis. Here are some opportunities to use the principles to do your own economic analysis.

1. ECONOMIC EXPERIMENT: Producing Foldits

Here is a simple economic experiment that takes about 15 minutes to run. The instructor places a stapler and a stack of paper on a table. Students produce "foldits" by folding a page of paper in thirds and stapling both ends of the folded page. There is an inspector who checks each foldit to be sure that it is produced correctly. The experiment starts with a single worker, who has one minute to produce as many foldits as possible. After the instructor records the number of foldits produced, the process is repeated with two students, three students, four students, and so on. The question is, "How does the number of foldits produced change as the number of workers increases?"

APPLICATIONS
2. What's the Cost?

Consider the following statements about costs. Are they correct? If not, provide a correct statement about the relevant cost.

- One year ago, I loaned $100 to a friend, and she just paid me back the whole $100. The loan didn't cost me anything.

- Our sawmill bought five truckloads of logs a year ago for $20,000. Today we'll use the logs to make picnic tables. The cost of using the logs is $20,000.

- Our new football stadium was built on land that a wealthy alum donated to our university. The university didn't have to buy the land, so the cost of the stadium equals the amount the university pays to the construction company that builds the stadium.

3. How Much RAM?

You are about to buy a personal computer and must decide how much random-access memory (RAM) to have in the computer. Suppose each 32-megabyte block of RAM costs $40. For example, a computer with two blocks of memory (64 MB) costs $40 more than a computer with one block (32 MB). The marginal benefit of memory is $320 for the first block and decreases by half for each additional block, to $160 for the second block, $80 for the third block, and so on. How many blocks of memory should you get in your computer? Illustrate your answer with a graph.

Summary

This chapter covers five key principles of economics, defined as simple, self-evident truths that most people would readily accept. If you understand these principles, you are ready for the rest of the book, which will show you how to do your own economic analysis. In fact, if you've done the exercises in this chapter, you're already doing economic analysis.

1. **Principle of opportunity cost.** The opportunity cost of something is what you sacrifice to get it.

2. **Marginal principle.** Increase the level of an activity if its marginal benefit exceeds its marginal cost: reduce the level if its marginal cost exceeds its marginal benefit. If possible, pick the level at which the marginal benefit equals the marginal cost.

3. **Principle of diminishing returns.** Suppose that output is produced with two or more inputs and that we increase one input while holding the other inputs fixed. Beyond some point—called the point of diminishing returns—output will increase at a decreasing rate.

4. **Spillover principle.** For some goods, the costs or benefits associated with the good are not confined to the person or organization that decides how much of the good to produce or consume.

5. **Reality principle.** What matters to people is the real value of money or income—its purchasing power—not the face value of money or income.

Key Terms

long run, 33
marginal benefit, 28
marginal cost, 28
marginal product of labor, 33

nominal value, 36
opportunity cost, 24
principle, 24
principle of diminishing returns, 30

real value, 36
short run, 33
spillover, 33
total product curve, 32

Problems and Discussion Questions

1. Suppose another year of college will increase your lifetime earnings by $30,000. The costs of tuition and books add up to only $8,000 for an additional year. Comment on the following statement: "Because the benefit of $30,000 exceeds the $8,000 cost, you should complete another year of college."

2. To celebrate its fiftieth anniversary, a gasoline station sells gasoline at the price it charged on its first day of operation: $0.10 per gallon. As you drive by the gasoline station, you notice a long line of people waiting to buy gasoline. What types of people would you expect to join the line?

3. You are the mayor of a large city, and you must decide how many police officers to hire. Explain how you could use the marginal principle to help make the decision.

4. Consider a city that must decide how many mobile cardiac arrest units (specially equipped ambulances designed to treat people immediately after a heart attack) to deploy. Explain how you could use the marginal principle to help make the decision.

5. Explain why the principle of diminishing returns does not occur in the long run.

6. You are the manager of a firm that makes computers. If you had to decide how much output to produce in the next week, would you use the principle of diminishing returns? If you had to decide how much output to produce ten years from now, would you use the principle of diminishing returns?

7. Your coffee shop has a single espresso machine. As the firm adds more and more workers, would you expect output (espressos per hour) to increase at a constant rate? Why or why not?

8. Use the spillover principle to discuss the following examples. Are there spillover costs or spillover benefits?

   • Logging causes soil erosion and stream degradation, harming fish.

   • An environmental group buys 50 acres of wetlands to provide a habitat for migrating birds.

   • Your office mate smokes cigarettes.

   • A person buys a dilapidated house in your neighborhood and fixes it up.

9. Explain this statement: The salaries of baseball players have increased in both real and nominal terms.

10. **Web Exercise.** Visit the Web site of the U.S. Environmental Protection Agency, accessing the page with answers to frequently asked questions [*http://www.epa.gov/history/faqs/index.htm*]. What is the EPA's mission, what are its goals, and how does it try to achieve these goals? Why do we need an organization like the EPA?

11. **Web Exercise.** The price of a gallon of gasoline was $0.42 in 1973 and had risen to $1.33 by 1999. How does the change in the price of gasoline compare to the cost of other goods? To answer, go to the

Web site of the Bureau of Labor Statistics [*http://www.bls.gov/cpi/*] and get information on the consumer price index (CPI). The CPI measures the cost of a standard market basket of goods in different years. The value of the CPI is 100 in the base year, and as prices increase, the value of the CPI increases. For example, a value of 123 means that prices have risen to the point where the cost of the standard market basket of goods is 23% higher than it was in the base year. How does the CPI figure for 1973 compare to that of 1999? Has the price of gasoline increased or decreased compared to the cost of other consumer goods?

Take It to the Net

We invite you to visit the O'Sullivan/Sheffrin page on the Prentice Hall Web site at: **http://www.prenhall.com/osullivan/** for additional World Wide Web exercises for this chapter.

Model Answers to Questions

Chapter-Opening Questions

1. To get a warship, we sacrifice something else, such as safe drinking water for 2.5 million Malaysians.

2. According to the marginal principle, the standard should be made stricter if the marginal benefit (the savings in health costs from a cleaner environment) exceeds the marginal cost (the cost of additional equipment and extra fuel).

3. According to the principle of diminishing returns, output will eventually increase at a decreasing rate.

4. The true cost (or what economists refer to as the economic cost) of paper equals the firm's cost (for material, labor, and the paper mill) and the cost associated with the pollution generated as a byproduct of paper.

5. Your income will buy the same quantity of goods and services, so you will be equally well off.

Test Your Understanding

1. False. This statement ignores the opportunity cost of time spent in school.

2. We need the opportunity cost of using the people in the army instead of in the civilian economy. One measure of the opportunity cost is the wages the people could have earned as engineers, teachers, doctors, lawyers, or factory workers.

3. One of the costs of a lunch is the time spent eating it. Even if someone else pays for your lunch, it is not truly free.

4. The marginal benefit is $150, and the marginal cost is only $100 (equal to $600 − $500), so it would be sensible to add the third bus.

5. It will be worthwhile if the opportunity cost of the time spent traveling is less than $40.

6. No. If the factory experiences diminishing returns, the additional output from the twenty-first worker will be smaller than the output from the additional output from the twentieth worker, and the extra output from the twenty-second worker will be even smaller than the output from the twenty-first worker. Therefore, hiring two more workers will increase total output by less than 10 tables.

7. False. The principle says that output increases but at a decreasing rate. Its does not say that hiring another worker decreases output, although this is a possibility with a very crowded factory.

8. *Obnoxious music:* Spillover cost. You must listen to what you consider awful music chosen by your roommate.

   Contaminated water: Spillover cost. People who bathe in the contaminated water risk being burned.

   Yard cars: Spillover cost. For most people, a bunch of partly restored cars (cars jacked up on the street or on the front lawn) is an eyesore.

   Food for the poor: Spillover benefit. Even noncontributors are happy if the poor receive holiday meals.

   Endangered species: Spillover benefit. Many people like the idea of preventing a species from becoming extinct.

9. The price of consumer goods increased faster than wages.

10. Your real wage hasn't changed, so you are just as well off.

Figure 2.A
How Much RAM?

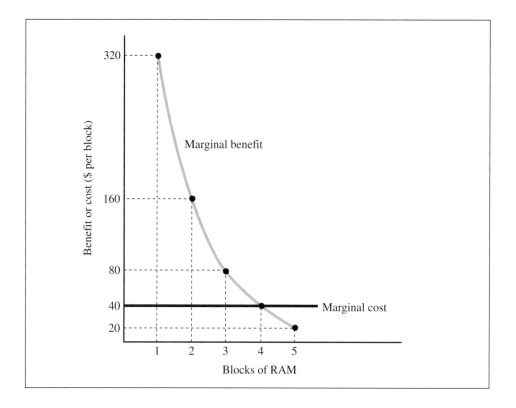

11. A set of goods that cost you $100 will cost you $103 today, so you must use $3 of your $4 interest earnings to cover the higher costs, leaving you with only $1 as actual interest earnings.

Using the Tools

2. What's the Cost? The opportunity cost of the loan to the friend is the interest the person could have earned if the $100 were in a bank account instead.

The opportunity cost of the logs is the amount of money the firm could get by selling the logs on the log market today. The opportunity cost of the land is the value of land in its next-best alternative, for example, a classroom building, a library, or a student center.

3. How Much RAM? See Figure 2.A. The marginal benefit of RAM equals the marginal cost at 4 blocks (128 MB).

 Notes

1. Gail Kinsey Hill, "Aluminum Industry Powering Down," *The Oregonian*, March 11, 2001, page C1; Gail Kinsey Hill, "Paying the Price for Power," *The Oregonian*, May 20, 2001, page A1; Gail Kinsey Hill and Alan Brettmann, "Alcoa OKs Deal with BPA," *The Oregonian*, May 17, 2001, page A1.

2. United Nations Development Program, *Human Development Report 1994* (New York: Oxford University Press, 1994).

3. Alan Riding, "The French Seek Their Own 'Peace Dividend,'" *New York Times,* July 15, 1990, p. 6.

4. Eric Schmitt, "Peace Dividend: Troops Turn to Teaching," *New York Times,* November 30, 1994, p. B1.

5. Jose de Cordoba, "Panama Has Plans for U.S. War Stuff: Turn It Into Hotels," *Wall Street Journal*, January 11, 2000, p. A1.

6. *USA Today*, April 19, 1999, p. 1.

7. World Health Organization, "Obesity: Preventing and Managing the Global Epidemic" (Geneva, 1997).

8. Virgina Postrel, "Economic Scene: Waistlines Are Now Victims of Economic Progress," *New York Times*, March 22, 2001; Tomas Philipson and Richard A. Posner, "Long Run Growth in Obesity as a Function of Technological Change," National Bureau of Economic Research Working Paper, 1999.

Markets and Government in the Global Economy

Imagine a housecleaning race between Shaquille O'Neal and his house cleaner. Shaq wouldn't have to stop vacuuming to move furniture; he could just lift up the chair or sofa with one hand and operate the vacuum with the other hand. With his massive hands and long reach, he could clean a window with one or two quick swipes. Given his 7-foot height and big vertical leap, he wouldn't need a stepladder to reach cobwebs in the ceiling corners.

If Shaq could clean his house faster than anyone else, why would he hire someone to do it? Although Shaq is a more productive cleaner than his house cleaner, he is also a more productive basketball player, and the difference in their basketball skills is enormous compared to the difference in their cleaning skills. Shaq will be better off specializing in the activity that is most productive relative to other people (basketball) and then using his basketball income to hire someone to clean his house. Stated another way, Shaq's opportunity cost of cleaning—the income he could earn playing basketball instead—is higher than his house cleaner's, so it is sensible for Shaq to play basketball and hire a cleaner.

n Chapter 1, we saw that a society makes three types of economic decisions: what products to produce, how to produce them, and who gets the products. In modern economies, most of these decisions are made in markets. In this chapter, we provide an overview of a modern market-based economy, explaining why markets exist, how they operate, and the role government plays in markets. We'll explain what the term *global economy* means, and we'll discuss the rationale for thinking in global terms.

The material we cover in this chapter will help you to understand how a market-based economy operates in today's global environment. Here are some of the practical questions we answer:

1. Why do markets exist?
2. Why do both rich and poor nations benefit from trade?
3. How do governments restrict international trade?
4. What are GATT, NAFTA, and the World Trade Organization?

Why Do Markets Exist?

In Chapter 1, we saw that a market is an arrangement that allows buyers and sellers to exchange things. A buyer exchanges money for a product (a good or service), while a seller exchanges a product for money. Before we explore how a market operates, let's think about why markets exist in the first place.

In the words of Adam Smith, "Man is the only animal that makes bargains: one dog does not exchange bones with another dog." We use markets to make our bargains, exchanging what we have for what we want. If each person were self-sufficient, producing everything he or she consumed, there would be no need for markets. Markets exist because we aren't self-sufficient but instead consume many products produced by other people. To get the money to pay for these products, each of us produces something to sell. Some people grow food; others produce goods such as clothing and bicycles; and others provide services such as medical care or legal advice. Because each of us specializes in one or two products, we need markets to sell what we produce and to buy other

The typical person is not self-sufficient but instead specializes by working at a particular job and uses his or her income to purchase goods and services.

products. Most of us use the labor market to sell our work time to employers and then use our labor income to buy food, housing, appliances, and other products.

Specialization and the Gains from Trade

Why do people specialize and trade? We can explain the rationale for specialization and trade with an example involving two people and two products: bread and shirts. The first two rows of Table 3.1 show how much of each good Brenda and Sam can produce in one hour. Brenda can produce either six loaves of bread or two shirts, while Sam can produce either one loaf of bread or one shirt.

We can use the principle of opportunity cost to explain the benefits from specialization and trade.

PRINCIPLE of Opportunity Cost

The opportunity cost of something is what you sacrifice to get it.

Opportunity cost is defined in terms of one unit of the good or, in our example, in terms of one shirt or one loaf of bread. The opportunity costs are shown in the third and fourth rows of Table 3.1.

1. Brenda's opportunity cost of one shirt is three loaves of bread; that's how many loaves of bread she could produce in the time it takes her to produce one shirt. She needs half an hour to produce a shirt, and during that half hour, she could produce three loaves of bread instead.

2. Brenda's opportunity cost of a loaf of bread is one third of a shirt; that's how many shirts she could produce in the time it takes her to produce a loaf of bread. She needs one sixth of an hour to produce a loaf of bread, and during that one sixth of an hour, she could produce one third of a shirt instead.

3. Sam's opportunity cost of a shirt is one loaf of bread.

4. Sam's opportunity cost of a loaf of bread is one shirt.

Each person could be self-sufficient. Brenda could produce all the bread and shirts she wants to consume, and Sam could produce everything for himself too. But what would happen if they decided to specialize and trade? Suppose they agree to trade at the rate of two loaves of bread for each shirt.

- Brenda could specialize in bread and trade for shirts. Instead of producing one shirt for herself, Brenda could use the time it would take to produce one shirt to produce three loaves of bread; that's her opportunity cost of a shirt. If she then trades two loaves of bread for one shirt, she will have one loaf of bread left over. Specialization and trade make Brenda better off because she gets the same number of shirts and one extra loaf of bread.

Table 3.1   Production per Hour and Opportunity Cost

	Brenda	Sam
Bread produced per hour	6	1
Shirts produced per hour	2	1
Opportunity cost of one loaf of bread	1/3 shirt	1 shirt
Opportunity cost of one shirt	3 loaves of bread	1 loaf of bread

• Sam could specialize in shirts and trade for bread. Instead of producing one loaf of bread for himself. Sam could use the time it would take to produce a loaf of bread to produce one shirt: that's his opportunity cost of a loaf of bread. If he trades the shirt for two loaves of bread, he will have two loaves of bread instead of the one he could have produced himself. Specialization and trade make Sam better off because he gets the same number of shirts and one extra loaf of bread.

This example shows the benefit of specialization and trade. By specializing and trading, each person can consume more.

Opportunity Cost and Comparative Advantage

Comparative advantage: The ability of one person or nation to produce a good at an opportunity cost that is lower than the opportunity cost of another person or nation.

We say that a person has a **comparative advantage** in producing a particular good if he or she has a lower opportunity cost than another person in producing that good. It is sensible for each person to produce the good for which he or she has a comparative advantage.

• **Shirts.** Sam's opportunity cost for shirts (one loaf) is lower than Brenda's (three loaves), so it is sensible for Sam to specialize in shirts and trade for bread.

• **Bread.** Brenda's opportunity cost for bread (one-third shirt) is lower than Sam's (one shirt), so Brenda should specialize in bread and trade for shirts.

As we saw in Table 3.1 specialization and trade—with each person producing the good for which he or she has a comparative advantage—allows each person to consume more.

You may have noticed that Brenda is more productive than Sam in producing both goods. Economists say that she has an **absolute advantage** in producing both goods. Despite her absolute advantage, Brenda gains from specializing in bread and trading some of her bread for shirts produced by Sam. In an hour Brenda can produce twice as many shirts as Sam, but she can produce *six* times as many loaves of bread. Brenda relies on Sam to make some of her shirts because that frees her to spend more time producing bread, the good for which she has the greatest productivity advantage over Sam and therefore a comparative advantage. The lesson is that trade results from comparative advantage (lower opportunity costs), not from absolute advantage.

Absolute advantage: The ability of one person or nation to produce a particular good at a lower absolute cost than that of another person or nation.

TEST Your Understanding

1. Tim's opportunity cost of producing one chair is five tables, while Carla's opportunity cost of producing one chair is one table. Compute each person's opportunity cost of tables. Which person should produce chairs, and which should produce tables?

2. In an hour, a financial planner can either produce three financial statements or answer twelve phone calls. What is the opportunity cost of a financial statement? What is the opportunity cost of a phone call?

3. Wally is the manager of a car wash and is more productive at washing cars than are any of the potential workers he could hire. Does that mean he should wash all the cars himself?

How Do Markets Operate?

Now that we know why markets exist, we're ready to discuss how they operate. In a modern economy, direct trade between two individuals is rare. Rather than producing one consumer good and trading directly with other consumers/producers, most exchanges occur in markets involving firms and other organizations. Markets allow us to exchange what we have for what we want. Most of us work in firms or other organizations for a paycheck, which we then use to buy goods and services from other firms.

The Circular Flow

Figure 3.1 is a **circular flow diagram** of a simple market-based economy. Exchanges occur in two markets:

Circular flow diagram: A diagram showing the flow of money and goods between markets.

- **Factor or input market.** The owners of the factors of production—natural resources, labor, physical capital (machines, buildings, and equipment), and human capital (the knowledge and skills acquired by a worker)—sell these inputs to organizations that use the inputs to produce goods and services.

- **Product or output market.** The organizations that produce goods and services sell their products to consumers.

There are two types of decision-makers in the circular flow model: households and firms.

Households as Sellers and Buyers

Households own the factors of production (inputs) and firms have the knowledge and the ability required to transform inputs into outputs. As shown by arrows B and J in Figure 3.1, the factor markets allow households and firms to exchange inputs and money: Households supply inputs to the factor market (arrow B), and firms pay households for these inputs (arrow J). There are three types of factor markets:

- In the labor market, firms hire workers, paying them wages or salaries in exchange for the output produced by the workers. In the United States, about three-fourths of the income earned by households comes from wages and salaries.

Figure 3.1
Circular Flow Diagram
The circular flow diagram shows the interactions between households (the suppliers of factors of production, or inputs) and firms (the producers of products) in the factor and product markets.

- In the capital market, households use their savings—money in bank accounts, mutual funds, and stock investments—to provide the funds that firms use to buy physical capital, for example, machines, buildings, and equipment. In exchange for the use of their savings, households receive interest payments or some portion of the firm's profits. In the United States, about 20% of the income earned by households comes from interest payments and profits.

- In the natural resource market, households own natural resources (for example, land, minerals, or oil) or own the firms that control the natural resources. These natural resources are sold to firms to use as inputs in the production process.

Households are also involved in the product market, where they purchase goods and services from firms. This interaction between households and firms is shown by arrows H and K in Figure 3.1: Households consume the products produced by firms (arrow H) and pay firms for these products (arrow K). To summarize, households are sellers in factor markets and buyers in product markets.

Firms as Sellers and Buyers

The purpose of a firm is to transform inputs into outputs—products—and then sell the products. Before a firm can produce anything, it must get the inputs required for production. As shown by arrow D in Figure 3.1, inputs flow from the factor markets to the firm, where they're used to produce output. As shown by arrow E, the money to pay for the inputs flows from the firm to the factor market on its way to households. In other words, the firm is a buyer in the factor markets. Once the firm produces a product, it brings it to the product market (shown by arrow F) and receives money when consumers buy it (arrow R).

Figure 3.1 shows that economic activity is circular. The inner circle shows physical flows (products and inputs), and the outer circle shows monetary flows (money exchanged for inputs or products). Firms pay money to households for their inputs. In the other direction, households pay money to firms when they buy the firms' products.

This circular flow diagram is a starting point for describing how an economy works, but it is incomplete for two reasons. First, the diagram does not show the role of government in the economy. As we'll see throughout the book, the government is a big part of a market-based economy: Government provides some goods and services, buys inputs, redistributes income, collects taxes, and regulates firms. Second, the diagram does not show the effects of international trade, which, as we'll see later in the chapter, is a large and growing part of most modern economies.

The Global Economy and Interdependence

In today's global economy, many products are produced in one country and sold in another. International trade is one component of the global economy. After introducing some of the language of international trade, we discuss the foreign-exchange market, which allows people to exchange currency, facilitating trade between nations with different currencies. Then we'll discuss global interdependence, exploring some of the economic ripple effects of changes in individual nations.

Markets and International Trade

Recall how Brenda and Sam benefited from specialization and trade. We saw that specialization and trade are beneficial if there are differences in opportunity costs that generate comparative advantages. Although our example consisted of two individuals, the same ideas apply to nations, which differ in their natural resources, climate, public infrastructure, physical capital, and labor forces. The resulting differences in productiv-

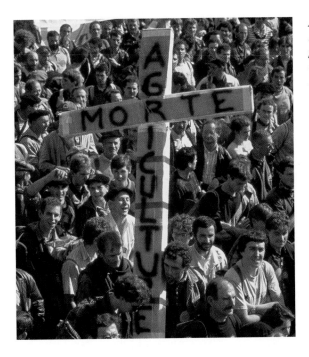

A proposal to lift trade restrictions is often met with opposition from people employed in protected domestic industries. French farmers protested against GATT.

ity mean that, like an individual, a nation has a comparative advantage in the production of particular products. When a nation specializes in production and engages in trade, it gives its citizens an opportunity to consume larger quantities of goods and services.

A nation will specialize in the product for which it has a comparative advantage. Like trade between individuals, international trade results from comparative advantage, not absolute advantage. This explains why a rich nation trades with a poor nation, even though a rich nation is more productive and has an absolute advantage in all products. For example, suppose the United States is more efficient than India in producing both computers and clothing but that the United States has a comparative advantage in computers while India has a comparative advantage in clothing. Both countries would be better off if each country specialized—the United States in computers and India in clothing—and traded. Remember, it is comparative advantage that matters. Even if the United States were absolutely more efficient in producing clothing, both countries would still benefit from specialization and trade.

International Trade: Exports and Imports

From the perspective of the United States, an **export** is a good produced in the United States and sold in another country, while an **import** is a good produced elsewhere and purchased in the United States. As shown in Figure 3.2, the leading U.S. exports are agricultural commodities, electrical machinery, and chemicals, while the leading imports are automated data-processing equipment (ADP) and office machinery, electrical machinery, vehicles, and crude oil. Figure 3.3 shows the volumes of trade between the United States and its major trading partners. The three largest partners are Canada, Japan, and Mexico.

Protectionist Policies

Despite the advantages from global specialization, most nations use trade barriers to restrict international trade. Why? Trade barriers are often designed to protect domestic firms from competition from foreign firms and to protect the jobs of workers in industries that would be adversely affected by trade. These industries are often very successful

Export: A good produced in the "home" country (for example, the United States) and sold in another country.

Import: A good produced in a foreign country and purchased by residents of the "home" country (for example, the United States).

Figure 3.2
Major Imports and Exports of the United States, 1999

Source: Statistical Abstract of the United States 2000 (Washington, DC: U.S. Government Printing Office, 2001).

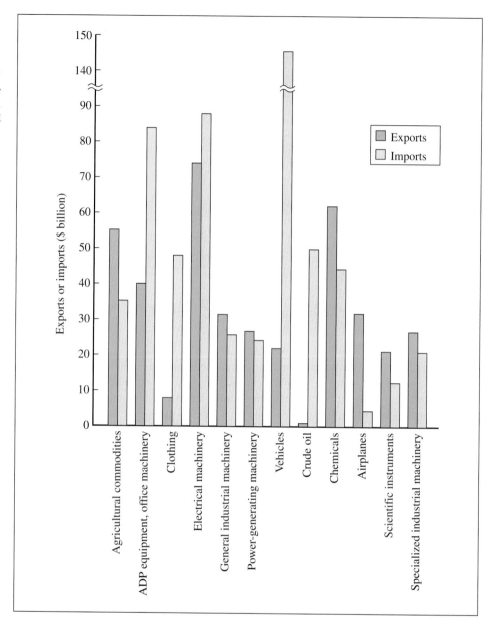

in lobbying politicians to obtain protections from trade. Policies that restrict trade are known as **protectionist policies**.

There are three common forms of protection:

- A quota is an absolute limit on the volume of a particular good that can be imported into a country. If a country imposed a quota on steel imports of 200,000 tons, only 200,000 tons of steel could enter that country.

- Under a voluntary export restraint, one country agrees to limit the volume of exports to another country. For example, the Japanese government agreed to limit the number of Japanese cars sold in the United States and Europe. Many nations use voluntary export restraints to avoid explicit quotas, which are often prohibited by treaties.

- A tariff is a special tax on imported goods. For example, a 10% tariff on imported television sets means that the tax on a $300 imported TV set is $30.

Protectionist policies: Rules that restrict the free flow of goods between nations, including tariffs (taxes on imports), quotas (limits on total imports), voluntary export restraints (agreements between governments to limit imports), and nontariff trade barriers (subtle practices that hinder trade).

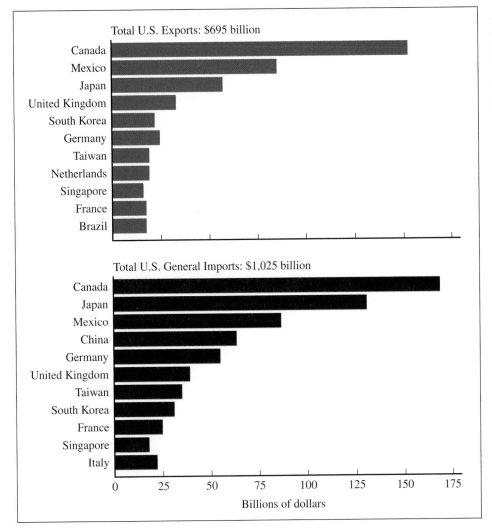

Figure 3.3
Major Trading Partners of the United States, 1999

Source: Statistical Abstract of the United States 2001 (Washington, DC: U.S. Government Printing Office, 2001).

Total U.S. Exports: $695 billion

Canada
Mexico
Japan
United Kingdom
South Korea
Germany
Taiwan
Netherlands
Singapore
France
Brazil

Total U.S. General Imports: $1,025 billion

Canada
Japan
Mexico
China
Germany
United Kingdom
Taiwan
South Korea
France
Singapore
Italy

0   25   50   75   100   125   150   175

Billions of dollars

There are other ways a nation can limit imports without an official trade barrier. One way is to target imports for extra-strict enforcement of health and safety laws. A foreign firm that is faced with stricter standards than domestic firms may decide to stay out of the market. Another way a country can restrict imports is to design or allow its customs system to be inefficient and sluggish. If it takes a lot of time and effort to pass imported goods through customs, foreign firms may drop out of the market. These are examples of nontariff trade barriers, practices that do not show up as official laws but have the same effects as tariffs and quotas.

History of Tariff and Trade Agreements

Since 1980, the average U.S. tariff has been about 5% of the value of imported goods, a rate that is close to the average tariffs in Japan and most European nations but very low by historical standards. Under the Smoot-Hawley tariffs of the 1930s, the average tariff in the United States was a whopping 59% of value. Tariffs are lower today because of several international agreements that reduce tariffs.

The first major trade agreement following World War II was the **General Agreement on Tariffs and Trade [GATT]**. This agreement was initiated in 1947 by the United States and 23

General Agreement on Tariffs and Trade [GATT]: An international agreement that has lowered trade barriers between the United States and other nations.

other nations and now has over 100 member nations. There have been eight rounds of GATT negotiations over tariffs and trade regulations, resulting in progressively lower tariffs for the member nations. The last set of negotiations, the Uruguay round, completed in 1994, decreased tariffs by about one-third of the previous level. In 1995 the **World Trade Organization [WTO]** was formed to enforce GATT and other international trade agreements. As explained in "A Closer Look: Video Piracy in China," an important international issue for WTO nations is the piracy of intellectual property such as videos.

In recent years, various groups of nations have formed trade associations to lower trade barriers and promote international trade.

- The **North American Free Trade Agreement [NAFTA]**. This agreement took effect in 1994 and will be implemented over a 15-year period. The agreement will eventually eliminate all tariffs and other trade barriers between Canada, Mexico, and the United States. NAFTA may soon be extended to other nations in the Western Hemisphere.

- A total of 15 nations have joined the **European Union [EU]**, an organization designed to remove all trade barriers within Europe and create a single market. Eleven of these nations have already committed to using a single currency, called the euro.

- The leaders of 18 Asian nations formed an organization called **Asian Pacific Economic Cooperation [APEC]** and in 1994 signed a nonbinding agreement to reduce trade barriers between their nations.

Currency Markets and Exchange Rates

The **foreign exchange market** allows people to exchange one nation's currency for another nation's currency, such as U.S. dollars for Japanese yen. Because each nation uses a different currency, international trade would not be possible without a foreign exchange market. A U.S. firm that sells computers in Japan is paid in yen but must pay its U.S. workers with dollars. The foreign exchange market allows the U.S. firm to exchange the

World Trade Organization [WTO]: An organization that oversees GATT and other international trade agreements.

North American Free Trade Agreement [NAFTA]: An international agreement that lowers barriers to trade between the United States, Mexico, and Canada (signed in 1994).

European Union [EU]: An organization of European nations that has reduced trade barriers within Europe.

Asian Pacific Economic Cooperation [APEC]: An organization of 18 Asian nations that attempts to reduce trade barriers between their nations.

Foreign exchange market: A market in which people exchange one currency for another.

A CLOSER LOOK   VIDEO PIRACY IN CHINA

The heart of China's home entertainment is the video compact disk (VCD), the analog of the videocassette used widely in the United States. Consumers rent disks from thousands of neighborhood video outlets. About 95% of the VCDs in China are pirated versions—illegal copies made from laserdisks or with handheld video cameras in theaters.[2] The copies made with video cameras—which often feature audience laughter and big heads blocking the screen—are released just days after the film is first screened in the United States or Hong Kong. At a price of $1 to $2, the pirated versions of movies like *The Grinch*, *Gladiator*, and *Mission Impossible-2* are bargains compared to the $20 price tag for legitimate versions.

The piracy problem is straining China's relations with its trading partners as the nation prepares to join the World Trade Organization (WTO). Once China joins the WTO, the member nations are expected to apply pressure on China to reduce the piracy problem.

yen it receives for dollars. The **exchange rate** is defined as the rate at which we can exchange one currency for another. At an exchange rate of 90 yen per dollar, if the U.S. firm sells a computer in Japan for 90,000 yen, it can exchange the yen for 1,000 U.S. dollars.

Exchange rate: The price at which currencies trade for one another.

Many newspapers publish information on foreign exchange rates. As shown in Table 3.2, exchange rates are quoted in two equivalent ways. First, the "value in dollars" indicates how many dollars a single unit of the foreign currency will buy. For example, the value in dollars of a German mark was $0.4332, meaning that 1 mark could be exchanged for $0.4332. Second, "the units per dollar" indicates how many units of the foreign currency are needed to buy 1 dollar. To get 1 dollar, you needed 2.3079 marks.

We can use the exchange rate between two currencies to determine the actual cost of a good produced in another nation. Suppose you are planning a trip to Mexico and want to determine the cost of staying in a hotel. If a hotel room in Mexico costs 450 pesos per night and the exchange rate is 9 pesos per dollar, the hotel room will cost you $50: To get the 450 pesos to pay for the room, you must sacrifice $50. If the exchange rate were 10 pesos per dollar instead, the hotel room would cost you only $45 a night: To get the 450 pesos, you would need only $45. The greater the exchange rate (pesos per dollar), the cheaper the hotel room in Mexico.

Global Interdependence

In the modern global economy, the nations of the world are intertwined. The fortunes of one nation affect those of its trading partners. Suppose the German economy goes through a bad spell and faces severe economic difficulties, including a high unemployment rate. As a result, German consumers will purchase fewer goods and services, including fewer imported goods from countries like Belgium. Firms in Belgium will produce less output and will hire fewer workers. The unemployment that began in Germany thus spreads to Belgium. Through international economic linkages. Germany's bad times can be transmitted to Belgium.

While trade brings the advantages of world specialization, it also creates vulnerabilities. The benefits of increased world productivity come at the cost of increased reliance

Table 3.2 Exchange Rates in July 2001

Nation	Currency	Value in Dollars (U.S. $ equivalent)	Units per Dollar (Currency per U.S. $)
Australia	Dollar	0.51	1.96
Brazil	Real	0.41	2.41
Britain	Pound sterling	1.41	0.71
Canada	Dollar	0.66	1.51
France	Franc	0.1291	7.74
Germany	Mark	0.4332	2.3079
Hong Kong	Dollar	0.1282	7.799
Ireland	Punt	1.07	0.92
Israel	Shekel	0.24	4.19
Japan	Yen	0.0079	125.75
Mexico	Peso	0.1095	9.12
Saudi Arabia	Rial	0.27	3.75

on the economic fortunes of economic neighbors. Large economic powers such as the United States, Germany, and Japan can have a large effect on the economies of other nations. The saying "When the U.S. sneezes, Canada catches a cold" expresses this idea. Countries that produce key raw materials, such as oil, can also have very large effects. During the 1970s, the oil-producing countries raised the world price of oil and inflicted much economic hardship on large countries such as the United States, Japan, and the countries of Western Europe.

The economies of the world are linked through the financial system as well as through trade in goods and services. One of the most important developments of the last decade has been the increase in the financial linkages between countries. For example, the residents of the United States can now routinely invest in firms in Asia and Latin America. A firm in Thailand that wants to undertake a major new venture might borrow funds in Western Europe, Japan, or the United States. Large banks in Japan have routinely made loans to firms throughout the world. In the past, many governments limited the ability of their citizens and businesses to borrow or lend in foreign countries. But in recent years, many economies have undergone a process of **financial liberalization**, opening up their financial markets to participants from foreign countries.

> **Financial liberalization:** The opening of financial markets to participants from foreign countries.

Financial liberalization creates many new opportunities for countries. They no longer need to rely on their own residents to finance important projects but instead can tap the resources from the entire world. Similarly, financial liberalization allows investors to scout the world for new and profitable investment opportunities and does not restrict them to their own country. In general, financial liberalization facilitates global specialization and leads to a more efficient world economy.

Financial liberalization creates opportunities and creates new vulnerabilities. Suppose investors have a bad experience in one developing country and become convinced that the economic prospects of that country have deteriorated. They begin to cut back on their loans to that country, slowing down economic activity there. At the same time, they may conclude, perhaps inaccurately, that similar difficulties plague a neighboring country, causing them to pull funds from that country too, also causing economic difficulties in the neighboring country. Before financial liberalization, neither country would have attracted the funds necessary to grow as rapidly as they did. But they would not have been subject to the changing opinions of the international financial markets either.

Because of the tighter linkages in product and financial markets, the economies of the world are becoming more and more interdependent. The greater flow of products across national boundaries and the increases in international financial transactions have increased the need for international institutions to help make the system work. The **International Monetary Fund**, headquartered in Washington, D.C., works closely with the governments of the world to promote efficient and effective financial policies to facilitate the growth in world trade and commerce.

> **International Monetary Fund:** An organization that works closely with national governments to promote financial policies that facilitate world trade.

TEST Your Understanding

4. What fraction of household income comes from wages and salaries?

5. What do firms do?

6. Nation T can produce either 3 tons of wheat or 9 tons of steel, while nation H can produce either 4 tons of wheat or 8 tons of steel. Which nation has a comparative advantage in wheat? Which has a comparative advantage in steel?

7. Complete the statement with *more* or *less*: If the exchange between U.S. dollars and French francs went from 5 francs per dollar to 3 francs per dollar, this would tend to make French goods _____ expensive to U.S. citizens.

Government in a Market Economy

Now that we know how markets operate, we can consider the role of government in a market-based economy. In most modern societies, the government has five general responsibilities.

1. Providing goods and services. The government provides all sorts of goods and services, including streets and highways, education, parks, public safety, national defense, and space exploration.
2. Redistributing income. In a market-based economy, some people earn much more income than others, and the government redistributes income to the poor.
3. Taxation. The government uses taxes on various goods and services to support its spending programs.
4. Regulation of business practices. The government uses regulations to control pollution, encourage competition among firms, and improve the safety of consumer goods.
5. Trade policy. The government uses various policies to control international trade, promoting some types of trade and restricting others.

Although it's convenient to speak of "the government," it's important to recognize that there are thousands of governments in the United States, and each citizen deals with at least three levels of government. Local governments pave the streets and run the primary and secondary schools, while state governments pave the highways and run the colleges and universities. The national government provides goods and services for the nation as a whole, including national defense and space exploration. In addition, the national government has the primary responsibility for income redistribution. All three levels of government impose taxes to pay for their spending programs, and all three regulate business practices.

Government Spending Programs

How do governments in the United States spend the money they collect from taxpayers? Figure 3.4 shows the budget breakdown for the three levels of government.

1. There are more than 80,000 local governments in the United States, including municipalities (city governments), counties, school districts, and special districts responsible for providing services such as water, fire protection, and libraries. Local governments spend most of their money on education (kindergarten through high school), public welfare and health (payments to poor households and support for public hospitals), highways, and police protection.
2. For states, the biggest spending programs are education (including colleges and universities), public welfare, highways, health and hospitals, and corrections (state courts and prisons).
3. For the federal government, the biggest spending programs are national defense, programs for the elderly (Social Security and Medicare), income security (payments to the poor), and interest on the national debt.

Criteria for a Tax System

If the government is to play a role in the market-based economy, taxes are necessary. The practical policy question is whether our current tax system is the best we can do. To most people, a good tax system is fair and easy to understand, and does not disrupt markets that otherwise operate effectively. Let's take a closer look at each one of these criteria.

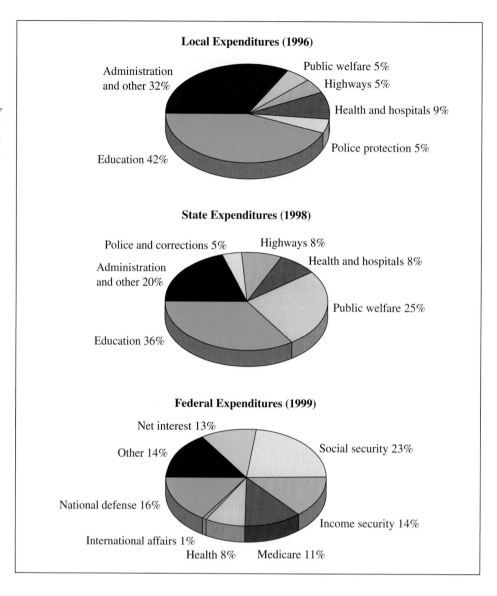

Figure 3.4

Percentages of Government Spending on Various Programs

Source: Statistical Abstract of the United States, 2000: Economic Report of the President (Washington, DC: U.S. Government Printing Office, 1998).

Local Expenditures (1996)

Administration and other 32%
Public welfare 5%
Highways 5%
Health and hospitals 9%
Police protection 5%
Education 42%

State Expenditures (1998)

Police and corrections 5%
Highways 8%
Health and hospitals 8%
Administration and other 20%
Public welfare 25%
Education 36%

Federal Expenditures (1999)

Net interest 13%
Other 14%
Social security 23%
National defense 16%
Income security 14%
International affairs 1%
Health 8%
Medicare 11%

Benefit-tax approach: The idea that a person's tax liability should depend on his or her benefits from government programs.

Horizontally equity: The idea that people in similar economic circumstances should pay similar amounts in taxes.

Vertical equity: The idea that people with more income or wealth should pay higher taxes.

There are two perspectives on the issue of fairness. The **benefit-tax approach** suggests that a person's tax liability should depend on his or her benefits from government programs. For example, the revenue from the gasoline taxes in the United States supports the construction and maintenance of highways. The more you drive, the more you use the highway system *and* the more gasoline taxes you pay. For many government programs, however, it would be difficult, if not impossible, to determine just how large a benefit a particular citizen receives. For example, all law-abiding citizens benefit from the criminal justice system (police, courts, prisons), but because we don't know how much each person benefits from the system, it would be impossible to determine just how much each person should pay for it.

The second perspective on fairness focuses on a citizen's ability to pay. A tax is **horizontally equitable** if people in similar economic circumstances pay similar amounts in taxes. For example, under a pure income tax, each person with a given amount of income would pay the same income tax. In contrast, the idea of **vertical equity** is that people with more income or wealth should pay higher taxes. The practical policy question is *how much* more they should pay. A tax system that is vertically equitable in the eyes of one citizen may be inequitable in the eyes of another.

The second criterion for evaluating a tax system is simplicity. If you've ever filled out an income tax form, you know that the tax system in the United States is very complex. The average household devotes about 27 hours per year to federal tax preparation. In addition, each household must contend with state and local taxes. Firms spend large sums of money to comply with the tax code, and pass on these costs to consumers in the form of higher prices. Despite the frequent calls for tax simplification, there is no sign that it will get any easier to comply with the tax system.

The third criterion for the tax system concerns its effects on market decisions. If a particular market does not generate any spillover benefits or costs, there is no reason to disrupt the market. When a tax is imposed, many people try to avoid the tax by changing their behavior. Taxes distort people's choices and disrupt markets, and one of the objectives of tax policy is to minimize these disruptions. One implication is that taxes should be spread over many goods and services rather than just a few. For example, a special tax on electricians would discourage people from becoming electricians and disrupt the market for electricians. In contrast, a general income tax would have roughly the same effect on occupations that generate the same income, so the market disruptions will be smaller.

There are many trade-offs associated with designing a tax system. A tax system that is pretty simple may not be equipped to deal with the many different circumstances of taxpayers, leading to horizontal inequities. A simple tax system may also be vertically inequitable in the eyes of many taxpayers, with high-income people paying either too much or too little. A tax that is considered vertically equitable is likely to distort peoples' decisions, causing disruptions in many markets. The challenge for policymakers is to develop a system with the appropriate balance among the three criteria.

The Revenue Sources of Local, State, and Federal Governments

Now that we know the criteria for a tax system, let's look at the tax structures of the three levels of government. Figure 3.5 shows the revenue sources for localities, states, and the federal government.

1. The major revenue source for local governments is the property tax. The property tax is a flat percentage of the value of residential, commercial, or industrial property. For example, if the tax rate is 2% and you own a property with a market value of $100,000, your annual tax would be $2,000 (0.02 times $100,000).

2. The major revenue sources for the states are sales taxes and individual income taxes. The sales tax is a fixed percentage of the purchase price of a consumer good. A person's state income tax liability is based on how much he or she earns, with tax rates that typically increase as income increases.

3. The major revenue sources for the federal government are individual income taxes and "social insurance and retirement receipts," which are taxes collected to support Social Security, Medicare, and workers' compensation.

To see how tax rates in the United States compare to those in other industrialized nations, read "Tax Rates in Different Nations."

Government Regulation of Markets

It is possible to imagine a world in which the government plays no role in the economy. In such a world, all economic decisions (what products to produce, how to produce them, and who gets the products) would be made in unregulated markets. This is

Figure 3.5
**Percentages of
Government
Revenue from
Different Sources**

*Source: Statistical Abstract of
the United States, 2000: Economic Report of the President*
(Washington, DC: U.S. Government Printing Office, 1998):
Census Bureau data at *http://
www.census.gov/govs/www/*.

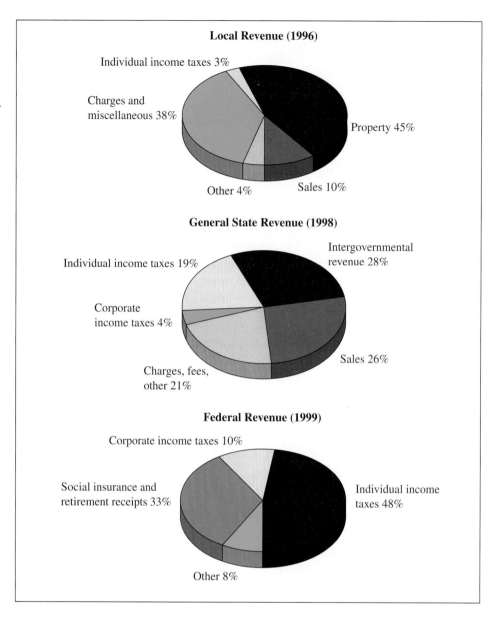

referred to as laissez-faire, which translates from French roughly as "let it happen." In
modern economies, however, the government plays an important role in many markets.

The government establishes a legal system to enforce property rights. If you buy
land to build a house, you must register your purchase with the appropriate government
agency and ensure that you are buying the land from the rightful owner and that no one
else has a claim on that property. The government's legal system also makes it possible
for one person to write a binding contract with another. A contract facilitates a transaction because each person involved in the transaction can be confident that the other person will fulfill his or her part of the deal. Without the legal system to enforce contracts,
it would be nearly impossible to conduct business.

Governments at all levels also regulate economic activity. At the national level, the
government regulates the purchase and sale of stocks and bonds, promotes competition
among firms by blocking some corporate mergers, promotes safety in food products and

TAX RATES IN DIFFERENT NATIONS

How does the United States rank in terms of tax revenue as a fraction of total income? The Figure shows tax rates for OECD nations, including the United States. The United States is at the low end, with only four nations (Turkey, Japan, Korea, and Mexico) with lower tax rates. One reason for the relatively low tax rate in the United States is that the government pays a relatively small share of its citizens' health-care costs.

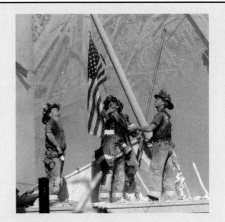

Tax Rates in OECD Nations, 1998

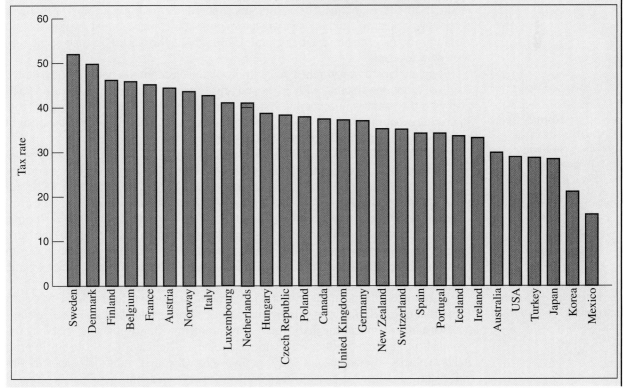

workplaces, and limits air and water pollution. The states regulate banking, transportation, education, land use, and many professions (physicians, lawyers, pharmacists, and house builders). Local governments use zoning and other regulations to control land use. It is difficult to think of a single area in which the government does not influence markets.

Because government plays such an important role in most modern market-based economies, most countries have what economists call **mixed economies**. Although most economic decisions are made in markets, these markets are regulated by the government, and the regulations differ from nation to nation and from state to state.

Mixed economy: A market-based economic system in which government plays an important role, including the regulation of markets, where most economic decisions are made.

Alternative Economic Systems

Centrally planned economy: An economy in which a government bureaucracy decides how much of each good to produce, how to produce the goods, and how to allocate the products among consumers.

An alternative to a market-based economy is a **centrally planned economy**, an economic system under which production and consumption decisions are made by a central government, not by individual producers and consumers in markets. In a pure centrally planned economy, there is no private property: everything is owned by the government.

In a centrally planned economy, a central bureaucracy makes all the decisions about what products to produce, how to produce them, and who gets the products. Bureaucrats tell each firm how much it should produce. One challenge for bureaucrats is to ensure that each firm has enough raw materials and workers to meet the firm's production goals. Another challenge for bureaucrats is to accurately assess the preferences of consumers so that the goods that are produced are actually desired by consumers.

Until the late 1980s, central planners ran the economies of the Soviet Union, most nations in Eastern Europe, and China. While some of these economies were effective in developing heavy industry, there were several major problems. The fundamental problem was that the bureaucrats lacked the information needed to make the millions of decisions required to allocate raw materials and other inputs to thousands of production facilities in the economy. The result was inefficiency and waste. Moreover, these economies lacked the flexibility of market economies. As computers and the information revolution transformed market economies throughout the world, planned economies were slow to adapt.

Transition: The process of shifting from a centrally planned economy toward a mixed economic system, with markets playing a greater role in the economy.

Many nations that had relied on centrally planned economies have recently shifted to mixed economic systems, with prices and private property. Two challenges are associated with the **transition** to economic systems in which markets play a much greater role in making economic decisions about production and consumption: the establishment of property rights and privatization of state-run firms.

The first challenge is to establish clear property rights and the rule of law. If property rights are uncertain, entrepreneurs will not be willing to make large investments and take risks because there will be no guarantee that they will benefit from successful projects. Entrepreneurs need law and order to prevent criminals from stealing the profits from legitimate enterprises. Russia has had severe problems with organized crime, making it difficult for ordinary businesses to exist without paying large sums for "protection." Entrepreneurs also need a legal system that prevents the government from unduly interfering with their everyday business activities. It will take time to develop the legal culture necessary to support a market-based economy.

Privatizing: The process of selling state firms to individuals.

A second challenge in the transition to a mixed economy is to **privatize** state-owned firms, that is, to sell the firms to individuals. Once a firm is sold off, it is allowed to compete with other firms in the marketplace. One problem with privatizing is that only the profitable production facilities will continue to operate. No one will want to buy unprofitable facilities, so many people will lose their jobs. Of course, other job opportunities will eventually appear as successful operations are expanded, but there may be a period when total employment drops. Another problem with privatizing is that there may be only one or two firms in a certain market, so even after the firms are privatized, there will be little competition between the privatized firms.

The difficulties for societies making the transition to a mixed economy make one thing clear. To have a successful market-based economy, the government must establish property rights, enforce laws, and provide a framework of regulation. Modern Western market economies have developed the roles of government gradually over many decades. Economies making the transition need to develop these roles more rapidly.

TEST Your Understanding

8. Match each trade restriction with its description.

Restriction	Description
A. Tariffs	1. Limits on total imports.
B. Quotas	2. Hidden impediments to trade.
C. Voluntary export restraints	3. Agreements between nations to restrict trade.
D. Nontariff trade barriers	4. Taxes on imports.

9. Complete the statement with GATT or NAFTA: _____ is a worldwide trade agreement, while _____ applies to a single continent.

Summary

This chapter has provided an overview of a market-based economy. In the factor markets, households provide labor and capital to firms in exchange for money. In the product markets, firms provide goods and services to households in exchange for money. In recent years, international trade agreements have lowered the barriers to trade, hastening the move to a global economy. Here are the main points of the chapter:

1. Most people are not self-sufficient but instead specialize to earn income, which they use to buy goods and services from others.

2. A system of international specialization and trade is sensible because people and nations have different opportunity costs of producing goods, giving rise to comparative advantage.

3. The foreign exchange market allows people to exchange one currency for another, facilitating international trade.

4. The free flow of goods can be hampered by barriers to trade, including tariffs, quotas, voluntary export restraints, and nontariff trade barriers. There are many international agreements designed to reduce trade barriers, including GATT, NAFTA, and the European Union.

Key Terms

absolute advantage, 44
Asian Pacific Economic Cooperation [APEC], 50
benefit-tax approach, 54
centrally planned economy, 58
circular flow diagram, 45
comparative advantage, 44
European Union [EU], 50
exchange rate, 51

export, 47
financial liberalization, 52
foreign exchange market, 50
General Agreement on Tariffs and Trade [GATT], 49
horizontal equity, 54
import, 47
International Monetary Fund, 52

mixed economy, 57
North American Free Trade Agreement [NAFTA], 50
privatizing, 58
protectionist policies, 48
transition, 58
vertical equity, 54
World Trade Organization [WTO], 50

Problems and Discussion Questions

1. Recall the example of Brenda and Sam shown in Table 3.1. Suppose a technological innovation increases shirt productivity of both people: Brenda can now produce three shirts per hour, while Sam can now produce two shirts per hour. Their productivity for bread has not changed. Suppose they agree to trade one shirt for each loaf of bread. Will both people gain from specialization and trade?

2. Consider two financial planners, Phil and Frances. In an hour Phil can either produce one financial

statement or answer ten phone calls, while Frances can either produce three financial statements or answer twelve phone calls. Does either person have an absolute advantage in producing both products? Should the two planners be self-sufficient (each producing statements and answering phones) or should they specialize?

3. Professor A is a better teacher than professor B for both an undergraduate course (U) and a graduate course (G). As the chair of the department, you measure teaching performance as the average grade received by students on standardized exams. How would you decide which course the professors should teach? Assume that students in course G will get 90 points if Professor A teaches it or 45 if Professor B teaches it. Students in course U will get 90 points if Professor A teaches it or 60 if Professor B teaches it.

4. Use the notion of comparative advantage to explain why two countries, one of which is less efficient in producing all products, will still find it advantageous to trade.

5. Suppose the prices of goods in Mexico and the United States remain unchanged while the exchange rate increases from 10 pesos per dollar to 20 pesos per dollar. Take the perspective of a U.S. consumer. Are Mexican goods more or less attrac-

tive? Take the perspective of a Mexican consumer. Are U.S. goods more or less attractive?

6. Some studies have suggested that industries in countries that receive protection from foreign trade are less efficient than the same industries in other countries that do not receive protection. Can you explain this finding?

7. **Web Exercise.** Visit the Web site of the Organization of Economic Cooperation and Development (OECD), an international organization of industrialized, market-economy countries (*http://www.oecd.org*). The site has all sorts of data on OECD countries, including data on trade at *http://www.oecd.org/publications/figures/*. Use the data to get figures for imports and exports of goods and services for the following countries: United States, Canada, Germany, France, Japan, and the Netherlands. In which of these countries do exports exceed imports? In which countries do imports exceed exports?

8. **Web Exercise.** Visit the Fortune Web site [*http://www.pathfinder.com/fortune/fortune500/500list.html*] and get a list of the world's largest corporations. How many corporations in the top 20 are U.S. firms?

9. **Web Exercise.** Visit the Web site of Accu-Rate Foreign Exchange Corporation [*http://www.accurate.ca/index.html*] to check the most recent exchange rates. If a hotel room in Lisbon costs 4,500 escudos, how much is that in dollars?

Take It to the Net

We invite you to visit the O'Sullivan/Sheffrin page on the Prentice Hall Web site at: **http://www.prenhall.com/osullivan/** for additional World Wide Web exercises for this chapter.

Model Answers to Questions

Chapter-Opening Questions

1. Markets exist because most people are not self-sufficient but instead specialize in producing one or two products and then buy other products from other people.

2. Comparative advantage makes trade between rich and poor nations beneficial for both.

3. The most common forms of protection are quotas, voluntary export restraints, and tariffs.

4. GATT is an international agreement that has lowered trade barriers between the United States and

other nations. NAFTA is an international agreement that lowers barriers to trade among the United States, Mexico, and Canada (signed in 1994). The WTO is the new organization that oversees GATT and other international trade agreements.

Test Your Understanding

1. Tim's opportunity cost of one table is one-fifth of a chair, while Carla's opportunity cost of one table is one chair. Carla has a lower opportunity cost of chairs, so she should produce chairs. Tim has a

lower opportunity cost of tables, so he should produce tables.

2. The opportunity cost of a financial statement is four phone calls, and the opportunity cost of a phone call is one-fourth of a financial statement.

3. No. If he has a comparative advantage at managerial tasks such as doing the books or marketing, he should hire some workers to wash the cars, allowing him to specialize in the tasks for which he has a comparative advantage.

4. About three-fourths.

5. They transform inputs into outputs—products—and then sell the products.

6. The opportunity cost of wheat is 2 tons of steel in H and 3 tons of steel in T. Therefore, H has a comparative advantage in wheat. The opportunity cost of steel is 1/2 ton of wheat in H and 1/3 ton of wheat in T. Therefore, T has a comparative advantage in steel.

7. More.

8. A4, B1, C3, D2.

9. GATT, NAFTA.

Notes

1. Rone Tempest, "Barbie and the World Economy," *Los Angeles Times,* September 22, 1996, page A1.

2. AP Worldstream, "In Time for Christmas, Chinese Video Piracy Thriving," December 12, 2000; *Los Angeles Times*, "Widespread DVD Piracy in China a Blow to Hollywood," August 31, 2000.

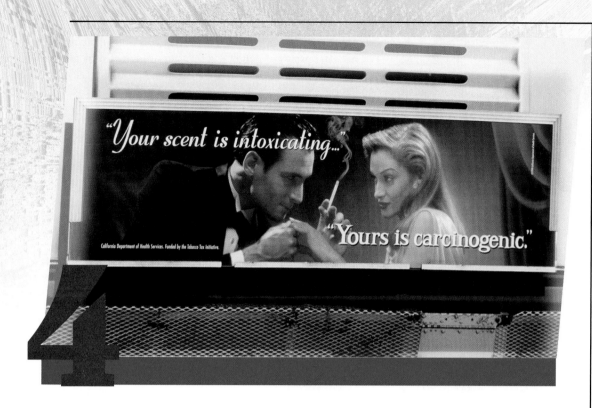

Supply, Demand, and Market Equilibrium

In 1998, cigarette makers in the United States signed agreements with all 50 states to settle lawsuits over smoking-related health-care costs. Over the next 25 years, the states will receive $246 billion from the tobacco makers. The agreement includes new restrictions on advertising and marketing of cigarettes, including the elimination of billboard ads, poster ads in buses and trains, and cigarette logos on jackets, T-shirts, and caps. Although the Marlboro man will continue to appear in ads, Joe Camel is retiring. A few weeks after the agreement was announced, the price of cigarettes increased by 40 cents per pack.

As a budget analyst for your state government, you monitor health-care programs dealing with tobacco-related illness. The annual budget for these programs equals the revenue from the tobacco settlement ($80 million per year) plus the revenue collected from the state's cigarette tax ($200 million in the year before the tobacco settlement). Two years after the tobacco settlement, you discover that the revenue from the state is only $250 million, or $30 million less than you expected. What happened? This sounds like a case for the economic detective.

e know that a market is an arrangement that allows buyers and sellers to exchange money and products. In this chapter we use a model of supply and demand—the most important tool of economic analysis—to see how markets work. We can use the model of supply and demand to see how the prices of goods and services are affected by all sorts of changes in the economy, such as bad weather, higher income, technological innovation, taxes, regulation, and changes in consumer preferences. This chapter will prepare you for the applications of supply and demand you'll see in this book. You'll also learn how to be an economic detective, using clues from the market to explain past changes in market prices. The first case for the economic detective is the puzzling revenue shortfall for health-care programs.

Perfectly competitive market: A market with a very large number of firms, each of which produces the same standardized product and is so small that it does not affect the market price of the good it produces.

We will use the model of supply and demand to explain how a perfectly competitive market operates. A **perfectly competitive market** has a very large number of firms, each of which produces the same standardized product and is so small that it does not affect the market price of the good it produces. The classic example of a perfectly competitive firm is a wheat farmer, who produces a tiny fraction of the total supply of wheat. No matter how much wheat the farmer produces, the market price of wheat won't change.

This chapter includes many applications of supply and demand analysis. Here are some practical questions we answer:

1. Would there be fewer travel deaths if parents traveling by airplane with infants were required to strap the infants into safety seats?
2. Ted Koppel, host of the ABC news program *Nightline,* once suggested that the prices of illegal drugs had fallen because the supply of illegal drugs had increased. Was he correct?
3. Some data published in your local newspaper seem to suggest that gasoline consumers violate the law of demand, buying more gasoline at higher prices. Should you be skeptical about the data?
4. Over the last few decades the consumption of chicken and turkey has increased. Why?

The Demand Curve

On the demand side of a product market, consumers buy products from firms. The main question concerning the demand side of the market is, How much of a particular product are consumers willing to buy during a particular period? A consumer who is "willing to buy" a particular product is willing to sacrifice enough money to purchase it. The consumer doesn't merely have a desire to buy the good but is willing to sacrifice something to get it. Notice that demand is defined for a particular period, for example, a day, a month, or a year.

We'll start our discussion of demand with the individual consumer. How much of a product is an individual willing to buy? It depends on a number of variables. Here is a list of the variables that affect a consumer's decision, using the pizza market as an example:

- The price of the product, for example, the price of a pizza
- Consumer income
- The price of substitute goods such as tacos or sandwiches
- The price of complementary goods such as beer or lemonade
- Consumer tastes and advertising
- Consumer expectations about future prices

Together, these variables determine how much of a particular product an individual consumer is willing to buy. We'll start our discussion of demand with the relationship between the price and quantity demanded, a relationship that is represented graphically by the demand curve.

The Individual Demand Curve and the Law of Demand

The starting point for a discussion of individual demand is a **demand schedule**, a table of numbers that shows the relationship between price and quantity demanded, ceteris paribus (the Latin phrase for "everything else held fixed"). The variables that are held fixed in the demand schedule are income, the prices of substitutes and complements, consumer tastes, advertising, and expectations about future prices. Table 4.1 shows Al's demand schedule for pizza. At a price of $2, Al buys 13 pizzas per month. As the price rises, he buys fewer pizzas: 10 pizzas at a price of $4, 7 pizzas at a price of $6, and so on, down to only 1 pizza at a price of $10.

The **individual demand curve** shows the relationship between the price and the **quantity demanded** by a consumer, ceteris paribus (everything else held fixed). To draw the curve, we assume that everything else that affects a consumer's demand for pizza (income, prices of substitutes, prices of complementary goods, his tastes, advertising, expectations about future prices) does not change. The only variable that changes is the price of pizza, and we use the numbers from the demand schedule to draw the individual demand curve. Figure 4.1 shows Al's demand curve for pizza.

The demand curve is negatively sloped, reflecting the **law of demand**. This law is not a legal restriction that sends violators to jail, but is a pattern of behavior that we observe in most consumers.

Demand schedule: A table of numbers that shows the relationship between price and quantity demanded by a consumer, ceteris paribus (everything else held fixed).

Individual demand curve: A curve that shows the relationship between price and quantity demanded by a consumer, ceteris paribus (everything else held fixed).

Quantity demanded: The amount of a good a consumer is willing to buy

Law of demand: The higher the price, the smaller the quantity demanded, ceteris paribus (everything else held fixed).

LAW OF DEMAND

The higher the price, the smaller the quantity demanded, ceteris paribus (everything else held fixed).

The words "ceteris paribus" provide a reminder that to isolate the relationship between price and quantity demanded, we assume that the other determinants of demand are unchanged. In Al's case we see that as the price of pizza increases, he consumes fewer pizzas. A movement along the demand curve is called a **change in quantity demanded**, a change in the quantity a consumer is willing to buy when the price of the good changes. For example, if the price increases from $8 to $10, we move along the demand curve from point c to point b, and the quantity demanded decreases from 4 pizzas per month to 1 pizza per month.

Change in quantity demanded: A change in the amount of a good demanded resulting from a change in the price of the good; represented graphically by movement along the demand curve.

Table 4.1   Al's Demand Schedule for Pizzas

Price ($)	Quantity of pizzas per month
2	13
4	10
6	7
8	4
10	1

Figure 4.1

The Individual Demand Curve

According to the law of demand, the higher the price, the smaller the quantity demanded, everything else being equal. Therefore, the demand curve is negatively sloped: When the price increases from $6 to $8, the quantity demanded decreases from 7 pizzas per month (point *d*) to 4 pizzas per month (point *c*).

Substitution affect: The change in consumption resulting from a change in the price of one good relative to the price of other goods.

Income affect: The change in consumption resulting from an increase in the consumer's real income.

To see why the law of demand is sensible, think about how Al might react to an increase in the price of pizza.

- **Substitution effect.** The more money Al spends on pizza, the less he has to spend on other products such as tacos, music, books, and travel. The price of pizza determines exactly how much of these other goods he sacrifices to get a pizza. If the price of pizza is $6 and the price of tacos is $1, Al will sacrifice 6 tacos for each pizza he buys. If the price of pizza increases to $8, he'll now sacrifice 8 tacos for each pizza. Given the larger sacrifice associated with buying pizza, he is likely to buy fewer pizzas, substituting tacos for pizza.

- **Income effect.** Suppose Al has a food budget of $100 per month and buys 10 pizzas at a price of $6 each (a total cost of $60) and spends $40 on other food. If the price of pizza rises to $7 each, the cost of his original food choices will be $110 ($70 for pizza and $40 on other items), well above his $100 food budget. To avoid exceeding his budget, Al must cut back on something and will probably cut back on pizza as well as other items. This is called the income effect because when the price of pizza increases, the purchasing power of Al's income (or budget) decreases, forcing him to consume smaller quantities.

From Individual to Market Demand

Market demand curve: A curve showing the relationship between price and quantity demanded by all consumers together, ceteris paribus (everything else held fixed).

The **market demand curve** shows the relationship between the price of the good and the quantity that all consumers together are willing to buy, ceteris paribus (everything else held fixed). As in the case of the individual demand curve, when we draw the market demand curve, we assume that the other variables that affect individual demand (income, the prices of substitute and complementary goods, tastes, and price expectations) are fixed. In addition, we assume that the number of consumers is fixed. The market demand curve shows the relationship between price and the quantity demanded by all consumers, everything else being equal.

Figure 4.2 shows how to derive the market demand curve when there are only two consumers. Panel A shows Al's demand curve for pizza, and panel B shows Bea's demand curve for pizza. At a price of $8, Al will buy 4 pizzas (point *c*) and Bea will buy 2 pizzas (point *g*), so the total quantity demanded at this price is 6 pizzas (4 + 2). In panel C, point

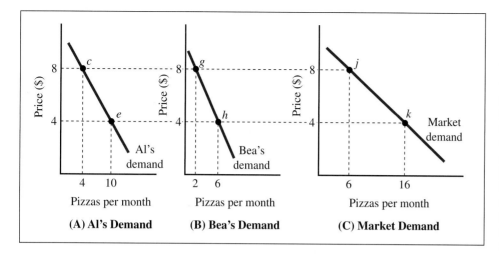

Figure 4.2

From Individual to Market Demand
The market demand equals the sum of the demands of all consumers. In this case there are only two consumers, so at each price, the market quantity demanded equals the quantity demanded by Al plus the quantity demanded by Bea. At a price of $8, Al's quantity is 4 pizzas (point *c*) and Bea's quantity is 2 pizzas (point *g*), so the market quantity demanded is 6 pizzas (point *j*). Each consumer obeys the law of demand, so the market demand curve is negatively sloped.

j shows the point on the market demand curve associated with a price of $8; at this price, the market quantity demanded is 6 pizzas. At a price of only $4, Al buys 10 pizzas and Bea buys 6 pizzas, for a total of 16 pizzas (shown by point *k* on the market demand curve).

The market demand is negatively sloped, reflecting the law of demand. This is sensible because if each consumer obeys the law of demand, consumers as a group will too. When the price increases from $4 to $8, there is a change in quantity demanded as we move along the demand curve from point *k* to *j*. The movement along the demand curve occurs if the price of pizza is the only determinant of demand that has changed.

The Supply Curve

On the supply side of a perfectly competitive market, firms sell their products to consumers. The main question for the supply side of the market is, How much of a particular product are firms willing to sell?

Here are the variables that affect the decisions of sellers, using the market for pizza as an example:

- The price of the product, such as the price of pizza
- The cost of the inputs used to produce the product, such as the wage paid to workers, the cost of electricity, and the cost of equipment
- The state of production technology, such as the knowledge used in making pizza
- The number of producers, such as the number of pizzerias
- Producer expectations about future prices
- Taxes or subsidies from the government

Together, these variables determine how much of a particular product producers are willing to sell. We'll start our discussion of market supply with the relationship between price of a good and quantity of that good supplied, a relationship that is represented graphically by the supply curve.

The Marginal Principle and the Output Decision

A perfectly competitive market has dozens or perhaps hundreds of firms, and we'll start our discussion of the supply curve with an individual firm. Nora's supply curve shows how many pizzas she is willing to produce at each price. Her decision about how many pizzas to produce is based on the marginal principle.

Marginal **PRINCIPLE**

Increase the level of an activity if its marginal benefit exceeds its marginal cost; reduce the level of an activity if its marginal cost exceeds its marginal benefit. If possible, pick the level at which the activity's marginal benefit equals its marginal cost.

Nora's activity is producing pizzas. If the price of pizza is $8, the marginal benefit of producing a pizza is the $8 Nora gets from selling it. In Figure 4.3 when the price is $8, the marginal benefit curve for pizza is horizontal at $8. Recall that marginal cost is the increase in total cost resulting from producing one more unit. In Figure 4.3 the marginal-cost curve for pizza is positively sloped, indicating that the more pizzas Nora produces, the higher the marginal cost of production.

When the price of pizza is $8, Nora satisfies the marginal principle at point p. She produces exactly 300 pizzas because that's the quantity at which the $8 marginal benefit equals the marginal cost of producing pizza. She stops at 300 pizzas because the marginal cost of producing the 301st pizza exceeds the $8 she could get from selling it. For example, if the marginal cost of the 301st pizza is $8.02. she would lose $0.02 on the 301st pizza.

How would Nora react to an increase in the price of pizza? If the price of pizza increased to $10, the marginal benefit of pizza production will increase to $10. At the higher price, it makes sense to produce the 301st pizza because the $10 benefit exceeds the $8.02 cost of producing it. In fact, when Nora applies the marginal principle with the higher price, she will increase production to 400 pizzas because that's the quantity at which the $10 marginal benefit equals the marginal cost. In Figure 4.3 the marginal-benefit curve for a price of $10 intersects the marginal cost curve at 400 pizzas (point q).

Individual Supply and the Law of Supply

Supply schedule: A table of numbers that shows the relationship between price and quantity supplied, ceteris paribus (everything else held fixed).

Quantity supplied: The amount of a good a firm is willing to sell.

A firm's **supply schedule** is a table of numbers that shows the relationship between price and the **quantity supplied** by the individual firm, ceteris paribus (everything else held fixed). The variables that are held fixed are input costs, technology, expectations, and government taxes or subsidies. Table 4.2 shows Nora's supply schedule for pizza. At a

Figure 4.3

The Marginal Principle and the Output Decision

The marginal benefit curve is horizontal at the market price. To satisfy the marginal principle, the firm produces the quantity at which the marginal benefit equals the marginal cost. An increase in the price shifts the marginal-benefit curve upward and increases the quantity at which the marginal benefit equals the marginal cost.

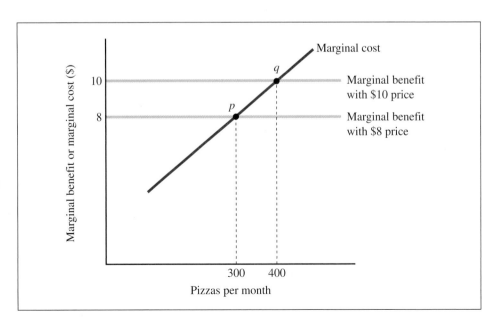

Table 4.2 Nora's Supply Schedule for Pizza

Price ($)	Quantity of pizzas per month
4	100
6	200
8	300
10	400
12	500

price of $4, she supplies 100 pizzas per month. As the price rises, she supplies more pizza: 200 pizzas at a price of $6, 300 pizzas at a price of $8, and so on, up to 500 pizzas at a price of $12.

The **individual supply curve** shows the relationship between the price and the quantity supplied by a single firm, ceteris paribus (everything else held fixed). To draw the curve, we assume that everything else that affects the supply of pizza (input costs, technology, price expectations, government taxes and subsidies) does not change. The only variable that changes is the price of pizza, and we use the numbers from the supply schedule to draw a supply curve. Panel A of Figure 4.4 shows Nora's supply curve for pizza.

Nora's supply curve is positively sloped, reflecting the **law of supply**, a pattern of behavior that we observe in producers.

Individual supply curve: A curve that shows the relationship between price and quantity supplied by a producer ceteris paribus (everything else held fixed).

Law of supply: The higher the price, the larger the quantity supplied, ceteris paribus (everything else held fixed).

LAW OF SUPPLY

The higher the price, the larger the quantity supplied, ceteris paribus (everything else held fixed).

The words "ceteris paribus" remind us that to isolate the relationship between price and quantity supplied, we assume that the other determinants of supply are unchanged. As the price of pizza increases, Nora produces a larger quantity of pizza. A

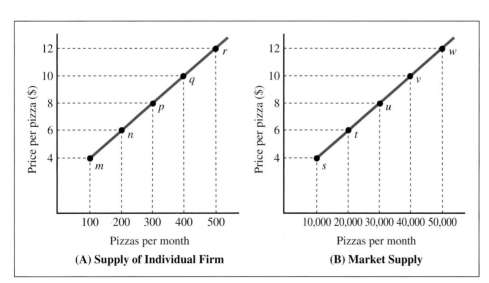

(A) Supply of Individual Firm

(B) Market Supply

Figure 4.4

Individual and Market Supply Curve
(A) Supply of individual firm. Nora supplies 300 pizzas at a price of $8 (point *p*) but 400 pizzas at a price of $10 (point *q*).
(B) Market supply. There are 100 identical pizzerias, so the market quantity equals 100 times the quantity supplied by Nora's, the typical pizzeria. At a price of $8, Nora supplies 300 pizzas (point *p*), so the market quantity supplied is 30,000 pizzas (point *u*).

Change in quantity supplied: A change in the quantity supplied resulting from a change in the price of the good; represented graphically by movement along the supply curve.

movement along the supply curve is called a **change in quantity supplied**, a change in the quantity a producer is willing to sell when the price of the good changes. For example, if the price increases from $8 to $10, Nora moves upward along her supply curve from point p to point q, and the quantity supplied increases from 300 pizzas per month to 400 pizzas per month.

Individual Supply to Market Supply

Market supply curve: A curve showing the relationship between price and quantity supplied by all producers together, ceteris paribus (everything else held fixed).

The **market supply curve** for a particular good shows the relationship between the price of the good and the quantity that all producers together are willing to sell, ceteris paribus (everything else held fixed). To draw the market supply curve, we assume that the other variables that affect individual supply are fixed. In addition, we assume that the number of producers is fixed.

Panel B of Figure 4.4 shows the market supply curve when there are 100 producers, each of which has the same individual supply curve as Nora. At a price of $8, Nora supplies 300 pizzas per month (point p), so the 100 firms together produce 30,000 pizzas (300 pizzas per firm times 100 firms), as shown by point u. If the price increases to $10, Nora supplies 400 pizzas (point q), so the quantity supplied by the market is 40,000 (point v).

The market supply curve is positively sloped, reflecting the law of supply. This is sensible because if each firm obeys the law of supply, firms as a group will too. When the price increases from $8 to $10, there is a change in quantity supplied as we move along the market supply curve from point u to point v. The movement along the supply curve occurs if the price of pizza is the only determinant of supply that has changed.

TEST Your Understanding

1. Complete the statement with "increase" or "decrease": When a price increases, the law of demand suggests that the quantity demanded will _____, while the law of supply suggests that the quantity supplied will _____.

2. List the variables that are held fixed in drawing a market demand curve.

3. List the variables that are held fixed in drawing a market supply curve.

Market Equilibrium

Market equilibrium: A situation in which the quantity of a product demanded equals the quantity supplied, so there is no pressure to change the price.

When the quantity of a product demanded equals the quantity supplied, this is called a **market equilibrium**. When a market reaches an equilibrium, there is no pressure to change the price. For example, if pizza firms produce exactly the quantity of pizza consumers are willing to buy, there will be no pressure for the price of pizza to change. The equilibrium price is shown by the intersection of the supply and demand curves. In Figure 4.5. at a price of $8, the supply curve shows that firms will produce 30,000 pizzas, which is exactly the quantity that consumers are willing to buy at that price.

Excess Demand Causes the Price to Rise

Excess demand: A situation in which, at the prevailing price, consumers are willing to buy more than producers are willing to sell.

If the price is below the equilibrium price, there will be **excess demand** for the product. Excess demand (sometimes called a shortage) occurs when consumers are willing to buy more than producers are willing to sell. In Figure 4.5 at a price of $6, there is an excess demand equal to 17,000 pizzas: Consumers are willing to buy 37,000 pizzas (point d), but producers are willing to sell only 20,000 pizzas (point c). This mismatch between supply and demand will cause the price of pizza to rise. Firms will increase the price they charge for their limited supply of pizza, and anxious consumers will pay the higher price to get one of the few pizzas that are available.

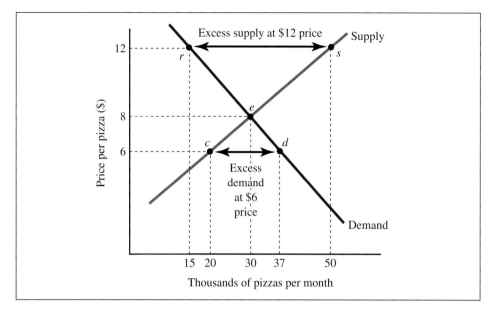

Figure 4.5

Supply, Demand, and Market Equilibrium
At the market equilibrium (point *e*, with price = $8 and quantity = 30,000), the quantity supplied equals the quantity demanded. At a price lower than the equilibrium price ($6), there is excess demand (the quantity demanded exceeds the quantity supplied). At a price above the equilibrium price ($12), there is excess supply (the quantity supplied exceeds the quantity demanded).

An increase in price eliminates excess demand by changing both the quantity demanded and quantity supplied. As the price increases, there are two effects.

- The market moves upward along the demand curve (from point *d* toward point *e*), *decreasing* the quantity demanded.

- The market moves upward along the supply curve (from point *c* toward point *e*), *increasing* the quantity supplied.

Because quantity demanded decreases while quantity supplied increases, the gap between the quantity demanded and the quantity supplied narrows. The price will continue to rise until excess demand is eliminated. In Figure 4.5, at a price of $8, the quantity supplied equals the quantity demanded.

In some cases, government creates an excess demand for a good by setting a maximum price (sometimes called a price ceiling). If the government sets a maximum price that is less than the equilibrium price, the result is a permanent excess demand for the good. The most prominent example in the United States is rent control, a maximum price for apartments. During World War II the federal government instituted a national system of rent controls. Although New York City was the only city to retain rent control after the war, rent control returned to dozens of cities in the 1970s. Since then several states have passed laws that have weakened rent control.

Excess Supply Causes the Price to Drop

What happens if the price is above the equilibrium price? **Excess supply** (sometimes called a surplus) occurs when producers are willing to sell more than consumers are willing to buy. This is shown by points *r* and *s* in Figure 4.5. At a price of $12, the excess supply is 35,000 pizzas: producers are willing to sell 50,000 pizzas (point *s*), but consumers are willing to buy only 15,000 pizzas (point *r*). This mismatch will cause the price of pizza to fall as firms cut the price to sell their pizza. As the price drops two things happen:

- The market moves downward along the demand curve, *increasing* the quantity demanded.

- The market moves downward along the supply curve, *decreasing* the quantity supplied.

Because the quantity demanded increases while the quantity supplied decreases, the gap between quantity supplied and demanded narrows. The price will continue to drop until

Excess supply: A situation in which, at the prevailing price, producers are willing to sell more than consumers are willing to buy.

excess supply is eliminated. In Figure 4.5, at price of $8, the quantity supplied equals the quantity demanded.

The government sometimes creates an excess supply of a good by setting a minimum price (sometimes called a price floor). If the government sets a minimum price that is greater than the equilibrium price, the result is a permanent excess supply. For several decades, the U.S. government set minimum prices for dozens of agricultural products such as corn and dairy products. These agricultural price-support programs ended in 1996. The European Community has price supports (minimum prices) for grains, dairy products, livestock, and sugar, and Japan has price supports for dairy products and sugar.

TEST Your Understanding

4. Complete the statement: The market equilibrium is shown by the intersection of the _____ curve and the _____ curve.

5. Complete the statement with "less" or "greater": Excess demand occurs when the price is _____ than the equilibrium price; excess supply occurs when the price is _____ than the equilibrium price.

6. Complete the statement with "supply" or "demand": A maximum price below the equilibrium price causes excess _____, while a minimum price above the equilibrium price causes excess _____.

Market Effects of Changes in Demand

We've seen that a market equilibrium occurs when the quantity supplied equals the quantity demanded, shown graphically by the intersection of the supply curve and the demand curve. In this part of the chapter, we'll see how changes on the demand side of the market affect the equilibrium price and equilibrium quantity.

Change in Quantity Demanded Versus Change in Demand

Earlier in the chapter we listed the variables that determine how much of a particular product consumers are willing to buy. One of the variables is the price of the product, and the law of demand summarizes the negative relationship between price and quantity demanded. We're ready to take a closer look at the other variables that affect demand— income, the prices of related goods, tastes, advertising, and the number of consumers— and see how changes in these variables affect the demand for the product and the market equilibrium.

If any of these other variables change, the relationship between price and quantity—shown numerically in the demand schedule and graphically in the demand curve—will change. That means we will have an entirely different demand schedule and a different demand curve. To convey the idea that changes in these other variables change the demand schedule and the demand curve, a change in any of these variables causes a **change in demand**. In contrast, a change in the price of the good causes *a change in quantity demanded*.

Change in demand: A change in the amount of a good demanded resulting from a change in something other than the price of the good; represented graphically by a shift of the demand curve.

Increases in Demand

We'll start with changes in the pizza market that increase the demand for pizza. An increase in demand means that at each price, consumers are willing to buy a larger quantity. In Figure 4.6 an increase in demand shifts the market demand curve from D_2 to D_3. At the initial price of $8, the quantity demanded increases from 30,000 pizzas

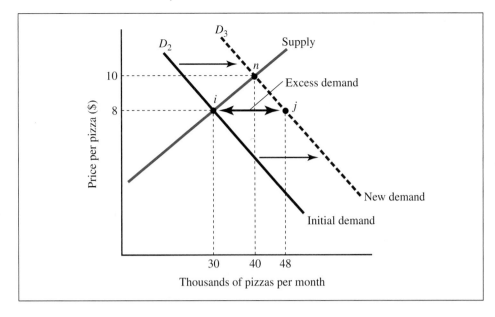

Figure 4.6
**Market Effects
of an Increase
in Demand**
An increase in demand shifts
the demand curve to the
right: At each price, the
quantity demanded
increases. At the initial price
($8), the shift of the demand
curve causes excess
demand, causing the price to
rise. Equilibrium is restored
at point n, with a higher equilibrium price ($10, up from
$8) and a larger equilibrium
quantity (40,000 pizzas, up
from 30,000 pizzas).

(point *i*) to 48,000 (point *j*). An increase in demand like the one represented in Figure 4.6 can occur for several reasons, which are listed in the first column of Table 4.3.

- **Increase in income.** Consumers use their income to buy products, and the more money they have, the more money they spend. For a **normal good** there is a positive relationship between consumer income and the quantity consumed.

- **Increase in price of a substitute good.** When two goods are **substitutes**, an increase in the price of the first good causes some consumers to switch to the second good.

Normal good: A good for which an increase in income increases demand.

Substitutes: Two goods that are related in such a way that an increase in the price of one good increases the demand for the other good.

Table 4.3   Changes in Demand Shift the Demand Curve

An increase in demand shifts the demand curve to the right when	A decrease in demand shifts the demand curve to the left when
The good is normal and income increases	The good is normal and income decreases
The good is inferior and income decreases	The good is inferior and income increases
The price of a substitute good increases	The price of a substitute good decreases
The price of a complementary good decreases	The price of a complementary good increases
Population increases	Population decreases
Consumer tastes shift in favor of the product	Consumer tastes shift away from the product
Favorable advertising	Unfavorable publicity
Consumers expect a higher price in the future	Consumers expect a lower price in the future

Tacos and pizzas are substitutes, so an increase in the price of tacos increases the demand for pizzas as some consumers substitute pizza for tacos, which are now more expensive relative to pizza.

Complements: Two goods that are related in such a way that an increase in the price of one good decreases the demand for the other good.

- **Decrease in price of a complementary good.** When two goods are **complements**, they are consumed together as a package, and a decrease in the price of one good decreases the cost of the entire package. As a result, consumers buy more of both goods. Pizza and beer are complementary goods, so a decrease in the price of beer decreases the cost of a beer and pizza meal, increasing the demand for pizza.

- **Increase in population.** An increase in the number of people means that there are more pizza consumers—more individual demand curves to add up to get the market demand curve—so market demand increases.

- **Shift in consumer tastes.** Consumers' preferences or tastes change over time, and when consumers' preferences shift in favor of pizza, the demand for pizza increases.

- **Favorable advertising.** The purpose of an advertising campaign is to shift consumers' preferences in favor of a product, so a successful pizza advertising campaign will increase the demand for pizza.

- **Expectations of higher future prices.** If consumers think next month's pizza price will be higher than they had initially expected, they may buy a larger quantity today (and a smaller quantity next month). That means that the demand for pizza today will increase.

Market Effects of an Increase in Demand

We can use Figure 4.6 to show the effects of an increase in demand on the equilibrium price and equilibrium quantity. An increase in the demand for pizza shifts the demand curve to the right, from D_2 to D_3. At the initial price of $8 (the equilibrium price with the initial demand curve), there will be an excess demand, as indicated by points i and j: Consumers are willing to buy 48,000 pizzas (point j), but producers are willing to sell only 30,000 pizzas (point i). Consumers want to buy 18,000 more pizzas than producers are willing to supply, so there is pressure to increase the price.

As the price rises, the excess demand shrinks because the quantity demanded decreases while the quantity supplied increases.

- The market moves upward along the supply curve to a larger quantity supplied.

- The market moves upward along the new demand curve to a smaller quantity demanded.

The supply curve intersects the new demand curve at point n, so the new equilibrium price is $10 (up from $8), and the new equilibrium quantity is 40,000 pizzas (up from 30,000).

Decreases in Demand

What sort of changes in the pizza market will decrease the demand for pizza? A decrease in demand means that at each price, consumers are willing to buy a smaller quantity. In Figure 4.7, a decrease in demand shifts the market demand curve from D_2 to D_1. At the initial price of $8, the quantity demanded decreases from 30,000 pizzas (point i) to 12,000 pizzas (point k). A decrease in demand like the one represented in Figure 4.7 can occur for several reasons, which are listed in the second column of Table 4.3.

- **Decrease in income.** A decrease in income means that consumers have less to spend, so they buy a smaller quantity of each normal good.

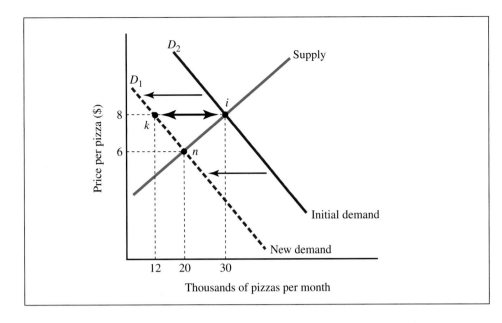

Figure 4.7

Market Effects of a Decrease in Demand

A decrease in demand shifts the demand curve to the left: At each price, the quantity demanded decreases. At the initial price ($8), the leftward shift of the demand curve causes excess supply, causing the price to fall. Equilibrium is restored at point *n*, with a lower equilibrium price ($6, down from $8) and a smaller equilibrium quantity (20,000 pizzas, down from 30,000 pizzas).

- **Decrease in price of a substitute good.** A decrease in the price of a substitute good such as tacos makes pizza more expensive relative to tacos, causing consumers to demand less pizza.

- **Increase in price of a complementary good.** An increase in the price of a complementary good such as beer increases the cost of a beer and pizza meal, decreasing the demand for pizza.

- **Decrease in population.** A decrease in the number of people means that there are fewer pizza consumers, so the market demand for pizza decreases.

- **Shift in consumer tastes.** When consumers' preferences shift away from pizza in favor of other products, the demand for pizza decreases.

- **Expectations of lower future prices.** If consumers think next month's pizza price will be lower than they had initially expected, they may buy a smaller quantity today, meaning the demand for pizza today will decrease.

Market Effects of a Decrease in Demand

We can use Figure 4.7 to show the effects of a decrease in demand on the equilibrium price and equilibrium quantity. The demand for pizza shifts the demand curve to the left, from D_2 to D_1. At the initial price of $8 (the equilibrium price with the initial demand curve), there will be an excess supply, as indicated by points *i* and *k*: Producers are willing to sell 30,000 pizzas (point *i*), but given the lower demand, consumers are willing to buy only 12,000 pizzas (point *k*). Producers want to sell 18,000 more pizzas than consumers are willing to buy, so there is pressure to decrease the price.

The excess supply means that there is pressure to reduce prices, and as the price falls, the excess supply shrinks because the quantity demanded increases while the quantity supplied decreases.

- The market moves downward along the supply curve to a smaller quantity supplied.

- The market moves downward along the new demand curve to a larger quantity demanded.

The supply curve intersects the new demand curve at point n, so the new equilibrium price is $6 (down from $8), and the new equilibrium quantity is 20,000 pizzas (down from 30,000 pizzas).

Normal Versus Inferior Goods

Up to this point, we've assumed that there is a positive relationship between income and the demand for a particular product such as pizza. The label for such a good is normal good, a label indicating that for most products there is a positive relationship between income and demand. For some goods there is a negative rather than a positive relationship between income and consumption. For an **inferior good** an increase in income decreases demand, shifting the demand curve to the left. In most cases an inferior good is an inexpensive good such as margarine that has an expensive alternative (butter). As income increases, some consumers switch from the inexpensive good to the expensive one, for example, buying less margarine and more butter. As a result, the demand for margarine decreases and the demand curve shifts to the left. Some other examples of inferior goods are potatoes, intercity bus travel, and used clothing.

Inferior good: A good for which an increase in income decreases demand.

TEST Your Understanding

7. Which of the following go together?
   a. Change in demand
   b. Change in quantity demanded
   c. Change in price
   d. Movement along the demand curve
   e. Shifting the demand curve
   f. Change in income

8. What's wrong with the following statement? "Demand increased because the demand curve shifted."

9. Complete the statement with "right" or "left": An increase in the price of cassette tapes will shift the demand curve for CDs to the _____; an increase in the price of CD players will shift the demand curve for CDs to the _____.

10. In the following list of variables, circle the ones that change as we move along the demand curve for pencils, and cross out the ones that are assumed to be fixed; quantity of pencils demanded, number of consumers, price of pencils, price of pens, consumer income.

Market Effects of Changes in Supply

We've seen that changes in demand shift the demand curve and change the equilibrium price and quantity. In this part of the chapter, we'll see how changes on the supply side of the market affect the equilibrium price and equilibrium quantity.

Change in Quantity Supplied Versus Change in Supply

Earlier in the chapter we listed the variables that determine how much of a particular product firms are willing to sell. One of the variables is the price of the product, and the relationship between price and quantity supplied is shown by the law of supply. We're ready to take a closer look at the other variables that affect supply—input costs, technology, the number of firms, and price expectations—and see how changes in these variables affect the supply of the product and the market equilibrium.

If any of these other variables changes, the relationship between price and quantity—shown numerically in the supply schedule and graphically in the supply curve—will change. That means that we will have an entirely different supply schedule and a different supply curve. To convey the idea that changes in these other variables change the supply schedule and the supply curve, a change in any of these variables causes a **change in supply**. In contrast, a change in the price of the good causes *a change in quantity supplied* (defined earlier in the chapter).

Change in supply: A change in the amount of a good supplied resulting from a change in something other than the price of the good; represented graphically by a shift of the supply curve.

Increases in Supply

We'll start with changes in the pizza market that increase the supply of pizza. An increase in supply means that at each price, producers are willing to sell a larger quantity. In Figure 4.8, an increase in supply shifts the market supply curve from S_2 to S_3. At the initial price of $8, the quantity demanded increases from 30,000 pizzas (point i) to 45,000 (point m). An increase in supply like the one represented in Figure 4.8 can occur for several reasons, which are listed in the first column of Table 4.4.

- **Decrease in input costs.** A decrease in the cost of labor or some other input will make pizza production less costly and more profitable at a given price, so producers will supply more.

- **Advance in technology.** A technological advance that makes it possible to produce pizza at a lower cost will make pizza production more profitable, so producers will supply more.

- **An increase in the number of producers.** The market supply is the sum of the supplies of all producers, so the larger number of producers, the greater the supply.

- **Expectations of lower future prices.** If firms think next month's pizza price will be lower than they had initially expected, they may be willing to sell a larger quantity today (and a smaller quantity next month). That means that the supply of pizza today will increase.

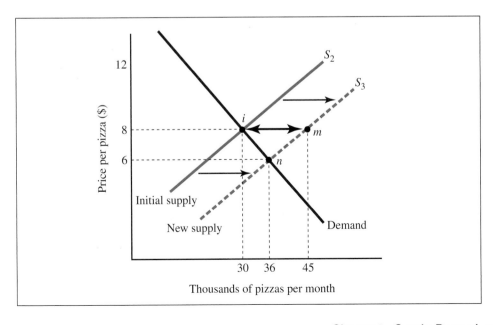

Figure 4.8
Market Effects of an Increase in Supply
An increase in supply shifts the supply curve to the right: At each price, the quantity supplied increases. At the initial price ($8), the rightward shift of the supply curve causes excess supply, causing the price to drop. Equilibrium is restored at point *n*, with a lower equilibrium price ($6, down from $8) and a larger equilibrium quantity (36,000 pizzas, up from 30,000 pizzas).

Table 4.4   Changes in Supply Shift the Supply Curve

An increase in supply shifts the supply curve to the right when	A decrease in supply shifts the supply curve to the left when
The cost of an input decreases	The cost of an input increases
A technological advance decreases production costs	
The number of firms increases	The number of firms decreases
Producers expect a lower price in the future	Producers expect a higher price in the future
Subsidy	Tax

- **Subsidy.** If the government subsidizes the production of the product (pays firms some amount for each unit produced), the subsidy will make the product more profitable, so firms will produce more.

Market Effects of an Increase in Supply

We can use Figure 4.8 to show the effects of an increase in supply on the equilibrium price and equilibrium quantity. An increase in the supply of pizza shifts the supply curve to the right, from S_2 to S_3. At the initial price of $8 (the equilibrium price with the initial supply curve), there will be an excess supply, as indicated by points i and m: Producers are willing to sell 45,000 pizzas (point m), but consumers are willing to buy only 30,000 (point i). Producers want to sell 15,000 more pizzas than consumers are willing to buy, so there is pressure to decrease the price.

As the price decreases, the excess supply shrinks because the quantity supplied decreases while the quantity demanded increases.

- The market moves downward along the new supply curve to a smaller quantity supplied.
- The market moves downward along the demand curve to a larger quantity demanded.

The new supply curve intersects the demand curve at point n, so the new equilibrium price is $6 (down from $8) and the new equilibrium quantity is 36,000 pizzas (up from 30,000).

How has technological change in electricity generation affected the supply of electricity from alternative sources, including wind power? To see the effects of technological innovation in the production of wind power, read "A Closer Look: Increasing the Supply of Wind Power."

Decreases in Supply

What sort of changes in the pizza market will decrease the supply of pizza? A decrease in supply means that at each price, producers are willing to supply a smaller quantity. In Figure 4.9, a decrease in supply shifts the market supply curve from S_2 to S_1. At the initial price of $8, the quantity supplied decreases from 30,000 pizzas (point i) to 14,000 pizzas (point p). A decrease in supply like the one represented in Figure 4.9 can occur for several reasons, which are listed in the second column of Table 4.4.

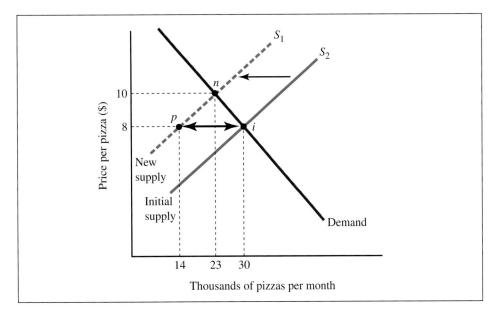

Figure 4.9

Market Effects of a Decrease in Supply
A decrease in supply shifts the supply curve to the left: At each price, the quantity supplied decreases. At the initial price ($8), the leftward shift of the supply curve causes excess demand, causing the price to rise. Equilibrium is restored at point *n*, with a higher equilibrium price ($10, up from $8) and a smaller equilibrium quantity (23,000 pizzas, down from 30,000 pizzas).

- **Increase in input costs.** A increase in the cost of labor or some other input will make pizza production more costly and less profitable at a given price, so producers will supply less.

- **A decrease in the number of producers.** The market supply is the sum of the supplies of all producers, so a decrease in the number of producers decreases supply.

- **Expectations of higher future prices.** If firms think next month's pizza price will be higher than they had initially expected, they may be willing to sell a smaller quantity today (and a larger quantity next month). That means that the supply of pizza today will decrease.

- **Tax.** If the government imposes a tax on producers (a firm pays the government some amount for each unit produced), the tax will make the product more costly and less profitable, so firms will supply less.

Market Effects of a Decrease in Supply

We can use Figure 4.9 to show the effects of a decrease in supply on the equilibrium price and equilibrium quantity. A decrease in the supply of pizza shifts the supply curve to the left, from S_2 to S_1. At the initial price of $8 (the equilibrium price with the initial supply curve), there will be an excess demand, as indicated by points *i* and *p*: Consumers are willing to buy 30,000 pizzas (point *i*), but producers are willing to sell only 14,000 pizzas (point *p*). Consumers want to buy 16,000 more pizzas than producers are willing to sell, so there is pressure to increase the price.

As the price increases, the excess demand shrinks because the quantity demanded decreases while the quantity supplied increases.

- The market moves upward along the demand curve to a smaller quantity demanded.

- The market moves upward along the new supply curve to a larger quantity supplied.

The new supply curve intersects the demand curve at point *n*, so the new equilibrium price is $10 (up from $8), and the new equilibrium quantity is 23,000 pizzas (down from 30,000).

A CLOSER LOOK | INCREASING THE SUPPLY OF WIND POWER

The year 2001 may be remembered as the year of the wind. Every few weeks, newspapers announced the development of another huge windfarm, a collection of turbines propelled by the wind and hooked up to the electric power system or electric grid. The United States Energy Department expects the supply of electricity from wind to double in just one year.[1]

The explosion in wind electricity resulted from technological innovations that decreased the cost of producing electricity from the wind. In the 1980s, the cost of wind electricity was about 50 cents per kilowatt hour. Several design innovations—including the replacement of small rapid rotors with large slow-moving blades and the development of monitoring systems that permit the turbines to change their direction and blade angle to more efficiently harness the wind—have decreased the cost of maintaining the turbines and increased the electricity output per hour. By 2001, the cost of wind power had dropped to about 4 cents per kilowatt hour, compared with 2.5 to 3 cents for electricity generated by conventional sources (natural gas and coal). Because the producers of wind power receive a fed-

eral tax credit of 1.5 cents per kilowatt hour, wind power is often competitive with conventional power sources.

In graphical terms, the technological innovations in the design of wind turbines decreased production costs, shifting the supply curve for wind electricity to the right, increasing the equilibrium quantity and decreasing the price. The federal tax credit amplified the rightward shift of the supply curve, leading to an even larger increase in quantity and decrease in price.

Market Effects of Simultaneous Changes in Demand and Supply

What happens to the equilibrium price and quantity when both supply and demand increase? It depends on which change is larger. In panel A of Figure 4.10, the increase in demand is larger than the increase in supply, meaning the demand curve shifts by a larger amount than the supply curve. The market equilibrium moves from point *i* to point *d*, and the equilibrium price increases from $8 to $9. This is sensible because an increase in demand tends to pull the price up, while an increase in supply tends to push the price down. If demand increases by a larger amount, the upward pull will be stronger than the downward push, and the price will rise.

We can be certain that when supply and demand both increase, the equilibrium quantity will increase. That's because both changes tend to increase the equilibrium quantity. In panel A of Figure 4.10, the equilibrium quantity increases from 30,000 to 44,000 pizzas.

Panel B of Figure 4.10 shows what happens when the increase in supply is larger than the increase in demand. The equilibrium moves from point *i* to *s*, meaning that the price falls from $8 to $7. This is sensible because the downward pull on the price resulting from the increase in supply is stronger than the upward pull from the increase in demand. As expected, the equilibrium quantity rises from 30,000 to 45,000 pizzas.

What about simultaneous *decreases* in supply and demand? In this case the equilibrium quantity will certainly fall because both changes tend to decrease the equilibrium

Figure 4.10
Market Effects of Simultaneous Changes in Supply and Demand
(A) Larger increase in demand. If the increase in demand is larger than the increase in supply (if the shift of the demand curve is larger than the shift of the supply curve), both the equilibrium price and the equilibrium quantity will increase.
(B) Larger increase in supply. If the increase in supply is larger than the increase in demand (if the shift of the supply curve is larger than the shift of the demand curve), the equilibrium price will decrease and the equilibrium quantity will increase.

quantity. The effect on the equilibrium price depends on which change is larger, the decrease in demand, which pushes the price downward, or the decrease in supply, which pulls the price upward. If the change in demand is larger, the price will fall because the force pushing the price down will be stronger than the force pulling it up. In contrast, if the decrease in supply is larger, the price will rise because the force pulling the price up will be stronger than the force pushing it down.

TEST Your Understanding

11. Which of the following items go together?
  a. Change in quantity supplied
  b. Change in input cost
  c. Change in price
  d. Shifting the supply curve
  e. Movement along the supply curve
  f. Change in supply

12. An increase in the wage of computer workers will shift the supply curve for computers to the left. True or false? Explain.

13. In the following list, circle the variables that change as we move along the market supply curve for housing, and cross out the variables that are assumed to be fixed: quantity of housing supplied, number of potential consumers, price of wood, price of houses, consumer income.

Applications

We can use the lessons from the pizza market to explore the effects of changes in other markets on equilibrium prices and quantities. Table 4.5 summarizes the effects of changes in demand and supply on equilibrium prices and quantities. When demand changes and the demand curve shifts, price and quantity change in the same direction.

- **Increase in demand.** Both the equilibrium price and the equilibrium quantity increase.

- **Decrease in demand.** Both the equilibrium price and the equilibrium quantity decrease.

Table 4.5 Market Effects of Changes in Demand or Supply

Change in Demand or Supply	Change in Price	Change in Quantity
Increase in demand	Increase	Increase
Decrease in demand	Decrease	Decrease
Increase in supply	Decrease	Increase
Decrease in supply	Increase	Decrease

When supply changes and the supply curve shifts, price and quantity change in opposite directions.

- **Increase in supply.** The equilibrium price decreases, but the equilibrium quantity increases.

- **Decrease in supply.** The equilibrium price increases, but the equilibrium quantity decreases.

Changes in Demand: Population Growth, Product Safety, Travel Modes

How will an increase in enrollment at a university affect the equilibrium price of apartments in the university town? In Figure 4.11, the initial equilibrium is shown by point *i*, with a monthly rent of $400 per apartment. An increase in university enrollment increases the number of students seeking apartments, shifting the demand for apartments to the right. The new equilibrium is shown by point *n*, with a price of $600 per apartment. The increase in demand increases the equilibrium price and the equilibrium quantity of apartments.

How does public information about the safety of products affect equilibrium prices and quantities? In 1999 a controversial report suggested that pesticide residue on apples made them unsafe for infants and small children. Although many experts disputed the report, it decreased the demand for apples. In Figure 4.12, the initial equilibrium is shown by point *i*, with a price of $0.60 per pound and a quantity of 26,000 pounds per

Figure 4.11

University Enrollment and Apartment Rent

An increase in university enrollment will increase the demand for apartments in the university town, shifting the demand curve to the right. Equilibrium is restored at point *n*, with a higher price ($600, up from $400) and a larger quantity (4,000 apartments, up from 3,000 apartments).

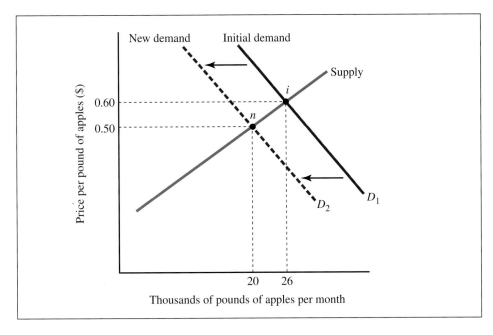

Figure 4.12
Market Effects of Pesticide Residue
A report of pesticide residue on apples decreases the demand for apples, shifting the demand curve to the left. Equilibrium is restored at point *n*, with a lower price ($0.50, down from $0.60) and a smaller quantity (20,000 pounds, down from 26,000 pounds).

month. The pesticide report shifted the demand curve to the left, leading to a new equilibrium at point *n*, with a lower equilibrium price ($0.50) and a smaller equilibrium quantity (20,000 pounds). The decrease in demand decreased the equilibrium price and the equilibrium quantity of apples.

How does an increase in the price of air travel affect automobile travel and highway deaths? For the answer, read "A Closer Look: Infant Airline Seats and Safety."

Changes in Supply: Technology, Weather

How do technological innovations affect equilibrium prices? Recent innovations in electronics have decreased the cost of producing personal computers. In Figure 4.13, the initial equilibrium is shown by point *i*. The decrease in production costs increases the

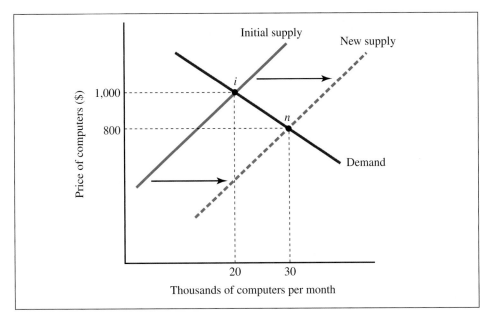

Figure 4.13
Technological Innovation and the Computer Market
Technological innovation decreases production costs, increasing supply and shifting the supply curve to the right. The equilibrium price decreases, and the equilibrium quantity increases.

supply of personal computers, shifting the supply curve to the right. The new equilibrium is shown by point n: The equilibrium price decreases from $1,000 to $800, and the equilibrium quantity increases from 20,000 to 30,000 computers per month. The personal computer is just one example of the many goods that are made affordable by technological innovations that decreased production costs and prices.

How does poor weather affect equilibrium prices? In 1992, several events combined to decrease the world supply of coffee and increase its price. Poor weather and insect infestations in Brazil and Colombia decreased the coffee-bean harvest by about 40%. In addition, a slowdown by dockworkers at Santos, Brazil's main coffee port, decreased the amount supplied to the world market. In Figure 4.14, the initial equilibrium is shown by point i, with a price of $0.60 per pound. The poor weather, insect infestations, and other supply disruptions shifted the supply curve to the left, and the new equilibrium is shown by point n. The equilibrium price of coffee increased to $0.72 per pound, and the equilibrium quantity decreased from 30 million to 22 million pounds per month.

Economic
Detective

The Economic Detective

We can use the information in Table 4.5 to play economic detective. Suppose we observe changes in the equilibrium price and quantity of a particular good, but we don't know what caused these changes. It could have been a change in demand or a change in supply. We can use the information in Table 4.5 to work backwards, using what we observe about changes in prices and quantities to discover the reason for the changes. We discuss three cases for the economic detective: an increase in the consumption of poultry products, a decrease in the price of illegal drugs, and the budgetary effects of the tobacco settlement.

The Mystery of Increasing Poultry Consumption
Why has the consumption of poultry (chicken and turkey) increased so much over the last several decades? One possibility is that consumers have become more health conscious and have switched from red meat to poultry as part of an effort to eat health-

Figure 4.14
Bad Weather and the Coffee Market
Bad weather decreases the supply of coffee beans, shifting the supply curve to the left. Equilibrium is restored at point n, with a higher price ($0.72, up from $0.60) and a smaller quantity (22 million pounds, down from 30 million pounds).

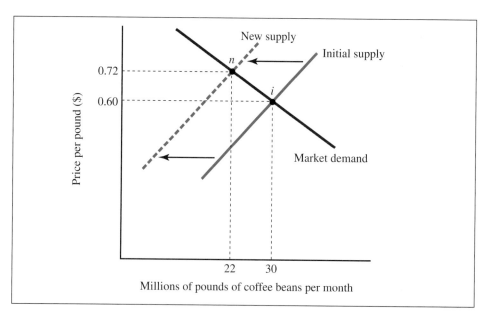

A CLOSER LOOK INFANT AIRLINE SEATS AND SAFETY

Should parents traveling by airplane be allowed to hold their infants in their laps? Or should they be required to buy a ticket for each infant and strap them into safety seats? A law requiring separate tickets and seats for infants would generate good news and bad news.

- Good news: Fewer infants would die in airline crashes because infants are safer in their own seats on aircraft.

- Bad news: More people would die in car crashes. A law requiring parents to buy tickets for infants would increase the cost of traveling by air, causing some parents to switch from flying to driving. Driving is actually more dangerous than flying: The number of people injured or killed per 100,000 miles traveled is much higher in cars.

There is an ongoing dispute between two federal agencies over infant safety seats for air travel. Since 1979 the National Transportation Safety Board has recommended that safety seats be mandatory, while the Federal Aviation Administration has used its regulatory authority to prevent such rules. Ultimately, the Congress will resolve this dispute.

The lesson from this example is that consumers respond to changes in prices. An increase in the price of one good (air travel) causes some consumers to switch to a substitute good (highway travel), leading to some unexpected results.

Source: "Effort Under Way to Revamp Laws on Child Safety," *Oregonian*, March 23, 1997, p. A20.

An increase in the price of air travel will cause some consumers to switch to highway travel, which is actually more dangerous.

ier food. In other words, the demand curve for poultry may have shifted to the right, increasing the equilibrium quantity of poultry. Of course, an increase in demand will increase the price too, so if this explanation is correct, we should also observe higher prices for poultry.

According to the U.S. Department of Agriculture, this popular explanation is incorrect.[2] In fact, the increase in poultry consumption was caused by an increase in supply, not an increase in demand. This conclusion is based on the fact that poultry prices have been decreasing, not increasing. Between 1950 and 1990, the real price of poultry (adjusted for inflation) decreased by about 75%. As shown in Figure 4.15, an increase in supply causes the market equilibrium to shift from point *i* (price = $2 and quantity = 50 million pounds) to point *n* (price = $0.80 and quantity = 90 million pounds). The increase in supply decreases the equilibrium price. The supply of poultry increased because innovations in poultry processing decreased the cost of producing poultry products. The lesson here is that we shouldn't jump to conclusions based on limited infor-

Figure 4.15

The Mystery of Increasing Poultry Consumption

Because the price of poultry decreased at the same time the quantity of poultry consumed increased, we know that the increase in consumption resulted from an increase in supply, not an increase in demand. Innovations in poultry processing decreased production costs, shifting the supply curve to the right.

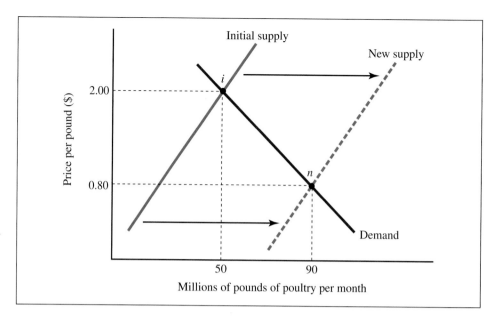

mation. A change in the equilibrium quantity could result from either a change in supply or a change in demand. To draw any conclusions, we need information about both price and quantity.

There may be a grain of truth in the popular explanation. It is possible that both demand and supply increased, shifting both curves to the right. Because the price of poultry decreased, however, we know that the shift of the supply curve (which tends to decrease the price) overwhelmed any shift of the demand curve (which tends to increase the price). Although changes in consumer preferences might contribute to increasing poultry consumption, the changes in consumption were caused largely by changes on the supply side of the market.

The Mystery of Falling Cocaine Prices

Ted Koppel, host of the ABC news program *Nightline*, once said. "Do you know what's happened to the price of drugs in the United States? The price of cocaine, way down, the price of marijuana, way down. You don't have to be an expert in economics to know that when the price goes down, it means more stuff is coming in. That's supply and demand."[3] According to Koppel, the price of drugs dropped because the government's efforts to control the supply of illegal drugs had failed. In other words, the lower price resulted from an increase in supply. According to the U.S. Department of Justice, the quantity of drugs consumed actually decreased during the period of dropping prices.[4] Is Koppel's economic detective work sound?

In this case, both the price and the quantity decreased. As shown in the second row of Table 4.5, when both the price and the quantity decrease, that means demand has decreased. In Figure 4.16, a decrease in demand shifts the demand curve to the left, and the market moves from point *i* (price = $15 and quantity = 400 units per day) to point *n* (price = $10 and quantity = 300 units per day). Koppel's explanation (an increase in supply) would be correct if the quantity of drugs increased at the same time that the price decreased. Because the quantity of drugs consumed actually decreased during the period of dropping prices, Koppel's explanation is incorrect. Lower demand—not a failure of the government's drug policy and an increase in supply—was responsible for the decrease in drug prices.

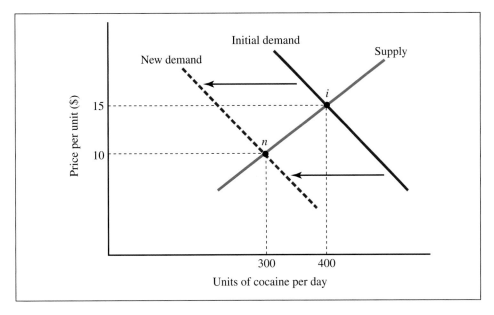

Figure 4.16

The Mystery of Lower Drug Prices
Because the quantity of cocaine consumed decreased at the same time the price of cocaine decreased, we know that the decrease in price resulted from a decrease in demand, not an increase in supply. A decrease in the demand for cocaine decreased the price and decreased the quantity consumed.

The Tobacco Settlement and Revenue for Health-Care Programs

At the beginning of this chapter, we presented a puzzle for a state budget analyst. The analyst expected the state support for programs dealing with tobacco-related illness to be $280 million per year, including $80 million from the tobacco settlement and $200 million from the state's cigarette tax. In fact, the state provided only $250 million. What happened?

The key to solving this mystery is the fact that the agreement will decrease the quantity of cigarettes purchased. Cigarette producers responded to the agreement by increasing the price of cigarettes by about 40 cents per pack. Consistent with the law of demand, the increase in price decreased the quantity demanded, decreasing the revenue from the cigarette tax. In Figure 4.17 an increase in price from $3.00 to $3.40 causes movement upward along the initial demand curve from point *i* to point *p*, decreasing the

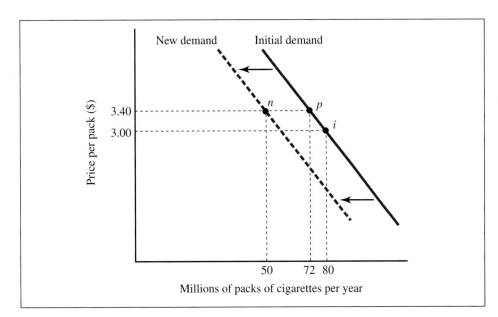

Figure 4.17

The Mystery of the Tobacco Money
The tobacco settlement increases the price of cigarettes from $3.00 to $3.40, causing movement upward along the original demand curve from point *i* to point *p*, decreasing the quantity consumed from 80 million to 72 million packs. The reduction in advertising and marketing shifts the demand curve to the left, reducing the quantity demanded at the new price ($3.40) from 72 million (point *p*) to 50 million packs (point *n*).

quantity sold from 80 million to 72 million packs per year. The agreement also required cigarette makers to reduce their advertising and marketing activities. As a result, the demand curve shifted to the left, as shown in Figure 4.17. The cutback in advertising reduced the quantity sold from 72 million packs per year (point p) to 50 million packs per year (point n). The net effect of the agreement is to decrease the quantity of cigarettes sold—and taxed—from 80 million to 50 million packs per year. With a tax of $1 per pack, that means that the state's revenue from the cigarette tax falls from $80 million to $50 million.

TEST Your Understanding

14. Complete the statement with "supply" or "demand": If the price and quantity change in the same direction, _____ is changing; if the price and quantity change in opposite directions, _____ is changing.

15. Suppose a freeze in Florida wipes out 20% of the orange crop. How will this affect the equilibrium price of Florida oranges? Defend your answer with a graph.

16. Suppose that between 2000 and 2001, the equilibrium price and the equilibrium quantity of amber both decrease. Draw a supply-demand diagram that explains these changes.

Using the TOOLS

In this chapter you learned how to use two tools of economics—the supply curve and the demand curve—to find equilibrium prices to predict changes in prices and quantities. Here are some opportunities to use these tools to do your own economic analysis.

1. ECONOMIC EXPERIMENT: MARKET EQUILIBRIUM

This simple experiment takes about 20 minutes. We start by dividing the class into two equal groups: consumers and producers.

- The instructor provides each consumer with a number indicating the maximum amount he or she is willing to pay (WTP) for a bushel of apples: The WTP is a number between $1 and $100. Each consumer has the opportunity to buy 1 bushel of apples per trading period. The consumer's score for a single trading period equals the gap between his or her WTP and the price actually paid for apples. For example, if the consumer's WTP is $80 and he or she pays only $30 for apples, the consumer's score is $50. Each consumer has the option of not buying apples. This will be sensible if the best price the consumer can get exceeds his or her WTP. If the consumer does not buy apples, his or her score will be zero.

- The instructor provides each producer with a number indicating the cost of producing a bushel of apples (a number between $1 and $100). Each producer has the opportunity to sell 1 bushel per trading period. The producer's score for a single trading period equals the gap between the selling price and the cost of producing apples. So if a producer sells apples for $20 and his or her cost is only $15, the producer's score is $5. Producers have the option of not selling apples, which is sensible if the best price the producer can get is less than his or her cost. If the producer does not sell apples, his or her score is zero.

Once everyone understands the rules, consumers and producers meet in a trading area to arrange transactions. A consumer may announce how much he or she is willing to pay for apples and wait for a producer to agree to sell apples at that price. Alternatively, a producer may announce how much he or she is willing to accept for apples and wait for a consumer to agree to buy apples at that price. Once a transaction has been arranged, the consumer and producer inform the instructor of the trade, record the transaction, and leave the trading area.

There are several trading periods, each of which lasts a few minutes. After the end of each trading period, the instructor lists the prices at which apples sold during that period. Then another trading period starts, providing consumers and producers another opportunity to buy or sell 1 bushel of apples. After all the trading periods have been completed, each participant computes his or her score by adding the scores from each trading period.

APPLICATIONS
2. Using Data to Draw a Demand Curve
The following table shows data on gasoline prices and gasoline consumption in a particular city. Is it possible to use these data to draw a demand curve? If so, draw the demand curve. If not, why not?

Year	Gasoline Price (per gallon)	Quantity Consumed (millions of gallons)
1999	1.20	400
2000	1.40	300
2001	1.60	360

3. Foreign Farm Workers and the Price of Berries
Current law allows thousands of Mexican workers to work on farms in the United States during harvest season. Suppose a new law outlaws the use of foreign farm workers. Assume that the resulting excess demand for labor increases the wage paid to farm workers by 20%. Use a supply-demand graph to predict the effects of the higher wage on the price of berries.

4. Market Effects of an Import Ban on Shoes
Consider a nation that initially imports half the shoes it consumes. Use a supply-demand graph to predict the effect of a ban on shoe imports on the equilibrium price and quantity of shoes.

5. The Mystery of Free Used Newspapers
In 1987 you could sell a ton of used newspapers for $60. Five years later, you could not sell them at any price. In other words, the price of used newspapers dropped from $60 to zero in just five years. Over this period the quantity of used newspapers bought and sold increased. What caused the drop in price? Defend your answer with a supply-demand graph.

Summary

In this chapter we've seen how supply and demand determine prices. And we saw how to predict the effects of changes in demand or supply on prices. Here are the main points of the chapter.

1. To draw a demand curve, we must be certain the other variables that affect demand (consumer income, prices of related goods, tastes, expectations, and number of consumers) are held fixed.

2. To draw a market supply curve, we must be certain the other variables that affect supply (input costs, technology, the number of producers, expectations, taxes and subsidies) are held fixed.

3. An equilibrium in a market is shown by the intersection of the demand curve and the supply curve. When a market reaches an equilibrium, there is no pressure to change the price.

4. A change in demand changes price and quantity in the same direction: An increase in demand increases the equilibrium price and quantity; a decrease in demand decreases the equilibrium price and quantity.

5. A change in supply changes price and quantity in opposite directions: An increase in supply decreases price and increases quantity; a decrease in supply increases price and decreases quantity.

Key Terms

Change in demand, 72
Change in quantity demanded, 65
Change in quantity supplied, 70
Change in supply, 77
Complements, 74
Demand schedule, 65
Excess demand, 70
Excess supply, 71

Income effect, 66
Individual demand curve, 65
Individual supply curve, 69
Inferior good, 76
Law of demand, 65
Law of supply, 69
Market demand curve, 66
Market equilibrium, 70

Market supply curve, 70
Normal good, 73
Perfectly competitive market, 64
Quantity demanded, 65
Quantity supplied, 68
Substitutes, 73
Substitution effect, 66
Supply schedule, 68

Problems and Discussion Questions

1. Figure 4.A shows the supply and demand curves for CD players. Complete the following statements.

a. At the market equilibrium (shown by point _____), the price of CD players is _____ and the quantity of CD players is _____.

b. At a price of $100, there would be excess _____, so we would expect the price to _____ (fill in with increase or decrease).

c. At a price exceeding the equilibrium price, there would be excess _____, so we would expect the price to _____ (fill in with increase or decrease).

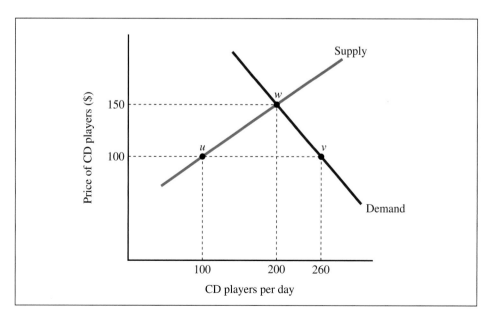

Figure 4.A
Supply and Demand for CD Players

2. The following table shows the quantities of corn supplied and demanded at different prices:

Price per Ton	Quantity Supplied	Quantity Demanded	Excess Demand or Excess Supply
$ 80	600	1,200	_____
$ 90	800	1,100	_____
$100	1,000	1,000	_____
$110	1,200	900	_____

  a. Complete the table.

  b. Draw the demand curve and the supply curve.

  c. What is the equilibrium price of corn?

3. Consider the market for personal computers. Suppose that the demand is stable: The demand curve doesn't change. Predict the effects of the following changes on the equilibrium price of computers. Illustrate your answer with a supply and demand diagram.

  a. The cost of memory chips (one component of a computer) decreases.

  b. The government imposes a $100 tax on personal computers.

4. Draw a supply-demand diagram to illustrate the effect of an increase in income on the market for restaurant meals.

5. Suppose that the tuition charged by public universities increases. Draw a supply-demand diagram to illustrate the effects of the tuition hike on the market for private college education.

6. Suppose that the government imposes a tax of $1 per pound of fish and collects the tax from fish producers. Draw a supply-demand diagram to illustrate the market effects of the tax.

7. As summer approaches, the equilibrium price of rental cabins increases and the equilibrium quantity of cabins rented increases. Draw a supply-demand diagram that explains these changes.

8. Suppose that the initial price of a pocket phone is $100 and that the initial quantity demanded is 500 phones per day. Depict graphically the effects of a technological innovation that decreases the cost of producing pocket phones. Label the starting point with an *i* and the new equilibrium with an *n*.

9. You've been hired as an economic consultant to evaluate the nation's airport security systems (metal detectors and machines that allow security people to see what's inside carry-on luggage). Suppose these security systems add $5 to the typical airplane ticket and require 10 minutes of extra time for each passenger. List the questions you will answer in your evaluation.

10. Suppose a freeze in Florida wipes out 20% of the orange crop. How will this affect the equilibrium price of California oranges? Defend your answer with a graph.

11. The Multifiber Agreement sets import quotas for various apparel products—including shirts—coming into the United States. Use a supply-demand graph to show the effects of the shirt quota on the equilibrium price of shirts in the United States.

12. Web Exercise: Visit the Web site of the National Association of Realtors [*http://www.realtor.com*]. Follow the "Find a Home" instructions and check housing prices for a three-bedroom, two-bath house in several cities, for example, San Francisco, California; Topeka, Kansas; Dallas, Texas; Concord, Massachusetts; and Seattle, Washington. Use supply and demand diagrams to explain why housing prices vary from city to city.

13. Web Exercise: Visit the Web site of eBay, a company that provides on-line auctions [*http://www.ebay.com*]. Suppose you want to buy a traditional 35mm camera. Access the listing of cameras being auctioned and check the most recent bids. Suppose someone develops a digital camera that takes better pictures than the traditional 35mm camera at half the cost. Predict the effects of the new camera on the supply of traditional 35mm cameras and the prices for cameras auctioned on the ebay site.

Take It to the Net

We invite you to visit the O'Sullivan/Sheffrin page on the Prentice Hall Web site at:
http://www.prenhall.com/osullivan/ for additional World Wide Web exercises for this chapter.

Chapter-Opening Questions

1. As is explained in A Closer Look on page 85, fewer infants would die in airplane crashes, but more people would die in automobile crashes as many parents responded to the higher cost of airline travel by switching to the alternative travel mode.

2. As is explained in one of the Economic Detective exercises, a lower price doesn't necessarily mean that supply has increased. The equilibrium quantity decreased at the same time, so the price drop was caused by a decrease in demand.

3. As is explained in one of the "Using the Tools" exercises, we can't draw a demand curve from a table of price and quantity data unless we know that the other determinants of demand (income, population, prices of substitutes and complementary goods, tastes, advertising) are fixed over the period covered by the data.

4. Innovations in poultry processing decreased the cost of producing poultry products. The resulting increase in supply decreased the equilibrium price, causing consumers to buy more poultry products.

Test Your Understanding

1. decrease, increase

2. Consumer income, the prices of substitute goods, the prices of complementary goods, consumer tastes, advertising, the number of consumers, and price expectations.

3. Input costs, technology, price expectations, number of producers, taxes and subsidies.

4. supply, demand

5. less, greater

6. demand, supply

7. One group is a, e, and f; another group is b, c, and d.

8. The statement is incorrect because it confuses the direction of causality. The correct statement is: "The demand curve shifted because demand increased." When something other than the price of the product changes, the relationship between price and quantity changes, causing the demand curve to shift.

9. right, left

10. Circle quantity of pencils demanded and price of pencils. Cross out number of consumers, price of pens, and consumer income.

11. One group is a, c, and e; another group is b, d, and f.

12. True. An increase in the wage increases production cost, so fewer computers will be supplied at each price.

13. Circle quantity of housing supplied and price of houses. Cross out number of consumers, price of wood, and consumer income.

14. demand, supply

15. The supply of oranges decreases, shifting the supply curve to the left. The equilibrium price will increase.

16. The demand decreases, shifting the demand curve to the left (an end to the Jurassic Park fad buying?), decreasing both the price and the quantity.

Using the Tools

2. Using Data to Draw a Demand Curve. It's tempting to use the data in the table to plot three combinations of price and quantity, connect the points with a curve, and call it a demand curve. That is not appropriate because we don't know what happened to the other determinants of the demand for gasoline over this period (consumer income, prices of substitutes and complements, tastes, advertising, price expectations). To draw a demand curve with these data, we must have additional data showing that these other variables did not change. If any of these other variables changed, we cannot draw a demand curve.

3. Foreign Farm Workers and the Price of Berries. The higher wage caused by the elimination of foreign farm workers will increase the production costs of berry farmers. The resulting decrease in supply of berries will shift the supply curve to the left. In Figure 4.B, the equilibrium price of berries increases from $0.60 to $0.73.

4. Market Effects of an Import Ban. An import ban has the same effect as a decrease in the number of firms in the market: supply decreases, shifting the market supply curve to the left. In Figure 4.C, the free-trade equilibrium is shown by point f, and the equilibrium with an import ban is shown by point b.

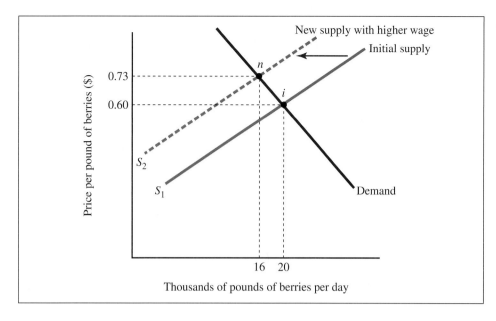

Figure 4.B
Market Effects of Higher Farm Wages
Reducing the number of foreign farm workers will increase the wage of farm workers, increasing the production costs of berry producers. The supply curve shifts to the left: At each price, a smaller quantity is supplied. Equilibrium is restored at point *n*, with a higher price ($0.73, up from $0.60) and a smaller quantity (16,000 pounds, down from 20,000 pounds).

The ban on imported shoes increases the price of shoes from $25 to $34.

5. The Mystery of Free Used Newspapers. Between 1987 and 1992 the price and quantity moved in opposite directions, meaning that the decrease in price was caused by an increase in supply. Over this five-year period, hundreds of communities adopted curbside recycling programs. These programs increased the supply of used newspapers, generating an excess supply of used newspapers that decreased the equilibrium price. In Figure 4.D, the increase in supply was so large that the equilibrium price fell to zero.

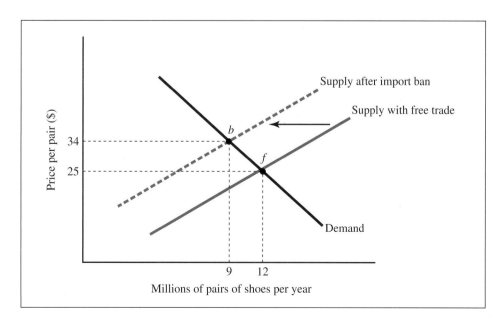

Figure 4.C
The Market Effects of an Import Ban
A ban on shoe imports decreases the supply of shoes, shifting the supply curve to the left. The free-trade equilibrium is shown by point *f*, and the equilibrium under the import ban is shown by point *b*. The import ban increases the price from $25 to $34 and decreases the quantity from 12 million to 9 million pairs of shoes.

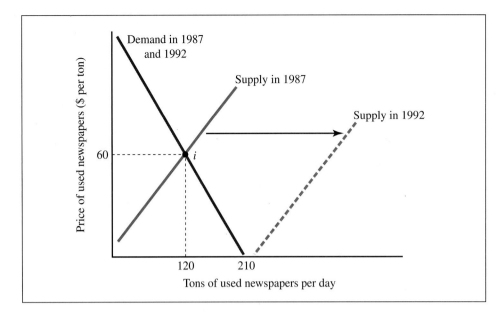

Figure 4.D

The Mystery of Free Used Newspapers
Between 1987 and 1992 the price of used newspapers decreased from $60 per ton to zero, a result of increases in supply caused by the expansion of curbside recycling programs.

Notes

1. *The News and Observer*, "Raleigh, N.C.-Based Companies Tap Growing Market for Wind Power," January 26, 2001; *Associated Press Online,* "Wind Farm to Power 70,000 Homes," January 10, 2001.

2. Mark R. Weimar and Richard Stillman, "Market Trends Driving Broiler Consumption," Livestock and Poultry Situation and Outlook Report LPS-44 (Washington, DC: U.S. Department of Agriculture, Economic Research Service, November 1990).

3. Kenneth R. Clark, "Legalize Drugs. A Case for Koppel," *Chicago Tribune*, August 30, 1988, sec. 5, p. 8.

4. U.S. Department of Justice, *Drugs, Crime, and the Justice System* (Washington, DC: U.S. Government Printing Office, 1992), p. 30.

Elasticity: A Measure of Responsiveness

In every large city in the United States, the public bus system runs a deficit: The total revenue from passenger fares is less than the cost of operating the bus system. Suppose your city wants to reduce its bus deficit and has decided to increase bus fares by 10%. Consider the following exchange between two city officials:

Buster: A fare increase is a great idea. We'll collect more money from bus riders, so revenue will increase and the deficit will shrink.

Bessie: Wait a minute, Buster. Haven't you heard about the law of demand? The increase in the bus fare will decrease the number of passengers taking buses, so we'll collect less money, not more, and the deficit will grow.

Who is right? As we'll see in this chapter, we can't predict how an increase in price will affect total revenue unless we know just how responsive consumers are to an increase in price. Like other consumers, bus riders obey the law of demand, but that doesn't necessarily mean that total fare revenue will fall.

Price elasticity of demand: A measure of the responsiveness of the quantity demanded to changes in price; computed by dividing the percentage change in quantity demanded by the percentage change in price.

From Chapter 4, we know that the quantity of a product demanded is determined by the price of the product, consumer income, and the prices of related goods. In this chapter, we'll use the concept of elasticity to measure the responsiveness of the quantity demanded to changes in these variables. The **price elasticity of demand** measures the responsiveness of quantity demanded to changes in the price of the product. We say that demand is elastic if a small change in price causes a large change in quantity demanded. Demand is inelastic if the quantity does not change very much as price changes. As we'll see later in the chapter, because the demand for bus service is inelastic, Buster is correct: An increase in the bus fare will increase total revenue. We can also use the concept of elasticity to measure the responsiveness of consumer demand to changes in the other factors that affect demand: consumer income, the price of substitute goods, and the price of complementary goods.

Switching to the supply side of the market, we can use elasticity to measure the responsiveness of the quantity supplied to changes in price. We know from Chapter 4 that an increase in price will increase the quantity supplied, but sometimes the question is, How much more will be supplied at the higher price? The **price elasticity of supply** measures the responsiveness of quantity supplied to changes in price. We say that supply is elastic if a small change in price causes a large change in the quantity supplied. In contrast, if producers are not very responsive, we say that supply is inelastic.

Price elasticity of supply: A measure of the responsiveness of the quantity supplied to changes in price; computed by dividing the percentage change in quantity supplied by the percentage change in price.

This chapter contains many applications of the concept of elasticity. Here are some practical questions that we answer:

1. How would a tax on beer affect the number of highway deaths among young adults?
2. Why is a bumper crop bad news for farmers?
3. If a firm wants to increase its total revenue, should it raise or lower its price?
4. Why do policies that limit the supply of illegal drugs increase the number of burglaries and robberies?
5. If the demand for a product increases, what information do we need to predict the resulting change in the equilibrium price?

The Price Elasticity of Demand

When the price of a good decreases, consumers will buy more of it, but how much more will they buy? The price elasticity of demand (E_d) measures the responsiveness of consumers to changes in price. We compute the price elasticity of demand by dividing the percentage change in the quantity demanded by the percentage change in price:

$$E_d = \frac{\text{percentage change in quantity demanded}}{\text{percentage change in price}}$$

As we saw in the appendix to Chapter 1, the simple way to compute the percentage change in a variable is to divide the change in the variable by the initial value of the variable. Suppose the price of milk increases from $2.00 to $2.20. (Later in the chapter, we'll see how to compute the price elasticity with the more precise midpoint formula described in the appendix to Chapter 1.)

We can use the numbers shown in Figure 5.1 to compute the price elasticity of demand for milk as follows:

- The percentage change in price equals the change in price (+$0.20) divided by the initial price ($2.00), or +10% (equal to +$0.20 divided by $2.00).

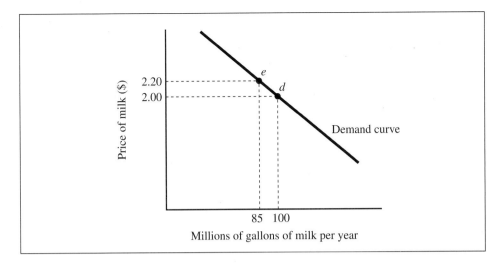

Figure 5.1

Market Demand Curve and Price Elasticity of Demand

A 10% rise in the price of milk (from $2 to $2.20) decreases the quantity demanded by 15% (from 100 to 85), so the price elasticity of demand is 1.50 = 15%/10%.

- The percentage change in quantity demanded equals the change in quantity (−15 million) divided by the initial quantity (100 million), or −15% (equal to −15 million divided by 100 million).

The conventional practice is to ignore any minus signs and compute the price elasticity as follows:

$$E_d = \frac{\text{percentage change in quantity demanded}}{\text{percentage change in price}} = \frac{15\%}{10\%} = 1.5$$

In this example, the price elasticity of demand, E_d, is equal to 1.5.

Why do we ignore the minus sign? The law of demand tells us that price and quantity move in opposite directions, so the percentage change in quantity will always have the opposite sign (+ or −) of the percentage change in price (− or +). In our example, a +10% change in price results in a −15% change in quantity. So to be absolutely precise, the price elasticity should be reported as a negative number. The conventional approach is to report all price elasticities as positive numbers. This means that a large number indicates that the quantity demanded is very elastic, or highly responsive to changes in price. As long as we remember the law of demand, there is no harm in dropping minus signs and reporting all price elasticities of demand as positive numbers.

The responsiveness of consumers to price changes varies from one good to another. An increase in the price of table salt doesn't change the quantity of salt demanded very much, but an increase in the price of a specific brand of corn flakes causes a large reduction in the quantity demanded. We can use the concept of price elasticity of demand to divide goods into three groups:

- **Elastic.** If the price elasticity of demand for a particular good is greater than 1.0, we say that demand is elastic. This is sensible because if the elasticity is greater than 1.0, the percentage change in quantity demanded exceeds the percentage change in price, meaning that consumers are very responsive to changes in price.

  Elastic demand: The price elasticity of demand is greater than one.

- **Inelastic.** If the price elasticity of demand is less than 1.0, consumers are not very responsive to changes in price, and we say that demand is inelastic.

  Inelastic demand: The price elasticity of demand is less than one.

- **Unitary elastic.** If the elasticity equals 1.0, the percentage change in quantity demanded equals the percentage change in price, and we say that demand is unitary elastic.

  Unitary elastic: The price elasticity demand equals one.

Elasticity and Substitutes

The price elasticity of demand for a particular good depends on the availability of substitutes. Consider two goods: insulin (a medicine for diabetics) and cornflakes. There are no good substitutes for insulin, so consumers are not very responsive to changes in price: An increase in price doesn't cause a large reduction in the quantity of insulin demanded. In other words, the lack of substitutes for insulin means that the demand is inelastic. In contrast, there are many substitutes for cornflakes, including different types of corn cereal and cereals made from other grains (wheat, rice, and oats). Therefore, a small increase in the price of cornflakes will cause a large decrease in quantity demanded as consumers switch to other types of cereal whose price has not changed. In other words, if substitutes are plentiful, demand is relatively elastic.

Table 5.1 shows the price elasticities of demand for various products. The different elasticities illustrate the importance of substitutes in determining the price elasticity of demand. Because there are no good substitutes for water and salt, it's not surprising that the elasticities are small. For example, the price elasticity of demand for water (0.20) means that a 10% increase in the price of water would decrease the quantity demanded by only 2%:

$$E_d = \frac{\text{percentage change in quantity of water demanded}}{\text{percentage change in price}} = \frac{2\%}{10\%} = 0.20$$

The demand for cigarettes, an addictive good, is also inelastic. The elasticity of 0.30 means that a 10% increase in price would cause a 3% decrease in quantity demanded.

Table 5.1   Price Elasticities of Demand for Selected Products

Product	Price Elasticity of Demand
Salt	0.1
Water	0.2
Coffee	0.3
Cigarettes	0.3
Shoes and footwear	0.7
Housing	1.0
Automobiles	1.2
Foreign travel	1.8
Restaurant meals	2.3
Air travel	2.4
Motion pictures	3.7
Specific brands of coffee	5.6

Sources: Frank Chaloupka, "Rational Addictive Behavior and Cigarette Smoking," *Journal of Political Economy,* August 1991, pp. 722–742; Gregory Chow, *Demand for Automobiles in the United States* (Amsterdam: North-Holland, 1957); David Ellwood and Mitchell Polinski, "An Empirical Reconciliation of Micro and Grouped Estimates of the Demand for Housing," *Review of Economics and Statistics,* vol. 61, 1979, pp. 199–205; H. F. Houthakker and Lester B. Taylor, *Consumer Demand in the United States: Analysis and Projections,* 2nd ed. (Cambridge, MA: Harvard University Press, 1970); John R. Nevin, "Laboratory Experiments for Estimating Consumer Demand: A Validation Study," *Journal of Marketing Research,* vol. 11, August 1974, pp. 261–268; Herbert Scarf and John Shoven, *Applied General Equilibrium Analysis* (New York: Cambridge University Press, 1984).

Because there are no good substitutes for coffee, the demand for coffee is inelastic (0.30). But because different brands of coffee are substitutes for one another, the demand for a specific brand of coffee is very elastic (between 5.6 and 8.9). An elasticity of 5.6 means that a 10% increase in price of a specific brand would decrease the quantity demanded by 56%. The change in quantity is large because consumers can easily switch to other brands.

For another example of the price elasticity of demand, consider the demand for trash disposal. Until recently, most cities charged a fixed monthly fee for trash collection. Under an alternative approach, called pay-to-throw, the more trash a household generates, the higher its trash bill. In 1991, Charlottesville, Virginia, switched 75 households from a fixed monthly fee to a price of $0.80 per 32-gallon bag of trash. The new pricing plan caused the following changes among the households participating in the experiment.[1]

- The volume of trash collected decreased by 37%, to 0.46 bag per person per week. The price elasticity of demand with respect to the volume of trash was 0.23.

- The weight of trash collected decreased by 14%, to 9.37 pounds per person per week. The weight decreased by a small amount because of the "Seattle stomp," a technique that allows a person to pack more trash into each bag. (Seattle had an early experiment in pay-to-throw pricing.) The price elasticity of demand with respect to the weight of trash was 0.08.

- The weight of recyclable materials (collected at no cost to the household) increased by 16%, to 4.27 pounds per person per week.

- Illegal dumping (littering and dumping household trash in commercial dumpsters) is difficult to measure. It appears that it may have increased by about 0.5 pound per person per week.

This study has some lessons for other communities that are considering a pay-to-throw plan: Although the total volume of trash would decrease, the total weight would decrease by a small amount, and illegal dumping would increase.

Other Determinants of Elasticity

We've seen that the availability of substitute goods affects the price elasticity of demand. Several other factors affect the price elasticity of demand:

- **Time.** Because it takes time to change consumption habits and find substitute goods, the more time we give consumers to respond to a price change, the larger their response. When the price of gasoline increases, consumers' immediate response is limited by their inability to immediately buy more fuel-efficient cars or move closer to their workplaces. Eventually, consumers can change cars and relocate, so we would expect a much larger reduction in gasoline consumption in the long run. As time passes, demand becomes more elastic because consumers have more options.

- **Importance in budget.** If a good represents a small part of the budget of the typical consumer, demand for it is relatively inelastic. If the price of pencils increases by 10% (from $0.50 to $0.55), there will be a relatively small decrease in the quantity demanded because the price change is trivial relative to the income of the typical consumer. In contrast, a 10% increase in the price of cars (from $20,000 to $22,000) will generate a much larger response because the change in price is large relative to consumer income. International comparisons of the price elasticity of demand for food suggest that demand is more price-elastic when the good represents a large part of the budget. In wealthy countries such as the United States, Canada, and

Germany, the price elasticity of demand for food is around 0.15.[2] In poor countries such as India, Nigeria, and Bolivia, people spend a larger fraction of their budget on food, so they are more responsive to changes in food prices; in these countries the price elasticity is around 0.34.

- **Necessities versus luxuries.** For necessities such as bread, rice, and potatoes, demand is relatively inelastic. For luxury goods such as restaurant meals and air travel, demand is relatively elastic. This is sensible because it is easier to do without luxury goods.

The price elasticity of demand for some goods varies with the age of the consumer. Although the overall price elasticity of demand for cigarettes is inelastic, the price elasticity for teenagers is elastic. For the implications for the effort to cut teenage smoking, read "A Closer Look: How to Cut Teen Smoking by 60%."

Elasticity Along a Linear Demand Curve

If a demand curve is linear—a straight line—does that mean that the elasticity of demand is the same at all points on the line? As shown in Figure 5.2, the price elasticity of demand decreases as we move downward along a linear demand curve.

- On the upper part of a linear demand curve, demand is elastic. In moving from point *r* to point *s,* the percentage change in quantity (20% = 2/10) is four times the percentage change in price (5% = 4/80), so the elasticity is 4.0.

- On the lower part of a linear demand curve, demand is inelastic. In moving from point *v* to point *w,* the percentage change in quantity (5% = 2/40) is one-fourth of the percentage change in price (20% = 4/20), so the elasticity is 0.25.

Why does the price elasticity vary along a linear demand curve? It's tempting to think the elasticity is constant because a straight line has a constant slope. But that's

A CLOSER LOOK   HOW TO CUT TEEN SMOKING BY 60%

Under the 1997 Tobacco Settlement, if smoking by teenagers does not decline by 60% by the year 2007, cigarette makers will face a fine of $2 billion.[3] The settlement is expected to increase cigarette prices by about 62 cents per pack, a percentage increase of about 25%. Will that be enough to reduce teen smoking by the target percentage? The answer depends on the price elasticity of demand for cigarettes.

The demand for cigarettes by teenagers is elastic: The teen elasticity is 1.3, meaning that a 10% increase in the price of cigarettes will decrease teen cigarette consumption by 13%.[4] About half the reduction results from fewer teen smokers, and the other half results from fewer cigarettes for each teen smoker. Although the teen demand for cigarettes is relatively elastic, a 25% price hike will not be enough to cut teen smoking

by the target amount. Given an elasticity of 1.3, the price of cigarettes must increase by about 46% (equal to 60% divided by 1.3).

Figure 5.2

Price Elasticity Along a Linear Demand Curve
The price elasticity of demand decreases as we move downward along a linear demand curve. Demand is elastic on the upper half of the demand curve and inelastic on the lower half.

	Percentage decrease in price	Percentage increase in quantity	Elasticity
Point r to point s	4/80 = 5%	2/10 = 20%	20%/5% = 4.0
Point v to point w	4/20 = 20%	2/40 = 5%	5%/20% = 0.25

incorrect because elasticity is measured by percentage changes, not absolute changes. As we move downward along the demand curve, we're moving in the direction of larger quantities, so the same absolute change in quantity (two units) becomes a smaller percentage change in quantity. Between points r and s, the percentage change in quantity is 20% (2/10), compared to only 5% (2/40) between points v and w. At the same time, the movement downward along the curve leads to a larger percentage change in price. As a result, the elasticity becomes smaller and smaller.

Using the Midpoint Formula to Compute Price Elasticity

The midpoint formula (Appendix, Chapter 1) provides a more precise way to compute percentage changes than the formula used in this chapter. Using the midpoint approach, we divide the change in a variable (for example, the change in price) by the average value of the variable (the average price). We can use this approach to compute the price elasticity associated with points d and e in Figure 5.1.

The percentage change in price equals the change (0.20) divided by the average price ($2.10), or 9.52%:

$$\text{percentage change in price} = \frac{\text{change}}{\text{average value}} = \frac{0.20}{(2.00 + 2.20)/2}$$

$$= \frac{0.20}{2.10} = 0.0952 = 9.52\%$$

The percentage change in quantity equals the change (-15) divided by the average quantity (92.5), or -16.22%:

$$\text{percentage change in quantity} = \frac{\text{change}}{\text{average value}} = \frac{-15}{(100 + 85)/2}$$

$$= \frac{-15}{92.5} = -0.1622 = 16.22\%$$

If we plug these percentage changes into the formula for the price elasticity of demand, the computed price elasticity is 1.70:

$$E_d = \frac{\text{percentage change in demand}}{\text{percentage change in price}} = \frac{16.22}{9.52} = 1.70$$

Why is this elasticity different from the elasticity we computed with the simple approach (1.50)? The midpoint approach measures the percentage changes more precisely, so we get a more precise measure of price elasticity. In this case, the percentage changes are relatively small, so the two elasticity numbers aren't too far apart. If the percentage changes were larger, however, the elasticity numbers generated by the two approaches would be quite different, and it would be wise to use the midpoint approach.

Extreme Cases: Perfectly Inelastic Demand and Perfectly Elastic Demand

Figure 5.3 shows two demand curves that show the extreme cases of demand elasticity. The demand curve in panel A of Figure 5.3 is a vertical line, indicating that regardless of price, the quantity demanded is 80 units. This is the case of **perfectly inelastic demand**, with a price elasticity of demand equal to zero. The numerator in the elasticity expression (the percentage change in quantity demanded) is zero, regardless of the percentage change in the price of the good.

The demand curve in panel B of Figure 5.3 is a horizontal line, indicating that the quantity demanded is infinitely responsive to any change in price. This is the case of **perfectly elastic demand**, with a price elasticity of demand equal to infinity. The numerator in

Perfectly inelastic demand: Price elasticity of demand equals zero.

Perfectly elastic demand: Price elasticity of demand is infinite.

Figure 5.3

Perfectly Inelastic Demand and Perfectly Elastic Demand

In panel A, the quantity demanded is the same at every price, so the price elasticity of demand is zero. In panel B, the quantity demanded is infinitely responsive to changes in price, so the price elasticity of demand is infinite.

(A) Perfectly Inelastic Demand

(B) Perfectly Elastic Demand

the elasticity expression (the percentage change in quantity demanded) is infinite, regardless of the percentage change in the price of the good. One implication of this demand curve is that if the price were to rise from $2 to any higher price, the quantity demanded would fall to zero.

TEST Your Understanding

1. Complete the statement: To compute the price elasticity of demand, we divide the percentage change in _____ by the percentage change in _____.

2. Complete the statement: If a 10% increase in price decreases the quantity demanded by 12%, the price elasticity of demand is _____.

3. Explain why the demand for prerecorded audio tapes is more elastic in the long run than in the short run.

4. If we are on the upper portion of the market demand curve and the price increases by 10%, will the quantity demanded decrease by more than 10% or by less than 10%?

Using the Price Elasticity of Demand

The price elasticity of demand is a very useful tool for economic analysis. We know from the law of demand that a decrease in price will increase the quantity demanded, ceteris paribus. If we know the elasticity of demand for a particular good, we can predict how much more of that good will be sold at the lower price. We can also predict whether an increase in price will increase or decrease total spending on the good.

Predicting Changes in Quantity Demanded

We can use the price elasticity of demand to predict what happens to the quantity demanded when the price increases. The formula for the elasticity has three variables: The price elasticity of demand (one variable) equals the percentage change in quantity (the second variable) divided by the percentage change in price (the third variable). If we know two of the three variables, we can compute the third. For example, suppose you run a campus film series and you've decided to increase your admission price by 15%. If you know the elasticity of demand for your movies, you could use the elasticity formula to predict how many fewer tickets you'll sell at the higher price. If the elasticity of demand is 2.0, a 15% price hike will decrease the quantity demanded by 30%:

$$E_d = 2.0 = \frac{\text{percentage change in quantity demanded}}{15\%} = \frac{30\%}{15\%}$$

Applications: College Education, Highway Deaths, Medical Care

How could university officials use the price elasticity of demand? Suppose a university increases its tuition from $4,000 to $4,400 and wants to predict how many fewer students will enroll in the university as a result of the higher price. The price elasticity of demand for higher education is about 1.40, so a 10% increase in tuition will decrease enrollment by 14%:

$$E_d = 1.4 = \frac{\text{percentage change in quantity demanded}}{10\%} = \frac{14\%}{10\%}$$

How would a tax on beer affect highway deaths among young adults? The price elasticity of demand for beer among young adults is about 1.30, and the number of highway deaths is roughly proportional to the group's beer consumption.[5] If a state imposes a beer tax that increases the price of beer by 20%, what will happen to the number of highway deaths among young adults? Using the elasticity formula, we predict that beer consumption will decrease by 26%:

$$E_d = 1.3 = \frac{\text{percentage change in quantity demanded}}{20\%} = \frac{26\%}{20\%}$$

If the number of highway deaths among young adults is proportional to their beer consumption, the number of highway deaths will also decrease by 26%. Of course, if young adults switch from beer to other alcoholic beverages, the number of highway deaths will decrease by a smaller amount.

If the price of medical care increases, how will consumers respond? The rising cost of medical care has forced many nations to take a closer look at programs that subsidize medical care for their citizens. If prices are increased to cover more of the costs of providing medical care, how will this affect poor and wealthy households? For an answer, read "A Closer Look: Pricing Medical Care in Developing Countries."

Predicting Changes in Total Revenue

If a firm increases the price of its product, will total sales revenue increase or decrease? The answer depends on the price elasticity of demand for the product. If we know the price elasticity, we can determine whether a price hike will increase or decrease the firm's total revenue.

A CLOSER LOOK — PRICING MEDICAL CARE IN DEVELOPING COUNTRIES

Many developing nations subsidize medical care, charging consumers a small fraction of the cost of providing the services. If a nation increased its price of medical care, how would the higher price affect its poor and wealthy households? In Côte d'Ivoire in Africa, the price elasticity of demand for hospital services is 0.47 for poor households and 0.29 for wealthy households. This means that a 10% increase in the price of hospital services would cause poor households to cut back their hospital care by 4.7%, while wealthy households would cut back by only 2.9%. In Peru, the differences between poor and wealthy households are even larger: The price elasticity is 0.67 for poor households but only 0.03 for wealthy households. The same pattern occurs in the demand for the medical services provided by physicians and health clinics. The poor are much more sensitive to price, so when prices increase, they suffer much larger reductions in medical care.

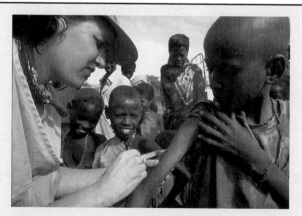

In developing nations, the poor are relatively sensitive to changes in the price of medical care.

Source: Paul Gertler and Jacques van der Gaag, *The Willingness to Pay for Medical Care: Evidence from Two Developing Countries* (Baltimore: Johns Hopkins University Press, 1990).

Let's return to the example of the campus film series. Suppose you are thinking about increasing the price of tickets from $4.00 to $4.40. An increase in the ticket price brings good news and bad news:

- **Good news.** You get more money for each ticket sold.
- **Bad news.** You sell fewer tickets.

Your total revenue will decrease if the bad news (fewer tickets sold) dominates the good news (more money per ticket). The elasticity of demand tells us how the good news compares to the bad news. If demand is elastic, consumers will respond to the higher price by purchasing many fewer tickets, so although you will collect more money per ticket, you'll sell so few tickets that your total revenue will decrease. For example, as Table 5.2 shows, if the price elasticity of demand is 2.0, a 10% increase in price will decrease the quantity demanded by 20%, from 100 to 80 tickets. Because the percentage decrease in quantity (the bad news) exceeds the percentage increase in price (the good news), total revenue decreases, from $400 to $352.

In general, an elastic demand means that the percentage change in quantity (the bad news from a price hike) will exceed the percentage change in price (the good news), so an increase in price will decrease total revenue.

We get the opposite result if the demand for the good is inelastic: An increase in price increases total revenue. If demand is inelastic, consumers are not very responsive to an increase in price, so the good news (more money per unit sold) dominates the bad news (fewer units sold). For example, suppose that the campus bookstore starts with a textbook price of $50 and a quantity of 100 books. If the bookstore increases its price by 10% (from $50 to $55 per book) and the elasticity of demand for textbooks is 0.40, the quantity of textbooks sold will decrease by only 4% (from 100 to 96). Therefore, the store's total revenue will be ($5,280 ($55 times 96), compared to only $5,000 at the lower price ($50 times 100). In general, an inelastic demand means that the percentage change in quantity will be smaller than the percentage change in price, so an increase in price will increase total revenue.

Table 5.3 summarizes the revenue effects of changes in prices for different types of goods:

- **Elastic demand.** There is a negative relationship between price and total revenue: An increase in price decreases total revenue: a decrease in price increases total revenue.
- **Inelastic demand.** There is a positive relationship between price and total revenue: An increase in price increases total revenue; a decrease in price decreases total revenue.
- **Unitary elastic demand.** Total revenue does not vary with price.

The relationship between elasticity and total revenue provides a simple test of whether demand is elastic or inelastic. Suppose that when a music store increases the price of its CDs, its total revenue from CDs drops. The negative relationship between price and total revenue means that demand for the store's CDs is elastic: Total revenue

Table 5.2 Price and Total Revenue with Elastic Demand

Price	Quantity of Tickets Sold	Total Revenue
4.00	100	$400
4.40	80	$352

Table 5.3 Elasticity and Total Revenue

Type of Demand	Value of Price Elasticity of Demand	Change in Quantity Versus Change in Price	Effect of Higher Price on Total Revenue	Effect of Lower Price on Total Revenue
Elastic	Greater than 1.0	Larger percentage change in quantity	Decreases	Increases
Inelastic	Less than 1.0	Smaller percentage change in quantity	Increases	Decreases
Unitary elastic	1.0	Same percentage changes in quantity and price	Does not change	Does not change

decreases because consumers are very responsive to an increase in price, buying a much smaller quantity. In contrast, suppose that when a city increases the price it charges for water, the total revenue from water sales increases. The positive relationship between price and total revenue suggests that the demand for the city's water is inelastic: Total revenue increases because consumers are not responsive to an increase in price.

We can use Figure 5.4 to reinforce what we've learned about price elasticity and total revenue. Panel A shows a linear demand curve (the same as the one in Figure 5.2), and Panel B shows the total revenue curve associated with the demand curve. We know that demand is elastic along the upper half of a linear demand curve; that means that a decrease in price will increase the quantity sold by a larger percentage amount. As a result, total revenue will increase, as shown by the positively sloped total-revenue curve between points *b* and *c*. In contrast, demand is inelastic along the lower half of a linear demand curve; that means that a decrease in price will increase the quantity sold by a smaller percentage amount. As a result, total revenue will decrease, as shown by the negatively sloped total-revenue curve between points *c* and *d*. The total-revenue curve will reach its maximum at the midpoint of the linear demand curve, where demand is unitary elastic. In Figure 5.4, demand is unitary elastic at point *t* on the demand curve, so total revenue reaches its maximum at $1,250 at point *c* on the total-revenue curve.

Applications: Transit Deficits, Property Crime

At the beginning of the chapter, we considered the question of whether increasing the price of bus rides would reduce a city's transit deficit. Now we know that to answer the question, we need to know the price elasticity of demand for bus service. The price elasticity in the typical city is 0.33, meaning that a 10% increase in fares will decrease ridership by about 3.3%.[6] Because demand for bus travel is elastic, the good news associated with a fare hike (more revenue per rider) will dominate the bad news (fewer riders), and total fare revenue will increase. In other words, an increase in fares will reduce the transit deficit.

What's the connection between antidrug policies and property crimes such as robbery, burglary, and auto theft? The government uses search-and-destroy tactics to restrict the supply of illegal drugs. If this approach succeeds, drugs become scarce and the price of drugs increases. Because the demand for illegal drugs is inelastic, the increase in price will increase total spending on illegal drugs. Many drug addicts support their habits by stealing personal property—robbing people, stealing cars, and burglarizing homes—so the increase in total spending on drugs means that drug addicts will commit more property crimes.[7] To support their more expensive drug habits, addicts will commit more burglaries, robberies, and auto thefts.

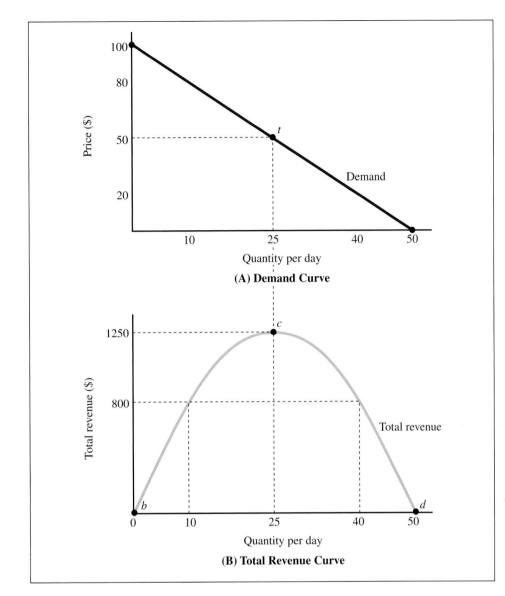

Figure 5.4

Elasticity and Total Revenue
Demand is elastic along the upper half of a linear demand curve, so a decrease in price increases total revenue. Demand is inelastic along the lower half of a linear demand curve, so a decrease in price decreases total revenue. Total revenue reaches its maximum at the midpoint of the demand curve, where demand is unitary elastic.

(A) Demand Curve

(B) Total Revenue Curve

The Video Elasticity Mystery

Economic Detective

The manager of a video-rental store has asked you to solve a mystery. According to national studies of the video-rental market, the price elasticity of demand for video rentals is 0.80: A 10% increase in price decreases the quantity of videos demanded by about 8%. In other words, the demand for videos is inelastic. Based on this information, the manager of the video store increased her price by 20%, expecting her total revenue to increase. She expected the good news (more money per rental) to dominate the bad news (fewer rentals). When her total revenue decreased instead of increasing, she was puzzled. Your job is to solve this mystery.

   The key to solving this mystery is to recognize that the manager can't use the results of a national study to predict the effects of increasing her own price. The national study suggests that if all video stores in the nation increased their prices by 10%, the nationwide quantity of videos demanded would drop by 8%. But when a single video store in a city increases its price, consumers can easily switch to other video stores in the city. As a result, a 10% increase in the price of video rentals at one store will decrease the quantity sold by that store by much more than 8%. The demand facing an individual store is elastic, so an increase in price will decrease total revenue.

TEST Your Understanding

Other Elasticities of Demand

We've seen that the price elasticity of demand measures the responsiveness of consumers to changes in the price of a particular good. Of course, the demand for a particular product also depends on other variables such as consumer income and the prices of related goods—substitutes and complements. We can use two other elasticities to measure the responsiveness of consumers to changes in these other variables that affect demand.

We saw in Chapter 4 that the demand for a particular product depends in part on the consumer's income. The income elasticity of demand measures the responsiveness of demand to changes in income, indicating how much more or less of a particular product is purchased as consumer income changes. The **income elasticity of demand** is defined as the percentage change in quantity demanded divided by the percentage change in income:

Income elasticity of demand: A measure of the responsiveness of the quantity demanded to changes in consumer income; computed by dividing the percentage change in the quantity demanded by the percentage change in income.

$$E_i = \frac{\text{percentage change in quantity demanded}}{\text{percentage change in income}}$$

For example, if a 10% increase in income increases the quantity of books demanded by 15%, the income elasticity of demand for books is 1.50 (equal to 15%/10%).

We can use the income elasticities of demand for various products to divide the products into different types. If the income elasticity is positive—indicating a positive relationship between income and demand—we say that the good is *normal*. If the income elasticity is negative—revealing a negative relationship between income and demand—we say that the good is *inferior*. Some examples of products with negative income elasticities are intercity bus travel and used clothing. We can divide the set of normal goods into two types. If the income elasticity is greater than 1.0—meaning that the percentage change in quantity demanded exceeds the percentage change in income—we say that the demand for a product is income-elastic. If the income elasticity is less than 1.0—indicating a smaller increase in quantity demanded—we say that demand is income-inelastic.

We saw in Chapter 4 that the demand for a particular product depends in part on the prices of related goods—substitutes and complements. The **cross elasticity of demand** measures the responsiveness of demand to changes in the prices of other goods, indicating how much more or less of a particular product is purchased as other prices change. The

Cross elasticity of demand: A measure of the responsiveness of the quantity demanded to changes in the price of a related good; computed by dividing the percentage change in the quantity demanded of one good (X) by the percentage change in the price of another good (Y).

cross elasticity is defined as the percentage change in quantity demanded of one good (X) divided by the percentage change in the price of a related good (Y):

$$E_{xy} = \frac{\text{percentage change in quantity of } X \text{ demanded}}{\text{percentage change in price of } Y}$$

As we saw in Chapter 4, two goods are considered substitutes if there is a positive relationship between the quantity demanded of one good and the price of the other good. For example, an increase in the price of bananas increases the demand for apples as consumers substitute apples for the more expensive bananas. For substitute goods, the cross elasticity is positive. In contrast, two goods are considered complements if there is a negative relationship between the quantity demanded of one good and the price of the other. For example, an increase in the price of ice cream increases the cost of apple pie with ice cream, causing consumers to demand fewer apples. For complementary goods, the cross elasticity is negative.

The Price Elasticity of Supply

Let's look at elasticity on the supply side of the market. The price elasticity of supply measures the responsiveness of producers to changes in price. We compute this elasticity by dividing the percentage change in quantity supplied by the percentage change in price:

$$E_s = \frac{\text{percentage change in quantity supplied}}{\text{percentage change in price}}$$

In Figure 5.5, when the price of milk increases from \$2.00 to \$2.20, the quantity supplied increases from 100 million gallons to 120 million gallons. In other words, a 10% increase in price increased the quantity supplied by 20%, so the price elasticity of supply is 2.0:

$$E_s = \frac{\text{percentage change in quantity supplied}}{\text{percentage change in price}} = \frac{20\%}{10\%} = 2.0$$

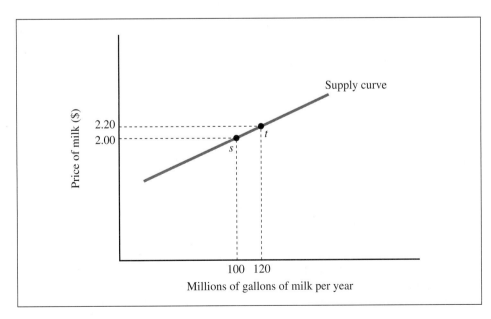

Figure 5.5

Market Supply Curve and Price Elasticity of Supply
A 10% increase in the price of milk (from \$2 to \$2.20) increases the quantity supplied by 20% (from 100 million gallons to 120 million), so the price elasticity of supply is 2.0 = 20%/10%.

Time is an important factor in determining the price elasticity of supply for a product. When the price of a particular product increases, the immediate response is that current producers produce more of the product in their existing production facilities (for example, factories, stores, offices, or restaurants). Although a higher price will certainly induce firms to produce more, the response is limited by the limited capacity of the firms' production facilities. Over time, however, new firms can enter the market and old firms can build new production facilities, so there will be a larger response in the long run. As time passes, supply becomes more elastic because more and more firms have the time to build production facilities and produce more output.

The milk industry provides a good example of the difference between short-run and long-run supply elasticities. The price elasticity of supply over a one-year period is 0.12: If the price of milk increases by 10% and stays there for a year, the quantity of milk supplied will rise by only 1.2%.[8] In the short run, dairy farmers can squeeze a little more output from their existing production facilities. Over a 10-year period, the price elasticity is 2.5: The same 10% rise in price will increase the quantity supplied by 25%. In the long run, dairy farmers can expand existing facilities and build new ones, so in the long run, there is a larger response to a higher price.

Productivity Changes in Quantity Supplied

We can use the price elasticity of supply to predict the effect of price changes on the quantity supplied. For example, suppose that the elasticity of supply is 0.80 and the price increases by 5%. Using the elasticity formula, we would predict a 4% increase in quantity supplied:

$$E_s = 0.80 = \frac{\text{percentage change in quantity supplied}}{5\%} = \frac{4\%}{5\%}$$

As we saw in Chapter 4, many governments establish minimum prices for agricultural products. The higher the minimum price, the larger the quantity supplied, consistent with the law of supply. If we know the price elasticity of supply, we can predict just how much more will be supplied at the higher price. For example, if the minimum price of cheese increases by 10% and the price elasticity is 0.60, the quantity of cheese supplied will rise by 6%:

$$E_s = 0.60 = \frac{\text{percentage change in quantity supplied}}{10\%} = \frac{6\%}{10\%}$$

Extreme Cases: Perfectly Inelastic Supply and Perfectly Elastic Supply

Perfectly inelastic supply:
Price elasticity of supply equals zero.

Perfectly elastic supply: Price elasticity of supply is infinite.

Figure 5.6 shows two supply curves that show the extreme cases of supply elasticity. The supply curve in panel A of Figure 5.6 is a vertical line, indicating that regardless of price, the quantity supplied is 50 units. This is the case of **perfectly inelastic supply**, with a price elasticity of supply equal to zero. The numerator in the elasticity expression (the percentage change in quantity supplied) is zero, regardless of the percentage change in the price of the good.

The supply curve in panel B of Figure 5.6 is a horizontal line, indicating that the quantity supplied is infinitely responsive to any change in price. This is the case of **perfectly elastic supply**, with a price elasticity of supply equal to infinity. The numerator in the elasticity expression (the percentage change in quantity supplied) is infinite, regardless of the percentage change in the price of the good. One implication of this supply curve is that if the price were to drop from $4 to any lower price, the quantity supplied would fall to zero.

Predicting Price Changes Using Price Elasticities

When supply or demand changes—when the supply curve or demand curve shifts—we can draw a supply and demand diagram to predict whether the equilibrium price will increase or decrease. In many cases, the simple diagram will show all we need to know about the effects of a change in supply or demand. But what if we want to predict how much a price will increase or decrease? We can use a simple formula to predict the change in the equilibrium price resulting from a change in supply or a change in demand.

In Figure 5.7, an increase in demand shifts the demand curve to the right and increases the equilibrium price. We explained in Chapter 4 that a demand curve shifts as a result of a change in something other than the price of the product—for example, a change in income, tastes, or the price of a related good. When demand increases, the immediate effect is excess demand: At the original price ($2.00), the quantity demanded exceeds the quantity supplied by 35 million gallons (135 million − 100 million). As the price increases, both consumers and producers help to eliminate the excess demand: Consumers buy less (the law of demand), and firms produce more (the law of supply). If both consumers and producers are very responsive to changes in price, it will take a small increase in price to eliminate the excess demand. In other words, an increase in demand will cause a small increase in price if both demand and supply are elastic.

We can use the following **price-change formula** to predict the change in the equilibrium price resulting from a change in demand. We divide the percentage change in demand by the sum of the price elasticities of supply and demand:

$$\text{percentage change in equilibrium price} = \frac{\text{percentage change in demand}}{E_s + E_d}$$

Price-change formula: A formula that shows the percentage change in equilibrium price resulting from a change in demand or supply, given values for the price elasticity of supply and price elasticity of demand.

Figure 5.7

Increase in Demand Increases the Equilibrium Price

An increase in demand shifts the demand curve to the right, increasing the equilibrium price. In this case, a 35% increase in demand increases the price by 10%. Using the price-change formula, we have 10% = 35%/(2.0 + 1.5).

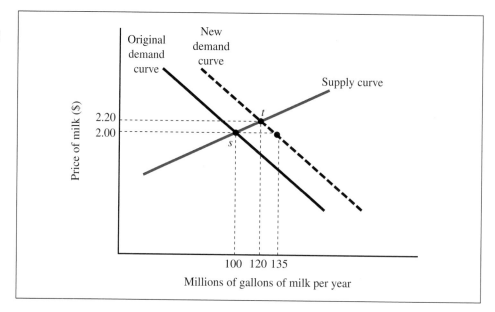

The numerator is the rightward shift of the demand curve in percentage terms. In Figure 5.7, the initial quantity demanded at a price of $2.00 is 100 million gallons (shown by the initial demand curve), while the new quantity demanded at the same price is 135 million gallons (shown by the new demand curve). The change in demand is 35% (35/100). The two price elasticities appear in the denominator. This is sensible because if consumers and producers are very responsive to changes in price (the elasticities are large numbers), excess demand will be eliminated with a relatively small increase in price.

We can use a simple example to see how to use the price-change formula. Suppose that demand increases by 35% (the demand curve shifts to the right by 35%). If the supply elasticity is 2.0 and the demand elasticity is 1.5, the predicted change in the equilibrium price is 10%:

$$\text{percentage change in equilibrium price} = \frac{\text{percentage change in demand}}{E_s + E_d}$$

$$= \frac{35\%}{2.0 + 1.5} = 10\%$$

In Figure 5.7, the equilibrium price increases by 10%, from $2.00 to $2.20. If either demand or supply were less elastic (if either of the elasticity numbers were smaller), the predicted change in price would be larger. For example, if the supply elasticity were 0.25 instead of 2.0, we would predict a 20% increase in price (35%/1.75).

What about the direction of the price change? We know from Chapter 4 that an increase in demand increases the equilibrium price and a decrease in demand decreases the equilibrium price. Therefore, the percentage change in price is positive when the change in demand is positive (when demand increases and the demand curve shifts to the right), and negative when the change in demand is negative (when demand decreases and the demand curve shifts to the left). For example, suppose the demand for a product decreases by 15% (the demand curve shifts to the left by 15%). If the supply elasticity is 1.0 and the demand elasticity is 0.50, the price-change formula shows that the equilibrium price will decrease by 10%:

$$\text{percentage change in equilibrium price} = \frac{\text{percentage change in demand}}{E_s + E_d}$$

$$= \frac{-15\%}{1.0 + 0.5} = -10\%$$

We can use a slightly different version of the price-change formula to predict the change in the equilibrium price resulting from a change in supply. As explained in Chapter 4, a change in supply results from changes in something other than the price of the product—for example, a change in the cost of labor or raw materials, a change in production technology, or a change in the number of firms. The immediate effect of an increase in supply is excess supply: At the original price, the quantity supplied exceeds the quantity demanded. As the price drops, consumers respond by purchasing more, and producers respond by producing less, so the gap between quantity supplied and demanded narrows. If both consumers and producers are very responsive to changes in price, it will take a small decrease in price to eliminate the excess supply. In other words, an increase in supply will cause a small decrease in price if both demand and supply are elastic.

To predict the change in price resulting from a change in supply, we just substitute supply for demand in the numerator of the price-change formula and add a minus sign. The minus sign indicates that there is a negative relationship between the equilibrium price and supply: When supply increases—when the supply curve shifts to the right—the price drops; when supply decreases, the price rises:

$$\text{percentage change in equilibrium price} = -\frac{\text{percentage change in supply}}{E_s + E_d}$$

For example, suppose the supply of milk increases by 10%. If the price elasticity of demand is 0.6 and the price elasticity of supply is 1.4, the equilibrium price will decrease by 5%:

$$\text{percentage change in equilibrium price} = -\frac{\text{percentage change in supply}}{E_s + E_d}$$

$$= -\frac{10\%}{1.4 + 0.6} = -5\%$$

TEST Your Understanding

8. Complete the statement: If a 10% increase in price increases the quantity supplied by 15%, the price elasticity of supply is _____ .

9. Suppose the price elasticity of a supply of cheese is 0.80. If the price of cheese rises by 20%, by what percentage will the quantity supplied change?

10. Suppose that the elasticity of demand for chewing tobacco is 0.70 and the elasticity of supply is 2.30. If an antichewing campaign decreases the demand for chewing tobacco by 30%, in what direction and by what percentage will the price of chewing tobacco change?

11. Suppose that the elasticity of demand for motel rooms in a town near a ski area is 1.0 and the elasticity of supply is 0.50. If the population of the surrounding area increases by 30%, in what direction and by what percentage will the price of motel rooms change?

Using the TOOLS

This chapter introduced several new tools of economics, including four different elasticities and a formula that can be used to predict the change in price resulting from a change in supply or demand. Here are some opportunities to use these tools to do your own economic analysis.

APPLICATIONS

1. Projecting Transit Ridership

As a transit planner, you must predict how many people ride commuter trains and how much money is generated from train fares. According to a recent study,[9] the short-run price elasticity of demand for commuter rail is 0.62 and the long-run elasticity is 1.59. The current ridership is 100,000 people per day. Suppose fares increase by 10%.

a. Predict the changes in train ridership over a one-month period (short run) and a five-year period (long run).

b. Over the one-month period, will total revenue increase or decrease? What will happen in the five-year period?

2. Bumper Crops

Your job is to predict the total revenue generated by the nation's corn crop. Last year's crop was 100 million bushels, and the price was $4.00 per bushel. This year's weather was favorable throughout the country, and this year's crop will be 110 million bushels, or 10% larger than last year's. The price elasticity of demand for corn is 0.50.

a. Predict the effect of the bumper crop on the price of corn, assuming that the entire crop is sold this year.

b. Predict the total revenue from this year's corn crop.

c. Did the favorable weather increase or decrease the total revenue from corn? Why?

3. Washington, D.C., Gas Tax

You are a tax analyst for Washington, D.C., and have been asked to predict how much revenue will be generated by the city's gasoline tax. The initial quantity of gasoline is 100 million gallons per month, and the price elasticity of demand for gasoline in the typical large city is 4.0. The tax, which is $0.10 per gallon, will increase the price of gasoline by 5%.

a. How much revenue will the gasoline tax generate?

b. In 1980, tax analysts in Washington, D.C., based their revenue predictions for a gasoline tax on the elasticity of demand for gasoline in the United States as a whole, which is 1.0. Would you expect the national elasticity to be larger or smaller than the elasticity for the typical large city? Would you expect the analysts to overestimate or underestimate the revenue from the gasoline tax?

4. College Enrollment and Housing

Consider a college town where the initial price of apartments is $400 and the initial quantity is 1,000 apartments. The price elasticity of demand for apartments is 1.0, and the price elasticity of supply of apartments is 0.50.

a. Use supply and demand curves to show the initial equilibrium, and label the equilibrium point *i*.

b. Suppose an increase in college enrollment is expected to increase the demand for apartments in a college town by 15%. Use your graph to show the effects of the increase in demand on the apartment market. Label the new equilibrium point *f*.

c. Predict the effect of the increase in demand on the equilibrium price of apartments.

Summary

This chapter deals with the numbers behind the laws of demand and supply. The law of demand tells us that an increase in the price of a product will decrease the quantity demanded, ceteris paribus. If we know the price elasticity of demand for that good, we can determine just how much less of it will be sold at the higher price. Similarly, if we know the price elasticity of supply for a product, we can determine just how much more of it will be supplied at a higher price. Here are the main points of the chapter.

1. The price elasticity of demand—defined as the percentage change in quantity demanded divided by the percentage change in price—measures the responsiveness of consumers to changes in price.

2. Demand is relatively elastic if there are good substitutes.

3. If demand is elastic, there is a negative relationship between price and total revenue. If demand is inelastic, there is a positive relationship between price and total revenue.

4. The price elasticity of supply—defined as the percentage change in quantity supplied divided by the percentage change in price—measures the responsiveness of producers to changes in price.

5. If we know the elasticities of supply and demand, we can predict the percentage change in price resulting from a change in demand or supply.

Key Terms

cross elasticity of demand, 108
elastic demand, 97
income elasticity of demand, 108
inelastic demand, 97

perfectly elastic demand, 102
perfectly elastic supply, 110
perfectly inelastic demand, 102
perfectly inelastic supply, 110

price-change formula, 111
price elasticity of demand, 96
price elasticity of supply, 96
unitary elastic, 97

Problems and Discussion Questions

1. When the price of compact discs (CDs) increased from $10 to $11, the quantity of CDs demanded decreased from 100 to 87. What is the price elasticity of demand for CDs? Is demand elastic or inelastic?

2. Explain why the demand for residential natural gas (gas used for heating, cooling, and cooking) is more elastic than the demand for residential electricity.

3. Would you expect the demand for a specific brand of running shoes to be more elastic or less elastic than the demand for running shoes in general? Why?

4. For each of the following goods, indicate whether you expect demand to be inelastic or elastic, and explain your reasoning: opera, foreign travel, local telephone service, video rentals, and eggs.

5. You observe a positive relationship between the price your store charges for CDs and the total revenue from CDs. Is the demand for your CDs elastic or inelastic?

6. Suppose the price elasticity of demand for a campus film series is 1.40. If the objective of the film society is to maximize its total revenue (price times the number of tickets sold), should it increase or decrease its price?

7. As the head of a state chapter of MADD (Mothers Against Drunk Driving), you are to speak in support of policies that discourage drunk driving. The number of highway deaths among young adults, which is roughly proportional to the group's beer consumption, is initially 100 deaths per year. You have scheduled a news conference to express your support for a beer tax that will increase the price of beer by 10%. The price elasticity of demand for beer is 1.30. Complete the following statement: "The beer tax will decrease the number of highway deaths among young adults by about _____ per year."

8. When the price of paper increases from $100 to $104 per ton, the quantity supplied increased from 200 to 220 tons per day. What is the price elasticity of supply?

9. Suppose that the government restricts logging to protect an endangered species. The restrictions increase the price of wood products and shift the supply curve for new housing to the left by 4%. The initial price of new housing is $100,000, the elasticity of demand is 1.0, and the elasticity of supply is 3.0. Predict the effect of the logging restriction on the equilibrium price of new housing. Illustrate your answer with a graph that shows the initial point (*i*) and the new equilibrium (*f*).

10. Web Exercise. Visit the Web site of Roll Back the Beer Tax (*www.beertax.com*). What are the arguments against beer taxes? Does this site ignore some of the benefits associated with beer taxes? What do you think about beer taxes?

11. Web Exercise. Visit the Web site of the Center for Disease Control (*http://www.cdc.gov*). Search for the facts on the price elasticity of demand for cigarettes. How are the estimated elasticities used by policy analysts?

Take It to the Net

We invite you to visit the O'Sullivan/Sheffrin page on the Prentice Hall Web site at:
http://www.prenhall.com/osullivan/ for additional World Wide Web exercises for this chapter.

Model Answers for This Chapter

Chapter-Opening Questions

1. A beer tax will increase the price of beer, decreasing beer consumption. Highway deaths are roughly proportional to beer consumption, so the tax will also decrease highway deaths. The actual change in highway deaths depends on the price elasticity of demand for beer.

2. As shown in "Using the Tools: Bumper Crops," a bumper crop of corn decreases the equilibrium price of corn by a relatively large amount because the demand for corn is inelastic. Although corn farmers will sell more bushels, they will receive much less per bushel, so total revenue will drop.

3. If demand is elastic, the firm should lower its price. If demand is inelastic, the firm should raise its price.

4. The policies increase the price of the illegal drug, which increases total spending on the drug because demand is inelastic. If drug addicts support their habits with property crime, they must commit more crime to support their more expensive habits.

5. The percentage change in demand, the price elasticity of supply, and the price elasticity of demand.

Test Your Understanding

1. Quantity, price.
2. 1.20.

3. An increase in the price of tapes will cause some consumers to buy CD players and switch from tapes to CDs, but this takes some time.

4. On the upper portion, demand is elastic, so quantity will decrease by more than 10%.

5. Decrease, 6.

6. The price elasticity is 1.0 (neither elastic nor inelastic).

7. Demand is elastic, so a decrease in price would increase total revenue.

8. 1.50 = 15%/10%.

9. The quantity supplied will increase by 16%.

10. Using the price-change formula, the price will decrease by 10% = 30%/3.

11. Using the price-change formula, the price will increase by 20% = 30%/1.50.

Using the Tools

1. Projecting Transit Ridership
   a. According to the elasticity formula, ridership will decrease by 6.2% in the short run (a loss of 6,200 riders) and 15.9% in the long run (a loss of 15,900 riders).
   b. Demand is inelastic in the short run, so total revenue will increase. Demand is elastic in the long run, so total revenue will eventually decrease.

2. Bumper Crops

    a. Using the price elasticity formula, to sell an additional 10% of corn, the price must decrease by 20%, to $3.20.

    b. Total revenue is 110 million × $3.20, or $352 million.

    c. Total revenue last year was $400 million, so the bumper crop decreased total revenue. This occurs because demand is inelastic, so the price decreases by a large amount.

3. Washington, D.C., Gas Tax

    a. Using the price elasticity formula, the 5% increase in price will decrease the quantity demanded by 20%, from 100 million gallons to 80 million gallons. The revenue is the tax per gallon ($0.10) × the quantity (80 million gallons), or $8 million.

    b. They will overestimate the revenue from the tax because they will underestimate the change in quantity demanded by the tax. Specifically, they will predict a quantity of 95 million gallons instead of 80 million gallons and revenue of $9.5 million instead of $8 million. Because it is relatively easy to buy gasoline in a nearby city, the demand for gasoline will be relatively elastic at the city level.

4. College Enrollment and Housing

    c. Use the price-change formula to compute the change in the equilibrium price. The price increases by 10% = 15%/(0.50 + 1.0).

Notes

1. Don Fullerton and Thomas Kinnaman, "Household Responses to Pricing Garbage by the Bag," *American Economic Review,* vol. 86, no. 4, 1996, pp. 971–984.

2. Chin-Fun Cling and James Peale, Jr., "Income and Price Elasticities," in *Advances in Econometrics Supplement,* edited by Henri Theil (Greenwich, CT: JAI Press, 1989).

3. Michael M. Phillips and Suein L. Hwang, "Why Tobacco Pact Won't Hurt Industry," *Wall Street Journal*, Sept. 12, 1997, page A2.

4. Frank J. Chaloupka and Michael Grossman, "Price, Tobacco Control Policies, and Smoking among Young Adults," *Journal of Health Economics* vol. 16, 1997, pp. 359–373.

5. Henry Saffer and Michael Grossman, "Beer Taxes, the Legal Drinking Age, and Youth Motor Vehicle Fatalities," *Journal of Legal Studies,* vol. 41, June 1987.

6. Kenneth A. Small, *Urban Transportation Economics* (Philadelphia, PA: Harwood Academic Publishers, 1992).

7. L. P. Silverman and N. L. Sprull, "Urban Crime and the Price of Heroin," *Journal of Urban Economics,* vol. 4, 1977, pp. 80–103.

8. Richard Klemme and Jean-Paul Chavas, "The Effects of Changing Milk Price on Milk Supply and National Dairy Herd Size," *Economic Issues,* University of Wisconsin, June 1985.

9. Richard Voith, "The Long Run Elasticity of Demand for Commuter Rail Transportation," *Journal of Urban Economics,* vol. 30, 1991, pp. 360–372.

6

Market Efficiency and Government Intervention

Consumer:	How much is this radio?
Salesperson:	It's $25, complete with headphones.
Consumer:	I'll take it. Here's the money.
Salesperson:	Thank you.
Consumer:	Thank you.

Every day, there are millions of mundane transactions like this one, most of them ending in a double "thank you." Are people being polite, or do they really mean it? The millions of "thank yous" remind us that both people in a voluntary transaction benefit; otherwise, they wouldn't make the trade. In this chapter, we'll see that a market equilibrium—with the quantity demanded equal to the quantity supplied—may generate the largest possible net benefits for buyers and sellers. In other words, the market equilibrium may be efficient. We'll explore the logic behind Adam Smith's metaphor of the invisible hand, the idea that individual buyers and sellers, each acting in his or her own self-interest, *frequently* promote the social interest.

The metaphor of the invisible hand is qualified by the word "frequently." In some markets, buyers and sellers acting in their own self-interest generate outcomes that are contrary to the social interest. We can rule out these sorts of markets by making four assumptions:

1. Informed Buyers and Sellers. We'll assume that both buyers and sellers have enough information to make informed decisions about buying and selling.

2. Perfect Competition. A perfectly competitive market has a very large number of firms, each of which is so small that it takes the market price as given. Firms are free to enter or exit the market, so whenever there is an opportunity to make a profit—that is, whenever the price of a product exceeds the cost of producing it— firms will enter the market and supply more of the product. The quantity supplied will continue to increase until the opportunity for profit is eliminated, which happens when the price is just high enough to cover the cost of providing the product, but no higher.

3. No Spillover Benefits. There is a spillover benefit when part of the benefits from some product go to someone who does not decide how much of the product to consume. For example, if your farm is in a flood plain and another farmer builds a dike to protect low-lying areas, you benefit from that farmer's decision to build a dam. The markets considered in this chapter do not have spillover benefits, meaning that the benefits of consumption are confined to the person who is deciding how much to consume.

4. No Spillover Cost. There is a spillover cost when part of the cost of producing some product is borne by someone who does not decide how much of the product to produce. For example, if you live downstream from a paper mill that dumps chemical waste into the river, you bear some of the cost of paper production because it makes the river unsafe for swimming and drinking. In the first part of this chapter, we consider markets without spillover costs, meaning that producers, who decide how much to produce, bear all the costs of production.

As we'll see in the last part of the chapter, when there are spillover costs—for example, water pollution—the market equilibrium will be inefficient, and government can guide buyers and sellers to make choices that promote the social interest. Later in the book, we'll examine the three other reasons for inefficiency: a small number of firms, spillover benefits, and poorly informed sellers and buyers.

This chapter also discusses the effects of government intervention in markets that would otherwise be efficient. We'll see that when government intervenes—controlling the price of the good or the quantity sold—it will prevent some voluntary transactions that would benefit both buyer and seller. For that reason, government intervention causes inefficiency. As we explore the efficiency of markets and the effects of government intervention, we answer the following practical questions:

1. If a college town uses a rent-control policy to cut the monthly rent on apartments, will some students be harmed by the policy?

2. If you want to operate a taxi in New York City, Toronto, or Boston, you must first buy a taxi medallion for over $100,000. Why?

3. Why is there a shortage (excess demand) for human organs for transplanting?

4. Who bears the cost of restrictions on textile imports, and what is the cost per textile job saved?

5. If a factory dumps chemical waste into a river, harming people downstream, what should the government do?

Consumer Surplus and Producer Surplus

We'll start our discussion of market efficiency by showing how to measure the benefits experienced by consumers and producers. We'll start with consumers, exploring the benefits they receive and how to measure them. Then we'll look at the supply side of the market.

The Demand Curve and Consumer Surplus

If you said "thank you" the last time you purchased a product, did you mean it? If you were willing to pay more than the price you actually paid, you received what's called **consumer surplus.** Consumer surplus is the difference between the maximum amount a consumer is willing to pay for a product and the price that he or she pays for the product. For example, if you are willing to pay $21 for a CD that you buy for $10, your consumer surplus is $11.

Let's start our discussion of consumer surplus with another look at the demand curve, which shows how much consumers are willing to pay for a product. Figure 6.1 shows the market demand curve for lawn cutting in a small town. The demand curve shows that no one will pay to have their lawn cut for $25 (point *t*), but the first consumer (Juan) will pay for a cut if the price drops to $22. This suggests that Juan is willing to pay up to $22 to have his lawn cut, but no more. Moving down the demand curve, the second

Consumer surplus: The difference between the maximum amount a consumer is willing to pay for a product and the price that he or she pays for the product.

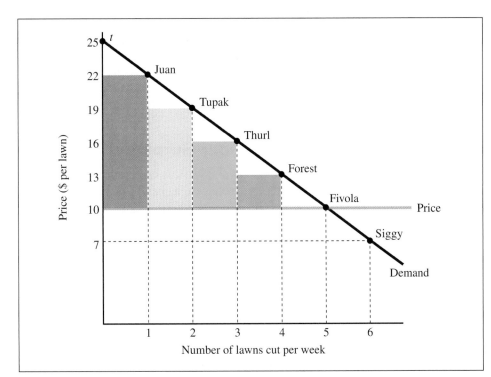

Figure 6.1

Demand Curve and Consumer Surplus
Consumer surplus equals the maximum amount a consumer is willing to pay (shown by the demand curve) minus the price paid. Juan is willing to pay $22, so if the price is $10, his consumer surplus is $12. The market consumer surplus equals the sum of the surpluses earned by all consumers in the market. In this case, the market consumer surplus is $30 = $12 + $9 + $6 + $3 + $0.

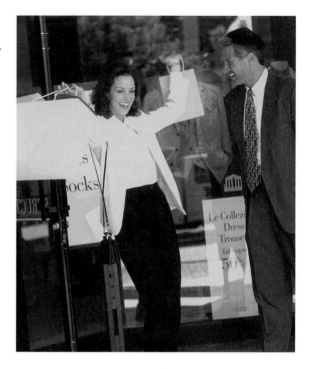

The price of a consumer good is less than or equal to the amount the consumer is willing to pay for the good. Consumer surplus measures the bonus or surplus received by the consumer.

consumer (Tupak) will pay for lawn cutting when the price drops to $19, suggesting that he is willing to pay up to $19. As we continue to move downward along the demand curve, other consumers are willing to pay less and less for each additional lawn cut.

We can use the demand curve to measure just how much of a net benefit or surplus consumers get. Suppose that the price of a lawn cut is $10, and everyone pays this price. Juan's consumer surplus is $12, the amount he is willing to pay ($22) minus the price. Similarly, Tupak's consumer surplus is $9, equal to the difference between the amount he is willing to pay ($19) and the market price. To compute the total consumer surplus in the lawn-cutting market, we simply add up the surpluses for each of the five consumers who buy lawn cutting at a price of $10. In this example, the market consumer surplus is $30, equal to $12 (Juan) + $9 (Tupak) + $6 (Thurl) + $3 (Forest) + $0 (Fivola). The fifth consumer (Fivola) gets no consumer surplus because the price equals the amount she is willing to pay. The sixth person (Siggy) doesn't have his lawn cut because the amount he is willing to pay is less than the price.

The Supply Curve and Producer Surplus

Like consumers, the people who produce goods and services say "thank you" when they sell their products. This suggests that they too receive a net benefit or surplus from voluntary transactions. **Producer surplus** is the difference between the price a producer receives for a product and the minimum amount the producer is willing to accept for the product. For example, if you are willing to cut someone's lawn for any amount over $4 and you do it for $10, your producer surplus is $6 ($10 − $4). The minimum amount a producer is willing to accept is the marginal cost of producing the product, so producer surplus is the difference between the price and the marginal cost.

Let's start our discussion of producer surplus with another look at the supply curve, which shows the marginal cost of production. Figure 6.2 shows the market supply curve for lawn cutting in a small town. Let's imagine that six people are willing to cut lawns if the price is right. Each potential cutter incurs the same cost for renting a lawn mower but different opportunity costs for their time. The marginal cost for the first producer (Abe) is $2:

Producer surplus: The difference between the price a producer receives for a product and the minimum amount the producer is willing to accept for the product.

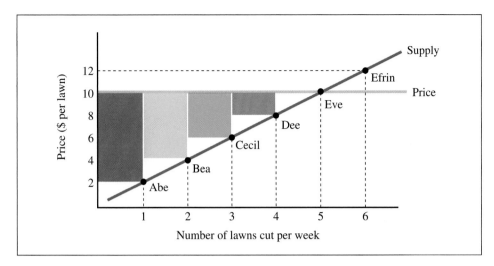

Figure 6.2

Supply Curve and Producer Surplus

Producer surplus equals the market price minus the producer's marginal cost (shown by the supply curve). Abe's marginal cost is $2, so if the price is $10, his consumer surplus is $8. The market producer surplus equals the sum of the surpluses earned by all producers in the market. In this case, the market producer surplus is $20 = $8 + $6 + $4 + $2 + $0.

He incurs a cost of $2, including the cost of renting a mower and the opportunity cost of his time. Therefore, Abe is willing to cut a lawn if he receives at least $2. On the supply curve, if the price is $2, one person—Abe—will cut lawns. Bea has a higher opportunity cost of time and therefore a higher marginal cost ($4): She won't cut a lawn unless she is paid at least $4. If the price is $4, two people—Abe and Bea—will cut lawns. Moving upward along the supply curve, the other potential lawn cutters have even higher marginal costs. The higher the price, the larger the number of people willing to cut lawns.

We can use the supply curve to measure just how much of a net benefit or surplus producers get. If the price of lawn cutting is $10, Abe's producer surplus for the first lawn is $8, the price he receives minus his marginal cost ($2). Similarly, Bea's producer surplus is $6, equal to the difference between the price and her marginal cost ($4). To compute the total producer surplus in the lawn-cutting market, we simply add up the surpluses for each of the five producers who cut lawns at a price of $10. In this example, the market producer surplus is $20, equal to $8 (Abe) + $6 (Bea) + $4 (Cecil) + $2 (Dee) + $0 (Eve). The fifth producer (Eve) gets no producer surplus because the price equals her marginal cost, and the sixth potential producer (Efrin) doesn't cut any lawns because the price is less than his cost.

Market Equilibrium and Efficiency

Figure 6.3 puts the demand and supply curves together to show the equilibrium in the market for lawn cutting. The demand curve intersects the supply curve at a price of $10 per lawn. At this price, five lawns are cut, meaning that there are five buyers and five sellers. The total surplus of a market is the sum of consumer surplus and producer surplus. In Figure 6.3, the consumer surplus is $30 and the producer surplus is $20, so the total surplus of the market is $50. As we'll see in this part of the chapter, the market equilibrium generates the highest possible total surplus. That's why we say that the market equilibrium is efficient: We can't do any better in terms of the total surplus of the market.

Total Surplus Is Lower with a Price Below the Equilibrium Price

To see why the market equilibrium maximizes the total surplus of the market, let's look at the total surplus of the market when the price is less than the equilibrium price. Suppose the government imposes a maximum price of $4 on lawn cutting. As

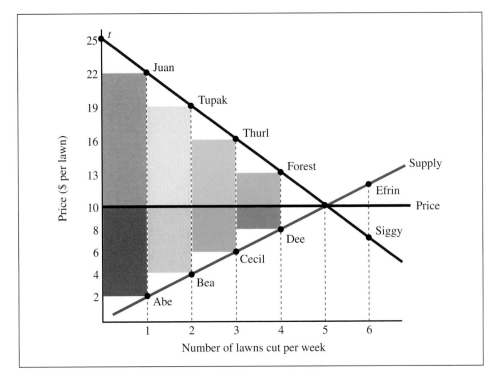

Figure 6.3

Market Equilibrium and the Total Value of the Market

The total surplus of the market equals consumer surplus (the lightly shaded areas) plus producer surplus (the darkly shaded areas). The market equilibrium generates the highest possible total market value, equal to $50 = $30 (consumer surplus) + $20 (producer surplus).

shown in panel A of Figure 6.4, at this price only two people cut lawns, and the producer surplus is shown by the darkly shaded area between the price line and the supply curve. Consumers can buy only as much as producers sell, so the market consumer surplus equals the surpluses for the first two consumers. This is shown as the lightly shaded areas between the price line and the demand curve. Comparing Figure 6.4 to Figure 6.3. we see that the maximum price reduces the total surplus of the market. For the first two lawns, consumers simply gain at the expense of producers. The maximum price also eliminates the surpluses from the third and fourth lawns, so the total surplus decreases.

The maximum price reduces the total surplus of the market because it prevents some mutually beneficial transactions. The third consumer (Thurl) is willing to pay $16 to have his lawn cut, and the third producer (Cecil) is willing to cut a lawn if he is paid at least $6. Thurl is willing to pay more than Cecil requires, so cutting Thurl's lawn would generate a net benefit of $10. If they split the difference, agreeing on a price of $11, each would get a surplus of $5. The maximum price prevents Thurl and Cecil from executing this transaction, so the maximum price decreases the total surplus of the market. The same logic applies to the fourth lawn: The maximum price prevents Forest and Dee from executing a transaction that would generate a net benefit of $5, equal to Forest's willingness to pay ($13) minus Dee's marginal cost ($8).

Total Surplus Is Lower with a Price Above the Equilibrium Price

What would happen if the government imposed a minimum price instead of a maximum price? If the minimum price is $19, as shown in panel B of Figure 6.4, the demand curve indicates that consumers would be willing to buy only two lawn cuts. The total surplus

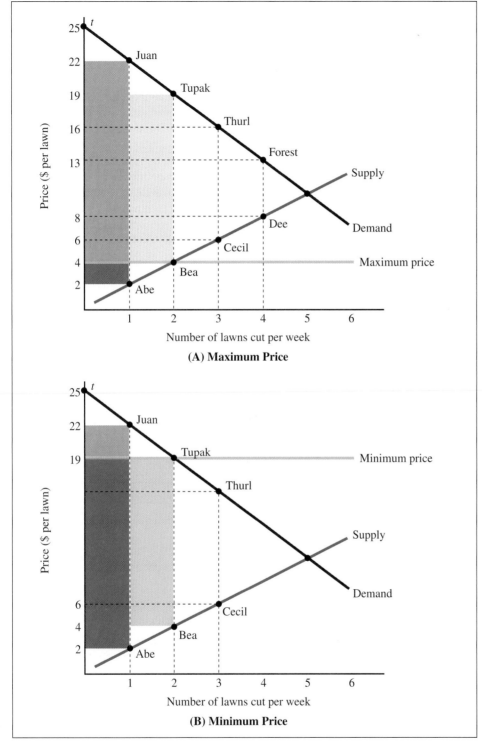

Figure 6.4

A Maximum Price or a Minimum Price Decreases the Total Surplus of the Market

(A) Maximum Price A maximum price of $4 reduces the total value of the market. The first two consumers gain at the expense of the first two producers. The consumer and producer surplus for the third and fourth lawns are lost entirely, so the total value of the market decreases.

(B) Minimum Price A minimum price of $19 reduces the total value of the market. The first two producers gain at the expense of the first two consumers. The consumer and producer surplus for the third and fourth lawns are lost entirely, so the total value of the market decreases.

of the market would be the sum of consumer and producer surplus for the first two lawns, the same as it was under the maximum price. The difference between the two policies is that under a maximum price, the first two consumers gain at the expense of the first two producers, while under the minimum price, the producers gain at the expense of consumers.

Efficiency and the Invisible Hand

The market equilibrium maximizes the total surplus of the market because it guarantees that all the mutually beneficial transactions happen. Once we reach the market equilibrium at point *e* in Figure 6.3, there are no more transactions that would benefit a buyer and a seller. The demand curve tells us that the potential buyer of the sixth lawn cut (Siggy) is willing to pay only $7, and the supply curve tells us that the potential seller of the sixth lawn cut (Efrin) has a marginal cost of $12. This transaction doesn't happen because the potential buyer is not willing to pay the cost of producing the good.

Our little example of the market for lawn cutting illustrates a general lesson about markets. The typical market has thousands of buyers and thousands of sellers, each acting in his or her own self-interest. If the market is perfectly competitive and has no spillovers, the market reaches the price and quantity that maximizes the total surplus of the market and is therefore efficient. Instead of using a bureaucrat to coordinate the actions of everyone in the market, we can rely on the actions of individual consumers and individual producers, each guided only by self-interest. This is the invisible hand in action.

The experience of the former Soviet Union demonstrates the importance of prices and the power of Adam Smith's ideas embodied in the metaphor of the invisible hand. The Soviet economy was a planned economy in the sense that bureaucrats—not individual producers—decided how much of each good to produce. There were no prices to guide the decisions of producers. When the Soviets discovered a persistent mismatch between what they were producing and what consumers wanted, they asked a team of experts to propose a solution to the problem. The experts told the bureaucrats to figure out the prices that would have occurred if the Soviet economy were a market economy instead of a planned one. Once the bureaucrats had these predicted prices, they could then base their production decisions on the predicted prices. In other words, the experts told the bureaucrats to base their decisions on the prices that would have emerged from a market economy.

TEST Your Understanding

1. Complete the statement: Consumer surplus equals _____ minus _____, while producer surplus equals _____ minus _____.

2. You are willing to pay $2,000 to have your house painted, and Pablo's marginal cost of painting a house is $1,400. If you split the difference, what's your consumer surplus? What's Pablo's producer surplus?

3. Looking back at Figure 6.4, how much is Forest willing to pay for the fourth cut lawn? What is Dee's marginal cost for cutting the fourth lawn? Describe a mutually beneficial transaction that would be blocked by a maximum price of $4.

4. The conclusion that a market equilibrium is efficient is based on four assumptions. What are they?

Government Intervention: Controlling Price

Now that we've seen that a perfectly competitive market without spillovers is efficient, we can discuss the effects of government intervention in such a market. We'll start with government policies that control the price of the product, setting either a maximum price or a minimum price. In each case, if the market is perfectly competitive and has no spillovers, government intervention reduces the total surplus of the market and thus causes inefficiency.

Maximum Prices: Rent Control

We've already seen two different effects of a maximum price. In Chapter 4, we saw that when the government sets a maximum price that is less than the equilibrium price, the result is excess demand for the product. The decrease in price reduces the quantity supplied and increases the quantity demanded, so at the controlled price, consumers want to buy more than producers want to sell. In this chapter, we see from panel A of Figure 6.4 that a maximum price decreases the total surplus of the market: Some consumers gain at the expense of producers, and the total surplus decreases. Here are some examples of goods that have been or may be subject to maximum prices:

- Rental housing. A **rent control** program establishes a maximum monthly rent.

- Gasoline. Price controls on gasoline in the 1970s established a maximum price.

- Medical goods and services. Some proposals to control medical costs include price controls.

Rent control: A policy under which the government specifies a maximum rent that is below the equilibrium rent.

In all three cases, a maximum price will cause excess demand and reduce the total surplus of the market.

Let's use rent control to discuss some of the subtle effects of a maximum price. As we saw in Chapter 4, a maximum price creates excess demand for the product. Rent control creates a gap between the number of consumers willing to rent housing and the number of apartments available. The excess demand for apartments means that consumers will spend more time searching for apartments. One cost of rent control is the opportunity cost of the extra time spent searching for apartments. Another example of the time cost of a maximum price is price controls for gasoline: Consumers spent hours waiting in line to buy gasoline, using time that could have been spent working, studying, or having fun.

We saw in this chapter that a maximum price is inefficient because it prevents mutually beneficial transactions between potential buyers and sellers. In the case of rent control, many people violate the spirit and the letter of the law by executing transactions of dubious legal merit. Consumers in some rent-control cities pay extra money to property owners to outbid other consumers for scarce apartments. These extra payments are often disguised as nonrefundable security deposits or "key money" (hundreds or thousands of dollars to get the key to the apartment when a consumer signs a lease).

Is rent control good for the poor? Many wealthy and famous people benefit from rent control,[1] suggesting that rent control is a very blunt instrument for helping the poor: You don't have to be poor to qualify for a rent-controlled apartment. As we explain later in the book, the government could use other policies to more effectively improve the economic circumstances of the poor.

Minimum Prices

We've already seen two different effects of a minimum price. In Chapter 4, we saw that when the government sets a minimum price that exceeds the equilibrium price, the result is excess supply of the product. The increase in price increases the quantity supplied as producers react to the higher price by producing more. The increase in price also decreases the quantity demanded as consumers react by purchasing less. At the minimum price, producers want to sell more than consumers want to buy.

As shown in panel B of Figure 6.4, a minimum price of $19 decreases the quantity sold from 5 lawns per hour to 2 lawns per hour. At the minimum price of $19, producers are willing to cut a large number of lawns, but at that price, they would have only two customers. The minimum price produces winners and losers. The winners are the two lucky producers who cut lawns at the higher price, and thus earn larger producer surpluses. The other three producers who would cut lawns at the equilibrium price are losers, as they lose their producer surpluses. Consumers are losers: two consumers still participate in the market, but get smaller surpluses; three consumers drop out of the market, and thus earn no consumer surplus. Because the gains of the winners are less than the losses of the losers, the total surplus of the market decreases.

Government Intervention: Restricting Quantity

What happens when the government controls the quantity of a particular product instead of its price? We'll consider two policies that control quantities. In the domestic economy, many state and local governments limit the number of firms in particular markets by limiting the number of business licenses to operate in those markets. As we saw in Chapter 3, national governments use a wide variety of policies to restrict imports, including import bans, import quotas, tariffs, and voluntary export restraints.

Licensing: Taxi Medallions

You may be surprised to learn the extent of business licensing programs used by state and local governments. There are limits on the number of taxicabs, dry cleaners, tobacco farms, liquor stores, bars selling liquor, appliance repairers, and dog groomers. Some people defend licensing schemes on the grounds that they protect consumers from high prices, low-quality products, and poor service. But studies of licensing show that most licensing programs increase prices without improving the quality of products and service.[2] We can use the licensing of taxis to explain the market effects of licensing. The analysis applies to other markets in which the government uses licenses to limit the number of firms.

Panel A of Figure 6.5 shows the market equilibrium in the taxi market. The demand curve intersects the supply curve at point *e*. The industry provides 10,000 miles of taxi service per day at a price of $3.00 per mile. Each taxi produces 100 miles of service per day, and there are 100 taxicabs in the market. The total surplus of the market equals the sum of consumer surplus and producer surplus, shown by the area between the demand curve and the supply curve.

Taxi medallion: A license to operate a taxi.

Suppose that the city passes a law requiring each taxicab to have a taxi license—also known as a **taxi medallion**—and limits the number of medallions to 80. The city gives the taxi medallions to the first 80 people who show up at City Hall. In panel B of Figure 6.5, the vertical line at 8,000 miles of service shows that this policy fixes the quantity of taxi service at 8,000 miles per day (80 taxis times 100 miles per taxi per day). The medallion policy creates an excess demand for taxi service: At the original price ($3.00), the quantity demanded is 10,000 miles, but the city's 80 taxicabs provide only 8,000 miles of service. The market moves upward along the demand curve to point *m*, where the price is $3.60 per mile of service. The medallion policy increases the price and decreases the quantity of taxi services.

Licensing and Market Efficiency

The medallion policy decreases the total surplus of the taxi market. In Figure 6.5, we see that the total surplus in panel B is less than the total surplus in panel A. The medallion policy decreases consumer surplus, a result of the higher price and smaller quantity. Producer surplus could increase or decrease, depending on the shapes of the supply and demand curves. In this example, it actually increases by a small amount. Like other policies such as maximum and minimum prices, the medallion policy decreases the quantity of goods sold, decreasing the total surplus of the market. The producers of the first

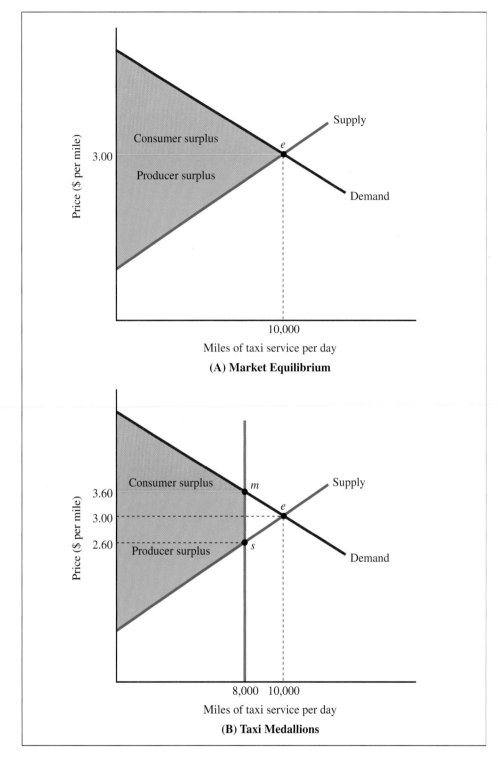

Figure 6.5
The Market Effects of Taxi Medallions
(A) Market Equilibrium The market equilibrium is shown by point *e,* with a price of $3.00 and a quantity of 10,000 miles per day. The total surplus is the area between the demand and supply curves.
(B) Taxi Medallions A medallion policy that fixes the number of taxis at 80 fixes the quantity of taxi service at 8,000 miles per day (100 miles per taxi) and increases the price to $3.60 (point *m*). The producers of the first 8,000 miles gain at the expense of consumers, but the surpluses on between 8,000 and 10,000 miles are lost entirely, so the total surplus decreases.

8,000 miles of service gain at the expense of consumers, but the surpluses on between 8,000 and 10,000 miles are lost entirely, so the total surplus of the market decreases.

Another way to see the inefficiency of taxi medallions is to look at the consumers and producers who are excluded from the market. Some of the excluded consumers would gladly pay the cost of providing taxi service. As shown by the points between m and e on the demand curve, many consumers are willing to pay between $3.00 and $3.60 per mile for taxi service. Although there are plenty of drivers who would be willing to provide taxi service at these prices, they can't do so without a medallion. Because the medallion policy prevents these riders and drivers from executing mutually beneficial transactions, the policy causes inefficiency.

Our analysis of taxi medallions applies to any market subject to quantity controls. State and city governments use licensing to limit many small businesses. Some cities limit the number of housing units by limiting the number of permits to build housing. These policies decrease the quantity supplied, increase prices, and cause inefficiency. Although some producers are willing to supply the good at a lower price, the government does not allow them to do so. Sometimes governments go beyond simply reducing the quantity produced, and outlaw markets for some goods. For an example, read "A Closer Look: A Market for Used Human Organs?"

Winners and Losers from Medallions

Who benefits and who loses from the city's medallion policy? The losers are consumers, who pay more for taxi rides. The winners are the people who receive a free medallion and the right to charge an artificially high price for taxi service. In some cities, people buy and sell taxi medallions, and the market value of a medallion reflects the profits it can earn its owner. The market price of a medallion is over $150,000 in New York City, $140,000 in Boston, and $100,000 in Toronto.[3] In cities such as Chicago, where medallions are more plentiful, the market price is much lower.

To be a winner in the medallion game, you must have received a medallion free of charge from the government. If you were to buy a medallion at the current market price (say, $100,000), you won't benefit from the medallion policy because the price you pay will be just high enough to offset any profits you'll earn with the medallion. In fact, you would be a big loser if, after you buy a medallion, the city issues more medallions. An increase in the number of medallions—and taxis—will decrease the price and profits of taxi service, decreasing the market price of your medallion. One reason that medallion schemes persist is that the current owners of medallions would lose a lot of money if the government allowed additional taxis to enter the market.

A CLOSER LOOK | A MARKET FOR USED HUMAN ORGANS?

Each year, thousands of Americans die waiting for replacement kidneys, hearts, livers, pancreases, and lungs. In the last decade, improvements in the effectiveness of organ transplants have increased the demand for used human organs. Because the supply hasn't increased along with demand, there are shortages of transplantable organs. In a normal market, the price would rise to eliminate the shortage, but because it is illegal to buy and sell human organs, there is no pricing mechanism to close the gap between the quantity supplied and the quantity demanded. The conventional approach to the organ shortage is to appeal to people's generosity, urging them to commit their organs to the transplant program. The failure of this approach led Nobel-winning economist Gary Becker to suggest monetary incentives for organ donors. Under his proposal, the federal government would pay organ donors and their survivors and would distribute the organs to hospitals for transplanting. This proposal raises all sorts of ethical questions and has not been embraced by many policy makers or health experts.

Source: Gary S. Becker, "How Uncle Sam Could Ease the Organ Shortage," *Business Week,* January 20, 1997, p. 18.

The Case of the Cheap Pet Salon

After 20 years of dog haircuts, perms, and pedicures, Doug wants to sell his pet-grooming salon. Several months earlier, a similar pet salon sold for $50,000. But Doug hasn't found anyone willing to buy his for more than $20,000. He suspects that the city has quietly increased the number of pet-grooming licenses, and that's why the price of grooming services dropped, pulling down the market price of pet salons like his. According to the local pet-grooming association, the quantity of grooming services (the number of haircuts, perms, and pedicures) has not changed in recent years. Why has the market price of a pet salon decreased so much? Has the city issued more licenses, or is there another explanation?

The key to solving this mystery is the fact that the quantity of grooming service hasn't changed. This means that the city hasn't issued any more licenses. In Figure 6.6, the vertical line at 300 indicates the fixed supply resulting from the city's limit on the number of grooming licenses. An increase in the number of licenses would shift this line to the right and increase the quantity of service. Therefore, the lower prices for grooming services— and lower prices for pet salons—must have been caused by a decrease in the demand for grooming services. The demand curve shifted to the left, decreasing the price of grooming services from $12 to $9. The lower price means that pet salons will be less profitable, meaning that Doug must accept a lower price for his salon.

Import Restrictions

We've seen that the government can control the quantity of a good produced by issuing a limited number of business licenses to producers. Another way to control quantity is to limit the imports of a particular good. Like a licensing scheme, an import restriction increases the market price and decreases the total surplus of the market.

To show the market effects of import restrictions, let's start with an unrestricted market. Panel A of Figure 6.7 shows the market equilibrium in a sugar market when

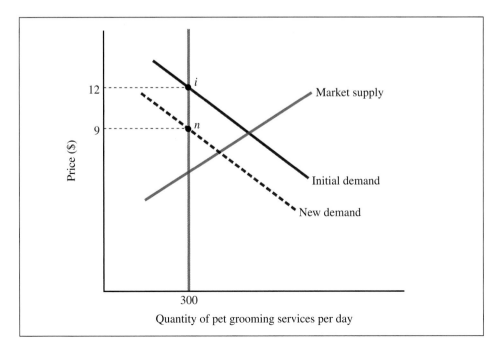

Figure 6.6

Decrease in Demand and the Price of Pet Grooming

If the quantity of grooming services hasn't changed, a decrease in price is a result of a decrease in demand, not an increase in the number of grooming licenses. The decrease in demand decreases the price from $12 to $9. The lower price of grooming services reduces the profits for pet salons, decreasing their market value.

Figure 6.7

The Effects of an Import Ban on Prices, Consumer Surplus, and Producer Surplus

(A) Free Trade with No Domestic Production With free trade, demand intersects the total supply curve at point *i,* with a price of 12¢ and a quantity of 360 million pounds. This price is below the minimum price of domestic suppliers (26¢, as shown by point *m*), so domestic firms do not participate in the market. The total surplus is shown by the shaded areas (consumer and producer surplus).

(B) Import Ban and Domestic Production If sugar imports are banned, the equilibrium is shown by the intersection of the demand curve and the domestic (U.S.) supply curve (point *d*). The price increases to 30¢. Although the ban generates a producer surplus for domestic producers, their gain is less than the loss of domestic consumers.

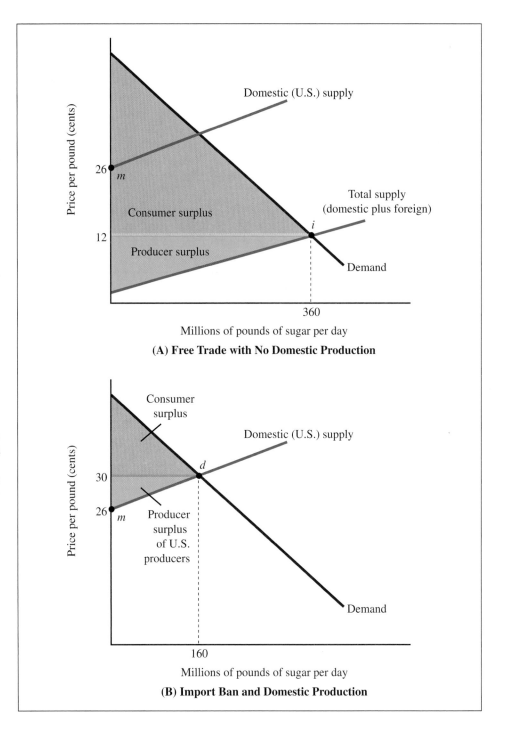

(A) Free Trade with No Domestic Production

(B) Import Ban and Domestic Production

there is free trade. The domestic supply curve shows the quantity supplied by domestic (U.S.) firms at different prices. Looking at point *m,* we see that U.S. firms will not supply any sugar unless the price is at least 26 cents per pound. The total supply curve, which shows the quantity supplied by both domestic and foreign firms, lies to the right of the domestic curve. At each price, the total supply exceeds the domestic supply because foreign firms also supply sugar. Point *i* shows the free-trade equilibrium: The domestic demand curve (showing the demand by U.S. consumers) intersects the total supply curve at a price of 12 cents per pound and a quantity of 360 million pounds per day. Because this price is below the minimum price for domestic firms, domestic firms do not supply any sugar.

What would happen if the United States banned sugar imports? Foreign suppliers would disappear from the market, so the total supply of sugar would be the domestic supply. In panel B of Figure 6.7, the new equilibrium is shown by point d: The demand curve intersects the domestic supply curve at a price of 30 cents per pound and a quantity of 160 million pounds. The decrease in supply resulting from the import ban increases the price and decreases the quantity, and domestic firms produce all the sugar for the domestic market.

The import ban decreases the total surplus of the market. The shaded areas in the two graphs show the consumer and producer surpluses with and without free trade. The import ban reduces consumer surplus, as shown by the two pink triangles in the two graphs. The ban also eliminates the producer surplus of foreign suppliers (shown by the blue triangle in panel A of Figure 6.7) and generates a producer surplus for domestic suppliers (shown by the blue triangle in panel B of Figure 6.7). The import ban causes domestic producers to gain at the expense of domestic consumers. Consumers lose more than domestic producers gain, so the import ban causes a net loss for people in the domestic economy.

Import restrictions are often defended on the grounds that they increase employment in the protected industries. The protection of these jobs increases consumer prices, so there is a trade-off: more jobs in the protected industry, but higher prices for consumers. According to one study, import restrictions in force in 1993 protected 56,464 jobs in the U.S. textile and apparel industries at a cost to consumers of about $178,000 per job, and protected 3,419 jobs in the motor-vehicle industry at a cost of about $271,000 per job.[4]

In many cases, policies that restrict imports are more subtle than an explicit ban. For some examples, read "A Closer Look: International Food Fights."

TEST Your Understanding

5. Why do tenants in rent-control cities voluntarily pay extra money for nonrefundable cleaning deposits and keys?

6. In Figure 6.5, consider a consumer who is represented by a point on the demand curve halfway between point m and point e. How much is the consumer willing to pay for a mile of taxi service? Consider a producer who is represented by a point on the supply curve halfway between point s and point e. What is the marginal cost of a mile of taxi service? Describe a mutually beneficial transaction between the consumer and the producer.

7. In Figure 6.7, how much sugar will domestic firms produce at a price of $0.15?

8. Complete the statement with *increases* or *decreases*: An import ban _____ the price of sugar, _____ the quantity of sugar, and _____ the output of the domestic sugar industry.

Spillovers and Market Inefficiency

Up to this point in the chapter, we have assumed that there are no spillovers in consumption or production. As we will see in this last part of the chapter, when there are spillover costs, the market equilibrium will be inefficient and government intervention may be beneficial.

In some cases, a country restricts imports indirectly, using rules and regulations to protect domestic firms from foreign competition. Japan requires foreign exporters of fruit to test their goods for the presence of harmful insects and diseases. In a case brought before the World Trade Association (WTO), the United States argued that Japan's quarantine testing system, which can take up to two years to complete, was not justified on scientific grounds. In 1999, the WTO ruled in favor of the United States, directing Japan to revise and simplify its quarantine procedures. The ruling is expected to increase the volume of apples, cherries, peaches, walnuts, and nectarines exported to Japan.

Australia and New Zealand were involved in a similar dispute. Australia claimed that apples imported from New Zealand posed a risk of spreading fireblight to Australian trees. New Zealand responded that the fireblight risk is trivial, estimating that there would be one case of fireblight every 10,000 years. Moreover, claimed the New Zealanders, fireblight was already present in Australia. This case is expected to be decided by the WTO.

Source: "Apple Export Ban Likely to Add Bite to Trade Talks," *Wellington Newspapers Limited,* December 16, 1998. p. 2.

Spillover **PRINCIPLE**

For some goods, the cost or benefit of the good is not confined to the person or organization that decides how much of the good to produce or consume.

In this section, we'll take a brief look at the implications of spillover costs for market efficiency. Later in the book, we'll take a more detailed look at spillovers—including spillover costs and benefits—and discuss several policy responses to them.

Spillover Costs

We can use the cardboard market to illustrate the inefficiency that occurs in a market with spillover costs. Suppose there are several cardboard mills along a river and that a city downstream from the mills draws water from the river for drinking. The city's water-treatment costs depend on how much chemical waste is dumped into the river. For each gallon of chemical waste from cardboard mills, the city's treatment costs increase by $2. There are spillover costs because the decision-makers in the cardboard mills ignore the costs incurred by people in the downstream city. In other words, some of the costs of producing cardboard are external to the firm, where decisions about how much cardboard to produce are made. Another word for spillover is *externality.*

Panel A of Figure 6.8 shows the market equilibrium in the cardboard market. The demand curve intersects the supply curve at point *e,* generating a price of $30 per ton and a quantity of 50 tons per day. The total surplus (the sum of consumer and producer surplus) is shown by the pink and blue triangles, the area between the demand curve and the supply curve. The total pollution cost depends on how much chemical waste is generated, which depends on how much cardboard is produced. If each ton of cardboard generates 5 gallons of waste at a cost of $2 per gallon to the city, the pollution cost per ton of cardboard is $10. In the market equilibrium with 50 tons of cardboard, the total pollution cost is $500, shown as the area of the brown rectangle.

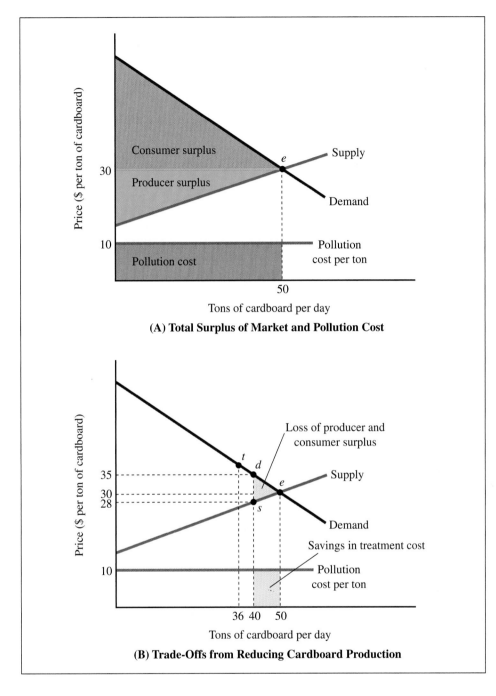

Figure 6.8
Market Inefficiency with Pollution Costs
(A) Total Surplus of Market and External Cost In the market equilibrium, shown by point *e,* the price is $30 per ton and the quantity is 50 tons. The triangles show the total surplus of the market (consumer surplus plus producer surplus). The rectangle shows the total pollution cost.
(B) Trade-Offs from Reducing Cardboard Production Reducing the quantity of cardboard generates good news and bad news. The triangle shows the bad news: the loss of consumer and producer surplus. The rectangle shows the good news: the savings in pollution cost. In this case, the good news is greater than the bad news, so reducing the quantity is sensible.

(A) Total Surplus of Market and Pollution Cost

(B) Trade-Offs from Reducing Cardboard Production

Trade-Offs from Producing Less

What are the trade-offs from reducing the quantity of cardboard? We know that the equilibrium quantity maximizes the sum of consumer and producer surplus, so producing less will decrease the surpluses. Suppose production drops from 50 tons to 40 tons. In panel B of Figure 6.8, the sum of consumer and producer surplus decreases by an amount shown by the yellow triangle. This is the bad news associated with reducing the quantity of cardboard by 10 tons. If there were no spillovers, there would be no good news from reducing cardboard production to offset this bad news. In the absence of spillovers, it would clearly be inefficient to produce less than the equilibrium quantity.

Because there are spillover costs from cardboard production, however, there is some good news from producing less. For each ton of cardboard not produced, the city's treatment costs decrease by $10. The savings in pollution costs from reducing paper production from 50 to 40 tons is $100 ($10 per ton times 10 tons), shown by the yellow rectangle in panel B of Figure 6.8. In this case, the good news (savings in pollution costs shown by the rectangle) is greater than the bad news (the reduction of the total surplus of the market, shown by the triangle), so it is sensible to reduce paper production. The rectangle is bigger than the triangle, meaning that the gain of the downstream city exceeds the loss of cardboard consumers and producers.

If cutting cardboard production by 10 tons is a good idea, what about eliminating the cardboard market? Of course, that means the elimination of the consumer and producer surplus of cardboard. This bad news is shown in panel A of Figure 6.8 as the pink and blue triangles (the total surplus of the market). The good news from eliminating the market would be that the city's treatment costs would decrease by $500 ($10 times 50 tons), shown by the brown rectangle in panel A of Figure 6.8. The elimination of the cardboard market is not sensible because the bad news (shown by the pink and blue triangles) exceeds the good news (shown by the brown rectangle). In this case, the gain of the downstream city is less than the loss of cardboard consumers and producers.

What is the socially efficient quantity of cardboard? We've seen that the market equilibrium generates too much cardboard, but the elimination of the market would not be sensible. We could use the marginal principle to decide how much to reduce cardboard production.

 Marginal **PRINCIPLE**

Increase the level of an activity if its marginal benefit exceeds its marginal cost, but reduce the level if the marginal cost exceeds the marginal benefit. If possible, pick the level at which the marginal benefit equals the marginal cost.

In the case of the cardboard, the activity mentioned in the principle is reducing the quantity produced.

We've already seen the benefits and costs of reducing cardboard production as the good news (benefits) and bad news (costs) from producing less. What about the marginal benefits and marginal costs?

- **Marginal benefit:** the savings in treatment cost from reducing cardboard production by one ton.

- **Marginal cost:** the loss in consumer and producer surplus from reducing cardboard production by one ton.

The marginal principle tells us that we should cut cardboard production as long as the $10 savings in treatment cost exceeds the loss of consumer and producer surplus.

Suppose we have already cut production to 40 tons. The question is, starting from 40 tons of cardboard, should we cut cardboard production by one more ton? As shown by point d in panel B of Figure 6.8, a consumer is willing to pay $35 for the 40th ton, so with a price of $30, the consumer surplus lost would be $5 (equal to $35 − $30). As shown by point s, the marginal cost of producing the 40th ton is $28, so the producer surplus lost by not producing the 40th ton would be $2 (equal to $30 − $28). When the losses in consumer and producer surplus are added, the marginal cost of cutting production from 40 to 39 tons is $7. Because this marginal cost is less than the $10 marginal benefit, it is sensible to cut production from 40 to 39 tons.

There is a simple graphical solution to the problem of finding the quantity of cardboard at which the marginal benefit of cutting back equals the marginal cost. The vertical difference between the demand curve and the supply curve shows the marginal cost of cutting output, the loss of consumer surplus plus the loss of producer surplus. If we find the quantity at which the vertical distance between the demand and supply curves equals the marginal benefit (the $10 savings in treatment cost), we have found the quantity that satisfies the marginal principle. In panel B of Figure 6.8, this happens at point *t*, with 36 tons of cardboard. Going beyond this point to a smaller quantity of cardboard would violate the marginal principle: The marginal benefit (the $10 savings in treatment cost) would be less than the marginal cost (the loss in consumer and producer surplus, as shown by the vertical difference between the demand and supply curves).

Market Effects of a Pollution Tax

We've seen that when there are spillover costs, the market equilibrium is inefficient in the sense that too much of the polluting good is produced. The economic approach to pollution is to force producers to pay for the pollution they generate, just as they pay for labor, raw materials, and machinery. In our cardboard example, the government could impose a pollution tax of $2 for each gallon of waste dumped into the river. The pollution tax internalizes the pollution externality: The tax means that the costs associated with the chemical waste from cardboard are no longer external to the firm (where decisions about how much to produce are made), but internal.

Figure 6.9 shows the market effects of the pollution tax. Because each ton of cardboard generates 5 gallons of chemical waste, a tax of $2 per gallon of waste increases the marginal cost of producing cardboard by $10 per ton ($2 per gallon times 5 gallons per ton). As shown in Figure 6.9, the pollution tax shifts the supply curve for cardboard up by $10. A new equilibrium is reached at point *t*, with a price of $37 and a quantity of 36 tons. It's not a coincidence that this is the same point we found to be socially efficient using the marginal principle. When firms bear the full cost of production, including the cost of pollution, the market equilibrium is socially efficient.

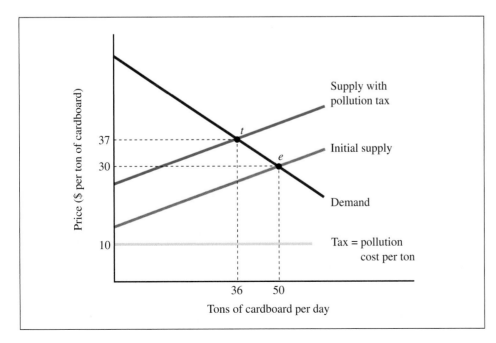

Figure 6.9

The Market Effect of a Tax on Pollution

A pollution tax of $2 per gallon of waste increases the marginal cost of producing cardboard by $10 per ton ($2 per gallon times 5 gallons of waste per ton of cardboard) and shifts the supply curve up by $10. The new equilibrium is shown by point *t*. The price increases from $30 to $37, and the quantity decreases to 36 tons per day.

TEST Your Understanding

Using the **TOOLS**

In this chapter, we used two of the tools of economics—the supply curve and the demand curve—to study the effect of government intervention in perfectly competitive markets with and without spillovers. Here are some opportunities to use these tools to do your own economic analysis.

1. ECONOMIC EXPERIMENT: Government Intervention

Recall the market-equilibrium experiment from Chapter 4. We can modify that experiment to show the various forms of government intervention in the market. After several trading periods without any government intervention, you can change the rules as follows:

• The instructor sets a maximum price for apples.

• The instructor sets a minimum price for apples.

• The instructor issues licenses to a few lucky producers.

• The instructor divides producers into domestic producers and foreign producers, and some of the foreign producers are excluded from the market.

APPLICATIONS
2. Price Controls for Medical Care

Suppose that in an attempt to control the rising costs of medical care, the national government imposes price controls on visits to physicians. The maximum price for a physician visit is 10% less than the equilibrium price. Assume that the price elasticity of demand for physician visits is 0.60 and the price elasticity of supply is 1.5.

a. By what percentage will the quantity of medical care supplied decrease?

b. By what percentage will the quantity of medical care demanded increase?

c. Illustrate your answer with a graph.

d. What sort of inefficiencies will occur as a result of the maximum price?

e. Would you expect patients and physicians to find ways around the maximum price?

3. Barber Licensing

Consider the market for haircuts in a city. In the initial equilibrium, the price is $6, and the quantity is 200 haircuts per day. The demand curve for haircuts is linear, with 200 haircuts demanded at a price of $6 and 100 haircuts demanded at a price of $12. Initially, there are 20 barbers, each of whom produces 10 haircuts per day. Suppose the city passes a law requiring all barbers to have a license and then issues only 15 barber licenses. Each licensed barber continues to provide 10 haircuts per day. Predict the new equilibrium price of haircuts and illustrate your answer with a supply-demand diagram.

Summary

In this chapter, we discussed the efficiency of markets and the consequences of government intervention in perfectly competitive markets. Government intervention in a market without spillovers prevents consumers and producers from executing beneficial transactions, meaning that intervention reduces the total surplus of the market and causes inefficiency. When there are spillover costs, it is sensible to intervene in markets to reduce the quantity produced. Here are the main points of the chapter:

1. The total surplus of a market equals the sum of consumer surplus and producer surplus.

2. In a perfectly competitive market without spillover costs, the market equilibrium maximizes the total surplus of the market, and is therefore efficient.

3. Price controls (a maximum or a minimum price) reduce the total surplus of a market because they prevent mutually beneficial transactions.

4. Quantity controls (licensing or import restrictions) decrease consumer surplus and the total surplus of the market.

5. When there are spillover costs from pollution, the market equilibrium is inefficient, but efficiency can be restored by imposing a tax on pollution.

Key Terms

consumer surplus, 121
producer surplus, 122

rent control, 127

taxi medallion, 128

Problems and Discussion Questions

1. What assumptions do we make to ensure that the market equilibrium in a perfectly competitive market is efficient? For each assumption, provide an example of a good for which the assumption is likely to be violated.

2. According to Ida, "I'm willing to buy a CD player for $50, but I can't find anyone willing to sell me one for that price." Does that mean that the market for CD players is inefficient?

3. Figure 6.A shows a supply curve and a demand curve and several areas between the curves. Identify the areas on the figure that represent the following:
   a. Consumer surplus in the market equilibrium
   b. Producer surplus in the market equilibrium

   c. Total surplus in the market equilibrium
   d. Consumer surplus under a maximum price of $10
   e. Producer surplus under a maximum price of $10
   f. Total surplus under a maximum price of $10
   g. Consumer surplus under a maximum quantity of 70
   h. Producer surplus under a maximum quantity of 70
   i. Total surplus under a maximum quantity of 70

4. Your city just announced a new rent-control program under which the maximum rent on apartments will be 20% below the equilibrium price. The price elasticity of supply of apartments is 0.50.
   a. Use a supply-demand diagram to show the effects of the rent-control program on the rental hous-

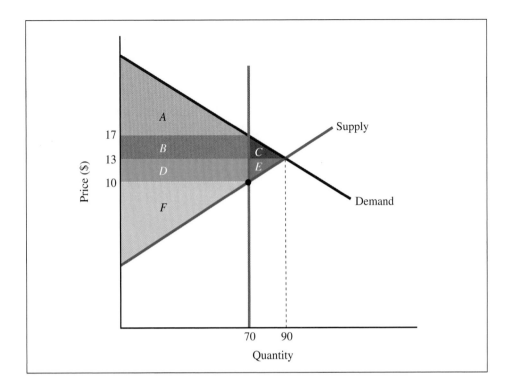

Figure 6.A
Identifying the Surpluses

ing market. The initial price is $300 per month and the initial quantity is 10,000 apartments. Label the initial equilibrium point with an *i* and the point that shows the quantity supplied under rent control with an *s*.

b. By what percentage will the quantity of apartments increase or decrease?

5. Why are local rent controls (a maximum price on rental housing in a city) more common than a maximum price on food or clothing sold in a city?

6. In the gasoline market, the equilibrium price is $2 and the equilibrium quantity is 100 million gallons per day. Suppose the government sets a maximum price of $1.80. The price elasticity of supply of gasoline is 2.0, and the price elasticity of demand is 1.0. Draw a graph and show the excess demand for gasoline. Compute the amount of excess demand.

7. In the example in the text of taxi medallions (Figure 6.5), suppose the city announces that it will issue 110 medallions instead of 80. Predict the market price of taxi service and the market price of medallions.

8. Using Figure 6.5 as a starting point, suppose the demand for taxi service decreases and the new demand curve intersects the supply curve at a quantity of 7,000 miles per day. If the government doesn't change the number of medallions, what happens to the price of a medallion?

9. Predict the effect of each of the following policies on the price of the relevant good. Then draw a supply-demand diagram to defend your answer.
  a. Licenses for dry cleaners
  b. Limit on building permits for housing
  c. Import restrictions on clothing

10. Suppose that initially there are no restrictions on importing kiwi fruit. The supply curves are the same as the supply curves for sugar shown in Figure 6.7. The initial price of kiwi fruit is 12 cents per piece. When imports are banned, the equilibrium price increases to 22 cents. Draw a market demand curve consistent with these numbers.

11. Suppose a new production process reduces the chemical waste per ton of cardboard to 3 gallons. Use a supply-demand diagram to predict the effect of a pollution tax ($2 per gallon of waste) on the price and quantity of cardboard. Compared to the initial situation with 5 gallons of waste per ton, is the price higher or lower? Is the quantity larger or smaller? Explain any differences between the two cases.

12. Suppose that in response to concerns about greenhouse gases and global warming, the government imposes a tax of $0.50 per gallon on gasoline. Use a supply-demand diagram to show the effects of the tax on the gasoline market.

13. **Web Exercise.** Visit the Web site of the Adam Smith Institute [*www.adamsmith.org.uk*]. Access the Policy Division and pick your favorite quote of Adam Smith. Explain the logic behind the quote.

14. **Web Exercise.** Visit the official Web site for New York City [*http://www.ci.nyc.ny.us/*]. Search the site for information on taxi medallions. You should find Web pages that describe what's involved in becoming a medallion owner and provide some data on the price of taxi medallions. Describe the process involved in becoming a taxi medallion owner or report the most recent price of a medallion.

Take It to the Net

We invite you to visit the O'Sullivan/Sheffrin page on the Prentice Hall Web site at: **http://www.prenhall.com/osullivan/** for additional World Wide Web exercises for this chapter.

Model Answers to Questions

Chapter-Opening Questions

1. The rent-control policy decreases the quantity of apartments supplied, forcing some students out of the market.

2. The city limits the number of taxi licenses or medallions, leading to higher taxi prices and large profits for people who own the medallions.

3. It is illegal to buy or sell human organs, so there is no pricing mechanism to close the gap between quantity demanded and quantity supplied.

4. Consumers pay higher prices, and the cost per job saved is about $178,000.

5. Impose a tax equal to the cost per unit of pollution.

Test Your Understanding

1. The willingness to pay, price, price, marginal cost.

2. The price would be $1,700, giving you and Pablo each a surplus of $300.

3. Forest is willing to pay $13, and Dee's marginal cost is $8. If they split the difference, the price would be $10.50, and each would get a surplus of $2.50.

4. No spillover costs, no spillover benefits, perfect competition, informed buyers and sellers.

5. Many consumers are willing to pay more than the controlled price for an apartment, and deposits and key money allow them to do so and get an apartment they could otherwise not get.

6. The consumer is willing to pay $3.30, and the producer's marginal cost is $2.80. If they split the difference, agreeing on a price of $3.05, each will get a surplus of $0.25.

7. Zero. This is below the minimum domestic price.

8. Increases, decreases, increases.

9. The consumer loses $2 ($32 − $30) and the producer loses $1 ($30 − $29), for a combined loss of $3.

10. Impose a tax on pollution equal to the cost generated by the pollution.

11. The tax increases cost per ton by $6 ($2 per gallon times 3 gallons per ton).

Using the Tools

2. Price Controls for Medical Care
   a. Using the supply elasticity formula, the quantity of doctor visits supplied will decrease by 15%: 1.5 = 15%/10%.
   b. Using the demand elasticity formula, the quantity of doctor visits demanded will increase by 6%: 0.60 = 6%/10%.
   c. In Figure 6.B, the initial equilibrium point (before the maximum price) is shown by point *i*: The price is $50 and the quantity is 1,000 visits. The maximum price is $45, so the new quantity supplied is 850 (point *s*), and the new quantity demanded is 1,060 (point *d*).
   d. The policy outlaws transactions that would benefit a buyer and a seller and causes a shortage (excess demand) that will increase the time spent waiting for doctors.
   e. Perhaps doctors can increase the prices charged for other services (X-rays, stitches, vaccinations, other office procedures).

3. Barber Licensing. See Figure 6.C. If there are 15 licenses. the maximum quantity is 150 haircuts per day. This quantity is halfway between 100 (at which

Figure 6.B
**Maximum Prices
for Medical Care**

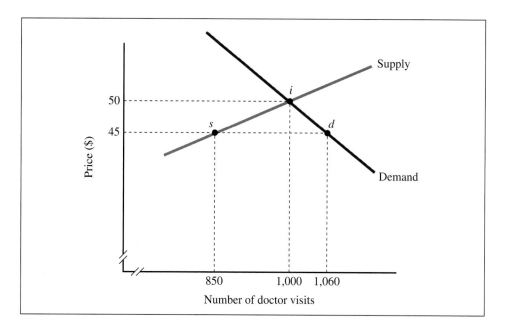

the price is $12) and 200 (at which the price is $6), so the new price is $9.

4. Bidding for a Boston Taxi Medallion. The new medallions will increase the quantity of taxi service supplied by 20% (300/1.500). The price of taxi service will drop by an amount large enough to increase the quantity demanded by 20%. According to the price-elasticity formula from Chapter 5, the price will decrease by 10%:

$$E_d = \frac{\text{percentage change in quantity demanded}}{\text{percentage change in price}}$$

$$= 2.0 = \frac{20\%}{10\%}$$

In other words, to close the gap between the quantity supplied and the larger quantity supplied, the price must drop by 10%, from $5.00 to $4.50. The

Figure 6.C
**Market Effects of
Barber Licenses**

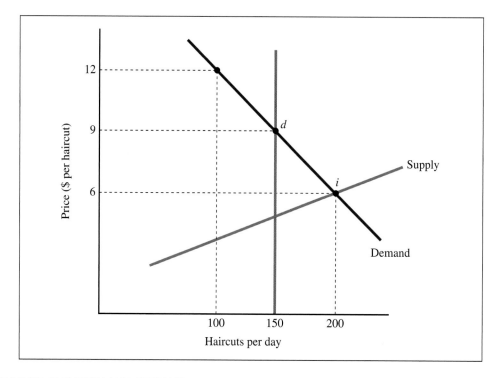

profit per mile of service drops from $1.00 (equal to the price of $5.00 minus the cost per mile of $4.00) to $0.50 (equal to $4.50 minus $4.00). Because the price of medallions reflects the profit earned from taxi service, cutting the profit per mile in half will cut the price of a medallion in half as well. Therefore, we expect the price of medallions to drop from $140,000 to $70,000.

 # Notes

1. William Tucker, "A Model for Destroying a City," *Wall Street Journal*, March 12, 1993, p. A8.

2. J. K. Smith, "An Analysis of State Regulations Governing Liquor Store Licensees," *Journal of Law and Economics*, October 1982, pp. 301–319; David Kirp and Eileen Soffer, "Taking Californians to the Cleaners," *Regulation*, September/October 1985, pp. 24–26; D. W. Taylor, "The Economic Effects of Direct Regulation of Taxicabs in Metropolitan Toronto," *Logistics and Transportation Review*, June 1989, pp. 169–182.

3. Taylor, "The Economic Effects of Direct Regulation of Taxicabs in Metropolitan Toronto."

4. *The Economic Effects of Significant U.S. Import Restraints* (Washington, DC: U.S. International Trade Commission, initial report in 1993: update in 1996).

5. Laura Brown, "Hub Cabbie Hopefuls Cry: The Russians Are Coming!" *Boston Herald*, Dec. 16, 1998, p. 1.

Consumer Choice

During the nineteenth century, some philosophers thought it was possible to measure the utility or satisfaction consumers receive from goods and services. The idea was to hook a person up to some sort of machine, let the person consume a product such as a pie, and then read from the machine's gauges the amount of additional happiness, or utility, generated by the pie. Because such a machine has not been invented, it is impossible to measure utility. Jeremy Bentham, one of these "utilitarians," died in London in 1832. He helped establish University College, London, and his fully clothed skeleton—with a wax head—is kept in a glass case there.

As we saw in Chapter 4, the demand curve shows the relationship between the price of a good and the quantity that a consumer is willing to buy. The demand curve is negatively sloped, reflecting the law of demand: The higher the price, the smaller the quantity demanded, ceteris paribus (everything else held fixed). In this chapter, we use some of the key principles of economics to explain the logic behind the demand curve and the law of demand.

This chapter takes a close look at the consumer's decision-making process. Here are some practical questions we'll answer:

1. How should a consumer divide his or her income among alternative goods and services?

2. Once you pay the admission fee to Disneyland, all the rides are free. Unfortunately, you may wait for two or three hours to get on your favorite ride. Why don't the managers of Disneyland shorten the lines by charging a dollar or two for each ride?

The Marginal Principle and Individual Demand

Let's consider a hypothetical market for burgers and examine the decisions of Bob, a consumer who has a fixed income of $30 per month to spend on two goods: burgers and tacos. Bob must decide how many burgers and tacos to buy each month. The quantity of burgers he buys is determined by a number of factors, including the price of burgers, the price of tacos, his income, and his tastes or preferences for the two goods.

The individual demand curve in Figure 7.1 shows the quantity of burgers Bob is willing to buy (demand) at each price. To find each point on the demand curve, we pick a price, say $3 per burger, and answer the question "How many burgers is Bob willing to buy at that price?" If the answer is 8 burgers per month, point *b* (with $3 on the price axis and 8 burgers on the quantity axis) is on Bob's demand curve. We can find a different point on the demand curve by choosing a different price, say $2, and asking the same question. If the answer is 11 burgers per month, point *c* is on Bob's demand curve too. We can find other points in the same way.

Each point on the individual demand curve is the result of a rational choice by the consumer. When we say "rational," we mean that the consumer considers the benefit and cost of buying the good, and buys the good only if the benefit exceeds the cost. We can use the marginal principle to show how consumers incorporate benefits and costs into their consumption decisions.

Marginal **PRINCIPLE**

Increase the level of an activity if its marginal benefit exceeds its marginal cost, but reduce the level if the marginal cost exceeds the marginal benefit. If possible, pick the level at which the marginal benefit equals the marginal cost.

Bob's activity is buying burgers, so he should pick the quantity of burgers at which the marginal benefit of burgers equals the marginal cost.

Total and Marginal Utility

Utility: The satisfaction the consumer experiences when he or she consumes a good.

Before we use the marginal principle, let's think about how to measure the benefit of buying a particular good. A consumer's benefit from a product is the **utility** from the product, defined as the pleasure or satisfaction from consuming the product. Although it's easy to define the benefit, it is difficult to measure: We can't hook Bob up to a satis-

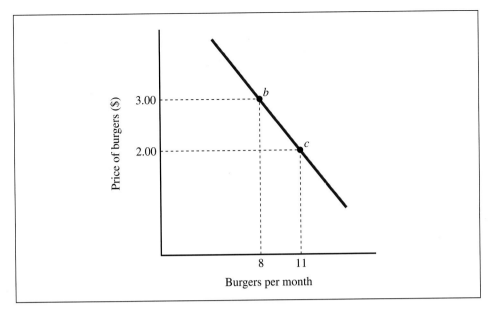

Figure 7.1

Individual Demand Curve

The individual demand curve is negatively sloped, consistent with the law of demand: The higher the price, the smaller the quantity demanded. If the price of burgers is $3, Bob consumes 8 burgers per month (point *b*). At a price of $2, he consumes 11 burgers per month (point *c*).

faction meter to determine how much happier he is after eating a burger. Nonetheless, suppose we can measure the consumer's benefit as the number of utils generated by the good (a **util** is one unit of utility or satisfaction).

The **total utility** from a product is defined as the utility or satisfaction from whatever quantity of the product the consumer gets. Panel A of Figure 7.2 shows the relationship between Bob's total utility from burgers and the number of burgers he buys. As the number of burgers increases, Bob's total utility increases, but at a decreasing rate. When Bob buys his first burger, his total utility increases from zero to 26 utils (point *u* on the total utility curve). When he buys the second burger, his utility increases from 26 to 50 utils (point *v*), so buying the second burger increases Bob's utility by 24 utils (50 − 26). Buying the second burger increases Bob's total utility, but the second burger adds less utility (24 utils) than the first (26 utils). Moving upward along the curve, the eighth burger increases Bob's utility by only 12 utils (152 minus 140). Eventually, additional burgers actually decrease Bob's utility level, as shown by the points beyond point *y* on the curve.

Panel B of Figure 7.2 shows Bob's marginal-utility curve. **Marginal utility** is defined as the change in utility resulting from buying one additional unit of the good. According to the **law of diminishing marginal utility,** as the consumption of a particular good increases, marginal utility decreases. In panel B of Figure 7.2, the marginal utility drops from 26 utils for the first burger to 24 utils for the second burger down to 12 utils for the eighth burger.

Util: A unit of utility.

Total utility: The utility (measured in utils) from whatever quantity of the product the consumer gets.

Marginal utility: The change in total utility from one additional unit of the good.

Law of diminishing marginal utility: As the consumption of a particular good increases, marginal utility decreases.

The Marginal Benefit Curve

To use the marginal principle, we must compute the marginal benefit for different quantities of burgers. We're measuring benefits in terms of utility, so the marginal benefit is the same as the marginal utility. Table 7.1 shows Bob's marginal benefits for the fifth through the ninth burgers, with the values of marginal utility drawn from Figure 7.2. The marginal benefit is 18 utils for the fifth burger, 16 utils for the sixth burger, and so on, to 10 utils for the ninth burger.

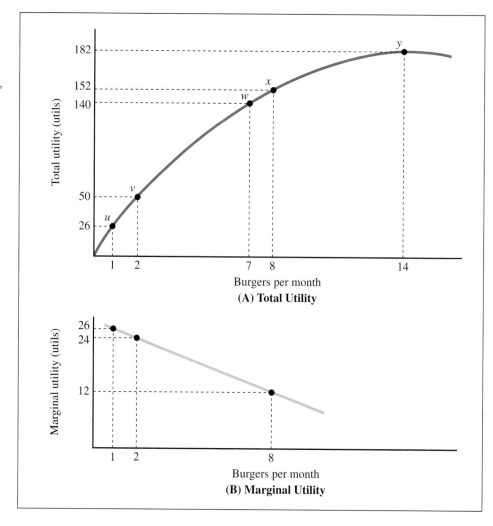

Figure 7.2
Total and Marginal Utility
In panel A, as the quantity of burgers consumed increases, the utility or satisfaction increases at a decreasing rate. In panel B, as the quantity of burgers increases, the marginal utility (the change in utility from one more burger) decreases. Both curves reflect the law of diminishing marginal utility.

The Marginal Cost Curve

Bob has a fixed budget to spend on burgers and tacos, so for each burger he buys, he sacrifices some tacos. To compute the marginal cost of burgers, we must determine how much utility from tacos he sacrifices by buying a burger rather than some tacos. Table 7.2 shows his marginal utility for different quantities of tacos. For example, the top row

Table 7.1   Marginal Utility of Burgers

Number of burgers	Marginal benefit (utility) of a burger
5	18
6	16
7	14
8	12
9	10

Table 7.2 Marginal Utility of Tacos

Number of tacos	Marginal benefit (utility) of a taco
3	5
6	4
9	3
12	2
15	1

shows that starting with 3 tacos, if Bob were to buy and eat one more taco, his total utility would increase by 5 utils. As we move down the table to larger quantities of tacos, the marginal utility decreases, consistent with the law of diminishing marginal utility.

Once we know the marginal-utility numbers for tacos, we can compute the marginal cost of burgers by following these five steps.

1. Pick a quantity of burgers, such as five burgers.
2. Determine how many tacos Bob could consume, given the following:
   - Assumed number of burgers
   - His income
   - The prices of the two goods

   In our example, Bob's income is $30 and the price of burgers is $3, so if Bob buys five burgers, he spends $15 on burgers, leaving $15 to spend on tacos. The taco price is $1, so if he buys five burgers he can afford 15 tacos.
3. In Table 7.2, find the marginal utility of tacos, given the quantity of tacos computed in step 2. For example, with 15 tacos, the marginal utility of tacos (the extra utility from buying one more taco—the sixteenth taco) is 1 util.
4. Use the prices of the two goods to compute the trade-off between burgers and tacos, that is, the number of tacos sacrificed per burger. If the burger price is $3 and the taco price is $1, the trade-off is three tacos per burger.
5. Compute the marginal cost of a burger by multiplying the marginal utility of tacos (1 util per taco) by the trade-off between tacos and burgers (three tacos per burger). The marginal cost associated with the fifth burger is 3 utils:

   marginal cost of fifth burger = 1 util per taco × 3 tacos sacrificed per burger

This gives us one point on the marginal-cost curve, point *q* in Figure 7.3.

To draw the rest of the marginal-cost curve in Figure 7.3, we simply repeat these steps for different quantities of burgers. For example, if Bob buys six burgers:

- He can afford 12 tacos (spending $18 on burgers leaves $12 for 12 tacos)
- At this quantity of tacos, the marginal utility is 2 utils per taco (from the fourth row of Table 7.2)
- The marginal cost of the sixth burger is 6 utils (2 utils per taco × 3 tacos sacrificed).

This gives us point *s* on the marginal-cost curve, with a marginal cost of 6 utils.

The marginal cost curve is positively sloped. For example, starting with 5 burgers, the marginal cost is 3 utils (point *q*), while starting with 6 burgers, the marginal cost is 6 utils (point *s*). Why does the marginal cost increase as burger consumption increases?

- The more burgers Bob buys, the fewer tacos he can afford.
- The fewer tacos he consumes, the higher the marginal utility of tacos—a result of diminishing marginal utility in reverse.

If the marginal utility of tacos is higher, for each additional burger Bob consumes, he will sacrifice more taco utility (the marginal utility times the trade-off of three tacos per burger). The marginal cost of a burger is the taco utility sacrificed for an additional burger, so the marginal-cost curve is positively sloped.

Finding a Point on the Demand Curve

Figure 7.3 shows the marginal-benefit curve (the same as the marginal-utility curve) and the marginal-cost curve. The marginal-cost curve intersects the marginal-benefit curve at eight burgers. In other words, to satisfy the marginal principle Bob should buy eight burgers. For each of the first eight burgers, the extra satisfaction from buying and eating the burger (the marginal benefit) is greater than or equal to the potential satisfaction from the three tacos he could have bought and eaten instead (the marginal cost).

Figure 7.3

Marginal Principle and Demand

The marginal benefit of burgers equals the marginal cost at eight burgers, so the marginal principle is satisfied at point *m*.

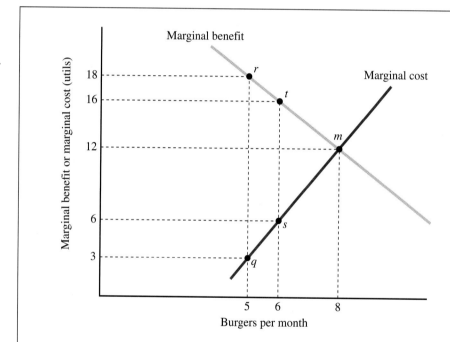

Quantity	Marginal benefit (utils)	Marginal cost (utils)
5	$18	$3
6	$16	$6
7	$14	$9
8	**$12**	**$12**

For example, the extra satisfaction from the fifth burger is 18 utils, compared to only 3 utils for the tacos he could have bought instead. Similarly, the marginal benefit is greater than the marginal cost for the sixth and seventh burgers; the marginal benefit equals the marginal cost for the eighth burger. Bob stops at eight burgers because the marginal benefit of the ninth burger (10 utils) is less than its marginal cost (15 utils from the tacos he could eat instead).

We've seen that one point on the demand curve satisfies the marginal principle. When the price of burgers is $3, Bob consumes eight burgers because that is the quantity at which the marginal benefit equals the marginal cost. If we repeated this exercise with different prices, we'd find that each point on the demand curve satisfies the marginal principle and therefore is a rational choice, given the price of the good.

Is it possible to measure the utility or satisfaction consumers receive from goods and services? As we saw in the chapter opener, utilitarians in the nineteenth century thought so. Unfortunately for the utilitarians, no one has invented a utility meter, so it is impossible to measure consumer utility. Nonetheless, utility theory is still useful as conceptual framework because it provides some insights into consumer decision-making. As explained in the Appendix to this chapter, economists have developed a different way to analyze consumer choices. This modern approach doesn't require the measurement of utility, but simply requires consumers to compare alternative bundles of goods and services.

The Utility-Maximizing Rule

We can use utility theory to introduce a general rule for consumer decisions. According to the **utility-maximizing rule,** a consumer will maximize his or her utility by picking the affordable combination of consumer goods that makes the marginal utility per dollar spent on one good equal to the marginal utility per dollar spent on a second good. In our example of burgers and tacos, this means that

$$\frac{\text{marginal utility of burgers}}{\text{price of burgers}} = \frac{\text{marginal utility of tacos}}{\text{price of tacos}}$$

To get the marginal utility per dollar spent on burgers, we divide the marginal utility of burgers by the amount of money spent on each burger (the price of burgers). For example, the marginal utility of the eighth burger is 12 utils and the price is $3, so the marginal utility for each dollar spent on the eighth burger is 4 utils. Looking back at the numbers in Tables 7.1 and 7.2, we see that Bob's choice of eight burgers and six tacos satisfies the utility-maximizing rule: The marginal utility per dollar spent on tacos is 4 utils per dollar (4 utils for the sixth taco divided by a price of $1), which is the same as the marginal utility per dollar spent on burgers (12 utils for the eighth burger divided by $3). The utility-maximizing rule is consistent with the marginal principle.

To see the logic behind the utility-maximizing rule, let's see what would happen if Bob picked a different combination of burgers and tacos. Would it be wise to pick 5 burgers and 15 tacos? In this case the marginal utility per dollar spent on burgers is 6 utils per dollar (18 utils divided by $3), while the marginal utility per dollar spent on tacos is only 1 util per dollar (1 util divided by $1). In other words, he gets a bigger marginal utility per dollar—or a bigger "bang per buck"—for the money he spends on burgers. Therefore, it would be sensible to spend more money on burgers and less on tacos. To maximize his utility, he should increase his burger consumption as long as an additional burger generates a larger bang per buck (a larger marginal utility per dollar). He should stop at eight burgers and six tacos because the bang per buck of the

Utility-maximizing rule: Pick the affordable combination of consumer goods that makes the marginal utility per dollar spent on one good equal to the marginal utility per dollar spent on a second good.

THE ECONOMICS OF DISNEYLINES

At Disneyland, you pay an admission fee ($45 for adults, $35 for kids), and once you're in the park, there is no extra charge for rides such as the Pirates of the Caribbean, Splash Mountain, and Indiana Jones Temple of the Forbidden Eye. With waiting times between one and three hours on the typical day, however, these rides are not free. Each ride has an opportunity cost equal to the time you'll spend in line. Once you're in the park, you don't have to worry about how to spend money on rides, but you must decide how to spend your limited time on them. You'll be helped out by the large signs that list the waiting times for all the rides and attractions.

Why doesn't Disney charge a price for each attraction according to its popularity, with the price of each high enough to reduce the time wasted in lines? Economists have developed three possible explanations:

- People don't like to think about money while they are vacationing. It is not a coincidence that the other examples of this type of pricing—cruise ships, ski resorts, and other theme parks—cater to vacationers.
- Waiting in line validates the consumer's decision. "If all these people are here," the consumer thinks, "I made a great choice to be here."

Part of the cost of a ride at Disneyland is the opportunity cost of time spent waiting in line.

- The lines allow parents to economize on expenses without having to say "No" to their kids. If Disney charged a price high enough to eliminate the lines, a family could spend hundreds of dollars on a day of fun. By forcing kids to wait in line, parents can save money without being held responsible for limiting the fun.

Source: Peter Passell, "Disneyland and the Old USSR: Sharing Something in Common," *New York Times,* April 24, 1996.

ninth burger (3.33 utils per dollar) would be less than the bang per buck of tacos (4 utils per dollar).

We've seen how consumers make decisions about how much to buy, given their income and the prices of alternative goods. For a discussion of consumer decisions involving limited time instead of limited money, read "A Closer Look: The Economics of Disneylines."

TEST Your Understanding

1. Betty bought five books in January, six books in February, and seven books in March. Her utility level from books was 30 utils in January, 45 utils in February, and 54 utils in March. Are these utility numbers consistent with the law of diminishing marginal utility?

2. As a person's consumption of a particular good increases, what happens to the marginal benefit of that good? Relate your answer to the law of diminishing marginal utility.

3. Suppose that Bob initially consumes 6 burgers and 12 tacos. Use the numbers in Tables 7.1 and 7.2 to compute the marginal utility per dollar spent for each good. Which good generates the larger bang per buck?

Using the **TOOLS**

In this chapter, we use some of the key principles of economics to explain the logic behind consumer choice and the law of demand. Here are some opportunities to do your own economic analysis.

APPLICATIONS

1. Consumer Metrics

You are the economist for Consumer Metrics, a consumer research firm that has developed a new device that measures the satisfaction level of a consumer before and after consuming a particular product. At the company's annual holiday party, people ate food and drank punch, and the firm paid for everything. By the end of the party, everything was consumed. Your job is to determine whether the company spent its party budget wisely. If you could hook the new device to the typical person at the party, what information would you collect, and how would you use it? What additional information would you need to determine whether the firm's chosen combination of food and punch maximized the utility of the typical partygoer?

2. Gasoline or Gasohol?

Consider the following statement: "My car can use either gasoline or gasohol (a mixture of methanol and gasoline). I use whatever fuel has a lower price per gallon." Is this a good rule for deciding what type of fuel to use in a car? If not, develop a rule that is consistent with the utility-maximizing rule.

Summary

We've seen that the market demand curve represents the rational decisions of individual consumers. We've also used utility theory to think about how people make consumption decisions. Here are the main points of the chapter.

1. Each point on the demand curve satisfies the marginal principle: The consumer increases the number of units consumed until the marginal benefit equals the marginal cost.

2. To maximize utility, a consumer should pick the affordable combination of goods that makes the marginal utility per dollar spent on one good equal to the marginal utility per dollar spent on a second good.

Key Terms

law of diminishing marginal utility, 147
marginal utility, 147

total utility, 147
util, 147

utility, 146
utility-maximizing rule, 151

Problems and Discussion Questions

1. Suppose the price of muffins is $2 and the price of cookies is $1. Use the following table to determine how many muffins Betty will consume, given a budget of $60.

Muffins		Cookies	
Number of muffins	Marginal benefit (utility) of a muffin	Number of cookies	Marginal benefit (utility) of a cookie
5	11	44	6
6	8	46	5
7	5	48	4
8	3	50	3

2. Suppose you have a fixed monthly budget for audio tapes and CDs. The price of CDs is $10, and the price of tapes is $5. Given your current choice of CDs and tapes, your marginal utility of CDs is 60, and your marginal utility of tapes is 15. Are you doing the best you can with your music budget? If not, should you buy more CDs (and fewer tapes) or more tapes (and fewer CDs)? Relate your answer to the marginal principle and the utility-maximizing rule.

3. Suppose you have a fixed budget of $3,000 per year to spend on food and music. The price of food is $1 per pound, and the price of music is $10 per CD. You currently spend $2,400 on food and $600 on music. If you want to determine whether you are spending your money wisely, what questions must you ask yourself?

4. **Web Exercise.** Visit the Web site for the Kelley Blue Book [*http://www.kbb.com*]. This site provides pricing information for new and used cars. Consider a Honda Accord LX Sedan with automatic transmission. How does the price of this model vary with age (the model year) and mileage? What's the price for a 1992 model with 90,000 miles? What's the price for a 1992 model with only 80,000 miles? From your perspective, is it worth spending the additional money to get a car with 10,000 fewer miles?

5. **Web Exercise.** Suppose you decide to buy a new digital camera. To get the facts on the alternative cameras, visit the Web site of *Consumers Digest* [*http://www.consumersdigest.com/*]. How does this site help consumers to decide between alternative products?

Take It to the Net

We invite you to visit the O'Sullivan/Sheffrin page on the Prentice Hall Web site at: **http://www.prenhall.com/osullivan/** for additional World Wide Web exercises for this chapter.

Model Answers to Questions

Chapter-Opening Questions

1. According to the utility-maximizing rule, the consumer should pick the affordable combination of consumer goods that makes the marginal utility per dollar spent on one good equal to the marginal utility per dollar spent on a second good.

2. "A Closer Look: The Economics of Disneylines," lists three possible explanations: Consumers like to avoid thinking about money on vacations; waiting in lines validates consumers' decisions; lines allow parents to economize on expenses without having to say "No."

Test Your Understanding

1. The marginal utility drops from 15 for the sixth book to 9 for the seventh book, consistent with the law of diminishing marginal utility.

2. The marginal benefit equals the marginal utility, which according to the law of diminishing marginal utility, decreases as consumption increases.

3. For burgers, 5.33 utils per dollar (16 utils divided by $3); for tacos, 2 utils per dollar (2 utils divided by $1). Burgers generate a larger bang per buck.

Using the Tools

1. Consumer Metrics. You could use the device to determine the marginal utility of food (the change in utility or satisfaction from eating the last ounce) and the marginal utility of punch (the change in utility or satisfaction from drinking the last ounce). If you get information on the prices of food and punch (prices per ounce), you could compute the marginal utility per dollar (bang per buck) for both food and punch. To maximize utility, the firm should equate the bang per buck on the two goods.

2. Gasoline or Gasohol? Applying the utility-maximizing rule, utility is the miles driven on a tank of fuel, and marginal utility is the miles per gallon of fuel (mpg). The rule suggests that to maximize utility, a driver should equate the mpg of gasohol divided by the price of gasohol to the mpg of gasoline divided by the price of gasoline. If the consumer picks one fuel or the other, she or he should pick the fuel that has the higher mpg divided by price. For example, suppose the price of gasohol is $1 per gallon and the price of gasoline is $1.25. If gasohol has an mpg of 18 and gasoline has an mpg of 25, gasoline is a better buy: It provides 20 miles per dollar, compared to 18 miles per dollar for gasohol. Although gasoline is more expensive, its higher mpg more than offsets the higher price per gallon. The rule suggested in the quote is misguided because it doesn't take into account differences in mpg.

APPENDIX

Consumer Choice Using Indifference Curves

In Chapter 7 we used utility theory to show that each point on the demand curve is the result of a rational choice by the consumer. In this appendix, we use a different model of consumer behavior to explain how the consumer makes this rational choice. The model is based on the notion that the consumer's objective is to maximize his or her utility, given the limitations dictated by his or her income and the prices of consumer goods. In contrast to the old-style utility theory discussed earlier, this modern approach does not require the measurement of utility or satisfaction. It just requires us to determine the rate at which a consumer is willing to trade one good for another. The modern approach is more realistic and useful because a consumer can easily answer the question, "How many tacos am I willing to give up to get one more burger?"

The Budget Set and Budget Line

Consider Bob, who has a fixed income of $30 per month, which he spends entirely on two goods: burgers and tacos. Bob must decide how many burgers and tacos to consume each month, given a $3 price per burger and a $1 price per taco.

Bob's ability to purchase burgers and tacos is limited by his income and the prices of the two goods. A consumer's **budget set** is defined as all the combinations of two goods the consumer can afford, given his or her income and the prices of two goods. Bob's budget set includes all the combinations of burgers and tacos that he can afford, given his income and the prices of burgers and tacos. In Figure 7A.1, the budget set is shown by the shaded triangle. A consumer's **budget line** shows all the combinations that exhaust his or her budget. In Figure 7A.1 the budget line connects points y and x. At point y, Bob spends his entire budget on tacos, getting 30 tacos ($30 = $1 per taco times 30 tacos); at point x, he spends his entire budget on burgers, getting 10 burgers ($30 = $3 per burger times 10 burgers). If Bob spends some money on each good, he can reach the points between y and x. For example, he could reach point e (eight burgers and six tacos) by spending $24 on burgers and $6 on tacos. The budget set is the shaded area below the budget line.

The slope of the budget line is the market trade-off between burgers and tacos. It shows the rate at which the consumer can trade burgers for tacos, given the market prices of the two goods. Starting from any point on the budget line, if Bob buys one

Budget set: A set of points that includes all the combinations of goods that a consumer can afford, given the consumer's income and the prices of the goods.

Budget line: The line connecting all the combinations of two goods that exhaust a consumer's budget.

**Budget Set
and Budget Line**
The budget set (the shaded triangle) shows all the afford-able combinations of burgers and tacos, and the budget line (with endpoints *x* and *y*) shows the combinations that exhaust the budget.

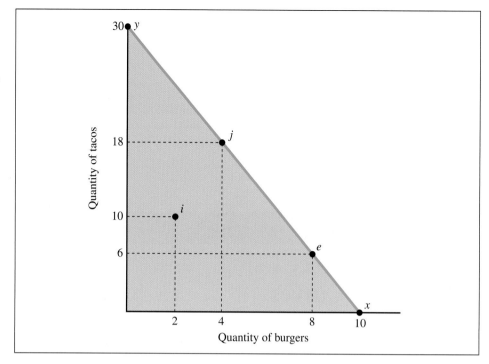

more burger, he uses $3 that he could have used instead to buy three tacos. The market trade-off is equal to the ratio of the two prices, the price of burgers divided by the price of tacos. The slope of the budget line is the negative of the price ratio, −3.0 tacos per burger in our example.

Indifference Curves

Indifference curve: The set of combinations of goods that generate the same level of utility or satisfaction.

We can represent the consumer's preferences or tastes with indifference curves. An **indifference curve** shows the combinations of the two goods that generate the same level of utility or satisfaction. In Figure 7A.2 the indifference curve passing through point *e* separates the combinations of burgers and tacos into three groups.

- **Superior combinations.** All the combinations above the indifference curve generate more satisfaction (higher utility) than combinations on the curve. Bob would prefer point *h* to point *e* or *f* because he gets more of both goods with point *h*.

- **Inferior combinations.** All the combinations below the indifference curve generate less satisfaction (lower utility) than do combinations on the curve. Bob would prefer point *e* to point *g* because he gets more of both goods with point *e*.

- **Equivalent combinations.** All combinations along the indifference curve generate the same satisfaction (the same utility) as combination *e*. Bob would be indifferent between combinations *e* and *f*.

An indifference curve shows the subjective preferences of an individual consumer, so indifference curves vary from one consumer to another. Nonetheless, the indifference curves of all consumers share two characteristics: They are negatively sloped, and they become flatter as we move downward along an individual curve.

Why is the indifference curve negatively sloped? If we increased Bob's burger consumption by one burger without changing his taco consumption, his utility would

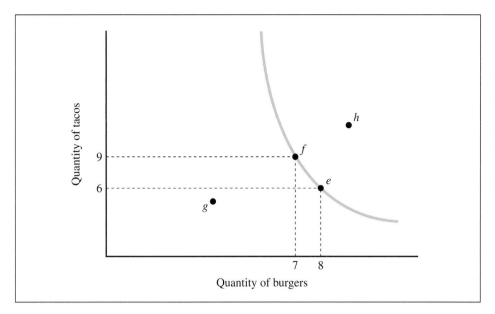

Indifference Curve and the Marginal Rate of Substitution
The indifference curve shows the different combinations of burgers and tacos that generate the same utility level. The slope is the marginal rate of substitution between the two goods (three tacos per burger between points *e* and *f*).

increase. To restore the original utility level, we must take away some tacos. In other words, there is a negative relationship between burgers and tacos, so the indifference curve is negatively sloped. The slope of the curve is the **marginal rate of substitution (MRS)** between the two goods, the rate at which a consumer is willing to substitute one good for another, that is, the subjective trade-off between the two goods. The marginal rate of substitution is the number of tacos we must take from Bob to offset the effect of giving him one more burger. In Figure 7A.2 if Bob starts at point *f* and we give him one more burger, we must take away three tacos to keep him on the same indifference curve. Therefore, the marginal rate of substitution near point *f* is three tacos per burger.

Marginal rate of substitution (MRS): The rate at which a consumer is willing to substitute one good for another.

The indifference curve becomes flatter as we move downward along the curve because of diminishing marginal utility. As we move down Bob's indifference curve, burger consumption increases and taco consumption decreases. The marginal rate of substitution decreases for two reasons:

- The larger the number of burgers, the lower the marginal utility of burgers, so we can take away fewer tacos to offset each additional burger.

- The smaller the number of tacos, the higher the marginal utility of tacos. Therefore, each taco we take away has a larger negative effect on Bob's utility, so we can offset any given increase in utility by taking away fewer tacos.

On the upper portion of the curve, Bob has many tacos and just a few burgers, so he is willing to trade several tacos to get another burger: The MRS is large, and the curve is steep. On the lower portion of the curve, he has many burgers and just a few tacos, so he is not willing to trade very many tacos to get another burger: The MRS is small, and the curve is flat.

An indifference map is a set of indifference curves, each with a different level of utility. Figure 7A.3 shows three indifference curves: C_1, C_2, and C_3. As Bob moves from a point on indifference curve C_1 to any point on C_2, his utility increases. This is sensible because he can get more of both goods on C_2, so he will be better off. In general, Bob's utility increases as he moves in the northeasterly direction to a higher indifference curve (from C_1 to C_2 to C_3, and so on).

Figure 7A.3

Indifference Map
An indifference map shows a set of indifference curves, with utility increasing as we move northeasterly to higher indifference curves.

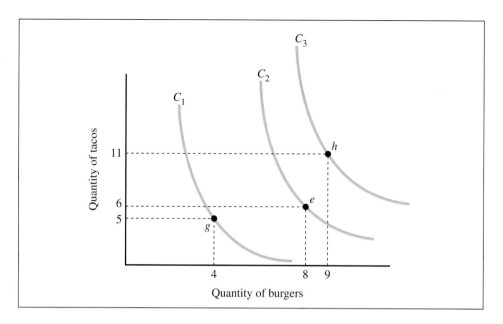

Maximizing Utility

Bob's objective is to maximize his utility, given his budget and the market prices. Bob can pick from many affordable combinations of burgers and tacos, and he will pick the one that generates the highest level of utility or satisfaction. In graphical terms, Bob will reach the highest indifference curve possible, given his budget set.

In Figure 7A.4, Bob will choose point e (eight burgers and six tacos) and will achieve the utility level associated with indifference curve C_2. Why does he choose point e instead of point i, j, or k?

- Point i. Bob doesn't choose this point for two reasons. First, it is not on the budget line, so it does not exhaust his budget: He has some money left over. Second, it is on a lower indifference curve—and generates less utility—than point e.

- Point j. Although point j exhausts Bob's budget, j lies on a lower indifference curve than e, so it generates less utility than point e. Starting from point j, Bob could reallocate his budget and buy more burgers and fewer tacos. As he moves down his budget line, he moves to progressively higher indifference curves, ultimately reaching point e on indifference curve C_2.

- Point k. Although point k generates a higher utility level than point e (it's on a higher indifference curve), it lies outside Bob's budget set, so he cannot afford it.

At point e, Bob reaches the highest indifference curve possible, given his budget set. The indifference curve touches—but does not pass through—the budget line: The indifference curve is tangent to the budget line. As we saw earlier in the discussion of point j, if Bob tentatively picked a point on the budget line whose indifference curve cuts through the budget line, he could increase his utility by moving along his budget line to a higher indifference curve. For the combination of goods that generates the highest possible utility, the indifference curve is tangent to the budget line.

What is the economic interpretation of the tangency condition? At the point of tangency, the slope of the indifference curve (the MRS) equals the slope of the budget line (the price ratio). Therefore, the consumer's subjective trade-off between the two goods (the MRS) equals the market trade-off (the price ratio). At point e in Figure 7A.4, the MRS (three tacos per burger) equals the price ratio (3.0). At any other combination of

Consumer Maximizes Utility at Tangency of Indifference Curve and Budget Line
To maximize utility, the consumer finds the combination of hamburgers and tacos at which an indifference curve is tangent to the budget line. At the utility-maximizing combination, the marginal rate of substitution equals the price ratio.

burgers and tacos, the MRS would not be equal to the price ratio, so the consumer could reallocate his budget and increase his utility. For example, starting at point j,

- Bob's MRS (the slope of the indifference curve) is 7.0: He is willing to give up seven tacos to get one burger.
- Given the prices of the two goods, the price ratio is 3.0, so Bob must give up only three tacos to get one burger.

To get one more burger (the fifth), Bob must give up only three tacos instead of the seven he is willing to give up, so he is better off buying one more burger and three fewer tacos. He will continue to reallocate his budget until the MRS equals the price ratio (until the slope of the indifference curve equals the slope of the budget line). This occurs at point e, where MRS is equal to three tacos per burger.

Drawing the Demand Curve

We can use the consumer choice model to draw Bob's demand curve for burgers. We've already derived one point on his demand curve: In Figure 7A.4, when the price of burgers is $3, he consumes eight burgers. To find another point on the demand curve, we change the price of burgers and find the utility-maximizing combination of burgers and tacos associated with the new price.

Figure 7A.5 shows what happens to the budget line when the price of burgers decreases to $2. The decrease in price tilts the budget line outward. The original vertical intercept (point y) is still in the budget set: If Bob spends his entire budget on tacos, he would be unaffected by the decrease in the price of burgers. The horizontal intercept moves outward from x (10 burgers) to z (15 burgers) because a given budget will buy more burgers. If Bob buys burgers and tacos (he chooses some point between the horizontal and vertical intercepts), he can afford more combinations of the two goods because he spends less money per burger.

Figure 7A.5

Consumer's Response to a Decrease in Price

A decrease in the price of burgers tilts the budget line outward. The indifference curve is tangent to the budget line at a larger quantity of burgers (11 burgers instead of 8). This is the law of demand: The higher the price, the smaller the quantity demanded.

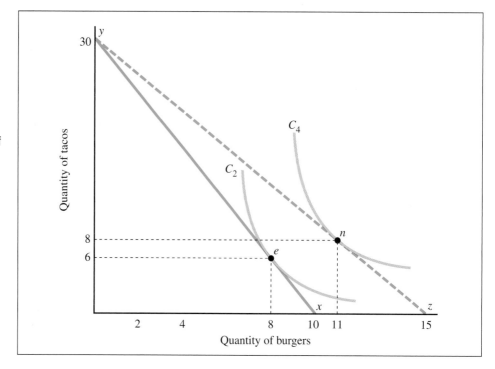

How will Bob respond to the lower price of burgers? Given the new budget line and the same set of indifference curves. Bob picks point *n*, where one of his indifference curves is tangent to the new budget line. In other words, he responds to the decrease in burger price by consuming 11 burgers instead of 8.

In Figure 7A.6, we can draw a second point on the demand curve: When the price is $2, Bob consumes 11 burgers. We can find other points on the demand curve by repeating this process for other prices: Draw the new budget line and find the point at which an indifference curve is tangent to the new budget line. When we do this, we'll find that the demand curve is negatively sloped, consistent with the law of demand: The lower the price, the larger the quantity demanded.

Figure 7A.6

Individual Demand Curve

At a price of $3 per burger, Bob maximizes his utility with 8 burgers (point *e* in Figure 7A.5 and point *b* in Figure 7A.6); at a price of $2 per burger, Bob maximizes his utility with 11 burgers (point *n* in Figure 7A.5 and point *c* in Figure 7A.6).

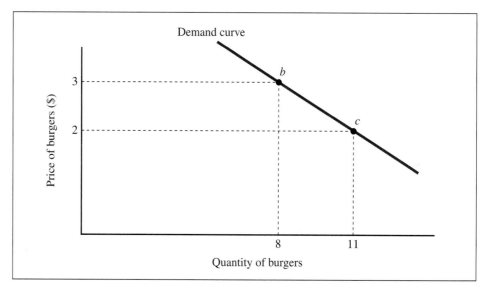

We've used the consumer choice model to find two points on the individual demand curve. For each price we found the quantity of burgers that generated the highest possible utility level, given the consumer's budget and the price of the other good (tacos). We have drawn a true demand curve because we changed the price of burgers but did not change the consumer's income or the prices of other goods.

Summary

We've used a model of consumer behavior to show how a consumer decides how much of a particular good to consume. The consumer's objective is to maximize his or her utility, given an income and the prices of consumer goods. Here are the main points of the appendix.

1. To maximize utility, the consumer finds the point at which one of her indifference curves is tangent to her budget line.

2. At the utility-maximizing combination of two goods, the marginal rate of substitution (the consumer's subjective trade-off between the two goods) equals the price ratio (the market trade-off).

Key Terms

budget line, 155
budget set, 155

indifference curve, 156

marginal rate of substitution (MRS), 157

Problems and Discussion Questions

1. Consider a person who spends a total of $200 on hats and violets. The price of hats is $20, and the price of violets is $5. Draw a budget line with hats on the horizontal axis and violets on the vertical axis.

   a. What is the slope of the budget line?

   b. Draw a conventional indifference curve (negatively sloped and convex to the origin) that intersects the budget line. Explain why the consumer can reach a higher utility level than the level shown by this indifference curve.

   c. Draw a second indifference curve that shows the highest possible utility level.

   d. Complete the statement: To maximize utility, the consumer finds the combination of hats and violets such that _____ equals 4.

2. Mistletoe, Inc. spent $500 on food and drink for this year's party. At the end of the party, there were no leftovers. The price of food (per ounce) is three times the price of drink. Your task is to figure out

   whether the firm could have spent the $500 more wisely.

   a. If you could conduct an exit poll as the employees leave the party, what question (only one) would you ask them?

   b. Provide an answer to your question that would suggest the firm should have spent more on food and less on drink.

3. Carla has a fixed budget for a new car and has tentatively decided to buy a car with 80 horsepower (hp) and 100 cubic feet (cf) of interior space. Given the current selection of cars and their prices, the price of horsepower is one-third the price of cubic feet. After some prompting from the used-car salesperson, Carla said, "To get an additional unit of horsepower, I would be willing to sacrifice 2 cubic feet of interior space." Does her tentative choice (80 hp and 100 cf) maximize her utility subject to her auto budget? If not, should she choose an auto with more or less horsepower?

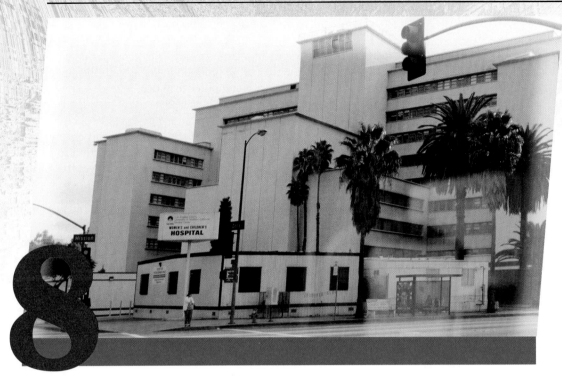

Production and Cost

Your small city is about to replace its aging 800-bed hospital with either a new 800-bed hospital or two new 400-bed hospitals. In a public hearing before the city council, an economic consultant made the following statement: "A big hospital is much more efficient than a small one, so it would be silly to build two 400-bed hospitals rather than a single 800-bed hospital. In fact, the cost per bed of an 800-bed hospital is about one-third of the cost per bed of a 400-bed hospital."

his chapter is about how production cost varies with the size of the production facility and the quantity of output produced in a given facility. Before the city council decides whether to build one or two new hospitals, it should take a careful look at the cost of providing hospital services in large and small hospitals. Similarly, before a firm builds a computer-chip factory, it should compare the production cost per chip in a large factory to the cost per chip in a small one. This chapter also explores how the cost of production varies with the quantity of output produced in a given facility. Before a computer firm decides how many chips to produce in its chip factory, it should take a careful look at the cost of producing different quantities of chips.

In later chapters, we'll use the cost curves discussed in this chapter to explain firms' decisions about whether to enter a market and how much output to produce once they enter. In this chapter, we'll see how to use cost curves to answer the following practical questions:

1. If the government breaks up a large aluminum producer into two smaller firms, by how much will the average cost of producing a given quantity of aluminum increase?

2. Are large trucking firms more efficient than smaller trucking firms? If so, how much more efficient?

3. Why is the typical short-run average cost curve shaped like the letter U, while the typical long-run average cost curve is shaped like the letter L?

4. Suppose that one electric utility has three times as many customers as another electric utility. Which utility has a higher unit cost of electricity, and how large is the cost difference?

Introduction

This chapter is about production cost in the short run and long run. Let's start with some definitions of cost and then review the difference between the short run and the long run.

Economic Cost Versus Accounting Cost

Explicit cost: The firm's actual cash payments for its inputs.

Our discussion of the firm's cost is based on the notion of economic cost. You may be surprised to hear that accountants and economists differ in the way they compute the cost of production. As we see in Table 8.1, a firm's total accounting cost equals the firm's **explicit cost**, defined as actual cash payments for inputs. For example, if the firm spends a total of $60,000 per year on labor, materials, rent, and machinery, its explicit cost would be $60,000, and this is the firm's total accounting cost.

The key principle underlying the computation of economic cost is the principle of opportunity cost.

PRINCIPLE of Opportunity Cost

> **The opportunity cost of something is what you sacrifice to get it.**

Implicit cost: The opportunity cost of nonpurchased inputs.

The firm's total economic cost equals explicit cost plus **implicit cost**. The firm's implicit cost is defined as the opportunity cost of nonpurchased inputs such as the entrepreneur's time or money.

Table 8.1 Accounting Versus Economic Cost

	Accounting Approach	Economic Approach
Explicit cost (purchased inputs)	$60,000	$60,000
Implicit: opportunity cost of entrepreneur's time		30,000
Implicit: opportunity cost of funds		10,000
Total cost	$60,000	$100,000

- **Opportunity cost of the entrepreneur's time.** An entrepreneur has less time to pursue other activities, and economic cost includes the opportunity cost of the time spent running the firm. If an entrepreneur could earn $30,000 per year in another job, the opportunity cost of his or her time is $30,000 per year.

- **Opportunity cost of funds.** Many entrepreneurs use their own funds to set up and run their businesses, and economic cost includes the opportunity cost of these funds. If an entrepreneur starts a business with some money withdrawn from his or her bank account, sacrificing $10,000 of interest income per year, the opportunity cost of the funds invested in the firm is $10,000 per year.

In this case, the implicit cost is $40,000 per year, and the **economic cost**—defined as the sum of the explicit and implicit cost—is $100,000. The economic cost is higher because the economist includes implicit cost, but the accountant does not. When we refer to the firm's production cost, we mean the economic cost of production, including both implicit and explicit cost.

Economic cost: Explicit cost plus implicit cost.

Short-Run Versus Long-Run Decisions

In later chapters, we'll see how firms use their cost curves to make two types of decisions:

- A firm that already has a production facility must decide how much output to produce in that facility. This is a short-run decision because one of the factors of production (the facility) is fixed.

- A firm that has decided to enter a market must decide how large a facility to build. Such a firm is making a long-run decision because none of the factors of production are fixed. The firm starts from scratch and can choose a production facility of any size.

In most cases, the long run is the time required for a firm to build a production facility and start producing output. For example, if it takes a firm in the garden-tool business one year to build a factory, the long run for that firm is one year, and the short run is any time less than a year. The long run varies across industries. If it takes one day to get a hot-dog cart and start selling hot dogs, the long run is a day. In contrast, it takes several years to design and build a computer chip factory, so the long run in that industry is several years.

Production and Cost in the Short Run

The short run is defined as a period of time over which at least one input to the production process is fixed. For most firms, the fixed input is its production facility, for example, a factory, store, office, or farm. In the short run, the firm cannot modify its production facility or build a new facility.

As we saw in Chapter 2, the key principle for short-run decision-making is the principle of diminishing returns.

PRINCIPLE of Diminishing Returns

Suppose that output is produced with two or more inputs and we increase one input while holding the other inputs fixed. Beyond some point—called the point of diminishing returns—output will increase at a decreasing rate.

A pizzeria experiences diminishing returns because its workers share a fixed production facility: a pizza oven. When the pizzeria adds a worker, each worker becomes less productive because he or she works with a smaller piece of the production facility. As the pizzeria adds more and more workers, output increases at a decreasing rate, meaning the marginal product of labor decreases.

Production and Marginal Product

Consider a firm that produces lawn rakes in a factory equipped with machines and other equipment. The firm's variable input is labor, and the firm's fixed input is its production facility, the fully equipped factory. As the number of workers increases—and the production facility doesn't change—what happens to the quantity of rakes produced?

Total product curve: A curve showing the relationship between the quantity of labor and the quantity of output produced.

Table 8.2 shows the relationship between the number of workers and the number of rakes produced per minute. The firm needs 8 workers to produce one rake per minute, 12 workers to produce 2 rakes per minute, and so on up to 130 workers to produce 10 rakes per minute. Figure 8.1 uses the numbers in Table 8.2 to show the firm's **total product curve**, the relationship between the quantity of labor and the quantity of output pro-

Table 8.2   Labor Input and Output

Labor: Number of Workers	Output: Rakes per Minute	Marginal Product of Labor
0	0	
8	1	1/8
12	2	1/4
15	3	1/3
20	4	1/5
27	5	1/7
36	6	1/9
48	7	1/12
65	8	1/17
90	9	1/25
130	10	1/40

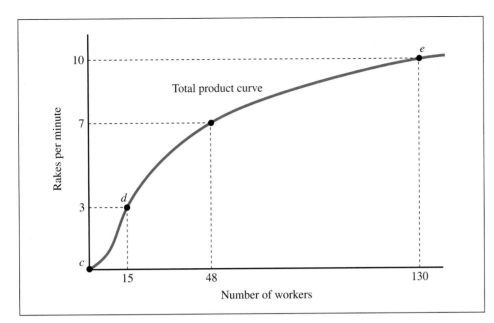

Figure 8.1
Total Product Curve
The total product curve
shows the relationship
between the quantity of labor
and the quantity of output,
given a fixed production facility. For the first 15 workers,
output increases at an
increasing rate: a result of
labor specialization. Point *d*
is the point of diminishing
returns. Beyond this point,
adding workers increases
output at a decreasing rate.

duced. Let's look at two different parts of the total product curve, starting with the part between points *d* and *e*.

The shape of the total product curve between points *d* and *e* is explained by diminishing returns. As the number of workers increases beyond 15, the curve becomes flatter; that is, output increases at a decreasing rate. The rake workers share the factory and all the machinery for making rakes, and as the number of workers increases, each worker has a smaller share of the facility. Eventually, adding a worker makes each worker in the factory less productive, so the marginal product of labor decreases and the total product curve becomes flatter. In Figure 8.1, this happens at point *d*, the point of diminishing returns.

To illustrate the notion of diminishing returns, consider the amounts of labor required to produce between 3 and 5 rakes per minute. In Table 8.2, to increase output from 3 to 4 rakes, the firm must increase its workforce from 15 to 20 workers, hiring 5 additional workers. To increase output from 4 to 5 rakes per minute, the firm must increase its workforce from 20 to 27 workers, hiring 7 additional workers. Because of diminishing returns resulting from sharing the production facility, it takes progressively more workers to increase output by one more rake.

What about the total product curve between points *c* and *d*? For a small workforce and a small quantity of output, the slope of the curve increases as the number of workers increases. In other words, the marginal product of labor increases for the first 15 workers. Although this may seem to be contrary to the principle of diminishing returns, remember that the principle says that eventually output will increase at a decreasing rate. So what's different when the firm produces a small quantity of output?

The difference is the possibility of labor specialization. Suppose there are 15 distinct tasks associated with making a rake. If the firm hires only 8 workers, some of the workers will be forced to perform more than one of these tasks. Together, the 8 workers will produce 1 rake per minute. Adding 4 more workers would allow some workers to specialize, each doing one of the 15 tasks. A worker with a single task will spend less time switching between tasks and also will become more skillful in the assigned task. In other words, specialization increases output per worker, so the firm can increase output from

1 to 2 rakes by adding only 4 workers. Adding 3 more workers—bringing the workforce to 15 workers—allows each worker to specialize in a single task, and increases output from 2 to 3 rakes per minute. In this example, there are benefits from specialization for the first 15 workers, so the firm's marginal product increases for the first 15 workers.

Short-Run Total Cost and Short-Run Marginal Cost

We've seen the production relationship between labor and output, so we're ready to show how the cost of production varies with the quantity of output produced. We can use the production data in Table 8.2 to derive several cost curves for our hypothetical rake producer. As we'll see, the shape of the total-product curve determines the shape of the total-cost curve, with a couple of twists. First, in drawing the total-product curve, we put output (rakes per minutes) on the vertical axis; to draw the total-cost curve, we put output on the horizontal axis. Second, the total-cost curve incorporates the fixed cost associated with the firm's production facility. Table 8.3 shows some hypothetical cost data for the rake producer whose total product curve is shown in Figure 8.2. The question is. How does the cost of producing rakes vary as the number of rakes produced *per minute* increases?

There are two types of production cost in the short run: fixed cost and variable cost.

Fixed cost [FC]: Cost that does not depend on the quantity produced.

• **Fixed cost [FC]** is defined as the cost that does not vary with the quantity produced. In our example, the fixed cost is the cost of the rake factory, including the cost of the building and all the machinery and equipment inside. We're interested not in the total output of the rake factory over its 30-year life, but in its output per minute. Therefore, we must translate the one-time $100 million expense for the factory into a cost per minute, for example, $36 per minute. As shown in the second column in Table 8.3, the fixed cost is $36 per minute, regardless of how much output is produced.

Table 8.3 Short-Run Production Costs

(1) Output: Rakes per Minute	(2) Fixed Cost (FC)	(3) Total Variable Cost (TVC)	(4) Short-Run Total Cost (STC)	(5) Short-Run Marginal Cost (SMC)	(6) Average Fixed Cost (AFC)	(7) Short-Run Average Variable Cost (SAVC)	(8) Short-Run Average Total Cost (SATC)
0	36	0	36	—	—	—	—
1	36	8	44	8.00	36.00	8.00	44.00
2	36	12	48	4.00	18.00	6.00	24.00
3	36	15	51	3.00	12.00	5.00	17.00
4	36	20	56	5.00	9.00	5.00	14.00
5	36	27	63	7.00	7.20	5.40	12.60
6	36	36	72	9.00	6.00	6.00	12.00
7	36	48	84	12.00	5.14	6.86	12.00
8	36	65	101	17.00	4.50	8.13	12.63
9	36	90	126	25.00	4.00	10.00	14.00
10	36	130	166	40.00	3.60	13.00	16.60

Figure 8.2

Short-Run Cost: Fixed Cost, Variable Cost, and Total Cost

The short-run total cost curve shows the relationship between the quantity of output and production costs given a fixed production facility. Short-run total cost equals fixed cost (the cost that does not vary with the quantity produced) plus total variable cost (the cost that varies with the quantity produced).

• Variable cost is defined as a cost that varies with the quantity produced. For example, to produce more rakes, the firm must hire more workers. If we assume that the firm pays each of its workers $1 per minute, the **total variable cost [TVC]** per minute is the same as the number of workers, $8 for one rake, $12 for two rakes, and so on.

The **short-run total cost [STC]** equals the sum of fixed and variable costs. Figure 8.2 shows the three cost curves. The horizontal line shows the fixed cost of $36, and the lower of the two positively sloped curves shows the total variable cost. The third curve shows short-run total cost as the sum of fixed cost and total variable cost. The vertical distance between the STC curve and the TVC curve equals the firm's fixed cost.

Economists like to think on the margin, and marginal cost is part of marginal thinking. The **short-run marginal cost [SMC]** is defined as the change in short-run total cost resulting from producing one more unit of the good. As shown in the fourth column of Table 8.3, if the firm decides to produce just one rake, its short-run total cost increases from $36 (the fixed cost) to $44, so the marginal cost of the first rake is $8. For the first three rakes, the marginal cost gets smaller and smaller, a result of the benefits of labor specialization. The firm needs eight workers to produce the first rake (a marginal cost of $8), but only four more workers to produce the second rake (marginal cost = $4), and only three more workers to produce the third rake. We saw earlier that specialization leads to increasing marginal productivity; now we know that it also leads to decreasing marginal cost. In Figure 8.3, the short-run marginal-cost curve is negatively sloped for the first three rakes.

Starting with the fourth rake, the short-run marginal cost increases as the number of rakes increases, a result of diminishing returns. Once the benefits of labor specialization are exhausted, diminishing returns set in, and it takes more and more workers to increase output by one rake. To increase output from three to four rakes, the firm needs five additional workers (marginal cost = $5, shown by point *c*). To increase output from four to five rakes, the firm needs seven additional workers (marginal cost = $7, shown by point *d*). Because the firm requires more and more workers to increase

Total variable cost [TVC]: Cost that varies as the firm changes its output.

Short-run total cost [STC]: The total cost of production in the short run, when one or more inputs (for example, the production facility) is fixed; equal to fixed cost plus variable cost.

Short-run marginal cost [SMC]: The change in short-run total cost resulting from producing one more unit of the good.

Figure 8.3

Short-Run Marginal Cost and Short-Run Average Cost

The positively sloped portion of the short-run marginal cost curve (SMC) results from diminishing returns. The short-run average total cost curve (SATC) is U-shaped, a result of spreading fixed cost (which pulls down the average total cost) and diminishing returns (which pulls up the average total cost). The SMC curve intersects each average-cost curve (SAVC and SATC) at the minimum point of the average curve.

production by one unit, the marginal cost of production increases. In Table 8.3 and Figure 8.3, marginal cost increases to $12 for the seventh rake, to $25 for the ninth rake, and so on.

Short-Run Average Cost Curves

It will often be useful to express the firm's cost of production as average cost. There are three types of short-run average cost:

- **Average fixed cost [AFC]:** fixed cost divided by the quantity produced.
- **Short-run average variable cost [SAVC]:** total variable cost divided by the quantity produced.
- **Short-run average total cost [SATC]:** total cost divided by the quantity produced: equal to the sum of AFC and SAVC.

Average fixed cost [AFC]: Fixed cost divided by the quantity produced.

Short-run average variable cost [SAVC]: Total variable cost divided by the quantity produced.

Short-run average total cost [SATC]: Short-run total cost divided by the quantity of output; equal to AFC plus SAVC.

The last three columns of Table 8.3 show these three types of average cost for our rake producer. To compute AFC, we simply divide the fixed cost by the quantity of rakes produced. In our example, AFC decreases from $36 per rake, to $18 per rake for two rakes, and so on. As output increases, the fixed cost ($36) is spread over more units, so AFC decreases.

To compute SAVC, we divide the total variable cost by the quantity of rakes produced. In Figure 8.3, the SAVC curve is negatively sloped for small quantities of output but positively sloped for larger quantities. The negative slope reflects the benefits of labor specialization when the firm produces a small quantity of output. Adding workers to a small workforce makes workers more productive on average, so the average cost of labor per rake drops. The SAVC curve is positively sloped for large quantities of output, a result of diminishing returns: adding more workers to a large workforce makes workers less productive on average, so the average cost of labor per rake rises.

Why is the SATC curve shaped like a U? At very small quantities of output, the curve is negatively sloped, a result of two forces that work together to pull SATC down as output increases:

- Spreading the fixed cost. For small quantities of output, a one-unit increase in output reduces AFC by a large amount because the fixed cost is pretty "thick," being spread over just a few units of output. For example, going from one rake to two rakes decreases AFC from $36 per rake to $18 per rake.
- Labor specialization. For small quantities of output, SAVC decreases as output increases, a result of labor specialization that increases worker productivity.

These two forces both pull SATC downward as output increases, so the curve is negatively sloped for small quantities of output.

What happens once the firm reaches the point at which the benefits of labor specialization are exhausted? As the firm continues to increase output, the average variable cost increases, a result of diminishing returns. There is a tug-of-war between two forces; the spreading of fixed cost continues to pull SATC down, while diminishing returns and rising SAVC pushes SATC up. In other words, the SATC curve could be negatively sloped or positively sloped, depending on the relative strengths of the two forces.

The outcome of the tug-of-war depends on the quantity produced, giving the SATC curve its U shape.

- Intermediate quantities of output (between three and seven rakes per minute). The tug-of-war is won by the spreading of fixed cost, so SATC decreases as output increases. In this case, the decrease in AFC is larger than the increase in SAVC because the fixed cost isn't too "thin" and diminishing returns are not too strong. As a result, short-run average total cost decreases as output increases.
- Large quantities of output (eight rakes per minute or more). The tug-of-war is won by diminishing returns and rising SAVC, so SATC increases as output increases. In this case, the reductions in AFC are relatively small because the fixed cost is so "thin" already, and diminishing returns are severe. As a result, short-run average total cost increases as output increases.

The Relationship Between Marginal and Average Curves

Figure 8.3 shows the relationship between short-run marginal cost and short-run average total cost. Whenever the marginal cost is less than the average total cost (for fewer than seven rakes), the average total cost is falling. In contrast, whenever the marginal cost exceeds the average total cost (for more than seven rakes), the average total cost is rising. Finally, when the marginal cost equals the average total cost, the average cost is neither rising nor falling (for seven rakes). In other words, the marginal-cost curve intersects the short-run average total cost curve at its minimum point.

We can use some simple logic to explain the relationship between average cost and marginal cost. Suppose that you start the semester with a cumulative GPA of 3.0 (a B average) and enroll in a single course this semester—a history course. If you receive a grade of C in history (2.0 for computing your GPA), your GPA will drop below 3.0. Your GPA decreases because the grade in the "marginal" course (the history course) is less than the "average" grade (the starting GPA), so the marginal grade pulls down your GPA. Suppose that you take an economics class the following semester and get a grade of A (4.0 for computing your GPA). In this case, your GPA will increase because the marginal grade (in economics) is higher than your average (your GPA), so the marginal grade pushes up your GPA. If you were to take a course the following semester and your grade in the course is the same as your GPA, your GPA wouldn't change. To summarize, whenever the marginal grade is less than the average grade, the average will fall; whenever the marginal grade exceeds the average grade, the average will rise; whenever the marginal grade equals the average grade, the average will not change.

In Figure 8.3, the SATC curve is negatively sloped for the first six rakes. Using the arithmetic of averages, the fact that the average cost is decreasing means that the marginal cost is less than the average cost: the lower marginal cost pulls down the average. In contrast, the SATC curve is positively sloped for eight or more rakes, which means that the marginal cost exceeds the average total cost: the higher marginal cost pulls up the average. If the average total cost is neither increasing nor decreasing, the marginal cost must equal the average total cost. In Figure 8.3, this happens at point m, the minimum point of the SATC curve. Using the same logic, the marginal cost equals the average variable cost at the minimum point of the SAVC curve (point c).

What is the relationship between average variable cost and average total cost? The total cost is the sum of fixed cost and variable cost, so the difference between the average total cost and the average variable cost is the average fixed cost. As output increases, the average fixed cost decreases because the fixed cost is spread over more and more rakes, decreasing the vertical distance between average total cost and average variable cost. In Figure 8.3, as output increases, the vertical distance between SAVC and SATC decreases.

Economic Detective

The Cost of Pencils

Mr. Big wants to enter the pencil-making business. He gathered some information from two existing pencil manufacturers: Sharp, Inc. and Pointy, Inc. The two firms have identical production facilities—identical factories and equipment. The two firms also pay the same wage to their workers and pay the same prices for materials. Although Sharp produces 1,000 pencils per minute and Pointy produces 2,000 per minute, each firm has a short-run average total cost of 10 cents per pencil. After building a production facility identical to the ones used by Sharp and Pointy, Mr. Big hired enough workers and bought enough materials to produce 2,500 pencils per minute. Based on the experience of Sharp and Pointy, he expected to produce at an average cost of 10 cents per pencil. After all, he thought, that's the average cost for 1,000 pencils and 2,000 pencils, so it should also be the average cost for 2,500 pencils. Much to his dismay, his average cost was 14 cents per pencil.

We can solve this mystery with a quick look at a typical short-run average total cost curve. In Figure 8.4, the U-shaped SATC curve shows an average cost of 10 cents for both

Figure 8.4

The Cost Mystery
Because the short-run average total cost curve is U-shaped, it is possible to have the same short-run average cost at two—but not three—different quantities of output.

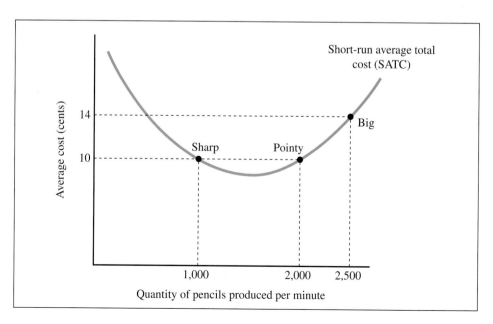

Sharp (1,000 pencils) and Pointy (2,000 pencils). Sharp produces on the negatively sloped portion of the average cost curve, while Pointy produces on the positively sloped portion. In contrast, Mr. Big produces 2,500 pencils at an average cost of 14 cents. Mr. Big thought that because Sharp and Pointy had the same average cost, the average cost curve must be horizontal. He didn't realize that the short-run average cost curve is U-shaped. Along a U-shaped curve, it is possible to have the same average cost for two different quantities of output. Unfortunately for Mr. Big, it's not possible to have the same average cost for three different quantities.

TEST Your Understanding

1. What key principle explains the positively sloped portion of the short-run marginal cost curve?

2. Comment on the following statement: "We're planning on increasing the output of our rubber-chicken factory by 10%. It's obvious that our short-run average total cost will decrease because we'll spread our fixed costs over more chickens."

3. According to the foreman in your chair factory, the short-run marginal cost of chairs is less than the short-run average cost. If you increase your output of chairs, will your short-run average cost increase or decrease?

4. Complete the statement with average or marginal: The short-run marginal cost curve intersects the short-run average cost curve at the minimum point of the _____ cost curve.

Production and Cost in the Long Run

Up to this point, we've been exploring short-run cost curves, which show the cost of producing different quantities of output in a given production facility. Let's turn next to long-run cost curves, which show the production costs in facilities of different sizes. The long run is defined as the period of time over which a firm is perfectly flexible in its choice of all inputs. In the long run, a firm can build a new production facility (factory, store, office, or restaurant) or modify an existing facility.

The key difference between the short run and the long run is that there are no diminishing returns in the long run. Remember that diminishing returns occur because workers share a fixed production facility, so the more workers in the facility, the smaller the piece of the facility available for each worker. In the long run, the firm can expand its production facility as its workforce grows.

Expansion and Replication

Continuing the example of rake production, consider a rake producer that has decided to replace its existing factory with a new one. The firm has been producing seven rakes per minute at a total cost of $84 per minute, or an average cost of $12 per rake. If the firm wants to produce twice as much output per minute in its new facility, what should it do?

One possibility is to simply double the original operation. The firm could build two factories that are identical to the original factory and hire two workforces, each identical to the original workforce. In this case, the firm's total cost will double with its output: each new factory will produce 7 rakes per minute at a cost of $84 per minute, so the firm can produce a total of 14 rakes per minute at twice the cost, $168 per minute. The firm's **long-run total cost** is defined as the total cost of production when the firm is perfectly flexible in its choice of all inputs, and can choose a production facility of any size. Table 8.4

Long-run total cost: The total cost of production in the long run when a firm is perfectly flexible in its choice of all inputs and can choose a production facility of any size.

Table 8.4 Long-Run Costs: Total and Average Cost

Output: Rakes per minute	Long-Run Total Cost	Long-Run Average Cost
3.5	$ 70	$20
7	$ 84	$12
14	$168	$12
28	$336	$12

shows the firm's long-run total cost for several different quantities, including 7, 14, and 28 rakes per minute. The replication process means the long-run total cost increases proportionately with the quantity produced, from $84 for 7 rakes per minute, to $168 for 14 rakes per minute, to $336 for 28 rakes per minute.

Long-run average cost of production [LAC]: Long-run total cost divided by the quantity of output produced.

The firm's **long-run average cost of production [LAC]** is defined as long-run total cost divided by the quantity of output produced. In Table 8.4, the long-run average cost is $12 per rake for 7 or more rakes per minute. Because long-run total cost is proportional to the quantity produced, the long-run average cost doesn't change as output increases. In Figure 8.5, the long-run average cost curve is horizontal for 7 or more rakes per minute.

For a firm that wants to double its output in the long run, replication is one option. Another possibility is to build a single larger factory, one that can produce the target quantity of output at a lower cost than would be possible by simply building two factories identical to the original. If so, the long-run average cost of producing the larger quantity (for example, 14 rakes per minute) would be less than $12.

Decrease in Output and Indivisible Inputs

Suppose that instead of expanding its operation, a rake producer wants to reduce its operation, producing half as many rakes per minute as it did in its original operation. Could the firm simply hire half as many workers, build a factory with half the floor area, and fill the factory with half as much machinery and equipment? Perhaps, but there may be a problem with indivisible inputs.

Figure 8.5

Long-Run Average Cost Curve

The long-run average cost curve is negatively sloped for up to seven rakes per minute, a result of indivisible inputs and the effects of labor specialization. If the firm replicates the operation that produces seven rakes per minute, the long-run average cost curve will be horizontal beyond seven rakes per minute.

The production of many goods and services involves indivisible inputs, such as this large ship for ocean cargo service.

An input is **indivisible** if it cannot be scaled down to produce a smaller quantity of output. For example, firms use industrial molds to make multiple copies of the same item, and a firm needs a mold regardless of how many copies it produces. Suppose the rake factory uses an industrial mold to shape plastic into the fan-shaped end of the rake. The firm needs the standard mold, regardless of how many rakes it produces, so cutting back from 7 rakes per minute to 3.5 rakes per minute won't affect the cost of the mold, so cutting output in half won't cut the firm's long-run total costs in half.

> **Indivisible input:** An input that cannot be scaled down to produce a smaller quantity of output.

Table 8.4 shows the implications of indivisible inputs for total and average cost. In the first row, the long-run total cost of producing 3.5 rakes per minute is $70, compared to $84 for 7 rakes per minute. That means the long-run average cost of 3.5 rakes is $20 per rake ($70/3.5), compared to $12 per rake for 7 rakes per minute. In Figure 8.5, the long-run average cost is negatively sloped between points *e* and *f*. In general, if there are indivisible inputs, the long-run average total cost curve will be negatively sloped.

Most production processes have at least one indivisible input. Here are some other examples of firms and their indivisible inputs:

- A railroad company providing freight service between two cities must lay a set of tracks between them. The company cannot scale down the tracks by laying a half set of tracks (a single rail).
- A cable TV firm uses a cable running throughout its territory.
- A computer-chip factory uses "clean rooms" and complex machines and testing equipment.
- A shipping firm uses a large ship to carry TV sets from Japan to the United States.
- A steel producer uses a large blast furnace.
- A hospital uses imaging machines (for X-rays, CAT scans, and MRIs).
- A pizzeria uses a pizza oven.

These indivisible inputs cannot be scaled down to produce a smaller quantity of output. For example, it is impractical to produce a small quantity of steel in a factory with a small blast furnace, just as it is impractical to transport a single TV set across the ocean

INDIVISIBLE INPUTS AND THE COST OF FAKE KILLER WHALES

Sea lions off the Washington coast eat steelhead and other fish, depleting some species threatened with extinction and decreasing the harvest of the commercial fishing industry. Rick Funk, a plastics manufacturer, thinks that a variation on the scarecrow would solve the sea lion problem. Killer whales love to eat sea lions, and Funk says that he could build a life-sized fiberglass killer whale, mount it on a rail like a roller coaster, and then send the whale diving through the water to scare off the sea lions. According to Funk, it would cost about $16,000 to make the first whale. Once the mold is made, however, each additional whale would cost an additional $5,000: It would cost a total of $21,000 for two whales, $26,000 for three whales, and so on.

This little story illustrates the effects of indivisible inputs on the firm's cost curves. The cost of the first whale ($16,000) includes the cost of the mold (the indivisible input). Once the firm has the mold, the additional cost for each whale is only $5,000, so the aver-

How much would it cost to make fake killer whales to scare away sea lions that feast on steelhead and other fish?

age cost per whale decreases as the number of whales increases.

Source: Sandi Doughton, "Killer Whale Latest Idea on Sea Lions," *The Oregonian*, January 7, 1995.

---

in a rowboat. For another example of indivisible inputs, read "A Closer Look: Indivisible Inputs and the Cost of Fake Killer Whales."

Decrease in Output and Labor Specialization

A second reason for higher average long-run costs in a smaller operation is that labor will be less specialized in the small operation. As the number of workers decreases, each worker will be forced to take on more production tasks. Labor productivity will be lower because workers spend more time switching between tasks and will be less proficient because they have less experience at each task. The workers in the smaller rake firm will be less specialized and thus less productive, so the workforce required to produce 3.5 rakes per minute will be more than half the workforce required to produce 7 rakes per minute. When the firm cuts back to only 3.5 rakes per minute, the firm's labor costs will not be cut in half, so the long-run average cost will increase to some amount greater than $12.

Two centuries ago, Adam Smith used the making of sewing pins to illustrate the benefits from specialization.[1]

> *A workman . . . could scarce, perhaps with his utmost industry, make one pin a day, and certainly could not make twenty. But the way in which this business is now carried on . . . one man draws out the wire, another straightens it, a third cuts it, a fourth points it, a fifth grinds the top for receiving the head; to make the head requires two or three distinct operations. . . . The . . . making of a pin is, in this manner, divided into about eighteen distinct operations. . . . I have seen a small manufactory of this kind where ten men . . . make among them . . . upward of forty eight thousand pins in a day.*

The idea of specialization is summarized in the old saying that a person who is a jack of all trades is a master of none. In a small operation, each worker is a jack of many tasks and is not very productive at any particular task. In a large operation, each worker concentrates on just a few tasks and becomes a master at those tasks.

Economies of Scale

A firm experiences **economies of scale** if its long-run average-cost curve is negatively sloped. In Figure 8.5, the rake producer experiences economies of scale between points *e* and *f*. For example, at point *e*, the long-run average cost of producing 3.5 rakes per minute is $20, compared to $12 for 7 rakes per minute (point *f*). An increase in output from 3.5 to 7 rakes per minute decreases the long-run average cost of production, so there are some economies (that is, cost savings) associated with scaling up the firm's operation. The economies of scale result from indivisible inputs and the benefits from labor specialization.

Economies of scale: A situation in which an increase in the quantity produced decreases the long-run average cost of production.

As we saw earlier in the book, recent technological innovations have decreased the cost of producing electricity from the wind, leading to the development of wind farms. There are scale economies in the production of electricity from wind because although large wind turbines are more costly than small ones, the higher cost is more offset by greater generating capacity. For the details, read "A Closer Look: Scale Economies in Wind Power."

A CLOSER LOOK | SCALE ECONOMIES IN WIND POWER

There are scale economies in the production of electricity from wind because the cost of purchasing, installing, and maintaining a wind turbine increases less than proportionately with the generating capacity of the turbine. This table shows the various costs of a small turbine (150 kilowatt capacity) and a large turbine (600 kilowatt capacity), each with an assumed lifetime of 20 years.[2]

Costs of Wind Turbines

	Small Turbine (150 kilowatt)	Large Turbine (600 kilowatt)
Purchase price of turbine	$150,000	$420,000
Installation cost	$100,000	$100,000
Operating and maintenance cost	$75,000	$126,000
Total cost	$325,000	$646,000
Electricity generated (kilowatt hours)	5 million	20 million
Average cost (per kilowatt hour)	$0.065	$0.032

The larger turbine has four times the generation capacity, but its purchase price is less than three times as large, its installation cost is the same, and its operating and maintenance costs are less than twice as large. Under typical wind conditions, the large turbine would produce about 20 million kilowatt hours over its lifetime, compared to 5 million kilowatt hours for the smaller turbine. The average cost per kilowatt hour is $0.032 for the large turbine, compared to $0.065 for the smaller turbine.

Figure 8.6

Long-Run Average Cost Curve for Electricity Generation

Source: Laurits Christensen and William H. Greene, "Economies of Scale in U.S. Electric Power Generation," *Journal of Political Economy,* vol. 84, 1976, pp. 655–676. Reprinted by permission of The University of Chicago Press.

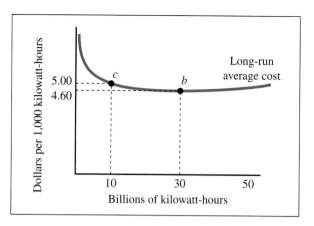

Actual Long-Run Average Cost Curves

What does the typical long-run average cost curve look like? Figures 8.6 through 8.9 show the actual long-run average cost curves for several products: electricity generation, aluminum production, truck freight, and hospital services. Each long-run average-cost curve is negatively sloped for small quantities of output and relatively flat (almost horizontal) over a large range of output. In addition, each curve has a slight positive slope for large quantities of output. In other words, these curves are L-shaped. Other studies suggest that the long-run cost curves of a wide variety of goods and services have the same shape.[3]

Why is the typical long-run average cost curve L-shaped? The average-cost curves are negatively sloped for small quantities of output because there are economies of scale resulting from indivisible inputs and labor specialization. The long-run average-cost curves are horizontal over a wide range of output because once a firm reaches a certain scale, long-run total cost increases proportionately with output, reflecting the ability to increase inputs and outputs proportionately.

Minimum Efficient Scale

Minimum efficient scale: The output at which the long-run average cost curve becomes horizontal.

One way to quantify the extent of scale economies in the production of a particular good is to determine the minimum efficient scale for producing the good. The **minimum efficient scale** is defined as the output at which scale economies are exhausted. In graphical

Figure 8.7

Long-Run Average Cost Curve for Aluminum Production

Source: Joel P. Clark and Merton C. Flemings, "Advanced Materials and the Economy," *Scientific American,* vol. 255, October 1986, pp. 51–60. Copyright © 1986 by Scientific American, Inc. All rights reserved.

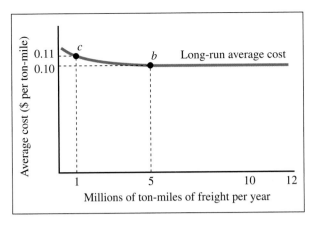

Figure 8.8

Long-Run Average Cost Curve for Truck Freight

Source: Roger Koenker, "Optimal Scale and the Size Distribution of American Trucking Firms," *Journal of Transport Economics and Policy*, January 1977, p. 62.

terms, the minimum efficient scale is the quantity at which the long-run average cost curve becomes horizontal, for example point *f* in Figure 8.5. If a firm starts out with a quantity of output below the minimum efficient scale, an increase in output will decrease its long-run average cost. Once the minimum efficient scale has been reached, an increase in output no longer decreases the long-run average cost.

Economists have estimated the minimum efficient scale for various industries. In Britain, the minimum efficient scale is 1 million tons of sulfuric acid per year (about 30% of the British market), 9 million tons for steel (about 33% of the British market), 10 million tons of oil per year (10% of the British market), and 300,000 tons of ethylene per year (9% of the British market).[4] In the United States, the minimum efficient scale for automobiles is between 200,000 and 400,000 autos per year.[5] This means that a production facility serving between 3% and 6% of the U.S. market would be large enough to fully exploit the economies of scale in auto production.

The possibility of economies of scale provides one reason why two companies may consider merging into one. There may be cost savings from using production facilities more efficiently, as well as savings in operating cost from combining the purchases of inputs and coordinating shipping operations.

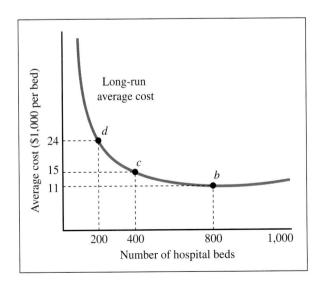

Figure 8.9

Long-Run Average Cost Curve for Hospital Services

Source: Harold A. Cohen, "Hospital Cost Curves with Emphasis on Measuring Patient Care Output," in *Empirical Studies in Health Economics*, edited by Herbert E. Klarman (Baltimore: Johns Hopkins University Press, 1970).

Diseconomies of Scale

Diseconomies of scale: A situation in which an increase in the quantity produced increases the long-run average cost of production.

If a firm's long-run average cost curve is positively sloped, the firm experiences **diseconomies of scale**, meaning that when the firm increases its output, the long-run average cost of production increases. Diseconomies of scale may arise for two reasons:

- **Coordination problems.** One of the problems of a large organization is that it requires several layers of management (a bureaucracy) to coordinate the activities of the different parts of the organization. If an increase in the firm's output requires additional layers of management, the long-run average cost curve may be positively sloped.

- **Increasing input costs.** When a firm increases its output, it will demand more of each of its inputs and may be forced to pay higher prices for some of these inputs. An increase in input prices will increase the long-run average cost of production, generating a positively sloped long-run average cost curve.

The long-run cost curves shown in Figures 8.6 through 8.9 suggest that diseconomies of scale are relatively mild. Once we reach a large quantity of output, the long-run average cost curves have a slight positive slope. The studies of other goods and services generate the same sort of L-shaped curves, suggesting that diseconomies of scale are not very severe, at least in the range output firms actually produce. This is sensible because if a firm experienced diseconomies of scale, it could decrease its long-run average cost by decreasing the quantity of output.

The experience of General Motors suggests there are diseconomies of scale in the production of automobiles, largely because of coordination problems.[6] General Motors, which is one-third bigger than Ford and larger than the two largest Japanese automakers combined (Toyota and Nissan), produces automobiles at an average cost that is between $200 and $2,000 higher than the average cost of Ford, Chrysler, and the Japanese. The Saturn project—an independent manufacturing operation with its own production facilities and its own input suppliers—is General Motors' response to these diseconomies of scale. By dividing its production into smaller pieces, General Motors hopes to avoid the high costs resulting from diseconomies of scale.

Firms recognize the possibility of diseconomies of scale and adopt various strategies to avoid them. An example of a firm that adjusts its operations to avoid diseconomies of scale is Minnesota Mining & Manufacturing, also known as 3M. According to Gordon Engdahl, the company's vice president for human resources, "We made a conscious effort to keep our units as small as possible because it keeps them flexible and vital. When one gets too large, we break it apart. We like to say that our success in recent years amounts to multiplication by division."[7]

Application: Hospital Services

At the start of this chapter, an economic consultant claims that the average cost per bed in an 800-bed hospital would be one-third the cost per bed in each 400-bed hospital. The long-run average cost curve shown in Figure 8.9 indicates that the consultant has overstated the scale economies in hospital services. For the 800-bed hospital the long-run average cost is $11,000 per bed (point *b*), compared to a long-run average cost of $15,000 per bed for a 400-bed hospital (point *c*). Although the larger hospital is more efficient, the difference in cost is not as large as the consultant suggested.

Short-Run Versus Long-Run Cost

Why is the firm's short-run average cost curve U-shaped, while the long-run average cost curve is L-shaped? For large quantities of output, the short-run curve is positively sloped because of diminishing returns and the resulting increases in the labor cost per unit of output. In the long run, the firm can scale up its operation by building a larger production facility, so the firm does not suffer from diminishing returns. If there are no diseconomies of scale, the long-run average cost curve will be negatively sloped or horizontal. If the firm experiences some diseconomies of scale, the long-run average-cost curve will eventually be positively sloped, but the short-run average-cost curve will be much steeper.

TEST Your Understanding

5. Draw a line connecting each item on the left with the appropriate item on the right.
- Diseconomies of scale
- Economies of scale
- Indivisible inputs
- Input specialization
- Coordination problems

- Negatively sloped long-run average cost curve
- Positively sloped long-run average cost curve

6. When you mention that most firms have L-shaped long-run average cost curves, your new boss says, "You're wrong. Haven't you heard of the principle of diminishing returns?" How should you respond?

7. As a child, you recorded the costs of your lemonade stand and drew your long-run average cost curve. Now you work in a computer-chip factory. Would you expect any similarities between the lemonade cost curve and the long-run average-cost curve for the chip factory? Would you expect any differences?

Using the TOOLS

You've learned all about the firm's short- and long-run cost curves. Here are some opportunities to use those curves as graphical tools in your own economic analysis.

APPLICATIONS

1. Production Consultant

A hammer manufacturer has just hired you to advise the firm on its production costs. In your first meeting with production managers, you hear the following statements. Are they true or false? Explain.

a. "If the production process is subject to diminishing returns, the long-run average cost curve will be positively sloped."

b. "At the current output level, this factory is subject to diminishing returns. Therefore, the firm is operating along the upward-sloping portion of its short-run marginal cost (SMC) curve."

c. "At the current output level, this factory is subject to diminishing returns. Therefore, the firm is operating along the upward-sloping portion of its short-run average total cost (SATC) curve."

d. "The short-run average total cost of producing 250 hammers is less than the short-run average cost of producing 260 hammers. Therefore, the short-run marginal cost of 260 hammers is less than the short-run average cost of 260 hammers."

2. Cost of Breaking Up an Aluminum Firm

Consider a large aluminum firm that initially produces two million pounds of aluminum per year. Suppose that an antitrust action breaks up the firm into two smaller firms, each of which produces half as much as the original firm. Use the information in Figure 8.7 to predict the effects on the long-run average cost of producing aluminum.

3. Deregulation and the Cost of Trucking

Consider the market for truck freight, which is currently served by a single regulated firm. If the market is deregulated, several new firms, unconstrained by regulations, will enter the market. At a public hearing on the issue of deregulation, the manager of the regulated firm issued a grim warning to the regulatory authorities: "If you deregulate this market, four or five firms will enter the market and the unit cost of truck freight will at least triple. There are big economies of scale in trucking services, so a single large firm is much more cost-efficient than several small firms would be. If you want firms in your city to pay three times as much for their truck freight, go ahead and deregulate this market." Use the information in Figure 8.8 to comment on this statement.

Summary

In this chapter, we looked at the cost side of a firm, explaining the shapes of the firm's short-run cost curves and long-run cost curves. Here are the main points of the chapter.

1. The positively sloped portion of the short-run marginal cost curve (SMC) results from diminishing returns.
2. The short-run average total cost curve (SATC) is U-shaped because of the conflicting effects of (a) fixed costs being spread over a larger quantity of output and (b) diminishing returns.
3. The long-run average cost curve (LAC) is horizontal over some range of output because replication is

an option, so doubling output will no more than double long-run total cost.

4. The long-run average cost curve (LAC) is negatively sloped for small quantities of output because there are indivisible inputs that cannot be scaled down and a smaller operation has limited opportunities for labor specialization.
5. Diseconomies of scale arise if there are problems in coordinating a large operation or higher input costs in a larger organization.

Key Terms

average fixed cost [AFC], 170
diseconomies of scale, 180
economic cost, 165
economies of scale, 177
explicit cost, 164
fixed cost [FC], 168
implicit cost, 164

indivisible input, 175
long-run average cost of production [LAC], 174
long-run total cost, 173
minimum efficient scale, 178
short-run average total cost [SATC], 170

short-run average variable cost [SAVC], 170
short-run marginal cost [SMC], 169
short-run total cost [STC], 169
total product curve, 166
total variable cost [TVC], 169

Problems and Discussion Questions

1. Suppose that the indivisible inputs used in the production of shirts have a cost per day of $400. To produce one shirt per day, the firm must also spend

a total of $5 on other inputs (labor, materials, and other capital). For each additional shirt, the firm incurs the same additional cost ($5). Compute the average cost for 40 shirts, 100 shirts, 200 shirts, and 400 shirts. Draw the long-run average cost curve for 40 to 400 shirts per day.

2. Consider a firm with the following short-run costs:

Quantity	Variable Cost	Total Cost
1	30	90
2	50	110
3	90	150
4	140	200
5	200	260

a. What is the firm's fixed cost?

b. Compute short-run marginal cost, short-run average variable cost, and short-run average total cost for the different quantities of output.

c. Draw the three cost curves. Explain the relationship between the SMC curve and the SATC curve and the relationship between the SAVC curve and the SATC curve.

3. Given the following relationship between labor input and the quantity produced, compute the marginal product of labor for the different input levels. Then draw the total product curve and the marginal-product curve.

Labor	Output
0	0
1	5
2	11
3	15
4	18
5	19

4. Consider a firm that has a fixed cost of $60 per minute. Complete the following table.

Output	FC	TVC	STC	SMC	AFC	SAVC	SATC
1	___	10	___	___	___	___	___
2	___	18	___	___	___	___	___
3	___	30	___	___	___	___	___
4	___	45	___	___	___	___	___
5	___	65	___	___	___	___	___
6	___	90	___	___	___	___	___

5. Consider a firm that has constant marginal returns. That means that the first worker is just as productive as the second, who is just as productive as the third, and so on. The same is true for all the firm's inputs.

a. Draw the firm's short-run marginal cost curve.

b. Explain why this firm's cost curve differs from the short-run marginal cost curve for rake production.

6. Beaverduck Bus Company wants to compute the cost of adding a third daily bus between Eugene and Corvallis. Comment on the following statement of Abby Abacus, the company accountant: "If we add the third bus, our total cost would increase from $700 to $780. Therefore, the marginal cost of the third bus is $260 ($780 divided by 3)."

7. You want to know the short-run marginal cost of producing a Chevrolet Caprice. Comment on the following statement from an analyst in the production department: "The marginal cost of a Caprice, given our current volume, is $12,500. Of course, the actual marginal cost depends on the number of cars produced. The larger the number produced, the lower the unit cost because we will spread out our design and tooling costs over more cars."

8. Explain the difference between diseconomies of scale and diminishing returns. Based on the cost curves you've seen in this chapter, which is more pervasive?

9. Suppose that one firm generates 30 billion kilo-watt-hours of electricity, which is about three times the output of a second electricity firm. Which firm will have a higher cost per kilowatt-hour? Use the information in Figure 8.6 to predict the difference in the average costs of the two firms.

10. Web Exercise. Visit the Web site of the Cooperative Administrative Support Unit (CASU), an organization that helps government agencies reduce their operating costs [http://www.dol.gov/dol/casu/welcome.html]. What economic concept allows CASU to help government agencies reduce their costs? Check out the details of CASU's "cost per copy" program. Are there economies of scale in photocopying?

11. Web Exercise. Visit the Web site of the Bureau of Labor Statistics [http://stats.bls.gov/] and do a key-word search of the site for information on compensation costs. How does the hourly compensation of U.S. workers compare with the compensation of workers in other countries?

Take It to the Net

We invite you to visit the O'Sullivan/Sheffrin page on the Prentice Hall Web site at:
http://www.prenhall.com/osullivan/ for additional World Wide Web exercises for this chapter.

Model Answers to Questions

Chapter-Opening Questions

1. As shown in Figure 8.7, the average cost for the large firm is $1.60 per pound (point c), compared to an average cost of $2.10 for each of the small firms.

2. As shown in Figure 8.8, although a larger trucking firm has lower average costs than a small one, the difference is relatively small, except for very small firms.

3. The short-run curve reflects diminishing returns, which pulls up short-run average cost as output increases. There are no diminishing returns in the long run.

4. In Figure 8.6, the larger firm (30 billion kwh) has an average cost that is 8% lower than the smaller firm (10 billion kwh).

Test Your Understanding

1. The principle of diminishing returns.

2. It's not obvious that the short-run average cost will decrease because diminishing returns pull up average cost as the quantity of output increases. If the initial quantity of output is large enough, the bad news associated with increasing output (diminishing returns) will dominate the good news (spreading out the fixed costs), so average cost will increase.

3. If the marginal cost is less than the average cost, the marginal pulls down the average, so the average cost curve is negatively sloped. Therefore, average cost will decrease, at least for small increases in output.

4. Average.

5. Draw lines from "diseconomies of scale" and "coordination problems" to "positively sloped long-run average cost curve." Draw lines from "economies of scale," "indivisible inputs," and "input specialization" to "negatively sloped long-run average cost curve."

6. Diminishing returns occur when we increase output in an existing production facility. The principle

of diminishing returns is applicable in the short run, not in the long run. To draw the long-run cost curve, we assume that we can change the size of the production facility.

7. There are some indivisible inputs for the lemonade stand (the pitcher and the sign), just as there are indivisible inputs for the chip factory (testing equipment, clean room). Therefore, both operations will have negatively sloped long-run average cost curves. Of course, the cost of these indivisible inputs is tiny for the lemonade stand and huge for the chip factory. Therefore, the average cost curve for the chip factory will be negatively sloped over a large range of output. If your lemonade stand was a one-person operation, you probably never experienced the benefits from input specialization. In contrast, input specialization will be important in the chip factory.

Using the Tools

1. Production Consultant
   a. False. The principle of diminishing returns is applicable to the short-run cost curves, not the long-run curves.
   b. True. Diminishing returns imply increasing short-run marginal cost.
   c. False. Diminishing returns imply increasing short-run marginal cost but do not imply increasing short-run average cost. If the output is small enough, the spreading of fixed costs will generate a negatively sloped short-run average-cost curve even if there are diminishing returns.
   d. False. The first sentence implies that the short-run average-cost curve is positively sloped. This means that the short-run marginal cost exceeds the short-run average cost.

2. Cost of Breaking Up an Aluminum Firm. In Figure 8.7, the average cost for the large firm is $1.60 per pound (point c), compared to an average cost of $2.10 for each of the small firms.

3. Deregulation and the Cost of Trucking. The cost curve for trucking service in Figure 8.8 suggests

that the manager has overstated the effects of deregulation on the average cost of trucking services. Suppose that the regulated firm provides 5 million ton-miles of trucking services per year at an average cost of $0.10 per ton-mile (point *b*). The entry of five firms would decrease the output per firm to 1 million ton-miles per year, increasing the cost per ton-mile to $0.11 (point *c*). In other words, deregulation would increase the average cost by only $0.01 per ton-mile.

 Notes

1. Adam Smith, *The Wealth of Nations* (New York: The Modern Library, 1937), pp. 4–5.

2. Danish Wind Turbine Manufacturers Association. Guided Tour of Wind Energy (*http: www.wind power.dk*).

3. John Johnson, *Statistical Cost Analysis* (New York: McGraw-Hill, 1960).

4. Aubrey Silberson, "Economies of Scale in Theory and Practice," *Economic Journal,* vol. 82, 1972, pp. 369–391.

5. Walter Adams and James W. Brock, "Automobiles," Chapter 4 in *The Structure of the American Economy,* 9th ed., edited by Walter Adams and James W. Brock (Upper Saddle River, NJ: Prentice Hall, 1995).

6. Walter Adams and James W. Brock, "Automobiles."

7. Frederick C. Klein, "At 3M Plants, Workers Have Flexibility, Involvement—And Their Own Radios," *Wall Street Journal,* February 5, 1982, p. 1.

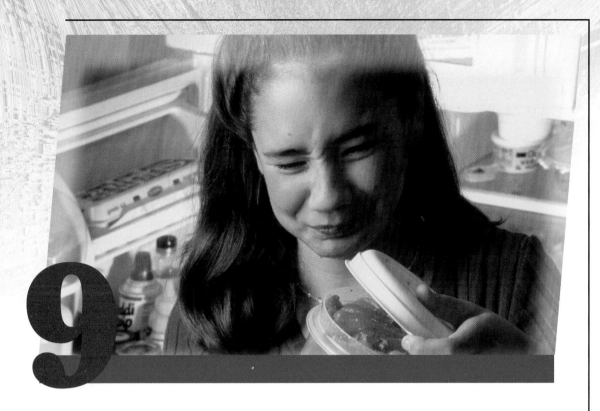

9

Perfect Competition: Short Run and Long Run

In 1992, Hurricane Andrew struck the southeastern United States, leaving millions of people without electricity for several days. Refrigerators stopped working, and thousands of people suddenly needed a lot of ice to cool and preserve their food. The price of a bag of ice immediately rose from $1 to $5. The same sort of price hikes occurred for chain saws (for clearing downed trees), bottled water, tarpaper (for repairing roofs), and plywood. If you had been the governor of Florida in 1992, what would you have done?

This is the first of 4 chapters exploring the decisions made by firms in different types of markets. Markets differ in the number of firms that compete against one another for customers. At one extreme is a monopoly: a market with a single seller. We'll explore the decisions of a monopolist in the next chapter. In this chapter, we'll look at the other extreme, a **perfectly competitive market**, a market with four features:

Perfectly competitive market:
A market with a very large number of firms, each of which produces the same standardized product and takes the market price as given.

- There are many firms.
- The product is standardized or homogeneous.
- Firms can freely enter or leave the market in the long run.
- Each firm takes the market price as given.

The first three features of perfect competition imply the fourth. If there are many firms selling a standardized product, each firm has a tiny fraction of the market, and no matter how much any individual firm produces and sells, the market price won't change. There is no incentive for any firm to cut the price because any firm can sell as much as it wants at the market price. There is no incentive to raise the price because a firm doing so would lose all its customers to other firms selling the standardized product at the market price. A perfectly competitive firm is a price taker: It takes the market price as given. For example, each corn farmer produces a tiny fraction of the total supply of corn, and no matter how much corn one farmer produces, the price of corn won't change.

If you're thinking that the model of perfect competition is not very realistic, you're right. Most firms have some control over their prices. When a firm increases its price slightly, it will certainly sell less, but the quantity sold will probably not go to zero. Although perfect competition is rare, it's a good starting point for the analysis of firms' decisions because a price-taking firm's decision is easy to understand. The firm doesn't have to worry about picking a price; it just decides how much to produce, given the market price. Once you understand this simple case, you will be ready to tackle the more complex decisions of firms that have some control over their prices.

In this chapter, you will see how firms use information on revenues and costs to decide how much output to produce. We'll consider both the short-run and the long-run responses to an increase in price, showing that the law of supply works in both the short run and the long run. Here are some practical questions that we answer:

1. What information does the firm need to decide how much output to produce?
2. If your firm's accountant reports that you are losing money, should you close your business or continue to operate at a loss?
3. How did Hurricane Andrew affect prices in the short run and in the long run?
4. Health concerns decreased the demand for butter. The price initially dropped but then rose. Why?

The Short-Run Output Decision

Total revenue: The money the firm gets by selling its product; equal to the price times the quantity sold.

The firm's objective is to maximize its profit, equal to revenue minus cost. A firm's **total revenue** is the money the firm gets by selling its product and is equal to the price times the quantity sold. For example, the total revenue for a farmer who sells 100 bushels of corn at $2 per bushel is $200. We know from Chapter 8 that a firm's total economic cost is the sum of its explicit costs (the firm's actual cash payments for its inputs) and implicit costs (the opportunity costs of no purchased inputs such as the entrepreneur's time or money). A firm's **economic profit** equals its total revenue minus its total economic cost. If our corn farmer has an economic cost of $180, the farmer's profit would be $20.

Economic profit: Total revenue minus total economic cost.

The Total Approach: Computing Total Revenue and Total Cost

The first approach to deciding how much output to produce involves computing the total revenue and total cost of different quantities of output. Table 9.1 shows the total revenue and total costs of a hypothetical rake producer. As shown in the third column, if the price of rakes is $25 per rake, the firm's total revenue equals $25 times the number of rakes produced, so total revenue increases by $25 for each additional rake produced and sold. The fourth column shows the short-run total costs associated with different quantities of rakes produced. The fifth column shows economic profit, defined as total revenue minus total cost. In this example, profit is maximized when the firm produces either 8 or 9 rakes per minute. In either case, total revenue exceeds total cost by $99. We'll assume that whenever profit is highest for two quantities of output (8 and 9 in this case), the firm produces the larger quantity.

Figure 9.1 shows how to choose the quantity of output that maximizes profit. We're looking for the largest profit, meaning the biggest gap between total revenue and total cost. In this case, profit is maximized when the firm produces either 8 or 9 rakes, with a profit equal to $99.

The Marginal Approach

The other way to decide how much output to produce involves the marginal principle, the general decision-making rule that is one of the key principles of economics.

Marginal **PRINCIPLE**

> **Increase the level of an activity if its marginal benefit exceeds its marginal cost, but reduce the level if the marginal cost exceeds the marginal benefit. If possible, pick the level at which the marginal benefit equals the marginal cost.**

Table 9.1 Deciding How Much Output to Produce

Output: Rakes per Minute	Price	Total Revenue	Total Cost	Profit	Marginal Revenue (Price)	Marginal Cost
0	25	0	36	−36	25	0
1	25	25	44	−19	25	8
2	25	50	48	2	25	4
3	25	75	51	24	25	3
4	25	100	56	44	25	5
5	25	125	63	62	25	7
6	25	150	72	78	25	9
7	25	175	84	91	25	12
8	25	200	101	99	25	17
9	25	225	126	99	25	25
10	25	250	166	84	25	40

Figure 9.1

Using the Total Approach to Choose an Output Level

Economic profit is shown by the vertical distance between the total-revenue curve and the total-cost curve. To maximize profit, the firm chooses the quantity of output that generates the largest vertical difference between the two curves.

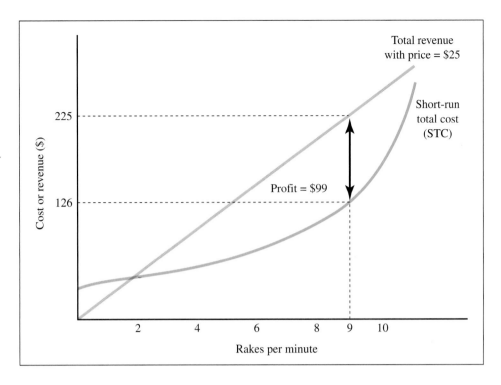

In our example, the firm's activity is producing rakes, so to use the marginal principle, the firm must compute the marginal benefit and the marginal cost of producing different quantities of rakes.

The benefit of producing and selling rakes is the revenue the firm collects. Therefore, the marginal benefit of producing rakes is the **marginal revenue** from rakes: the change in total revenue that results from selling one more rake. As shown in columns two and three in Table 9.1, the perfectly competitive rake firm can sell as much as it wants at the $25 market price, so if the firm sells one more unit of output, its total revenue increases by $25. This means that

Marginal revenue: The change in total revenue that results from selling one more unit of output.

$$\text{marginal benefit} \ = \ \text{marginal revenue} \ = \ \text{market price}$$

The marginal principle tells us that the firm will maximize its profit by choosing the quantity at which marginal revenue (the market price) equals marginal cost:

$$\text{price} \ = \ \text{marginal cost}$$

Figure 9.2 illustrates the use of the marginal principle for the firm's output decision. In panel A, the market supply and demand curves represent the collective choices of all rake producers and consumers. The market supply curve intersects the market demand curve at a price of $25. In panel B, the horizontal line shows the market price—the marginal revenue for the perfectly competitive firm. The marginal-revenue line intersects the marginal-cost curve at a quantity of 9 rakes per minute, so that's the quantity that maximizes profit (where marginal revenue equals marginal cost).

To see that an output of 9 rakes per minute maximizes the firm's profit, imagine the firm produced only 4 rakes per minute. Could the firm make more profit by producing 5 rakes instead of 4?

1. From the seventh row of numbers in Table 9.1 and point *d* in Figure 9.2, we know that the marginal cost of the 5th rake is $7.

2. The price of rakes is $25, so the marginal benefit (marginal revenue) is $25.

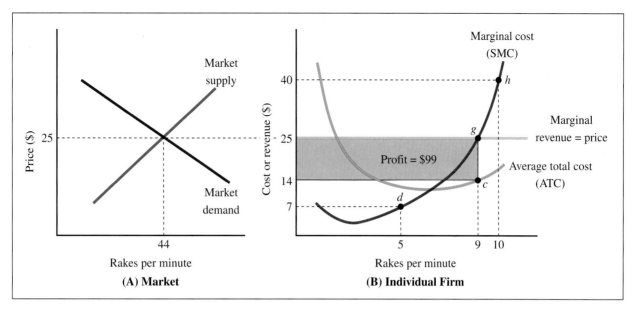

Figure 9.2 The Marginal Approach to Picking an Output Level
A perfectly competitive firm takes the market price as given. In panel A, the market supply curve intersects the market demand curve at a price of $25. In panel B, using the marginal principle, the typical firm will maximize profit at point g, where the market price ($25) equals the marginal cost. Economic profit equals the difference between price and average cost ($11 = $25 − $14) times the quantity produced (nine rakes per minute), or $99 per minute.

Because the extra revenue from the 5th rake (price = $25) exceeds the extra cost (marginal cost = $7), the production and sale of the 5th rake increases the firm's total profit by $18 (equal to $25 − $7). Therefore, it is sensible to produce the 5th rake. The same logic applies, with different numbers for marginal cost, for the 6th through the 8th rakes. For the 9th rake, marginal revenue equals marginal cost, so the firm's profit doesn't change. To be consistent with the marginal principle, we'll assume that the firm goes to the point at which marginal revenue equals marginal cost. In this case, the firm produces the 9th rake.

The same logic applies for producing any quantity greater than 9 rakes per minute. Imagine the firm produced 10 rakes. Would its profit be higher if it produced one fewer rake (9 rakes instead of 10)? From Table 9.1 and the marginal cost curve in Figure 9.2, we see that the marginal cost of the 10th rake is $40 (point h), which exceeds the marginal revenue (the market price) of $25. The 10th rake adds more to cost ($40) than it adds to revenue ($25), so producing the rake decreases the firm's profit by $15 (equal to $40 − $25). The marginal principle suggests that the firm should choose point g, with an output of 9 rakes.

Economic Profit

We've seen that the perfectly competitive firm maximizes its profit by producing the quantity at which its marginal revenue (price) equals its marginal cost. How much profit does the firm earn? The firm's economic profit equals its total revenue minus its total cost. The easiest way to compute a firm's total economic profit is to multiply the average profit per unit produced (the gap between the price and the average cost) by the quantity produced:

economic profit = (price − average cost) × quantity produced

In Figure 9.2, the average cost of producing 9 rakes is $14 (point *c*), so the economic profit is $99:

$$\text{economic profit} = (\$25 - \$14) \times 9 = \$99$$

In Figure 9.2, the firm's profit is shown by the area of the shaded rectangle. The height of the rectangle is the average profit ($11 per rake), and the width of the rectangle is the quantity produced (9 rakes).

Economic Detective

The Turnaround Artist

Emilio knows how to turn an unprofitable company into a profitable one. His latest project was a firm that was losing money producing and selling hammers. The firm sold 100 hammers per day at a price of $20 each and lost $500 per day. Emilio showed up at the factory on Monday and told the factory manager to increase production to 101 hammers on Tuesday. After a brief conversation with the factory manager on Wednesday, Emilio gave his advice, collected his fee, and disappeared. One week later, the firm was producing fewer hammers but making a profit of $2 on each hammer. What is Emilio's secret formula for success? What was his advice on Wednesday?

The key to answering these questions is the marginal principle. The purpose of Emilio's experiment was to compute the marginal cost of hammers. He compared the total cost of producing 101 hammers to the total cost of 100 hammers, and must have discovered that the marginal cost of the 101st hammer was greater than the market price ($20). According to the marginal principle, if the marginal cost exceeds the marginal benefit (the price), a decrease in output will increase profit. Emilio's formula for success is the marginal principle.

TEST Your Understanding

1. Explain why a perfectly competitive firm takes prices as given.

2. Complete the statement: A perfectly competitive firm will produce the quantity of output at which _____ equals _____.

3. Suppose the market price of sugar is 22 cents per pound. If a sugar farmer produces 100,000 pounds, the marginal cost of sugar is 30 cents per pound. Is the farmer maximizing profit? If not, should the farmer produce more sugar or less sugar?

The Shut-Down Decision

Consider next the decisions faced by a firm that is losing money. Suppose the market price is so low that the firm's total revenue is less than its total cost, even though the firm used the marginal principle to decide how much to produce. For an unprofitable firm like this one, the question is, Should we continue to operate at a loss or should we shut down? This may seem like a silly question. Why would any firm continue to operate if it is losing money? As we'll see, it will be sensible to operate at a loss if the firm would lose even more money by shutting down.

Figure 9.3 shows the situation faced by an unprofitable firm. Suppose the market price of rakes drops to $9 per rake. If the firm continues to operate, it will produce 6 rakes per minute (shown by point *z*, where the marginal revenue (the price) equals marginal cost). The firm's problem is that the average total cost of production ($12, as shown by point *t*) is less than the price ($9), so economic profit is negative. The average

Figure 9.3
Shut-Down Decision
With a price of $9, the marginal principle indicates that the firm should pick point z, producing 6 rakes per minute. The average cost exceeds the price by $3, so the firm loses $18 per minute ($3 per rake times 6 rakes per minute). The average variable cost is $6 per rake, which is less than the $9 price, so total revenue exceeds total variable cost, and it is sensible to continue operating.

cost exceeds the price by $3, so the firm will lose $18 per minute ($3 per rake times 6 rakes per minute). Should the firm continue to operate at a loss, or shut down?

Total Revenue Versus Total Variable Cost

The firm should continue to operate if the benefit of operating exceeds the cost of operating. The benefit equals the firm's total revenue, or the price times the quantity produced. In Figure 9.3, the firm can sell 6 rakes at a price of $9 per rake, so the total revenue from operating is $54. The firm's cost of operating—as opposed to shutting down—equals the firm's total variable cost. As shown by point u, when the firm produces 6 rakes, its average variable cost is $6 per rake. Therefore, its total variable cost is $36 ($6 per rake times 6 rakes). Because the benefit of operating (total revenue of $54) exceeds the variable cost ($36), it is sensible for the firm to continue to operate.

We can use a shortcut to determine whether total revenue exceeds the total variable cost. Total revenue is the price times the quantity produced, and total variable cost is the average variable cost times the quantity produced. Therefore, if the price exceeds the average variable cost, total revenue will exceed total variable cost. The firm should continue to operate if price exceeds the average variable cost; otherwise, it should shut down.

Operate: price > average variable cost

Shut down: price < average variable cost

In Figure 9.3, the price is $9 and the average variable cost of 6 rakes is $6 per rake, so it is sensible to continue operating, even at a loss.

The firm's **shut-down price** is defined as the price at which the firm is indifferent between operating and shutting down. In Figure 9.3, the shut-down price is $5 (shown by point s). If the market price of rakes drops below the shut-down price, the firm would be better off shutting down. At the shut-down price, marginal cost equals price (the marginal principle) and average variable cost also equals the price (for total revenue to equal total variable cost). Therefore, marginal cost equals average variable cost, and as we saw in Chapter 8, that happens at the minimum point of the average variable cost curve. That means that the shut-down price is the minimum average variable cost.

Shut-down price: The price at which the firm is indifferent between operating and shutting down.

A firm should shut down an unprofitable facility if its total revenue is less than its total variable cost.

Why Operate an Unprofitable Facility?

If the idea of operating an unprofitable facility is puzzling, think about what would happen if the firm shut down. Although the firm would no longer pay for labor and materials, it would still pay for its idle production facility, for example, a factory full of machinery and equipment. The cost of the production facility is a **sunk cost**, defined as a cost the firm has already paid or has agreed to pay some time in the future. For example, a firm with a $1 million production facility has a sunk cost of $1 million, regardless of whether the firm paid for the facility in the past or will pay for it in the future. What matters is that the firm cannot do anything about this sunk cost.

Sunk cost: The cost a firm has already paid or has agreed to pay some time in the future.

If a firm shuts down its production facility, it will still pay its sunk costs—the cost of the production facility. In our example, the sunk cost is the same as the fixed cost, which is $36 per minute (see the first row of numbers in Table 9.1, where the total cost with zero output is $36). Therefore, the firm will lose $36 per minute if it shuts down. But if the firm operates, it will lose only $18 per minute. Because the firm loses less money if it operates, it is sensible to continue operating.

How long should a firm continue to operate at a loss? Let's think about what happens when the firm must decide whether to build a new production facility. The firm will build a new facility—and produce output to stay in the market—only if the price of rakes exceeds the average total cost of production. In other words, the firm will stay in the market only if the market price is high enough that total revenue is high enough to cover all the costs of production, including the cost of a new facility. Although a firm may operate an existing facility at a loss, it won't replace it if the new facility would be unprofitable too.

TEST Your Understanding

4. Complete the statement with a number: If a lamp producer can sell 40 lamps per day at a price of $20 per lamp, the benefit of operating its production facility is _____ per day.

5. Complete the statement with *operate* or *shut down*: Consider a firm with total revenue of $500, total cost of $700, and variable cost of $400. The firm should _____ its production facility.

6. Complete the statement: A firm that is losing money should continue to operate if the market price exceeds _____.

Short-Run Supply Curves

Now that we've explored the output decision of a price-taking firm, we're ready to show how firms respond to changes in the market price of output. We'll represent the relationship between price and quantity supplied with two short-run supply curves, one for the individual firm and one for the entire market.

The Short-Run Supply Curve of the Firm

The firm's **short-run supply curve** shows the relationship between the market price and the quantity supplied by the firm over a period of time during which one input—the production facility—cannot be changed. In the case of rake producers, the firm's supply curve answers the following question: At a given price of rakes, how many rakes will the firm produce? We have already used the marginal principle and the marginal-cost curve to answer this question for two different prices. At a price of $9, the marginal revenue (price) equals marginal cost when the firm produces 6 rakes per minute; at a price of $25, price equals marginal cost with 9 rakes.

The firm's short-run supply curve is the part of the firm's short-run marginal cost curve above the shut-down price. The shut-down price for the rake firm is $5, so as shown in Figure 9.4 the short-run supply curve is the marginal cost curve starting at $5. For any price above the shut-down price, the firm will choose the quantity at which price equals marginal cost, so we can read the firm's quantity supplied from its marginal cost curve. If the price is $12, the firm will supply 7 rakes per minute (point m). As the price increases, the firm responds by supplying more rakes: 8 rakes when the price is $17.

What about prices below the shut-down price? If the price drops below the shut-down price, the firm's total revenue will not be high enough to cover its total variable cost, so the firm will shut down and produce no output. In panel A of Figure 9.4, the firm's supply curve starts at point s, indicating that the quantity supplied is zero for any price less than $5.

What's the shut-down price for a corn farmer? What's the break-even price? We can answer these questions with the actual short-run cost curves for corn farmers shown in Figure 9.5 (in 1971 dollars). The break-even or zero-profit price is $0.72 per bushel. At any higher price, the farmer will make a profit. If the price is $1.00, the farmer will pro-

Short-run supply curve: A curve showing the relationship between the price of a product and the quantity of output supplied by a firm in the short run.

(A) Individual Firm

(B) Industry with 100 Identical Firms

Figure 9.4

Short-Run Supply Curves

In panel A, the firm's short-run supply curve is the part of the marginal-cost curve above the shut-down price ($5). For prices below the shut-down price, the firm shuts down, so the quantity supplied is zero. In panel B, there are 100 firms in the market, so the market supply at a given price is 100 times the quantity supplied by the typical firm. At a price of $9, each firm supplies 6 rakes per minute (point z), so the market supply is 600 rakes per minute (point w).

Figure 9.5

Shut-Down Price for Corn Farmer

The corn farmer's shut-down price is $0.44, while the break-even price is $0.72.

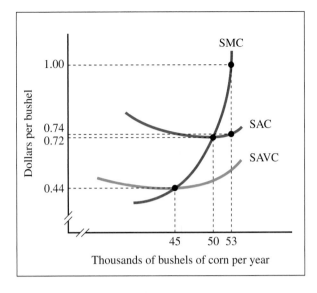

Thousands of bushels of corn per year

duce 53,000 bushels at an average cost of about $0.74 and earn a profit of about $13,780. The shut-down price is $0.44: At prices between $0.44 and $0.72, the farmer will lose money but will continue to operate at a loss because the price exceeds the average variable cost; at prices below $0.44, the farmer will shut down the unprofitable operation.[1]

The Market Supply Curve

Short-run market supply curve: A curve showing the relationship between price and the quantity of output supplied by all firms in the short run.

The **short-run market supply curve** shows the relationship between the market price and the quantity supplied by all firms in the short run. Panel B of Figure 9.4 shows the short-run market supply curve when there are 100 identical rake firms. For each price, we get the quantity supplied for the entire market by multiplying the quantity supplied by the typical firm (from the individual supply curve) by 100. At a price of $9, each firm produces 6 rakes (point z), so the market supply is 600 rakes (point w). If the price increases to $17, each firm produces 8 rakes, so the market supply is 800 rakes (point y).

What happens if firms are not identical but instead have different individual supply curves? To compute the market supply in this case, we would add the quantities supplied by the dozens (or hundreds) of firms in the market. The assumption that firms are identical is harmless: It makes it easier to derive the market supply curve from the supply curve of the typical firm, but it does not change the analysis.

In many parts of the developing world, people cannot afford their own phones, and have traditionally relied on pay phones. The recent development of mobile phones has generated a new competitive industry in many developing nations. Read "A Closer Look: Wireless Women."

TEST Your Understanding

7. Complete the statement: The firm's short-run supply curve shows the relationship between _____ and _____.

8. Suppose that you want to draw the firm's short-run supply curve. What information do you need?

9. Suppose there are 100 identical firms in a perfectly competitive industry. At a price of $22, the typical firm supplies 50 units of output. What is the market quantity supplied at a price of $22?

WIRELESS WOMEN

In Pakistan, many poor villagers cannot afford their own phones, and phone service is provided by thousands of "wireless women," entrepreneurs who invest $310 in a Village Phone package, which includes wireless phone equipment (transceiver, battery, charger), a signboard, a calculator, and a stopwatch. Then they sell phone service to their neighbors, charging by the minute and second. On average, their net income is about $2 per day, about three times the average per-capita income in Pakistan.

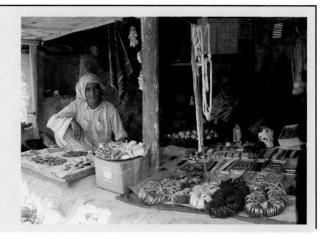

The Long-Run Supply Curve for an Increasing-Cost Industry

In the long run, firms can enter or leave an industry, and existing firms can modify their facilities or build new facilities. A market reaches a long-run equilibrium when three conditions hold:

1. The quantity of the product supplied equals the quantity demanded.
2. Each firm in the market maximizes its profit, given the market price.
3. Each firm in the market earns zero economic profit, so there is no incentive for other firms to enter the market.

The first two conditions are actually the two conditions for short-run equilibrium, so the only difference between the short run and the long run is that in the long run, economic profit is zero. When a firm earns zero economic profit, its total revenue equals its total economic cost. The total economic cost includes opportunity cost of the firm's inputs, including the entrepreneur. A firm earning zero economic profit stays in business because it isn't losing any money, and the entrepreneur receives a wage equal to the opportunity cost of his or her time.

Figure 9.6 shows a market in long-run equilibrium. The demand curve intersects the short-run market supply curve at a price of $12 and a quantity of 700 rakes per minute (condition 1). There are 100 firms, each of which produces 7 rakes per minute. Each firm maximizes its profit by choosing the quantity at which the marginal revenue (the price) equals the marginal cost, producing 7 rakes per minute (condition 2). At the quantity chosen by each firm, price equals short-run average total cost, so each firm makes zero economic profit (condition 3).

Production Costs and the Size of the Industry in the Long Run

Let's look at the **long-run market supply curve**, which shows the relationship between the market price and the quantity supplied by all firms in the long run, a period long enough that firms can enter or leave the market. Suppose the typical rake firm produces 7 rakes

Long-run market supply curve: A curve showing the relationship between the market price and quantity supplied by all firms in the long run.

Figure 9.6

Long-Run Market Equilibrium

In panel A, the market demand curve intersects the short-run market supply curve at a price of $12. In panel B, given the market price, the typical firm satisfies the marginal principle at point *m*, producing 7 rakes per minute. Because price equals the average cost at the chosen quantity, economic profit is zero, and no other firms will enter the market.

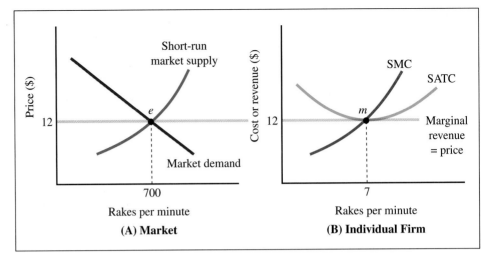

(A) Market

(B) Individual Firm

Increasing-cost industry: An industry in which the average cost of production increases as the total output of the industry increases; the long-run supply curve is positively sloped.

per minute, using a standard set of inputs, including a factory, some workers, and raw materials (wood and plastic). In a perfectly competitive industry, there are no restrictions on entry, so anyone can use the standard set of inputs to produce 7 rakes per minute.

Table 9.2 shows hypothetical data on the cost of producing rakes. Let's start with the first row, which shows the firm's production costs in an industry with 50 firms and a total of 350 rakes (with 7 rakes per firm). To compute the total cost for the typical firm, we add the cost of the firm's production facility (the cost of the rake factory), the cost of labor, and the cost of materials. In the first row, the total cost of the typical firm producing 7 rakes per minute is $70, and the average cost is $10 per rake ($70 divided by 7 rakes).

The rake industry is an example of an **increasing-cost industry**, defined as an industry in which the average cost of production increases as the total output of the industry increases. In the last column of Table 9.2, the average cost is $10 per rake in an industry that produces 350 rakes, $12 per rake in an industry that produces 700 rakes, and so on. The average cost increases as the industry grows for two reasons:

- **Increasing input prices.** As an industry grows, it competes with other industries for limited amounts of various inputs, and this competition drives up the prices of these inputs. For example, suppose that the rake industry competes against other industries for a limited amount of special wood. To get more of that wood to produce more rakes, firms in the rake industry must outbid other industries for the limited amount available, and this competition drives up the price of wood.

Table 9.2   Industry Output and Average Production Cost

Number of Firms	Industry Output	Rakes per Firm	Total Cost for Typical Firm	Average Cost per Rake
50	350	7	$70	$10
100	700	7	84	12
150	1,050	7	96	14

- **Less productive inputs.** A small industry will use only the most productive inputs, but as the industry grows, firms may be forced to use less productive inputs. For example, a small rake industry will use only the most skillful workers. As the industry grows, it will have to rely on less skillful workers. As the average skill level of the industry's workforce decreases, the average cost of production increases: In a large rake industry, it will take more hours of labor—and more money—to produce each rake. Another example is the production of agricultural products such as sugar. Because of variation in climate and soil conditions, it is cheaper to grow sugar in some areas than in others. As the quantity of sugar produced increases, growers are forced to produce sugar in areas with higher costs.

Drawing the Long-Run Market Supply Curve

The long-run supply curve tells us how much output will be produced at each price in the long run, when the number of firms in the market can change. Given a market price, we determine the total output of the industry by multiplying the output per firm (7 rakes in our example) by the number of firms in the industry. So the key question for the long-run supply curve is, How many firms will be in the market at that price?

Let's think about the incentive for a firm to enter the market. Economic profit is positive when total revenue exceeds total cost or when price exceeds the average cost. Whenever there is an opportunity to make a profit in a market—whenever the price exceeds average cost—firms will enter the market. Firms will continue to enter a market until economic profit is zero, which happens when the price equals average cost. When economic profit is zero, the firm's revenue is high enough to cover all its costs—including the opportunity cost of all its inputs—but not high enough to cause additional firms to enter the market. Each firm that is already in the market makes just enough money to stay in business, so there is no incentive for new firms to enter the market, and no incentive for existing firms to leave.

As a starting point, suppose the price of rakes is $12. There are no restrictions on entry into the industry, so any firm can use the standard set of inputs to produce 7 rakes per minute. The information in Table 9.2 suggests that there will be 100 firms in the market. To explain why 100 is the correct number, think about what would happen if there were either fewer firms or more firms:

- **Fewer firms.** If there were fewer than 100 firms, the average cost per rake would be less than the $12 price. If there were only 50 firms (producing a total of 350 rakes per minute), the average cost would be only $10 per rake. At that average cost, the profit per rake would be $2 (a price of $12 minus an average cost of $10). Firms would start to enter this profitable market, and entry would continue until the average cost reached the $12 market price. This occurs when there are 100 firms producing a total of 700 rakes.

- **More firms.** If there were more than 100 firms, the average cost per rake would exceed the $12 price. If there were 150 firms (producing a total 1,050 rakes per minute), the average cost would be $14 per rake. Each firm would lose $2 per rake (an average cost of $14 minus a price of $12). Firms would start to leave this unprofitable market, and exit would continue until the average cost dropped to the $12 market price, which occurs when there are 100 firms producing a total of 700 rakes.

To find the number of firms in the market, we find the number of firms at which the average cost per rake equals the $12 market price. If the price equals the average cost, each of the 100 firms makes zero economic profit, so there is no incentive for new firms to enter the market and no incentive for existing firms to leave.

Each point on the long-run supply curve shows the quantity of rakes supplied at a particular price. To find a point on the supply curve, we pick a price and then determine how many rakes the industry will produce at that price. At a price of $12, there will be 100 firms producing 700 rakes, so one point on the supply curve shown in Figure 9.7 is point *h*. To find the other points on the long-run supply curve, we pick other prices and use the data in Table 9.2 to determine the quantity at which price equals the average cost of production. At a price of $10, the quantity is 350 rakes (point *e*), and at a price of $14, the quantity is 1,050 (point *j*).

The long-run supply curve in Figure 9.7 is positively sloped, as it will be for any increasing-cost industry. This is another example of the law of supply. The higher the price of rakes, the larger the quantity supplied. An increase in the price of rakes makes rake production more profitable, so firms enter the market, increasing the quantity supplied to the market. Firms will continue to enter the market until the average cost per rake reaches the market price. Each firm gets just enough revenue to cover its production costs, so economic profit is zero.

For an example of the law of supply, let's look at what happened to the supply of wolfram during World War II. Wolfram is an ore of tungsten, an alloy required to make heat-resistant steel for armor plate and armor-piercing shells. During World War II, the United States and its European allies bought up all the wolfram produced in Spain, thus denying the Axis powers (Germany and Italy) access to Spanish wolfram.[2] The idea was to hamper the Axis war effort by denying them a vital input to the production of military equipment and weapons. This buying program was very costly to the Allied powers for two reasons:[3]

- The Allied powers had to outbid the Axis powers for the Spanish wolfram, and the price of wolfram increased from $1,144 per ton to $20,000 per ton.

- Spanish firms responded to the higher prices by supplying more wolfram. Workers poured into the Galatia area in Spain, where they used simple tools to gather wolfram from the widely scattered outcroppings of ore. The quantity of wolfram supplied increased tenfold. Because wolfram miners obeyed the law of supply, the Allied powers were forced to buy a huge amount of wolfram, much more than they had expected.

Figure 9.7
Long-Run Market Supply Curve
The long-run market supply curve shows the relationship between the price and quantity supplied in the long run, when firms can enter or leave the industry. At each point on the supply curve, the market price equals the long-run average cost of production. The market supply curve for an increasing-cost is positively sloped.

The supply of rental housing is relatively inelastic because most local governments restrict the amount of land available for building apartments.

Examples of Increasing-Cost Industries: Sugar, Rental Housing

The sugar industry is an example of an increasing-cost industry. If the price of sugar is only 11 cents per pound, sugar production is profitable in areas with relatively low production costs, including the Caribbean, Latin America, Australia, and South Africa.[4] At a price of 11 cents, the world supply of sugar equals the amount produced in these areas. As the price increases, sugar production becomes profitable in areas where production costs are higher, increasing the quantity of sugar supplied as these other areas join the world market. For example, at a price of 14 cents per pound, sugar production is profitable in the European Community; and at a price of 24 cents, production is profitable even in the United States. The law of supply works in the world sugar market: The higher the price, the larger the number of areas that produce sugar, so the larger the quantity of sugar supplied.

Another example of an increasing-cost industry is rental housing. Local governments use land-use zoning to restrict the amount of land available for apartments. When housing producers decide to build more apartments, there is fierce competition for the small amount of land zoned for apartments, so the cost of land—and the cost per apartment—increases by a large amount.[5]

TEST Your Understanding

10. Complete the statement: The long-run supply curve shows the relationship between _____ (on the horizontal axis) and _____ (on the vertical axis).

11. Use Table 9.2 to compute the average cost in a 75-firm industry, assuming the total cost of the typical firm in such an industry is $70.

12. Circle the three items in the following list that go together: positively sloped supply curve, horizontal supply curve, increasing-cost industry, increasing average cost of production, constant average cost of production.

Market Equilibrium Revisited

We can use what we've learned about the short-run supply curve and the long-run supply curve to get a deeper understanding of perfectly competitive markets. Let's use the two supply curves to explore the short-run and the long-run effects of a change in demand.

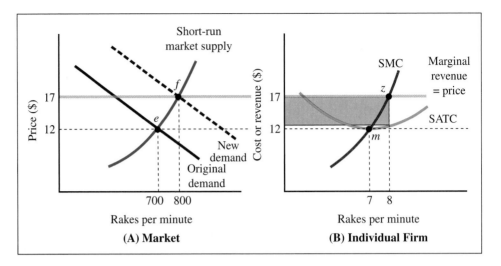

Figure 9.8
Short-Run Effects of an Increase in Demand

An increase in demand increases the market price to $17, causing the typical firm to produce 8 rakes instead of 7. Price exceeds the short-run average total cost at the chosen quantity, so economic profit is positive. Firms will enter the profitable market.

(A) Market

(B) Individual Firm

Increase in Demand and the Incentive to Enter

Figure 9.8 shows the short-run effects of an increase in the demand for rakes. Panel A shows what's happening at the market level. Let's start with the initial equilibrium shown by point e: The original demand curve intersects the short-run market supply curve at a price of $12 per rake and a quantity of 700 rakes. When demand increases, the market demand curve shifts to the right, and it intersects the supply curve at a price of $17 and a quantity of 800 rakes. In panel B, an increase in price from $12 to $17 increases the output per firm from 7 rakes to 8 rakes. At this quantity, the $17 price now exceeds the average total cost, so the typical firm makes an economic profit (shown by the shaded rectangle). At the market level shown in panel A, the new short-run equilibrium has a price of $17 and a quantity of 800 rakes.

This is not a long-run equilibrium because each firm is making a positive economic profit. Firms will enter the profitable market and as they compete for customers, the price of rakes will decrease. New firms will continue to enter the market until the price drops to the point at which economic profit is zero. The question is, How far does the price drop?

The Long-Run Effects of an Increase in Demand

We can use the long-run supply curve to determine the long-run price. In Figure 9.9, the short-run effect of the increase in demand is shown by the move from point e to point f: The price increases from $12 to $17, and the quantity increases from 700 to 800. The new long-run equilibrium is shown by point s, where the new demand curve intersects the long-run supply curve. Starting with a price of $17 (the new short-run equilibrium), firms will continue to enter the market until the price drops to $14 and the quantity is 1,050 rakes per minute. At this price and quantity, each of the 150 firms produces 7 rakes per minute and earns zero economic profit.

Figure 9.9 shows how the price of rakes changes over time. An increase in demand causes a large upward jump in the price (from point e to point f), followed by a slide downward to the new long-run equilibrium price (from point f to point s). In the short run, firms respond to an increase in price by squeezing more output from their existing production facilities. Because of diminishing returns, it is costly to increase output in the short run, so the price increases by a large amount. The higher price causes new firms to enter the market, and as they enter, the price gradually drops to the point at which each firm makes zero economic profit. The long-run supply curve is relatively flat because firms enter the industry and build new factories, so there are no diminishing returns.

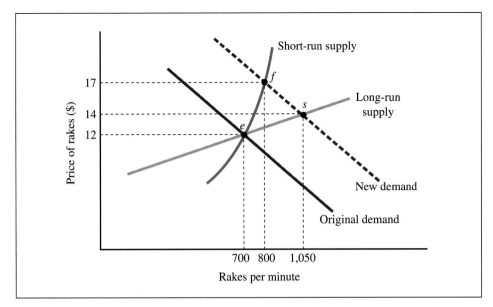

Figure 9.9
Short-Run and Long-Run Effects of an Increase in Demand
The short-run supply curve is steeper than the long-run supply curve because there are diminishing returns in the short run. In the short run, an increase in demand increases the price from $12 (point *e*) to $17 (point *f*). In the long run, firms enter the industry, and the price drops to $14 (point *s*). The large upward jump in price is followed by a downward slide to the new long-run equilibrium price.

Long-Run Supply for a Constant-Cost Industry

As the rake industry expanded, the average cost of production increased, a result of higher input costs. In other words, the rake industry is an increasing-cost industry. In contrast, as a **constant-cost industry** grows, it continues to buy its inputs at the same prices. For this to happen, the industry doesn't have a big enough effect on the input market to affect input prices. As a result, the average cost of production for the typical firm doesn't change as the industry grows. In Table 9.2 the rake industry would be a constant-cost industry if the average cost of rakes were constant at $10, regardless of how many rakes were produced.

Constant-cost industry: An industry in which the average cost of production is constant; the long-run supply curve is horizontal.

As an example of constant-cost industry, consider the taxi industry in a city. As the taxi industry grows, it will use more gasoline, more workers, and more cars, but because the industry is such a small part of the markets for gasoline, labor, and cars, the prices of these inputs won't change. As a result, the average cost of production won't change as the industry grows.

The long-run supply curve for a constant-cost industry is horizontal at the constant average cost of production. If the average cost of taxi service is $3 per mile (including the cost of gasoline, the taxicab, and the driver), the long-run supply curve for taxi service is horizontal at $3, as shown in Figure 9.10. At any lower price, the quantity of taxi service supplied would be zero because no rational firm would provide taxi service at a price less than the average cost of providing the service. At any higher price, firms would enter the taxi industry in droves, and entry would continue until the price dropped to the constant average cost of taxi service ($3).

Hurricane Andrew and the Price of Ice

For an example of the short-run and long-run effects of an increase in demand, let's look at the short-run and long-run effects of a hurricane. In 1992, Hurricane Andrew struck the southeastern United States, leaving millions of people without electricity for several days. Figure 9.11 shows the short and long-run effects of the hurricane on the price of ice, which was used to cool and preserve food in areas without electricity. Before the hurricane, the market was at point e, with a price of $1 per bag of ice. The long-run supply curve is horizontal, indicating that the ice industry is a constant-cost industry.

Figure 9.10

Long-Run Supply Curve for a Constant-Cost Industry

In a constant-cost industry, input prices do not change as the industry grows, so the average production cost is constant and the long-run supply curve is horizontal. For the taxi industry, the cost per mile of taxi service is constant at $3, so the supply curve is horizontal at $3 per mile of service.

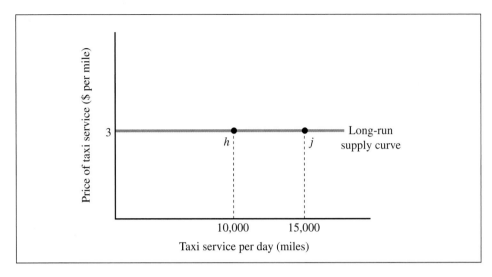

In the short run (a day or two), the number of ice suppliers is fixed. The increase in demand caused by the hurricane moved the market from point *e* to point *f*, and the price rose to $5 per bag of ice. In the long run, firms responded to the higher price by entering the market. Many people trucked ice from distant locations and sold it from trucks parked on streets and highways. As these firms entered the ice market in the days after the hurricane, the price of ice gradually dropped, and the market eventually reached the intersection of the new demand curve and the long-run supply curve (point *s*), with a price equal to the prehurricane price.

This pattern of price changes following the hurricane was observed in other markets. Immediately after the hurricane, $200 chain saws were sold for $900, but the price dropped steadily as new roadside firms entered the market. The same sort of price changes occurred for bottled water, tarpaper, and plywood. The basic pattern was a large upward jump in price followed by a downward slide to the long-run equilibrium price.

Public officials are often tempted to pass laws prohibiting what's called *price gouging*, charging high prices for scarce goods after a natural disaster. One effect of such laws is to slow the transition from the short run to the long run. The people who set up roadside stands to sell ice were motivated by the high price. If the price were controlled at $1

Figure 9.11

Hurricane Andrew and the Price of Ice

A hurricane increases the demand for ice, shifting the demand curve to the right. In the short run, the supply curve is steep, so the price rises by a large amount. In the long run, firms enter the industry, pulling down the price. Because this is a constant-cost industry, the supply curve is horizontal, and the large upward jump in price is followed by a downward slide back to the original price.

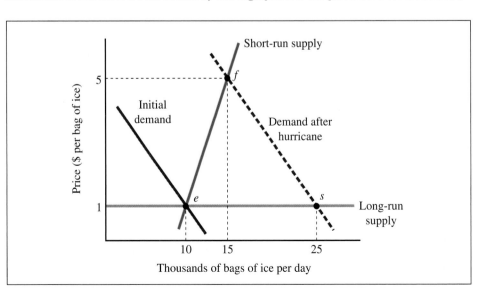

per bag, few people would have incurred the large expenses associated with trucking the ice from distant locations and setting up roadside stores. The result would have been less ice and more spoiled food. An alternative to a law regulating prices is to leave prices to the market and help to ease the transition from short run to long run by making it easier for entrepreneurs to enter the market.

Butter Prices

Several years ago, people became concerned about the undesirable health effects of eating butter. The demand for butter dropped, decreasing its price. Some time later, the price of butter started rising steadily, although demand hadn't been changing. After several months of price hikes, the price of butter was getting close to the price observed before demand decreased. According to a consumer watchdog organization, the rising price of butter was evidence of a conspiracy on the part of butter producers. Is there some other explanation for the rising price of butter?

The key to solving this puzzle is the distinction between the short run and the long run. In Figure 9.12, the short-run effect of a decrease in demand is shown by the move from point e (price = $2.00) to point f (price = $1.44). In the short run, not many firms will leave the market when the price drops, so the decrease in demand will cause a large price drop. Although many of the remaining firms will lose money, they will stay in the market if their total revenue covers their total variable cost. In the long run, however, unprofitable firms will leave the market, causing the price to rise. In Figure 9.12, the new long-run equilibrium is shown by point s, with a price of $1.80. The pattern of a large price drop followed by a gradual increase in price is a normal pattern for a perfectly competitive market.

TEST Your Understanding

13. Explain why the short-run supply curve is steeper than the long-run supply curve.

14. Describe the short-run price effect and the long-run price effect of a decrease in the demand for rakes.

15. Under what circumstances would an increase in demand for a particular good not affect the price of the good in the long run?

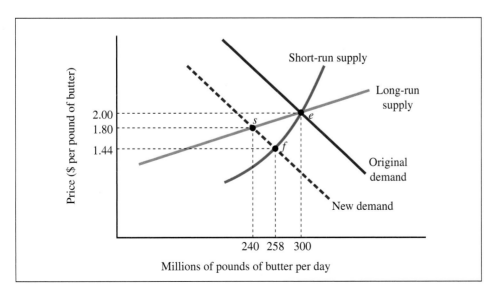

Figure 9.12

The Short-Run and Long-Run Effects of a Decrease in the Demand for Butter
The short-run supply curve is steeper than the long-run supply curve because there are diminishing returns in the short run. In the short run, a decrease in demand decreases the price from $2.00 (point e) to $1.44 (point f). In the long run, firms leave the industry, and the price rises to the new equilibrium price of $1.80 (point s).

Using the **TOOLS**

We've seen how a perfectly competitive firm can use its cost curves to decide how much to produce and whether to continue operating an unprofitable operation. We've also explored the short- and long-run effects of changes in demand. Here are some opportunities to do your own economic analysis.

APPLICATIONS

1. Advice for an Unprofitable Firm

You've been hired as an economic consultant to a price-taking firm that produces shirts. The firm already has a shirt factory, so it is operating in the short run. The price of shirts is $5, the hourly wage is $12, and each shirt requires $1 worth of material. At the current level of output (20 workers and 70 shirts per hour), the firm is losing money: Its total cost exceeds its total revenue. The firm has experimented with different numbers of workers and discovered that 21 workers would produce 72 shirts; 15 workers would produce 60 shirts; and 16 workers would produce 63 shirts. Your job is to tell the firm which of these four options to take:

- **Option 1:** Shut down the unprofitable operation.
- **Option 2:** Continue to produce 70 shirts per hour.
- **Option 3:** Produce more shirts.
- **Option 4:** Produce fewer shirts.

2. Maximizing the Profit Margin

According to the marginal principle, the firm should choose the quantity of output at which price equals marginal cost. A tempting alternative is to maximize the firm's profit margin, defined as the difference between price and short-run average total cost. Use the firm's short-run cost curves to evaluate this approach. Draw the firm's short-run supply curve and compare it to the supply curve of a firm that maximizes its profit.

3. Market Effects of an Increase in Housing Demand

Consider the market for apartments in a small city. In the initial equilibrium, the monthly rent (the price) is $500 and the quantity is 10,000 apartments. Suppose that the population of the city suddenly increases by 24%. The price elasticity of demand for apartments is 1.0. The short-run price elasticity of supply is 0.20, and the long-run price elasticity of supply is 0.50.

a. Depict graphically the short- and long-run effects of the increase in population.

b. By what percentage will the price increase in the short run? (Use the price-change formula from Chapter 5.)

c. By what percentage will the price increase in the long run?

Summary

In this chapter, we explored the decisions made by perfectly competitive firms and the implications of these decisions for the supply side of the market. In the short run, a firm uses the marginal principle to decide how much output to produce. In the long run, a firm will enter a market if the price exceeds the average cost of production. Here are the main points of this chapter:

1. A price-taking firm should produce the quantity of output at which the marginal revenue (the price) equals the marginal cost of production.

2. An unprofitable firm should continue to operate if its total revenue exceeds its total variable cost.

3. The long-run supply curve will be positively sloped if the average cost of production increases as the industry grows.

4. The long-run supply curve is flatter than the short-run supply curve because there are diminishing returns in the short run, but not in the long run.

5. An increase in demand causes a large upward jump in price, followed by a downward slide to the new long-run equilibrium price.

 ## Key Terms

constant-cost industry, 203
economic profit, 188
increasing-cost industry, 198
long-run market supply curve, 197

marginal revenue, 190
perfectly competitive market, 188
short-run market supply curve, 196
short-run supply curve, 195

shut-down price, 193
sunk cost, 194
total revenue, 188

 ## Problems and Discussion Questions

1. In the following table, provide the numbers for marginal cost. Then use the data to draw the short-run supply curve for tables.

Tables per hour	Total cost	Marginal cost
3	120	—
4	155	—
5	200	—
6	270	—

2. The following table shows short-run marginal costs for a perfectly competitive firm:

Output	100	200	300	400	500
Marginal cost	$5	$10	$20	$40	$70

a. Use this information to draw the firm's marginal-cost curve.

b. Suppose the shut-down price is $10. Draw the firm's short-run supply curve.

c. Suppose there are 100 identical firms with the same marginal-cost curve. Draw the short-run industry supply curve.

3. You've been hired by an unprofitable firm to determine whether it should shut down its unprofitable operation. The firm currently uses 70 workers to produce 300 units of output per day. The daily wage (per worker) is $100, and the price of the firm's output is $30. Although you don't know the firm's fixed cost, you know that it is high enough that the

firm's total cost exceeds its total revenue. Should the firm continue to operate at a loss?

4. Consider the choices facing an unprofitable (and perfectly competitive) firm. The firm currently produces 100 units per day and sells them at a price of $22 each. At the current output quantity, the total cost is $3,000 per day, the variable cost is $2,500 per day, and the marginal cost is $45.

a. Evaluate the following statement from the firm's accountant: "Given our current production level, our variable cost ($2,500) exceeds our total revenue ($2,200). We should shut down our production facility."

b. Illustrate your answer with a graph showing short-run cost curves and the revenue curve of a perfectly competitive firm.

5. Consider the following statement from a wheat farmer to his workers: "The price of wheat is very low this year, and the most I can get from the crop is $35,000. If I paid you the same amount as I paid you last year ($30,000), I'd lose money, because I also have to worry about the $20,000 I paid three months ago for seed and fertilizer. I'd be crazy to pay a total of $50,000 to harvest a crop I can sell for only $35,000. If you are willing to work for half as much as last year ($15,000), my total cost will be $35,000, so I'll break even. If you don't take a pay cut. I won't harvest the wheat." Is the farmer bluffing, or will the farmworkers lose their jobs if they reject the proposed pay cut?

6. Consider a firm that uses the following rule to decide how much output to produce: If the profit margin (price minus short-run average total cost) is positive, the firm will produce more output. Use the firm's short-run cost curves to evaluate this approach. Draw the firm's short-run supply curve and compare it to the short-run supply curve of a profit-maximizing firm.

7. Consider the following data on the relationship between the price of gasoline (in real terms, adjusted for inflation) and the quantity of gasoline sold per day in the city of Ceteris Paribus:

Year	Price	Gallons per Day
1995	1.00	50,000
1996	1.10	53,000

If possible, draw the industry supply curve and compute the price elasticity of supply.

8. Between 1980 and 1990, the percentage of U.S. households with videocassette recorders (VCRs) increased from 1% to 70%. The rapid growth in the number of VCRs increased the demand for video rentals. Predict the effect of this increase in demand on the price of video rentals in the short run and the long run.

9. Suppose each lamp manufacturer produces 10 lamps per hour. In the following table, fill in a number wherever you see a _____. Then use the data in the table to draw the long-run supply curve for lamps.

Number of Firms	Industry Output	Total Cost for Typical Firm	Average Cost per Lamp
40	_____	$300	$_____
80	_____	$360	$_____
120	_____	$420	$_____

10. Suppose that a new technology decreases the amount of labor time required to produce a particular good. Would you expect all firms eventually to adopt the new technology?

11. Draw a long-run supply curve for haircutting that is consistent with the following statement: "The haircutting industry in our city uses a tiny fraction of the electricity, scissors, and commercial space available on the market. In addition, the industry uses only about 100 of the 50,000 people who could cut hair."

12. Draw a long-run supply curve for pencils and explain why you drew it as you did.

13. Web Exercise. Visit the Web site of Agricultural Weather dot Com [*http://www.agriculturalweather.com*]. How might the information available at this Web site be useful to someone involved in the market for Florida orange juice?

14. Web Exercise. Visit the Web site of the Florida Agricultural Statistics Service [*http://www.nass.usda.gov/fl/*]. Access the reports provided to get some data on recent trends in the price of some Florida citrus products. Draw a supply-demand graph consistent with the recent changes in prices and quantities.

Take It to the Net

We invite you to visit the O'Sullivan/Sheffrin page on the Prentice Hall Web site at: **http://www.prenhall.com/osullivan/** for additional World Wide Web exercises for this chapter.

Model Answers to Questions

Chapter-Opening Questions

1. To use the marginal principle, the firm needs the price (marginal benefit or marginal revenue) and the marginal cost of production for different levels of output.

2. It would be sensible to shut down if your total revenue is less than your variable cost. Otherwise, it would be sensible to continue operating.

3. Hurricane Andrew increased the demand for goods such as ice, chain saws, and plywood. In the short run, the supply curve for ice is steep, so the price increased by a relatively large amount. Over time, the price dropped as new firms entered the market to supply ice.

4. The large drop in price was a short-run effect, reflecting the steep short-run supply curve. As firms dropped out of the market and production decreased, the price started to rise.

Test Your Understanding

1. The firm is such a tiny part of the market that no matter how much output it produces, it will not affect the market price.

2. Marginal revenue (or price), marginal cost.

3. The farmer is not maximizing profit because the marginal revenue (price) is less than the marginal cost. The farmer should produce less sugar.

4. $800 ($20 per lamp times 40 lamps).

5. Operate.

6. Average variable cost.

7. Price, quantity supplied.

8. You need the short-run marginal cost curve and the shut-down price. If you have the average variable cost curve and the marginal cost curve, you can figure out the shut-down price by finding the price at which the two curves intersect.

9. 5,000 units (50 units per firm times 100 firms).

10. Quantity supplied, price.

11. The average cost per rake is $10 ($70/7 rakes).

12. The related terms are positively sloped supply curve, increasing-cost industry, and increasing average cost of production.

13. There are diminishing returns in the short run, so production costs increase rapidly as a firm increases its output.

14. In the short run, the price would drop by a large amount. Then the price would start to rise. If the rake industry is an increasing-cost industry, the new long-run price would be less than the original price.

15. If the good is produced by a constant-cost industry, one with a horizontal long-run supply curve.

Using the Tools

1. Advice for an Unprofitable Firm. At the current output level (70 shirts), the marginal cost of production is $7 per shirt: To produce one more shirt, the firm must use 0.50 hour of labor, which would cost $6 (half of the hourly wage) and $1 worth of material. Because the marginal cost exceeds the price ($5), the firm is not maximizing its profit.

At an output level of 60 shirts, the marginal cost of production is only $5 per shirt: To produce one more shirt, the firm must use one-third of an hour of labor, which would cost $4 (one-third of the hourly wage) and $1 worth of material. At this quantity of output, the price equals marginal cost, so the firm is maximizing profit. Total revenue ($300 = $5 per shirt × 60 shirts) exceeds variable cost ($240 = $180 for labor [$12 per hour × 15 hours]) plus $60 for materials ($1 per shirt × 60 shirts), so it is sensible to continue to operate, even if total cost exceeds total revenue.

2. Maximizing the Profit Margin. To maximize the profit margin, the firm will choose the quantity that generates the largest possible gap between the price and average cost, and this occurs at the minimum point of the average cost curve. In Figure 9.A, the average total cost curve reaches its minimum point at point *b*, with a quantity of 7 rakes and an average cost of $12. With a price of $17, the firm would produce 7 rakes per minute and earn a profit of $5 per rake or $35 per minute.

As shown in Figure 9.A at a price of $17, the firm would earn more profit by using the marginal principle. The price equals marginal cost with 8 rakes, and profit is $38.40 (an average cost of $12.20 means profit per unit is $4.80). The profit-margin approach is misguided because it looks at only one part of the profit picture: Total profit equals the profit margin times the quantity produced. Although the profit margin will be lower with 8 rakes, total profit will be higher.

As shown in Figure 9.A, the supply curve is a vertical line starting at the minimum point of the average-cost curve. Suppose the firm will shut down if the profit margin is negative. At any price less than $12, price will be less than average cost, so the profit margin will be negative and the firm will shut down. To maximize the gap between price and average cost, the firm will choose the quantity associated with the minimum point of the average cost curve (7 rakes), regardless of the price of rakes. Therefore, as long as the price exceeds $12, the firm will produce 7 rakes. In contrast, the supply curve of a profit-maximizing firm is the marginal cost curve above the shut-down price.

3. Market Effects of an Increase in Housing Demand

  a. See Figure 9.B.

  b. Use the price-change formula from Chapter 5: percentage change in price = % change in demand/(Es + Ed) = 24/1.20 = 20%.

  c. Percentage change in price = 24/1.50 = 16%.

Figure 9.A
Short-Run Supply Curve with Maximizing the Profit Margin

A firm that maximizes its profit margin (the difference between price and average cost) will produce the quantity at which average cost is at its minimum. The supply curve is a vertical line starting at the minimum of the average-cost curve.

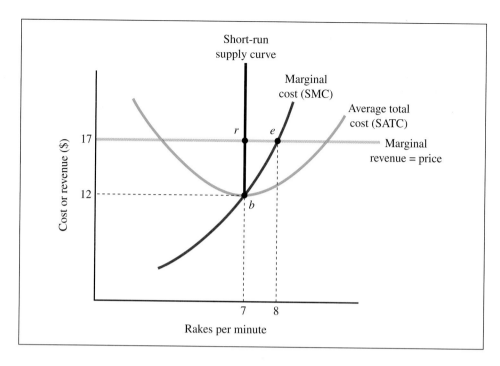

Figure 9.B
Short- and Long-Run Effects of Population Growth

The initial equilibrium is shown by point *i*. The increase in demand moves the market to point *s* in the short run and to point *f* in the long run.

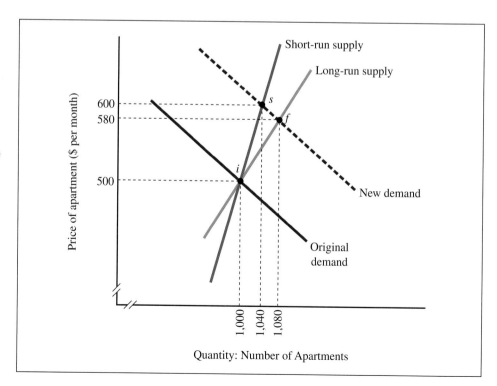

Notes

1. *The Structure of the American Economy,* 8th ed., Walter Adams, ed., © 1990. Adapted by permission of Prentice-Hall, Inc., Upper Saddle River, NJ.

2. TeleCommons Development Group, "Grameen Telecom's Village Phone Programme: A Multi-Media Case Study," (*http://www.telecommons.com/villagephone*).

3. D.I. Gordon and R. Dangerfield, *The Hidden Weapon* (New York: Harper & Brothers, 1947), pp. 105–116.

4. Frederic L. Hoff and Max Lawrence, *Implications of World Sugar Markets, Policies, and Production Costs for U.S. Sugar*, Agricultural Economic Research Report 543 (Washington, DC: U.S. Department of Agriculture, Economic Research Service, November 1985).

5. Frank De Leeuw and Nkanta Ekanem. "The Supply of Rental Housing," *American Economic Review*, vol. 61, 1971, pp. 806–817.

Monopoly

The Coca-Cola Company recently built a new football scoreboard for a large state university. Now football fans can enjoy the latest in scoreboard graphics as they watch the game. In addition, Coca Cola gave $2.3 million dollars to remodel the university's student center,[1] providing students with a comfortable place to meet, eat, talk, and relax. What explains this outburst of generosity? Does it have anything to do with the fact that Coca-Cola was recently given the exclusive right to sell beverages on campus—a monopoly? Who is really paying for the scoreboard and the student center?

Monopoly: A market in which a single firm serves the entire market.

Patent: The exclusive right to sell a particular good for some period of time.

Franchise or licensing scheme: A policy under which the government picks a single firm to sell a particular good.

n Chapter 9, we explored the decisions made by firms in a perfectly competitive market, a market where there are dozens or perhaps hundreds of firms. This chapter deals with the opposite extreme: a **monopoly**, a market, served by a single firm. In contrast with a perfectly competitive or price-taking firm, a monopolist can pick any price it wants. Of course, the higher the price it charges, the smaller the quantity it will sell, because consumers obey the law of demand.

A monopoly occurs when there is one firm and a barrier to entry—a barrier that prevents other firms from entering a market. Here is a list of possible barriers to entry:

- A **patent** is granted by the government, giving an inventor the exclusive right to sell a new product for some period of time. Under a GATT agreement that took effect in 1995, patents in the United States and other GATT nations are now issued for 20 years from the time the inventor applies for a patent. To receive a patent, the inventor must prove the product is useful and novel (a true innovation, not just a slight modification of an existing product) and must provide a working model. Patent holders in many European countries pay an annual renewal fee for their patents, and the longer an inventor holds a patent, the higher the annual fee. In the United States, there are no renewal fees, so by paying a one-time fee, an inventor can prevent anyone else from selling the product for 20 years.

- In some cases, the government implicitly grants monopoly power by allowing industrial associations to restrict the number of firms in the market. For example, the U.S. government allows sports associations such as the major-league baseball leagues to restrict the number and location of teams.

- Under a **franchise or licensing scheme**, the government designates a single firm to sell a particular good. Here are some examples of franchise and licensing schemes:
  - Some cities select a single firm to provide off-street parking.
  - The National Park Service picks a single firm to sell food and other goods in Yosemite National Park.
  - The Federal Communications Commission issues licenses for individual radio and television stations.

- In some markets, there are large economies of scale in production (average cost decreases as the firm's output increases), so a single firm will be profitable, but a pair of firms would lose money. A natural monopoly occurs when the entry of a second firm would make price less than average cost, so a single firm serves the entire market.

- As we'll see later in the book, some firms use illegal means to exclude other firms from the market.

To explain how a monopoly works, we'll start with an example of a monopoly that results from a patent. We'll see that a monopolist can use the marginal principle to find the price that generates the highest possible profit. Later in this chapter, we'll explore the policy implications of a natural monopoly. Here are some of the practical questions relating to monopoly that we will answer:

1. What are the trade-offs associated with patents and other policies that grant monopoly power?

2. When the patent on a popular pharmaceutical drug expires, what happens to the price of the drug?

3. Should the government allow an electric utility (a monopolist in the market for electricity) to charge any price it wants?

Because the indivisible inputs required to generate electric power are very costly, there are large economies of scale in power generation.

4. It costs about $1.5 billion to set up the satellites for a satellite radio system. How many firms are likely to set up such a system and provide satellite radio service?

The Monopolist's Output Decision

A monopolist must decide what price to charge and how much output to produce. Like other firms, the monopoly's objective is to maximize profit, defined as the difference between total revenue and total cost. We learned about production costs in an earlier chapter, so we start our discussion with the revenue side of the monopolist's profit picture. Then we show how a monopolist picks a price and a quantity.

Total Revenue and Marginal Revenue

A firm's total revenue—the money it gets by selling its product—equals the price times the quantity sold. Table10.1 shows how to use a demand schedule (in the first two columns) to compute a firm's total revenue (in the third column). At a price of $16, the firm doesn't sell anything, so its total revenue is zero. To sell 1 unit, the firm must cut its price to $14, so its total revenue is $14. To get consumers to buy 2 units instead of just one, the firm must cut its price to $12. The total revenue associated with selling 2 units is $24. As the price continues to drop and the quantity sold increases, total revenue

Table 10.1 Demand, Total Revenue, and Marginal Revenue

Price	Quantity Sold	Total Revenue	Marginal Revenue
$16	0	0	—
$14	1	$14	$14
$12	2	$24	10
$10	3	$30	6
$ 8	4	$32	2
$ 6	5	$30	−2
$ 4	6	$24	−6

Figure 10.1

Total Revenue and Marginal Revenue
As the firm cuts its price to sell more output, its total revenue rises for the first 4 units sold, but then decreases for the 5th and 6th units. Therefore, marginal revenue (the change in total revenue from selling one more unit) is positive for the first 4 units and then becomes negative.

increases for a while but then starts falling. To sell 5 units instead of 4, the firm cuts its price from $8 to $6, and total revenue decreases from $32 to $30. The total revenue associated with selling 6 units is even lower ($24). The top panel in Figure 10.1 shows the relationship between total revenue and the quantity sold.

The firm's marginal revenue is defined as the change in total revenue that results from selling one more unit of output. In Table 10.1, we compute marginal revenue by taking the difference between the total revenue from selling a certain quantity of output (for example, 3 units), and the total revenue from selling one fewer unit of output (for example, 2 units). As shown in the fourth row in the table, the total revenue from selling 3 units is $30 and the total revenue from selling 2 units is only $24, so the marginal revenue from selling the third unit is $6. As shown in the table and in the lower panel of Figure 10.1, marginal revenue is positive for the first 4 units sold. Beyond 4 units, selling an additional unit results in lower total revenue, so marginal revenue is negative. For example, the marginal revenue for the fifth unit is –$2, and the marginal revenue for the 6th unit is –$6.

Table 10.1 and Figure 10.1 illustrate the trade-offs associated with cutting a price to sell a larger quantity. When the firm cuts its price from $12 to $10, there is good news and bad news:

- **Good news.** The firm collects $10 from the new customer (the third), so revenue increases by $10.

- **Bad news.** The firm cuts the price for all its customers, so it gets less revenue from the customers who would have been willing to pay the higher price ($12). Specifically, the firm collects $2 less from each of the two original customers, so revenue decreases by $4.

The combination of good news and bad news leads to a net increase in total revenue of only $6, resulting from the $10 gained from the new customer minus the $4 lost on the first two customers. Because of the bad news associated with selling an additional unit of output, a firm's marginal revenue is always less than its price.

Figure10.2 shows the demand curve and marginal revenue curve for the data shown in Table 10.1. Because the firm must cut its price to sell more output, the marginal revenue curve lies below the demand curve. For example, the demand curve shows that the firm will sell 3 units at a price of $10 (point *d*), but the marginal revenue for this quantity is only $6 (point *i*). For quantities of 5 units and greater, marginal revenue is negative because when the firm cuts its price to sell one additional unit, the bad news dominates the good news: The amount the firm loses on its original customers exceeds the amount it gains on the new one, so total revenue drops.

The Marginal Principle and the Output Decision

We use a simple example to explain how a monopolist decides how much output to produce. Sneezy, who holds a patent on a new drug that cures the common cold, must decide how much of the drug to produce and what price to charge for it. These two decisions are related because according to the law of demand, the higher the price, the smaller the quantity demanded. Sneezy can use the marginal principle to choose how much to produce and what price to charge.

Marginal **PRINCIPLE**

Increase the level of an activity if its marginal benefit exceeds its marginal cost, but reduce the level if the marginal cost exceeds the marginal benefit. If possible, pick the level at which the marginal benefit equals the marginal cost.

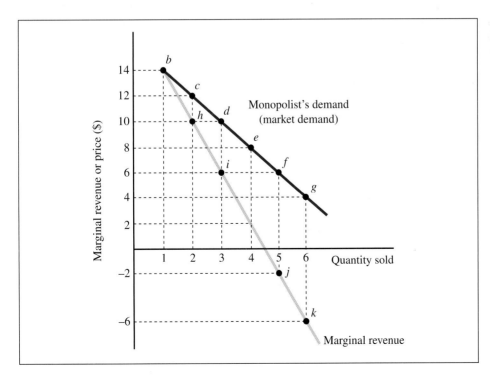

Figure 10.2
Demand Curve and Marginal Revenue Curve
Marginal revenue is equal to the price for the first unit sold, but is less than the price for all other units sold. To increase the quantity sold, a firm cuts its price and receives less revenue on the units that could have been sold at the higher price. Therefore, beyond the first unit sold, the marginal revenue curve lies below the demand curve.

Sneezy's activity is producing the cold drug, and he will pick the quantity at which the marginal revenue from selling one more unit (the marginal benefit) equals the marginal cost associated with that unit:

$$\text{marginal revenue} = \text{marginal cost}$$

The first two columns in Table10.2 show the relationship between the price of the cold drug and the quantity demanded. We can use these numbers to draw the market demand curve, as shown in Figure 10.3. Because Sneezy is a monopolist—the only seller of the drug—the market demand curve shows how much he will sell at each price. The demand curve is negatively sloped, consistent with the law of demand. For example, at a price of $18 per dose, the quantity demanded is 600 doses per hour (point h), compared to 900 doses at a price of $15 (point m).

Like other monopolists, Sneezy must cut his price to sell a larger quantity. Therefore, marginal revenue is less than price, as shown in the third column in Table 10.2. In Figure 10.3 the marginal revenue curve lies below the demand curve. For example, with a price of $18, Sneezy will sell 600 doses (point h), and the marginal revenue for this quantity is $12 (point i). In other words, if he cuts his price by an amount large enough to sell just one more dose, his total revenue would increase by $12. Similarly, with a price of $15, he will sell 900 doses (point m), and the marginal revenue is $6 (point n). Figure 10.3 also shows some of Sneezy's cost curves.

Picking a Quantity and a Price

We're ready to show how a monopolist can use the marginal principle to pick a quantity and price. To maximize his profit, Sneezy should produce the quantity at which the marginal revenue equals marginal cost. By looking at the numbers in Table 10.2, we can see that this happens with a quantity of 900 doses and a price of $15, as shown in the fourth row. In Figure 10.3, the marginal revenue curve intersects the marginal cost curve at point n with a quantity of 900 doses, so that's the quantity that maximizes profit. To get consumers to buy this quantity, the price must be $15 (point m on the demand curve). The average cost of production is $8 per dose (shown by point c), so the profit per dose is $7 ($15 minus $8). Sneezy's profit equals the profit per dose ($7) times the quantity sold (900 doses), or $6,300 per hour.

To show that a price of $15 and a quantity of 900 doses maximizes Sneezy's profit, let's see what would happen if he picked some other quantity. Suppose he decided to produce 599 doses per hour at a price just above $18 (just above point h on the demand

Table 10.2 Using the Marginal Principle to Pick a Price and Quantity

Price (per Dose)	Quantity Sold (Doses)	Marginal Revenue	Marginal Cost	Total Revenue	Total Cost	Profit
$18	600	$12	$4.00	$10,800	$5,710	$5,090
$17	700	$10	$4.60	$11,900	$6,140	$5,760
$16	800	$8	$5.30	$12,800	$6,635	$6,165
$15	900	$6	$6.00	$13,500	$7,200	$6,300
$14	1,000	$4	$6.70	$14,000	$7,835	$6,165
$13	1,100	$2	$7.80	$14,300	$8,560	$5,740
$12	1,200	0	$9.00	$14,400	$9,400	$5,000

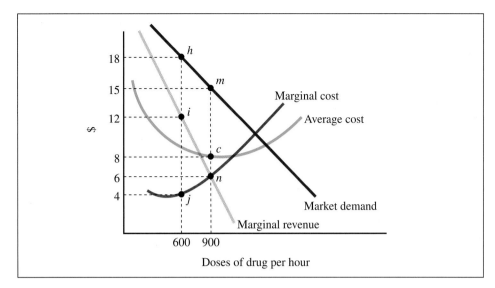

Figure 10.3
Monopolist Picks a Quantity and a Price
To maximize profit, the monopolist picks point *n*, where marginal revenue equals marginal cost. The monopolist produces 900 doses per hour at a price of $15 (point *m*). The average cost is $8 (point *c*), so the profit per dose is $7 (equal to the $15 price minus the $8 average cost) and the total profit is $6,300 (equal to $7 per dose times 900 doses).

curve). Could he make more profit by cutting his price by enough to sell one more dose? Sneezy should answer two questions:

- What is the extra cost associated with producing dose number 600? As shown by point *j* on the marginal cost curve, the marginal cost of the 600th dose is $4.

- What is the extra revenue associated with dose number 600? As shown by point *i* on the marginal revenue curve, the marginal revenue is $12.

If Sneezy wants to maximize his profit, he should produce the 600th dose because the $12 extra revenue exceeds the $4 extra cost, so his total profit will increase by $8. The same argument applies, with different numbers for marginal revenue, and marginal cost, for doses 601, 602, and so on, up to 900 doses. Sneezy should continue to increase the quantity produced as long as the marginal revenue exceeds the marginal cost. The marginal principle is satisfied at point *n*, with a total of 900 doses.

Why should Sneezy stop at 900 doses? Beyond 900 doses, the marginal revenue from an additional dose will be less than the marginal cost associated with producing it. Although Sneezy could cut his price and sell a larger quantity, an additional dose would add less to revenue than it adds to cost, so his total profit would decrease. As shown in the fifth row in Table 10.2, Sneezy could sell 1,000 doses at a price of $14, but the marginal revenue at this quantity is only $4, while the marginal cost at this quantity is $6.70. Producing the 1,000th dose would decrease Sneezy's profit by $2.70. For any quantity exceeding 900 doses, the marginal revenue is less than the marginal cost, so Sneezy should produce exactly 900 doses.

Formula for Marginal Revenue

There are two ways to compute a firm's marginal revenue. One way, shown in Table 10.1, involves computing the total revenue from selling two different quantities of output. A second way uses a simple formula that incorporates the good news and bad news associated with cutting prices:

$$\text{marginal revenue} = \text{price} - (\text{quantity} \times \text{slope of demand curve})$$

The first part of the formula's right side shows the good news. When a firm cuts its price by just enough to sell one more unit (the last unit sold), the firm's revenue increases by an amount equal to the new price. Recall that the bad news equals the previous quantity sold (one less than the current quantity) times the price cut. The slope of the demand curve is the change in price divided by the resulting change in quantity. In other words, the slope is the price cut required to sell just one more unit of output. To keep the arithmetic simple, we'll use the current quantity—not the previous quantity—to compute the bad news, so the bad news equals the current quantity times the slope of the demand curve.

We can use our earlier example to show how to use this marginal revenue formula. At point h on Sneezy's demand curve, the price is $18 and the quantity is 600 doses. The slope of the demand curve is $0.01 per dose: If we use points h and m, the rise is $3 (equal to $18 – $15) and the run is 300 doses (equal to 900 – 600), so the slope is $0.01 per dose (equal to $3/300 doses). This means that to sell the 600th dose, Sneezy cuts his price by $0.01. We can plug these values into the marginal revenue formula:

$$\text{marginal revenue} = \text{price} - (\text{quantity} \times \text{slope of demand curve})$$

$$\text{marginal revenue} = \$18 - (600 \text{ doses} \times \$0.01 \text{ per dose}) = \$12$$

This is shown by point i on the marginal revenue curve: At the quantity 600 doses, the marginal revenue is $12. This formula provides an approximate value for marginal revenue because it uses the current quantity (600) instead of the previous quantity (599). If the quantity is large, the one-unit difference between the current quantity and the previous quantity won't matter much, and the formula provides a good approximation of the true marginal revenue.

The Costs of Monopoly

What are the trade-offs—the costs and benefits to society as a whole—associated with a monopoly? This is an important question because in many cases, a monopoly results from government policy. If the costs exceed the benefits, it may be sensible to remove the barriers to entry and allow other firms to enter the market. We discuss the costs of monopoly in this part of the chapter and explore the benefits in the next part.

Monopoly Versus Perfect Competition

How does a monopoly differ from a perfectly competitive market? To show the difference, let's consider an example of an arthritis drug that could be produced by a monopoly or a perfectly competitive industry. Let's take the long-run perspective, a period of time long enough that a firm is perfectly flexible in its choice of inputs and firms can enter or leave a perfectly competitive market.

Consider the monopoly outcome first. Let's assume that the long-run average cost of producing the arthritis drug is constant at $8 per dose. As we saw in Chapter 8, if average cost is constant, the marginal cost equals average cost. In panel A of Figure 10.4, the long-run marginal cost curve is the same as the long-run average cost curve. Given the demand and marginal revenue curves in panel A of Figure 10.4, the monopolist will maximize profit where marginal revenue equals marginal cost (point n), producing 200 doses per hour at a price of $18 per dose. The monopolist's profit is $2,000 per hour (a $10 profit per dose ($18 – $8) times 200 doses).

Consider next the market for the arthritis drug under perfect competition. We're assuming that the arthritis drug industry is a constant-cost industry: Input prices do not change as the industry grows, so the long-run market supply curve is horizontal at the long-run average cost of producing the drug ($8 per dose). In panel B of Figure 10.4, the horizontal long-run supply curve intersects the demand curve at point p, with an equi-

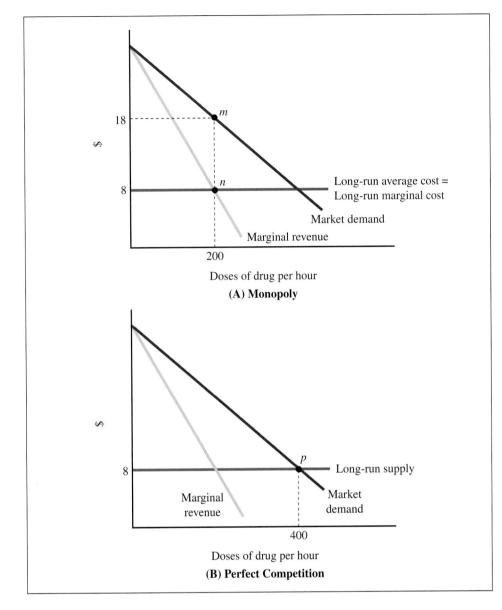

Figure 10.4

Monopoly Versus Perfect Competition

(A) Monopoly The monopolist picks the quantity at which long-run marginal cost equals marginal revenue (200 doses per hour, as shown by point *n*). As shown by point *m* on the demand curve, the price associated with quantity is $18 per dose.

(B) Perfect Competition The long-run supply curve of a perfectly competitive, constant cost industry intersects the demand curve at point *p*. The equilibrium price is $8, and the equilibrium quantity is 400 doses per hour.

librium price of $8 and an equilibrium quantity of 400 doses per hour. Compared to a monopoly outcome, the perfectly competitive outcome has a lower price ($8 instead of $18) and a larger quantity (400 doses instead of 200).

To examine the social cost of monopoly power, let's imagine that we start with a perfectly competitive market and then switch to a monopoly. Consumers will be worse off under monopoly, and we can use the concept of consumer surplus to determine just how much worse off they are. As we saw in Chapter 6, consumer surplus is shown by the area between the demand curve and the horizontal price line. In Figure10.5, the monopoly price is $18, so the consumer surplus associated with the monopoly is shown by triangle *C*. In contrast, the perfectly competitive price is $8, so the consumer surplus with perfect competition is shown by the larger triangle consisting of triangle *C*, rectangle *R*, and triangle *D*. In other words, a switch from perfect competition to monopoly decreases consumer surplus by the areas *R* and *D*.

Figure 10.5

Deadweight Loss from Monopoly

A switch from perfect competition to monopoly increases the price from $8 to $18 and decreases the quantity sold from 400 to 200 doses. Consumer surplus decreases by an amount shown by the areas *R* and *D*, while profit increases by the amount shown by rectangle *R*. The net loss to society is shown by triangle *D* (the deadweight loss of monopoly).

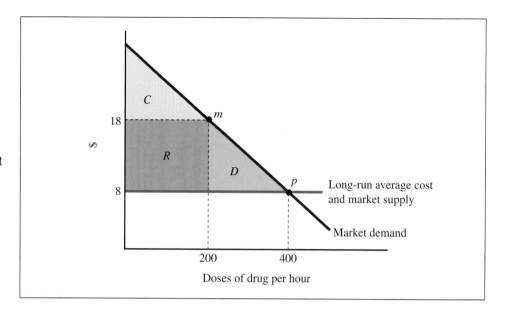

Let's take a closer look at the loss of consumer surplus resulting from a switch to monopoly:

- **Rectangle *R*.** The switch to monopoly increases the price by $10 per dose. Consumers buy 200 doses from the monopolist and pay $10 extra on each of these doses, for a loss of $2,000 per hour.

- **Triangle *D*.** The switch to monopoly decreases the quantity consumed because the price increases and consumers obey the law of demand. Consumers lose consumer surplus on the doses they would have consumed at the lower price. This loss is shown by triangle *D*, with an area of $1,000 (one half the base of the triangle (200 doses) times the height ($10)).

The total loss of consumers is the sum of the areas of rectangle *R* and triangle *D*, or $3,000.

How much better off are firms under perfect competition? Under perfect competition, each firm makes zero economic profit, while a monopolist earns positive economic profit. In Figure 10.5, the monopolist's profit is shown by rectangle *R*: The profit margin is $10 (a price of $18 minus an average cost of $8) and the quantity is 200 doses per hour, for a total profit of $2,000 per hour. The switch to monopoly means that the monopolist gains rectangle *R* at the expense of consumers: They pay an additional $10 per dose, while the monopolist gets a profit of $10 per dose.

Only part of the loss experienced by consumers is recovered by the monopolist, so there is a net loss from switching to monopoly. Consumers lose rectangle *R* and triangle *D*, but the monopolist gains only rectangle *R*. That leaves triangle *D* as the net loss or **deadweight loss from monopoly** The word *deadweight* indicates that this loss is not offset by a gain to anyone. In contrast, Rectangle *R* is lost by consumers but gained by the monopolist. Consumers lose triangle *D* because in a perfectly competitive market, they would receive some consumer surplus from the 201st through 400th doses, which of course a monopolist would not produce. The lesson is that monopoly is inefficient because, compared to a perfectly competitive market, the monopolist produces less output.

Deadweight loss from monopoly: A measure of the inefficiency from monopoly; equal to the difference between the consumer-surplus loss from monopoly pricing and the monopoly profit.

Rent Seeking: Using Resources to Get Monopoly Power

Another source of inefficiency from a government-sanctioned monopoly is that firms use resources to acquire monopoly power. A firm that gets a monopoly on a particular product will earn a large profit, so firms are willing to spend large sums of money in an effort to persuade the government to erect barriers to entry (licenses, franchises, and industrial associations). In Figure 10.5, a firm would be willing to spend up to $2,000 per hour to get a monopoly on the arthritis drug. One way to get monopoly power is to hire lobbyists to persuade legislators and other policymakers to grant monopoly power. This is known as **rent seeking.**

> **Rent seeking:** The process under which a firm spends money to persuade the government to erect barriers to entry and pick the firm as the monopolist.

Rent seeking is inefficient because it uses resources that could be used in other ways. For example, the people employed as lobbyists could instead produce goods and services. In Figure 10.5, if a monopolist spent all its potential profit ($2,000 per hour) on rent-seeking activity, the net loss to society would be areas R and D, not just area D. The classic study of rent seeking found that firms in some industries spent up to 30% of their total revenue to get monopoly power.[2]

At the beginning of this chapter, we saw that Coca-Cola helped a state university to build a new football scoreboard and remodel the student center. Was this an act of generosity? In return for the scoreboard and the remodeled student center, Coca-Cola earned the exclusive right to sell beverages on campus. Just like any monopolist, Coca-Cola will use its monopoly power to charge higher prices for beverages, so the cost of the scoreboard and student center actually comes out of the pockets of students.

TEST Your Understanding

1. Why is a monopolist's marginal revenue less than its price?
2. Complete the statement with a number: At a price of $15 per CD, a firm sells 80 CDs per day. If the slope of the demand curve is $0.10 per CD, marginal revenue is _____.
3. You want to determine the quantity of output produced by a monopolist. What information do you need, and how would you use it?
4. At a price of $18 per CD, the marginal revenue of a CD seller is $12. If the marginal cost of CDs is $9, should the firm increase or decrease the quantity produced? Should it increase or decrease its price?

Patents and Monopoly Power

Are there benefits associated with a government-sanctioned monopoly? As we'll see, a patent or another entry barrier encourages innovation because the innovator knows he or she will earn monopoly profits on a new product for some specific period of time. If the monopoly profits are large enough to offset the substantial research and development costs of a new product, a firm will develop the product and become a monopolist.

Incentives for Innovation

Let's use the arthritis drug to show why a patent encourages innovation. Suppose that Hanna hasn't yet developed the drug and she computes the potential benefits and costs of developing the drug as follows:

- The cost of research and development would be $14 million.
- The estimated annual profit from a monopoly would be $2 million (in today's dollars).

- Hanna's competitors will need three years to develop and produce their own versions of the drug, so if Hanna isn't protected by a patent, her monopoly will last only three years.

Based on these numbers, Hanna won't develop the drug unless she receives a patent that lasts at least seven years. That's the length of time she needs to recover her research and development costs ($2 million per year times seven years is $14 million). If there is no patent and she loses her monopoly in three years, she will earn a profit of $6 million, which is less than her research and development costs. On the other hand, with a 20-year patent she will earn $40 million, which is more than enough to recover her costs.

Trade-Offs from Patents

Is the patent for Hanna's drug beneficial from the social perspective? The patent grants monopoly power to Hanna, and she responds by charging a higher price and producing less than the quantity that would be produced in a perfectly competitive market (200 doses per hour instead of 400). From society's perspective, 400 doses would be better than 200 doses, but we don't have that choice. Hanna won't develop the drug unless a patent protects her from competition for at least seven years. Therefore, society's choice is between 200 doses (the patent and monopoly outcome) and zero doses. Because 200 doses is clearly better than none, the patent is beneficial from society's perspective.

What about a product that would be developed without the protection of a patent? Suppose Marcus could develop a new drug with a research and development project costing $5 million. If Marcus does not have a patent for his new drug, he would earn monopoly profits of $2 million per year for three years, a total of $6 million. Because his research and development costs are low relative to the monopoly profit, a three-year monopoly will generate enough profit to cover his costs, so he will develop the new drug even without a patent. Therefore, if the government issues a 20-year patent, the only effect is to prolong Marcus's monopoly, and that means the patent would be inefficient from society's perspective.

There are trade-offs with patents: The monopoly power causes higher prices for consumers but encourages firms to invest in research and development to develop new drugs.

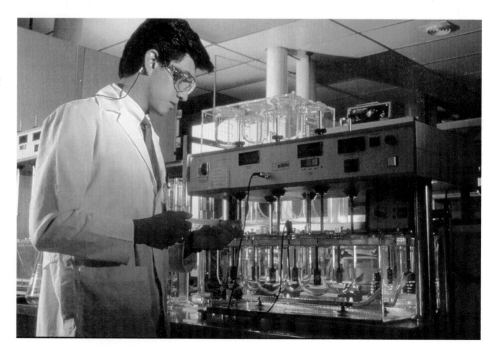

What are the general conclusions about the merits of the patent system? As usual, there are some trade-offs. It is sensible to grant a patent for a product that would otherwise not be developed but not sensible to grant one for a product that would be developed even without a patent. Unfortunately, no one knows in advance whether a particular product would be developed without a patent, so the government can't be selective in granting patents. Therefore, some patents will merely prolong a firm's monopoly power and generate higher prices. There is no consensus among economists on whether the benefits of patents (from the development of new products) exceed the costs (from prolonging monopoly power).

What happens when a patent expires? New firms will enter the market, and the resulting competition for consumers will decrease prices. The transition from monopoly to competition is not always a smooth one, as you'll see in "A Closer Look: Barriers to Generic Drugs."

Do the Benefits Exceed the Costs?

From the efficiency perspective, we cannot make a clear-cut case for or against a government-sanctioned monopoly. As usual, there are both benefits and costs associated with using patents, licenses, franchises, and industrial associations to establish monopolies:

- On the cost side, a monopolist produces less output than a perfectly competitive market, and people also waste resources trying to get and keep monopoly power.

- On the benefit side, a patent or a license increases the payoff from research and development, and firms respond by developing new products.

In some cases—when research and development costs are substantial and other firms could quickly imitate a new product—the benefits will dominate the costs, and public policies that support a monopoly are sensible. In other cases, it would be more efficient to eliminate the artificial barriers to entry.

A CLOSER LOOK | BARRIERS TO GENERIC DRUGS

When the patent for a popular pharmaceutical drug expires, other firms introduce generic versions of the drug. The generics are virtually identical to the original branded drug, but they sell at a much lower price. The producers of branded drugs have an incentive to delay the introduction of generic drugs, and sometimes use illegal means to do so.

In 1999, the Federal Trade Commission (FTC) launched a probe of four large pharmaceutical companies to determine whether they unfairly stifled competition from generic producers. The FTC is investigating allegations that the makers of branded drugs made deals with generic suppliers to keep generics off the market. The alleged practices include cash payments and exclusive licenses for new versions of the branded drug.[3] Eli Lilly and Company announced a deal under which Sepracor, Inc. would have the exclusive right to sell a purified version of Prozac (the antidepressant with annual sales of $2.8 billion). In effect, this deal would extend Lilly's monopoly over the drug for another 15 years. Abbott Laboratories was accused of paying $24 million per year to Ivax Corporation and an undisclosed amount to Novartis AG to delay the launch of their generic versions of Hytrin, Abbott's hypertension drug. Similar allegations of payoffs to generic suppliers have been levied against Hoechst AG in connection with its annual payment of $40 million to Andrx Corporation, which had produced—but not sold—a generic version of Cardizem, Hoechst's heart medication. Another tactic used by the producers of branded drugs is to claim that generics are not as good as the branded drug. Dupont has asserted that generic versions of its Coumadin (a blood thinner) are not equivalent to Coumadin, and may pose risks to patients.

Natural Monopoly

Up to this point, we have considered a monopoly that results from artificial barriers to entry. In some monopolized markets, a second firm could enter a market, but if it did, both firms would lose money. That's why a single firm serves the entire market in what's called a **natural monopoly**. The classic examples of natural monopolies are public utilities (sewerage, water, and electricity generation) and transportation services (railroad freight and mass transit). We'll use the example of electricity generation to explain why a natural monopoly occurs.

Natural monopoly: A market in which the entry of a second firm would make price less than average cost, so a single firm serves the entire market.

Picking an Output Level

Figure 10.6 shows the long-run average cost curve for electricity generation, using real data from Chapter 8. The curve is negatively sloped and steep, reflecting the large economies of scale associated with generating electric power. These economies of scale occur because the indivisible inputs required to generate power (the power plant or hydroelectric dam) are very costly.

What about the long-run marginal cost of generating electricity? As we learned in Chapter 8, if the average cost of production is decreasing (if the average cost curve is negatively sloped), the marginal cost is less than the average cost. In Figure 10.6, the long-run marginal-cost curve of electricity lies below the long-run average-cost curve.

Figure 10.6 shows how to use the cost curves and revenue curves to pick the output level that maximizes profit. If a single firm—a monopolist—provides electricity, the monopolist's demand curve is the same as the market demand curve: To determine how much electricity the monopolist will sell at a particular price, we look at the market demand curve. The demand curve is negatively sloped, and the marginal-revenue curve lies below the demand curve. The marginal principle is satisfied at point n, with 3 billion units of electricity (thousands of kilowatt-hours). The price associated with this quantity is $8.20 per unit of electricity (shown by point m) and the average cost is $6.20 per unit (shown by point c), so the profit per unit of electricity is $2.00. The price exceeds the average cost, so the electric company will earn a profit.

Will a Second Firm Enter?

If there are no artificial barriers to entry, a second firm could enter the electricity market. What would happen if a second firm entered the market? In Figure 10.7 the entry of

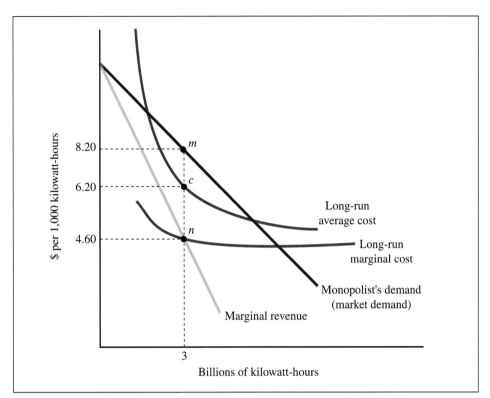

Figure 10.6

Natural Monopolist Uses the Marginal Principle to Pick a Price and Quantity

Because of scale economies in production (indivisible inputs), the long-run average cost curve is negatively sloped. The monopolist chooses point n (where marginal revenue equals marginal cost), supplying 3 billion units at a price of $8.20 per unit (point *m*) and an average cost of $6.20 per unit (point *c*). The profit per unit of electricity is $2.00

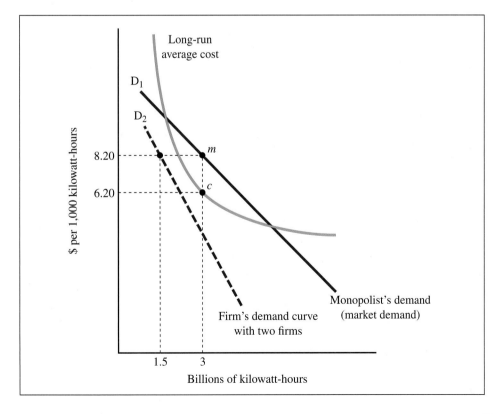

Figure 10.7

Why Won't a Second Firm Enter the Market?

The entry of a second electricity firm would shift the demand curve facing the typical firm to the left. In this example, after entry, the firm's demand curve lies entirely below the long-run average cost curve. No matter what price the typical firm charges, it will lose money. Therefore, a second firm will not enter the market.

a second firm would shift the demand curve facing the first firm—the former monopolist—to the left, from D_1 to D_2: At each price, the first firm will sell a smaller quantity of electricity because it now shares the market with another firm. For example, at a price of $8.20, the total quantity of electricity sold is 3 billion units, or 1.5 billion units for each firm. In general, the larger the number of firms, the lower the demand curve facing the typical firm. D_2 is the demand curve for the typical firm in a two-firm market, so it is also the demand curve for the potential entrant.

Will a second firm enter the electricity market? The demand curve of the typical firm in a two-firm market lies entirely below the long-run average-cost curve, so there is no quantity at which the price exceeds the average cost of production. No matter what price the typical firm charges, it will lose money. The firm's demand curve lies below the average cost curve because the average cost curve is steep, reflecting the large economies of scale in generating electricity. A second firm—with half the market—would have a very high average cost and wouldn't be able to charge a price high enough to cover its high average cost. Therefore, the second firm will not enter the market, so there will be a single firm, a natural monopoly. For an example of a potential new natural monopoly, read "A Closer Look: Will Satellite Radio Be a Natural Monopoly?"

A CLOSER LOOK — WILL SATELLITE RADIO BE A NATURAL MONOPOLY?

The biggest development in radio since the emergence of the FM band is satellite radio. Two firms—Sirius Satellite Radio and XM Satellite Radio—will provide dozens of national radio channels for people traveling in automobiles.[4] The quality of the reception will be on par with compact disks, and be the same throughout the continental United States. Sirius will initially provide 17 rock and pop channels, five country/western channels, six R&B channels, five Latin channels, and three classical channels. Its information channels will include the Bloomberg News Radio, CNBC, C-SPAN, BBC WorldService, NPR Talk, and Public Radio International.

What's the cost of listening to satellite radio? To listen, you must first buy a satellite receiver for about $200, and then pay about $10 per month for the service. The advantage of satellite radio is that most stations will be free of those annoying commercials that clutter most broadcast radio stations. The music channels on the Sirius system will be free of commercials, while the information channels will have just a few minutes of commercials per hour. About half the XM channels will be commercial free, and the others will have no more than 6 minutes of commercials per hour. In contrast, the typical broadcast radio station has about 20 minutes of commercials per hour.

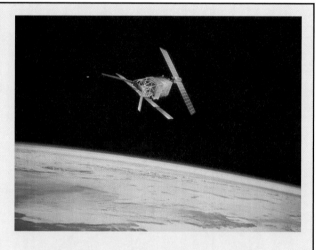

How many satellite radio systems can the market support? For each system, the cost of building and launching satellites is about $1.5 billion. Although the fixed costs are large, the potential market is large as well, with about 200 million motor vehicles on the road as potential subscribers. The CEO of Sirius suggests that his company will break even—cover its fixed and operating costs—with just 2 million subscribers, only 1% of the market. The CEO of XM estimates a larger break-even level of 4 million subscribers.

Price Controls for a Natural Monopoly

When a monopoly is inevitable—the case of natural monopoly—the government often sets a maximum price for the monopolist. There are many examples of natural monopolies that are subject to maximum prices. Local governments regulate utilities and firms that provide water, electricity, and local telephone service. State governments use public utility commissions (PUCs) to regulate the electric-power industry.

Let's use the electricity market to explain the effects of government regulation of a natural monopoly. Suppose the government sets a maximum price for electricity and forces the electric company to serve all the consumers who are willing to pay the maximum price. In other words, the government—not the firm—picks a point on the market demand curve. Under an **average-cost pricing policy**, the government picks the price at which the market demand curve intersects the monopolist's long-run average cost curve. In Figure10.8, the original average cost curve intersects the demand curve at point *i*, with a price of $5.20 per unit of electricity. Although consumers would prefer a lower price, the electric company would lose money at any price less than $5.20, so lower prices are not feasible.

How will this regulatory policy affect the monopolist's production costs? Under average-cost pricing, a change in the monopolist's production cost will not affect its profit because the government will adjust the regulated price to keep the price equal to the average cost. The government will increase the regulated price when the monopolist's cost increases, and decrease the price when its cost decreases. Because there is no reward for cutting its costs and no penalty for higher costs, the monopolist has little incentive to control its cost, so its costs will increase, pulling up the regulated price.

Average-cost pricing policy: A regulatory policy under which the government picks the point on the demand curve at which price equals average cost.

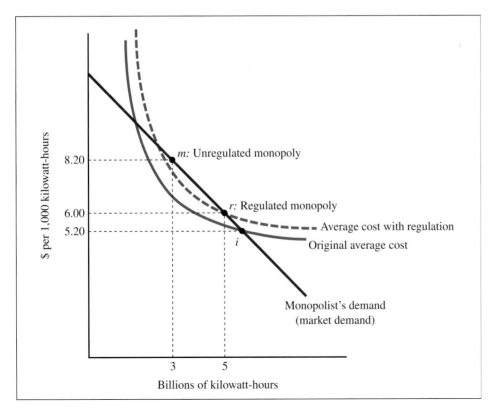

Figure 10.8
Regulation Using Average-Cost Pricing
Under an average-cost pricing policy, the government chooses the price at which the demand curve intersects the average cost curve. Regulation shifts the long-run average cost curve upward, so the government picks point *r*, with a price of $6.00 per unit.

The average-cost policy causes the market to move along the market demand curve in two steps:

- **Downward slide.** Starting from the price and quantity resulting from an unregulated monopoly (point *m*), we slide down the demand curve to point *i* (*i* stands for impossible dream), the point that would occur if regulation did not increase the monopolist's cost.
- **Upward climb.** As the monopolist's cost increases because of regulation, the regulator increases the price to cover the extra costs, so we climb part way back up the market demand curve, from point *i* to point *r*.

In this example the net effect of this regulatory policy is a lower price of electricity ($6.00 instead of $8.20) and a larger quantity (5 billion units instead of 3 billion units). In other words, the regulatory policy moves the market downward along the market demand curve, from point *m* to point *r*.

Economic Detective

A Decrease in Demand Decreases the Price?

When the population of Powerland decreased, the demand for all sorts of goods—including housing, clothing, and electricity—decreased as well. The decrease in the demand for housing decreased the price of housing, consistent with simple supply and demand analysis. In contrast, the price of electricity increased, a result that seems to defy the laws of supply and demand. What explains the puzzling increase in the price of electricity?

The key to solving this mystery is the fact that electricity is a regulated natural monopoly, with prices set by government regulators. The government of Powerland uses an average-cost pricing policy to set the price of electricity: the regulated price equals the average cost of production. Any decrease in the quantity of electricity produced will lead to a higher average cost as the producer moves upward along the negatively sloped average cost curve. Under average-cost pricing, the higher the average cost, the higher the regulated price. In graphical terms, the demand curve for electricity shifted to the left, so it intersected the negatively sloped average cost curve at a smaller quantity of electricity and a higher average cost. The regulated price is shown by the intersection of the demand curve and the average cost curve, so a leftward shift in demand increases the regulated price.

TEST Your Understanding

9. Complete the statement: A natural monopolist picks the quantity of output at which _____ equals _____.

10. Explain the effects of the entry of a second firm on the demand curve facing the original monopolist.

11. Complete the statement with *above* or *below*: A natural monopoly occurs when the long-run cost curve lies entirely _____ the demand curve of the typical firm in a two-firm market.

Using the TOOLS

APPLICATIONS
1. Textbook Pricing: Publishers Versus Authors
Consider the problem of setting a price for an economics textbook. The marginal cost of production is constant at $20 per book. The publisher knows from experience that the

slope of the demand curve is $0.20 per textbook: Starting with a price of $48, a price cut of $0.20 will increase the quantity demanded by 1 textbook. For example, here are some combinations of price and quantity:

Price per textbook	$44	$ 40	$ 36	$ 32	$ 30
Quantity of textbooks	80	100	120	140	150

a. What price will the publisher choose?

b. Suppose that the author receives a royalty payment equal to 10% of the total sales revenue from the book. If the author could choose a price, what would it be?

c. Why do the publisher and the author disagree about the price for the book?

d. Design an alternative author-compensation scheme under which the author and the publisher would choose the same price.

2. Payoff for Casino Approval

In 1996, developers interested in building an American Indian casino in Creswell, Oregon, placed a curious announcement in the local newspaper. If local voters approved the casino, the developers promised to give citizens $2 million per year. Given an adult population of about 1,600, each adult in Creswell would receive a cash payment of $1,250 per year.

a. Why did the developers propose this deal? Why aren't similar deals proposed for new clothing stores, music stores, or auto-repair shops?

b. If the deal goes through and you moved to Creswell, would you expect to get $1,250 per year?

3. Environmental Costs for Regulated Monopoly

The Bonneville Power Administration (BPA) is a regulated monopoly that uses dozens of hydroelectric dams to generate electricity. The dams block the path of migrating fish and thus contribute to the decline of several species of fish. Suppose that BPA spends $100 million to make its hydroelectric dams less hazardous for migrating fish. Who will bear the cost of this program?

Summary

In this chapter, we've seen some of the subtleties of monopolies and their pricing policies. Compared to a perfectly competitive market, a monopoly means a higher price, a smaller quantity, and resources wasted in the process of seeking monopoly power. On the positive side, some of the products we use today might never have been invented without the patent system and the monopoly power it grants. Here are the main points of the chapter:

1. Compared to a perfectly competitive market, a market served by a monopolist will have a higher price and a smaller quantity of output.

2. A switch from perfect competition to monopoly decreases consumer surplus by more than it

increases profits, so there is a net loss or a deadweight loss to society.

3. Some firms spend money and use resources to acquire monopoly power, a process known as rent-seeking.

4. Patents protect innovators from competition, leading to higher prices for new products but a greater incentive to develop new products.

5. A natural monopoly occurs when there are large-scale economies in production, so the market can support only one firm.

6. Under an average-cost pricing policy, the regulated price for a natural monopoly is equal to the average cost of production.

Key Terms

average-cost pricing policy, 229
deadweight less from monopoly, 222
franchise or licensing scheme, 214

monopoly, 214
natural monopoly, 226

patent, 214
rent seeking, 223

Problems and Discussion Questions

1. Consider a restaurant that charges $10 for all you can eat and has 30 customers at this price. The slope of the demand curve is $0.10 per meal, and the marginal cost of providing a meal is $3. What price will satisfy the marginal principle and maximize the restaurant's profit?

2. The National Park Service grants a single firm the right to sell food and other goods in Yosemite National Park. Discuss the trade-offs associated with this policy.

3. Since 1963, many state governments that outlaw commercial lotteries have introduced state lotteries to raise revenue for state and local governments. In 1994, the net revenue from state lotteries was about $10 billion. Would you expect the state lotteries to have higher or lower paybacks (total prize money divided by the total amount of money collected) than commercial games of chance such as horse racing and slot machines? Explain.

4. Consider the Slappers, a hockey team that plays in an arena with 8,000 seats. The only cost associated with staging a hockey game is a fixed cost of $6,000: The team incurs this cost regardless of how many people attend a game. The demand curve for hockey tickets has a slope of $0.001 per ticket ($1 divided by 1,000 tickets): Each $1 increase in price decreases the number of tickets sold by 1,000. For example, here are some combinations of price and quantity:

Price per ticket	$4	$5	$6	$7
Quantity of tickets	8,000	7,000	6,000	5,000

The owner's objective is to maximize the profit per hockey game (total revenue minus the $6,000 fixed cost).

a. What price will maximize profit?

b. If the owner picks the price that maximizes profit, how many seats in the arena will be empty?

c. Is it rational to leave some seats empty?

5. The government allows professional sports associations (collections of teams) to restrict the number of teams. How do these barriers to entry affect the price of tickets to professional sporting events and the number of tickets sold? If we eliminated these barriers to entry, what would happen to ticket prices and total attendance at sporting events?

6. Consider a natural monopolist. Here are some data on prices and quantities:

Price per unit	$20	$19	$18	$17	$16
Quantity (units)	100	120	140	160	180
Marginal revenue	—	—	—	—	—

a. Complete the table: For each quantity, use the formula for marginal revenue to compute the marginal revenue.

b. Draw the monopolist's demand curve and the monopolist's marginal revenue curve.

c. Suppose that the monopolist's long-run marginal cost is $9. How much output should the monopolist produce?

7. Consider a regulated natural monopoly with an initial price (equal to average cost) of $3 per unit. Suppose the demand for the monopolist's product decreases. What will happen to the price? How does this differ from the effects of a decrease in demand for a product produced in a perfectly competitive market?

8. Consider a monopolist who owns a natural spring that produces water that, according to nearby residents, has a unique taste and healing properties. The monopolist has a fixed cost of installing plumbing to tap the water but no marginal cost. The demand curve for the spring water is linear. Depict graphically the monopolist's choice of a price and quantity. At the profit-maximizing quantity, what is the price elasticity of demand? If the spring were owned by the government, what price would it charge?

9. In the board game "Monopoly," when a player gets the 3rd deed for a group of properties (for example, the 3rd orange property: St. James, New York, and Tennessee Avenues), he or she doubles the rent charged on each property in the group. Similarly, a player who has a single railroad charges a rent of $25, while a player who has all 4 railroads charges a rent of $200 for each railroad. Are these rules consistent with the analysis of monopoly in this chapter?

10. Adam Smith predicted that a monopolist would charge "the highest price which can be got." Do you agree?

11. Suppose the drug company Bristol-Meyers-Squibb announces that it will increase the price of Taxol, the cancer-fighting drug, by 10%. According to a consumer advocate, "The price hike will increase Bristol's total revenue from Taxol by 10%." Do you agree? What is the advocate assuming about the price elasticity of demand for Taxol? Is this assumption realistic?

12. Web Exercise. How much does it cost to get a patent on an invention? To find out, visit the Web site of the U.S. Patent and Trademark Office [*http://www.uspto.gov*]. A patent on an invention is called a utility patent. How much does it cost to file for a patent? How much do you pay when it is issued? How much do you pay to maintain your patent?

13. Web Exercise. Visit the Web site of the U.S. Postal Service, one of the world's largest government-sanctioned monopolies [*http://www.usps.gov/*]. Perform a site search to find the annual performance plan. List some of the facts and some of the postal service's goals and objectives.

Take It to the Net

We invite you to visit the O'Sullivan/Sheffrin page on the Prentice Hall Web site at: **http://www.prenhall.com/osullivan/** for additional World Wide Web exercises for this chapter.

Model Answers to Questions

Chapter-Opening Questions

1. The bad news is that a monopolist charges a higher price. The good news is that monopoly profits encourage innovation.

2. In response to competition from generic equivalents, the producer of the branded drug usually decreases its price, but the price of the branded drug is still higher than the price of generic drugs.

3. An unregulated monopolist will charge a high price and earns a large profit, so the government often sets a maximum price.

4. The substantial fixed cost means that the market will be able to support only a few firms.

Test Your Understanding

1. To sell one more unit, the monopolist must cut the price. The marginal revenue equals the price minus the revenue lost from selling goods at a lower price to the original customers.

2. MR = $15 – (80 units times $0.10 per unit) = $7.

3. You need the marginal revenue curve and the marginal cost curve. The monopolist will pick the quantity at which the two curves intersect.

4. Marginal revenue exceeds marginal cost, so the firm should increase the quantity produced. To increase the quantity, the firm must cut its price.

5. The profit per space is $5 ($35 – $30), so the daily profit is $2,500 ($5 per space times 500 spaces). You are willing to pay up to $2,500 per day for the monopoly.

6. If Hanna's monopoly profit lasts five years, she'll earn a total of $10 million, which is still less than the cost of the research and development project ($14 million). She won't develop the drug.

7. It will be sensible to develop the product even without a patent if the inventor maintains his monopoly position long enough. Suppose it takes other firms five years to develop an imitation product and the original inventor earns a profit of $30 million per year. In this case, the monopoly profit will more than cover the costs of research and development.

8. The absence of a patent will discourage innovation in gambling devices. Perhaps this is an indirect way of discouraging gambling.

9. Marginal revenue, marginal cost.

10. The firm's demand curve shifts to the left: At each price, the firm sells a smaller quantity.

11. Below.

Using the Tools

1. Textbook Pricing: Publishers Versus Authors

   a. To maximize profit, the publisher picks the quantity at which marginal revenue equals marginal cost. Using the marginal revenue formula, we can compute the marginal revenue at each price and quantity. Here are the numbers for marginal revenue:

Price	$44	$40	$36	$32	$30
Quantity	80	100	120	140	150
MR	$28	$20	$12	4	0

   If the marginal cost is $20, the publisher will pick a price of $40 and a quantity of 100 books.

   b. The author's objective is to maximize total revenue (price times quantity), not profit (total revenue minus total cost). From the author's perspective, the marginal cost of selling another textbook is zero, so to satisfy the marginal principle, the author will choose the price at which marginal revenue is zero. In this case, the author would choose a price of $30.

   c. They disagree because the authors ignore production costs.

   d. If the author received a share of profits instead of a share of revenue, he or she would choose the same price as the publisher.

2. Payoff for Casino Approval

   a. The proposal to pay residents a total of $2 million per year is an example of rent seeking. The developers anticipate a profit of at least $2 million per year from their casino monopoly and are willing to pay at least this amount to get the monopoly. There are no such offers of cash for stores and repair shops because the city doesn't regulate entry into these other activities, so there are no monopoly profits and rent seeking.

   b. The prospect for a big annual cash payment will attract people to Creswell, so we would expect the population to grow and the per-capita payment to shrink.

3. Environmental Costs for a Regulated Monopoly. The environmental costs will increase the monopolist's costs, and the higher costs will result in a higher regulated price. In graphical terms, the long-run average-cost curve will shift upward, and the demand curve will intersect the cost curve at a higher price. Consumers will bear the costs of environmental protection.

Notes

1. Jeannie Donnelly, "OSU Beverages Will Be Provided Exclusively by Coca-Cola," *The Daily Barometer,* May 27, 1994, p. 1.

2. Richard A. Posner, "The Social Costs of Monopoly and Regulation," *Journal of Political Economy,* vol. 83, 1975, pp. 807–827.

3. Ralph T. King, Jr., "FTC Widens Probe into Generic-Drug Barriers," *Wall Street Journal,* March 9, 1999, p. B8.

4. Tim Jones, "Satellite Radio Sends Signal," *Chicago Tribune,* January 18, 2001; Florida Today Space Online, September 18, 2000 (*http://www.flatoday.com/space/explore/stories/2000b/*); Richard McCaffery, "TMF Interview with XM Satellite Radio President and Chief Executive Officer Hugh Panero," The Motley Fool (*http://www.fool.com*); Hilary Chipba, "Sirius Satellite Radio Surges on Daimler Deal, Upcoming Deals and More," Stockhouse.com (*http://www.investorlinks.com*).

11

Entry and Monopolistic Competition

Tweeter just inherited a lot of money, enough to start her own car-stereo business. Woofer owns the only car-stereo store in town and sells stereos at a price of $230 with an average cost of $200 per stereo, for a profit of $30 per stereo. Should Tweeter use her inheritance to open her own car-stereo store? If she does, will she make a profit of $30 per stereo, just like Woofer?

Entrepreneur: A person who has an idea for a business and coordinates the production and sale of goods and services, taking risks in the process.

weeter wants to become a successful entrepreneur. An **entrepreneur** comes up with an idea for a business and puts the idea into practice by acquiring a production facility (a factory, store, or office building), buying raw materials, and hiring workers. An entrepreneur takes risks, committing time and money to a business without any assurance that it will be profitable.

Like entrepreneurs around the world, Tweeter has a difficult decision to make. Before she decides whether or not to enter the car-stereo market, she must predict how much she would be able to charge for her car stereos and how much it would cost her to supply them. Before she enters the market, there is a $30 gap between price and average cost, but the gap is likely to shrink when she enters the market. The price will fall as Woofer and Tweeter compete for customers. In addition, Tweeter may have a higher average cost than Woofer. If the price drops below her average cost, Tweeter would lose money, so she would be better off using her inheritance some other way.

In this chapter, we explore how entrepreneurs make decisions about entering a market. We also explain the effects of market entry on consumers and other firms in the market. Here are some practical questions that we answer:

1. If the entry of a firm into a market would increase the average production cost of firms already in the market, should the government prevent the firm from entering?
2. How did the deregulation of trucking services affect the prices and the profits of trucking firms?
3. What happened when Network Solutions, Inc. lost its government-sanctioned monopoly in the market for registering Internet addresses?
4. De Beers, the dominant firm in the world diamond market, is thinking about etching its logo and a serial number on each of its gems. Why?
5. How did the entry of Wal-Mart affect retail prices in Germany?

The analysis in this chapter is based on two assumptions. First, we assume there are no barriers to entry: There are no patents or government licensing programs that limit the number of firms. Second, we assume that firms do not act strategically: Each firm acts on its own, taking the actions of other firms as given. This means that firms already in the market do not conspire to fix prices and do not try to prevent other firms from entering the market.

The Effects of Market Entry

Consider a market served by a single profitable firm, a monopolist. We saw in Chapter 10 that if there are large economies of scale in production, the entry of a second firm would drive the market price below average cost, meaning that each firm would lose money, with its total cost exceeding its total revenue. Because no firm will enter a market where it will lose money, the market will remain a monopoly. In this chapter, we will see that if there are not large economies of scale, additional firms will enter the market, driving down prices and profit.

Output and Entry Decisions

As we saw earlier in the book, a firm in any market can use the marginal principle to decide how much output to produce.

Marginal **PRINCIPLE**

> **Increase the level of an activity if its marginal benefit exceeds its marginal cost, but reduce the level of the activity if the marginal cost exceeds the marginal benefit. If possible, pick the level of the activity at which the marginal benefit equals the marginal cost.**

Consider a firm whose activity is producing toothbrushes. The marginal benefit of producing toothbrushes is the marginal revenue from selling one more brush. In Figure 11.1, if a single firm produces toothbrushes, the demand curve facing the firm is the market demand curve. The marginal cost of producing toothbrushes is simply the marginal cost of production.

A firm that is considering entering the toothbrush market must make a long-run decision about what size and type of production facility to build. Therefore, the long-run cost curves—which show production costs for a firm that hasn't committed to a particular production facility—are relevant for the firm's entry decision. In Figure 11.1 the long-run average cost curve is L-shaped, which, as we saw in Chapter 8, is consistent with empirical studies of production costs. If the average cost of production is decreasing (if the average cost curve is negatively sloped), the marginal cost is less than the average cost. In Figure 11.1, the marginal-cost curve lies below the average-cost curve.

As we saw in Chapter 10, the monopolist will maximize profit by picking the quantity at which marginal revenue equals marginal cost. In Figure 11.1, this happens at point n, with a quantity of 300 toothbrushes. From the market demand curve, the price associated with this quantity is $2.00. Given an average cost of $0.90 per toothbrush, the monopolist's profit per unit is $1.10 (equal to $2.00 minus $0.90), so the total profit (shown by the shaded area) is $330. Given the large profits in the toothbrush market, will a second firm enter the market?

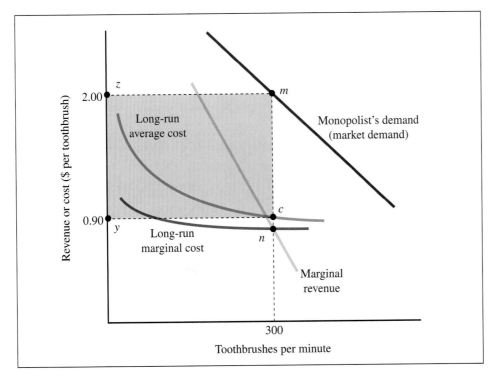

Figure 11.1
Short-Run Equilibrium in Monopolistic Competition: A Single Toothbrush Producer

The single toothbrush producer (a monopolist) picks point n (where marginal revenue equals marginal cost), supplying 300 toothbrushes per minute at a price of $2.00 (point m) and an average cost of $0.90 (point c). The profit per brush is $1.10.

When a second firm enters a market, the demand curve facing the original firm shifts to the left. At any particular price, some consumers will patronize the new firm, so there will be fewer consumers who are willing to purchase toothbrushes from the first firm. In other words, the first firm will sell fewer brushes at each price. In Figure 11.2, the demand curve facing the first firm—the original monopolist—shifts to the left, and profit decreases for three reasons:

1. **The market price drops.** The marginal principle is satisfied at point *x*, so the first firm produces 200 toothbrushes at a price of $1.85 (point *e*). The competition between the two firms causes the price to drop, from $2.00 to $1.85.

2. **The quantity produced by the first firm decreases.** The first firm produces only 200 toothbrushes, down from 300 produced as a monopolist.

3. **The first firm's average cost of production increases.** The decrease in the quantity produced causes the firm to move upward along its negatively sloped average-cost curve to a higher average cost (from $0.90 to $1.00).

The combination of a lower price, a higher average cost, and a smaller quantity means that the first firm earns less profit. The profit rectangle (shown by points *z, m, c,* and *y* in Figure 11.1) shrinks because the top of the rectangle (determined by the price) sinks, the bottom of the rectangle (determined by the average cost) rises, and the right side of the rectangle (determined by the quantity) moves to the left. In our example, the profit drops from $330 to $170.

What about the second firm? If we assume that the second firm has access to the same production technology as the first firm and pays the same prices for its inputs, the cost curves for the second firm will be identical to the cost curves for the first firm. If the second firm produces the same product as the first firm, the demand curve facing the second firm will be identical to the demand curve facing the first firm. As a result, we can use Figure 11.2 to represent both firms. Each firm produces 200 toothbrushes at an average cost of $1.00 per toothbrush and sells them at a price of $1.85.

Figure 11.2

Entry Decreases Price and Increases Average Cost

The entry of a second toothbrush producer shifts the demand curve for the original firm to the left: A smaller quantity is sold at each price. The marginal principle is satisfied at point *x*, so the firm produces a smaller quantity (200 instead of 300 toothbrushes) at a higher average cost ($1.00 instead of $0.90 per toothbrush) and sells at a lower price ($1.85 instead of $2.00).

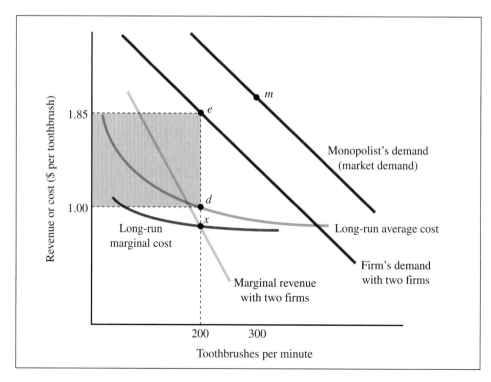

Application: Woofer and Tweeter

For an example of the effects of entry on price, cost, and profit, recall Tweeter's entry decision described at the beginning of the chapter. Woofer the monopolist initially sells 10 stereos per day at a price of $230 and an average cost of $200 per stereo. Suppose that if Tweeter enters the market, the price will drop to $225 and her average cost will be $205, so she could earn a profit of $20 per stereo. Although Tweeter's entry squeezes profit from both sides—decreasing the market price and increasing the average cost—there is still some profit to be made, so she will enter the market. Of course, other firms may also enter the market, so Tweeter should not count on making a $20 profit per stereo for very long.

Entry in the Real World

Empirical studies of real markets provide overwhelming evidence that entry decreases market prices and firms' profit.[1] In one study of the retail pricing of tires, a market with only two tire stores had a price of $55 per tire, compared to a price of $53 in a market with three stores, $51 with four stores, and $50 with five stores.[2] In other words, the larger the number of stores, the lower the price of tires.

A recent change in public policy shows what happens when the government eliminates artificial barriers to entry. The Motor Carrier Act of 1980 eliminated the government's entry restrictions on the trucking industry, most of which had been in place since the 1930s. New firms entered the trucking market, and freight prices dropped by about 22%.[3] The market value of a firm's trucking license reflects the profit the firm can earn in the market. As a result of increased competition and lower prices from deregulation, the average value of a trucking license dropped from $579,000 in 1977 to less than $15,000 in 1982.[4]

European nations are also deregulating their markets. Until recently, most nations in Western Europe had national monopolies in telecommunication equipment and services. That changed in 1988, when the European Union deregulated telecommunication markets, starting with the market for data communication in 1990, followed by the market for voice communication in 1998. European and U.S. companies are preparing to enter the deregulated markets, with many of the companies forming transatlantic alliances. For example, Deutsche Telekom and France Telecom have an alliance with Sprint (the third largest U.S. long-distance carrier), while MCI and AT&T each have their own alliances with other European companies. The increase in competition is expected to improve service and decrease prices, perhaps cutting the cost of international calls by as much as 50%.[5]

There have also been changes in the retail industry in Europe. The American retail giant Wal-Mart entered the German grocery market in 1997, and by 2001 had 95 stores and over 18,000 workers, placing it as one of the top three food retailers in Germany. To find out the effects of Wal-Mart's entry on competition and prices, read "A Closer Look: Wal-Mart and Retail Prices in Germany."

For another example of the effects of entry, consider the market for registration of Web addresses. In 1999, Network Solutions Inc. had a government-sanctioned monopoly in the registration of domain names, and its price for a standard 2-year registration was $140. After the U.S. Commerce Department eliminated the barriers to entering the market, several firms entered, resulting in lower prices and more options for consumers.[6] Two new competitors, Register.com and Tucows.com, cut prices to between $10 and $15 per year. In addition, the new firms offered registration periods of up to 10 years (compared to 2 years under the monopoly) and permitted up to 63 characters in each domain name (compared to a limit of 26 characters under the monopoly). Network Solutions, the original monopolist, quickly matched its competitors' lower prices and expanded service options.

WAL-MART AND RETAIL PRICES IN GERMANY

The entry of Wal-Mart into the German retail market triggered widespread price cutting.[7] When Wal-Mart announced price cuts of 20% in early 2000, other large grocery chains responded in kind. Rewe closed its stores for a week in February to reorganize its operation around "permanent bargain prices." In June, Aldi announced selective price cuts of 25%.

The price competition among the large food retailers ran afoul of German law concerning retail pricing. In 2001, German authorities concluded that Wal-Mart and its two competitors sold several products (milk, sugar, butter, flour, rice, and cooking oil) for below their cost, which is illegal under German law. The retailers, faced with fines of 1 million marks ($445,000) per product, agreed to raise their prices. Wal-Mart announced that it would "orient" its pricing policies to comply with German law, but vowed to offer products "at the lowest possible prices." The German Retail Trade Association, which represents 475,000 businesses with over 3 million workers, praised the decision as "a hopeful signal of the end of ruinous, cutthroat competition."

TEST Your Understanding

1. Complete the statement: A firm picks the quantity of output at which _____ equals _____.

2. Draw a graph showing the effect of the entry of a second firm on the demand curve facing the original firm (a monopolist).

3. Complete the statement with "increases" or "decreases": The entry of an additional firm _____ the profit per unit of output because entry _____ the price and _____ the average cost of production.

4. Suppose that when Tweeter enters the car-stereo market, the price drops by $20 and the average cost increases by $15. Is it sensible to enter the market?

Monopolistic Competition

Now that we know the effects of entry into a monopolized market, let's think about how many firms will actually enter a particular market. The extreme case of market entry is monopolistic competition, a situation in which dozens of firms enter the market. Here are the characteristics of a market that is subject to **monopolistic competition**.

Monopolistic competition: A market served by dozens of firms selling slightly different products.

1. **Many firms.** Because there are relatively small economies of scale, small firms can produce at about the same average cost as large firms. Therefore, even a small firm can cover its costs, and the market can support many firms.

Product differentiation: A strategy of distinguishing one product from other similar products.

2. **Differentiated product.** The firms sell slightly different products. **Product differentiation** may be in the form of differences in physical characteristics, location, services, and the aura or image associated with the product.

3. **No artificial barriers to entry.** There are no patents or government regulations preventing firms from entering the market.

What's the logic behind the label *monopolistic competition*? Although it may seem like an oxymoron, there are good reasons for the label. Each firm differentiates its product from the products of other firms in such a way that each firm is the sole seller of a narrowly defined good. For example, each firm in the toothbrush market uses a unique design for its toothbrushes, so each is a monopolist for its unique toothbrush. That's the reason for the word *monopolistic* in monopolistic competition. The *competition* in the label results from the keen competition among firms for customers to buy products that are close but not perfect substitutes. When one firm increases its price, many of its consumers will switch to the products of other firms because they are close substitutes. In other words, the demand for the product of a monopolistically competitive firm is very price elastic: An increase in price decreases the quantity demanded by a relatively large amount because consumers can easily switch to another firm selling a similar product.

Let's take a closer look at the notion of product differentiation, one of the key features of monopolistic competition. Firms in such a market differentiate their products in several ways:

- **Physical characteristics.** A firm can distinguish its products from the products of other firms by offering a different size, color, shape, texture, or taste. For example, toothpastes differ in flavor, color, texture, whitening capability, and alleged ability to fight decay and plaque. Some other examples of goods that are differentiated by their physical characteristics are athletic shoes, dress shirts, appliances, and pens.

- **Location.** Some products are differentiated by where they are sold. Some examples are gas stations, music stores, grocery stores, movie theaters, and ice-cream parlors. In each case, firms sell the same product at different locations.

- **Services.** Some products are distinguished by the services that come with them. For example, some stores provide informative and helpful salespeople, while others require consumers to make decisions on their own. Other examples of services that can differentiate products are home delivery (for appliances and pizza) and free technical assistance (for computer hardware and software).

- **Aura or image.** Some firms use advertising to make their products stand out from a group of nearly identical products. In this case, product differentiation is a matter of perception rather than reality. Some examples are aspirin, designer jeans, and motor oil.

An unusual product-differentiation strategy is being considered by De Beers, the dominant firm in the world diamond market.[8] The demand for diamonds has decreased in recent years, in large part because of the Asian economic crisis. For example, Japan's demand for diamonds, which had tripled in the preceding 15 years, decreased by 20% during 1998. At the same time, new suppliers have entered the market and have not cooperated with De Beers in keeping prices high. The result is lower profits for De Beers and concern that diamonds may eventually become another standardized commodity in the global market, with much lower prices and profits. To differentiate its diamonds, De Beers is experimenting with etching, in script that is invisible to the naked eye, its logo and a serial number on each of its gems. Will customers be willing to pay a premium for a gem from the biggest name in diamonds? We'll see.

Short-Run and Long-Run Equilibrium

We'll use the toothbrush example to illustrate the features of monopolistic competition. The producers of toothbrushes differentiate their products with respect to color, bristle design, handle size and shape, and durability. We saw earlier that after a second firm enters the toothbrush market, both firms still make a profit. Will a third firm enter this lucrative market? The entry of a third firm will shift the demand curve facing each firm farther to the left, decreasing the market price, decreasing the quantity produced per firm, and increasing the average cost per toothbrush. If after the third firm enters the market, profit would still be positive for all three firms, then the third firm will enter the market. This entry process will continue until the entry of one more firm would make the profit of each firm negative.

Because there are no barriers to entering the toothbrush market, firms will continue to enter the market until each firm makes zero economic profit. Figure 11.3 shows the long-run equilibrium from the perspective of the typical firm in a monopolistically competitive market. As more firms enter the market, the market share of the typical firm decreases, so its demand curve shifts to the left. The typical firm satisfies the marginal principle at point *g* and sells 55 brushes per minute at a price of $1.35 (point *h*) and an average cost of $1.35. The price equals the typical firm's average cost, so the typical firm makes zero economic profit. Each firm's revenue is high enough to cover all its costs—including the opportunity cost of all its inputs—but not enough to cause additional firms to enter the market. In other words, each firm makes just enough money to stay in business.

Trade-Offs with Monopolistic Competition

There are some trade-offs associated with monopolistic competition and product differentiation. Let's compare the monopoly outcome (shown in Figure 11.1) with the long-run equilibrium under monopolistic competition (Figure 11.3). There are many more toothbrush producers with monopolistic competition, and that brings good news and bad news:

- **Good news: lower price.** Competition among firms decreases the price of toothbrushes from $2.00 to $1.35.

- **Good news: greater variety.** The large number of toothbrush firms—each selling a toothbrush with a unique design—means more choice for consumers.

Figure 11.3

Long-Run Equilibrium with Monopolistic Competition: Toothbrushes

In a monopolistically competitive market, new firms will continue to enter the market until economic profit is zero. The typical firm picks the quantity at which its marginal revenue equals its marginal cost (point *g*). Economic profit is zero because the price equals the average cost (shown by point *h*).

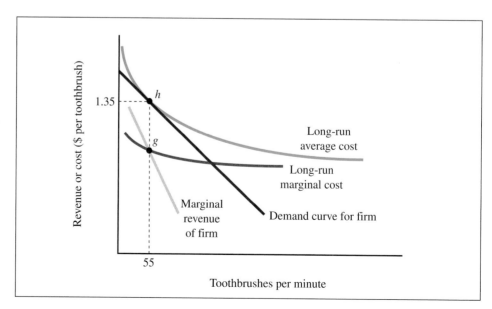

- **Bad news: higher average cost.** Each of the firms in the monopolistically competitive market produces less output than the monopolist and has a higher average cost of production: $1.35 per toothbrush, compared to $0.90 for the monopolist.

Given these trade-offs, it's impossible to make a clear-cut case for or against monopolistic competition. Although a market with many brands of toothbrushes has lower prices and more variety, it also has a higher average cost of production because more factories, machinery, and equipment may be used to produce toothbrushes. Looking at the trade-offs from the other perspective, a nation that limited the number of toothbrush firms to one would have a lower average cost of producing toothbrushes, but prices would be higher and consumers would have fewer toothbrush options.

For another example of the trade-offs from monopolistic competition, consider restaurant meals. The typical large city has dozens of Italian restaurants, each of which has a slightly different menu and prepares its food in slightly different ways. In this example, the benefit of product differentiation is variety: Consumers can pick from restaurants offering a wide variety of menus and preparation techniques. Although a city with a single Italian restaurant would have a lower average cost of preparing Italian meals—a result of scale economies in producing meals—there would be less variety for restaurant patrons.

The same logic applies to articles of clothing such as jeans and shirts, which are differentiated according to their fit, color, design, and durability and the aura associated with the label. There is a trade-off between production cost and variety: If we all wore uniforms, the average cost of producing clothing would be lower, but most people prefer to wear a variety of clothes.

Spatial Differentiation and Competition

Some products are differentiated by where they are sold. Your city probably has several music stores, each of which sells a particular CD at about the same price. Everything else being equal, you are likely to purchase CDs from the most convenient store, but if a store across town offers lower prices, you might purchase your CDs there instead. In other words, each music store has a monopoly in its own neighborhood but competes with music stores in the rest of the city.

Figure 11.4 shows the long-run equilibrium in the market for CDs. Because there are no barriers to entering the market, new music stores will enter the market until each music store makes zero economic profit. The typical music store satisfies the marginal principle at point *g*, selling 70 CDs per hour at a price of $14 per CD (point *h*) and an average cost of $14 per CD. The price equals the store's average cost, so the typical store makes zero economic profit. Each store's revenue is high enough to cover all its costs—including the opportunity cost of all its inputs—but not enough to cause additional stores to enter the market. In other words, the firm makes just enough money to stay in business.

We saw earlier that there are trade-offs with monopolistic competition. The larger the number of firms, the lower the price and the greater the product variety, but the higher the average cost of production. When firms differentiate their products by offering them at more locations, the benefit of having more firms is that consumers travel shorter distances to get the product. If a large metropolitan area had only one music store, the average cost of production would be lower, but prices would be higher and music consumers would spend much more time traveling to buy CDs.

There are many differentiated products that are sold in monopolistically competitive markets. We've seen that CDs from different stores are differentiated according to location or accessibility. This sort of differentiation occurs for other retail products that

Figure 11.4

Long-Run Equilibrium with Monopolistic Competition: Music Stores

Music stores and other retailers differentiate their products by selling them at different locations. The typical firm chooses the quantity of CDs at which its marginal revenue equals its marginal cost (point *g*). Economic profit is zero because the price equals average cost (shown by point *h*).

require consumers to travel, such as groceries, hardware, drugs, dry cleaning, and bank services. Different firms sell essentially the same product at different locations.

How Many Gas Stations?

Consider a city that initially allowed only one gasoline station to operate. When Jane, a staff member of a local employment agency, heard that the city had decided to relax its restrictions and allow more gasoline stations to operate in the city, she decided to identify some unemployed workers who could apply for the new station-manager jobs. She knew that the city's single gas station pumped 20,000 gallons of gasoline per hour and the long-run average cost curve reaches its minimum point with an output of 5,000 gallons per hour. Therefore, Jane reasoned, the city would soon have a total of four gas stations (20,000 gallons divided by 5,000 gallons per station) and would need three new station managers.

You can imagine Jane's surprise when she discovered that there would be five new gas stations instead of three. She had to scramble to find five unemployed workers to apply for the new manager jobs. Your job is to solve this puzzle. Why did Jane underestimate the number of new gasoline stations?

There are two keys to solving the gas-station puzzle:

- The law of demand means a larger quantity of gasoline sold. The entry of firms will increase competition in the gasoline market, so the market price will drop and the quantity of gasoline demanded will rise. The total quantity of gasoline demanded will exceed the initial quantity of 20,000 gallons per hour.

- Entry means a smaller quantity per gas station. The typical firm operates along the negatively sloped portion of its average cost curve, not the horizontal portion, so we would expect each gas station to pump less than 5,000 gallons per hour.

If the total demand is greater than 20,000 gallons and the output per station is less than 5,000 gallons, there will be more than four stations. For example, suppose that the total quantity demanded rises to 24,000 gallons per hour and each station pumps only 4,000 gallons per hour. In this case, there will be six gas stations (24,000 gallons divided by 4,000 gallons per station) instead of just four.

TEST Your Understanding

5. Explain the logic behind the label *monopolistic competition*. What is monopolistic, and what form does the competition take?

6. Explain the trade-offs associated with monopolistic competition and product differentiation.

7. Suppose each new firm in the car-stereo market in Tweeter's town decreases the price by $5 per stereo and increases the average cost per stereo by $5. How many firms will enter the market?

Using the TOOLS

We've used the tools of economics to explore the firm's entry decision, showing that a firm will enter a market if the price will exceed the average cost of production. Here are some opportunities to use these tools to do your own economic analysis of markets.

1. ECONOMIC EXPERIMENT: BUSINESS LICENSES

Here is an experiment that shows the effects of entry on prices and average cost. Students play the role of entrepreneurs who must decide whether to enter a market and how much to pay for a business license.

- The class is divided into groups of three to five students. Each group represents a firm that has the option of buying a business license to produce and sell tables.
- The following table shows how the market price, the quantity per firm, and the average cost of production vary with the number of firms in the market.

Number of Firms	Price	Quantity per Firm	Average Cost
1	$20	10	$9
2	$18	9	$10
3	$16	8	$11
4	$14	7	$12
5	$12	6	$13
6	$10	5	$14
7	$8	4	$15

- A business license allows a firm to operate the business for one day. Each license will be auctioned to the highest bidder. Each firm can buy only one license.
- For the first three rounds of the experiment, the instructor auctions up to seven business licenses. The instructor will continue to auction licenses as long as someone bids a positive amount for one of the licenses.
- Once the license auction is complete (everyone who wants to buy a license gets one), each firm can use the table to compute its daily profit:

$$\text{profit} = [(\text{price} - \text{average cost} \times \text{quantity}] - \text{price of license}$$

- After three rounds of auctioning seven licenses in each round, the instructor auctions only two licenses for rounds four and five.
- At the end of the experiment, we compute the profit of each firm by adding up its profit over the five rounds.

APPLICATIONS

2. How Many Music Stores?

Consider the city of Discville, where zoning laws allow only one music store. The city's music store sells CDs at a price of $20 with an average cost of $12. Suppose the city eliminates its restrictions on music stores, allowing additional stores to enter the market. According to an expert in the music market, "Each additional music store will decrease the price of CDs by $2 per CD and increase the average cost of selling CDs by $1 per CD." How many music stores will enter the market?

3. Opposition to a New Drugstore

The city of Drugville is evaluating a request by a drugstore chain to open a new drugstore in the city. Consider the following statement from a citizen at a public hearing: "The output of the typical drugstore in our city is about 80% of the output at which its long-run average cost is minimized, so the average cost of drugs is higher than the minimum cost. The new drugstore would increase the average cost of production even further, so all our drugstores—including the new one—would be unprofitable, and consumers would pay higher prices for drugs." Assume that the citizen is correct in stating that the typical drugstore produces at 80% of the output at which average cost is minimized. Do the citizen's conclusions (all stores will be unprofitable and consumers will pay higher prices) follow logically from the facts?

4. ECONOMIC EXPERIMENT: Fixed Costs and Entry

Here is an experiment that shows the implications of entry for prices and profits. Students play the role of entrepreneurs who must decide whether to enter the market for lawn cutting. If they decide to enter the market, they must then decide how much to charge for cutting lawns.

- There are eight potential lawn-cutting firms (each represented by one to three students). There are two sorts of costs for firms: a fixed cost per day, and a marginal cost of cutting each lawn. Each firm can cut up to two lawns per day.
- There are 16 potential consumers who are willing to pay different amounts to have their lawns cut.
- The experiment has two stages. In the first stage, each potential firm decides whether to enter the market. The entry decision is sequential: The instructor will go down the list of potential firms, one at a time, and give each firm the option of entering the market. The entry decisions are public knowledge. When a firm enters the market, it incurs a fixed cost of $14.
- Each firm in the market posts a price for lawn cutting, and consumers shop around and decide whether to purchase lawn care at the posted prices. Each trading period lasts several minutes, and each firm can change its posted price up to three times (a total of three prices per trading period).
- A consumer's score in a trading period equals the difference between the amount that he or she is willing to pay for lawn care and the price actually paid.
- A firm's score equals its profit, which is its total revenue minus its total cost (the fixed cost of $14 plus the variable cost equal to $3 per lawn times the number of lawns cut).

Summary

This chapter is about market entry and monopolistic competition. In a monopolistically competitive market, entry continues until each firm in the market makes zero economic profit. Firms can differentiate their products by picking a distinct physical design, level of service, location, or product aura. Here are the main points of the chapter:

1. As firms enter a market, the market price drops because of competition among firms for consumers, and the average cost of production increases because each firm produces less output.

2. In a monopolistically competitive market, firms compete for customers by producing differentiated products.

3. There are some trade-offs associated with monopolistic competition: An increase in the number of firms decreases price and increases variety, but it also increases the average cost of production.

Key Terms

Problems and Discussion Questions

1. Consider the city of Discville, where zoning laws limit the number of video arcades to one. The city's only video arcade has a price of 50 cents per game with an average cost of 34 cents per game. Suppose that the city eliminates its restrictions on video arcades, allowing additional firms to enter the market. According to an expert in the arcade market, "Each additional video arcade will decrease the price of games by 2 cents and increase the average cost of providing video games by 3 cents." What is the equilibrium number of video arcades?

2. Jean-Luc owns the only wig store in town and sells 30 wigs per week at a price of $70 per wig with an average cost of $35 per wig. Some experts have reported the following facts on the wig market: (a) The average cost of wig selling increases by $2 for every 1-unit decrease in the number of wigs sold. For example, if Jean-Luc sold only 29 wigs per week, his average cost would be $37. (b) The price of wigs decreases by $1 for every 1-unit increase in the number of wigs sold: the slope of the market demand curve is $1. Suppose Sinead opens a second wig store in town and sells her wigs at a price of $60 each. If Jean-Luc sells wigs at the same price as Sinead, will the profit per firm be positive or negative?

3. The city of Zoneville currently uses zoning laws to restrict the number of pizzerias. Under a proposed

law, the restrictions on pizzerias would be eliminated. Consider the following statement by an expert in the pizza industry: "A pizzeria reaches the horizontal portion of its long-run average cost curve at an output of about 1,000 pizzas per day. The city's existing pizzeria sells 3,000 pizzas per day. Based on these facts, I predict that if the city eliminates the restrictions on pizzerias, we will soon have three pizzerias (3,000 pizzas divided by 1,000 pizzas per pizzeria)." If we assume that the expert's facts about production costs are correct, is the expert's conclusion (three pizzerias) correct?

4. A prominent feature of Mao's Communist China was the blue uniform worn by all citizens.
   a. Explain the trade-offs associated with the use of uniforms. What were the benefits, and what were the costs?
   b. Suppose people had a choice among ten types of uniforms rather than being required to wear a single type. Would you expect the benefits of requiring uniforms to decrease by a little or a lot?

5. Consider the "Fixed Costs and Entry" experiment. Suppose the fixed cost per day is $18 per firm and the marginal cost is $4. Each firm can cut up to 3 lawns per day. The market demand curve is linear, with a vertical intercept of $70 and a slope of –$1 per lawn. Predict the outcome of the experiment,

including the equilibrium price, quantity, and number of firms. Explain the reasoning behind your predictions.

6. Under a franchising arrangement, a firm such as McDonald's sells the right to operate retail outlets. Your job is to determine how many franchises McDonald's should sell in Burgerburg.

   a. List the information you need and explain how you would use it.

   b. Provide a numerical example such that McDonald's should sell four franchises.

   c. If you purchase one of the four franchises, would you be better off if McDonald's sold fewer or more franchises? Use your numerical example to defend your answer.

7. Consider a city that issues licenses for pet groomers. Initially, the city does not allow the licenses to be bought and sold. Shortly after an economist joins the city licensing authority, the city decides to allow the licenses to be bought and

sold on the open market. Much to the surprise of the licensers, the price of the licenses was zero: No one was willing to pay a positive amount for a pet grooming license.

   a. Explain why the price of grooming licenses is zero.

   b. Illustrate your answer with a supply-demand diagram.

8. **Web Exercise.** Is the market for outdoor backpacks monopolistically competitive? Visit the Web site of Fog Dog Sports [*http://www.fogdog.com*]. Do a site search and check how many types of backpacks are available from this site. How are the alternative backpacks differentiated?

9. **Web Exercise.** Do a Web search using the word "franchising" to find some sites that provide information on franchising opportunities. One possible site is The Franchise Doctor [*http://www.franchisedoc.com/*]. What sort of franchising opportunities exist?

Take It to the Net

We invite you to visit the O'Sullivan/Sheffrin page on the Prentice Hall Web site at: **http://www.prenhall.com/osullivan/** for additional World Wide Web exercises for this chapter.

Model Answers to Questions

Chapter-Opening Questions

1. The entry of a firm will increase average cost but will also decrease price and increase the variety of products on the market, so it's not clear that preventing it from entering is sensible.

2. Because many firms entered the market, prices dropped by about 22% and the profit per license decreased.

3. The entry of new firms (initially a maximum of five additional firms) increased competition and decreased prices.

4. Recent decreases in demand and increases in supply have led to fears that diamonds will become another standard commodity. The purpose of etching the logo and a serial number on each diamond is to differentiate De Beers products from the gems of other suppliers.

5. The entry of Wal-Mart triggered widespread price-cutting. German authorities forced Wal-Mart to increase its prices on some products, including milk, sugar, flour, rice and cooking oil.

Test Your Understanding

1. Marginal revenue, marginal cost.

2. The firm's demand curve shifts to the left: At each price, the firm sells a smaller quantity.

3. Decreases, decreases, increases.

4. No. The new price would be $210 per stereo, which would be less than the new average cost of $215 per stereo.

5. Each firm has a monopoly in the sale of its differentiated product, but the firms compete with firms that sell similar products.

6. The larger the number of firms, the lower the price and greater the variety of products. On the other hand, having more firms means less output per firm and a higher average cost.

7. With four firms in the market, the price is $215 per stereo and the average cost is $215 per stereo, so each firm makes zero economic profit.

Using the Tools

2. **How Many Music Stores?** Based on the information from the expert, we expect two additional music stores to enter the market. The following table shows price and average cost for different numbers of music stores:

Number of stores	1	2	3	4
Price	$20	$18	$16	$14
Average cost	$12	$13	$14	$15

In a 3-store market, price exceeds average cost by $2. In a four-store market, price is $1 less than average cost. Therefore, we would expect three firms in the music market.

3. **Opposition to a New Drugstore.** In all the examples we have considered, the typical firm operates along the negatively sloped portion of its long-run average cost curve, yet profit is still positive. A firm will enter the market only if it expects to earn a positive profit, so the statement that the new drugstore would make profit negative for all drugstores is puzzling. We know that entry decreases prices as firms compete for customers, so the statement that consumers would pay higher prices is also puzzling.

Notes

1. Leonard W. Weiss, ed., *Concentration and Price* (Cambridge, MA: MIT Press, 1989).

2. Timothy F. Bresnahan and Peter C. Reiss, "Entry and Competition in Concentrated Markets," *Journal of Political Economy*, vol. 99, October 1991, pp. 977–1009.

3. Theodore E. Keeler, "Deregulation and Scale Economies in the U.S. Trucking Industry: An Econometric Extension of the Survivor Principle," *Journal of Law and Economics*, vol. 32, October 1989, pp. 229–253.

4. Thomas Gale Moore, "Rail and Truck Reform—The Record So Far," *Regulation*, November/December 1983.

5. Richard L. Hudson, "European Companies Speed Shift to Phone Competition," *Wall Street Journal*, June 24, 1994, p. B4. Reprinted by permission of the *Wall Street Journal*, © 1994 Dow Jones & Company, Inc. All Rights Reserved Worldwide.

6. "Tucows.com to Slash Domain Name Registration Rates," *News Bytes News Network*, January 11, 2000; "Network Solutions Offers 10-Year .Com Registrations," *News Bytes News Network*, January 18, 2000; "Register.com Latest to Offer Long Domain Names," *News Bytes News Network*, January 11, 2000.

7. "Europe's Largest Supermarket Chain Goes on Discounting Spree," *AP Worldstream*, February 8, 2000; "Price Wars Put Pressure on Germany's Restrictive Retail Laws," *AP Worldstream*, June 27, 2000; Carol J. Williams, "Germany Refuses to Bargain on Wal-Mart's Below-Cost Sales," *Los Angeles Times*, September 9, 2000.

8. "De Beers Is It," *Economist*, December 19, 1998.

12

Oligopoly and Strategic Behavior

When Paul Allen, one of the billionaire founders of Microsoft, announced the grand opening of the Experience Music Project museum in Seattle, there was an outbreak of messages on the Internet chat site dedicated to Jimi Hendrix, the rock legend. Four Hendrix fanatics who had been exchanging messages on the chat site for several months decided to travel to Seattle to meet each other and celebrate the opening of the museum. They all flew in for the occasion, and the discussion among the Web pals eventually turned to the cost of their airline tickets. Although each of the four traveled about the same distance to Seattle, they paid very different prices for their airline tickets.

- Katrina is puzzled and upset: "Brian lives in a city that is served by a single airline, and so do I. But Brian paid $370 and I paid $400." Why is the price lower in Brian's city?
- Jason is puzzled and upset too: "Melissa lives in a city that is served by two airlines, and so do I. But Melissa paid $350 and I paid $400." Why is the price higher in Jason's city?

n this chapter, we explain these puzzling differences in prices. The monopolist in Brian's city could be charging a low price to discourage other firms from entering the market. The two airlines in Jason's city could have a price-fixing scheme under which they do not compete with one another but instead collude and charge the same high price.

This is the fourth chapter on decision-making by firms. In earlier chapters, we looked at perfect competition (many firms selling a homogeneous product), monopoly (a market with a single firm), and monopolistic competition (a market with dozens of firms). In this chapter, we look at an **oligopoly**, a market with just a few firms. Table 12.1 shows the facts on five oligopolies in the United States. The numbers in parentheses are the U.S. market shares of the different companies. For example, Coca-Cola has 45% of the U.S. beverage market, compared to 31% for Pepsi and 14% for Cadbury Schweppes.

Oligopoly: A market served by a few firms.

Concentration ratio: A measure of the degree of concentration in a market; the four-firm concentration ratio is the percentage of the market output produced by the 4 largest firms.

Economists use **concentration ratios** to measure the degree of concentration in a market. For example, a four-firm concentration ratio is the percentage of total output in a market produced by the four largest firms. In Table 12.2, the four-firm concentration ratio for cigarettes is 93%, indicating that the largest four firms produce 93% of the cigarettes in the United States. According to one rule of thumb, if the four-firm concentration ratio is greater than 40%, the market is considered an oligopoly.

In this chapter, we explore the decisions of oligopolists and the role of public policy in markets with just a few firms. Here are some of the practical questions we answer:

1. You've probably heard an advertisement that goes like this: "If you buy a stereo from us and find the same stereo for sale somewhere else for a lower price, we'll pay you the difference in price." Does this refund policy lead to higher or lower stereo prices?

2. Suppose two airlines agree to charge the same high price for air travel between two cities. Will this pricing agreement persist?

3. Will the spread of electronic commerce on the Internet lead to higher or lower prices?

4. In the last few years, a new option for college textbooks has emerged: You can now purchase textbooks on the Internet. How will your favorite monopoly—the campus bookstore—respond to competition from Web booksellers?

Table 12.1 Oligopolies in the United States

Beverages	Music	Tobacco	Phone Service	Cars
Coca-Cola (45%)	Universal/Polygram (26%)	Philip Morris (49%)	AT&T/TCI (47%)	General Motors (29%)
Pepsi (31%)	Warner Music (18%)	RJR Nabisco (24%)	Bell Atlantic/GTE (24%)	Ford (25%)
Cadbury Schweppes (14%)	Sony Music (17%)	Brown and Williamson (15%)	SBC/Ameritec (18%)	Chrysler (16%)
	EMI Group PLC (13%)		MCI WorldCom (12%)	
	BMG Entertainment (12%)			

Source: G. Pascal Zachary, "Let's Play Oligopoly!," *Wall Street Journal,* March 8, 1999, p. B1.

Table 12.2 Concentration Ratios in Selected Manufacturing Industries

Industry	Four-Firm Concentration Ratio (%)	Eight-Firm Concentration Ratio (%)
Cigarettes	93	Not available
Guided missiles and space vehicles	93	99
Beer and malt beverages	90	98
Batteries	87	95
Electric bulbs	86	94
Breakfast cereals	85	98
Motor vehicles and car bodies	84	91
Greeting cards	84	88
Engines and turbines	79	92
Aircraft and parts	79	93

Source: U.S. Bureau of the Census, *1992 Census of Manufacturing, Concentration Ratios in Manufacturing* (Washington, DC: U.S. Government Printing Office, 1995).

You may be surprised by the answers to some of these questions. Perhaps you should write down your own answers now and look at them after you've read the chapter.

The key feature of an oligopoly is that firms act strategically. The firms in an oligopoly are interdependent in the sense that they sell similar products and consumers can easily switch from one firm to another. As a result, the actions of one firm affect the profits of other firms in the oligopoly. For example, if one airline cuts its fares, the other airlines in the market will lose customers to the low-price airline unless they cut their prices too. We'll discuss two types of strategies used by oligopolists: price fixing (conspiring to keep prices high) and entry deterrence (preventing additional firms from entering the market).

Most firms in an oligopoly earn economic profit, yet additional firms do not enter the market. An oligopoly—a market with just a few profitable firms—occurs for three reasons:

- **Economies of scale in production.** As you saw in Chapter 10, a natural monopoly occurs when there are relatively large economies of scale in production, so a large firm can produce at a much lower cost than a small firm. In some cases, scale economies are not large enough to generate a natural monopoly but are large enough to generate a natural oligopoly, with a few firms serving the entire market.

- **Government barriers to entry.** As you saw in Chapter 10, government may limit the number of firms in a market by issuing patents or controlling the number of business licenses.

- **Advertising campaign.** In some markets, a firm cannot enter without a substantial investment in an advertising campaign. The result is the same as economies of scale in production: Just a few firms will enter the market.

Cartel Pricing and the Duopolists' Dilemma

One of the virtues of a market economy is that firms compete with one another for customers, and this leads to lower prices. But in some markets, firms cooperate instead of competing with one another. The eighteenth-century economist Adam Smith recognized the possibility that firms would conspire to raise prices: "People of the same trade seldom meet together, even for merriment and diversion, but the conversation ends in a conspiracy against the public, or in some contrivance to raise prices."[1] We'll see that raising prices is not simply a matter of firms getting together and agreeing on higher prices. An agreement to raise prices is likely to break down unless the firms find some way to punish a firm that violates the agreement.

We'll use a market with two firms—a duopoly—to explain the key features of an oligopoly. The basic insights from a duopoly apply to oligopolies with more than two firms. Consider a duopoly in the market for air travel between two hypothetical cities. The two airlines can compete for customers on the basis of price, or they can cooperate and conspire to raise prices. To simplify matters—and to keep the numbers manageable—let's assume that the average cost of providing air travel is constant at $300 per passenger. As shown in Figure 12.1, the average cost is constant, which means that marginal cost equals average cost.

Cartel: A group of firms that coordinate their pricing decisions, often by charging the same price.

A **cartel** is a group of firms that coordinate their pricing decisions, often charging the same price for a particular good or service. In our airline example, the two airlines could form a cartel and choose the price that a monopolist would choose. In Figure 12.1, the demand curve facing a monopolist is the market demand curve, and the marginal-revenue curve intersects the marginal-cost curve at a quantity of 150 passengers per day (point *f*). If the two airlines act as one, they will pick the monopoly price of $400 and split the monopoly output, each serving 75 passengers per day. The average cost is $300, so each airline earns a daily profit of $7,500 (a profit of $100 per passenger × 75 passengers). An arrangement under which the two firms act as one, coordinating their pricing

Figure 12.1

A Cartel Picks the Monopoly Price

Point *c* shows the outcome with a successful price-fixing arrangement (a cartel). The total output is 150 passengers and the price is $400 per passenger, so each firm serves 75 passengers at an average cost of $300 per passenger (shown by point *f*) and earns a profit of $7,500 per day.

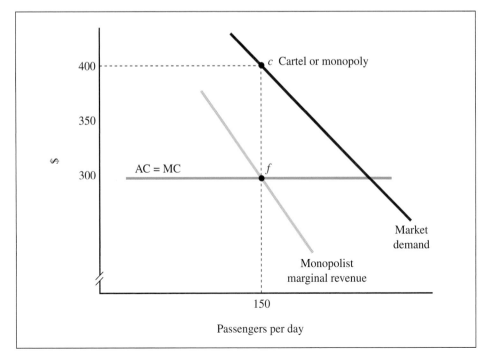

decisions, is also known as **price fixing**. As we'll see later in the chapter, cartels and price-fixing are illegal under U.S. antitrust laws.

Price fixing: An arrangement in which two firms coordinate their pricing decisions.

What would happen if the two firms competed against one another? If they do, each firm faces its own demand curve. The firm's demand is to the left of the market demand curve because consumers are divided between the two firms: At a given price, the number of passengers served by a single firm will be less than the number served by both firms together. In Figure 12.2, panel A shows the perspective of the individual firm. Given the firm's demand curve and marginal-revenue curve, the marginal principle is satisfied at point c, where marginal revenue equals marginal cost. Each firm serves 100 passengers at a price of $350 (point d). Panel B shows the market perspective: The price is $350, and the quantity is 200 passengers. Given an average cost of $300, each firm earns a profit of $5,000 (equal to $50 per passenger × 100 passengers). When the two firms compete, each earns only $5,000, compared to $7,500 each when they conspire to fix the price.

The Game Tree

Each firm would earn more profit under a price-fixing agreement, but will the firms reach such an agreement? We can answer this question with the help of a **game tree**, a graphical tool that provides a visual representation of the consequences of alternative strategies. Each firm must choose a price for airline tickets, either a high price (the cartel price of $400) or a low price (the duopoly price of $350). Each firm can use the game tree to develop a pricing strategy, knowing that the other firm is also choosing a price.

Game tree: A graphical representation of the consequences of different strategies.

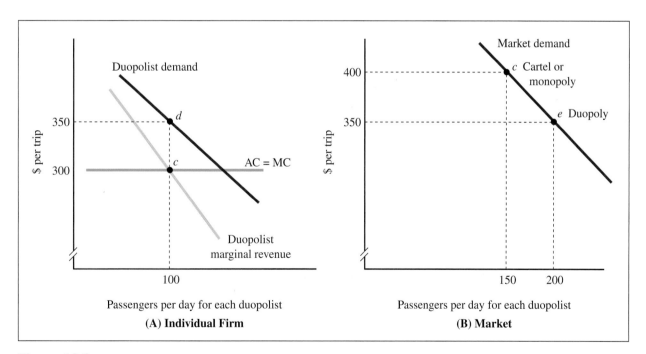

Figure 12.2 Competing Duopolists Pick a Lower Price
At the individual firm (duopolist) level, marginal revenue equals marginal cost at point c, so each firm serves 100 passengers at a price of $350 per passenger (shown by point d in panel A). Given an average cost of $300 per passenger, each duopolist earns a profit of $5,000. At the market level (panel B), the duopoly outcome has a quantity of 200 passengers (100 passengers per firm × 2 firms) at a price of $350 (point e).

Figure 12.3
Game Tree for Price-Fixing Game
The path of the game is square X to square Z to rectangle 4: Each firm picks the low price and earns a profit of $5,000. The duopolists' dilemma is that each firm would make more profit if both picked the high price, but neither firm will do so, fearing that the other firm would pick the low price.

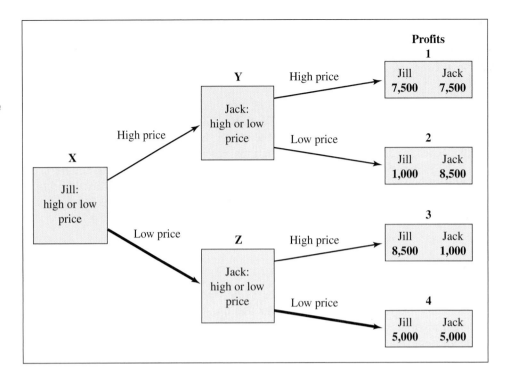

Figure 12.3 shows the game tree for the price-fixing game. Let's call the managers of the airlines Jack and Jill. The game tree has three components:

- The squares are decision nodes. For each square, there is a player (Jack or Jill) and a list of the player's options. For example, the game starts at square X, where Jill has two options: the high price or the low price.

- The arrows show the path of the game from left to right. Jill chooses her price first, so we move from square X to one of Jack's decision nodes, either square Y or square Z. If Jill chooses the high price, we move from square X to square Y. Once we reach one of Jack's decision nodes, he chooses a price (high or low), and then we move to one of the rectangles. For example, if Jack chooses the high price too, we move from square Y to rectangle 1.

- The rectangles show the profits for the two firms. When we reach a rectangle, the game is over, and the players receive the profits shown in the rectangle.

There is a profit rectangle for each of the four possible outcomes of the price-fixing game.

We've already computed the profits for two profit rectangles. The first rectangle shows what happens when each firm chooses the high price. This is the cartel or price-fixing outcome, with each firm earning $7,500. The fourth rectangle shows what happens when each firm chooses the low price. This is the duopoly outcome, with each firm earning $5,000.

What would happen if the two firms chose different prices? If Jill chooses the low price and Jack chooses the high price, Jill will capture a large share of the market and gain at Jack's expense. In the first column of Table 12.3, Jill serves 170 passengers at a price of $350 each and an average cost of $300 per passenger, so her profit is $8,500 (a $50 profit per passenger × 170 passengers). In the second column, Jack serves only 10 passengers at a price of $400 each and the same average cost, so his profit is $1,000 (a $100 profit per passenger × 10 passengers). This is shown by rectangle 3 in Figure 12.3:

Table 12.3 Profits When Firms Choose Different Prices

	Jill: Low Price	Jack: High Price
Price	$ 350	$ 400
Quantity	170	10
Average cost	$ 300	$ 300
Profit per passenger	$ 50	$ 100
Profit	$8,500	$1,000

The path of the game is square X to square Z to rectangle 3. The other underpricing outcome is shown by rectangle 2. In this case. Jill chooses the high price and Jack chooses the low price, so Jack gains at Jill's expense. The roles are reversed, and so are the numbers in the profit rectangle.

The Outcome of the Price-Fixing Game

We can predict the outcome of the price-fixing game by a process of elimination. We'll eliminate the rectangles that would require one or both of the firms to act irrationally, leaving us with the rectangle showing the outcome of the game.

- If Jill chooses the high price, we'll move along the upper branches of the tree and eventually reach rectangle 1 or 2, depending on what Jack does. Although Jill would like Jack to choose the high price too, this would be irrational for Jack, because he can make more profit by choosing the low price. Therefore, we can eliminate rectangle 1.

- If Jill chooses the low price, we'll move along the lower branches of the tree, eventually reaching rectangle 3 or 4, depending on Jack's choice. Jack won't choose the high price because then Jill would gain at his expense. Therefore, we can eliminate rectangle 3.

We've eliminated the two rectangles involving a high price for Jack. This means that the low price is a **dominant strategy** for Jack: Regardless of what Jill does, Jack will choose the low price.

There are two rectangles left (2 and 4), and Jill's action will determine which rectangle we'll reach. Jill knows that Jack will choose the low price regardless of what she does, so she can either choose a high price and allow Jack to gain at her expense (rectangle 2) or choose the low price too (rectangle 4). It would be irrational for Jill to allow herself to be underpriced, so we can eliminate rectangle 2. The remaining rectangle shows the outcome of the game: Each person chooses the low price. The thick arrows show the path of the game, from square X to square Z to rectangle 4.

Both firms will be unhappy with this outcome because each could earn a higher profit with rectangle 1. To get there, however, each firm must choose the high price. The **duopolists' dilemma** is that although both firms would be better off if they chose the high price, each firm chooses the low price. Jill won't choose the high price because Jack would underprice her and gain at her expense. Jack won't choose the high price because then Jill would gain at his expense. As we'll see later, the firms can avoid this dilemma, but only if they find some way to punish a firm that underprices. For a description of how music distributors tried to keep prices high, read "A Closer Look: Price Fixing for Music CDs."

Dominant strategy: An action that is the best choice under all circumstances.

Duopolists' dilemma: A situation in which both firms in a market would be better off if both chose the high price but each chooses the low price.

The big-five music distributors—Universal Music, Sony Corporation, Time-Warner, EMI Music, and Bertelsmann Music Group (BMG)—collectively sell 85% of the nation's CDs. The firms subsidize the advertising campaigns of music retailers, covering a portion of retail advertising costs. In 1997, the distributors decided to tie advertising subsidies to the retailers' pricing decisions. The distributors specified a set of minimum advertised prices (MAP) and announced that any retailer that advertised a CD for less than the MAP would lose all of its "cooperative advertising" funds from the distributor. Under the MAP policy, a large retailer could lose millions of dollars in cooperative advertising funds, even if the advertisement of a sub-MAP price was funded entirely by the retailer.

In May 2000, the Federal Trade Commission reached an agreement with music distributors to end their MAP policy. Here is an excerpt from the FTC press release:

> In the 1990s, many new music retailers, including major consumer electronics stores, started to sell CDs at low prices to gain customers and market share. The more traditional music retailers also lowered their prices to compete. This retail "price war" led to lower CD prices for U.S. consumers, as prices for popular CDs fell as low as $9.99. The record companies adopted the MAP policies in 1995—96 to extinguish this "price war."
>
> The FTC alleges these MAP policies achieved their unlawful objective. The "price war" ended

shortly after the policies were adopted and the retail price of CDs increased. The distributors increased their own prices, and since 1997 wholesale prices for music have increased.

The FTC estimates that U.S. consumers may have paid as much as $480 million more than they should have for CDs and other music because of these policies over the last three years. These settlements will eliminate these policies and should help restore much-needed competition to the retail music market. Today's news should be sweet music to the ears of all CD purchasers.

Source: Federal Trade Commission, "Record Companies Settle FTC Charges of Restraining Competition in CD Music Market," Press Release, May 10, 2000.

The Prisoners' Dilemma

The duopolists' dilemma is similar to the prisoners' dilemma. Consider two people, Bonnie and Clyde, who have been accused of committing a crime. The police give each person an opportunity to confess to the crime, with Bonnie speaking first and Clyde second. The traditional version of the story involves simultaneous decision-making: The two are put in separate rooms, and each makes a choice without the other person knowing what that choice is. The results are the same with sequential or simultaneous decision-making; we'll use the sequential approach to emphasize the similarities to the price-fixing scenario.

The police confront the two criminals with the game tree shown in Figure 12.4. If both confess, each gets 5 years in prison. If neither confesses, the police can convict them on a lesser charge, and each gets 2 years. If only one confesses and implicates the other, the confessor is rewarded with a 1-year prison sentence and the other gets 10

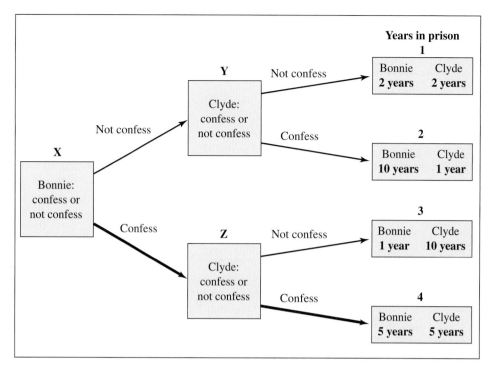

Figure 12.4

Game Tree for Prisoners' Dilemma
The path of the game is square X to square Z to rectangle 4: Each person confesses and gets 5 years in prison. The prisoners' dilemma is that each person would be better off if neither confessed, but both actually confess.

years. Clyde, who goes second, will confess no matter what Bonnie does, and Bonnie knows this. The rational choice for each person is to confess, so each serves 5 years. Although both criminals would be better off if they both kept quiet, they implicate each other because the police reward them for doing so. There is an incentive for squealing, just as there is an incentive for one duopolist to underprice the other.

Avoiding the Dilemma: Price Matching

The duopolists' dilemma occurs because the two firms are unable to coordinate their pricing decisions and act as one. Each firm has an incentive to underprice the other firm because the low-price firm will capture a larger share of the market and earn a larger profit. One way to avoid this dilemma is to develop a system of price matching.

Guaranteed Price Matching

To eliminate the incentive for underpricing, one firm can guarantee that it will match its competitor's price. Suppose Jill places the following advertisement in the local newspaper: "If you buy a plane ticket from me and then discover that Jack offers the same trip at a lower price, I will pay you the difference between my price and Jack's price. If I charge you $400 and Jack's price is only $350, I will pay you $50." This pricing scheme is known as **guaranteed price matching**: Jill guarantees that she will match Jack's price. It is also known as a *meet-the-competition policy*. Jill's promise to match Jack's lower price is credible because she announces it in the newspaper.

How will Jack respond to Jill's price-matching scheme? In effect, Jill tentatively chooses the high price but will instantly switch to the low price if Jack picks the low price. After a $50 refund, Jill's price will be $350, the same as Jack's. Jack will respond to Jill's price-matching scheme in one of two ways:

Guaranteed price matching: A scheme under which a firm guarantees that it will match a lower price by a competitor; also known as a meet-the-competition policy.

1. **Choose the high price.** If Jack matches Jill's announced high price, each firm will earn a profit of $7,500 (rectangle 1 in the game tree in Figure 12.3).
2. **Choose the low price.** If Jack tries to underprice Jill, she will switch to the low price, and each will earn a profit of only $5,000 (rectangle 4 in the game tree).

Jack's decision is easy: A pair of high prices is more profitable than a pair of low prices, so he will choose the high price, just like Jill.

Jill's price-matching scheme eliminates the duopolists' dilemma and makes cartel pricing possible, even without a formal cartel. The duopolists' dilemma disappears because underpricing is no longer possible. The motto of the price-matching scheme is "High for one means high for all, and low for one means low for all." It would be irrational for Jack to choose the low price because he knows that Jill would match it. Once the possibility of underpricing has been eliminated, the duopoly will be replaced by an informal cartel, each firm charging the price that would be charged by a monopolist.

To most people, the notion that guaranteed price matching leads to higher prices is surprising. After all, Jill promises to give refunds if her price exceeds Jack's, so we might expect her to keep her price low to avoid giving out a lot of refunds. In fact, she doesn't have to worry about refunds because she knows that Jack will also choose the high price. In other words, Jill's promise to issue refunds is an empty promise. Although consumers might think Jill's refund policy will protect them from high prices, the policy guarantees that they will pay the high price.

Price Fixing in Cyberspace?

What are the implications of electronic commerce on the Internet for competition and prices? Will the spread of electronic commerce lead to higher or lower prices for consumer goods such as books, CDs, and cameras? The Internet gives consumers an unprecedented opportunity to almost instantly compare the products and prices of different sellers and could promote competition and lead to lower prices. Unfortunately, the Internet also gives firms an unprecedented opportunity to engage in price matching to maintain a cartel price.

A firm has an incentive to cut price if the firm could sell more output at the lower price, as consumers switch from rival sellers. But if a rival can instantly respond to a price cut on the Internet, the price-cutting firm won't gain many consumers. That could mean that a firm won't cut its prices in the first place, and a cartel price may persist. The same logic applies to a potential entrant, who might be tempted to enter the market with a price below the cartel price. If the original firms can instantly match the entrant's lower price, the entrant won't sell very much, and the payoff from entering may be so low that the firm won't enter the market.

Application: Different Ticket Prices

At the beginning of this chapter, we saw that Jason paid more for his plane ticket than Melissa did for hers, even though both live in cities that are served by two airlines. The two airlines in Melissa's city may suffer from the duopolists' dilemma: Although they would prefer the high price ($400), they both choose the low price ($350). In contrast, an airline in Jason's city could use a guaranteed price-matching scheme, promising to refund the difference between its price and the price of the other airline. The price-matching scheme eliminates underpricing, so each airline will choose the high price ($400). Jason pays a higher price because the price-matching scheme allows the airlines in his city to engage in cartel pricing (price fixing).

Many stores advertise their guaranteed price-matching policies. Focus Camera goes beyond matching a lower price, promising to refund the difference plus 10%. This empty promise promotes price fixing by camera stores.

At **FOCUS CAMERA**, we guarantee you the lowest prices. If you purchase a camera from us and within 30 days find the same camera at a lower price, we'll **REFUND** the difference **PLUS** 10%. For example, if you buy a camera from us for $300 and find it elsewhere for $280, we'll give you $22, making our actual price only $278!

TEST Your Understanding

1. Complete the statement with *e* or *c*: Rectangle 1 in Figure 12.3 is associated with point _____ in Figure 12.2, while rectangle 4 is associated with point _____.

2. Use Figure 12.3 to complete the statement: If each firm picks the low price, the path of the game is square _____ to square _____ to rectangle _____, and each firm earns a profit of _____.

3. Suppose Jack promises that if Jill chooses the high price, he will too. If Jack's objective is to maximize his profit, what will he do after Jill chooses the high price?

4. If you were Jill, would you believe Jack's promises to choose the high price? Which price would you choose?

Repeated Pricing and Retaliation for Underpricing

Up to this point, we've assumed that the price-fixing game is played only once. Each firm chooses a price and sticks with that price for the lifetime of the firm. What happens when two firms play the price-fixing game repeatedly, setting prices over an extended period of time? We'll see that repetition makes price fixing more likely because firms can punish a firm that cheats on a price-fixing agreement.

Retaliation Strategies

Grim trigger: A strategy under which a firm responds to underpricing by choosing a price so low that each firm makes zero economic profit.

Tit-for-tat: A strategy under which the one firm in a duopoly starts out with the cartel price and then chooses whatever price the other firm chose in the preceding period.

Firms use several strategies to maintain a price-fixing agreement. We explore three, all of which involve punishing a firm that underprices the other firm. Continuing the airline example, suppose Jack and Jill choose their prices at the beginning of each month. Jill chooses the cartel price ($400) for the first month and then waits to see what price Jack chooses. Jill could use one of the following schemes to punish Jack if he underprices her:

1. Duopoly price. Jill continues to choose the high price until Jack underprices her. Once that happens, she chooses the duopoly price ($350 in our example) for the remaining lifetime of her firm. Jill allows herself to be underpriced only once and then abandons the idea of cartel pricing and accepts the duopoly outcome, which is less profitable than the cartel outcome but more profitable than being underpriced by the other firm.

2. Grim trigger. When Jack underprices Jill, she responds by dropping her price to a level at which each firm will make zero economic profit forever. This is called the grim-trigger strategy because grim consequences are triggered by Jack's underpricing.

3. Tit-for-tat. Starting in the second month. Jill chooses whatever price Jack chose the preceding month. As long as Jack chooses the cartel price, the cartel arrangement will persist, but if Jack underprices Jill, the cartel will break down. In Figure 12.5. Jack

Figure 12.5
Tit-for-Tat Pricing
Under a tit-for-tat retaliation scheme, the leading firm (Jill, the square) chooses whatever price the other firm (Jack, the circle) chose the preceding month.

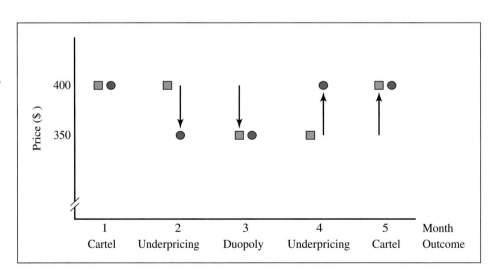

underprices Jill in the second month, so Jill chooses the low price for the third month, resulting in the duopoly outcome. To restore the cartel outcome. Jack must eventually choose the high price, allowing Jill to underprice him for one month. This happens in the fourth month, so the cartel is restored in the fifth month. Although Jack can gain at Jill's expense in the second month, if he wants to restore cartel pricing, he must allow Jill to gain at his expense during the fourth month.

These three pricing schemes promote cartel pricing by penalizing the underpricer. To decide whether to underprice Jill, Jack must weigh the short-term benefit against the long-term cost:

1. The short-term benefit is the increase in profit in the current period. If Jack underprices Jill, he can increase his profit from $7,500 (Jack's profit if both firms pick the high price) to $8,500 (Jack's profit if he chooses the low price and Jill chooses the high price). Therefore, the short-term benefit of underpricing is $1.000.

2. The long-term cost is the loss of profit in later periods. Jill will respond to Jack's underpricing by cutting her price, and this decreases Jack's profit. For example, if Jill pulls the grim trigger, Jack will lose the opportunity for a monthly profit of $7,500 for the remaining lifetime of his firm.

If the two firms expect to share the market for a long time, the long-term cost of underpricing will exceed the short-term benefit, so underpricing is less likely. The threat of punishment makes it easier to resist the temptation to cheat on the cartel.

Price Fixing and the Law

Under the Sherman Anti-Trust Act of 1890 and subsequent legislation, explicit price fixing is illegal. It is illegal for firms to discuss their pricing strategies or their methods of punishing a firm that underprices other firms. In one of the early price-fixing cases (Addyston Pipe, 1899), six manufacturers of cast-iron pipe met to fix prices in certain geographical areas. Several months after the Supreme Court ruled that their cartel pricing was illegal, the firms merged into a single firm, so instead of acting like a monopolist, which was illegal, they became a monopolist. Here are some other examples of price fixing:

1. **GE/Westinghouse (1961).** General Electric and Westinghouse were convicted of fixing prices for electrical generators, resulting in fines of over $2 million and imprisonment or probation for 30 corporate executives.

2. **Coca-Cola (1986).** The Coca-Cola Bottling Company of North Carolina paid a fine and issued discount coupons to its customers to settle a case involving a conspiracy to fix the prices of soft drinks.

3. **Infant formula (1993).** The three major producers of infant formula (together serving 95% of the market) paid a total of $200 million to wholesalers and retailers to settle lawsuits claiming that they had conspired to fix prices.

4. **Plastic wrap in Japan (1993).** A Tokyo court found eight Japanese companies guilty of conspiring to fix the prices of the plastic film used for wrapping food. The companies received fines of $54,000 to $73,000, and 15 executives were given suspended jail sentences of six months to one year.

5. **Airline pricing (1994).** In an antitrust lawsuit filed in 1992, the U.S. Justice Department alleged that the nation's airlines used advanced price listing to fix airline ticket prices. Before an airline increased its price, it could post a "suggested" price on a central computer and see whether the other airlines would increase their prices. By March 1994, eight of the nation's largest airlines (United Airlines, USAir Group,

American Airlines, Delta Airlines, Northwest Airlines, Continental Airlines, Trans-World Airlines, and Alaska Air) had agreed to drop this practice. According to Ann Bingaman of the antitrust division of the Justice Department, advance price listing allowed airlines to fix prices at an artificially high level, costing consumers an extra $1.9 billion for airline tickets.[2]

6. **Steel beam pricing in Europe (1994).** The European Union Commission fined 16 steel companies a total of 104 million Euros units ($116 million) for conspiring to fix the price of steel beams.

7. **Carton board pricing in Europe (1994).** The European Union Commission fined 19 manufacturers of carton board a total of 132 million Euros units ($165 million) for operating a cartel that fixed prices at secret meetings in luxury Zurich hotels.

8. **Food additives (1996).** An employee of Archer Daniels Midland (ADM), a huge food company that likes to call itself "the supermarket to the world," provided audio and video tapes of ADM executives scheming to fix prices. ADM pleaded guilty to the charges of price fixing and was fined $100 million.

Price Leadership

Price leadership An implicit agreement under which firms in a market choose a price leader, observe that firm's price, and match it.

Because explicit price fixing is illegal, firms often rely on implicit pricing agreements to fix prices at the monopoly level. Under a **price leadership** arrangement, a group of firms selects a firm to serve as a price leader, observes the price chosen by the leader, and then matches it. Such an agreement allows firms to cooperate without actually discussing their pricing strategies.

The problem with an implicit pricing agreement is that it relies on indirect signals that are often garbled and misinterpreted. Suppose that two firms have cooperated for several years, both sticking to the cartel price. When one firm suddenly drops its price, the other firm could interpret the price cut in one of two ways:

Advance price listing allowed airlines to fix prices, costing consumers an extra $1.9 billion for airline tickets. The airlines agreed to stop this practice in 1994.

1. Change in market conditions. Perhaps the first firm has observed a change in demand or production cost and decides that both firms would benefit from a lower price.

2. Underpricing. Perhaps the first firm is trying to increase its market share and profit at the expense of the second firm.

The first interpretation would probably cause the second firm to match the lower price of the first firm, and price fixing would continue at the lower price. In contrast, the second interpretation could trigger a price war, destroying the price-fixing agreement. Because firms often pull the grim trigger when a more moderate response would be appropriate, implicit pricing agreements are difficult to maintain.

Kinked Demand Curve

The **kinked demand model** of oligopoly gets its name from its assumptions about how firms in an oligopoly respond when one firm changes its price. Figure 12.6 shows the demand curve facing Kirk, one of three firms in the oligopoly. Suppose each of the three firms starts out with a price of $6, so Kirk sells 30 units of output (point *k*).

Kinked demand model: A model under which firms in an oligopoly match price reductions by other firms but do not match price increases by other firms.

1. If Kirk increases his price, the other two firms will not change their prices. Kirk will have a higher price than the other firms, so his quantity will decrease by a large amount (from 30 to 10 units).

2. If Kirk decreases his price, the other firms will decrease their prices. Kirk will have the same (lower) price as other firms, so his quantity will increase by a small amount (from 30 to 33 units).

These assumptions mean that the demand curve of the typical firm has a kink at the prevailing price: It is relatively flat (price-elastic) for higher prices because other firms won't match a higher price but relatively steep (price-inelastic) for lower prices because other firms will match a lower price. Once a price has been established, it will tend to persist because there is a large penalty for a firm that picks a higher price (a large decrease in the quantity sold) and a small benefit for a firm that picks a lower price (a small increase in the quantity sold).

Figure 12.6

Kinked Demand Curve Model

Under the kinked demand model, when one firm increases its price, the other firms don't change their prices, so the quantity sold by the firm will decrease by a large amount. But when one firm decreases its price, the other firms cut their prices too, so the quantity sold by the firm will increase by a small amount.

The model of kinked demand is really a model of pessimism. Each firm assumes the worst about how its fellow oligopolists will respond to a change in price: The other firms will not go along with a higher price but will match a lower price. Although this model may have some intuitive appeal, there is no evidence that firms really act this way. Starting in 1947, various studies of oligopolies have failed to find compelling evidence to support the kinked-demand model of oligopoly.[3]

TEST Your Understanding

7. Which retaliation strategy, the duopoly price or the grim trigger, provides a greater incentive to maintain cartel pricing? Explain.

8. Suppose that Jack and Jill use a tit-for-tat scheme to encourage cartel pricing and Jill chooses the low price for a single month. How long will the two firms deviate from cartel pricing? Explain.

9. Complete the statement with cost or benefit: If two firms expect to be in the market together for a long time, the _____ of underpricing will be large relative to the _____.

Entry Deterrence by an Insecure Monopolist

You've seen what happens when two duopolists try to act as one, fixing the price at the monopoly level. Now let's think about how a monopolist might try to prevent a second firm from entering its market. In other words, we look at a potential oligopoly. To explain how a monopolist tries to protect a monopoly, we use some of the numbers from our airline example, although we look at a different city with a different cast of characters.

Suppose that Jane initially has a secure monopoly in the market for air travel between two cities. When there is no threat of entry, Jane uses the marginal principle (marginal revenue = marginal cost) to pick a quantity and a price. In Figure 12.7, we

Figure 12.7

Entry Deterrence and Limit Pricing

Moving downward along the demand curve, point *m* shows the secure monopoly, point *i* shows the insecure monopoly, and point *d* shows the duopoly. Point *h* shows what happens if the insecure monopolist produces a large quantity but a second firm enters anyway.

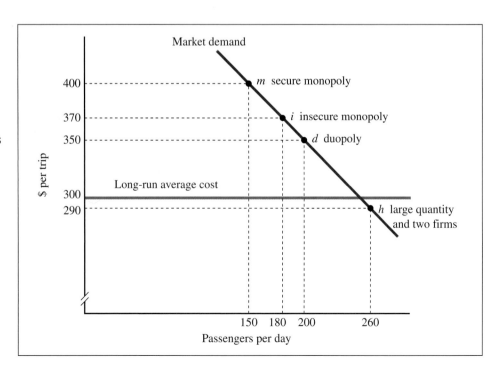

start at point m, with a quantity of 150 passengers per day and a price of $400 per passenger. Her profit per passenger is $100 ($400 minus the average cost of $300), so her daily profit is $15,000. If Jane discovers that the manager of a second airline is thinking about entering the market, what will she do? Now that she has an **insecure monopoly**, she has two options: She can be passive and allow the second airline to enter the market, or she can try to prevent the second airline from entering.

Insecure monopoly: A monopoly that is faced with the possibility that a second firm will enter the market.

Game Tree for the Entry Game

Let's look first at the passive strategy. By producing a small quantity of output. Jane will leave room in the market for the second airline. If the second airline enters the market, Jane will be forced to cut her price to compete with the new airline for customers. In Figure 12.7, the market will move downward along the demand curve from point m to point d (the duopoly outcome). The price is lower ($350 instead of $400), and Jane will have only 100 passengers per day (half of the 200 passengers served at a price of $350). Her profit per passenger will be $50 ($350 minus the average cost of $300), so her daily profit will be $5,000. In Figure 12.8, the path of the game is square X to square Y to rectangle 1: If Jane is passive, Dick will enter the market and each firm will receive a profit of $5,000.

What must Jane do to prevent Dick from entering the market? One possibility is to buy a large fleet of airplanes and sign labor contracts that force her to hire a large workforce. These actions would commit Jane to serve a large number of passengers at a low price. If Dick enters the market, he will be forced to charge a low price too, and both firms would lose money. This is shown in the lower branches of the game tree in Figure 12.8.

- If Jane produces a large quantity and Dick enters anyway, the total output of the two firms will be very large. In Figure 12.7, the market would move downward along the demand curve to point h, with a price of $290 and a quantity of 260 passengers.

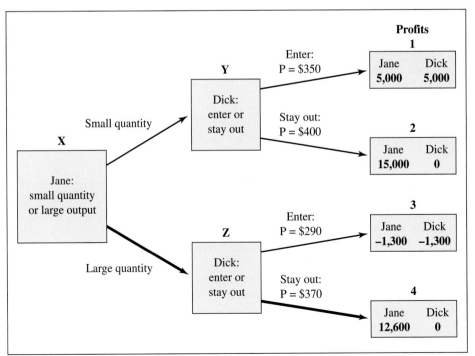

Figure 12.8
Game Tree for the Entry Game
The path of the game is square X to square Z to rectangle 4: Jane chooses a large quantity, so Dick decides to stay out. Jane earns a profit of $12,600, and Dick gets nothing.

Consumers would be happy with this outcome, but the two firms would not: The price would be less than the average cost of each firm, so each firm would lose $1,300 (rectangle 3 in Figure 12.8).

- If Jane produces a large quantity and Dick stays out of the market, the total output of the market will be 180 passengers, as shown by point i in Figure 12.7. Jane's profit would be $12,600 ($70 per passenger × 180 passengers). This outcome is shown by rectangle 4 in Figure 12.8).

The Outcome of the Entry Game

Let's use a process of elimination to predict the outcome of the entry-deterrence game. We've already eliminated rectangle 2: If Jane is passive and chooses a small quantity, Dick will enter. We've also eliminated rectangle 3: If Jane produces a large quantity. Dick would lose money in the market, so he will stay out.

Rectangles 1 and 4 are left, and Jane's action will determine which rectangle we'll reach. If Jane produces a large quantity, she can prevent Dick from entering the market, but is this sensible? Jane's profit from the passive approach (rectangle 1) is lower than the profit from entry deterrence (rectangle 4), so we can eliminate rectangle 1. The remaining rectangle shows the outcome of the game: Jane will maintain her insecure monopoly by producing a large quantity. The thick arrows show the path of the game, from square X to square Z to rectangle 4.

The entry-deterrence game generates a market price that is between the price of a secure monopolist and the duopoly price. Before Dick threatened to enter the market, Jane was a secure monopolist and charged $400 (point m in Figure 12.7). Once Dick threatens to enter the market, point m will no longer be an option because if Jane continues to act like a secure monopolist (choosing a small quantity of output), Dick will enter the market and the price will fall to $350 (point d). Jane can avoid sharing the market by committing herself to produce a large quantity and accepting the lower price associated with an insecure monopolist ($370, as shown by point i).

Limit pricing: A scheme under which a monopolist accepts a price below the normal monopoly price to deter other firms from entering the market.

The strategy of picking a price that is lower than the normal monopoly price to deter entry is known as **limit pricing**. For a discussion of limit pricing by Microsoft Corporation, read "A Closer Look: What's the Monopoly Price for Microsoft Windows?"

Although our example shows that deterrence is the best strategy for Jane, it won't be the best strategy for all monopolists. Suppose Rod could prevent Leah from entering

A CLOSER LOOK WHAT'S THE MONOPOLY PRICE FOR MICROSOFT WINDOWS?

The Windows operating system from Microsoft, Inc. runs about 90% of the world's personal computers, so it is natural to think that Microsoft has a monopoly in the market for operating systems. According to economist Richard Schmalensee, an expert on oligopoly and monopoly, Microsoft's profit-maximizing monopoly price is between $900 and $2,000. That's the amount Microsoft would charge if it acted like a regular monopolist.[4]

So why does Microsoft charge only $99 for Windows? One possibility is limit pricing. Perhaps Microsoft is an insecure monopolist and picks a low price to discourage entry and preserve its monopoly. If Microsoft charged $2,000 for its operating system, there would be an incentive for other firms to develop alternative operating systems.

his market but only by increasing his output by a very large amount and thus accepting a much lower price. A low price means a small profit, so the deterrence strategy could generate less profit than simply sharing the market with Leah. In general, entry deterrence will not be profitable if the price required to prevent entry is relatively low.

Applications: Aluminum, Plane Tickets, Campus Bookstores

Between 1893 and 1940, the Aluminum Company of America (Alcoa) had a monopoly on aluminum production in the United States.[5] During this period, Alcoa kept other firms out of the market by producing a large quantity and keeping its price low. Although a higher price would have generated more profit in the short run, other firms would have entered the market, so Alcoa's profit would have been lower in the longer run.

At the beginning of this chapter, we saw that Katrina paid more for her plane ticket than Brian paid for his, even though they both live in cities that are served by a single airline. If the monopolist in Katrina's city is secure, meaning that there is no threat that another airline would enter the market, the airline will charge the normal monopoly price of $400. In Brian's city, an insecure monopolist prevents a second airline from entering the market by committing itself to produce a large quantity and accepting a low price. Brian pays a lower price because he buys his ticket from an insecure monopolist.

We can apply the notion of entry deterrence to your favorite monopoly: your campus bookstore. On most college campuses the campus bookstore has a monopoly on the sale of textbooks. Other organizations are prohibited, usually by the state government or the college, from selling textbooks on campus. The recent growth of Internet commerce has given students another option: Order textbooks over the Web and have them shipped by mail, UPS, Federal Express, or Airborne Express. Several Web booksellers charge less than the campus bookstore, and the growth of Web book sales threatens the campus bookstore monopoly. If your campus bookstore suddenly feels insecure about its monopoly position, it could cut its prices to prevent Web booksellers from capturing too many of its customers. If it does this, you will pay lower prices even if you don't patronize the Web seller.

Entry Deterrence and Contestable Markets

We've seen that an insecure monopolist may cut its price to prevent other firms from entering the market. The threat of entry moves the market price closer to the price that would occur in a market with two firms. The same logic applies to a monopolized market that could potentially have many firms: The threat of entry will force the monopolist to charge a price that could be close to the one that would occur in a market with many firms. The mere existence of a monopoly does not mean that it will charge high prices and earn large profits. To protect its monopoly, a monopolist may act like a firm in a market with many firms, picking a low price and earning a small profit.

The threat of entry underlies the theory of market contestability. Firms can enter or leave a **contestable market** without incurring large costs. The few firms in a contestable market will be threatened constantly by the entry of new firms, so prices and profits will be low. In the extreme case of perfect contestability, firms can enter and exit a market at zero cost. In this case, the price will be the same as the price that would occur in a perfectly competitive market, one with dozens of firms. Although few markets are perfectly contestable, many markets are contestable to a certain degree, and the threat of entry tends to decrease prices and profits.

Contestable market: A market in which the costs of entering and leaving are low, so the firms that are already in the market are constantly threatened by the entry of new firms.

BallPoint Pens

In 1945, Reynolds International Pen Corporation introduced a revolutionary product: the ballpoint pen. The new type of pen could be produced with a very simple production technology.[6] For three years, Reynolds earned enormous profits on this innovative product. In 1948, Reynolds stopped producing pens, dropping out of the market entirely. What happened?

The key to solving this mystery is the fact that Reynolds earned enormous profits for a short time. The simple technology of the ballpoint pen could be easily copied by other producers, so the price required to deter entry was very low. The entry-deterring price was so low that it was better for Reynolds to charge a high price and squeeze out as much profit as possible from a short-lived monopoly. Reynolds sold its pens for $16, about 20 times the average production cost ($0.80). By 1948, a total of 100 firms had entered the ballpoint market, and the price had fallen close to the production cost.

Review: Four Types of Markets

This is the fourth of four chapters on decision-making by firms in different market settings. We can use Table 12.4 to review the characteristics of the four types of markets we've discussed in Chapters 9 though 12.

   1. **Perfect Competition.** There are very many firms, each selling a standardized or homogeneous product. Each firm is such a small part of the market that the firm takes the market price as given: The demand for the individual firm's product is perfectly elastic.

Table 12.4   Characteristics of Different Types of Markets

	Perfect Competition	Monopolistic Competition	Oligopoly	Monopoly
Number of firms	Very large number	Many	Few	One
Type of product	Standardized (homogeneous)	Differentiated	Standardized or differentiated	Unique
Demand faced by individual firm	Price taker: demand is perfectly elastic	Demand is price elastic but not perfectly elastic	Demand is less elastic than demand facing monopolistically competitive firm	Firm faces market demand curve
Entry conditions	No barriers	No barriers	Large barriers from economies of scale or government policies	Large barriers from economies of scale or government policies
Examples	Wheat, soybeans	Toothbrushes, music stores, clothing	Air travel, automobiles, beverages, cigarettes, long-distance phone services	Local phone service, patented drugs

2. **Monopolistic competition.** There are many firms, each selling a slightly different product. Some examples are restaurants, retail stores, gas stations, and clothing. This contrasts with perfect competition, in which each firm sells a standardized product. Because the products sold by different firms in a monopolistically competitive market are not perfect substitutes, the demand for the firm's product is not perfectly elastic. There are no barriers to entering the market, so there are many firms.

3. **Oligopoly.** There are just a few firms in the market, a result of two sorts of barriers to entry: economies of scale and government policies limit the number of firms in the market. The demand for an individual firm's product is less elastic than it would be in a monopolistically competitive market because there are fewer firms in the oligopoly. Some examples are automobiles, airline travel, and breakfast cereals.

4. **Monopoly.** A single firm serves the entire market. A monopoly occurs when the barriers to entry are very large, which could result from very large economies of scale or a government limit on the number of firms. The demand for a monopolist's product is shown by the market demand curve. Some examples of goods with large scale economies are local phone service and electric power generation. Some examples of monopolies established by government policy are drugs covered by patents and concessions in national parks.

TEST Your Understanding

10. Complete the statement: Suppose that Jane picks a small quantity of output. In Figure 12.8, the path of the game would be square _____ to square _____ to rectangle _____.

11. In Figure 12.8, Jane would prefer rectangle 2 to rectangle 4. Why can't she get to rectangle 2?

12. Why does a secure monopolist charge a higher price than an insecure monopolist does?

Using the TOOLS

We've used one of the tools of economics—the game tree—to predict the outcomes of price-fixing and entry-deterrence games. Here are some opportunities to use this tool to do your own economic analysis of markets.

1. ECONOMIC EXPERIMENT: Price-Fixing

Here is a price-fixing or cartel game for the classroom. You'll have an opportunity to conspire to fix prices in a hypothetical market with five firms.

- The instructor divides the class into five groups. Each group represents one of five firms that produce a particular good.
- Each group must develop a pricing strategy for its firm, recognizing that the other groups are choosing prices for their firms at the same time. There are only two choices: a high price (the cartel price) or a low price.
- The profit of a particular firm depends on the price chosen by the firm and the prices chosen by the four other firms. Here is the profit matrix:

Number of High-Price Firms	Number of Low-Price Firms	Profit for Each High-Price Firm	Profit for Each Low-Price Firm
0	5	—	$ 50
1	4	$20	70
2	3	40	90
3	2	60	110
4	1	80	130
5	0	100	—

1. From the second row, if one of the five firms chooses the high price and the other four firms choose the low price, the high-price firm earns a profit of $20, and each low-price firm earns a profit of $70.

2. The game is played for several rounds. In the first three rounds, the firms make their choices without talking to each other in advance. In the fourth and fifth rounds, the firms discuss their strategies, disperse, and then make their choices.

3. The group's score equals the profit earned by the firm.

APPLICATIONS

2. Advertising and Price Fixing

Consider two sellers of CD players (Cecil and Dee) who suffer from the duopolists' dilemma. Although both Cecil and Dee would be better off if both chose the high price, they both choose the low price. Cecil recently discovered that Dee is planning a big advertising campaign, the purpose of which is to increase her sales at Cecil's expense (without changing her price). Suppose that Cecil has the opportunity to launch his own advertising campaign before Dee starts hers. What sort of advertising campaign should he launch?

3. Entry Deterrence

Your firm sells a very popular children's toy. The manager of another firm is thinking about introducing a similar toy. You have the following facts:

- Your average cost of production is constant at $2 per toy.
- At the current monopoly price of $5 per toy, you sell 120 toys per day.
- You could prevent the entry of the second firm by increasing your output to 150 toys per day and cutting your price to $4 per toy.
- If the second firm enters the market, your price would decrease to $3 per toy, and you would sell only 80 toys per day.

Should you prevent entry of the second firm?

Summary

In this chapter, we've seen that when a few firms share a market, they have an incentive to act strategically. Firms may use cartel pricing or price fixing to avoid competition and keep prices high. If another firm threatens to enter a monopolist's market, the monopolist may cut its price to discourage other firms from entering a market. Here are the main points of the chapter.

1. Each firm in an oligopoly has an incentive to underprice the other firms, so price fixing (also known as cartel pricing) will be unsuccessful unless firms have some way of enforcing a price-fixing agreement.

2. One way to maintain price fixing is a guaranteed price-matching scheme: One firm chooses the high

price and promises to match a lower price offered by its competitor.

3. Price fixing is more likely to occur if firms choose prices repeatedly and can punish a firm that chooses a price below the cartel price.

4. To prevent a second firm from entering the market, an insecure monopolist may commit itself to produce a relatively large quantity and accept a relatively low price.

Key Terms

cartel, 254
concentration ratio, 252
contestable market, 269
dominant strategy, 257
duopolists' dilemma, 257

game tree, 255
grim trigger, 262
guaranteed price matching, 259
insecure monopoly, 267
kinked demand model, 265

limit pricing, 268
oligopoly, 252
price fixing, 255
price leadership, 264
tit-for-tat, 262

Problems and Discussion Questions

1. Consider two firms, Speedy and Hustle, that provide land transportation from the downtown area to the airport. The practice of guaranteed price matching is illegal.
   - If the two firms act independently (they do not engage in price fixing or any other collusive behavior), each firm will serve 100 passengers per day at a price of $20 per passenger and an average cost of $15 per passenger.
   - Under a price-fixing or cartel arrangement, each firm would serve 75 passengers at a price of $28 and an average cost of $18 per passenger.
   - If one firm charges $20 and the other firm charges $28, the low-price firm will earn a profit of $900 and the high-price firm will earn a profit of $400.
   - Speedy chooses a price first, followed by Hustle.
   Draw a game tree for the price-fixing game and predict the outcome.

2. Recall the example of the repeated pricing game between Jack and Jill. Suppose that each firm uses the grim-trigger strategy to punish underpricing. Each person expects to go out of business in one month, meaning that each person is about to choose a price for the last time. Which price will each person choose?

3. Many firms have going-out-of-business sales with remarkable bargains. What insights does the material in this chapter provide about such sales?

4. Consider the example of entry deterrence shown in Figure 12.8. Suppose that just one number changes: If Jane chooses a large quantity and Dick

stays out, Jane's profit would be $4,500. All the other numbers are the same as those shown in Figure 12.8. Draw a new game tree and predict the outcome: Will Jane choose a large or a small quantity, and will Dick enter or stay out?

5. On Wa-ki-ki beach, there are two hotels, Weird and Bizarre. The practice of guaranteed price matching is illegal. If the two firms act independently (they do not engage in price fixing or any other collusive behavior), each firm will rent 50 rooms per day at a price of $50 per room and an average cost of $45 per room. Under a price-fixing or cartel arrangement, each hotel would rent 30 rooms per day at a price of $60 and an average cost of $48. If one firm charges $50 and the other firm charges $60, the low-price firm will earn a profit of $500, and the high-price firm will earn a profit of $150. Bizarre picks a price first, followed by Weird.

   a. Suppose each firm must pick a price and maintain its chosen price for the remaining lifetime of the firm. Draw a game tree and predict the outcome.

   b. Suppose the two firms can change their prices daily, and expect to be in business for three more days. Weird announces that he will start with the high price and maintain the price as long as Bizarre does too. If Bizarre undercuts Weird, however, Weird will pick the low price for the remainder of the game. Predict the outcome of the game.

6. Consider the market for air travel between Madison and Chicago. The long-run average cost is constant at $200 per passenger, and the demand curve is lin-

ear, with a slope of −$1 per passenger. A secure monopolist would charge a price of $280 and serve 70 passengers per day. The other possible prices are $260 for an insecure monopolist, $250 for the duopoly outcome, and $180 for the case in which one firm picks a large quantity and a low price but a second firm enters anyway.

a. Use these numbers to draw two figures, one like Figure 12.7 and a second like Figure 12.8. Provide a complete set of numbers, and briefly explain how you got them. Label any curves you draw, and identify the relevant points on your graph.

b. Use your second figure to predict the outcome of the entry-deterrence game. What is the price of air travel?

7. In the state of Turnover, the typical car-stereo seller stays in business for one year. In the state of Longtime, the typical car-stereo seller stays in business for five years. Which state is likely to have higher prices for car stereos?

8. Consider the Jack and Jill repeated price game described in the text. Suppose Jill uses the duopoly-pricing strategy, and the two firms expect to be in business for three periods.

a. In the current period, what are Jack's costs and benefits of underpricing?

b. Will Jack underprice in the final period? If Jill can predict Jack's behavior in the last period, what will she do? What are the implications for the second period?

9. Web Exercise. Visit the Web site of the U.S. Federal Trade Commission to get the facts on the most recent price-fixing cases [*http://www.ftc.gov/*]. Click on the Search icon, and do a search of News Releases using the words "price fixing." Write a brief description of three recent price-fixing cases.

10. Web Exercise. To check out the competition for your campus bookstore, visit the Web sites of a few Internet book sellers. (Here are some URLs: [*http://www.eFollet.com*], [*http://www.Varsitybooks.com*], and [*http://www.Bigwords.com*].) How do the prices, including shipping charges, compare to those charged by the campus bookstore? What's the story on renting books instead of buying them?

Take It to the Net

We invite you to visit the O'Sullivan/Sheffrin page on the Prentice Hall Web site at: **http://www.prenhall.com/osullivan/** for additional World Wide Web exercises for this chapter.

Model Answers to Questions

Chapter-Opening Questions

1. It is likely to lead to higher prices because it eliminates the possibility of underpricing. The promise to issue refunds is an empty promise.

2. The price-fixing arrangement is more likely to persist if the airlines pick prices repeatedly over time, giving the airlines the opportunity to punish anyone who cheats on the price-fixing agreement.

3. The Internet gives consumers more opportunities to shop for low prices but also gives rival firms more opportunities to match prices and promote cartel pricing.

4. The growth of the off-campus firms threatens the campus bookstore monopoly, and the bookstore might cut its prices to prevent off-campus booksellers from extending their services to your town.

Test Your Understanding

1. *c, e.*

2. X, Z, 4, $5,000.

3. He will choose the low price and gain at Jill's expense.

4. Jack's promise is not credible because once Jill chooses the high price, he will earn more profit by choosing the low price. Jill should ignore the incredible promise and choose the low price.

5. $50 ($400 − $350).

6. They are common in appliance and electronics stores and in hardware stores. Many grocery stores honor the coupons of other stores. Although these schemes appear to be good news for consumers, they actually facilitate price-fixing and lead to higher prices.

7. The grim trigger makes profit zero, while the duopoly price leaves each firm with a positive profit. The costs of underpricing are higher with the grim trigger, so there is a greater incentive to charge the cartel price.

8. Two months. In the first month. Jill underprices Jack. In the second month. Jill chooses the high price but is underpriced by Jack, who is punishing her for underpricing him in the first month. In the third month, they both choose the high price.

9. Cost, benefit.

10. X, Y, 1.

11. If she chooses a small quantity. Dick will enter.

12. To prevent the entry of a second firm, an insecure monopolist commits itself to produce a large quantity of output and accepts a low price. A secure monopolist doesn't have to worry about other firms entering the market.

Using the Tools

2. Advertising and Price Fixing. The first option is the duopolist strategy. To prevent losing sales to Dee, Cecil could neutralize Dee's advertising campaign with an identical campaign of his own. Cecil and Dee would probably continue to sell about the same quantities at the same prices, but their profits would be lower because the advertising campaign costs money. The second option is a guaranteed price-matching scheme. Cecil could advertise the monopoly price and promise to match any lower price by Dee. If Dee recognizes the opportunity for price fixing, she will also advertise the monopoly price, and both firms will earn more profit.

3. Entry Deterrence. The profit from entry deterrence is $300 per day: Profit is the quantity (150) × the gap between price and average cost ($2 = $4 − $2). The profit from allowing entry is only $80 per day: The profit is the quantity (80) × the gap between price and average cost ($1 = $3 − $2). The deterrence strategy generates a higher price and a larger quantity with no change in average cost, so profits are higher.

Notes

1. Adam Smith, *The Wealth of Nations* (New York: Modern Library, 1994).

2. Sharon Walsh, "Six Airlines to Halt Advance Price Listing," *New York Times News Service*, printed in *The Oregonian*, March 18, 1994, p. B1.

3. George Stigler, "The Kinked Oligopoly Demand Curve and Rigid Prices," *Journal of Political Economy*, vol. 55, 1947, pp. 432–449.

4. "Big Friendly Giant," *The Economist*, January 30, 1999, p. 72.

5. Leonard W. Weiss, *Economics and American Industry* (New York: Wiley, 1963), pp. 189–204.

6. Thomas Whiteside, "Where Are They Now?" *New Yorker*, February 17, 1951, pp. 39–58.

Using Market Power: Price Discrimination and Advertising

The day after his 60th birthday, George took his granddaughter to the movies. He got a $3 senior-citizen discount for admission but paid the full price for popcorn. George's experience raises two questions about the pricing decisions of firms:

- Is a senior-citizen discount an act of generosity or an act of profit maximization?
- If a senior discount is sensible for admission to a movie, why isn't it sensible for popcorn?

n Chapter 10 through Chapter 12, we saw that many firms have market power in the sense that their actions affect market prices. In this chapter, we take a closer look at the behavior of firms with market power. We'll explain why some firms charge different prices for different types of consumers. We'll also explore the firm's decision to advertise, and we'll look at the trade-offs—the costs and benefits—of advertising. Here are some practical questions that we'll answer:

1. Why do faculty members pay more than students for on-campus movies?
2. Why are hardback books so much more expensive than paperback books?
3. How does a firm decide how many TV commercials to use?
4. If you want to advertise on the Internet, what are the possible pricing arrangements?

Price Discrimination

Price discrimination: The process under which a firm divides consumers into two or more groups and picks a different price for each group.

Up to this point in the book, we've assumed that a firm charges the same price to all its consumers. In some markets, firms divide consumers into two or more groups and charge a different price to each group, a practice known as **price discrimination**. One approach is to offer a discount (resulting in a lower price) to some types of consumers. The firm identifies a group of customers who are not willing to pay the regular price and then offers a discount to people in that group.

Here are some examples of price discrimination with discounts for certain groups of consumers:

- Discounts on airline tickets for travelers who spend Saturday night away from home. An airline passenger who spends a Saturday night away from home is likely to be a tourist, not a business traveler. The typical tourist is not willing to pay as much for air travel as is the typical business traveler.

- Discount coupons for groceries and restaurant food. The typical coupon-clipper is not willing to pay as much as the typical consumer.

- Manufacturers' rebates for appliances. A person who takes the trouble to mail a rebate form to the manufacturer is not willing to pay as much as the typical consumer.

- Senior-citizen discounts on airline tickets, restaurant food, drugs, and entertainment.

- Student discounts on movies and concerts.

The only legal restriction on price discrimination is that a firm cannot use it to drive rival firms out of business.

Price discrimination is not always possible. A firm has an opportunity for price discrimination if three conditions are met:

1. **Market power.** The firm must have some control over its price. Therefore, price discrimination does not occur in a perfectly competitive market, in which each firm takes the market price as given.

2. **Different consumer groups.** Consumers must differ in their willingness to pay for the product or in their responsiveness to changes in price (as measured by the price elasticity of demand).

3. **Resale is not possible.** It must be impractical for one consumer to resell the product to another consumer. As a counterexample, suppose a bar sells drinks to women at a discount price and women can easily resell drinks to men. In this case, women are likely to buy extra drinks and sell them to men, so the bar won't sell

many drinks at the regular price and price discrimination won't be profitable. In general, the possibility of resale causes price discrimination to break down, so a firm will be better off with a single price.

Senior Discounts in Restaurants

Consider a restaurant whose patrons can be divided into two groups, senior citizens and others. In Figure 13.1, the demand curve for senior citizens is lower than the demand curve for other citizens, reflecting the assumption that the typical senior is willing to pay less than the typical nonsenior.

What happens if the restaurant picks a single price for its meals, charging the same amount to seniors and nonseniors? Suppose the most profitable single price is $5. If the average cost of producing meals is constant at $1 per meal, the restaurant will make a profit of $4 on each meal served. At a price of $5, the restaurant will have 100 senior customers (point *s*) and 300 nonsenior customers (point *n*). As shown in Table 13.1, the firm gets a profit of $400 from seniors and $1,200 from nonseniors, for a total profit of $1,600.

Under a price-discrimination scheme, the restaurant will divide its customers into two groups and offer a lower price to senior citizens. This is sensible because the two groups have different demands for restaurant meals, so the restaurant should treat them differently. Panel A of Figure 13.1 shows how to pick a price for senior citizens. The marginal principle (marginal revenue = marginal cost) is satisfied at point *e*, with 280 senior meals per day. Therefore, the appropriate price for seniors is $3 (point *d* on the senior demand curve). The profit per senior meal is $2 (the $3 price minus the $1 average cost), and the restaurant's profit from its senior customers is $560 per day ($2 per meal times 280 meals). The senior discount increases the restaurant's profit from its senior customers from $400 to $560.

We can also use the marginal principle to find the appropriate price for nonseniors. In panel B of Figure 13.1, the marginal principle is satisfied at point *c*, with 260 nonsenior meals per day. Therefore, the restaurant should charge $6 for nonseniors (point *f* on the demand curve). The profit per nonsenior meal is $5 (the $6 price minus the $1 average cost) and the restaurant's profit from nonseniors is $1,300 per day ($5 per meal × 260 meals). The higher price for nonseniors increases the restaurant's profits from its nonsenior customers from $1,200 to $1,300.

By treating the two groups of consumers differently, the restaurant can earn more profit. The switch from a single-price policy to price discrimination generates a lower

(A) Senior Citizens

(B) Nonseniors

Figure 13.1

Price Discrimination

A firm that picks a single price of $5 (for both seniors and nonseniors) reaches point *n* on the nonsenior demand curve (300 customers) and point *s* on the senior demand curve (100 customers). Under a price-discrimination scheme, the price for nonseniors is $6 (point *f*), and the price for the seniors is $3 (point *d*).

Table 13.1 A Senior Discount Increases Total Profit

	Single Price Policy		Senior Discount	
	Seniors	Nonseniors	Seniors	Nonseniors
Price	$5	$5	$3	$6
Average cost per meal	$1	$1	$1	$1
Profit per meal	$4	$4	$2	$5
Number of meals	100 meals	300 meals	280 meals	260 meals
Profit	$400	$1,200	$560	$1,300
Total profit	$1,600		$1,860	

price for seniors and a higher price for nonseniors. The switch in pricing increases the restaurant's profit in both segments of the market, and its total profit increases from $1,600 to $1,860 per day.

Price Discrimination and the Elasticity of Demand

We can use the concept of price elasticity of demand to explain why price discrimination increases the restaurant's profit. Compared to other consumers, senior citizens have more elastic demand for restaurant meals, in part because they have lower income and more time to shop around for low prices. Starting with the single-price policy, the demand for restaurant meals by seniors is elastic, while the demand by nonseniors is inelastic. What are the implications for the switch to the new pricing scheme, with a higher price for nonseniors and a lower price for seniors?

A higher price for nonseniors, who have inelastic demand, increases the restaurant's profit. We know from Chapter 5 that if demand is inelastic, an increase in price will increase total revenue: The good news (more revenue per customer) dominates the bad news (fewer customers). Therefore, an increase in the nonsenior price will increase the revenue from nonseniors. At the same time, the higher price means that the restaurant will serve fewer meals to nonsenior customers, so the restaurant's production costs will decrease. Because the restaurant's nonsenior revenue increases while the cost of serving nonseniors decreases, profit from nonseniors will increase.

A lower price for senior customers, who have elastic demand, increases the restaurant's profit. We know that if demand is elastic, a decrease in price will increase total revenue: The good news (more customers) dominates the bad news (less revenue per customer). At the same time, the lower price means the restaurant will serve more meals to seniors, so the restaurant's total cost will increase. If demand is very elastic, the increase in revenue will more than offset the increase in total cost and the restaurant's profit from senior citizens will increase.

The same logic applies to other cases of price discrimination. A firm will charge a higher price to consumers with relatively inelastic demand. For example, local pharmacies pay up to five times as much as hospitals for common drugs.[1] The demand for drugs by pharmacies is relatively inelastic because pharmacies stock a wide variety of drugs to fill individual prescriptions, and they buy much smaller quantities of each drug. The inelastic demand by pharmacies encourages pharmaceutical firms to discriminate against them. For an example of price discrimination based on weather conditions, read "A Closer Look: Interacting with a Soda Vending Machine on a Hot Day."

INTERACTING WITH A SODA VENDING MACHINE ON A HOT DAY

On a hot day, are you willing to pay more for an ice-cold can of coke? If so, you're the type of consumer Coca-Cola Company had in mind when it developed a high-tech vending machine, complete with heat sensors and microchips, that charges a higher price when the weather is hot.[2] According to Douglas Ivester, the head of Coca-Cola, the desire for a cold drink increases when it is hot, so "it is fair that it should be more expensive. The machine will simply make the process more automatic."

The announcement of the new vending machine led to howls of protest from consumers. In response, Coca-Cola Company said that it would not actually use the new machine, but was "exploring innovative technology and communication systems that can actually improve product availability, promotional activity and even offer consumers an interactive experience when they purchase a soft drink from a vending machine." Based on the reaction to the news of the heat-sensing vending machine, you can imagine the "interactive experience" when a hot and thirsty consumer discovers the higher price for a cold drink on a hot day.

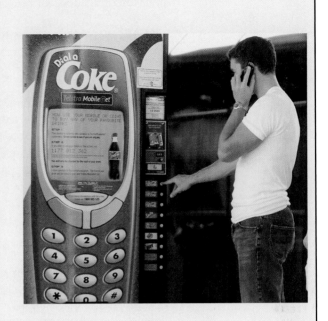

Application: Movie Admission and Popcorn

We're ready to answer the two questions in the opening paragraph of the chapter. A senior discount for movie admission is not an act of generosity by a firm, but part of the firm's pricing strategy designed to increase profit. Senior citizens are typically willing to pay less than other citizens for movies, so a theater divides its consumers into two groups—seniors and others—and offers a discount to seniors. This price discrimination in favor of senior citizens increases the theater's profit.

Why don't theaters offer a senior discount for popcorn? Unlike admission to the theater, popcorn can be easily transferred from one customer to another. If senior citizens could buy popcorn at half the regular price, many nonseniors would get seniors to buy popcorn for them, so the theater wouldn't sell as much popcorn at the regular price. Price discrimination for popcorn would not be profitable.

Why Are Hardback Books So Expensive?

Economic Detective

Most novels are published in two forms—hardback and paperback—the paperback edition being published and available for sale several weeks or months later than the hardback edition. The cost of producing a hardback book is only about 20% higher than the cost of producing the same book as a paperback, but the price of a hardback book is about three times the price of a paperback book. Why is the price difference so large when the cost difference is so small?

The key to solving this puzzle is the fact that hardback books are published first, followed by the paperback edition. Booksellers use hardbacks and paperbacks to distinguish between two types of consumers: those who are willing to pay a lot and those who are willing to pay a little. The people who are willing to pay the most are eager to read the book as soon as it comes out, so they pay $18 for a hardback book. The people who are willing to pay less are more patient and are willing to wait a few weeks for the $6 paperback version. The pricing of hardback and paperback books is another example of price discrimination, with consumers with less elastic demand paying a higher price.

TEST Your Understanding

1. Why is aspirin sold in airports so much more expensive than aspirin sold in grocery stores?

2. Complete the statement with "increase" or "decrease": Suppose a firm starts with a single price and then switches to a price-discrimination scheme. The firm will _____ the price for the group of consumers with relatively inelastic demand and _____ the group with relatively elastic demand.

3. Many cocktail lounges and bars that have cover charges have lower cover charges for women than for men. Why?

Advertising

In most modern economies, firms spend enormous amounts of money on advertising to increase the demand for their products. In the United States, firms spend about $45 billion each year on television advertisements, and much more on print advertisements in newspapers and magazines. The total spending on Internet advertising is about $3 billion per year and growing rapidly.

Advertising and the Marginal Principle

How do firms decide how much to spend on advertising and where to spend it? Consider a producer of laundry detergent that has decided to advertise on television. The firm can use the marginal principle to decide how many 30-second slots to buy each week.

 Marginal **PRINCIPLE**

Increase the level of an activity if its marginal benefit exceeds its marginal cost, but reduce the level if the marginal cost exceeds the marginal benefit. If possible, pick the level at which the marginal benefit equals the marginal cost.

The marginal benefit of advertising depends on how many more boxes of detergent are sold as a result of the TV ad. The second column of Table 13.2 shows the quantities of detergent sold with different numbers of TV ads. If the firm does not advertise, it sells 100,000 boxes. As the number of ads increases, so does the quantity sold: from 110,000 for one ad, to 119,000 for two ads, and so on. The marginal benefit of advertising (shown in the third column) is the change in quantity sold resulting from the last ad times the firm's net revenue (revenue less cost) per unit sold. Let's assume that the net revenue is $1 per box. The first ad increases the quantity sold by 10,000 boxes, so the marginal benefit of the first ad is $10,000. Moving down the third column, the marginal benefit decreases to $9,000 for the second ad, $8,000 for the third ad, and so on.

Before we can use the marginal principle, we must determine the marginal cost of advertising. In our example, the marginal cost is simply the price of each 30-second advertising slot. In the last column of Table 13.2, the marginal cost is constant at $7,000 per slot. According to the marginal principle, the firm should buy 4 ads, because that's

Table 13.2 Advertising and the Marginal Principle

Number of Advertisements	Quantity of Detergent Sold (Boxes)	Marginal Benefit (Assuming Net Revenue of $1 per Box)	Marginal Cost
0	100,000		
1	110,000	$10,000	$7,000
2	119,000	$9,000	$7,000
3	127,000	$8,000	$7,000
4	134,000	$7,000	$7,000
5	140,000	$6,000	$7,000
6	145,000	$5,000	$7,000

the number at which the marginal benefit equals the marginal cost. Starting with any smaller quantity, the marginal benefit of another ad exceeds the cost, so an additional ad would increase the firm's profit.

What sort of firms will advertise? For advertising to be profitable, the increase in sales must be large relative to the cost of advertising, meaning that consumers' choices must be sensitive to advertising. Several brands of laundry detergent are close but not perfect substitutes, and advertising causes many consumers to switch from one brand to another. The same is true for pain medications: Advertising causes consumers to switch among Tylenol, Advil, Bayer Aspirin, and Excedrin. Some other examples of heavily advertised products are cough medicines, antacids, and cold remedies. In contrast, there is little to be gained from advertisements for standardized goods such as wheat or notebook paper.

The Prices of Advertising Slots

A firm that has decided to launch an advertising campaign must decide where and when to run the advertisements. A firm advertising on radio or television must decide when to run the ad. A firm advertising in newspapers or on the World Wide Web must decide where to place the ad in the newspaper or on the Web. If the prices were the same for all ad slots (all times and locations), the firm's decision would be simple: Pick the slot that generates the greatest exposure to potential customers.

Of course, the prices of advertising slots vary, being determined by the laws of supply and demand. Advertisers are willing to pay the most for slots that have the biggest audience, so the price for television advertising slots is highest during the most popular programs. The most expensive slots are during major sporting events such as the Super Bowl and the Academy Awards; the least expensive slots are for the early morning hours (3:00 A.M. to 5:00 A.M.), when most consumers are asleep. For an example of different systems for pricing Internet advertising, read "A Closer Look: Cost per Impression, Click, or Customer?"

The Missing Ads for Generic Drugs

Economic Detective

The sellers of brand-name pain medication (such as Bayer Aspirin, Tylenol, Advil, Excedrin) spend millions of dollars every year on advertising. The same is true for the manufacturers of brand-name cough syrup and cold medications. But the sellers of generic versions of these products—which are chemically equivalent—do not advertise at all. Why?

The key to solving this mystery is to recognize the difference between the consumers of generics and the consumers of branded products. The potential purchasers of generic drugs recognize the chemical equivalence of generic and branded drugs, so they are sensitive to price and generally pick the product with the lowest price. An advertisement for a generic aspirin wouldn't increase sales by very much. In fact, if a producer of a generic product increased the price of its product to cover the costs of an advertising campaign, the quantity sold might actually decrease. In contrast, the consumers of branded drugs and medications are sensitive to advertising and less sensitive to price, so advertising increases total sales, even if the price of a branded drug increases to cover the cost of advertising.

The Advertisers' Dilemma

Up to this point, we have looked at a firm's decision to advertise in isolation, without considering the possible responses of rival firms. What happens when a second firm selling a competing product has the opportunity to react to the first firm's advertising campaign? In Chapter 12, we used game trees to explore the interdependence of firms concerning pricing and market entry. We can use the same tool to look at interactions concerning advertising. As we'll see, firms might get caught in an advertisers' dilemma: Although each firm would be better off if neither advertised, both firms advertise.

Consider the producers of two brands of aspirin. Each firm must decide whether to spend $7 million on an advertising campaign for its product. In Table 13.3, the first two columns of numbers show what happens if neither firm advertises. Each earns $8 million in net revenue (revenue minus production costs) and spends no money on advertising, so the profit per firm is $8 million. The third and fourth columns of numbers show what happens if each firm spends $7 million on advertising. Net revenue increases from $8 million to $13 million, a benefit of $5 million. The benefit of advertising ($5 million) is less than the cost ($7 million), so the profit earned by each firm falls, from $8 million to $6 million.

Table 13.3   Advertising and Profit

	Neither Advertises		Both Advertise		Jack Advertises	
	Jack	Jill	Jack	Jill	Jack	Jill
Net revenue from sales ($ million)	8	8	13	13	17	5
Cost of advertising ($ million)	0	0	7	7	7	0
Profit ($ million)	8	8	6	6	10	5

What happens if one firm advertises and the other does not? The last two columns of numbers in Table 13.3 show that advertising is profitable for the advertising firm. If Jack spends $7 million on advertising and Jill spends nothing, Jack's net revenue increases from $8 million to $17 million. The benefit of advertising (a $9 million increase in net revenue) exceeds the $7 million cost, so Jack's profit increases to $10 million ($17 million – $7 million).

Jack's advertising allows him to gain at Jill's expense. Jack's advertising causes some of Jill's consumers to switch to Jack, and Jill's net revenue drops from $8 million to $5 million. Jill's profit falls from $8 million to $5 million.

We can use the data in Table 13.3 to construct a game tree for the advertising game. In Figure13.2, Jack makes his decision first, followed by Jill.

- If neither firm advertises, we go from square X to square Z to rectangle 4, and the payoff (profit) is $8 million for each firm.

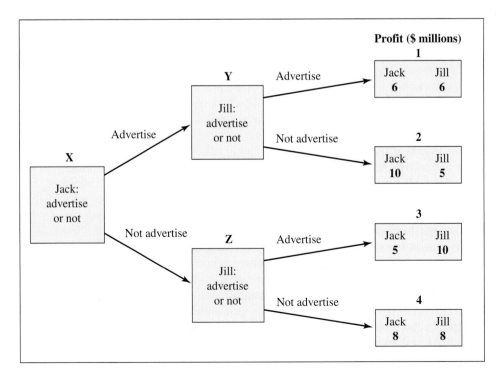

Figure 13.2
Game Tree for Advertisers' Dilemma
Jack moves first, choosing to advertise or not. Jill's best response is to advertise no matter what Jack does. Knowing this, Jack realizes that the only possible outcomes are shown by rectangles 1 and 3. From Jack's perspective, rectangle 1 ($6 million) is better than rectangle 3 ($5 million), so his best response is to advertise too. Both Jack and Jill advertise, and each earns a profit of $6 million.

Some types of advertising are wasteful because the campaign of one firm simply cancels out the campaign of another firm.

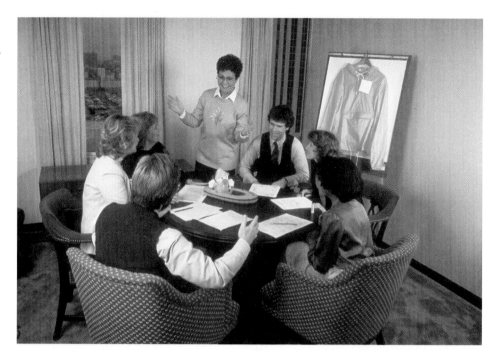

- If both firms advertise, we go from square X to square Y to rectangle 1, and each firm earns a profit of $6 million.

- If Jack advertises and Jill does not, we go from square X to square Y to rectangle 2, and Jack earns $10 million, while Jill earns $5 million. If the roles are reversed, we end up in rectangle 3, with Jill the advertiser earning $10 million, while Jack earns $5 million.

What is the outcome of this advertising game? Suppose Jack decides to advertise, meaning that we move along the upper branches of the game tree from square X to square Y. Jill will earn $6 million if she matches Jack's advertising campaign (rectangle 1) but only $5 million if she does not (rectangle 2). The best response is to match Jack's campaign. If Jack does not advertise, we go from square X to square Z, and Jill chooses between rectangle 3 and rectangle 4. Jill can use advertising to take sales away from her rival Jack, earning a profit of $10 million in the process. If she does not advertise, her profit will be $8 million. To summarize, Jill's best response is to advertise no matter what Jack does. In other words, for Jill, advertising is a dominant strategy.

Jack can figure out that advertising is a dominant strategy for Jill. Knowing this, Jack realizes that the only possible outcomes are shown by rectangles 1 and 3. From Jack's perspective, rectangle 1 ($6 million) is better than rectangle 3 ($5 million), so his best response is to advertise too. Both firms advertise, and each earns a profit of $6.

What is the advertisers' dilemma? Both Jack and Jill would be better off if neither advertised: Each would get a profit of $8 million if neither advertised, compared to $6 million when both advertise. Each firm has an incentive to use advertising to increase its net revenue at the expense of the other. Knowing this, each firm spends $7 million to counter the advertising campaign of the other firm. Stuck in the dilemma, each firm earns $2 million less than it would if neither advertised.

The advertisers' dilemma occurs when advertising causes a relatively small increase in the total sales of the industry but allows a firm that advertises to gain at the expense of firms that don't advertise. In our example, a pair of advertising campaigns costing a total of $14 million increases the industry's net revenue by only $10 million—from $16 million ($8 million each) to $26 million ($13 million each). If the increase in industry net revenue were larger, advertising could benefit both firms. We'll see an example of that type of advertising in the Using the Tools exercise, "Got Milk?"

Trade-Offs from Advertising

What are the trade-offs associated with advertising? There is no doubt that advertising influences consumer choices; otherwise, firms would not spend billions of dollars each year on it. What do firms and consumers get for the billions of dollars worth of resources used for advertising? Let's take a look at some of the issues in the spirited debate over the merits of advertising.

One benefit of advertising is that it helps consumers to make informed decisions. Some advertisements contain factual information about product characteristics, and this information helps consumers to choose among products that are similar but not identical. For example, a car advertisement that discloses the car's fuel efficiency could help a fuel-conscious consumer to make a decision about what car to buy. Advertisements can also help by providing information about where to go to buy a product.

Another benefit is that advertising provides consumers with information on the prices and promotes competition. The market for eyeglasses provides a test of the effects of advertising on prices. Some states outlaw advertising for eyeglasses, while most allow it. One study found that states that outlawed advertising for eyeglasses had eyeglass prices that were 20% higher than prices in states that allowed advertising.[4] Advertising promotes competition by providing new firms with a means of quickly and efficiently spreading information about their products. This encourages firms to enter profitable markets, leading to lower prices.

The game tree shown in Figure 13.2 shows one possible negative aspect of advertising. If the industry's net revenue increases by an amount that is less than the cost of the advertising campaigns, advertising will decrease profit. In this case, the two firms are trapped in an advertisers' dilemma. Because the advertising campaigns cancel out each other, the resources used in the advertising campaigns—workers' time, raw materials, and equipment—are wasted.

On the negative side, some advertisements give the impression that there are real differences between products when there are none. The purpose of some advertising is to establish an image or aura for the product. Many advertisements for beer, soft drinks, cigarettes, and designer jeans don't discuss ingredients and other features of the product. Instead, they show people having a wonderful time while drinking, smoking, or wearing the product. The message is that people who use the product are more popular and happy, and you too could be more popular and happy if you consumed the product.

We can summarize the trade-offs from advertising as follows: In some cases, advertising campaigns of rival firms simply cancel each other out, so the resources used in the process are wasted. In other cases, the purpose of advertising is to suggest there are differences in products when there are none or to establish an image or aura for the product. On the other hand, advertising can provide information about product characteristics, prices, and locations, and help consumers to make informed decisions. Some types of advertising promote competition and decrease prices.

TEST Your Understanding

4. In Table 13.2, suppose the cost of a 30-second TV ad increases to $9,500. How many ads should the firm use?

5. In Table 13.2, suppose the net revenue per box of detergent decreases to $0.80. How many ads should the firm use?

6. If the percentage of Web users who click on advertisements increased, how would that affect the price of Internet banner ads?

Using the **TOOLS**

In this chapter, we've seen examples of firms using their market power to increase their profit. Many firms charge different prices to different types of consumers, a practice known as price discrimination. Firms spend billions of dollars each year on advertising, with the idea of increasing the demand for their products and their profit. Here are some opportunities to do your own economic analysis.

1. ECONOMIC EXPERIMENT: Price Discrimination

Here is an experiment that shows how a monopolist—a museum—picks different prices for different consumer groups. Some students play the roles of consumers, and others play the roles of museum managers. Here is how the experiment works:

- The instructor picks a small group of students (three to five) to represent the museum. There is a fixed marginal cost of each museum patron (for ticket-takers, guides, cleanup, and other tasks).
- There are 40 consumers (potential museum patrons), and half the consumers are senior citizens with senior-citizen cards. Each consumer receives a number indicating how much he or she is willing to pay for a trip to a museum.
- In each round of the experiment, each museum posts two prices: one for senior citizens and one for nonseniors. Consumers then decide whether to buy a ticket at the relevant posted price.
- A consumer's score in a particular round equals the difference between his or her willingness to pay and the amount actually paid for a museum admission.
- A museum's score equals its profit, equal to its total revenue minus its total cost ($2 times the number of patrons).
- The experiment is run for five rounds. At the end of the experiment, each consumer computes his or her score by adding up his or her consumer surpluses. The museum's score equals the sum of the profits from the five rounds.

APPLICATIONS

2. Price Discrimination in a Campus Film Series

You manage a campus film series and charge different prices to students and faculty members. The current prices and numbers of viewers are as follows:

	Price	Number of viewers	Slope of demand curve
Students	$3	100	$0.01 per viewer
Faculty	$4	50	$0.10 per viewer

The marginal cost of another viewer is zero. Does the current pricing scheme maximize your total revenue? If not, how should you change your prices?

3. Pricing First-Run Movies and Early Apples

If you see a movie when it first comes out, you pay much more than you would if you waited a month or two for the movie to appear at a second-run movie theater. If you buy apples early in the harvest season, you pay more than you would if you waited until the middle of the harvest season. Are both movies and apples subject to price discrimination?

4. Picking a Web Page for a Banner Ad

You sell books on the Internet, and your net revenue is 20% of total sales revenue. You are looking for a Web page on which to place a banner advertisement and have narrowed your choices to 2 pages with the following characteristics:

	Web Page A	Web Page B
Clicks per 1,000 Impressions	50	30
Average Income of Viewers	$2,000	$5,000
Price per 1,000 Impressions	$ 35	$ 35

One of every 10 people who actually see your advertisement (after clicking on the banner ad) order some books, and the average order is 2% of the customer's monthly income. Which of the two Web pages should you choose for your banner ad?

5. Advertising with Spillover Benefits: Got Milk?

Bessie and George are milk producers, and each must decide whether to spend $7 million on an advertising campaign. If neither advertises, each will earn $10 million in net revenue from sales (net revenue). If both advertise, each will earn $20 million in net revenue and $13 million in profit ($20 million – $7 million for advertising). If only one producer advertises, that firm will earn $16 million in net revenue, and the other firm will earn $15 million in net revenue. Prepare a game tree like Figure 13.2 (assume that Bessie decides first) and predict the outcome of this advertising game. If there is an advertisers' dilemma, how does it differ from the advertisers' dilemma discussed earlier in the chapter? How might the dairy industry solve this dilemma? (*Hint:* Think white mustaches.)

Summary

In this chapter, we've seen two ways in which firms use their market power to increase their profits. Many firms charge different prices to different types of consumers, a practice known as price discrimination. Firms spend billions of dollars per year on advertising, with the idea of increasing the demand for their products and their profit. Here are the main points of the chapter:

1. To engage in price discrimination, a firm divides its customers into two or more groups and charges lower prices to groups with more elastic demand.

2. Price discrimination is not an act of generosity; it's an act of profit maximization.

3. A firm can use the marginal principle to decide how many advertisements to purchase.

4. Rival firms may get caught in an advertisers' dilemma: Although each would be better off if neither advertised, both advertise.

5. The prices of advertising slots are determined by supply and demand; the most expensive slots are the ones with the greatest exposure to potential consumers.

Key Term

price discrimination, 278

Problems and Discussion Questions

1. Consider an airline that initially has a single price ($300) for all consumers. At this price, it has 120 business travelers and 80 tourists. The airline's marginal cost is $100. The slope of the business demand curve is –$2 per traveler and the slope of the tourist demand curve is –$1 per traveler. Does the single-price policy maximize the airline's profit? If not, how should it change its prices?

2. Comment on the following statement from a member of a city council: "Several of the merchants in our city offer discounts to our senior citizens. These discounts obviously decrease the merchants' profits, and we should decrease the merchants' taxes to offset their losses on senior-citizen discounts."

3. An advertisement for an early-bird sale at a fabric store notes that people who buy fabric between 6:00 and 7:00 A.M. receive a 40% discount, and people who shop between 7:00 and 8:00 A.M. receive a 20% discount. What is the rationale for such a pricing scheme?

4. Why are senior-citizen discounts common for services such as admission to museums and other entertainment but uncommon for consumer goods such as hardware, appliances, and automobiles?

5. Car companies offer many options on new cars, including automatic transmissions, CD players, leather trim, and heated seats. The markup on these options (the difference between the price consumers pay and the cost incurred by the car company) is higher for leather trim and CD players than it is for automatic transmissions. Why?

6. Your bicycle shop makes a profit of $20 on each bike sold. Advertisements on the local radio station cost $250 per 30-second slot. If you don't advertise, you'll sell 200 bikes per month. The first advertisement will increase sales by 80 bikes (from 200 to 280), and each additional ad will increase bike sales by half as much as the previous ad: The second ad increases sales by 40 bikes, the third increases sales by 20 bikes, and so on. How many radio ads should you purchase?

7. Comment on the following rule for advertising: "You should increase your advertising budget as long as one additional dollar of advertising increases your sales by at least one dollar."

8. Consider two automobile companies that are considering advertising campaigns. If neither firm advertises, each will earn net revenue of $5 million. If each spends $10 million on advertising, each firm's net revenue will be $12 million. If one advertises and the other does not, the firm that advertises will earn $17 million in net revenue, while the firm that does not will earn $1 million. Draw a game tree and predict the outcome. From the industry perspective, do the benefits of advertising exceed the costs?

9. Web Exercise. Visit the Web site of Coupons.com, an organization that provides information on all sorts of coupons [*http://www.coupons.com/*]. What sort of coupons are available, and how much do they cost? How much do firms providing these coupon packs charge?

10. Web Exercise. Visit the Web site of the Manitoba Milk Producers [*http://www.milk.mb.ca/*]. What sort of promotion does this association do? Why do the producers of milk band together to advertise milk rather than staging individual advertising campaigns?

Take It to the Net

We invite you to visit the O'Sullivan/Sheffrin page on the Prentice Hall Web site at:
http://www.prenhall.com/osullivan/ for additional World Wide Web exercises for this chapter.

Model Answers to Questions

Chapter-Opening Questions

1. Compared to students, faculty members are willing to pay more for campus movies (their demand is less elastic), so a profit-maximizing monopolist will charge them a higher price.

2. Consumers who are eager to read a book are willing to pay more, so they buy the expensive hardback version because it comes out first. People who are willing to pay less wait for the cheaper paperback version a few months later.

3. Using the marginal principle, the firm picks the number of ads at which the marginal benefit (the increase in net sales revenue) equals the marginal cost (the cost per ad).

4. You can pay (1) a fee per 1,000 impressions, (2) a fee per "click," or (3) a fee per acquisition (paying customer).

Test Your Understanding

1. People looking for aspirin in airports usually have a headache or expect one. They are willing to pay more than a headache-free grocery shopper: The airport shopper has a less elastic demand. Firms engage in price discrimination, charging a higher price to the group of consumers with the less elastic demand (airport customers).

2. Increase, decrease.

3. If women are willing to pay less than men for admission into a cocktail lounge or bar (they have a more elastic demand), price discrimination may increase the bar's profit. A discounted cover charge works well because the good purchased (admission) cannot be transferred to men.

4. One ad. The marginal benefit of the first ad exceeds the higher marginal cost, but the marginal benefit of the second ad ($9,000) is less than the marginal cost.

5. Two ads. The marginal benefit of the first ad is $8,000, and the marginal benefit of the second ad is $7,200, compared to a marginal cost of $7,000. The marginal benefit of the third ad is only $6,400, which is less than the marginal cost.

6. The price will increase. The more clickers, the greater the consumer exposure to banner ads, so the larger the increase in sales and the more money an advertiser is willing to pay for a banner ad.

Using the Tools

2. Price Discrimination in a Campus Film Series. We can use the formula for marginal revenue (explained in Chapter 10) to compute the marginal revenue for the two types of consumers. At the current prices, the marginal revenue for students is $2 = $3 − (100 viewers × $0.01 per viewer), which exceeds the marginal cost, so you should decrease the price for students. In contrast, the marginal revenue for faculty is −$1 = $4 − (50 viewers × $0.10 per viewer). Marginal revenue is negative, so an increase in price for faculty will increase total revenue.

3. Pricing First-Run Movies and Early Apples. The price pattern for movies is another example of price discrimination. Eager moviegoers are willing to pay a large amount of money for a movie when it first comes out, while patient moviegoers are willing to wait for the movie to appear in a second-run theater at a lower price.

The price pattern for apples is unlikely to be a case of price discrimination because the apple market is perfectly competitive: Each farmer takes the market price as given. Price discrimination isn't possible unless the firm has some control over its price. The price pattern for apples reflects the forces of supply and demand: Early in the harvest season, there aren't many apples available for sale, so the equilibrium price is relatively high. As supply increases over the course of the harvest season, the price drops. At the end of the season, the price rises again.

4. Picking a Web Page for a Banner Ad. The following table shows how to compute the net benefits for each Web page. If one of ten clickers purchases something, the number of orders (per 1,000 impressions) is 5 for A and 3 for B. If each customer spends 2% of his or her income, the average order is $40 for A and $100 for B. Total revenue equals the number of orders times the amount of the average order, and the net revenue equals 20% of total revenue. The net revenue is $40 for A and $60 for B, so the net benefit for A is $5 and the net benefit for B is $25. B is a better choice.

	Page A	Page B
Clicks per 1,000 impressions	50	30
Income of viewers	$2,000	$5,000
Orders	5	3
Average order	$40	$100
Revenue	$200	$300
Net revenue	$40	$60
Cost per 1,000 impressions	$35	$35
Net benefit	$5	$25

5. Advertising with Spillover Benefits: Got Milk? Figure 13.A shows the game tree. For George (the second mover), not advertising is a dominant strategy. If Bessie advertises, George earns a profit of $15 if he does not advertise, compared to only $13 if he does. If Bessie does not advertise, George earns a profit of $10 if he does not advertise, compared to $9 if he does. Knowing that George will not advertise no matter what she does, Bessie's best response is not to advertise: She earns a profit of $10 if she does not advertise, compared to $9 if she does. The advertisers' dilemma is that each firm would benefit if both firms advertised: Each would earn a profit of $13 million instead of $10 million, but neither will advertise. In this case, there are

Figure 13.A
Game Tree for Advertising with Spillover Benefits

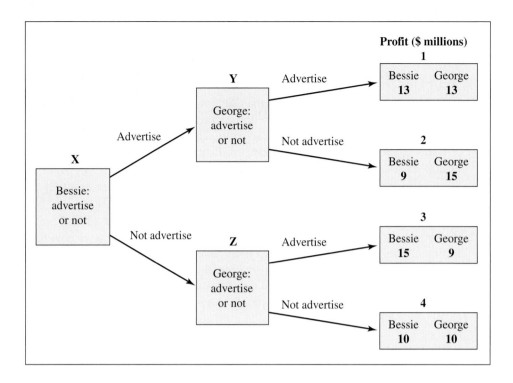

spillover benefits from advertising, while in the earlier example, the advertising campaign of one firm reduced the net revenue of a nonadvertising firm. An industry association might form to solve this problem by providing general advertising for milk, each firm sharing the cost of the campaign. The next time you see one of those "Got Milk?" advertisements, check to see who pays for it.

 Notes

1. William Comanor and Stuart O. Schweitzer, "Pharmaceuticals," Chapter 7 in *The Structure of the American Economy,* 9th ed., edited by Walter Adams and James W. Brock (Upper Saddle River, NJ: Prentice Hall, 1995).

2. Rance Crain, "Is Thirst for Alpha Status Behind Coke's High-Tech Talk?" *Advertising Age*, vol. 70, November 22, 1999, p. 26.

3. John C. Dvorak, "State of the Banner," *Forbes*, December 25, 2000, p. 273.

4. Lee Benham, "The Effects of Advertising on the Price of Eyeglasses," *Journal of Law and Economics,* vol. 15, 1972, pp. 337–352.

Controlling Market Power: Antitrust Policy and Deregulation

In January 2001, the lights went out in California. The statewide demand for electricity exceeded the supply, and electric utilities across the state used a system of rolling blackouts to cut the power to blocks of customers in turn. The blackouts snarled traffic, forced people to shop and eat by candlelight, caused manufacturers to send their workers home, and made life miserable for everyone. At the same time, the utilities lost money on every kilowatt hour they sold. The utilities lost a total of $12 billion, and Pacific Gas and Electric filed for bankruptcy.

The California energy debacle came just a few years after the state reformed its heavily regulated electricity market, deregulating parts of the market. Was the energy debacle caused by too little deregulation, or too much?

his chapter explores two policy issues concerning firms in concentrated markets. We'll start with a look at antitrust policies, which are designed to promote competition in markets dominated by a few large firms. Under federal antitrust rules, the government can break up monopolies into several smaller companies, prevent corporate mergers that would reduce competition, and regulate business practices that tend to reduce competition. The second policy issue is deregulation. We'll discuss recent deregulation of three markets: air travel, telecommunications, and electricity. In these cases, the government recently reversed a long history of regulation in an attempt to promote competition. Here are some practical policy questions that we answer:

1. Why did the government prevent the proposed merger between Office Depot and Staples, two office-supply chains?
2. What was the government's antitrust case against Microsoft Corporation all about?
3. How did the deregulation of air travel affect the price of air travel?
4. In what sense was the California energy crisis of 2000–2001 a good example of the "perfect storm" theory of disasters?

Antitrust Policy

The purpose of antitrust policy is to promote competition among firms, with the idea that competition leads to lower prices and better products. Table 14.1 provides a brief summary of the history of antitrust policy. The first legislation was the Sherman Antitrust Act of 1890, which made it illegal to monopolize a market or to engage in practices that result in a restraint of trade. Because the act did not specify which practices were illegal, it led to conflicting court rulings.

Many of the ambiguities of the Sherman Act were resolved by the Clayton Act of 1914. The Clayton Act outlawed specific practices that discourage competition, including tying contracts (requiring a consumer who buys one product to buy a second product) and price discrimination that reduces competition. The act also outlawed mergers resulting from the purchase of a competitor's stock when such a merger would substantially reduce competition. Also in 1914, the government established the Federal Trade Commission to enforce antitrust laws.

Table 14.1 Brief History of Antitrust Legislation

1890	Sherman Act: Made it illegal to monopolize a market or to engage in practices that result in a restraint of trade.
1914	Clayton Act: Outlawed specific practices that discourage competition, including tying contracts, price discrimination for the purpose of reducing competition, and stock-purchase mergers that would substantially reduce competition.
1914	Federal Trade Commission Act: Established to enforce antitrust laws.
1936	Robinson-Patman Act: Prohibited selling products at "unreasonably low prices" with the intent of reducing competition.
1950	Celler-Kefauver Act: Outlawed asset-purchase mergers that would substantially reduce competition.
1980	Hart-Scott-Rodino Act: Extended antitrust legislation to proprietorships and partnerships.

More recent legislation has clarified and extended antitrust law. The Robinson-Patman Act of 1936 prohibited selling products at unreasonably low prices with the intent of reducing competition, a practice known as predatory pricing. The Celler-Kefauver Act of 1950 closed a loophole in the Clayton Act by outlawing mergers through the purchase of another firm's physical assets (for example, buildings and equipment) when such a merger would reduce competition substantially. The Hart-Scott-Rodino Act of 1980 extended antitrust legislation to proprietorships and partnerships. Before this act, antitrust legislation applied only to corporations.

Two government organizations, the Antitrust Division of the Department of Justice, and the Federal Trade Commission, are responsible for initiating actions against individuals or firms that may be violating antitrust laws. The courts have the power to impose penalties on the executives found to be in violation of the laws, including fines and prison sentences. In some cases, the government seeks no penalties but directs the firm to discontinue illegal practices and take other measures to promote competition.

Breaking Up Monopolies

One form of antitrust policy is to break up a monopoly into several smaller firms. A **trust** is an arrangement under which the owners of several companies transfer their decision-making powers to a small group of trustees, who then make decisions for all the participating firms. Firms in a trust act as a single firm, so an industry that appears to have many firms may in fact be a virtual monopoly.

Trust: An arrangement under which the owners of several companies transfer their decision-making powers to a small group of trustees, who then make decisions for all the firms in the trust.

The label *antitrust* comes from early cases that involved breaking up trusts. The classic example is John D. Rockefeller's Standard Oil Trust, which was formed in 1882 when the owners of 40 oil companies empowered nine trustees to make the decisions for all 40 companies. The trust controlled over 90 percent of the market for refined petroleum products, and the trustees ran it like a monopoly. In 1911, the government ordered the breakup of the Standard Oil Trust. The Supreme Court found that Rockefeller had used "unnatural methods" to maintain his monopoly power and drive his rivals out of business. He coerced railroads to give him special rates for shipping and spied on his competitors. The government broke up Standard Oil into 34 separate companies, including the corporate ancestors to Exxon, Mobil, Chevron, and Amoco.

After the American Tobacco Company bought 30 of its competitors, it controlled 95% of the U.S. cigarette market. The Supreme Court found that American Tobacco maintained its monopoly power by driving rivals out of business and agreeing to exclusive contracts with wholesalers that prevented them from purchasing cigarettes from other companies. The court-ordered breakup in 1911 led to several new companies, including several of today's big cigarette companies: Reynolds, Liggett and Meyers, and P. Lorillard.

In 1982, the government broke up American Telephone and Telegraph (AT&T) into seven regional phone companies. AT&T had used its legal monopoly in local telephone service to prevent competition in the markets for long-distance service and communications equipment. After an eight-year legal battle, AT&T agreed to form seven Regional Bell Operating Companies, transforming "Ma Bell" into seven "Baby Bells." The new AT&T was allowed to compete in the market for long-distance service, where it faced competition from newcomers MCI and Sprint. AT&T was also allowed to operate in the market for communications equipment, where it faced competition from newcomers Mitel and Northern Telecom.

Blocking Mergers

A **merger** occurs when two firms combine their operations. A second type of antitrust policy is to block corporate mergers that would reduce competition and lead to higher prices. We saw in Chapter 11 that as the number of firms in a market increases, compe-

Merger: A process in which two or more firms combine their operations.

tition among firms drives down prices. Because a merger decreases the number of firms in a market, it is likely to lead to higher prices. In 1994, Microsoft tried to purchase Intuit, the maker of Quicken, a personal-finance software package that was a substitute for a similar Microsoft product. The merger would have reduced competition in the personal-finance software market, so the government blocked the merger.

Of course, the government does not oppose all corporate mergers. One possible benefit from a merger is that the new firm could combine production, marketing, or administrative operations and thus produce its products at a lower average cost. In 1997, the Justice Department and the Federal Trade Commission released new guidelines for proposed mergers. The new guidelines allow companies involved in a proposed merger to present evidence that the merger would reduce costs and lead to lower prices, better products, or better service. If the evidence for greater efficiency is convincing, the government might allow a merger that reduces the number of firms in a market. FTC Chairman Robert Pitofsky assessed the effects of the new guidelines as follows:[1]

> There may be some deals that go through which otherwise would not have. But it won't change the result in a large number of cases [rather it will have] the greatest impact in a transaction where the potential anticompetitive problem is modest and efficiencies that would be created are great.

The new guidelines will bring the U.S. antitrust rules closer to those of Europe and Canada, and could help U.S. companies compete in those markets.

In recent years, the analysis of proposed mergers has shifted from counting the number of firms in a market to predicting how a particular merger would affect price effects. The data generated by retail checkout scanners provides an enormous amount of information about prices and quantities sold. Using this data, economists can determine how one firm's pricing policies affect the sales of that firm and its competitors. Economists can use this information to predict whether a merger would lead to higher prices. Two recent antitrust cases illustrate how this new approach works.

Wonder Bread

In 1995, Interstate Bakeries (the nation's third largest wholesale baker) tried to buy Continental Baking (the maker of Wonder Bread). Based on grocery-store scanner data, the government concluded that Wonder Bread is a close substitute for Interstate's bread: The demand for Wonder Bread increases when the price of Interstate's bread increases, and vice versa.[2] The scanner data showed that when Interstate increased its price, many consumers switched to Wonder Bread, so their bread money went to Continental instead of Interstate. The substitutability of the two brands discouraged Interstate from increasing its prices.

Figure 14.1 shows the pricing decisions for each firm when each acts independently. Each firm uses the marginal principle, picking the quantity at which the marginal revenue from bread equals the marginal cost. Given a constant marginal cost of $1.00, each firm charges a price of $1.50 and sells 500 loaves per minute. The profit per loaf is $0.50, so the total profit for each firm is $250 ($0.50 per loaf times 500 loaves).

How would a merger affect Interstate's incentives to raise its prices? After a merger, a single company (let's call it Wonderstate) would earn the profits from both brands (Wonder and Interstate) and pick both prices. Suppose Wonderstate increased the price of Interstate bread to $1.60 but kept the price of Wonder Bread at $1.50. The price hike would bring bad news and good news for Wonderstate, the new firm:

- **Bad news: Less profit on Interstate Bread.** As shown in Figure 14.1, at the higher price, only 400 loaves of Interstate Bread would be sold. As we see by multiplying

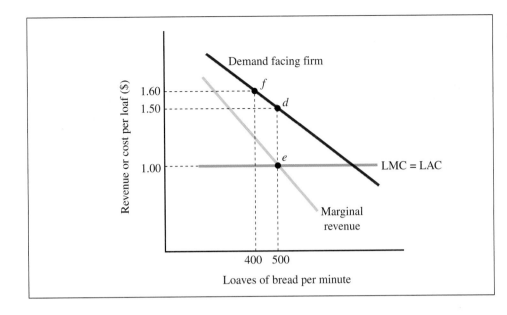

Figure 14.1

The Marginal Principle and Pricing of White Bread
Using the marginal principle, each bread firm picks the quantity at which marginal revenue equals marginal cost. At the profit-maximizing price of $1.50 per loaf, each firm sells 500 loaves and earns a profit of $0.50 per loaf, for a profit of $250.

the new profit per loaf ($0.60) by the new quantity (400 loaves), profit from the Interstate brand would decrease to $240, down from $250.

- **Good news: More profit on Wonder Bread.** Suppose the increase in the price of Interstate Bread increases the quantity of Wonder Bread sold from 500 to 560 loaves per minute. The profit per loaf is still $0.50 per bread, so the profit on Wonder Bread increases to $280, up from $250.

In this case, the good news ($30 more in profit from Wonder Bread) exceeds the bad news ($10 less profit from Interstate Bread), so the price hike for Interstate Bread would increase the profit of Wonderstate, the new firm. Before a merger, the good news would be experienced by another firm (the firm making Wonder Bread). A merger means that this good news stays within the larger firm, encouraging that firm to increase prices.

The lesson from this example is that a merger of two firms selling close substitutes may lead to higher prices. That's what the Department of Justice concluded in the case of Interstate Bakeries and Continental Bakery. The government allowed the merger between the two companies but forced Interstate to sell some of its brands and bakeries. For example, Interstate sold the rights to sell its Weber brand bread to Four-S Banking Company. The idea is to ensure that other companies will compete with the new merged company in the market for white bread.

Staples and Office Depot

Pricing data were also used to predict the price effects of a merger between two office-supply chains, Staples and Office Depot, in 1997. Economists with the Federal Trade Commission (FTC) examined the prices and quantities of each item sold by the two chains. With the help of computers, the economists found an interesting pattern: The prices charged by Staples were lower in cities where Office Depot also had a store.[3]

Figure 14.2 shows the economics behind higher prices in cities without an Office Depot. The figure shows Staples' revenue and cost curves for one specific product: file folders. Panel A shows what happens when Staples faces no competition from an Office Depot, and panel B shows what happens when it does. The demand curve facing Staples is lower in the city where it faces competition with Office Depot because the two firms share the market. Using the marginal principle, Staples picks the quantity and price

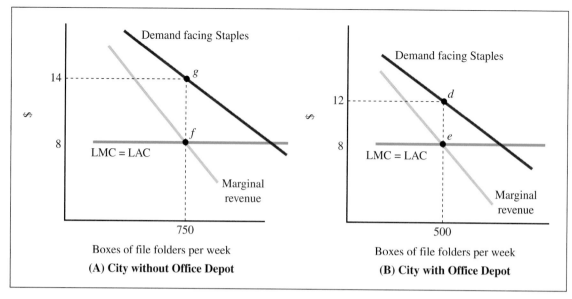

(A) City without Office Depot

Boxes of file folders per week

(B) City with Office Depot

Boxes of file folders per week

Figure 14.2 **Pricing by Staples Office Supplies in Different Cities**
Using the marginal principle, Staples picks the quantity at which its marginal revenue equals its marginal cost. In a city without a competing firm, Staples picks the monopoly price of $14. In a city where Staples competes with Office Depot, the demand facing Staples is relatively low, so the profit-maximizing price is only $12.

where its marginal revenue equals its marginal cost. The profit-maximizing price is $14 in a city without an Office Depot, and $12 in a city with one.

The FTC used this logic to convince the court that the proposed merger of Staples and Office Depot would lead to higher prices. The judge in the case observed that, "direct evidence shows that by eliminating Staples' most significant, and in many markets, only, rival, this merger would allow Staples to increase prices or otherwise maintain prices at

Pricing data showed that the prices charged by Staples were lower in cities where Office Depot also had a store. The Department of Justice blocked a proposed merger of the two firms.

A CLOSER LOOK | ANTITRUST POLICY IN ASIA

Many nations in Asia have a history of weak antitrust policy. A few years ago during negotiations between two Hong Kong companies, a junior member of one of the negotiating teams passed a note to his boss suggesting that he remind his adversary of Hong Kong's open and competitive markets.[4] The boss scribbled his response: "Nonsense (expletive modified)! Hong Kong was built on cartels and don't ever forget it."

In recent years, several Asian countries have strengthened their antitrust laws. Japan is investigating the telecom giant NTT, and South Korea recently fined two industrial groups, Posco and Samsung, for anti-competitive practices. Indonesia and Malaysia are in the process of developing antitrust laws and enforcement mechanisms.

Despite this recent activism, antitrust laws and enforcement in Asia are much weaker than in Europe and America. Hong Kong and Singapore still do not have general laws against cartels. There are special challenges in implementing antitrust policy in Asia because economic power is concentrated in fewer hands. In South Korea, many markets are dominated by family-

owned conglomerates, or *chaebol*. In other countries many businesses are controlled by a small number of tycoons with close ties to local governments. It remains to be seen whether Asian countries will strengthen their antitrust policies to match those of Europe and America.

an anti-competitive level."[5] Evidence from the companies' pricing data showed that the merger would have allowed Staples to increase its prices by about 13%. By blocking the merger, the FTC saved consumers an estimated $1.1 billion over five years.[6]

In some cases, the government acts after the fact, seeking remedies for an earlier merger that increased prices. In 1981, the Federal Trade Commission brought an antitrust suit against Xidex Corporation for its earlier acquisition of two rivals in the microfilm market. By acquiring Scott Graphics, Inc. in 1976 and Kalvar Corporation in 1979, Xidex increased its market share of the U.S. microfilm market from 46% to 71%. As a result, the price of microfilm increased: The price of one type of microfilm (diazo) increased by 11%, and the price of a second type (vesicular) increased by 23%. These price hikes were large enough that Xidex recovered the cost of acquiring its two rivals ($4.2 million for Scott Graphics and $6 million for Kalvar) in less than two years.[7]

This is a classic case of a merger that leads to higher prices and more profits for a dominant firm. To settle the antitrust lawsuit, Xidex agreed to license its microfilm technology—at bargain prices—to other firms. The idea is that if other firms have access to the microfilm technology, the competition between Xidex and the competing firms will decrease the price of microfilm.

Check the Yellow Pages

Economic Detective

On Katrina's first day on the job as an economist with the Federal Trade Commission, she was put on a team examining a proposed merger between the country's second and fourth largest hardware-store chains. Her job was to predict whether a merger would increase hardware prices. Her boss handed her some disks with checkout scanner data from the second largest chain. Each disk contained scanner data from one small town, listing the prices and quantities of hammers, wrenches, nuts, bolts, rakes, glue, drills, and hundreds of other hardware products. Her boss also gave her the telephone yellow pages for each small town. What can she do with the disks and the yellow pages?

The key to solving this mystery is to recognize the similarity to the case of Staples and Office Depot. A merger of the country's second and fourth largest hardware chains could reduce competition and lead to higher prices. If the scanner data show that prices are lower in some towns, Katrina could look in the yellow pages to see which towns have hardware stores from both chains and which don't. If the towns that are served by both chains have lower prices, the proposed merger would probably decrease competition and increase prices.

Regulating Business Practices

The third type of antitrust policy involves the regulation of business practices. The government may intervene when a specific business practice increases market concentration in an already concentrated market. Among the practices that are subject to scrutiny are price fixing (discussed in Chapter 12), **tying** (forcing consumers of one product to purchase another), and price discrimination that reduces competition.

The Robinson-Patman Act prohibits selling products at "unreasonably low prices" with the intent of reducing competition, a practice known as **predatory pricing**. The idea is that a firm sells a product at a price below its production costs, forcing its rivals to do the same or leave the market. Once the predator's rivals drop out of the market, the firm then charges a monopoly price, well above its production cost. This will be a profitable strategy if the firm can charge the monopoly price for a long enough period to offset the losses it experienced while driving its rival out of business.

Is there a reason to be skeptical about a claim of predatory pricing? Consider a market with two firms, one of which is determined to have the market to itself. By cutting its price below its cost, the firm can drive its competitor out of business, losing perhaps $10 million in the process. If it increases its price next year, there may be nothing to prevent a new firm from entering the market. If so, it would have to cut its price below its cost again to drive the new firm out. The problem with predatory pricing is that it never ends; the firm must repeatedly lose money to drive out an endless series of competitors.

The Microsoft Case

In recent years, the most widely reported antitrust actions have involved Microsoft Corporation, the software giant. Microsoft receives royalties from computer makers that install the Microsoft operating software on their computers. The curious—and illegal—feature of the original arrangement was that Microsoft received a royalty for every computer made by the firm, even if the firm installed other operating systems on some of its computers. This scheme discouraged computer makers from using software from Microsoft's rivals, and the courts declared it illegal in 1994.

The case of *United States* v. *Microsoft Corporation* demonstrated that Microsoft stifled competition in the software industry. In the initial ruling, Judge Jackson ruled that Microsoft [i] used illegal practices to protect its monopoly in the market for operating systems, [ii] illegally tied the operating system to Internet Explorer, the Microsoft browser, and [iii] used its monopoly in operating systems to gain a monopoly in the browser market. As a remedy, the judge ordered Microsoft to be split into two companies, one producing the Windows operating system and a second producing application software.

Tying: A business practice under which a consumer of one product is required to purchase another product.

Predatory pricing: A pricing scheme under which a firm decreases its price to drive a rival out of business and increases the price when the other firm disappears.

The U.S. Court of Appeals for the Washington, D.C. Circuit Court overruled Judge Jackson on the issue of the browser monopoly, but upheld the judge's ruling that Microsoft violated the Sherman Antitrust Act by employing anticompetitive practices to protect its operating-system monopoly. The Appeals Court ordered a lower court to reexamine the issue of tying the operating system to the browser. Most important, the Appeals Court overturned the breakup remedy and directed the courts to develop an alternative remedy.

For the latest on the case, check the Web site for the U.S. Department of Justice (*http://www.usdoj.gov*).

TEST Your Understanding

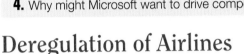

1. List three types of antitrust policies.
2. Why was the federal government concerned about the merger of Interstate Bakeries and Continental Baking?
3. What are the essential provisions of the new guidelines for corporate mergers?
4. Why might Microsoft want to drive competing browsers out of the market?

Deregulation of Airlines and Telecommunications

In this part of the chapter, we explore the recent deregulation of two markets: air travel and telecommunications. In both cases, the motivation behind deregulation was to increase competition and decrease prices. The Airline Deregulation Act of 1978 eliminated entry restrictions and price controls in the market for air travel. The Telecommunications Act of 1996 eliminated most price controls for cable television and established a framework for entry into the markets for cable television service, local telephone service, and Internet service.

Deregulation of Airlines

Before 1978, the Civil Aeronautics Board (CAB) regulated interstate air travel by limiting entry into the market and controlling prices. About 90% of the markets were monopolized, with prices that were between 30% and 50% higher than the prices that would have occurred in a more competitive environment.[8] The Airline Deregulation Act of 1978 eliminated most of the entry restrictions and price controls, and the CAB eventually disappeared.

In the first few years after deregulation, a large number of firms entered the market, and competition among airlines serving individual markets (individual routes) increased. Since then, many of the firms that entered the market just after deregulation have disappeared. Some firms went out of business, and others merged with other airlines. Some of the airline mergers have led to lower production costs and prices, while others have reduced competition and led to higher prices.[9] Some cities now have a dominant airline, and fares are actually higher than they were before deregulation.[10]

A single firm controls at least 55% of airline traffic at 10 of the largest 15 U.S. airports.[11] Among the cities with the most dominant firms are Cincinnati (Delta controls 91% of the market), Pittsburgh (United, 88%), Minneapolis–St. Paul (Northwest, 82%), Atlanta (Delta, 80%), Houston (Continental, 78%), Denver (United, 70%), and Dallas–Fort Worth (American, 66%).

The consensus among economists is that airline deregulation generated net benefits for consumers.[12] On average, fares have decreased by about 33% in real terms since deregulation, and the frequency of service has increased. Several factors contributed to lower prices: competition from incumbent carriers (18% of the savings), competition from Southwest Airlines (31%), competition from other entrants (10%), and improvements in carriers' operating efficiencies (41%).

Deregulation of Telecommunication Services

The Telecommunications Act of 1996 established new rules for firms involved in the transmission of video, voice, and data. The basic idea is to promote competition in the markets for telecommunications services. Several provisions of the act will affect the Regional Bell Operating Companies (the Baby Bells) that were formed as a result of the breakup of AT&T in 1982. Here are the most important provisions of the act:

- **Local telephone service.** The act opened local telephone service to competition, with the idea that new firms would compete with the Baby Bells for local service. In addition, cable-TV firms might eventually provide telephone service over their cables.

- **Cable-TV service.** Price controls for cable-TV services were eliminated, and telephone companies are to be allowed to enter the market for cable-TV services.

- **Long-distance service.** Once there is sufficient competition for local telephone service, the Baby Bells will be allowed to enter the market for long-distance service.

One purpose of the act is to open local telephone service to real competition. The challenge is to develop a set of rules that would allow new competitors to get access to the copper wires leading into residences. These wires are controlled by the Baby Bells, which of course are not eager to give their new competitors access to their facilities. Although the Federal Communication Commission has developed pricing rules governing access to the copper wires, the rules have been tied up in court for several years. Therefore, there has been little progress in opening up local telephone service to competition. Consequently, the Baby Bells have not yet been allowed to enter the market for long-distance service.

The policy objective is to negotiate an access fee for ISPs that is high enough for the telephone companies to recover the costs of installing and maintaining the system. The Baby Bells would like to enter the market for Internet services themselves but are prohibited from entering any market for long-distance services—for voice or data—until there is more competition in local phone service.

We can summarize our discussion of deregulation of telecommunications as follows. In the telecommunications market, competition requires rival firms to share facilities (copper wires and cables leading into residences). The challenge for policymakers is to develop a set of pricing rules that allows rival firms to share these facilities. Once those rules are in place and households have more options for the transmission of voice, data, and video, we can expect more competition, lower prices, and better service.

Electricity Deregulation

The electricity industry has been regulated as a natural monopoly since its early days. There are three stages of producing electricity: generation in power plants, transmission along high-voltage lines, and distribution to final users along low-voltage lines. The transmission stage is subject to economies of scale because a market (for example, a city) can be served by one set of transmission lines from power-generating facilities. Substantial fixed costs are associated with laying the transmission lines, so it is sensible to lay one set of lines and regulate the single firm as a natural monopolist. The same logic applies to the distribution system: The substantial fixed costs of a distribution network mean that it is sensible to have a single network managed by a natural monopolist.

Until recently, there were also substantial economics of scale in electricity genera- tion. The minimum efficient scale for power plants was large relative to the size of the markets they served, meaning that a single firm could supply the market more effi- ciently than several small firms. Recent technological innovations have reduced the economies of scale in electricity generation, so generation is no longer a true natural monopoly. For example, the minimum efficient scale for combined cycle gas turbine technology (CCGT) is about one-fifth the scale of a traditional power plant.

Traditional Regulation and Pressure to Deregulate

Under traditional electricity regulation, public and private utilities were responsible for all three phases of electricity production: They generated electricity in their own power plants and then used their own transmission and distribution systems to deliver electricity to consumers. State and local governments granted each utility a monopoly over a particular geographical area and set the price of electricity at a level so the utility earned a reasonable or "fair" accounting profit. Because utilities were responsible for all three stages of pro- duction, there was just one price to control—the retail price charged to consumers.

In the 1990s, there was growing pressure to deregulate the electricity market. There were three forces behind the pressure to deregulate.

- As we saw earlier in the book, if the controlled price is set equal to the firm's aver- age cost of production, the regulated firm has less incentive to control its costs, which leads to higher costs and higher prices.

- There was substantial variation in electricity prices across regions and states. For example, the price was 10 cents per kilowatt hour (kwh) in some northeastern states (Massachusetts, Connecticut, and New York), 6 cents in some central states (Indiana and Wisconsin), and 5 cents in northwestern states (Oregon and Washington). In California, the price was 9.5 cents per kwh. Consumers in high-price states called for deregulation to allow electricity to be transmitted across state lines.

- The development of alternative technology reduced the economies of scale in elec- tricity generation, so generation is no longer considered a natural monopoly. Instead of a single power source for a city, there could be many generators, with competition among alternative producers leading to lower prices.

From an economist's perspective, the ideal deregulation plan would have five features.

1. Get utilities out of the generation business. The utilities would be responsible for transmission and distribution, with the regulated price of transmission and distri- bution being just high enough to allow the utilities to cover their costs.

2. Open electricity generation to competition, allowing generators to sell their power in an open market to any energy firm.

3. Open the retailing market to competition. Each consumer would choose a firm to supply power. Each retail firm would buy power from a generator and pay the reg- ulated price for using the utilities' wires to transmit electricity to their consumers.

4. Allow the retail price to be determined by the market. In this ideal situation, com- petition among power generators would lead to lower wholesale prices (paid by electricity retailers to generators) and lower retail prices (paid by consumers to retailers).

5. Eliminate any geographical limits on power supply. Electricity retailers could buy their power from out-of-state generators. For example, California retailers could buy cheap hydroelectric power from Oregon generators. In this case, the delivered price in California would reflect higher transmission costs, but that's all.

The California Experience

The state of California reformed its electricity regulation program in 1998. Although the plan is often labeled "California's Deregulation Plan," the label is inaccurate because although some regulations were eliminated, others remained in force. In an attempt to foster competition at the generation level, the state's utilities sold off their generating facilities to the highest bidders. The wholesale price (paid by utilities and other energy retailers to generators) was allowed to fluctuate with market forces, but the retail price was subject to strict controls. The retail price was rolled back by 10% and was to be maintained at this level for several years.

Two years after the reform program was implemented, the California electricity market was in disarray. Utilities did not have enough power to meet demand, and were forced to implement rolling blackouts—cutting off the power supply for an hour in each designated area in turn. The wholesale price for electricity was about 500% higher than it was the previous year, while the retail price was stuck at the regulated level. Electric utilities lost money on each kilowatt hour of electricity they sold, and their losses were measured in the billions of dollars. In the period June from 2000 to December 2000, the wholesale price was between $103 and $385 per megawatt hour (Mwh), while the retail price was controlled at roughly $60 per Mwh.[13] The expected entry of new retailers didn't happen because any entering firm would lose money, experiencing the same fate as the utilities. By 2001, the retailer/utilities had lost $12 billion, and in early 2001 one of the state's largest utilities, Pacific Gas and Electric, filed for bankruptcy.

The disarray in the electricity market was caused in part by a mismatch between supply and demand.[14] Between 1996 and 2000, the total demand for electricity increased by about 17%. In the 1990s, the state's economy grew quickly, with especially rapid growth in power-hungry "new economy" activities such as electronics manufacturing and Internet commerce. While the economy was growing, the already small reserve capacity of the electricity-generating industry shrunk. In the 10 years preceding the demand surge in the late 1990s, no new generating facilities were built in the state. Between 1996 and 2000, the state's generating capacity actually dropped by 4%. An additional factor on the supply side was an increase in the price of natural gas, the most widely used fuel for electricity generation.

Normally, an increase in demand increases prices, which encourages consumers to consume less and producers to supply more. Why didn't this happen in California in 2001? Given the maximum retail price, consumers didn't have much of an incentive to reduce their power consumption. On the supply side, it takes a year or two to bring a generating facility on line, so even in the best of circumstances, the generating capacity couldn't increase immediately. In addition, the financial problems experienced by utilities could lead to bankruptcy, meaning that some generators might never be paid for the electricity generated in their new facilities. This risk reduced the incentive for new firms to enter the generating market. In addition, the utilities' financial problems caused some small independent generators to refuse to sell electricity to the utilities. In other words, the maximum retail price caused problems on both sides of the market: Consumers had less incentive to conserve, and producers had less incentive to supply power.

What about importing electricity from other states? One of the purposes of the reform plan was to encourage the purchase of power from other states. Although the excess demand for power in California increased imports somewhat, the surrounding states—most with rapidly growing economies—didn't have much excess capacity. In the Northwest, a drought reduced the generating capacity of hydroelectric sources, causing excess demand for power in Oregon and Washington.

An additional factor in the California energy crisis was price manipulation by generators large enough to exercise their market power. The objective of the reform plan was to promote competition in the generating market, but after the utilities sold their power plants to the highest bidders, a few companies controlled most of the power generated in the state. As we saw earlier in the book, firms in oligopolies have the power to charge a price higher than the competitive price, and there is evidence that's what happened in California.[15] One study suggests that the competitive price in June 2000 would have been about $70 per Mwh, while the actual price was about $120 per Mwh. In other words, the actual price was almost double the competitive price. In computing the competitive price, the study took into account the costs of producing electricity (including pollution-control costs and fuel costs) and demand conditions. The same study provides evidence that generators used a strategy of supply withholding (taking plants off line to create an artificial shortage) to manipulate prices.

It's important to note that power shortages might have occurred even without the California reform plan. In a traditional regulatory environment, an increase in demand with nearly zero excess capacity would cause excess demand and either higher prices or quantity restrictions such as brownouts or rolling blackouts. Of course, a utility that got power from its own plant wouldn't experience the financial problems of a utility that must buy power in an unregulated wholesale market. Nonetheless, some power shortages might have occurred even under the traditional regulatory environment.

The California energy crisis is an example of the "perfect storm" view of disasters. Several factors contributed to the crisis—an increase in demand for electricity, stagnant supply, rising fuel costs, retail price controls, price manipulation, and drought in the Pacific Northwest. Although none of these factors by itself would have caused major problems, their convergence in the year 2001 led to soaring wholesale prices, billions of dollars lost by utilities, and rolling blackouts that disrupted the economy.

Deregulation in Other States

In the middle 1990s, Pennsylvania and New York restructured their electricity markets, with both moving toward deregulated markets. Under both plans, consumers can choose from several electricity retailers. Some retailers also generate their own power, while others buy power from generators and transmit the electricity to business and residential users. There are Web sites where consumers can provide their Zip codes and get a list of alternative suppliers. By April 2001, almost 800,000 Pennsylvanians had selected alternative electricity suppliers.[16]

The early experience with electricity deregulation in the two states is mixed. Prices are lower in Pennsylvania, but much higher in New York.[17] Under the New York plan, utilities sold off their generating plants to the highest bidders. The plants were sold to a small number of firms and the purchase prices were much higher than expected, reflecting the expectations that in the deregulated market with a small number of generators, each firm could charge a high price. Over a one-year period, the average bill for Con Ed increased by about 38%, reflecting higher fuel costs and perhaps some exercise of market power by generators.

It is too early to determine the long-term effects on electricity deregulation. The energy debacle in California has provided some important lessons for policymakers in other states. Many other states are at earlier stages of the deregulation process, and may modify their plans to avoid some of the problems generated by the perfect storm in California.

5. Did the deregulation of the airline industry lead to low prices in all cities?

6. Under what conditions will the Baby Bells be allowed to provide long-distance service?

7. List the factors that contributed to the California energy crisis.

Using the **TOOLS**

In this chapter, we've explored some policy issues concerning firms in concentrated industries. We've explored the incentives for predatory pricing, seen the price effects of mergers, and considered the effects of deregulation on competition and prices. Here are some opportunities to do your own economic analysis.

APPLICATIONS

1. Cost Savings from a Merger

Consider the following statement from a firm that has proposed a merger between two companies: "The two companies could save about $50 million per year by combining our production, marketing, and administrative operations. In other words, we could realize substantial economies of scale. Therefore, the government should allow the merger." In light of the new guidelines concerning mergers, how would you react to this statement?

2. Willingness to Pay for New Airport Gates

Your city is considering an airport expansion project that would increase the number of airport gates and allow additional airlines to serve your city. According to a recent report, the additional competition made possible by the new gates would decrease the average airline fare from $220 to $200 and increase the number of passengers from 400 to 600 per day. The city would borrow money to finance the project, and the daily payment required to pay off the loan (over 20 years) would be $8,100. Is the project worthwhile from the social perspective?

Summary

In this chapter, we've explored two types of policy issues concerning firms in concentrated industries: antitrust policy and deregulation. The purpose of antitrust policy is to promote competition among the few firms in a concentrated market. In the airline industry and the telecommunication industry, deregulation has generated mixed results. Here are the main points of the chapter:

1. Under antitrust policies, the government breaks up some dominant firms, prevents some corporate mergers, and regulates business practices that reduce competition.

2. The modern approach to merger policy doesn't simply look at the number of firms in an industry but uses data on prices and quantities sold to predict the price effects of a merger.

3. In most circumstances, predatory pricing is unprofitable because the monopoly power is costly to acquire and doesn't last very long.

4. The deregulation of the airline industry has led to more competition and lower prices on average but higher prices in some markets.

5. The purpose of the deregulation of the telecommunications industry is to promote competition in phone service, cable television, and Internet access.

Key Terms

merger, 295
predatory pricing, 300

trust, 295

tying, 300

Problems and Discussion Questions

1. Consider a market that is initially served by two firms, each of which charges a price of $10 and sells 100 units of the good. The long-run average cost of production is constant at $9 per unit. Suppose a merger would increase the price to $14 and reduce the total quantity sold from 200 to 150. Compute the consumer loss associated with the merger. How does it compare to the increase in profit? What is the net loss from the merger?

2. Consider an allegation that a firm is engaging in predatory pricing, picking a price below its average cost in an attempt to drive its competitors out of business. Why might you be skeptical about such a claim?

3. The construction project at your city's airport is nearing completion, and your job is to decide how to use the 10 new gates of the airport. The city is currently served by Gotcha Airlines, which has offered the city $20 million to help cover the cost of the airport construction project. In return, the new gates would be designated for the exclusive use of Gotcha. What trade-offs are associated with accepting Gotcha's offer?

4. As the recently appointed head of the Federal Communications Commission, your job is to develop a set of rules for the use of the cables laid by cable-television companies. You must decide whether the ISPs should have access and, if so, at what price.

5. Web Exercise. Visit the Web site of the U.S. Federal Trade Commission [*http://www.ftc.gov/*]. Access the Antitrust/Competition part of the Web site, and in the Antitrust Menu, open the document *Promoting Competition, Protecting Consumer: A Plain English Guide to Antitrust Laws*. What is the difference between a vertical merger and a horizontal merger? What is a Potential Competition merger and why might the FTC block one?

2. Web Exercise. Visit the Web site of the U.S. Federal Communications Commission [*http://www.fcc.gov/*]. Do a search of the site for the latest news and analysis of the issue of broadband Internet access. What is the FCC doing to promote competition in Internet access?

Take It to the Net

We invite you to visit the O'Sullivan/Sheffrin page on the Prentice Hall Web site at:
http://www.prenhall.com/osullivan/ for additional World Wide Web exercises for this chapter.

Model Answers to Questions

Chapter-Opening Questions

1. Pricing data showed that the prices charged by Staples were lower in cities where Office Depot also had a store, suggesting that competition between the two firms kept prices low. A merger would eliminate the competition, leading to higher prices.

2. The government alleged that Microsoft used its monopoly power in operating systems to try to gain a monopoly in the Internet browser market. In addition, the government alleged that Microsoft tried to dominate the browser market to protect its monopoly in operating systems. A "findings of fact" accepted these allegations.

3. Deregulation decreased prices on average, but increased concentration in some cities led to higher fares in those cities.

4. None of the individual factors contributing to the crisis would have been enough to cause big problems, but their convergence caused disaster.

Test Your Understanding

1. Breaking up monopolies, blocking mergers, and regulating business practices (price fixing, tying, and price discrimination).

2. Scanner data showed that the white breads produced by the two firms were close substitutes. An unregulated merger would have reduced competition and led to higher prices.

3. Companies that are involved in a proposed merger can present evidence that the merger would reduce costs and lead to lower prices, better products, or better service. If the evidence for this is convincing, the government might allow a merger that reduces the number of firms in a market.

4. If Microsoft succeeded in driving competing browsers out of the market, the browser threat to Internet Explorer would disappear.

5. No. On average, prices decreased, but travelers to and from some cities that are served by only one or two airlines pay higher prices.

6. Sufficient competition in the market for local telephone service.

7. An increase in demand for electricity, stagnant supply, rising fuel costs, retail price controls, price manipulation, and drought in the Pacific Northwest.

Using the Tools

1. **Cost Savings from a Merger.** The new guidelines allow companies to present evidence that a merger would reduce costs. If the evidence for greater efficiency is convincing, the government might allow a merger that reduces the number of firms in a market. As is shown in the quote from FTC Chairman Pitofsky, the increased efficiency must be large enough to offset concerns about the reduction in competition. The question is whether reduced competition and higher prices might offset the $50 million savings in cost.

2. **Willingness to Pay for New Airport Gates.** We can compute the gain in consumer surplus resulting from the decrease in price generated by the expansion project (Chapter 7). In Figure 14.A, the gain in consumer surplus is shown by trapezoid *ABCD*, with area equal to $9,000 per day. The area of the shaded rectangle is $8,000, and the area of the shaded triangle is $1,000. The change in consumer surplus exceeds the cost of the project, so the project is worthwhile.

Figure 14.A

Consumer Surplus and Airport Expansion Project
A decrease in price from $220 to $200 increases the consumer surplus by the area of the trapezoid *ABCD*, or $9,000.

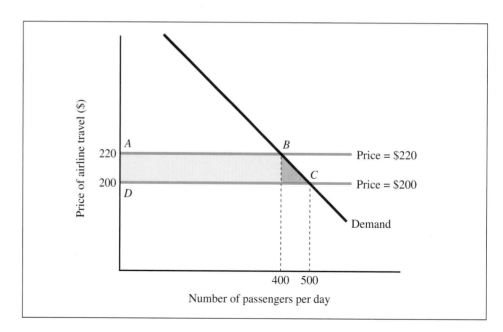

Notes

1. John R. Wilke, "New Antitrust Rules May Ease Path to Mergers," *Wall Street Journal,* April 9, 1997, pp. A3–A4.

2. "The Economics of Antitrust: The Trustbuster's New Tools," *The Economist,* May 2, 1998, pp. 62–64.

3. "The Economics of Antitrust: The Trustbuster's New Tools."

4. "Antitrust in Asia: Regulation Speed," *The Economist*, January 20, 2001, p. 63.

5. *Federal Trade Commission v. Staples, Inc.,* 970 F. Supp. 1066 (D.D.C. 1997, Hogan, J).

6. U.S. Federal Trade Commission, *Promoting Competition, Protecting Consumers: A Plain English Guide to Antitrust Laws (http://www.ftc.gov/bc/compguide/index.htm).*

7. David M. Barton and Roger Sherman, "The Price and Profit Effects of Horizontal Merger: A Case Study," *Journal of Industrial Economics,* vol. 33, December 1984, pp. 165–177.

8. William G. Shepherd and James W. Brock, "Airlines," Chapter 10 in *The Structure of American Industry,* edited by Walter Adams and James W. Brock (Upper Saddle River, NJ: Prentice Hall, 1995).

9. Clifford Winston, "U.S. Industry Adjustment to Economic Deregulation," *Journal of Economic Perspectives,* vol. 12, no. 3, Summer 1998, pp. 89–110.

10. Paul MacAvoy, *Industry Regulation and the Performance of the American Economy* (New York: W. W. Norton, 1992).

11. Richard W. Barsness, "No More Friendly Skies," *San Francisco Chronicle*, February 18, 1999, p. A23; Laurence Zukerman, "Firing on Fortress Northwest," *New York Times*, August 25, 1999, p. C1.

12. Clifford Winston, "U.S. Industry Adjustment to Economic Deregulation," *Journal of Economic Perspectives*, vol. 12, no. 3, Summer 1998, pp. 89–110; Alfred E. Kahn, "Airline Deregulation—A Mixed Bag But a Clear Success Nonetheless," *Transportation Law Journal,* vol. 16, 1988, pp. 229–252.

13. Paul Joskow and Edward Kahn, "A Quantitative Analysis of Pricing Behavior in California's Wholesale Electricity Market During Summer 2000," NBER Working Paper 8157, March 2001.

14. "California's Power Crisis: A State of Gloom," *The Economist*, January 20, 2001.

15. Paul Joskow and Edward Kahn, "A Quantitative Analysis of Pricing Behavior in California's Wholesale Electricity Market During Summer 2000," NBER Working Paper 8157, March 2001.

16. *http://www.electricchoice.com.*

17. Maria Guzzo, "Electricity Deregulation Has Created a Brand-New Marketplace the Local Businesses Now Must Learn to Navigate," *Pittsburgh Business Times*, February 26, 1999; Neela Banerjee and Richard Perez-Peña, "A Failed Energy Plan Catches up to New York," *New York Times*, June 1, 2000.

Imperfect Information and Disappearing Markets

Otto is about to buy his first car. He has decided to buy a 10-year-old model X—the same make, model, and model year all of his friends have. According to several consumer magazines, half the model X cars on the road are lemons. A lemon is a car that breaks down frequently and costs a lot to repair. Otto figures that there is a 50% chance he will get a lemon. Before buying, Otto asks his friends about their experiences with their model X cars. To his surprise, 9 of 10 friends purchased cars that turned out to be lemons! Given the conflicting information from the consumer magazines and his friends, Otto doesn't know what to think. Is there a 50% chance of getting a lemon or a 90% chance?

n this chapter, we show why Otto is likely to buy a lemon, just like most of his friends. Although half the model X cars on the road may be high-quality cars, few of the high-quality cars will be offered for sale in the used-car market, so most buyers will get lemons. To understand this, think about who is more likely to sell a used car: the owner of a lemon or the owner of a high-quality car—let's call it a plum. Because people with lemons are more likely to sell their cars, most of the cars for sale will be lemons. Buyers realize this, so they won't be willing to pay very much for used cars, and the price of used cars will be relatively low. The low price makes the owners of the plums even less likely to sell their cars, so the average quality of cars decreases further. In the market equilibrium, most of the used cars on the market are lemons.

We'll see that a market will break down if either buyers or sellers are unable to distinguish between low-quality goods and high-quality goods. As we saw earlier in this book, the model of supply and demand is based on several assumptions. One of the assumptions is that buyers and sellers have enough information to make informed choices. In a world of fully informed buyers and sellers, markets operate smoothly, generating an equilibrium price and an equilibrium quantity for each good. In a world with imperfect information, some goods will be sold in very small numbers or not sold at all.

This chapter explores the effect of imperfect information on several types of markets. Here are some of the practical questions that we answer:

1. Where can you get information about the quality of automobile repair shops?
2. Why do some sellers of used cars offer money-back guarantees?
3. Why do we rely on volunteer blood donors instead of paying people to donate blood?
4. Why do professional baseball pitchers who switch teams spend so much time on the disabled list, nursing their injuries instead of playing?
5. The federal government is expected to spend $200 billion to cover the losses incurred by dozens of Saving and Loan Associations (S&Ls). How did the S&Ls get into so much trouble?

The Mixed Market for Used Cars

The classic example of a market with imperfect information is the market for used cars.[1] Suppose prospective buyers cannot distinguish between low-quality cars (lemons) and high-quality cars (plums). Although a buyer can get some information about a particular car by looking at the car and taking it for a test drive, the information gleaned from this kind of inspection is not enough to determine whether the car is a lemon or a plum. In contrast, the seller (the current owner of a used car) knows from experience whether the car is a lemon or a plum. We say that there is **asymmetric information** in a market if one side of the market—either buyers or sellers—has better information than the other. For example, the sellers of used cars know more about the cars being sold than buyers do. Because buyers cannot distinguish between lemons and plums, there will be a single market: Lemons and plums will be sold together in a mixed market for the same price.

Asymmetric information: One side of the market—either buyers or sellers—has better information about the good than the other.

We begin our discussion with an extreme case, a market in which all the cars on the market will be lemons. This extreme case is unrealistic, but it provides a useful starting point for a discussion of the implications of asymmetric information. This extreme case shows that one possibility is the disappearance of the market for the high-quality good. As we'll see later, a more realistic case is a situation in which most—but not all—the used cars are lemons, so there is a small chance that a buyer will get a high-quality car.

Ignorant Consumers and Knowledgeable Sellers

How much is a consumer willing to pay for a used car that could be either a lemon or a plum? To determine the price in a mixed market—with both high-quality and low-quality goods—we must answer three questions:

1. How much is the consumer willing to pay for a plum (a high-quality car)?
2. How much is the consumer willing to pay for a lemon (a low-quality car)?
3. What is the chance that a used car purchased in the mixed market will be a lemon?

Suppose the typical buyer is willing to pay $4,000 for a plum and $2,000 for a lemon. In addition, the consumer has neutral expectations about the used-car market. That means that the consumer assumes that half the used cars are lemons and the other half are plums, so there is a 50% chance of getting a lemon. How much is the consumer willing to pay for a car that has a 50% chance of being a lemon? A reasonable assumption is that she or he is willing to pay the average value of the two types of cars, or $3,000.

Sellers of used cars are knowledgeable about what they are selling. The current owner of a used car knows from everyday experience whether the car is a lemon or a plum. Given a single market price for all used cars, lemons and plums alike, each current owner must decide whether or not to sell his or her car. We can use the supply curves for lemons and plums to show how many plums and lemons will be supplied at a particular price.

Figure 15.1 shows two hypothetical supply curves: one for plums and another for lemons. The minimum price for plums is $2,500: At any price less than $2,500, no plums will be supplied. As shown by the plum supply curve, the number of plums supplied increases with the price of used cars. For example, 4 plums will be supplied at a price of $3,000 (point n). The minimum price for lemons is $500: At any price less than $500, no lemons will be supplied. Lemons have a lower minimum price because they are worth

Figure 15.1
Market for Used Cars
If buyers have neutral expectations (assume that there is a 50% chance of getting a lemon), they are willing to pay $3,000 for a used car. At this price, the supply of plums is 4 (point n) and the supply of lemons is 16 (point m). At a price of $2,000, only lemons will be supplied (9 lemons, as shown by point p).

less to their current owners. As shown by the lemon supply curve, the number of lemons supplied increases with the price of used cars. For example, 16 lemons will be supplied at a price of $3,000 (point *m*).

Equilibrium in the Mixed Market

Table 15.1 shows two scenarios for our hypothetical used-car market, with numbers consistent with the supply curves shown in Figure 15.1. In the first column we assume that buyers have neutral expectations about the chance of getting a lemon. If buyers assume that half the used cars on the market are lemons and half are plums, the typical buyer will be willing to pay $3,000 for a used car. At this price, 4 plums and 16 lemons will be supplied, so 80% of the used cars (16 of 20) will be lemons. In this case, consumers underestimate the chance of getting a lemon.

What will consumers do when they realize that they've underestimated the chance of getting a lemon? They certainly won't be willing to pay $3,000 for a used car. In general, the greater the chance of getting a lemon, the smaller the amount that consumers are willing to pay. As a result, the price of used cars will decrease. As was explained earlier in the book, a market reaches an equilibrium when there is no pressure to change the price. Therefore, the scenario represented by the data in the first column is not an equilibrium.

Suppose that after observing the outcome in the first column, buyers become very pessimistic. They assume that all the used cars on the market are lemons. Under this assumption, the typical buyer will be willing to pay only $2,000 (the value of a lemon) for a used car. This price is less than the $2,500 minimum price for supplying plums, so plums will disappear from the used-car market. This is shown in Figure 15.1: At a price of $2,000, the quantity of plums supplied is zero, but the quantity of lemons is 9 (point *p*). In other words, all the used cars will be lemons, so consumers' pessimism is justified. Because consumers' expectations are consistent with their actual experiences in the market, the equilibrium price of used cars is $2,000. The equilibrium in the used-car market is shown in the second column of Table 15.1.

In this equilibrium, no plums are bought or sold, so every buyer will get a lemon. The domination of the used-car market by lemons is an example of the **adverse-selection problem**. The uninformed side of the market (buyers in this case) must choose from an undesirable or adverse selection of goods (used cars in this example). The asymmetric information in the market generates a downward spiral of price and quantity: A decrease in price decreases the quantity of plums supplied, decreasing the price further when

Adverse-selection problem: The uninformed side of the market must choose from an undesirable or an adverse selection of goods.

Table 15.1   All Used Cars Are Lemons

	Neutral Expectations	Pessimistic Expectations
Assumed chance of lemon	50%	100%
Willingness to pay for lemon	$2,000	$2,000
Willingness to pay for plum	$4,000	$4,000
Willingness to pay for used car	$3,000	$2,000
Number of lemons supplied	16	9
Number of plums supplied	4	0
Total number of used cars	20	9
Actual chance of lemon	80%	100%

buyers realize that most of the cars on the market are lemons, which leads to even fewer plums on the market. In the extreme case, this downward spiral continues until all the cars on the market are lemons, so every buyer will get a lemon.

TEST Your Understanding

1. Complete the statement with *buyers* or *sellers*: There is asymmetric information in the used-car market because _____ cannot distinguish between lemons and plums but _____ can.

2. Suppose the typical consumer is willing to pay $3,000 for a plum and $1,000 for a lemon. If there is a 50% chance of getting a lemon, how much is the consumer willing to pay for a used car?

3. Why do goods of different qualities (such as used cars) sell for the same price, but goods of different sizes (such as apples) sell for different prices?

4. When buyers assume that there is a 40% chance of getting a lemon, 8 lemons and 2 plums are supplied. Is this an equilibrium? Explain.

5. Complete the statement: The fact that a buyer must pick a used car from an undesirable selection of cars is called the _____ problem.

Reviving the High-Quality Market

The disappearance of high-quality cars from our hypothetical market is an extreme—and unrealistic—case. In most used-car markets, some high-quality cars are offered for sale, so there is at least a small chance that a buyer will get a high-quality car. There are some high-quality cars on the market because some plum owners are willing to sell their cars at a low price, a result of changes in their transportation needs or a desire to buy a new car.

Thin Market for Plums

In our earlier example, the market for high-quality used cars disappears because informed suppliers refuse to participate in the mixed market for used cars. Specifically, the $2,500 minimum price for high-quality cars is so high that no plums are supplied at the equilibrium price of $2,000. If the minimum price for plums is lower, say $1,800, some plums will be supplied when the market price is $2,000. Although most of the used cars will be lemons, some lucky buyers will get plums. In this case, we say that asymmetric information generates a **thin market**: Some high-quality goods are sold, but fewer than would be sold in a market with perfect information.

Thin market: A market in which some high-quality goods are sold but fewer than would be sold in a market with perfect information.

We can use a simple example to show how we get a thin market for plums. In Table 15.2, consumers assume that there is a 90% chance of getting a lemon (worth $2,000 to the consumer) and a 10% chance of getting a plum (worth $4,000 to the consumer). Let's assume that each consumer is willing to pay $2,200 for a used car under these circumstances. Consumers are willing to pay a little more than the value of a lemon because there is a small chance of getting a plum. Figure 15.2 shows the supply curves for this example: At a price of $2,200, there will be 2 plums (shown by point *s*) and 18 lemons (shown by point *t*). In this case, consumers accurately assess the chance of getting a lemon: 90% of the used cars sold (18 of 20) turn out to be lemons. Therefore, the equilibrium price of used cars is $2,200 and the equilibrium quantity is 20 cars, 10% of which are plums.

Table 15.2 Thin Market for Plums	
Assumed chance of lemon	90%
Willingness to pay for lemon	$2,000
Willingness to pay for plum	$4,000
Willingness to pay for used car	$2,200
Number of lemons supplied	18
Number of plums supplied	2
Total number of used cars	20
Actual chance of lemon	90%

Applications: Otto's Puzzle, the Supply of Blood

This chapter started with Otto's puzzle. Is there a 50% chance of getting a lemon, as suggested by a casual reading of the data from consumer magazines, or a 90% chance, as suggested by the experiences of Otto's friends? As we see in Table 15.2 and Figure 15.2, the answer is 90%. To assess his chances of getting a lemon, Otto should listen to his friends. The price of model X cars is so low that just a few plum owners sell their cars.

For another example of a good with asymmetric information, think about blood used for transfusions. About 30 years ago, a large fraction of the blood used for transfusions in the United States came from paid donors ("commercial" blood). Today, all the blood for transfusions comes from volunteer donors. During the 1960s, Japan made similar changes in its blood supply system, moving from a largely commercial supply to one that relies to a much greater extent on volunteer donors.[2] What explains these shifts away from commercial blood supply in favor of a volunteer supply? The answer is adverse selection.

Hospitals cannot always distinguish between bad blood (from donors with infectious diseases such as hepatitis) and good blood. Thirty years ago, 30% of heart-surgery patients contracted hepatitis from tainted blood. According to Dr. Harvey G. Klein, the

Figure 15.2

Thin Market for Plums

If buyers assume that there is a 90% chance of getting a lemon, they are willing to pay $2,200 for a used car. At this price, the supply of plums is 2 (point *s*) and the supply of lemons is 18 (point *t*), so the actual chance of getting a lemon is 90%, the same as the assumed chance of getting a lemon.

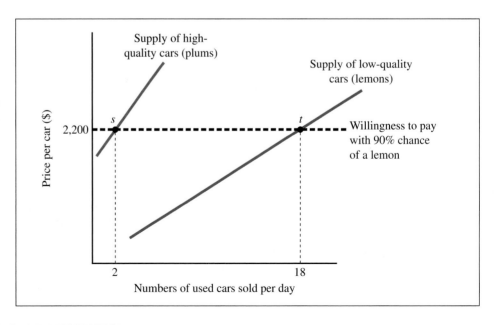

chief of the department of transfusion medicine at the National Institutes of Health, blood from paid donors was a big factor in the hepatitis problem.[3] The monetary incentives caused a large number of people with "bad" blood to give blood—and be less than completely honest about their health histories. The elimination of paid donors in the last 30 years has decreased the chance of contracting hepatitis during heart surgery to only 2%.

Money-Back Guarantees and Warranties

The domination of the used-car market by lemons provides an opportunity for clever sellers. Buyers are willing to pay $4,000 for a plum, and some plum owners would gladly sell their cars if they could get more than $2,200 for them. This large gap between the willingness to pay and the willingness to accept provides a profit opportunity for clever entrepreneurs who can somehow persuade a skeptical consumer that a particular used car is a plum, not a lemon.

A supplier could identify a particular car as a plum in a sea of lemons by offering one of the following guarantees:

- Money-back guarantee. The seller could promise to refund the $3,500 price if the car turned out to be a lemon. Because the car is in fact a plum—a fact known by the seller—the buyer will not ask for a refund, and buyer and seller will be happy with the transaction.

- Warranties and repair guarantees. The seller could promise to cover any extraordinary repair costs for one year. Because the car is a plum, there won't be any extraordinary repair costs, so buyer and seller will be happy with the transaction.

Car consumers also have an incentive to get information about the quality of used cars. A consumer who identified a plum could buy the high-quality car for a price below his or her willingness to pay ($4,000). There is a big payoff from information that enables the consumer to distinguish between lemons and plums. It may be rational for a car consumer to hire a mechanic to inspect a particular car for defects.

Lemons Laws

Many states have laws that require automakers to buy back cars that experience frequent problems in the first year of use. For example, under California's Song-Beverly Consumer Warranty Act, also known as the lemons law, auto dealers are required to repurchase vehicles that have been brought back for repair at least four times for the same problem or have been in the mechanic's shop for at least 30 calendar days in the first year following purchase. A vehicle repurchased under the lemons law must be fixed before it is sold to another customer and must be identified as a lemon with a stamp on the title and a sticker on the car that says "lemons law buyback."

Do state lemons law work? Mr. Reynoso, a Los Angeles dental technician purchased a used 1996 Astro van for $22,000. He didn't find out until much later that the vehicle had been repurchased by the dealer under the lemons law after the original owner had brought the van in for repairs 44 times in just a few months.[4] Four years earlier, the California Department of Motor Vehicles claimed that General Motors, the maker of the Astro van, had violated the lemons law by reselling lemons to consumers without identifying them as lemons. GM paid $330,000 to settle those charges, but it didn't admit to any wrongdoing. Mr. Reynoso's experience led to a class-action lawsuit against General Motors.

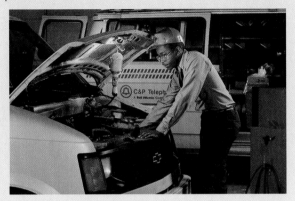

A CLOSER LOOK · CONSUMER SATISFACTION SCORES FROM VALUESTAR

If you live in the San Francisco Bay area, you can get information about the performance of firms providing consumer services such as medical and dental care, gardening and landscaping, pet grooming, auto repair, and home improvement. ValueStar uses customer-satisfaction surveys to determine how well a firm does relative to its competitors in providing quality service.[6] To get the right to display a Customer-Rated seal, a firm must prove that it has all the required licenses and insurance and must agree to pay for a survey of its past customers. ValueStar uses consumer surveys to compute a consumer-satisfaction score for each company. Any company receiving a score of at least 85 out of 100 has the right to dis-

play a Customer-Rated Gold seal for a one-year period.

Another problem with enforcing these laws is that lemons can cross state lines without a paper trail. For example, a Dodge Caravan with a leaky roof was bought and repurchased under state lemons laws three times in three different states: Virginia, Minnesota, and Illinois.[5] The interstate commerce in lemons has led to new laws requiring the branding of lemons on vehicle titles to follow the car when it crosses state lines.

The problems associated with asymmetric information occur for some types of consumer services. Most consumers can't easily determine the quality of service they will receive from an auto-repair shop, a landscaper, or a housing remodeler. How can a high-quality service provider distinguish itself from low-quality providers? For a recent approach to solving this problem, read "A Closer Look: Consumer Satisfaction Scores from ValueStar."

TEST Your Understanding

6. When buyers assume that there is a 70% chance of getting a lemon, 7 lemons and 3 plums are supplied. Is this an equilibrium? Explain.

7. Explain why it would not be rational for a lemon owner to offer a buyer a money-back guarantee.

8. Suppose that the minimum price of plums decreases. Would you expect the market to become "thinner" or "thicker"?

9. Explain why there are profit opportunities in a thin market.

Applications

The most important lesson of this chapter is that if one side of a market cannot distinguish between high- and low-quality goods, the mixed market will be dominated by low-quality goods. The adverse-selection problem is caused by imperfect information. Let's look at three other examples of mixed markets that suffer from the adverse-selection problem: used baseball pitchers, malpractice insurance, and medical insurance.

Used Baseball Pitchers

Professional baseball teams compete with each other for players. After six years of play in the major leagues, a player has the option of becoming a free agent and offering his services to the highest bidder. A player is likely to switch teams if the new team offers him a higher salary than his original team. One of the puzzling features of the free-agent market is that pitchers who switch teams are more prone to injuries than pitchers who don't. On average, pitchers who switch teams spend 28 days per season on the disabled list; pitchers who do not switch teams spend only 5 days per season on the disabled list.[7] This doesn't mean that all the switching pitchers are lemons: Many of them are injury-free and are terrific additions to their new teams. But on average, the switching pitchers spend five times longer recovering from injuries.

This puzzling feature of the free-agent market for baseball players is explained by asymmetric information and adverse selection. Because the coaches, physicians, and trainers from the player's original team have interacted with the player on a daily basis for several years, they know from experience whether he is likely to suffer from injuries that prevent him from playing. In contrast, the new team has much less information: Its physicians can examine the pitcher, but a single exam is not the same as several years of daily experience with the pitcher. Suppose the market price for pitchers is $1 million per year and a pitcher who is currently with the Chicago Cubs is offered this salary by another team. If the Cubs think the pitcher is likely to spend a lot of time next season recovering from injuries, they won't try to outbid another team for the pitcher: they will let the pitcher switch teams. But if the Cubs think the pitcher will be injury-free and productive, he will be worth more than $1 million to the Cubs, so they will outbid other teams and keep the pitcher. In general, an injury-prone pitcher is more likely to switch

Baseball pitchers who switch teams are more prone to injuries than those who don't switch.

teams: Like the used-car market, there are many "lemons" on the used-pitcher market. The market for baseball players playing other positions (outfield, infield) does not suffer from the adverse selection, perhaps because the injuries that affect their performance are easier for a potential new team to detect.

Although you may think it's bizarre to compare baseball pitchers to used cars, people in baseball don't think so. They recognize the similarity between the two markets. Jackie Moore, who managed a free-agent camp where teams looking for players can see free agents in action, sounds like a used-car salesman:[8] "We want to get players off the lot. We want to cut a deal. How many camps can you go into where you can look at a player and take him home with you?"

Malpractice Insurance

So far, we've discussed markets in which sellers have better information than buyers, but what happens when buyers are better informed than sellers? Consider the market for insurance. A person who buys an insurance policy knows much more about his or her risks and needs for insurance than the insurance company knows. For example, when you buy an auto-insurance policy, you know more than your insurance company about your driving habits and your chances of getting in an accident. We'll see that insurance markets suffer from the adverse-selection problem: Insurance companies must pick from an adverse or undesirable selection of customers.

Let's look at the market for malpractice insurance. To keep things simple, suppose there are only two types of physicians: careful and reckless. On average, the cost of settling malpractice suits against careful doctors is $4,000 per doctor per year, while the cost of settling malpractice suits against reckless doctors is $30,000 per doctor per year. If the doctor is insured, these costs are paid by an insurance company. Uninsured physicians will have to pay these costs themselves. Suppose insurance companies cannot distinguish between careful doctors and reckless doctors, but each doctor knows whether he or she is careful or reckless. This means that there is asymmetric information in the insurance market: Buyers (physicians) have better information than sellers (insurance companies).

If insurance companies cannot distinguish between careful doctors and reckless doctors, there will be a mixed market and a single price for malpractice insurance. Suppose all insurance companies are initially neutral in their expectations about what type of doctors will buy malpractice insurance. Insurance companies assume that half the doctors who buy insurance are careful and half are reckless. If the typical insurance company gets equal numbers of careful doctors and reckless doctors, the average cost of providing insurance will be $17,000 per doctor. Therefore, if the insurance company charges $17,000 per year for insurance and its expectations about the mixture of careful doctors and reckless doctors are correct, the company's total revenue will cover its total cost. In other words, the company will earn zero economic profit.

The expectations of the insurance company are unlikely to be realized. At a price of $17,000, none of the careful physicians will buy malpractice insurance. They won't buy it because the premium is over four times the average cost of settling malpractice suits against a careful doctor, so malpractice insurance is not a very good deal for them. A careful doctor would rather take the risk, knowing that he or she will pay an average of $4,000 per year to settle malpractice suits. This is the adverse-selection problem: Insurance companies get an undesirable (adverse) selection of doctors. To ensure zero economic profit, the price of insurance must increase to $30,000, the average cost of serving the reckless physicians.

In this example, careful physicians do not buy malpractice insurance because insurance companies are unable to distinguish between careful doctors and reckless doctors. The reckless doctors in the mixed market increase the cost of providing insurance and increase the price of insurance. In fact, insurance companies try to identify careful doctors and offer them lower insurance rates. When a doctor applies for an insurance policy, the insurance company gathers information about the doctor and the history of his or her medical practice. Although these actions help insurance companies to distinguish between careful and reckless physicians, they are by no means perfect, so the adverse-selection problem persists.

The same logic applies to the markets for other types of insurance, including life insurance, health insurance, and theft insurance. Life-insurance companies try to distinguish between high-risk and low-risk folks. Because the companies are unable to distinguish between the two types with sufficient precision, the adverse selection persists. For an example of how insurance companies might use new technology to more precisely identify people with higher risks of death, read "A Closer Look: Genetic Testing, Thrill Seekers, and Insurance."

Pricing Health Insurance

Our discussion of adverse selection provides some insights into recent changes in the pricing of medical insurance. Until recently, most insurance prices were based on **community rating**. In a given community or metropolitan area, every firm paid the same

Community rating: In a given community or metropolitan area, every firm pays the same price for medical insurance.

A CLOSER LOOK — GENETIC TESTING, THRILL SEEKERS, AND INSURANCE

You probably know someone who is impulsive and excitable, a thrill seeker who keeps life interesting for those of us who are more relaxed and mellow. Scientists recently identified one of the genes responsible for novelty-seeking behavior, and discovered that about 15% of the people in Israel, Europe, and the United States carry the gene.[9] About half of the novelty-seeking variation among people is linked to genes, so the fact that a particular person has the novelty-seeking gene suggests that the person is more inclined to take up skydiving and bungee jumping, and engage in other risky behavior.

If you managed a life-insurance company, would you like to know whether each customer has the novelty-seeking gene? It would reduce the problem of asymmetric information and allow you to charge different prices for insurance, with lower prices for people who are less inclined to take risks. The same is true for other genetic information that reveals an individual's likelihood of developing heart disease or cancer: An insurance company with genetic information could charge different prices, with lower prices for consumers whose genetic makeup makes them less likely to develop health problems.

The development of genetic tests has led to fears that insurance companies will use the results of the tests to engage in genetic discrimination—denying insurance or charging higher prices to people with unfavorable genes. Federal employees are protected by an executive order that forbids genetic discrimination. For the public at large, there are proposals in Congress to outlaw genetic discrimination.

price for the medical insurance for its employees, with the price equal to the average cost of providing medical coverage to the entire community. A firm providing medical coverage to its employees through an insurance company would pay the insurance company an amount equal to the number of employees times the community price.

Most insurance companies now use **experience rating** to set their prices. Under this system, they charge different prices to different firms, depending on the past medical bills of the firm's employees. A firm whose employees have low medical bills pays a low price for its employees' insurance. The switch from community rating to experience rating occurred when insurance companies were able to identify employers with low medical costs. Eventually, most insurance companies switched to experience rating.[10]

Experience rating gives firms an incentive to decrease the health costs of their workers. Firms are more likely to invest in safety and health programs for their workers. Firms will also make a greater effort to avoid hiring applicants with health problems. Under experience rating, a firm that hires a worker with above-average medical costs will soon face an increase in the price of its insurance. Among the workers who might suffer as a result are older workers and the disabled.

Experience rating: Each firm pays a different price for medical insurance, depending on the past medical bills of the firm's employees.

Moral Hazard

Does insurance affect people's risk-taking behavior? Insurance causes people to take greater risks because part of the cost of an undesirable outcome will be borne by the insurance company. Here are some examples of people taking greater risks because they have insurance:

- Irma could buy a fire extinguisher for her kitchen. If she had to pay for any property damage caused by a fire, she would definitely buy a fire extinguisher. But because her homeowner's insurance covers property damage from fires, she doesn't buy a fire extinguisher.

- Harry decides how carefully to drive his car. If he had to pay for any repairs resulting from a collision, he would drive very carefully. But his auto insurance covers all repair costs, so he drives recklessly.

- Flo can either fly on a commercial airline or hitch a ride with her pilot friend in a 4-seat airplane. Traveling in small airplanes is much riskier, and if Flo dies in an airplane crash, her family would lose the income she would otherwise earn. If she didn't have life insurance to offset these income losses, she wouldn't take the risk of harming her family in that way. But because her family would collect $1 million in life insurance, she is willing to take the risk.

The **moral hazard problem** is that insurance encourages risky behavior. More precisely, moral hazard occurs when an insured party takes an unobserved action (not observed by the insurer) that affects the probability of the event that triggers payment from the insurer. For example, Harry's unobserved action is reckless driving, which increases the probability of a collision, an event that triggers payment from his auto insurance company.

The moral-hazard problem is pervasive. The availability of fire insurance decreases investment in fire-prevention programs and other investment that reduces the risk of fire. Collision insurance increases risky behavior on the roads. The availability of life insurance encourages risky activities such as flying small airplanes, parachuting, and bungee jumping.

For another example of moral hazard, consider insurance provided for bank insurance. Suppose you deposit $10,000 in a Savings and Loan (S&L) and a year later the S&L goes bankrupt. The Federal Deposit Insurance Corporation (FDIC) insures the first $100,000 of your deposit, so if the S&L goes bankrupt, you'll still get your money back. The federal

Moral hazard problem: Insurance encourages risky behavior.

deposit insurance law was enacted in 1933 in response to the bank failures of the Great Depression.

Deposit insurance for S&Ls causes a moral hazard problem. If you know you will get your money back no matter what happens to the S&L, you may deposit your money in the S&L without evaluating the S&L's performance and the riskiness of its investments. If you and other depositors don't monitor the bank's performance, an S&L with a very risky investment strategy will continue to attract deposits because the depositors don't face any risk. That means the manager of an S&L will be more likely to take on risky investments, knowing that if the investments don't pay off and the S&L goes bankrupt, the federal government will bear the cost, paying off all the depositors. Recognizing this moral-hazard problem, the federal government historically limited S&Ls to relatively safe investments.

In the 1980s, the federal government loosened some of the restrictions on S&L investments, and the managers of S&Ls started taking on very risky investments, including high-risk commercial mortgages and junk bonds. When these risky investments failed, many S&Ls that had invested heavily in these high-risk investments went into bankruptcy. The government bailed out the failed S&Ls, at a total cost to taxpayers of about $200 billion.

Bicycle Theft Insurance

Economic Detective

At Wheeler State University, 1 out of every 10 bicycles was stolen in 1998. When a group of young entrepreneurs discovered that no one on campus had bicycle-theft insurance, they decided to go into the insurance business, offering one-year theft insurance for $15 per bike. They sold 100 policies in 1999 and expected 10 of their 100 customers (10% of them) to lose their bicycles to theft. The entrepreneurs figured that their total revenue would more than cover the cost of replacing 10 bicycles, leaving a tidy profit. By the end of 1999, a total of 20 insured bicycles had been stolen, and the students lost a bundle of money on their little enterprise. What happened?

The key to solving this puzzle is the fact that the 10% theft rate occurred in 1998, when no one had theft insurance. When the entrepreneurs offered theft insurance, they expected the same theft rate. Because of moral hazard, however, the students who bought theft insurance were less careful in protecting their bikes from theft, perhaps using less secure locks or leaving their bikes on campus overnight. As a result, the theft rate for insured bikes was 20%, not 10%. The entrepreneurs lost money because they did not anticipate that insurance would increase risk-taking.

TEST Your Understanding

10. Your favorite baseball team just announced that it signed two pitchers from the free-agent market. What's your reaction?

11. Complete the statement with numbers: Suppose that the average annual malpractice cost is $40,000 for reckless doctors and $2,000 for careful doctors. If half the insured doctors are reckless, the insurance company will earn zero economic profit if the price of insurance is _____. If careful doctors are not willing to pay any more than $5,000 for insurance, the price required for zero economic profit is

_____.

12. Many professional athletes purchase insurance against career-ending injuries. Would you expect the insured players to act differently from those who don't have insurance?

Using the **TOOLS**

We've seen what happens when one side of the market—either buyers or sellers—has better information than the other side. In a market for a used good, sellers know more than buyers, and the market will be dominated by low-quality goods. In an insurance market, buyers know more than sellers, and the market will be dominated by high-risk consumers. Here are some opportunities to do your own economic analysis of markets with asymmetric information.

1. ECONOMIC EXPERIMENT: LEMONS

In this experiment, students play the role of consumers purchasing used cars. Over half the used cars on the road (57%) are plums, and the remaining cars (43%) are lemons. Each consumer offers a price for a used car and then rolls a pair of dice to find out whether he or she gets a lemon or a plum. In general, rolling a big number is good news: To get a plum, you need to roll a big number. The higher the price you offer, the smaller the number you must roll to get a plum. Here is how the experiment works:

- Each consumer tells the instructor how much he or she is offering for a used car and then rolls the dice.
- The instructor tells the consumer whether the number she rolled is large enough to get a plum. If the number is not large enough, she gets a lemon.
- The consumer's score equals the difference between the maximum amount she is willing to pay for the type of car she got ($1,200 for a plum and $400 for a lemon) and the price she actually paid. For example, if Otto offers $500 and gets a plum, his score is $700. If Carla offers $600 and gets a lemon, her score is –$200.
- The instructor announces the result of each transaction to the class.
- There are three to five buying periods. At the end of the last trading period, each consumer adds up his or her surpluses.

APPLICATIONS

2. Rising Insurance Rates

At a large state university, an insurance company provides group medical coverage for university employees. When the company discovered that some of the younger employees had switched to insurance companies with lower rates, the company increased its rates. This is puzzling because you might think that the insurance company would drop its rates to prevent other employees from switching to other companies. Indeed, the rate hike caused more employees to switch. Did the insurance company act irrationally?

3. Purchasing a Fleet of Used Cars

You are responsible for buying a fleet of 10 used cars for your employees and must pick either brand B cars or brand C cars. For your purposes, the two brands are identical except for one difference: Based on your market experience with the two brands, you figure that 50% of B cars are lemons and only 20% of C cars are lemons. You are willing to pay $1,000 for a known lemon and $3,000 for a known plum. If the price of B cars is $1,800 and the price of C cars is $2,200, which brand of car should you pick?

4. State Auto Insurance Pool

Consider a state in which automobile drivers are divided equally into two types of drivers: careful and reckless. The average annual auto-insurance claim is $400 for a careful driver and $1,200 for a reckless driver. Suppose the state adopts an insurance system under which all drivers are placed in a common pool and allocated to insurance companies randomly. An insurance company cannot refuse coverage to any driver it is assigned, but a driver who is unhappy with the insurance company has the option of being reassigned (randomly) to another insurance company. By law, each insurance company must charge the same price to all its customers. Predict the price of auto insurance under two alternative policy scenarios:

a. Auto insurance is mandatory.

b. Auto insurance is voluntary.

5. ECONOMIC EXPERIMENT: BIKE INSURANCE

This experiment shows the effect of asymmetric information on the market for bicycle insurance. Consider a city with two types of bike owners; some face a relatively high probability of bike theft, and others face a relatively low probability of bike theft. Bike owners know from experience whether they face a high probability or a low probability of theft, but the insurance company cannot distinguish between the two types of owners. For the city as a whole, 20% of bicycles are stolen every year. Here is how the experiment works:

- The class is divided into small groups, each of which represents an insurance company that must pick a price at which the firm will offer bike theft insurance. The insurance company must pay $100 for each insured bike that is stolen.

- The instructor has a table showing, for each price of bike insurance, how many owners of each type (high probability and low probability) will purchase insurance. Using the numbers supplied by the instructor, each insurance company can compute its total revenue (the price per bike insured times the number of insured bikes), the number of bikes stolen, and the company's total replacement cost.

- The group's score for a trading period equals the company's profit, which is the total revenue less the total replacement cost for stolen bikes.

- The experiment runs for several trading periods, and a group's score equals the sum of its profits over these trading periods.

Summary

In this chapter, we've seen what happens when one of the assumptions underlying most supply and demand analysis—that people make informed decisions—is violated. If either buyers or sellers don't have reliable information about a particular good or service, the market will suffer from the adverse-selection problem. The uninformed side of the market picks from an adverse selection of goods or customers. Here are the main points of the chapter:

1. If one side of the market cannot distinguish between high-quality and low-quality goods, both types of goods will be sold in a mixed market at the same price.

2. The markets for many used goods suffer from the adverse-selection problem because sellers have better information than buyers.

3. If sellers of high-quality goods have a relatively low minimum price, some high-quality goods will be sold, but most of the goods will be of low quality.

4. Insurance markets suffer from adverse selection because buyers have better information than sellers.

5. The moral-hazard problem is that insurance encourages risky behavior because part of the cost of an unfavorable outcome will be paid by an insurance company.

Key Terms

adverse-selection problem, 314
asymmetric information, 312

community rating, 321
experience rating, 322

moral hazard problem, 322
thin market, 315

Problems and Discussion Questions

1. Use the notion of adverse selection to explain a classic quip from Groucho Marx: "I won't join any club that is willing to accept me as a member."

2. The following table shows some scenarios for different used-car markets. Which markets are in equilibrium? Graph each equilibrium, using Figure 15.1 as a model.

	Scenario A	Scenario B	Scenario C
Assumed chance of lemon	60%	80%	95%
Willingness to pay for used car	$6,000	$5,000	$4,500
Number of lemons supplied	70	40	90
Number of plums supplied	30	10	10
Total number of used cars	100	50	100

3. You are thinking about buying a used camera at a price of $60. You are willing to pay $20 for a lemon and $100 for a plum. Under what circumstances would it be wise to buy a used camera? Are these circumstances likely to occur? Explain.

4. Suppose that both buyers and sellers of used cars are ignorant: No one can distinguish between lemons and plums. Would you expect the market to be dominated by lemons?

5. Suppose that a new lie detector is 100% accurate. Discuss the implications for the adverse-selection problem in the used-car market.

6. When a person applies for life insurance, the insurance agent asks the applicant about his or her occupation. Why should this matter to the insurance company?

7. Scientists have recently developed new genetic tests that could be used by an insurance company to determine whether a potential customer is likely to develop certain diseases. Discuss the trade-offs associated with allowing insurance companies to use these tests.

8. On the campus of Bike University, half the bikes are expensive (replacement value = $100), and half are cheap (replacement value = $20). There is a 50% chance that any particular bike—expensive or cheap—will be stolen in the next year. Suppose a firm offers bike-theft insurance for $40 per year: The firm will replace any insured bike that is stolen. If the firm sells 20 insurance policies, will the firm make a profit? Explain.

9. In a given year, there is a 10% chance that a fire in Ira's warehouse will cause $100,000 in property damage. If Ira spent $5,000 on a fire-prevention program, the probability of a fire would drop to zero. If Ira doesn't have fire insurance, will he spend the money on the prevention program? If he has an insurance policy that covers 80% of the property damage from a fire, will he spend the money on the prevention program? At what coverage rate (40%, 50%, 60%, 70%), will Ira be indifferent about spending money on the prevention program?

10. As Kira tries to decide whether or not to do a bungee jump, she asks to make one phone call. If there is a moral hazard problem, whom will she call?

11. **Web Exercise.** Visit the Web site of Carfax [*http://www.carfax.com*] and check out the sample reports. What sort of deception occurs in the market for used cars? How much does it cost to get a report on a used car you are considering buying? Do you think the information is worth the price?

12. **Web Exercise.** Visit the Web site of the Red Cross (*http://www.redcross.org/*) and get the facts on donating blood. Go to "Help Now" and then click on "Give Blood." Are you eligible to give blood? Where would you go to donate blood?

Take It to the Net

We invite you to visit the O'Sullivan/Sheffrin page on the Prentice Hall Web site at: **http://www.prenhall.com/osullivan/** for additional World Wide Web exercises for this chapter.

Model Answers to Questions

Chapter-Opening Questions

1. In San Francisco, information about various consumer services is available from Value Star.

2. They are trying to distinguish their high-quality cars from low-quality cars.

3. Hospitals cannot always distinguish between bad blood (from donors with infectious disease such as hepatitis) and good blood. Monetary incentives for blood caused a large number of people with "bad" blood to give blood—and be less than completely honest about their health histories.

4. Like the used-car market, the used-pitcher market has asymmetric information: the pitcher's original team has more information than the new team. A team is more likely to be outbid by another team for a pitcher's services, if the pitcher has health problems that make him worth less to the original team.

5. This is another example of the moral-hazard problem. The problem was caused by federal deposit insurance, which encouraged the managers of S&Ls to take on very risky investments. When these risky investments failed, many S&Ls that had invested heavily in these high-risk investments went into bankruptcy.

Test Your Understanding

1. Buyers, sellers.

2. $2,000, the average value of the two types of cars.

3. It is easy to determine the size of an apple but not easy to determine the quality of a car.

4. No: 80% of the used cars are lemons, meaning consumers underestimate the chance of getting a lemon.

5. Adverse-selection.

6. Yes: 70% of the cars are lemons.

7. The buyer will eventually return the car and get a full refund, perhaps after putting a lot of miles on it or abusing it.

8. Thicker: The lower the minimum price, the larger the quantity supplied at each price, so the more plums in the market.

9. There will be a large gap between the amount a buyer is willing to pay for a true plum and the amount a plum owner is willing to accept.

10. You may be skeptical about the new player because free-agent pitchers who switch teams spend a long time on the disabled list. Before reading this chapter, you might have been more optimistic about the pitchers.

11. $21,000 (the average of the two cost figures), $40,000 (the cost for reckless doctors).

12. Insured athletes are likely to spend less effort in avoiding injuries, knowing that the insurance company will compensate them for a career-ending injury.

Using the Tools

2. Rising Insurance Rates. The medical costs of younger employees are usually lower than the average medical cost for all university employees. When the youngsters switched to a different insurance company, the average age—and the average medical costs—of the original insurance company increased. The insurance company increased its rates to cover its higher costs, fully anticipating that this would cause other low-cost employees to switch to other companies. The insurance company faced a progressively more adverse selection of customers, and the higher price of medical insurance reflects the adverse selection.

3. Purchasing a Fleet of Used Cars. The following table shows how to compute the benefits and costs of the two brands. For brand B, you expect half the cars to be lemons and half to be plums, so the total value of a brand B fleet is $20,000 (5 lemons together worth a total of $5,000 and 5 plums together worth a total of $15,000). At a price of $1,800, the total cost of a B fleet is $18,000 ($1,800 per used car × 10 cars). Therefore, the value of a B fleet exceeds its cost by $2,000. We can do the same computations for the C fleet. The only difference is that you would get 2 lemons and 8 plums with a C fleet. The value of a C fleet exceeds its cost by $4,000, so the C fleet is a better deal. Although you pay $400 more per C car, the extra cost is more than offset by the smaller number of lemons in the C fleet.

	Brand B	Brand C
Number of lemons	5	2
Value of lemons	$5,000	$2,000
Number of plums	5	8
Value of plums	$15,000	$24,000
Total value of fleet	$20,000	$26,000
Total cost of fleet	$18,000	$22,000
Surplus (value − cost)	$2,000	$4,000

4. **State Auto Insurance Pool**
   a. Under the pooling policy, there will be a single mixed market and a single price for auto insurance. If auto insurance is mandatory, the pooling policy will increase the price to $800—the average cost per driver for each insurance company.
   b. If auto insurance is voluntary, the long-run equilibrium price will exceed $800 and may even approach $1,200. If insurance companies initially have neutral expectations about the mixture of careful drivers and reckless drivers, the price of insurance will be $800 per driver. If this price exceeds the maximum price of some careful drivers, they will drop out of the market, so more than 50% of the insured drivers are reckless. Given the larger percentage of reckless (high cost) drivers, insurance companies will lose money at a price of $800 per driver, so they will increase the price. The price of insurance will increase until the insurance company's expectations about the mixture of careful drivers and reckless drivers are realized. If all the careful drivers drop out of the market, the price of insurance will increase to $1,200, the cost per reckless driver.

Notes

1. George Akerlof, "The Market for 'Lemons': Quality Uncertainty and the Market Mechanism," *Quarterly Journal of Economics*, August 1970, pp. 488–500.
2. Alvin W. Drake, Stan N. Finkelstein, and Harvey M. Sapalsky, *The American Blood Supply* (Cambridge, MA: MIT Press, 1982).
3. Oz Hopkins Koglin, "U.S. Blood 'Extremely Safe' as Volunteer Donors Cut Risks," *The Oregonian*, November 7, 1994, p. B1.
4. Kathryn Kranhold, "Lawsuit Accuses General Motors of Violating State Lemon Law," *Wall Street Journal*, Oct. 1, 1997.
5. Andrea Adelson, "Pushing Lemons over State Lines," *New York Times*, August 27, 1996, p. C1.
6. http://valuestar.com.
7. Kenneth Lehn, "Information Asymmetries in Baseball's Free Agent Market," *Economic Inquiry*, vol. 22, January 1984, pp. 37–44.
8. Chris Sheridan, "Free Agents at End of Baseball's Earth," Associated Press, printed in *Corvallis Gazette-Times*, April 15, 1995, p. B1.
9. "Genetic Discrimination Feared," Associated Press Online, June 26, 2000; Malcolm Ritter, "A Thrill a Minute: Geneticists Find Personality Link," *The Oregonian*, January 2, 1996, p. A1.
10. Henry J. Aaron, "Issues Every Plan to Reform Health Care Financing Must Confront," *Journal of Economic Perspectives*, vol. 8, no. 3, Summer 1994, pp. 31–43.

Public Goods, Taxes, and Public Choice

Here is the text from a TV newscast in the year 2070:

Boomer, the 200-meter asteroid on a collision path with the earth, is expected to land at about 10:00 tomorrow morning in the heart of the world's breadbasket, the American Midwest. The energy to be released by the impact will exceed the total explosive yield of all the nuclear weapons on the planet. Although Boomer is much smaller than the asteroid that caused the extinction of the dinosaurs about 65 million years ago, it is large enough to cause significant changes in the world's climate. The collision will generate a stratospheric dust cloud that will inhibit photosynthesis and retard plant growth, resulting in lower agricultural yields and higher food prices throughout the world.

Could this catastrophe have been averted? Yes, according to scientists at the National Aeronautics and Space Administration. In 1996, scientists developed the technology for an asteroid-diversion system: Large optical telescopes would detect an asteroid on a collision course with the earth, and an orbiting gossamer mirror of coated polyester would focus a tight beam of sunlight on the asteroid, vaporizing enough of its surface to change its path. In the U.N. debate over the asteroid-diversion system, everyone agreed that the potential benefits of the system would outweigh the costs, but no one was willing to pay for the system. Why couldn't the nations of the world agree on such an important program, one that would have prevented tomorrow's catastrophe?

n this chapter, we'll see that if a particular good generates spillover benefits, government intervention can make beneficial transactions happen. For example, the cost of an asteroid-diversion program is so high that no single person would provide such a program. We will never have such a program—even if its benefits exceed its costs—unless we make a collective decision about what sort of diversion program to develop and how to pay for it. The purpose of government is to help make this sort of collective decision. That hypothetical newscast suggests that some sort of multinational arrangement will be necessary to launch an asteroid-diversion program.

This chapter explores the economic challenges associated with providing—and paying for—goods that generate spillover benefits. We also take a look at some alternative theories on how governments operate. Here are some practical questions that we answer:

1. Should we eliminate taxes and pay for government programs with voluntary contributions instead?
2. Is it sensible to pay landowners to host endangered wildlife such as wolves and spotted owls?
3. How will a monthly apartment tax of $80 affect the monthly rent on apartments?
4. It often seems that there is little difference between the candidates in an election. Why?

Spillover Benefits

In Chapter 6, we saw that a market in which there are neither spillover benefits nor costs is an efficient market. Government intervention in an efficient market can only make it less than efficient. In this chapter, we'll see that a market with spillover benefits is inefficient, so there is an opportunity for government to promote efficiency. Recall the spillover principle.

Spillover **PRINCIPLE**

For some goods, the costs or benefits associated with the good are not confined to the person or organization that decides how much of the good to produce or consume.

To illustrate the idea of spillover benefits, consider a dam built for flood-control purposes. There are 100,000 people in the valley below the dam, and each person gets a $5 benefit from the dam. The total benefit of the dam is $500,000 (equal to 100,000 people times $5 per person), which exceeds the $200,000 total cost of the dam. Because the total benefit exceeds the total cost, the dam should be built. The problem is that no single person will build the dam because the $200,000 cost exceeds his or her $5 personal benefit. In other words, if we rely on the forces of supply and demand, with each person considering only the personal benefits and costs of a dam, no dam will be built.

The government can solve this problem by collecting enough taxes to pay for the dam. Suppose the government offers to build the dam and pay for it with a tax of $2 per person. The tax raises $200,000 in tax revenue ($2 per person times 100,000 people), which is just high enough to pay the $200,000 cost of the dam. Every person will support this proposal because the $2 tax per person is less than the $5 benefit per person. The government can use its taxing power to provide a good that would otherwise not be provided.

Public Goods

The dam is an example of a **public good**, a good that is available for everyone to consume, regardless of who pays and who doesn't. In contrast, a **private good** is consumed by a single person or household. For example, only one person can eat a hot dog. If a government hands out free cheese to the poor, is the free cheese a public good or a private good? Although anyone can get in line for the cheese, only one person can actually consume a particular piece of cheese, so the free cheese is a private good that happens to be available free of charge from the government. Similarly, an apartment in a public housing project can be occupied by a single household, so it is a private good provided by the government.

We can be more precise about the difference between public and private goods:

- Private goods are rival in consumption (only one person can consume the good) and excludable (it is possible to exclude a person who does not pay for the good).

- Public goods are nonrival in consumption (available for everyone to consume) and nonexcludable (it is impractical to exclude people who don't pay).

Here are some other examples of public goods:

National defense	Preservation of endangered species
Law enforcement	Protecting the earth's ozone layer
Space exploration	Income transfers to the poor

If someone refuses to pay for one of these public goods, it would be impractical to prevent that person from consuming the good. One role of government is to use its taxing power to collect money to pay for public goods.

Public good: A good that is available for everyone to consume, regardless of who pays and who doesn't.

Private good: A good that is consumed by a single person or household.

Private Goods with Spillover Benefits

There are some private goods that generate spillover benefits. One example is education, a good that generates two sorts of spillover benefits.

- Workplace spillovers. In most workplaces, people work in groups, and teamwork is important. A well-educated person understands instructions readily and is more likely to suggest ways to improve the production process. When a well-educated person joins a work team, the productivity of everyone on the team increases, leading to higher wages for everyone on the team.

- Civic spillovers. Citizens in a democratic society make collective decisions by voting in elections, and each citizen must live with these decisions. A well-educated person is more likely to vote intelligently, so there are spillover benefits for other citizens.

Because of these spillover benefits from education, the government uses various policies to encourage people to become educated. Local governments provide free education through high school. States subsidize students at public colleges and universities, providing college education at a fraction of the actual cost of the education. In addition, the federal government provides financial aid to students in both public and private schools.

The government subsidizes other goods that generate spillover benefits. For example, many firms use government subsidies to support on-the-job training and education. This is sensible because some of the benefits of education and training go to other firms: When a worker trained by one firm switches to another firm, the second firm also benefits. This is the rationale for subsidizing some types of education and training programs. Another example is research at universities and other nonprofit organizations. If a research project provides knowledge or technology that leads to the development of new products or the improvement of old ones, the benefits from the project spill over onto consumers and producers. This is the rationale for subsidizing basic research in the sciences.

Voluntary Contributions and the Free-Rider Problem

Most public goods are supported by taxes. What would happen if we eliminated taxes and asked people to contribute money to pay for national defense, dams, city streets, and the police? Would people contribute enough money to support these programs at their current levels?

Free-rider problem: Each person will try to get the benefit of a public good without paying for it, trying to get a free ride at the expense of others who do pay.

The problem with using voluntary contributions to support public goods is known as the **free-rider problem**. Each person will try to get the benefits of a public good without paying for it, trying to get a free ride at the expense of others who do pay. Of course, if everyone tries to get a free ride, there will be no money to support the public good, so it won't be provided. The flip side of the free-rider problem is the chump problem: No one wants to be the chump—the person who gives free rides to other people—so no one contributes any money. The free-rider problem suggests that if taxes were replaced with voluntary contributions, the government would be forced to cut back or eliminate many programs.

A Classroom Experiment in Free Riding

Do people really try to get free rides? Or would most people contribute at least some money to support a public good? Here is a classroom experiment that helps to answer this question.

- The instructor selects 10 students at random and gives each student 10 dimes (or play money).
- Each student can contribute money to support a public good by dropping 1, 2, or 3 dimes into a public-good pot. Each student has the option of keeping all the dimes and not contributing anything. The contributions are anonymous; none of the students knows how much the other students contribute.
- For each dime in the pot, the instructor adds 2 dimes. For example, if the students contribute a total of 40 dimes, the instructor adds 80 dimes, for a total of 120 dimes in the pot. The 2-for-1 match represents the idea that the benefits of public goods exceed the costs. In this case, the benefit-cost ratio is 3 to 1.
- The instructor divides the money in the public-good pot equally among the 10 students. For example, if there are 120 dimes in the pot, each student receives 12 dimes.
- Steps 2 through 4 can be repeated 4 or 5 times.

If your instructor does this experiment in your course, you'll see how much money your fellow students contribute to the public good. You'll also see the payoffs earned by students with different contribution strategies.

If your instructor does not do the experiment, you can learn something from the instructions from the experiment by answering the following questions:

- How much would you contribute?
- If your fellow students acted in the same way as you, how much money would you have at the end of 5 rounds?

- If your fellow students acted differently (contributing more or less than you contributed), how much money would you have?

We can change the experiment to mimic the compulsory tax system. The instructor could require each student to contribute three dimes, the maximum amount, each round. Would a switch to a compulsory tax system make the students better off or worse off?

The Mystery of the Three-Clock Tower

Economic
Detective

Back in the days before the inexpensive wristwatch, most people did not carry their own timepieces. Many towns built clock towers in the center of town so that their citizens could know the time. The towns paid for the clock towers with voluntary contributions from citizens. One town in the northeastern United States built a four-sided tower but put clock faces on only three sides of the tower. To most people, this seems bizarre. If you build a clock tower, why not put clock faces on all four sides?

The key to solving this puzzle is the free-rider problem. It turns out that one of the town's wealthy citizens refused to contribute money to help build the clock tower. The town officials decided that because he did not pay, they should not put a clock face on the side of the tower facing his house. In other words, the citizen tried—unsuccessfully—to get a free ride. The problem is that other citizens on the same side of town also suffered from not seeing the clock. In this case, preventing a free ride by one citizen caused problems for other citizens.

Overcoming the Free-Rider Problem

Many organizations, including public radio and television, religious organizations, and charitable organizations, raise money through voluntary contributions. So it appears that some people overcome their inclination to be free riders and contribute voluntarily to organizations that provide public goods. The successful organizations use a number of techniques to encourage people to contribute, such as the following:

- Give contributors private goods such as coffee mugs, books, musical recordings, and magazine subscriptions. People are more likely to contribute if they get something for it.

- Arrange matching contributions. You are more likely to contribute if you know that your $30 contribution will be matched with a contribution from another person.

- Appeal to people's sense of civic or moral responsibility.

It's important to note, however, that these organizations are only partly successful in mitigating the free-rider problem. Public radio is one of the success stories, but the typical public-radio station gets contributions from fewer than a quarter of its listeners.

TEST Your Understanding

1. Explain why the free-rider problem occurs for public goods but not for private goods.

2. Margie, one of the students participating in the free-rider experiment, thinks in marginal terms and asks the following question: "If I contribute one dime, how will that affect my payoff from the experiment?" Answer her question, assuming that her contribution does not affect the contribution of other students.

3. Suppose Margie uses the marginal principle to make all her decisions. Will she contribute the extra dime?

Applications: Asteroids and Wildlife

Now that we've discussed some of the economic challenges associated with providing public goods, let's think about two unconventional public goods: the diversion of asteroids and the preservation of wolves.

Asteroid Diversion

How do we apply the concepts of public goods to the issue of protecting the earth from catastrophic collisions with asteroids? On average, the earth is hit by a 200-meter asteroid every 10,000 years, by a 2-kilometer asteroid every million years, and by a 10-kilometer asteroid every 100 million years.[1] As was explained at the beginning of the chapter, we have the technology to divert approaching asteroids.

The diversion of asteroids is a public good in the sense that it is available for everyone to consume, regardless of who pays and who doesn't. As with any public good, the key to developing an asteroid-diversion program is to collect money to pay for the program. According to NASA scientists, the program would require several new telescopes, which would cost about $50 million to install and about $10 million per year to operate.[2] The cost of the gossamer mirror or the nuclear weapons required to change the path of the asteroid would be $100 million to $200 million. Although it would be sensible to finance the program with contributions from all earthlings, it may be impossible to collect money from everyone. A more likely outcome is that one or more developed countries will finance their own diversion systems.

Preservation of Wolves

We can also apply the concepts of public goods and free riding to the issue of preserving wildlife. There are some trade-offs associated with preserving wolves and other wildlife in Yellowstone Park. To environmentalists, wolves are a part of the ecosystem, and the purpose of preserving wolves is to maintain the natural ecosystem. Ranchers, whose livestock is often eaten by wolves, consider the wolf a pest that should be eliminated or tightly controlled. In other words, there are costs as well as benefits associated with the preservation of wolves, just as there are costs and benefits associated with other public goods such as dams, fireworks, national defense, and space exploration.

One response to the wolf-preservation problem comes from Defenders of Wildlife, an environmental group in Montana. The organization collects money from its members and uses the money to reward landowners who allow wolves to live on their properties. The host landowner receives a payment of $5,000 for each litter of wolf pups reared on the property.[3] In addition, the organization compensates ranchers for livestock killed by wolves. As a result of these programs, ranchers in the Yellowstone area are more likely to support efforts to maintain the wolves as part of the ecosystem of Yellowstone Park. The programs treat preservation as a public good, one that is supported by money collected from the people who benefit from preservation.

Financing Government: Taxes

In this part of the chapter, we'll look at the market effects of taxes and answer two important questions about taxes. First, who really bears the burden of a tax? As we'll see, it is not necessarily the person who actually pays the tax to the government. Second, is the total burden of a tax equal to the revenue collected by the government? As we'll see, a tax changes people's behavior, so the total burden actually exceeds the revenue collected. We'll start with the issue of who bears the tax burden.

Tax Shifting: Forward and Backward

We can use supply and demand curves to look at the market effects of taxes. Suppose that your city imposes a tax of $80 per apartment and collects the tax from housing firms. You may think the burden of the tax falls exclusively on the housing firm, since that's who mails the check to the government. But some simple supply and demand analysis will show why this is incorrect. The housing firm will charge more for apartments and pay less for its inputs, so the tax will actually be paid by consumers and input suppliers.

Figure 16.1 shows the market effects of an $80 tax on apartments. We saw in Chapter 4 that an increase in the cost of producing a good shifts the supply curve to the left. In a perfectly competitive industry, in the long run, the equilibrium price equals the average cost of production. That means each firm makes just enough money to stay in the market. The original price of $200 was just high enough to cover the monthly cost of providing an apartment. The tax increases the average cost per apartment by $80, shifting the market supply curve up by $80.

Because of the tax, the $200 original price is now less than the $280 average cost ($200 + $80 tax). At the $200 price, housing firms will lose money on their apartments, so they will withdraw some apartments from the market and build fewer new apartments to replace old ones. As a result, the supply curve will shift to the left: At each price, fewer apartments will be supplied.

The leftward shift of the supply curve increases the equilibrium price of apartments. At the $200 price, there will be an excess demand for apartments, and the price will increase to eliminate the excess demand. In Figure 16.1, the market moves from point *i* to point *f*: The demand curve intersects the new supply curve at a price of $230, compared to $200 before the tax. In other words, housing firms shift part of the tax forward to consumers, who pay $30 of the $80 tax. Although housing firms pay the entire $80 tax in a legal sense, they get some of the money to pay the tax by charging consumers $30 more for apartments.

The apartment tax also affects the people who supply inputs to the housing industry. The tax decreases the output of the industry, so the industry needs smaller quantities of all the inputs used to produce apartments. Therefore, the tax causes an excess supply of

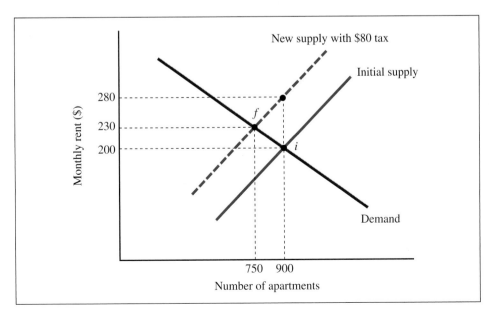

Figure 16.1

Market Effects of an Apartment Tax
A tax of $80 per apartment shifts the supply curve to the left, moving the market equilibrium from point *i* to point *f*. The equilibrium price increases from $200 to $230, and the equilibrium quantity decreases from 900 to 750 apartments.

each of the inputs used to produce housing, such as labor and land. To eliminate the excess supplies, input prices drop, meaning that housing firms pay less for their inputs, and part of the $80 tax is shifted backward to input suppliers: Housing firms pay lower wages and less for land. Although housing firms pay the apartment tax in a legal sense, they get some of the money to pay the tax by paying less to workers and landowners.

So who really pays the apartment tax? Although the housing firm actually sends the money to the government, the housing firm collects more money from consumers and pays less money to input suppliers, so consumers and input suppliers indirectly pay the tax. Recall that at every point on the long-run supply curve, economic profit per firm is zero. Each housing firm makes zero profit before and after the tax, so the housing firm doesn't pay the tax in an economic sense. This is possible because the firm shifts part of the tax forward to consumers and shifts the rest of the tax backward to input suppliers.

We can use Figure 16.1 to show just how much of the $80 apartment tax is paid by consumers and how much is paid by input suppliers. After the tax is imposed, the typical apartment owner charges $230 to consumers, pays a tax of $80 to the government, leaving $150 to pay all the people who supply the inputs required to produce the apartment. Before the tax, the apartment owner charged $200 and gave it all to input suppliers. Therefore, the tax makes input suppliers worse off by $50 per apartment ($200 received before the tax minus $150 received after the tax). If we add the $50 burden imposed on input suppliers to the $30 price hike experienced by consumers, we get a total of $80, an amount equal to the apartment tax.

Predicting the Amount of Forward Shifting

How much of a tax will be shifted forward to consumers, and how much will be shifted backward to input suppliers? No one likes to pay taxes, so everyone will try to avoid paying a particular tax by changing his or her behavior. We've already seen that housing firms avoid paying the tax by shifting part of the tax to consumers. Firms can shift the tax forward because they produce fewer apartments, causing an excess demand for apartments that increases the price of apartments. If consumers want to avoid paying too much of the tax, they must change their behavior.

The amount of the tax shifted forward to consumers depends on the price elasticity of demand for the taxed good. If the demand for apartments is inelastic—meaning that consumers are not very responsive to price changes—we need a large price hike to eliminate the excess demand for housing caused by the tax. Therefore, consumers will be hit by a large increase in price, and so they will pay the bulk of the tax. This is shown in panel A of Figure 16.2. Demand is inelastic—the demand curve is steep—and a $5 tax increases the equilibrium price by $4 (from $10 to $14). Consumers pay four-fifths of the tax. In panel B, demand is elastic—the demand curve is nearly flat—and consumers pay a small part of the tax. A $5 tax increases the equilibrium price by only $1 (from $10 to $11), so consumers pay only one-fifth of the tax.

The amount of backward shifting to input suppliers depends on their responsiveness to changes in input prices. We know that a tax on a product causes an excess supply of the inputs used to produce that product, and input prices must drop to eliminate the excess supply. If input suppliers are not very responsive to price changes—meaning that the supply of inputs is very inelastic—a large decrease in input prices will be needed to eliminate the excess supply of inputs. Therefore, input suppliers will pay the bulk of the tax.

Why should we care about tax shifting? An important policy question is, Who actually pays the taxes that support public goods? We've seen that the easy answer—the people who are legally responsible for paying the tax—is often wrong. A tax increases consumer prices and decreases input prices, so we must look beyond the taxpayer to

Figure 16.2

Elasticities of Demand and Tax Effects
If demand is inelastic (panel A), a tax will increase the market price by a large amount, so consumers will bear a large share of the tax. If demand is elastic (panel B), the price will increase by a small amount and consumers will bear a small share of the tax.

determine who actually bears the cost of a tax. The subtleties of tax shifting are often missed by the people who design our tax policy and the media folks who report on it.

Applications: Cigarette Tax and Luxury Tax

We can use what we've learned about tax shifting to discuss some recent episodes in tax policy. In 1994, President Clinton proposed an immediate $0.75 per pack increase in the cigarette tax. The tax had two purposes: to generate revenue for Clinton's health-care reform plan and to decrease medical costs by discouraging smoking. Figure 16.3 shows the effects of the proposed tax on the cigarette market. The tax would decrease the supply of cigarettes and increase the equilibrium price from $2.00 per pack to $2.45. Cigarette producers would charge $2.45 per pack and pay a tax of $0.75, leaving only $1.70 to pay input suppliers, including the owners of tobacco-growing land. This is less than input suppliers received before, so some of the $0.75 tax would come out of the pockets of people who own land suitable for growing tobacco.

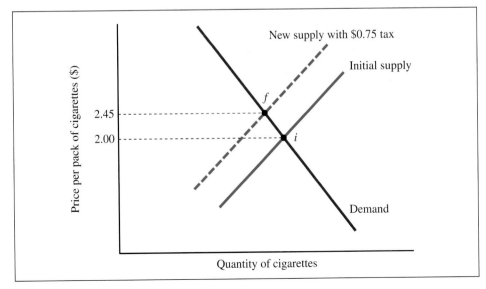

Figure 16.3

Market Effects of a Cigarette Tax
A tax of $0.75 per pack of cigarettes shifts the supply curve to the left, moving the market equilibrium from point *i* to point *f*. The equilibrium price increases from $2.00 to $2.45, and the equilibrium quantity decreases.

It appears that tobacco farmers and landowners understand the economics of cigarette taxes. Led by a group of representatives and senators from tobacco-growing areas in North Carolina, Kentucky, and Virginia, the Congress scaled back Clinton's proposed tax hike from $0.75 to $0.05. Although the government would collect the tax from cigarette producers, savvy tobacco farmers realized the tax would decrease their income and the price of the land used to grow tobacco. The representatives of tobacco-growing areas, acting on behalf of tobacco farmers and landowners, used their power in Congress to scale back the President's proposed tax hike.

Another lesson on backward shifting comes from a special luxury tax passed by the U.S. Congress in 1990 and repealed a few years later. The idea was to raise money from wealthy consumers by taxing luxury goods such as expensive boats. For example, the luxury tax on a $300,000 boat was $20,000. In fact, the luxury tax was shared by consumers and input suppliers, including people who worked in boat factories and boat yards. The tax decreased the quantity of boats produced, so the boat industry needed fewer workers, leading to layoffs and lower wages for the remaining workers. Although the idea behind the luxury tax was to "soak the rich," the tax actually harmed low-income workers in the boat industry.

Tax Burden and Deadweight Loss

We've seen that people respond to a tax by changing their behavior, causing the tax to be shifted to other people. These changes in behavior also have implications for the total burden of a tax. If people change their behavior in response to a tax, the total burden of a tax will exceed the amount of money the government actually collects from the tax. To see why, suppose the government imposes a tax on No. 3 pencils and the tax is large enough that everyone who initially used No. 3 pencils switches to other types of pencils or other writing implements. If no one purchases No. 3 pencils, the tax won't raise any revenue for the government, but the tax generates a burden because some people who would prefer to use No. 3 pencils have switched to other writing implements.

We'll use the fish market to explore the total burden of a tax. In Figure 16.4 the initial supply curve for fish is a horizontal line, indicating that the fish market is a constant-cost industry. This means that input prices don't change as the industry grows or

A luxury tax on expensive boats will harm wealthy consumers as well as the people who work in boat factories and boat yards.

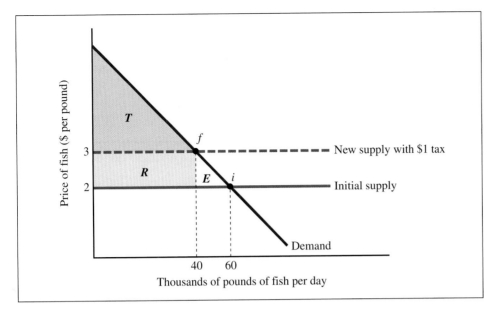

Figure 16.4
Total Burden of a Tax
In a constant-cost industry, a tax increases the equilibrium price by the tax ($1 per pound in this example). Consumer surplus decreases by areas *R* and *E*. Total tax revenue is shown by rectangle *R*, so the total burden exceeds tax revenue by triangle *E*, sometimes known as the deadweight loss or excess burden of the tax.

shrinks. The demand curve intersects the initial supply curve at point *i*, so the price is $2 per pound and the quantity is 60,000 pounds of fish per day. If the government imposes a tax of $1 per pound of fish, the supply curve will shift upward by $1. In addition to paying $2 for the inputs required to produce one pound of fish, the fish producer must also pay a $1 tax, so the price required to cover all expenses is now $3 instead of $2.

In Figure 16.4 the fish tax increases the equilibrium price of fish from $2 to $3. Why does the price increase by an amount equal to the tax? In a constant-cost industry, input prices are fixed, so there is no opportunity to shift the tax backward onto input suppliers: They get the same prices for their inputs, regardless of how much output is produced. Therefore, consumers bear the full cost of the tax.

We can use the concept of consumer surplus to determine just how much consumers lose as a result of the tax. Before the fish tax, the consumer surplus is shown by the area between the initial supply curve and the demand curve, or areas *T, R,* and *E.* When the price increases to $3, the consumer surplus shrinks to the area of triangle *T,* so the loss of consumer surplus (the **total burden of the tax**) is shown by rectangle *R* and triangle *E.* Let's take a closer look at these two areas:

Total burden of the tax: The loss in consumer surplus resulting from a tax (assuming a constant-cost industry).

- Rectangle *R* shows the extra money consumers must pay for the 40,000 pounds of fish they purchase. The tax increases the price by $1 per pound, so consumers pay an extra $40,000.

- Triangle *E* shows the loss of consumer surplus on the fish that are not consumed because of the tax. Consumers obey the law of demand, so when the price rises, they cut their purchases, buying 20,000 fewer pounds of fish. As a result, they give up the consumer surplus they would have received on these 20,000 pounds of fish.

How does the total burden of the tax compare to the tax revenue raised by the government? The total tax revenue is the tax per pound ($1) times the quantity consumed (40,000 pounds), or $40,000. This is shown by rectangle *R*: Part of the loss experienced by consumers is the revenue gain for government. In addition to losing rectangle *R,* consumers also lose triangle *E,* so the consumer's total burden of the tax exceeds the tax revenue. Triangle *E* is sometimes known as the **deadweight loss from taxation** or the

Deadweight loss from taxation: The difference between the total burden of a tax and the amount of revenue collected by the government.

excess burden of a tax. Because the tax causes consumers to change their behavior—they consume less fish at the higher price—there is a deadweight loss or excess burden.

The essential reason for excess burden is that taxes cause people to change their behavior, making choices to avoid taxes. For another example of changes in behavior in response to taxes, read "A Closer Look: Taxes and December Babies."

TEST Your Understanding

4. Complete the statement with *right* or *left*: A tax on a particular good shifts the market supply curve to the _____.

5. How will a tax on backpacks affect the equilibrium price and quantity of backpacks?

6. Complete the statement with *excess supply* or *excess demand*: A tax on chairs will initially cause _____ in the market for chairs and _____ in the markets for the inputs used to make chairs.

Public Choice

We have discussed the challenges associated with providing and paying for goods that generate spillover benefits. In this part of the chapter, we look at how governments actually operate, exploring four contrasting views of government that have emerged from a field of study known as **public choice economics**.

Public choice economics: A field of economics that explores how governments actually operate.

Governments Take Actions to Promote Efficiency

The public-interest view of government is based on the idea that governments make the economy more efficient. For example, governments provide public goods, including dams, national defense, and space exploration. Because of the free-rider problem, a system of voluntary contributions for public goods is unlikely to raise enough money to support public goods at the efficient levels. The alternative to voluntary contributions is to give government the power to collect taxes.

Voters Tell Governments What to Do

The second view of government focuses on voters and how they affect government decisions. We vote directly on ballot measures and budget elections, both of which may impose constraints on government. We also vote for people to represent our viewpoints

---

A CLOSER LOOK   TAXES AND DECEMBER BABIES

The current tax law includes a tax credit for children: A child born on or before December 31 reduces the household's tax liability in that year and every subsequent year until the child reaches 18. A recent study shows that the higher the tax credit, the larger the percentage of children born in the last week of the year and the smaller the percentage of children born in the first week of the year.[4] It appears that couples time the births of their children to take advantage of the tax credit. The authors estimate that increasing the tax benefit of having a child by $500 raises the probability of having the child in the last week of December by about 27%.

in legislative bodies (city councils, state legislatures, Congress) and in executive positions (mayor, governor, president). The basic idea of a democracy is that the government will take actions that are approved by the majority of citizens. If governments are responsive to voters, the voting public ultimately makes all the important decisions, and the actions of government reflect the preferences of voters.

One result of public choice economics is known as the median-voter rule. According to the **median-voter rule**, the choices made by government will reflect the preferences of the median voter, defined as the voter who splits the voting population into two halves, one half wanting more of something (for example, a larger government budget) and the other half wanting less (a smaller government budget). As we'll see, this rule has some interesting implications for decision-making and politics.

Median-voter rule: A rule suggesting that the choices made by government will reflect the preferences of the median voter.

To see the logic of this rule, consider a state where there are two candidates for governor—Penny and Buck—and the only issue in the election is how much the state should spend on education. Each citizen will vote for the candidate whose proposed education budget is closest to the citizen's preferred budget. Figure 16.5 shows citizens' preferences for education spending, with different preferred budgets on the horizontal axis and the number of voters with each preferred budget on the vertical axis. For example, 2 citizens have a preferred budget of $1 billion, 4 have a preferred budget of $2 billion, and so on. The median budget, which splits the rest of the voters into two equal groups (20 voters on either side), is $5 billion.

Suppose the two candidates start out with very different proposed education budgets. Penny proposes a budget of $3 billion, and Buck proposes $7 billion. The 20 citizens with preferred budgets less than or equal to $4 billion will vote for Penny because her proposed budget is closest to their preferred budgets. Buck's supporters include the 20 citizens with preferred budgets greater than or equal to $6 billion. The two candidates will split the 10 voters with a preferred budget of $5 billion (halfway between the two proposed budgets), so each candidate will get a total of 25 votes, resulting in a tie.

Penny could increase her chance of being elected by increasing her proposed budget. Let's say she proposes $4 billion instead of $3 billion. The voters with a preferred budget of $5 billion will switch to Penny because Penny's $4 billion proposal is now closer to their $5 billion preferred budget than Buck's $7 billion. Penny won't lose any of her other votes, so she will win the election by a vote of 30 (2 + 4 + 6 + 8 + 10) to 20 (8 + 8 + 4). If Buck is smart, he will realize that he could get more votes by moving toward the median budget. For example, if he decreases his proposed budget to $6 billion, the election would result in a tie vote again. Penny and Buck will continue to move their

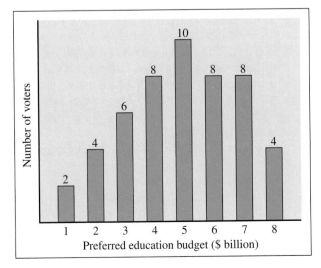

Figure 16.5
Median Voter Rule
If Penny proposes a $3 billion budget and Buck proposes a $7 billion budget, the election will result in a tie. By moving toward the median budget, Penny can increase her chance of being elected. Both candidates will propose a budget close to the $5 billion preferred budget of the median voter.

proposed budgets toward the median budget ($5 billion) until they both actually propose budgets that are very close to the median budget.

There are powerful forces pulling the two candidates toward the preferences of the median voter. As long as Penny proposes a smaller budget than Buck, the people with small preferred budgets will continue to vote for her. The benefit of moving toward the median is that she can take some votes from Buck. Similarly, Buck doesn't have to worry about people with large preferred budgets but can concentrate instead on the battle for voters in the middle. The result is that by election day, the 2 candidates have adopted virtually the same position: the position of the median voter. The median-voter rule says that the choices made by government will reflect the preferences of the median voter. In other words, there isn't much of a choice.

The logic of the median-voter result also applies to competition among some types of sellers. Read the "A Closer Look: Are Politicians Like Ice-Cream Vendors?"

It is also possible to "vote with your feet." The economist Charles M. Tiebout suggested that a household's choice of which community to live in is based in part on the tax and spending policies of different communities. Households express their preferences by moving to communities that offer the best package of services and taxes. A community with inefficient public services will experience a loss in population, perhaps causing the local officials to make the public services more efficient.

It is clear that people vote with their ballots and with their feet. In both cases, citizens can express their preferences for public goods, taxes, and public policies. These two sources of citizen power limit the ability of governments to take actions that are inconsistent with the preferences of most voters.

Government Officials Pursue Their Own Self-Interest

Several economists, including Nobel laureate James Buchanan, have suggested a model of government that focuses on the selfish behavior of government officials. According to this view, politicians and bureaucrats pursue their own narrow interests, which of course may differ from the public interest. For example, politicians or bureaucrats may

A CLOSER LOOK ARE POLITICIANS LIKE ICE-CREAM VENDORS?

Imagine a one-mile stretch of beach with 120 swimmers and sunbathers distributed evenly along the beach. Suppose each person on the beach will purchase one ice-cream cone. If there are two ice-cream vendors on the beach selling an identical product, where will they locate? The most efficient arrangement would be to divide the beach into two half-mile territories and locate each vendor at the middle of his or her territory. Lefty would be at the quarter-mile mark, and Righty would be at the three-quarter mile mark. Each vendor will sell 60 ice-cream cones. If beach people patronize the closest vendor, this arrangement will minimize the total travel costs of ice-cream patrons.

Is this an equilibrium arrangement? If Lefty were to move to the right—to the half-mile mark, the median location—he would not lose any of his customers to his left but would capture part of Righty's market: Lefty would now be the closest vendor for the people located between the half-mile mark and the five-eighths mark, so he would sell 75 ice-cream cones instead of only 60. Righty would now sell only 45 cones. To protect her market, Righty would move to the median location too. In the equilibrium, both vendors pick the median location, with equal numbers of customers on each side (60 for each vendor). The outcome of the ice-cream vendors' game is the same as the politicians' game. Like the politicians, the vendors have an incentive to move to the median location, so there is no real difference between the two vendors.

gain prestige from starting a new spending program even if the cost of the program exceeds its social benefit. Because voters don't have much information about the costs and benefits of public services, they may not be in a position to evaluate the actions of politicians or bureaucrats and vote accordingly.

The self-interest theory of government explains why voters sometimes approve explicit limits on taxes and government spending. For example, most states have limits on the amount of property taxes that can be raised, and many states also limit total government spending. According to the self-interest theory of government, limitations on taxes and spending are necessary safeguards against politicians and bureaucrats who benefit from larger budgets.

The theory of rent seeking, which we described in Chapter 10, also applies to governments. Many public policies cause one group of citizens to gain at the expense of others, and a citizen group may try to persuade government officials to implement policies that are favorable to members of the group. Resources are expended in the attempts to influence the decisions of politicians and bureaucrats, and from a social point of view, much of this expenditure is wasteful.

Special-Interest Groups Manipulate the Government

Another model of government is based on the idea that small groups of people manipulate government for their own gain. Suppose the total benefit of a dam is less than its total cost, so the project is inefficient, but a few farmers reap large benefits from the dam, while the costs are spread over a million taxpayers. The farmers have a strong incentive to spend time and money to convince policymakers to build the dam. If the tax is only $1 per person, not many taxpayers will make their preferences known to policymakers. If politicians listen to people who express their preferences and contribute money to political campaigns, the inefficient project may be approved. This is an example of a special-interest group (farmers) that manipulates government at the expense of a larger group (all taxpayers). In general, when a few people share the benefit from a project and a large number of people share the cost, government is more likely to approve inefficient projects.

In general, whenever benefits are concentrated on a few citizens but costs are spread out over many citizens, we expect special-interest groups to form. Special-interest organizations often use lobbyists to express their views to government officials and policymakers.

The European Union (EU), with 15 member nations, makes decisions that affect people and firms throughout Europe. As the power of the union has grown, so has the number of lobbyists expressing their points of view. By 1995, there were 10,000 lobbyists trying to influence decision-makers on the European Commission (the executive branch), the Council of Ministers (the representatives of member states), and the European Parliament (popularly elected representatives).[5] The fear of manipulation by lobbyists representing special interests has led some officials to advocate a formal registration process: Each lobbyist would be required to provide a list of his or her clients and the amount of money spent on the behalf of each client. Under another proposal, lobbyists would be issued color-coded entry badges that would allow them to enter only certain parts of the parliament building, limiting their access to officials of the EU.

Which Theory Is Correct?

Which of these theories best describes the actual practices of governments? This is a very difficult question. Economists and political scientists have studied many dimensions of the decision-making processes underlying tax policies and spending policies. There is evidence that people do vote with ballots and with their feet and that these two forms of voting make a difference. There is also evidence that government officials sometimes pursue their own interests and those of special-interest groups. The field of public choice is a very active area of research involving economists and political scientists.

TEST Your Understanding

7. In Figure 16.5, suppose that 32 additional citizens enter the state and each has a preferred budget of $2 billion. How will the new citizens affect the election?

8. Do you think all citizens have the same opportunity to vote with their feet, picking the community that provides the best package of goods and services?

9. In the 1960s and 1970s, many people greeted Vietnam War protesters with signs that read "America: Love It or Leave It." Does your ability to vote with your feet vary with the level of government?

Using the TOOLS

In this chapter, we explain why the government provides public goods. Because of the free-rider problem, we can't rely on voluntary contributions to support public goods and subsidies, so we use taxes to support public programs. Here are some opportunities to do your own economic analysis of public goods and taxes.

1. ECONOMIC EXPERIMENT: Voluntary Contributions

In this voluntary-contribution experiment, students play the role of citizens who have the opportunity to contribute money to support public education. Here is how the experiment works:

- The class is divided into groups of three to five students per group, with each group representing a citizen. Each group starts with $30.

- Each time period each citizen decides how much to contribute to public education. The maximum contribution is $10 per time period. The group records this amount on its report card.

- The instructor computes the total contributions to public education. Each dollar contributed to public education decreases the cost of the city's welfare system and criminal-justice system by $3, so the city's budget savings from the contributions equals the total contributions times 3. The tax refund per citizen equals the budget savings divided by the number of citizens. Here are some examples of contributions and tax refunds for a city with 20 citizens:

Total Contributions	Decrease in Budget	Tax Refund per Citizen
$ 20	$ 60	$ 6
$100	$300	$30
$200	$600	$60

- The experiment is run for five rounds. A group's score for the experiment equals the amount of money it has at the end of five rounds.

APPLICATIONS

2. Stream Preservation

Consider a trout stream that is threatened with destruction by a nearby logging operation. Each of the 10,000 local fishers would be willing to pay $5 to preserve the stream. The owner of the land would incur a cost of $20,000 to change the logging operation to protect the stream.

a. Is the preservation of the stream efficient from the social perspective?

b. If the landowner has the right to log the land any way he wants, will the stream be preserved?

c. Propose a solution to this problem. Describe a transaction that would benefit the fishers and the landowner.

d. Will your proposed solution work?

3. Shifting a Housecleaning Tax

Consider a city where people from poor households clean the houses of rich households. Initially, firms charge households $10 per hour, keep $1 per hour for administrative costs, and pay their workers $9 per hour. Like many luxury goods, the demand for housecleaning service is very elastic. Housecleaning workers are not very responsive to changes in the wage.

a. Use supply and demand curves to show the initial equilibrium in the market for cleaning services (price = $10 per hour; quantity = 1,000 hours of cleaning per week), and label the equilibrium point with an *i*.

b. Suppose the city imposes a tax of $3 per hour of cleaning services, and one-third of the tax is shifted forward to consumers. Use your graph to show the effects of the tax on the housecleaning market. Label the new equilibrium point with an *f*. What is the new price?

c. Is it reasonable that only one-third of the tax is shifted forward? Explain.

d. Suppose that firms continue to keep $1 per hour for administrative costs. Predict the new wage.

e. Who bears the bulk of the housecleaning tax: wealthy households or poor households?

 Summary

In this chapter, we've seen that governments can solve the problems caused by spillover benefits. We also saw that taxes affect the prices of consumer goods and inputs, and that we must look beyond the taxpayer to determine who actually bears the cost of a tax. We've also examined three different views on how governments actually operate. Here are the main points of the chapter:

1. If the cost of a particular good exceeds its per capita benefit, that good will not be provided by a market, even if the total benefit of the good exceeds its total cost. We can use government—with its taxing authority—to make a collective decision about whether to provide such a good.

2. A system of voluntary contributions suffers from the free-rider problem: People will voluntarily contribute only a small fraction of the amount that would be generated under a compulsory taxation to pay for the public good.

3. A tax on a good will be shifted forward to consumers and backward to input suppliers.

4. Because a tax causes people to change their behavior, the total burden of the tax exceeds the revenue generated by the tax.

 Key Terms

Problems and Discussion Questions

1. A three-person city is considering a fireworks display. Bertha is willing to pay $100 for the proposed fireworks display; Marian is willing to pay $30; Sam is willing to pay $20. The cost of the fireworks display is $120.

   a. Will any single citizen provide the display on his or her own?

   b. If the cost of the fireworks display is divided equally among the citizens, will a majority vote in favor of the display?

   c. Describe a transaction that would benefit all three citizens.

2. Churches collect substantial sums of money through voluntary contributions. What explains their ability to overcome the free-rider problem at least partially?

3. Suppose the students in the chapter's free-rider experiment make the following agreement: If any single person does not contribute three dimes, all the contributions will be returned, each contributor receiving a refund equal to the amount that he or she contributed. How will this agreement affect the outcome of the experiment?

4. The spotted owl is an endangered creature that lives in old-growth forests. Logging in the old-growth forests destroys the habitat of the owls. Explain how the lessons from the wolf-preservation program might be applied to the issue of preserving the spotted owl.

5. Each of the 80,000 citizens in a particular county would be willing to pay $0.10 to increase the number of wolf litters by one. Each litter of wolves imposes costs on ranchers (from livestock losses) of $5,000.

   a. Is the provision of an additional litter of wolves efficient from the social perspective?

   b. If ranchers have the right to kill any wolves on their property, will an additional litter be protected?

   c. Propose a solution to this problem. Describe a transaction that would benefit the wolf lovers and ranchers.

6. Contributions to organizations such as United Way and the American Cancer Society are tax deductible: For each dollar contributed, a person's tax liability decreases by $0.15 to $0.31. Explain the rationale for this tax policy.

7. Under a special luxury tax passed by Congress in 1990, buyers of expensive cars pay a 10% tax on the portion of the purchase price above $30,000.

   a. Will the luxury car tax be paid exclusively by the wealthy consumers who buy expensive cars?

   b. What information do you need to determine the share of the tax paid by wealthy consumers?

8. In the words of Will Rogers, "The trouble with land is that they're not making it any more." In other words, the supply of land is fixed, and the supply curve is a vertical line.

   a. If the government imposes a tax on land, which side of the market—land consumers or landowners—will pay a larger part of the tax?

   b. Will the land tax generate a deadweight loss?

9. Consider the example of the governor's election shown in Figure 16.5. Suppose 18 new people move into the state and each newcomer has a desired education budget of $9 billion.

   a. Will the two candidates change their proposed education budget? If so, how much will each candidate propose?

   b. How would your answer to part (a) change if each newcomer had a desired budget of $15 billion instead of $9 billion?

10. Consider the market effects of a tax on hotel rooms. The market is perfectly competitive, with an initial equilibrium price of $50 per night and an initial equilibrium quantity of 100 rooms rented out per day. Draw a supply and demand graph such that a $10 tax per room increases the equilibrium price from $50 to $56 and decreases the equilibrium quantity from 100 rooms to 80 rooms. How is the tax divided between consumers and input suppliers?

11. **Web Exercise.** Visit the Web site of the U.S. Department of Treasury [*http://www.ustreas.gov*]. Access the most recent annual report, and list the 10 largest expenditure categories. Identify the categories with the most rapid increases in the last few years.

12. **Web Exercise.** Visit the Web site of the Census Bureau that has data on government finance [*http://www.census.gov/govs/www*]. Click the link entitled "State and Local Government Finances" and get the most recent data on your state's tax and expenditures. How does the percentage of your state's revenue from income taxes compare to the percentage shown for all states in Figure 3.5.

Take It to the Net

We invite you to visit the O'Sullivan/Sheffrin page on the Prentice Hall Web site at: **http://www.prenhall.com/osullivan/** for additional World Wide Web exercises for this chapter.

Model Answers to Questions

Chapter-Opening Questions

1. A system based on voluntary contributions would suffer from the free-rider problem, with few people contributing money to support the public good.

2. The payments to host landowners treat preservation as a public good supported by money collected from the people who benefit from preservation.

3. The housing firm will collect more money from consumers (the price of apartments will be higher) and pay less money to input suppliers (the prices of inputs will be lower), so consumers and input suppliers will indirectly pay the tax.

4. A liberal candidate who moves toward the center won't lose the votes of liberal citizens but will gain some votes from moderate citizens. A conservative candidate who moves toward the center won't lose conservative votes but will gain moderate votes. Both candidates are likely to adopt the position favored by the median voter.

Test Your Understanding

1. The producer of a private good collects money from each consumer. If you don't pay, you don't get the good. In contrast, it is impossible to prevent people who don't pay from consuming a public good.

2. If Margie adds a dime to the pot, the instructor adds 20 cents and then divides the 30 cents equally among the 10 students, so Margie gets back 3 cents for every dime she puts in.

3. She will not contribute the extra dime because the marginal benefit (3 cents) is less than the marginal cost (10 cents).

4. Left.

5. The equilibrium price increases and the equilibrium quantity decreases.

6. Excess demand, excess supply.

7. The median voter now has a preferred budget of $3 billion: A total of 38 voters have a lower preferred budget ($1 or $2 billion), and a total of 38 voters

have a higher preferred budget. Both candidates will propose the median budget ($3 billion).

8. Low-income households cannot afford housing in many neighborhoods, so they have fewer options. Many suburban communities have zoning policies that limit high-density housing, restricting the choices of low-income households. If there is racial discrimination, minority households will have fewer options.

9. At the local level, the typical metropolitan area has many municipalities to choose from, so foot voting is not very costly. At the national level, voting with your feet means renouncing your citizenship and moving far away, so it is more costly.

Using the Tools

2. Stream Preservation
    a. The benefit is $50,000 (10,000 fishers time $5 per fisher), which exceeds the cost of $20,000. Because the benefit exceeds the cost, the preservation of the stream is socially efficient.
    b. No. If the landowner is also a fisher, the $20,000 cost exceeds the $5 benefit.
    c. The citizens could contribute to a stream-preservation fund to cover the landowner's cost. If each fisher contributed $3 (60% of his or her benefit), together they could raise a total of $30,000. The landowner would be better off by $10,000, and each fisher would be better off by $2.
    d. The free-rider problem may make it difficult to raise enough money to pay off the landowner.

3. Shifting a Housecleaning Tax
    a. See Figure 16.A.
    b. See Figure 16.A. The tax shifts the supply curve to the left, and the new price is $11.
    c. We know that demand is very elastic and input suppliers are not very responsive, so a one-third shift is reasonable.

Figure 16.A
Market Effects of Cleaning Tax

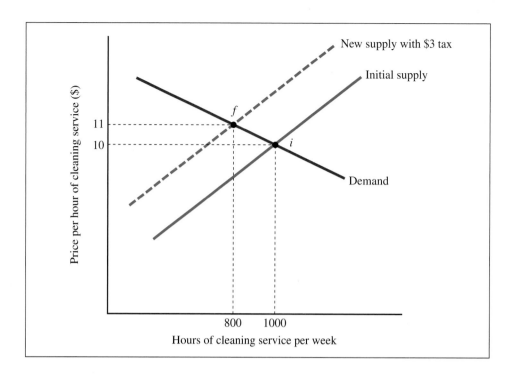

d. The firm collects $11 from consumers, pays the $3 tax, and pays its $1 administrative cost, leaving only $7 for workers. The wage decreases from $9 to $7.

e. Workers experience a wage cut of $2 per hour, while consumers pay an additional $1 per hour for cleaning services.

 Notes

1. Carl Sagan, "A Warning for Us?," *Parade*, June 5, 1994, p. 8; John Boudreau, "Collision Course: Scientists Say There's a Big Asteroid Bang in Our Future," *Washington Post*, April 6, 1994, p. C1.

2. "Mirror Beam Could Deflect Killer Asteroid, Theory Says," *New York Times*, November 9, 1994, p. C6.

3. Terry L. Anderson, "A Carrot to Save the Wolf," *The Margin*, Spring 1992, p. 28.

4. Stacy Dickert-Conlin and Amitabh Chandra, "Taxes and the Timing of Births," *Journal of Political Economy*, 107, February 1999, pp. 161-77.

5. Charles Goldsmith, "The EU Is Beset by Swarms of Lobbyists," *Wall Street Journal*, April 14, 1995, p. A6.

Environmental Policy

Under the Climate Control Accord of 1994, electric utilities in the United States agreed to do their part in the battle against global warming. Arizona Public Service provides electricity to the rapidly growing population in the southwestern United States. Although the utility could decrease its emissions of the pollutants responsible for global warming, it would be very costly to do so. Instead, Arizona Public Service paid for projects that will decrease air pollution in India, China, and other developing countries, where pollution abatement costs less than it does in developed countries.[1] In addition, Arizona Public Service paid for a reforestation project in Mexico, which will help in the battle against global warming because forests absorb some of the pollutants responsible for global warming.

his story of Arizona Public Service provides an introduction to recent innovations in environmental policy. Governments around the world are setting pollution targets and letting polluters decide how to meet those targets. This approach contrasts sharply with the traditional regulatory policy under which the government gets involved in the details of pollution abatement. In the case of global warming, Arizona Public Service can meet its pollution-abatement responsibility by paying for abatement projects elsewhere, even projects in other countries. Indeed, our most pressing environmental problems—global warming, the depletion of the ozone layer, and acid rain—cross international boundaries, and so do the solutions.

As we saw in the previous chapter, the government has a role in markets with spillover benefits. In this chapter, we'll see that the government also plays a role in markets with spillover costs.

Spillover **PRINCIPLE**

> **For some goods, the costs or benefits associated with the good are not confined to the person or organization that decides how much of the good to produce or consume.**

One of the lessons from Chapter 6 that if a particular good generates spillover costs, the market equilibrium will be inefficient and a tax on pollution will make the market efficient. In this chapter, we take a closer look at spillover costs, exploring several environmental problems that result from spillover costs and evaluating alternative policies to deal with spillover costs. You've seen the headlines and read the stories about global warming, the hole in the ozone layer, acid rain, and urban smog. Now you'll learn why these problems occur and what we can do about them. Here are some practical questions that we answer:

1. How would a switch from a traditional regulatory policy to a pollution tax affect the price of a polluting good and the amount of pollution?
2. What is a carbon tax, and how would a tax of $100 per ton of carbon affect the equilibrium price of gasoline?
3. Why do we want to protect the ozone layer in the upper atmosphere but get rid of ozone (also known as smog) near the earth's surface?
4. What is the rationale for the cash-for-clunkers program, under which firms buy old cars and destroy them?

Pollution Tax Versus Regulation

As we saw in Chapter 6, the economist's response to a pollution problem is to impose a pollution tax. A pollution tax forces firms to pay for the waste they generate, causing firms to produce less of the polluting good. In this chapter, we'll take a closer look at a firm's response to a pollution tax, showing that a pollution tax also encourages firms to spend money to abate pollution. We'll also look at some alternatives to a pollution tax.

Pollution tax: A tax or charge equal to the spillover cost per unit of waste.

Suppose there are several paper mills along a river and a city downstream from the mills uses the river water for drinking. Each gallon of chemical waste from paper mills increases the city's water-treatment costs by $4. Therefore, the appropriate **pollution tax,** equal to the spillover cost per ton of waste, is $4 per gallon of waste. Assume that each paper mill produces one ton of paper per day.

The Firm's Response to a Pollution Tax

Most polluting firms can control the amount of waste they dump into the environment. For example, a paper firm could install filters and other abatement equipment, or it could switch to raw materials that generate less chemical waste. The first two columns of Table17.1 show a hypothetical relationship between the volume of waste generated and the cost of producing one ton of paper. For example, the cost per ton is $60 if the firm generates 5 gallons of waste per ton of paper but $61 if the firm generates only 4 gallons of waste per ton of paper. In other words, when the firm decreases its waste by 1 gallon, the production cost per ton increases by $1.

Pollution abatement is subject to diminishing returns. As the firm continues to decrease the volume of waste, it becomes progressively more expensive to decrease it further. This makes sense because the firm must use progressively more expensive abatement equipment to decrease the volume of waste. For example, the cost of eliminating the last gallon of waste is $30 ($116 minus $86)

The third and fourth columns of Table 17.1 show the tax cost per ton and the total cost per ton of paper with different volumes of waste. The tax is $4 per gallon of waste, so the tax cost is $20 if the firm generates 5 gallons of waste per ton of paper but only $16 for 4 gallons, $12 for 3 gallons, and so on. The fourth column of Table 17.1 shows the firm's total cost per ton of paper, equal to the sum of the production cost per ton and the tax cost per ton. If the firm generates 5 gallons of waste, the production cost will be $60 and the tax cost will be $20, so the total cost per ton is $80. As the firm continues to decrease the volume of waste, the production cost increases while the tax cost decreases. The total cost per ton initially decreases (from $80 to $77 to $76) but eventually increases, reaching $116 if the firm generates no waste.

How will the typical paper firm respond to a pollution tax? The question for the firm is: Should we continue to generate 5 gallons of waste per ton of paper and pay $20 in pollution taxes or should we spend some money to reduce our waste? In Table 17.1, the total cost per ton is minimized at $76 with 3 gallons of waste. Therefore, the typical firm will decrease its waste from 5 to 3 gallons per ton of paper.

We can use the marginal principle to explain why it is sensible to generate only 3 gallons of waste.

Table 17.1 Cost per Ton of Paper with Varying Amounts of Pollution

Waste per Ton (Gallons)	Average Production Cost per Ton	Tax Cost per Ton	Average Total Cost per Ton with Tax
5	$ 60	$20	$ 80
4	$ 61	$16	$ 77
3	$ 64	$12	$ 76
2	$ 71	$ 8	$ 79
1	$ 86	$ 4	$ 90
0	$116	$ 0	$116

Marginal **PRINCIPLE**

Increase the level of an activity if its marginal benefit exceeds its marginal cost, but reduce the level if the marginal cost exceeds the marginal benefit. If possible, pick the level at which the marginal benefit equals the marginal cost.

In this case, the activity is reducing waste, so the firm should continue to cut its waste as long as the marginal benefit (the $4 savings in taxes) exceeds the marginal cost (the extra production cost from cutting waste by 1 gallon). Starting with 5 gallons of waste, it is sensible to cut back to 4 gallons because the $4 marginal benefit exceeds the $1 marginal cost. Similarly, it is sensible to cut back to 3 gallons because the $4 marginal benefit exceeds the $3 marginal cost. The firm will not cut back to 2 gallons because the $4 marginal benefit is less than the $7 marginal cost.

The Market Effects of a Pollution Tax

We're ready to study the market effects of a pollution tax. Suppose that each firm produces 1 ton of paper per day and has the production costs shown in Table 17.1. Figure 17.1 shows the effects of the $4 pollution tax ($4 per gallon of waste) on the industry supply curve. In a perfectly competitive industry, the equilibrium price equals the average cost of production, so each firm makes just enough money to stay in the market. The original price of $60 per ton was just high enough to cover the cost of producing a ton of paper without the pollution tax. The tax increases the cost of producing paper because the typical firm pays some pollution taxes and incurs some additional costs when it cuts back its pollution from 5 gallons to 3 gallons per ton of paper. Therefore, the $60 price will not be high enough to cover the higher production costs, so some firms will leave the market. As a result, the supply curve will shift to the left: At each price, a smaller quantity of paper will be supplied.

The leftward shift of the supply curve increases the equilibrium price of paper. In Figure 17.1, the market moves from point *i* to point *f*, where the demand curve intersects the new supply curve. The price of paper increases from $60 to $68 per ton, and consumers respond to the higher price by decreasing the quantity of paper demanded,

Figure 17.1

Market Effects of a Pollution Tax

The pollution tax increases the cost of producing paper, shifting the market supply curve to the left. The equilibrium moves from point *i* to point *f*. The tax increases the equilibrium price from $60 to $68 per ton and decreases the equilibrium quantity from 100 to 80 tons per day.

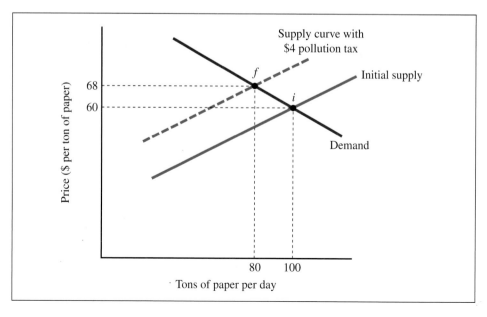

from 100 to 80 tons per day. Like other taxes, the pollution tax is partially shifted to consumers in the form of a higher price, and they respond by consuming less paper. When consumers face the full cost of producing paper, they decide to consume less of it.

How does the pollution tax affect the total volume of waste dumped into the river? The volume of waste decreases for two reasons:

- **Abatement.** There is less waste per ton of paper: 3 gallons instead of 5 gallons per ton.

- **Lower output.** The industry produces less paper: 80 tons instead of 100 tons per day.

In this example, the volume of water pollution decreases from 500 gallons per day (100 tons of paper times 5 gallons per ton) to 240 gallons per day (80 tons of paper times 3 gallons per ton). In general, we can clean up the environment by producing less of a polluting good and generating less waste per unit of the good.

Traditional Regulation: Command and Control

An alternative to a pollution tax is a system of regulations that control the amount of pollution generated by each firm. The label for a traditional regulatory policy is a **command-and-control policy**. The government commands each firm to produce no more than a certain volume of pollution and controls the firm's production process by forcing the firm to use a particular pollution-control technology. In our paper example, the government would tell each firm to produce no more than 4 gallons of chemical waste per ton of paper and force each firm to install a particular type of filter to meet the pollution target.

One problem with this approach is that the mandated abatement technology—the control part of the policy—is unlikely to be the most efficient technology. There are two reasons for this:

- The regulatory policy specifies a single abatement technology for all firms. Because the producers of a polluting good often use different materials and production techniques, an abatement technology that is efficient for one firm is likely to be inefficient for others.

- The regulatory policy decreases the incentives to develop more efficient abatement technologies. The command part of the policy specifies a maximum volume of waste for each firm (for example, 4 gallons per ton), and there is no incentive to cut the volume of waste below the maximum volume. There is a small benefit from developing new technology because there is no payoff from using it. In contrast, a pollution tax provides the right incentives: If the firm develops a new technology that cuts the firm's waste below 4 gallons per ton, the firm will pay less in pollution taxes.

Because a command-and-control policy causes firms to use inefficient abatement technology, the policy will increase firms' costs by a large amount.

Figure 17.2 shows the market effects of a command-and-control policy. Assume that the maximum volume of waste is 4 gallons per ton of paper. This policy increases the cost of producing paper, so it shifts the market supply curve to the left. For the reasons explained earlier, the mandated technology will be less efficient—and more costly—than the technology developed under a pollution tax. That means that the supply shift resulting from the regulatory policy will be larger than the supply shift from the pollution tax. To see this, compare Figure 17.2 with Figure 17.1. The regulatory policy has a larger supply shift even though firms generate more waste (4 gallons per ton instead of the 3 gallons per ton under the tax). In Figure 17.2, the new supply curve intersects the demand curve at point *f*: The price of paper increases to $74, and the quantity of paper decreases to 70 tons per day. The total volume of pollution is 280 gallons per day (70 tons times 4 gallons per ton).

Command-and-control policy: A pollution-control policy under which the government commands each firm to produce no more than a certain volume of pollution and controls the firm's production process by forcing the firm to use a particular pollution-control technology.

Figure 17.2
Market Effects of Command and Control

The command-and-control policy increases the cost of producing paper, shifting the market supply curve to the left. The equilibrium price increases to $74 per ton, and the equilibrium quantity decreases to 70 tons per day. Compared to the pollution-tax policy, the command-and-control policy leads to a higher price and a smaller quantity.

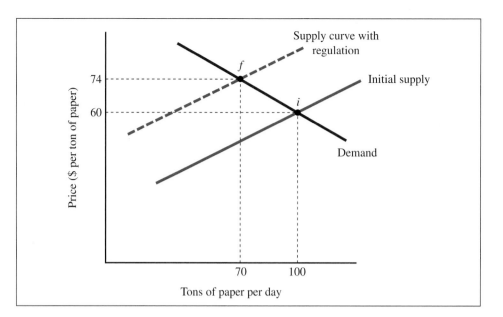

How does the regulation outcome compare to the pollution-tax outcome? Comparing Figure 17.1 with Figure 17.2, we see the following under regulation:

- The price of paper is higher: $74 instead of $68 with the tax.

- The quantity of paper produced is lower: 70 tons per day instead of 80 tons per day with the tax.

- There is more pollution: 280 gallons per day instead of 240 gallons per day with the tax.

The command-and-control policy generates more pollution at a higher cost to consumers because the mandated abatement technology is inferior—and more costly—than the technology developed under the tax policy.

We've seen that one problem with traditional environmental policy is that it is inflexible, not allowing firms to use the most efficient abatement methods. For an example of different abatement strategies, read "A Closer Look: Dear Abby and Environmental Policy."

Another advantage of the tax policy is that it generates tax revenue. The money raised from a pollution tax could be used to cut other taxes or increase spending on public programs. In some European nations—Germany, France, and the Netherlands—the revenue from pollution taxes is used to clean up polluted rivers.

A command-and-control policy does have one advantage over a pollution tax. The response to a command-and-control policy is predictable: The policy specifies how much waste each firm can produce, so we can predict the total volume of waste. In contrast, we don't know how firms will respond to the pollution tax—they could pollute a little or a lot, depending on the tax and the cost of abating pollution—so it is difficult to predict the total volume of waste.

Marketable pollution permits: A system under which the government picks a target pollution level for a particular area, issues just enough pollution permits to meet the pollution target, and allows firms to buy and sell the permits.

Marketable Pollution Permits

In recent years, policymakers have developed a new approach to environmental policy. Here is how a government runs a system of **marketable pollution permits**:

- Pick a target pollution level for a particular area.

- Issue just enough pollution permits to meet the pollution target.

- Allow firms to buy and sell the permits.

DEAR ABBY AND ENVIRONMENTAL POLICY

A person with the moniker "Dreading Winter" wrote to advice columnist Abigail Van Buren with a pollution problem.[2] Her neighbors heated their home with a wood-burning stove, and the smell and smoke from the wood fire gave Dreading Winter burning eyes, a stuffy nose, and painful sinuses. She offered the neighbors $500 to stop burning wood, but they declined the offer. The readers of "Dear Abby" offered the following suggestions to Dreading Winter.

1. Buy the neighbors a catalytic add-on for the wood stove or a wood-chip gasifier for an oil furnace. In either case, there would be much less air pollution from burning wood.
2. Soak a towel in water, swish it around the room, and watch the smoke disappear.
3. Leave a saucer of vinegar in each room to eliminate the smoke odor.
4. Pay your neighbors to hire a chimney sweep to clean their flue.
5. Seal and caulk your windows to keep the smoke outside (at a cost less than $500).
6. Use the $500 to purchase an air purifier for your home.

These suggestions demonstrate a fundamental idea in environmental economics: There is usually more than one way to deal with a pollution problem. The economic question is, What is the most efficient (least costly) way to reduce the problem? In some cases, it may be more efficient to prevent the pollution (switch to an alternative fuel or install a catalytic add-on to the stove) than to deal with it (seal and caulk windows or install an air purifier). In other cases, treatment will be more efficient than prevention.

For example, if the target pollution level in the paper industry is 400 gallons of waste per day, the government would issue a total of 400 permits, each of which entitles a firm to generate 1 gallon of waste per day. The key innovation is that these permits are marketable: Firms can buy and sell the permits. In fact, an environmental group could decrease the amount of pollution by purchasing a permit and then retiring it.

Marketable Permits

To explain the effects of marketable pollution permits, let's extend our example of the paper industry to include firms that have higher pollution-abatement costs. Specifically, there are two types of paper mills, each of which produces 1 ton of paper per day:

- Half the paper mills can abate pollution at a low cost, as shown in the second column of Table 17.2. For example, the production cost per ton is $61 with 4 gallons of waste, compared to $60 with 5 gallons of waste.

- Half the paper mills have high abatement costs, as shown in the third column of Table 17.2. For example, if a high-cost firm generates 4 gallons of waste, the cost per ton is $67, compared to $61 for a low-cost firm generating the same volume of waste.

The differences in abatement costs could result from differences in raw materials or production techniques. For some types of raw materials and some production techniques, the cost of abating pollution is relatively high.

Table 17.2   Abatement Costs: Low-Cost Firm Versus High-Cost Firm

Waste per Ton (Gallons)	Production Cost per Ton: Firm with Low Abatement Cost	Production Cost per Ton: Firm with High Abatement Cost
5	$ 60	$ 60
4	$ 61	$ 67
3	$ 64	$ 82
2	$ 71	$112
1	$ 86	$172
0	$116	$300

Suppose the government issues four marketable permits to each paper mill. If a particular firm wants to generate 5 gallons of waste per day, it can buy a fifth permit from another firm. Of course, a firm that sells one of its permits can generate only 3 gallons of waste per day. Each firm with low abatement cost will sell a permit to a firm with high abatement cost. Such an exchange benefits both the buyer and the seller because the buyer is willing to pay more than the seller is willing to accept.

- **Willingness to pay.** Each firm with high abatement cost is willing to pay up to $7 for a permit. If such a firm gets a fifth permit, it can generate 5 gallons of waste per ton and produce a ton of paper for $60, compared to a cost of $67 per ton when the firm has only four permits. Getting a fifth permit saves the firm $7 on the ton of paper it produces, so the firm is willing to pay up to $7 for a permit.

- **Willingness to accept.** Each firm with low abatement cost is willing to accept any amount above $3 for one of its permits. If such a firm gives up one of its four permits, it could generate only 3 gallons of waste, so its production cost for the ton of paper it produces would increase by $3 (from $61 to $64). Giving up a permit costs the firm $3, so the firm is willing to accept any amount greater than $3 for a permit.

The actual price of the permit depends on the negotiating skills of the two firms. A plausible outcome of the bargaining process is a price halfway between the buyer's $7 willingness to pay and the seller's $3 willingness to accept. If the buyer and the seller split the difference, the price will be $5.

Allowing firms to sell their permits decreases the total cost of achieving any abatement target. For each permit sold, a firm with high abatement cost saves $7 in abatement costs. The firm with low abatement cost will have one less permit, so it must abate one more unit of pollution, at a cost of $3. For each permit sold, the total cost of abatement decreases by $4, the difference between the $7 cost saved by the high-cost firm and the $3 cost incurred by the low-cost firm.

Why is the total cost of abatement lower with marketable permits? By allowing firms to trade their permits, the government exploits the differences in abatement costs, relying on firms with low abatement cost to do the abatement. As a result, we can achieve the same volume of pollution abatement at a lower cost. In a perfectly competitive market, these cost savings will be passed on to consumers in the form of a lower price of paper.

Experiences with Marketable Permits

The first program of marketable pollution permits, started in 1976 by the U.S. Environmental Protection Agency, allowed limited trading of permits for several airborne pollutants. Trading was later extended to lead in gasoline (in 1985) and the chemicals that are responsible for the depletion of the ozone layer (in 1988). The 1990 Clean Air Act established a trading system for sulfur dioxide, which is responsible for acid rain. In the early 1990s, a trading system was introduced in the Los Angeles Basin for the pollutants that are responsible for urban smog.

The first pollution permit was sold in 1977, and thousands of exchanges have occurred since then. Here are some examples:

- Duquesne Light Company paid $3,750,000 to Wisconsin Power and Light for the rights to dump 15,000 tons of sulfur dioxide. In this transaction, the price of a ton of sulfur dioxide emissions was $250.

- Mobil Oil Corporation paid $3,000,000 for the rights to dump 900 pounds of reactive vapors per day. Mobile paid this sum to the city of Torrance, California, which had earlier acquired the pollution rights from General Motors.

- A firm in Los Angeles installed a new incinerator that decreased its hydrocarbon emissions by 100 tons per year and offered to sell the rights to emit 100 tons of hydrocarbons for $400,000.

A system of marketable permits may lead to severe pollution in some areas. For example, if you live in Torrance, California, you probably don't like the idea that Mobil Oil will use a marketable permit to generate more pollution at its refinery. You probably don't care that the marketable permit system is more efficient than a command-and-control system that would limit the refinery's pollution to its current level. This "hot spot" problem suggests that the marketable permit system may be inappropriate for pollutants that generate large local effects. Alternatively, the number of permits issued for a particular geographical area could be limited to prevent severe pollution.

The government can use marketable permits to reduce air and water pollution over time. A common practice is to issue marketable permits with a one-year life and then decrease the number of permits issued each year. For example, under an air-quality management plan for the Portland, Oregon, metropolitan area, the number of permits will decrease by 10% each year. This approach was also used by the Environmental Protection Agency to phase out lead in gasoline and the chemicals that are responsible for the depletion of the ozone layer.

No Market for Marketable Permits

Economic Detective

A state issued some marketable permits for sulfur dioxide emissions to several electricity generators and set up a special marketing office to help firms buy and sell the permits. Most of the permits were given to the utilities with the oldest generating facilities. One year later, none of the permits had been bought or sold. This was puzzling to the state officials and the people in the marketing office. The idea of issuing marketable permits was to get a market going. Your job is to solve this mystery. Why didn't the marketable-permit program work? How could the program be changed to encourage trading?

A careful reading of the description of the permit policy reveals a clue that will help solve this mystery. Old electricity-generating facilities usually have old pollution-abatement technology, so they have higher abatement costs than newer plants. When a utility sells one of its permits, it must reduce its emissions, and this would be costly for old

MARKETABLE POLLUTION PERMITS IN SOUTHERN CALIFORNIA

Under RECLAIM, the clean-air program implemented in Southern California in 1994 the volume of nitrogen-oxide pollution decreases by 8% per year.[3] Between 1994 and 2003, the volume of pollution will be sliced by 75%. Under the program, the number of marketable pollution permits (aka credits) decreases every year. In the period 1999 to 2001, a booming California economy increased production and the demand for permits. Because demand increased while supply decreased, the equilibrium price of permits increased, from $0.13 per pound of nitrogen oxide gas to $13.

The response to the higher permit price was predictable. Large polluters like the Los Angeles Department of Water and Power developed plans to install new pollution-abatement equipment to reduce its emissions by 90%. Although the abatement equipment will cost $40 million, it is less expensive than buying pollution permits. A few years ago, Libbey Glass Company installed low-pollution burners in its plant, dropping its emissions below the volume allowed by its permits. The company sold its extra permits to other firms, generating income for Libbey and allowing other firms with more expensive abatement technology to continue production.

facilities with high abatement costs. By issuing most of the permits to old facilities with high abatement costs, the state inadvertently gave most of the permits to the utilities that had the greatest incentive to keep them. These utilities kept all their permits rather than selling them.

A simple example will show why a utility with high abatement costs will hold onto its permit. Suppose a 1-ton reduction in sulfur dioxide emissions would increase abatement costs by $1,000 in an old facility but by only $200 in a new facility. In this case, the old facility would be willing to accept no less than $1,000 for one of its pollution permits, while a new facility would be willing to pay no more than $200 for a permit. The two utilities can't make a deal because the minimum amount the old facility is willing to accept exceeds the maximum amount the new facility is willing to pay. To encourage trading, the state could redesign its permit policy to spread the permits more evenly among old and new facilities.

TEST Your Understanding

1. Complete the statement with *low* or *high*: Under a system of marketable pollution permits, a firm with _____ abatement costs will buy permits from a firm with _____ abatement costs.

2. Why will a switch to marketable pollution permits decrease total abatement costs?

3. Looking back at Table 17.2, suppose that for the low-cost firm, the production cost per ton with 3 gallons of waste is $69 (instead of $64). If the government issues four permits per firm, will trading still occur? Explain.

4. Looking back at Table 17.2, suppose that after the high-cost and low-cost firms finish buying and selling permits, an environmental group appears. If the group is willing to pay $10 for each gallon of waste reduction, how many permits will the group purchase?

Global Warming and Public Policy

Now that we've discussed the policy options for dealing with environmental problems, we are ready to discuss some environmental problems. We look at global warming first and then discuss ozone depletion, acid rain, and urban smog.

The Causes of Global Warming

Here is a simple experiment that explains global warming. On a warm day, park your car in a sunny spot, close the windows, and wait. Solar energy in the form of visual and ultraviolet light will come through the car windows and heat the air in the car. This is the greenhouse effect: If all the windows are closed, there is no way for the heat to escape, so the temperature in the car (or in a greenhouse) will increase.

The windows of the car are like the earth's atmosphere. Solar energy comes through the atmosphere and heats the air near the earth's surface. Certain types of gases in the atmosphere (called greenhouse gases) trap this heat close to the earth's surface and are beneficial. Without these gases, the earth's surface temperature would be far below freezing, so most forms of life would die off. Unfortunately, we are pumping more of these greenhouse gases into the atmosphere, so the earth's temperature is increasing. Just as rolling up a window in a parked car increases the temperature in the car, increasing the volume of greenhouse gases increases the temperature near the earth's surface.

Carbon dioxide is by far the most important greenhouse gas. To explain why the volume of carbon dioxide is increasing, let's look at the carbon cycles, the movement of carbon between the earth's atmosphere and the plant material on the earth's surface. When a plant grows, it converts carbon dioxide from the atmosphere into carbon and stores this carbon in its tissue. When we burn oil, coal, and gas (the fossilized remains of old plants), the carbon stored in the plant material combines with oxygen to form carbon dioxide, which is released back into the atmosphere. To put it bluntly, plants suck in carbon dioxide, and we blow it back out when we burn plant material. In the last century, we have blown out more carbon than plants have been able to suck in, and the volume of carbon dioxide in the atmosphere has increased by about 25%. By digging up stored carbon and burning it, we've thrown the carbon cycle out of whack, and the resulting increase in greenhouse gases has increased global temperatures.

How does the destruction of tropical rain forests affect the volume of carbon dioxide in the atmosphere? The plants in these forests absorb some of the carbon dioxide we generate when we burn fossil fuels. The destruction of tropical rain forests has two effects:

- If trees and plants are burned to clear the land, the carbon stored in these plants is converted into carbon dioxide.

- Once the forest is cleared, there is less plant material to convert carbon dioxide into stored carbon.

As we'll see later in the chapter, one approach to dealing with global warming is to protect existing rain forests and promote the recovery of damaged forests.

The Consequences of Global Warming

Scientists agree that greenhouse gases are accumulating. The volume of atmospheric carbon dioxide is now about 25% above the preindustrial level, and it is increasing at a rate of about 1.6% per year,[4] so the volume of greenhouse gases will double in about 60 years. Most scientists agree that a doubling of atmospheric carbon dioxide will increase global temperatures, but they don't agree just how large the increase in temperature will be. Because we know so little about how the earth's ecosystems will respond to a rapid increase in carbon dioxide, the actual change in temperature could be small or large. The practical policy question is: Should we wait to find out the consequences of a doubling of atmospheric carbon dioxide or do something now to reduce the accumulation of greenhouse gases?

How would an increase in temperatures affect the earth's environment and the global economy? Most scientists expect total rainfall to increase, with some areas getting more and others getting less. The increase in carbon dioxide will make all plants—crops and weeds alike—grow faster. Overall, the net effect on agriculture is likely to be negative because scientists expect less rainfall in areas with fertile soil and more rainfall in areas with less productive soil.

An increase in global temperatures would also melt glaciers and the polar ice caps, raising sea levels. As a result, a large amount of land currently used for agriculture or living space could be inundated. Of course, we could build dikes to protect low-lying areas, but such protective measures are very expensive. The Netherlands has launched a multibillion-dollar program to increase the height of its sea walls. According to a recent report from the Climate Institute, by the year 2070, much of the metropolitan area in Manila, Philippines, could be under 1 meter of water, and rising sea levels could force the relocation of 3.3 million people in Jakarta, Indonesia.[5]

A Carbon Tax

The economist's response to the accumulation of greenhouse gases is to impose a tax on fossil fuels. The spillover cost of a particular fuel depends on how much carbon dioxide is released into the atmosphere, so the **carbon tax** for a particular fuel would be determined by the fuel's carbon content.

Carbon tax: A tax based on a fuel's carbon content.

Figure 17.3 shows the effects of a carbon tax on the market for coal in China. Coal provides about three-fourths of the primary energy in China and is used in small industrial boilers, household stoves, and room heaters. In contrast, most of the coal consumed in developed countries such as the United States is used to generate electricity. A carbon tax will add to the expenses incurred by coal producers, so some of them will lose money at the initial price, and some suppliers will leave the market. The resulting decrease in the supply of coal will shift the supply curve to the left. In Figure 17.3 the carbon tax leads to a higher price for coal ($42 instead of $35 per ton) and a smaller quantity (78 instead of 100 tons per day).

Table 17.3 shows some of the effects of two carbon taxes—a low one and a high one—on the prices of fossil fuels. For example, the high tax would more than double the price of coal (a fuel with a high carbon content), but it would increase the price of gasoline by only 23%. In Table 17.3, we see that a carbon tax of $100 per ton of carbon would decrease greenhouse emissions by 43%, a result of three types of changes:

- The tax will increase the price of energy and increase the cost of producing energy-intensive goods. Consumers will respond by demanding smaller quantities of these goods, in part by switching to goods produced with less energy.

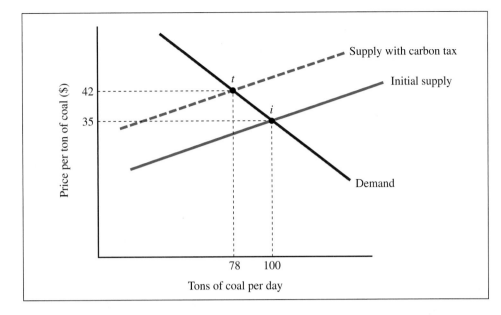

Figure 17.3

Market Effects of a Carbon Tax on Coal
A carbon tax shifts the supply curve to the left, moving the equilibrium from point *i* to point *t*. A tax of $10 per ton of carbon increases the equilibrium price of coal from $35 per ton to $42 per ton and decreases the equilibrium quantity from 100 to 78 tons per day.

- Some energy producers will switch to noncarbon energy sources such as the wind, the sun, and geothermal sources.
- Energy producers will improve the efficiency of carbon-based fuels, squeezing out more energy per ton of coal or oil.

One concern about a carbon tax is that it would impose a large burden on the poor. In Table 17.3, we see that the low carbon tax would generate $10 billion per year, while the high tax would generate $125 billion per year. This money could be used to reduce income taxes or payroll taxes, reducing the burden of the carbon tax on the poor.

Table 17.3 Effects of Different Carbon Taxes

	Low Tax	High Tax
Tax per ton of carbon	$5.00	$100.00
Effect on price of coal		
Tax per ton	$3.50	$70.00
Percentage increase	10	205
Effect on price of oil		
Tax per barrel	$0.58	$11.65
Percentage increase	2.8	55
Effect on price of gasoline		
Tax per gallon	$0.014	$0.28
Percentage increase	1.2	23
Percentage reduction in greenhouse emissions	10	43
Total tax revenue per year, U.S. (billions)	$10.00	$125.00

Source: William D. Nordhaus, "Economic Approaches to Greenhouse Warming," in *Global Warming: Economic Policy Responses*, edited by Rudiger Dornbusch and James M. Poterba (Cambridge, MA: MIT Press, 1991).

The Kyoto Agreement and Developing Nations

The United Nations officially recognized the greenhouse effect in 1995, when its International Panel on Climate Change noted that human activity had a "discernible influence" on global temperatures. In 1997, the Kyoto Conference on global warming produced an agreement under which the largest industrial nations pledged to reduce their carbon dioxide emissions to just below the 1990 levels by the year 2008. In 2001, the United States government announced that it would not participate in the **Kyoto Agreement**. To meet the abatement targets, the participating nations must make large and costly changes in their energy systems.

Kyoto Agreement: An agreement among industrial nations to reduce carbon dioxide emissions.

The developing nations were exempted from the Kyoto deal, over the strenuous objections of some industrialized nations. As the economies of developing nations grow over the next few decades, they are likely to rely on coal, which is inexpensive and easy to transport, as a major source of energy. Because coal generates about twice as much carbon dioxide as natural gas, the developing nations will produce a large volume of carbon dioxide emissions. The exemption of the developing nations is a stumbling block in the effort to control the accumulation of greenhouse gases.

TEST Your Understanding

5. Use a supply and demand diagram to show the effects of a carbon tax on the market for an energy-intensive good such as aluminum or steel.

6. Explain how a carbon tax would decrease the total volume of greenhouse gases.

7. In Chapter 16, you learned the rationale for subsidizing goods that generate spillover benefits. Does the same sort of reasoning apply to trees?

Other Environmental Problems

The problem of global warming is not the only environmental problem that we face today. There are many other problems, including the depletion of the ozone layer, acid rain, and urban smog. Let's look at each of these problems separately.

Ozone Depletion

A layer of ozone in the upper atmosphere prevents most of the sun's harmful ultraviolet light from reaching the surface of the earth. Ultraviolet light causes living cells to mutate, causing skin cancer and eye disease in humans and the death of marine organisms at the base of the food web. It also disrupts plant growth and hastens the decay of plastics. The ozone layer in the upper atmosphere is essential to life on this planet because it protects us from the harmful effects of ultraviolet light.

A 1991 report suggests that human-made chemicals had depleted the ozone layer by about 3% overall, with a 50% depletion in the atmosphere over Antarctica. The primary culprit is a family of chemicals known as chlorofluorocarbons (CFCs), which were once used in refrigeration, air conditioning, spray products, foam injection, and industrial solvents. When these chemicals reach the upper atmosphere, they act as catalysts, converting ozone into oxygen, which does not block ultraviolet light. The depletion over Antarctica is much greater because the presence of ice crystals accelerates this chemical reaction.

The nations of the world have agreed to stop producing CFCs altogether. Under the Montreal Protocol (of 1990), the production of these chemicals will stop by 2010. Because CFCs take a long time to break down, however, scientists expect the depletion of the ozone layer to continue for at least 50 more years. The ban on CFCs will increase the equilibrium prices of the goods that were produced with these chemicals. For example, refrigerator producers will switch from CFCs to other chemicals that don't harm the ozone layer but are more expensive and less efficient as coolants. The resulting increase in production costs will increase the equilibrium price of refrigerators.

Acid Rain

In the 1970s and 1980s, there were persistent reports of sterile lakes and withering trees in the northeastern United States, eastern Canada, Scandinavia, and Germany. The sulfur dioxide emissions (SO_2) of coal-burning power plants combined with nitrogen oxides and other chemicals in the atmosphere to form **acid rain**. The rainfall in the areas downwind from the power plants changed the acidity of soil and water, causing problems for trees, fish, and other forms of aquatic life. Power plants in the eastern and midwestern United States caused acid rain in the northeastern United States and eastern Canada, while power plants in the United Kingdom and Germany caused acid rain in Scandinavia.

Acid rain: Precipitation with an acidic combination of sulfur dioxides and nitrogen oxides.

The Clean Air Act of 1990 established a system of marketable pollution permits for SO_2. Each utility will receive enough permits to generate between 30% and 50% of the volume of SO_2 it produced 10 years earlier. Overall, the permit system will decrease SO_2 emissions by about 10 million tons per year, a reduction of about 40%. Under the first permit trade, a Wisconsin utility sold permits to the Tennessee Valley Authority at a price of $250 per ton of sulfur dioxide. A report from the National Acid Precipitation Assessment Program (NAPAP) estimated the cost of reducing sulfur dioxide emissions under two alternative systems: one with marketable permits and one with nonmarketable permits. The cost with marketable permits is 15 to 20% lower.[6]

Although the SO_2 permits were expected to sell for about $300 per ton, by 1999 the price was only $140. The price was lower than expected for two reasons:[7]

- **Overinvestment in scrubbers.** One way to reduce the emissions of a power plant is to install scrubbers, which reduce the amount of sulfur that exits the smokestacks. The decisions to install scrubbers were made in 1992, three years before the new policy took effect. Many firms' scrubber decisions were based on an assumed permit

The sulfur dioxide emissions (SO_2) of coal-burning power plants combine with nitrogen oxides and other chemicals in the atmosphere to form acid rain.

price of $300 to $400 per ton. At this price, scrubbing would be cheaper than buying permits, so many utilities installed scrubbers. Once installed, the marginal cost of operating the scrubber equipment is only $65 per ton of SO_2. If a permit has a price of $140 per ton, it is less costly to scrub than to buy a permit. The large investment in scrubbers reduced the demand for permits (used by firms that did not install scrubbers), leading to lower permit prices.

- **Lower price for low-sulfur coal.** The other way to reduce SO_2 emissions is to switch to low-sulfur coal. In the mid-1990s, the price and transport costs of low-sulfur coal dropped, making it less expensive to switch to low-sulfur coal. The resulting decrease in the demand for SO_2 permits decreased their price.

Utilities responded to the lower than expected price of permits by canceling plans for additional investment in scrubber equipment.

Urban Smog: Emissions Standards and Cash for Clunkers

Urban smog is one of our most persistent environmental problems. Smog results from the mixing of several pollutants, including nitrogen oxides, sulfur dioxide, and volatile organic compounds. Another name for smog is ground-level ozone. Although atmospheric ozone is beneficial because it blocks harmful ultraviolet light, ozone is harmful when it comes in contact with living things, as it does at ground level. Smog causes health problems in human beings and animals. It also retards plant growth and decreases agricultural productivity. The Environmental Protection Agency (EPA) has established standards for the concentrations of urban smog. About one-third of the U.S. population lives in areas where the concentrations of smog often exceed the EPA standards.

The automobile is by far the biggest source of the pollutants that lead to smog. We currently use a command-and-control approach to regulate automobile pollution: The Environmental Protection Agency tells automakers what emissions equipment to install in cars. There are several problems with this approach:

- If a car is not properly maintained, the emissions equipment quickly loses its effectiveness. Although many states have inspection programs to monitor emissions equipment, many of the programs are not very effective.

- Many of the cars on the road were built before the emissions controls were implemented, and these cars are responsible for a large share of automobile emissions.

- The emissions equipment does not control the total emissions of the car, just the emissions per mile driven. If people drive more miles in a cleaner car, total emissions can actually increase.

An alternative to the current policy is to levy an annual pollution tax on each car.[8] At the end of the year, a car would be tested to determine the volume of pollution per mile driven. The tax per mile would equal the volume of pollution per mile times a tax per unit of pollution. The annual tax would be computed by multiplying the tax per mile by the number of miles driven in the last year. For example, if a car generated 5 units of pollution per mile and the tax per unit of pollution were $0.01, the tax per mile would be $0.05. If the car were driven 10,000 miles each year, the annual pollution tax would be $500. The pollution tax would encourage people to buy cleaner cars, maintain their emissions equipment, drive less, and use alternative modes of transportation. The tax is consistent with the idea that people should pay the full cost of driving an automobile, including the spillover costs.

One of the problems with the current policy is that it does nothing to decrease the pollution from cars that don't have pollution-control equipment. In 1992, the Environmental Protection Agency (EPA) designed a program that would allow many types of firms to meet their pollution-abatement responsibilities by purchasing and destroying old cars. A disproportionate amount of automobile air pollution comes from cars that were built before modern emissions equipment was required. The EPA has a booklet that shows how much pollution each type of car generates. Under a cash-for-clunkers program, a firm can meet its pollution abatement responsibility by retiring enough cars so the volume of automobile pollution avoided equals the amount the firm would otherwise abate itself. There have been several successful experiments with cash-for-clunkers programs in Los Angeles, Denver, and the state of Texas.

TEST Your Understanding

8. Use a supply-demand diagram to show the effects of a ban on CFCs on the market for refrigerators.

9. Explain how a carbon tax will affect the urban smog problem.

10. The policy of buying and destroying heavy polluting cars is called "Cash for Clunkers," not "Cash for Cars." Why?

Using the TOOLS

You've learned about several environmental policies, including a pollution tax, pollution regulations, and marketable pollution permits. Now you can use what you've learned to do your own economic analysis of environmental problems.

APPLICATIONS

1. Market Effects of a Carbon Tax
Consider the market for gasoline. In the initial equilibrium, the price is $2.00 per gallon and the quantity is 100 million gallons. The price elasticity of demand is 1.0, and the price elasticity of supply is 2.0. Suppose the government imposes a carbon tax and the tax is expected to shift the gasoline supply curve to the left by 24%.

a. Use a supply-demand diagram to show the market effects of the carbon tax.

b. Predict the new equilibrium price and quantity of gasoline.

2. Predict the Price of Pollution Permits
Consider the example of marketable pollution permits discussed in this chapter. Suppose that instead of issuing 4 permits to each firm, the government issues only 3 permits to each firm.

a. How much money is a high-cost firm willing to pay to get one additional permit?

b. How much money is a low-cost firm willing to accept in exchange for one of its permits?

c. If firms split the difference between the willingness to pay and the willingness to accept for a permit, what will be the price of a permit?

3. *Hot Rod*, *Motor Trend*, and Cash for Clunkers
Several car-hobby magazines, including *Hot Rod* and *Motor Trend*, have run editorials in opposition to the cash-for-clunkers program. Why would car-hobby magazines oppose the program? Can you imagine any way to overcome their objections?

4. ECONOMIC EXPERIMENT: Pollution Permits

In the pollution-permit experiment, students play the role of paper firms that buy or sell pollution permits. The experiment, which extends over five trading periods, works as follows:

- The class is divided into groups of three to five students, each group representing a firm that produces 1 ton of paper per period. The instructor provides each firm with data about its cost of production. The cost depends on how much waste the firm generates: The smaller the volume of waste, the higher the production cost. Here is an example:

Gallons of waste	2	3	4
Production cost per ton	$66	$56	$50

- Each firm receives three pollution permits for each of the five trading periods. A firm that does not sell any of its permits to other firms has the right to generate 3 gallons of waste in that period. A firm that sells one of its three permits can generate only 2 gallons of waste, and a firm that buys a permit from another firm can generate 4 gallons of waste.

- At the beginning of each trading period, firms meet in the trading area to buy or sell pollution permits for that day. Each firm can buy or sell one permit per day. Once a transaction has been arranged, the buyer and the seller inform the instructor of the transaction, record the transaction on their report cards, and then leave the trading area.

- In each trading period, we compute the firm's profit with the following equation:

$$\text{profit} = \text{price of paper} - \text{production cost} + \text{revenue from permit sold} - \text{cost of permit purchased}$$

- In each period, a firm will either buy or sell a permit, so we compute the firm's profit with just 3 numbers. For example, using the production-cost numbers from the table shown, if the price of paper is $70 per ton and a firm buys a permit for $5, the firm's profit is

$$\text{profit} = \$70 - \$50 + 0 - \$5 = \$15$$

- If another firm sold a permit for $12, the firm's profit would be $16:
- profit = $70 − $66 + $12 − 0 = $16
- For the fourth and fifth trading periods, several environmental groups have the option of buying pollution permits. Each environmental group is given a fixed sum of money to spend on permits, and the objective is to get as many permits as possible, reducing the total volume of pollution in the process.

Summary

We started this chapter by showing the market effects of a pollution tax. Because a traditional command-and-control policy discourages innovation in pollution abatement technology, it is less efficient—and more costly—than a pollution tax or a system of marketable permits. Here are the main points from the chapter:

1. A pollution tax, which forces firms to pay for pollution, decreases the total volume of pollution because firms produce less of the polluting good and generate less pollution for each unit produced.

2. Compared to a pollution tax, a command-and-control policy is likely to lead to higher consumer prices and more pollution (less abatement).

3. A system of marketable permits is predictable because the government issues just enough permits to reach a target level of pollution. The system is efficient because the firms with the lowest abatement costs will do the abatement.

4. One approach to the problem of carbon dioxide emissions is a carbon tax.

5. Urban smog is a continuing problem, in part because we use command-and-control policies. An annual pollution tax would be more effective at reducing smog.

Key Terms

acid rain, 363
carbon tax, 360

command-and-control policy, 353
Kyoto Agreement, 362

marketable pollution permits, 354
pollution tax, 350

Problems and Discussion Questions

1. Use a supply-demand graph to show a situation in which the equilibrium quantity of a polluting good is 20 tons but a pollution tax decreases the equilibrium quantity of the good to zero. Is this situation likely to occur?

2. Suppose paper firms have access to the abatement technology shown in the first two columns of Table 17.1 and the government imposes a pollution tax of $8 per gallon of waste.

  a. Compute new values for the third and fourth columns of the table. How much waste will the typical firm generate?

  b. Use a supply-demand diagram to show the market effects of the tax.

  c. Would you expect the volume of pollution to be larger or smaller than the volume generated with the $4 tax (shown in Figure 17.1)?

3. Suppose the government adopts a zero-tolerance pollution policy for the production of paper. In other words, the government requires each paper mill to eliminate all its water pollution. Suppose the paper firms have access to the abatement technology shown in the first two columns of Table 17.1.

  a. What is the production cost per ton under the zero-tolerance policy?

  b. If the government uses a pollution tax to implement its zero-tolerance policy, what is the smallest tax that would cause the typical firm to voluntarily pick zero pollution?

4. To predict the market price of a marketable pollution permit, what information do you need? Explain how you would use this information.

5. Use a supply-demand diagram to show the market effects of a cash-for-clunkers program on the market for used cars.

6. Consider the use of marketable pollution permits for the control of sulfur dioxide emissions from two electric utilities: Old Power and Light (OPL) and Young Power and Light (YPL). The following table shows the production cost for the two utilities with different volumes of sulfur dioxide emissions.

Tons of Sulfur Dioxide	Production Cost for OPL	Production Cost for YPL
10	$1,000	$1,000
9	$1,100	$1,020
8	$1,300	$1,060
7	$1,600	$1,120

Assume that the government issues 10 marketable pollution permits to OPL and 8 marketable permits to YPL.

- Will any permits be traded? Explain.
- Suppose the government had issued 9 permits to YPL and 9 permits to OPL. Will any permits be traded? If so, predict the equilibrium price for a permit.

7. One of the objections to a carbon tax is that it would be regressive: Poor people would pay a large fraction of their incomes for carbon taxes. How could we overcome this objection?

8. You are the economic consultant to a member of Congress. Someone has just introduced a bill that would impose a $50 carbon tax, which will of course affect the market for home-heating oil. Would you expect the entire tax to be paid by consumers? Why or why not? Your job is to determine which side of the market—consumers or input suppliers—will pay the larger part of the tax. What additional information do you need?

9. Web Exercise. Visit the Web site for the U.S. Environmental Protection Agency [*http://www.epa.gov*]. Search the site for information on electric vehicles. How do the costs of electric cars compare to the costs of gas-powered vehicles? What about performance?

10. Web Exercise. Visit the part of the Web site of the U.S. Environmental Protection Agency that describes acid-rain programs [*http://www.epa.gov/airmarkets*]. Click on "SO_2 Market Analysis." Imagine that you are a member of an environmental group that wants to buy a pollution permit (an allowance). How would you do it? How much are you likely to pay for a one-ton allowance for SO_2? You may have to do some digging—or clicking. *Hint:* Check the auction web pages.

 Take It to the Net

We invite you to visit the O'Sullivan/Sheffrin page on the Prentice Hall Web site at: **http://www.prenhall.com/osullivan/** for additional World Wide Web exercises for this chapter.

Model Answers to Questions

Chapter-Opening Questions

1. Figure 17.1 and Figure 17.2 show that compared to a command-and-control policy, a pollution tax generates a lower price of paper, more output, and less pollution.

2. As shown in Table 17.3, a $100 tax on carbon would increase the price of gasoline by $0.28 per gallon.

3. Atmospheric ozone is beneficial because it blocks harmful ultraviolet light. Ozone is harmful when it comes in contact with living things, as it does at ground level.

4. A disproportionate amount of automobile air pollution comes from cars built before modern emissions equipment was required. The cash-for-clunkers program removes these heavy-polluting cars from the road.

Test Your Understanding

1. High, low.

2. Under a system of marketable permits, low-cost firms do most of the abating.

3. No. The low-cost firm is willing to accept any amount greater than $8 (equal to $69 – $61), which exceeds the $7 willingness to pay by the high-cost firm.

4. The group will buy one permit from each low-cost firm (the willingness to accept for one of the firm's three permits is $7 = $71 – $64) and one from each of the high-cost firms (the willingness to accept for one of the firm's 5 permits is $7 = $67 – 60).

5. The tax will increase production costs, shifting the supply curve to the left. The new supply curve will intersect the demand curve at a higher price and a smaller quantity.

6. Consumers will buy a smaller quantity of the good. Energy producers will switch to noncarbon energy sources and improve the efficiency of carbon fuels.

7. A tree decreases the volume of carbon dioxide in the atmosphere and diminishes the problem of global warming, so there is a spillover benefit. A subsidy internalizes the externality, encouraging people to plant and maintain trees.

8. The tax will increase production costs, shifting the supply curve to the left. The new supply curve will intersect the demand curve at a higher price and a smaller quantity.

9. The tax will increase the price of gasoline, causing people to drive fewer miles and generate smaller volumes of the pollutants that cause urban smog.

10. The word *clunker* suggests an old car in poor repair, which is the sort of car that is likely to be destroyed under the policy.

Using the Tools

1. Market Effects of a Carbon Tax
   a. See Figure 17.A.
   b. According to the price-change formula from Chapter 6, the percentage change in price is 8% = % change in demand/$(E_s + E_d)$ = 24%/(2.0 + 1.0).

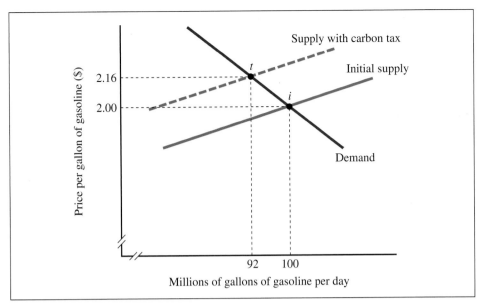

Figure 17.A
**Market Effects
of a Carbon Tax**

Therefore, the price increases from $2.00 to $2.16 per gallon. According to the formula for demand elasticity, the tax causes the market to move upward along the demand curve, so we can use the formula for the price elasticity of demand to predict the change in quantity: E_d = % change in quantity/% change in price. The percentage change in quantity is 8%: 1.0 = 8%/8%. Therefore, the quantity decreases from 100 million gallons to 92 million gallons.

2. Predict the Price of Pollution Permits

   a. A high-cost firm is willing to pay up to $15 for one more permit because a fourth permit would allow the firm to generate 4 gallons (with production cost = $67 for a ton of paper) instead of 3 gallons (production cost = $82 for a ton of paper).

   b. A low-cost firm is willing to accept any amount greater than $7 for one of its three permits. If a low-cost firm sold one of its permits, the firm could generate only 2 gallons of waste and its production cost would increase from $64 to $71 per ton of paper.

   c. A price of $11 for a permit is halfway between the $15 willingness to pay by the high-cost firm and the $7 willingness to accept by the low-cost firm.

3. *Hot Rod, Motor Trend*, and Cash for Clunkers. The hobby magazines are written for car hobbyists, many of whom like to buy old cars and fix them up—or at least try to fix them. The cash-for-clunkers program will decrease the supply of fix-up cars and increase their price. This will make the car-restoration hobby more expensive, so we can expect fewer people to buy old cars and hobby magazines. One way to overcome this problem would be to use the clunkers program to destroy only the engine of the high-pollution cars, giving hobbyists the opportunity to buy the rest of the car and install a cleaner engine.

Notes

1. Peter Pasell, "For Utilities, New Clean-Air Plan," *New York Times*, November 18, 1994, p. C1; Brad Knickerbocker, "Trading Pollutants Is a Big First Step Toward Cleaner Air," *Christian Science Monitor*, November 22, 1994, p. 12.

2. Abigail Van Buren, "Aid for Reader's Winter Woe," *Sacramento Bee*, February 15, 1984.

3. Gary Polakovic, "Cost of Clean Air Credits Soars in Southland," *Los Angeles Times*, September 5, 2000.

4. Andrew R. Solow, "Is There a Global Warming Problem?" in *Global Warming: Economic Policy Responses*, edited by Rudiger Dornbush and James M. Poterba (Cambridge, MA: MIT Press, 1991).

5. Eduardo Lachica, "Asia Faces Increasing Pressure to Act as Global Warming Threatens Its Coasts," *Wall Street Journal*, August 22, 1994, p. A5C.

6. *1990 Integrated Assessment Report* (Washington, DC: U.S. National Acid Precipitation Assessment Program, 1991).

7. Richard Schmalensee, Paul L. Joskow, A. Denn Ellerman, Juan Pablo Montery, and Elizabeth M. Bailey, "An Interim Evaluation of Sulfur Dioxide Emission Trading," *Journal of Economic Perspectives*, vol. 12, 1998, pp. 53–68.

8. Edwin S. Mills and Lawrence J. White, "Government Policies Towards Automobile Emissions Control," in *Approaches to Air Pollution Control*, edited by Anne Frielaender (Cambridge, MA: MIT Press, 1978).

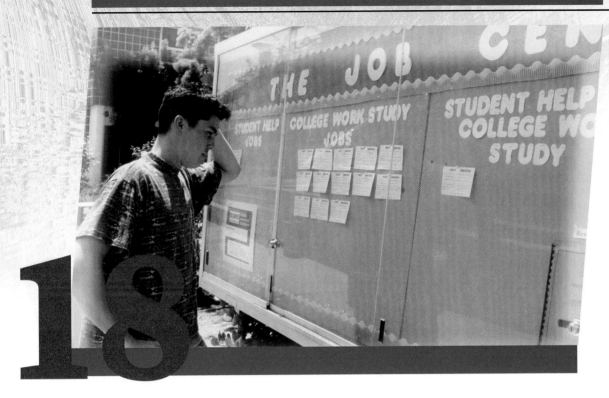

The Labor Market

Recent reports on the earnings of college graduates have made the jobs of college recruiters easier:[1]

- In 1972. the typical college graduate earned 43% more than a high-school graduate.
- In 1999, the typical college graduate earned 80% more than a high-school graduate.

These facts raise two questions: First, why do college graduates earn so much more than high-school graduates? Second, why did the earnings gap almost double during the last 27 years?

n this chapter, we use a model of supply and demand to answer these and other practical questions about the labor market. You may be surprised by the answers. Here are some of the other issues that we address:

1. If the wage increases, will an individual work more hours or fewer hours?
2. If a worker switches from a relatively safe factory job to a job in a steel mill, by how much will his or her wage increase?
3. Why do women, on average, earn only about 75% as much as men?
4. How have companies such as Nike and Disney responded to allegations that their products are produced in foreign sweatshops with dreadful working conditions and low wages?
5. In 1913, Henry Ford increased the wage of his autoworkers from $3 per day (the wage paid by other automakers) to $5. Was he being generous or was he trying to maximize his profit?

The Demand for Labor

We can use supply and demand curves to show how wages are determined and show how public policies affect wages and employment. We'll start with the demand side of the labor market, looking first at how an individual firm can use the key principles of economics to decide how many workers to hire.

The demand for labor and other productive inputs is different from the demand for consumer products such as stereos, books, haircuts, and pizza. Firms use workers to produce the products demanded by consumers, and so economists say that labor demand is a *derived demand,* that is, derived from the demand for the products produced by workers. As we'll see in this chapter, the demand for labor is determined by the demand for consumer products and the price of those products.

Labor Demand by an Individual Firm in the Short Run

Consider a perfectly competitive firm that produces rubber balls. Because this firm is perfectly competitive, it takes the price of its output and the prices of its inputs as given. Because it hires a tiny fraction of the workers in the labor market, it takes the market wage as given and can hire as many workers as it wants at that wage. In addition, the firm produces a tiny fraction of the rubber balls sold in the market, so it takes the price of its output as given. Let's say the price of rubber balls is $0.50.

Consider the firm's hiring decision in the short run, defined as the period during which at least one input—for example, the factory—cannot be changed. We can use two of the key principles of economics to explain the firm's hiring decision. Recall the marginal principle:

Marginal **PRINCIPLE**

Increase the level of an activity if its marginal benefit exceeds its marginal cost, but reduce the level if the marginal cost exceeds the marginal benefit. If possible, pick the level at which the marginal benefit equals the marginal cost.

This firm's activity is hiring labor to produce rubber balls, and the firm will pick the quantity of labor at which the marginal benefit of labor equals the marginal cost of labor. The firm can hire as many workers as it wants at the market wage, so the marginal cost of labor equals the hourly wage. If the wage is $8 per hour, the extra cost associated with one more hour of labor—the marginal cost—is $8, regardless of how many workers the firm hires.

What is the marginal benefit of labor? The firm hires labor to produce balls, so the marginal benefit equals the monetary value of the balls produced with an additional hour of labor. Table 18.1 shows how to compute the marginal benefit associated with different quantities of labor. The first two columns show the relationship between the number of workers and the quantity of balls produced. As the number of workers increases, the number of balls increases, but at a decreasing rate, consistent with the principle of diminishing returns.

PRINCIPLE of Diminishing Returns

> **Suppose that output is produced with two or more inputs and we increase one input while holding the other inputs fixed. Beyond some point—called the point of diminishing returns—output will increase at a decreasing rate.**

As we saw in Chapter 8, because of diminishing returns, the marginal product of labor (the change in output from one additional worker) decreases as the number of workers increases, from 26 for the first worker, to 24 for the second worker, and so on.

The marginal benefit of labor equals the **marginal revenue product of labor [MRP]**, defined as the extra revenue generated by one additional worker. To compute the MRP, we multiply the marginal product of labor by the price of output ($0.50 per ball in this example):

$$MRP = \text{price of output} \times \text{marginal product}$$

Marginal revenue product of labor [MRP]: The extra revenue generated from one more unit of labor; equal to price of output times the marginal product of labor.

Figure 18.1 shows the marginal revenue product curve. Because the marginal product drops as the number of workers increases, the MRP curve is negatively sloped, falling from $11 for the third worker (point n) to $8 for the fifth worker (point m), and so on.

A firm can use its MRP curve to decide how much labor to hire at a particular wage. In Figure 18.1, the marginal-cost curve is horizontal at the market wage ($8). The perfectly competitive firm takes the wage as given, so the marginal-cost curve is also the labor-supply curve faced by the firm. The marginal principle is satisfied at point m, where the marginal cost equals the marginal revenue product. The firm will hire 5 work-

Table 18.1   The Marginal Principle for Labor Decision

Number of Workers	Balls per Hour	Marginal Product	Price per Ball	Marginal Benefit = Marginal Revenue Product	Marginal Cost when Wage = $8
1	26	26	$0.50	$13	$8
2	50	24	0.50	$12	$8
3	72	22	0.50	$11	$8
4	92	20	0.50	$10	$8
5	108	16	0.50	$ 8	$8
6	120	12	0.50	$ 6	$8
7	128	8	0.50	$ 4	$8
8	130	2	0.50	$ 1	$8

Figure 18.1

The Marginal Principle and the Firm's Demand for Labor

Using the marginal principle, the firm picks the quantity of workers at which the marginal benefit (the marginal revenue product of labor) equals the marginal cost (the wage). The firm's short-run demand curve for labor is the marginal revenue product curve.

Short-run demand curve for labor: A curve showing the relationship between the wage and the quantity of labor demanded over the short run, the period when the firm cannot change its production facility.

ers because for the first 5 workers, the marginal benefit (the MRP) is greater than or equal to the marginal cost (the $8 wage). It would not be sensible to hire another worker because the additional revenue from the 6th worker ($6) would be less than the $8 additional cost of that worker. If the wage increases to $11, the firm will satisfy the marginal principle at point *n*, hiring only 3 workers.

The MRP curve is also the firm's **short-run demand curve for labor,** which shows the relationship between the wage and the quantity of labor demanded in the short run, the period when the firm cannot change its production facility. The demand curve answers the following question: At each wage, how many hours of labor does the firm want to hire? We've already used the MRP curve to answer this question for two different wages ($11 and $8), and we can do the same for any other wage. Because the MRP curve is a marginal-benefit curve and the firm uses the marginal principle to decide how much labor to hire, the MRP curve is the same as the firm's demand curve. If you pick a wage, the MRP curve tells you exactly how much labor the firm will demand.

What sort of changes would cause the demand curve to shift? To draw the labor demand curve, we hold fixed the price of the output and the productivity of workers. Therefore, an increase in the price of output will increase the MRP of workers, shifting the entire demand curve to the right: At each wage, the firm will hire more workers. This is shown in Figure 18.2. An increase in the price of balls shifts the labor demand curve to the right. At a wage of $8, the firm hires 7 workers instead of 5. Similarly, if workers become more productive, the increase in the marginal product of labor will increase the MRP and shift the demand curve to the right. Conversely, a decrease in price or labor productivity would shift the demand curve to the left.

Market Demand in the Short Run

To draw the short-run market demand curve for labor, we add the labor demands of all the firms that use a particular type of labor. In the simplest case, all firms are identical, and we simply multiply the number of firms by the quantity of labor demanded by the typical firm. If there were 100 firms and each hired 5 workers at a wage of $8, the mar-

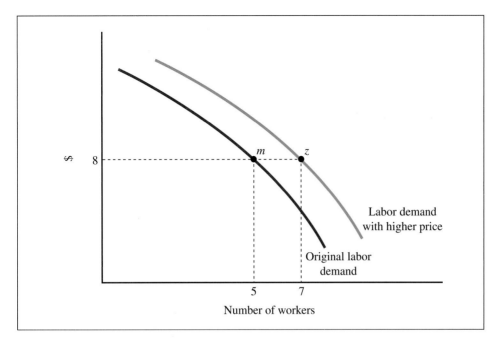

Figure 18.2

An Increase in the Price of Output Shifts the Labor Demand Curve

An increase in the price of the good produced by workers (balls) increases the marginal revenue product at each quantity of workers, shifting the demand curve to the right. At each wage, the firm will demand more workers. For example, at a wage of $8, the demand for labor increases from 5 workers (point *m*) to 7 workers (point *z*).

ket demand for labor would be 500 workers. Similarly, if the typical firm hired 3 workers at a wage of $11, the market demand would be 300 workers.

What About Labor Demand in the Long Run?

Recall that in the long run, firms can enter or leave the market and firms already in the market can change all their inputs, including their production facilities. The **long-run demand curve for labor** shows the relationship between the wage and the quantity of labor demanded over the long run, when the number of firms in the market can change and firms in the market can modify their production facilities.

Although there are no diminishing returns in the long run, the market demand curve is still negatively sloped. As the wage increases, the quantity of labor demanded decreases for two reasons:

- The **output effect**. An increase in the wage will increase the cost of producing balls, and firms will pass on at least part of the higher labor cost to their consumers: Prices will increase. According to the law of demand, firms will sell fewer balls at the higher price, so they will need less of all inputs, including labor.

- The **input-substitution effect**. An increase in the wage will cause the firm to substitute other inputs for labor. At a wage of $4, it may not be sensible to use much machinery in the ball factory, but at a wage of $20, it may be sensible to mechanize the factory, using more machinery and fewer workers.

The output effect reinforces the input-substitution effect, so the market demand curve is negatively sloped.

The notion of input substitution applies to other labor markets as well. For the most graphic examples of factor substitution, we can travel from a developed country such as the United States, Canada, France, Germany, or Japan to a less developed country in South America, Africa, or Asia. Wages are much lower in the less-developed countries, so production tends to be more labor intensive. In other words, labor is less costly relative

Long-run demand curve for labor: A curve showing the relationship between the wage and the quantity of labor demanded over the long run, when the number of firms in the market can change and firms already in the market can modify their production facilities.

Output effect: The change in the quantity of labor demanded resulting from a change in the quantity of output produced.

Input-substitution effect: The change in the quantity of labor demanded resulting from a change in the relative cost of labor.

to machinery and equipment, so labor is substituted for these other inputs. Here are some examples:

- Mining. U.S. firms use huge earth-moving equipment to mine for minerals, while many firms in less-developed countries use thousands of workers, digging by hand.

- Furniture. Firms in developed countries manufacture furniture with sophisticated machinery and equipment, while many firms in less-developed countries make furniture by hand.

- Accounting. Accountants in developed countries use computers and sophisticated software programs, while some accountants in less-developed countries use simple calculators and ledger paper.

Short-Run Versus Long-Run Demand

How does the short-run demand curve for labor compare to the long-run demand curve? There is less flexibility in the short run because firms cannot enter or leave the market, and firms in the market cannot modify their production facilities. As a result, the demand for labor is less elastic in the short run. That means the short-run demand curve is steeper than the long-run demand curve. You may recall that we used the same logic to explain why the short-run supply curve for a product (lawn rakes) was steeper than the long-run supply curve for the product.

TEST Your Understanding

1. The coach of a professional basketball team wants to hire a new player for $3 million per year. Under what circumstances would it be sensible to hire the player?

2. Complete the statement with *increase* or *decrease*: According to the output effect, a decrease in the wage will _____ production costs, so the price of output will _____. The quantity of output produced will _____, so the demand for labor will _____.

3. Explain the input-substitution effect associated with a decrease in the wage.

The Supply of Labor

The labor supply curve answers the following question: How many hours of labor will be supplied at each wage? When we speak of a labor market, we are referring to the market for a specific occupation in a specific geographical area. Consider the supply for nurses in the city of Florence. The supply question is, How many hours of nursing services will be supplied at each wage? To answer, we must think about how many nurses are in the city and how many hours each nurse works.

The Individual Decision: How Many Hours?

Let's start with an individual's decision about how many hours to work. The decision to work is a decision to sacrifice some leisure time: Each hour of work reduces leisure time by one hour. Therefore, the demand for leisure is the flip side of the supply of labor. The price of leisure time is the income sacrificed for each hour of leisure, that is, the hourly wage.

We know from Chapter 4 that an increase in the price of a good has two effects: a substitution effect and an income effect. An increase in the wage—the price of labor—has the following effects on the demand for leisure:

- Substitution effect. The worker faces a trade-off between leisure time and consumer goods such as music, books, food, and entertainment. For each hour of leisure time Leah takes, she loses 1 hour of work time, and her income drops by an amount equal to the wage. Therefore, she has less money to spend on consumer goods. For example, if the wage is $8 per hour, each hour of leisure decreases the amount of income available to spend on consumer goods by $8. When the wage increases to say $10, Leah will sacrifice more income—and consumer goods—for each hour of leisure. Given the larger sacrifice of consumer goods per hour of leisure time, she will demand less leisure time. That means that she will work more hours and earn more money for consumer goods. In other words, as the wage increases, she will substitute income—and the consumer goods it buys—for leisure time.

- Income effect. For most people, leisure is a normal good in the sense that the demand for leisure increases as real income increases. An increase in the wage increases Leah's real income in the sense that she can afford more of all goods, including leisure time. Suppose Leah has a total of 100 hours per week to divide between leisure and work. At a wage of $10, she works 36 hours and has 64 hours of leisure. She also earns $360 ($10 per hour × 36 hours of work) and spends that amount on consumer goods. If her wage increases to $15, her real income increases because she can have more consumer goods *and* more leisure time. For example, if she worked only 30 hours, she could buy $450 worth of consumer goods ($15 per hour × 30 hours) and have 70 hours of leisure (100 hours per week –30 hours of work). The increase in real income causes Leah to consume more of all goods, including leisure time. That means that an increase in real income causes her to demand more leisure and supply less labor.

For the demand for leisure, the income and substitution effects of an increase in the wage work in opposite directions: The substitution effect decreases the desired leisure time, while the income effect increases the desired leisure time. Therefore, we can't predict whether an increase in the wage will cause Leah to demand more leisure time (supply less labor) or less leisure (supply more labor).

A simple example will show why we can't predict a worker's response to an increase in the wage. Suppose each nurse initially works 36 hours per week at an hourly wage of $10 and the wage increases to $12. Here are three reasonable responses to the higher wage:

1. Lester works fewer hours. If Lester works 30 hours instead of 36 hours, he gets 6 hours of extra leisure time and still earns the same income per week ($360 = 30 hours × $12 per hour).

2. Sam works the same number of hours. If Sam continues to work 36 hours per week, he gets an additional $72 of income ($2 per hour × 36 hours) and the same amount of leisure time.

3. Maureen works more hours. If Maureen works 43 hours instead of 36 hours, she sacrifices 7 hours of leisure time but earns a total of $516, compared to only $360 at a wage of $10 per hour.

Empirical studies of the labor market confirm that each of these responses is reasonable. When the wage increases, some people work more, others work less, and others work about the same amount.[2] In most labor markets, the average number of hours per worker doesn't change very much as the wage changes because the increases in work hours from people like Maureen are nearly offset by decreases in work hours from people like Lester.

The Market Supply Curve

Market supply curve for labor:
A curve showing the relationship between the wage and the quantity of labor supplied.

Now that we know how individual workers respond to changes in wages, we're ready to consider the supply side of the labor market. The **market supply curve for labor** shows the relationship between the wage and the quantity of labor supplied. In Figure 18.3, the market supply curve for labor is positively sloped, consistent with the law of supply: The higher the wage (the price of labor), the larger the quantity of labor supplied. An increase in the wage affects the quantity of nursing supplied in three ways:

1. **Change in hours per worker.** When the wage increases, some nurses will work more hours, while others will work fewer hours, and others will work the same number of hours. We don't know for certain whether the average number of work hours will increase, decrease, or stay the same, but the change in the average number of hours is likely to be relatively small.

2. **Occupational choice.** An increase in the nursing wage will cause some workers to switch from other occupations to nursing and motivate more new workers to pick nursing over other occupations.

3. **Migration.** Some nurses in other cities will move to Florence to earn the higher wages offered there.

The second and third effects reinforce one another, so an increase in the wage causes movement upward along the market supply curve. If the wage of Florence nurses increases from $10 to $15 per hour, the quantity of nurses supplied increases from 8,000 hours per day (point *b*) to 16,000 hours per day (point *e*). Although individual workers may not work more hours as the wage increases, the supply curve is positively sloped because an increase in the wage changes workers' occupational choices and causes migration.

Figure 18.3

Supply, Demand, and Market Equilibrium

At the market equilibrium (point *e*, with wage = $15 per hour and quantity = 16,000 hours), the quantity supplied equals the quantity demanded, so there is neither excess demand for labor nor excess supply of labor.

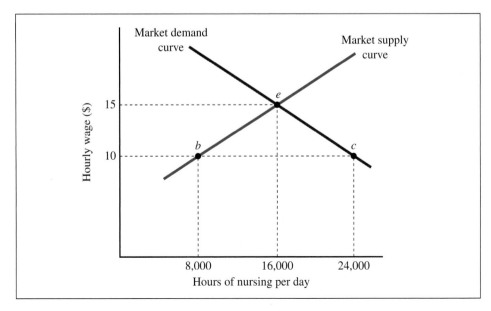

Market Equilibrium

We're ready to put supply and demand together to think about equilibrium in the labor market. A market equilibrium is a situation in which there is no pressure to change the price of a good or service. Figure 18.3 shows the equilibrium in the market for nurses. The supply curve intersects the demand curve at point *e*, so the equilibrium wage is $15 per hour, and the equilibrium quantity is 16,000 hours of nursing per day. At this wage, there is neither an excess demand for labor nor an excess supply of labor, so the market has reached an equilibrium.

How would a change in the demand for nurses affect the equilibrium wage of nurses? We know from Chapter 4 that a change in demand causes the equilibrium price and the equilibrium quantity to move in the same direction: An increase in demand increases the equilibrium price and quantity, while a decrease in demand decreases the equilibrium price and quantity. For example, suppose that the demand for medical care increases. Nurses help provide medical care, so an increase in the quantity of medical care demanded will shift the demand curve for nurses to the right: At each wage, firms will demand more hours of nursing services. As shown in Figure 18.4, an increase in demand increases the equilibrium wage and the equilibrium quantity of nursing services.

How would a change in supply of nurses affect the equilibrium wage of nurses? We know from Chapter 4 that a change in supply causes price and quantity to move in opposite directions: An increase in supply decreases the equilibrium price but increases the equilibrium quantity, while a decrease in supply increases the equilibrium price but decreases the equilibrium quantity. Suppose a new television program makes nursing look like an attractive occupation, causing a large number of youngsters to become nurses rather than accountants, lawyers, or doctors. The supply curve for nurses will shift to the right: At each wage, more nursing hours will be supplied. The equilibrium wage will decrease, and the equilibrium quantity will increase.

How do immigration policies affect wages? A recent program that provides special treatment for highly skilled immigrants has generated a great deal of controversy. Read "A Closer Look: H-1B Visas for High-Tech Workers."

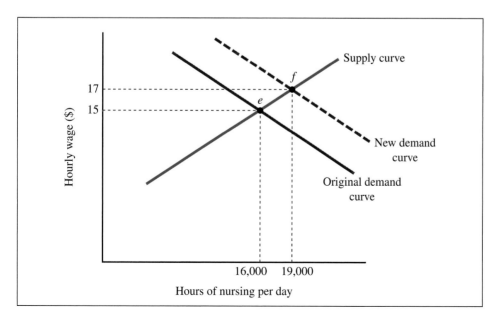

Figure 18.4
Market Effects of an Increase in Demand for Labor
An increase in the demand for nursing services shifts the demand curve to the right, moving the equilibrium from point *e* to point *f*. The equilibrium wage increases from $15 to $17 per hour, and the equilibrium quantity increases from 16,000 hours to 19,000 hours.

A CLOSER LOOK: H-1B VISAS FOR HIGH-TECH WORKERS

Under the H-1B visa program, American companies can attract highly skilled foreign workers to the United States.[3] The renewable visa allows a person to work in the United States for up to 6 years, and often leads to a green card and permanent residence. The program is motivated by an excess demand for skilled workers, with a gap between demand and supply estimated to be about 850,000 workers. Most H-1B visas are issued to people with at least a Master's Degree. Although the process of getting a H-1B visa for a prospective worker is costly (about $5,000), for many firms it is the least costly way to hire high-skilled workers such as engineers and software developers. In 2000, Congress increased the number of H-1B visas from 115,000 to 195,000 per year.

What are the economic effects of immigration? When more workers are admitted into a country, there is greater competition for certain types of occupations and jobs, and wages decrease. That's why the Institute of Electrical and Electronics Engineers, an organization that represents high-tech engineers, argued against increasing the number of H-1B visas.

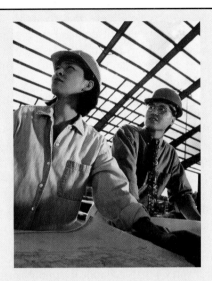

The existing evidence suggests that the effects of immigration on the wages of native workers is relatively small. On the positive side, immigration decreases production costs, increasing profits and decreasing prices for consumers.

TEST Your Understanding

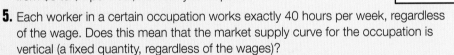

4. Your objective is to earn exactly $120 per week. If your wage decreases from $6 to $4 per hour, how will you respond?

5. Each worker in a certain occupation works exactly 40 hours per week, regardless of the wage. Does this mean that the market supply curve for the occupation is vertical (a fixed quantity, regardless of the wages)?

6. Complete the following: A decrease in the supply of nurses will _____ the equilibrium wage and _____ the equilibrium quantity of nursing services.

Explaining Differences in Wages and Income

Now that we know how the equilibrium wage for a particular occupation is determined, we're ready to explain why wages vary from one job to another. Let's think about why some occupations pay more than others, why women earn less than men, and why college graduates earn more than high-school graduates.

Why Do Wages Differ Across Occupations?

There is substantial variation in wages across occupations. Most professional athletes earn more than medical doctors, who earn more than college professors, who earn more than janitors. We'll see that the wage for a particular occupation will be high if the supply of workers in that occupation is small relative to the demand for those workers. This is shown in Figure 18.5, where the supply curve intersects the demand curve at a high wage.

The supply of workers in a particular occupation could be small for four reasons:

1. **Few people with the required skills.** To play professional baseball, people must be able to hit balls thrown at them at about 90 miles per hour. The few people who have this skill are paid a lot of money because baseball owners compete with one another for skillful players, bidding up the wage. The same logic applies to other professional athletes, musicians, and actors. The few people who have the skills required for these occupations are paid high wages.

2. **High training costs.** The skills required for some occupations can only be acquired through education and training. For example, the skills that are required of a medical doctor can be acquired in medical school, and legal skills can be acquired in law school. If it is costly to acquire these skills, a relatively small number of people will become skilled, and they will receive high wages. The higher wage compensates workers for their training costs.

3. **Undesirable job features.** Some occupations are dangerous, and only a relatively small number of people are willing to work in dangerous occupations. The workers with the greatest risk of losing their lives on the job are lumberjacks, boilermakers, taxicab drivers, and mine workers. The workers who choose dangerous occupations receive high wages, so they are compensated for the danger associated with their jobs. Each year, 1 in 10,000 steelworkers is killed on the job. To compensate for the higher risk of getting killed on the job, steelworkers receive a wage premium of 3.7%, or about $700 per year.[4] The same logic applies to other undesirable job features. For example, wages are higher for jobs that are stressful or dirty or that force people to work at odd hours.

4. **Artificial barriers to entry.** As we'll see later, government and professional licensing boards restrict the number of people in certain occupations, and labor unions restrict their membership. These supply restrictions increase wages.

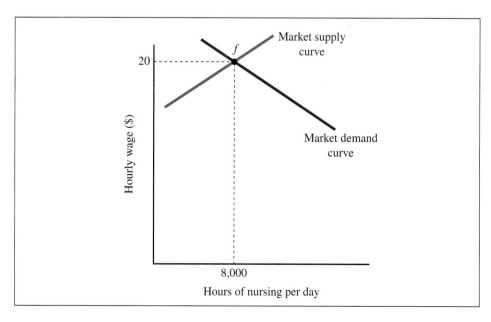

Figure 18.5

Supply Is Low Relative to Demand

If supply is low relative to demand—because few people have the skills, training costs are high, or the job is undesirable—the equilibrium wage will be high.

Gender and Racial Discrimination

Why do women, on average, earn less than men? In the United States, the typical woman earns about 75% as much as the typical man. The gender gap is smaller in European nations but much larger in Japan.

Why is the gender gap so large? Part of the gender gap is explained by differences in skills and productivity. On average, women in many occupations have less education and less work experience, so they are less productive and are paid less. Another reason for the wage gap is occupational discrimination: Women have been denied access to many occupations, causing them to flood a small number of female-dominated occupations such as teaching, nursing, and clerical work. Given the plentiful supply of workers in these female-dominated occupations, wages are low compared to the wages in male-dominated occupations. Given the distribution of men and women in different occupations in the 1990s, about half of female workers would have to change occupations to achieve equal gender representation in all occupations.[5]

What about differences in earnings by race? In 1995, black males who worked full time earned 73% as much as their white counterparts earned, while black females earned 86% as much as their white counterparts. Hispanic males earned 62% as much as white males, while Hispanic females earned 73% as much as white females.[6] For both males and females, part of the earnings gap is caused by differences in productivity: On average, whites have more education and work experience, so they are paid higher wages. Part of the wage gap is caused by racial discrimination. Some black and Hispanic workers are paid lower wages for similar jobs, and others are denied opportunities to work in some high-paying jobs.

How much of the earnings gap is caused by discrimination? A recent study suggests that racial discrimination decreases the wages of black men by about 13 percent.[7] Another study[8] shows that black-white earnings differences have decreased over the last few decades and that the differences are now small enough that "most of the disparity in earnings between blacks and whites in the labor market of the 1990s is due to the differences in skills they bring to the market, and not to discrimination within the labor market."

Why Do College Graduates Earn Higher Wages?

In 1997, the typical college graduate earned 78% more than the typical high-school graduate. Over the last 25 years, this wage gap, or "college premium," has almost doubled. There are two explanations for the college premium.

The first explanation is based on supply and demand analysis. A college education provides the skills necessary to enter certain occupations, so a college graduate has more job options than a high-school graduate. Both high-school grads and college grads can fill jobs that require only a high-school education, so the supply of workers for these low-skilled jobs is plentiful, and the equilibrium wage for these jobs is low. In contrast, there is a smaller supply of workers for jobs that require a college education, so the wages in these high-skill jobs are higher than the wages for low-skilled jobs. This is the **learning effect** of a college education: College students learn the skills required for certain occupations, increasing their human capital.

Learning effect: The increase in a person's wage resulting from the learning of skills required for certain occupations.

The second explanation of the college premium requires a different perspective on college and its role in the labor market. Suppose certain skills are required for a particular job but an employer cannot determine whether a prospective employee has these skills. For example, most managerial jobs require the employee to manage his or her time efficiently, but it is impossible for an employer to determine whether a prospective employee is a good manager of time. Suppose that these skills are also required to complete a college degree. For example, to get passing grades in all your classes, you must be able to use your time efficiently. When you get your college degree, firms will conclude that you have some of the skills they require, so they may hire you instead of an equally skilled high-school graduate. This is the **signaling effect** of a college education: A person who completes college provides a signal to employers about his or her skills. This second explanation suggests that colleges simply provide a testing ground where students can reveal their skills to potential employers.

Signaling effect: The increase in a person's wage resulting from the signal of productivity provided by completing college.

The most important factor in doubling the college premium over the last 25 years is technological change. Changes in technology have increased the demand for college graduates relative to the demand for other workers. In all sectors of the economy, firms are switching to sophisticated machinery and equipment that require highly skilled workers. The share of jobs that require the skills of a college graduate has increased steadily, increasing the demand for college graduates and increasing their wages. Another factor in the growing college premium is the pace of technological change. Workers with more education can more easily learn new skills and new jobs, so firms are willing to pay more for college graduates.

TEST Your Understanding

7. Complete the statement with *demand* or *supply*: The wage for a particular occupation will be low if _____ is small relative to _____.

8. The wages of police officers vary from city to city. What could explain the wage differences?

9. In some countries, it is customary to tip restaurant waiters. What are the implications for the wages paid to waiters?

10. Would you expect people who work between midnight and 8:00 A.M. to earn higher or lower wages than people who work from 9:00 A.M. to 5:00 P.M.? Explain.

Public Policy and Labor Markets

We can use the model of the labor market to show the effects of public policies on wages and employment. We'll look at two policies: the minimum wage and occupational licensing. Each of these policies affects one side of the labor market—supply or demand—leading to changes in the equilibrium wage and total employment.

Effects of the Minimum Wage

In 2001, the federal minimum wage was $5.15 per hour. Figure 18.6 shows the effects of a minimum wage on the market for restaurant workers. The market equilibrium is shown by point *e*: The supply of restaurant workers equals demand at a wage of $4.70 and a quantity of 50,000 worker hours per day. Suppose a minimum wage is established at $5.15 per hour. At this wage, the quantity of labor demanded is only 49,000 hours (point *d* on the demand curve). In other words, the minimum wage decreases the quantity of labor used by restaurants by 1,000 hours per day.

What are the trade-offs associated with the minimum wage? From the perspectives of restaurant workers and restaurant diners, there is good news and bad news:

- Good news for some restaurant workers. Some workers keep their jobs and receive a higher wage ($5.15 per hour instead of $4.70 per hour).

- Bad news for some restaurant workers. Some workers lose their jobs. If the typical workday for restaurant workers is 5 hours, the loss of 1,000 hours of restaurant work per day translates into a loss of 200 jobs.

Figure 18.6

The Market Effects of a Minimum Wage

The market equilibrium is shown by point *e*. The wage is $4.70 per hour, and the quantity of labor is 50,000 labor hours per day. A minimum wage of $5.15 per hour decreases the quantity of labor demanded to 49,000 hours per day. Although some workers receive a higher wage, others lose their jobs or work fewer hours.

• Bad news for diners. The increase in the wage increases the cost of producing restaurant meals, increasing the price of meals.

There are winners and losers from the minimum wage: Workers who keep their jobs gain at the expense of other workers and at the expense of diners.

In recent years, there has been growing concern in the United States about poor working conditions and low wages for foreign workers who produce products for U.S. consumers. For a discussion of this issue, read "A Closer Look: Foreign Sweatshops and Codes of Conduct."

Occupational Licensing

In some occupations, the number of workers is limited by government-sanctioned licensing boards. A licensing board establishes requirements for working in a particular occupation. For example, a person may be prohibited from working in an occupation unless she or he (1) completes a given educational program, (2) passes an examination, (3) has a certain amount of work experience, and/or (4) has lived in a particular area for some time. Among the workers who are subject to occupational licensing are physicians, dentists, beauticians, plumbers, and pharmacists. In the United States, there are over 1,500 occupational licensing boards.[9]

Occupational licensing is controversial. In principle, the licensing requirements are designed to protect consumers from incompetent workers. However, occupational licensing has been criticized on three grounds:

1. Weak link between performance and licensing requirements. In many cases, the licensing requirements seem arbitrary, and there is a weak link between the requirements and the likely performance of the worker.

2. Alternative means of protection. There are other ways to protect consumers from incompetent workers. The government could provide consumers with information about the past performance of workers. Or consumers can spread the word about workers' performance, just as they spread the word for other goods and services. Of course, the dissemination of information will work better for some occupations (for example, plumbers and beauticians) than they do for others (such as doctors).

FOREIGN SWEATSHOPS AND CODES OF CONDUCT

Several widely publicized reports have documented poor working conditions and low wages in foreign factories that produce shoes, clothing, and toys for U.S. corporations. In 1996, a report revealed that part of Wal-Mart's Kathie Lee Collection was produced in Honduras by people working 20 hours per day for 31 cents per hour.[10] Similar reports suggested that goods sold by Nike, Disney, and Mattel were produced in overseas sweatshops. Some human-rights activists have organized protests to publicize what they consider unethical business practices and have organized consumer boycotts.

The corporations have responded to the uproar by monitoring the firms that produce their goods and establishing codes of conduct for foreign suppliers.[11] The Council on Economic Priorities, an interest group in New York, inspects workplaces and awards the "Social Accountability 8000" to businesses that meet its criteria for wages and working conditions. The Apparel Industry Partnership, a group that includes social activists and apparel firms, is developing a code of conduct for apparel producers. The group was pleased to see the results of a survey suggesting that three-fourths of America's shoppers would be willing to pay higher prices for clothes and shoes bearing a "No Sweat" label. Some companies have hired accounting firms such as Price Waterhouse Coopers to audit their foreign suppliers. On campus, the United Students Against Sweatshops is developing a code of conduct for companies that produce products bearing university logos.

The efforts to monitor the labor practices of foreign suppliers raise several questions:

- How will better working conditions and higher wages affect the cost of producing the products and their prices?
- How will consumers respond to the higher prices?

- How much more are consumers willing to pay for "No Sweat" products?
- Will firms selling "No Sweat" products lose customers to firms selling products produced in factories that don't meet the codes of conduct?

Corporations with overseas production facilities responded to the uproar over sweatshops by monitoring the foreign firms that produce the goods for the corporations and establishing codes of conduct for foreign suppliers.

3. Entry restrictions. The licensing requirements increase the cost of entering the occupation, decreasing the supply of workers and increasing the wage paid to workers subject to occupational licensing.

Figure 18.7 shows the market effects of occupational licensing for retail pharmacists. Most of the drugs dispensed by retail pharmacists have already been prepared for use by drug companies, so the principal tasks for a retail pharmacist are counting pills and pasting labels on bottles. To be licensed as a retail pharmacist, a worker can complete a

Figure 18.7

The Market Effects of Occupational Licensing

Occupational licensing increases the cost of entering an occupation, shifting the supply curve to the left. An increase in the required education for pharmacists increases the equilibrium wage from $15 to $17 and decreases the equilibrium quantity from 32,000 to 24,000 hours of pharmacist labor.

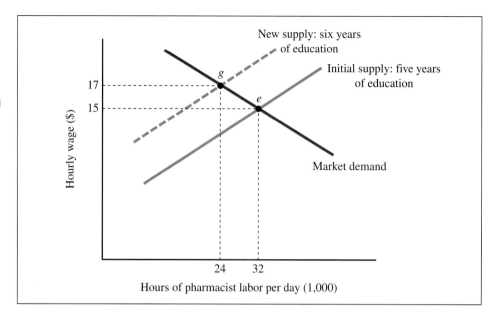

Hours of pharmacist labor per day (1,000)

5-year baccalaureate or a 6-year doctorate. The market equilibrium with this educational requirement is shown by point *e*: The wage of retail pharmacists is $15 per hour.

What would be the market effects of increasing the educational requirement for retail pharmacists? In 1991, three labor organizations representing over 170,000 pharmacists proposed changes in the licensing of pharmacists, changes that would force all new pharmacists to complete the 6-year doctorate program.[12] The increase in the education requirement (from 5 years to 6) would increase the cost of entering the occupation, shifting the supply curve to the left: At every wage, fewer pharmacist hours would be supplied. In Figure 18.7, the market would move from point *e* to point *g*, increasing the equilibrium wage to $17. In addition, the increase in the wage would increase the cost of producing and selling drugs, increasing the price of drugs. The general lesson is that occupational licensing increases wages, increases production costs, and increases prices.

If occupational licensing leads to higher prices, why does it persist for workers such as plumbers, beauticians, and retail pharmacists? Perhaps it persists because consumers believe that licensing protects them from incompetent and unscrupulous workers and because consumers are willing to pay higher prices for this perceived protection. Or perhaps the workers who receive higher wages are better organized than consumers and are therefore more effective in influencing public policy. This could be another example of public policy that benefits special-interest groups at the expense of the general public.

TEST Your Understanding

11. Imelda works 20 hours per week in a shoe store and is paid the minimum wage. When the government increases the minimum wage by $1, she rejoices, saying, "I will be better off by $20 per week." Is her calculation correct?

12. Comment on the following statement: It's silly to suggest that an increase in the minimum wage will decrease the quantity of labor demanded by fast-food restaurants. It's impossible to substitute machines for workers, so the restaurants will hire the same number of workers at the higher wage.

Labor Unions

We've used a simple model of labor supply and labor demand to explain differences in wages. Our analysis is based on the assumption that workers take the market wage as given. A **labor union** is an organized group of workers, the objectives of which are to increase job security, improve working conditions, and increase wages and fringe benefits.

A Brief History of Labor Unions in the United States

As shown in Figure 18.8, about one-sixth of all workers in the United States belong to a union, down from about one-third of workers 40 years ago. Among private-sector workers, the unionization rate is less than 10%, while over 37% of public-sector workers belong to unions. There are two types of labor unions:

- A **craft union** includes workers from a particular occupation, for example, plumbers, bakers, or electricians.

- An **industrial union** includes all types of workers from a single industry, for example, steelworkers or autoworkers.

There are also umbrella organizations that include many individual unions. The largest of these "unions of unions" is the AFL-CIO (the American Federation of Labor–Congress of Industrial Organizations).

Let's take a brief look at the history of labor organizations in the United States. In the nineteenth century, there were all sorts of craft unions, and the main umbrella organizations were the Knights of Labor (founded in 1869) and the AFL (founded in 1881). The CIO (formed in 1931) was a collection of industrial unions that represented semi-skilled workers in mass production, including workers in the automobile, rubber, and

Labor union: An organized group of workers; the objectives of the organization are to increase job security, improve working conditions, and increase wages and fringe benefits.

Craft union: A labor organization that includes workers from a particular occupation, for example, plumbers, bakers, or electricians.

Industrial union: A labor organization that includes all types of workers from a single industry, for example, steelworkers or autoworkers.

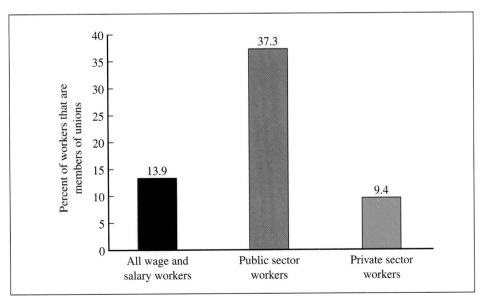

Figure 18.8
Unionization Rates in the United States, 1999
Overall, 14% of all wage and salary workers are members of unions. Over 37% of public-sector workers are members of unions.

Source: *Statistical Abstract of the United States*, 2000.

steel industries. The CIO merged with the AFL in 1955. The most important recent trend has been the expansion of unions serving workers in the public sector. In the last 30 years, the number of government workers in unions and employee associations has more than doubled.

Labor unions get their power to influence labor markets from the states and the federal government. Let's take a brief look at the most important pieces of labor legislation:

- The Wagner Act (1935) guaranteed workers the right to join unions and required each firm to bargain with a union formed by a majority of its workers. The National Labor Relations Board (NLRB) was established to enforce the provisions of the Wagner Act.

- The Taft-Hartley Act (1947) gave government the power to stop strikes that "imperiled the national health or safety" and gave the states the right to pass right-to-work laws. These laws, which are currently in force in 21 states, outlaw union shops, defined as workplaces where union membership is required as a condition of employment.

- The Landrum-Griffin Act (1959) was a response to allegations of corruption and misconduct by union officials. This act guaranteed union members the right to fair elections, made it easier to monitor union finances, and made the theft of union funds a federal offense.

Labor Unions and Wages

One goal of a union is to increase the wages of its members, and there is evidence that unions raise the wages of union workers. One study of unions concluded that unionized workers earn 20% to 30% more than nonunion workers doing the same work.[13] Let's look at three ways in which a union could try to increase the wages of its members.

One approach is to organize workers and negotiate a higher wage. Suppose workers in a particular industry form an industrial union and agree on a union wage that exceeds the equilibrium wage. Like a minimum wage imposed by a government, a wage negotiated by a union means that some workers will earn higher wages but other workers who are willing to work will not have the opportunity to work. To deal with this problem, the union can reduce the number of workers by restricting membership or can share the smaller number of jobs among its members.

Another way in which a union can increase the wage of its members is to promote the products produced by union workers. You've probably seen advertisements encouraging people to buy products with the union label. The demand for labor is a derived demand, so an increase in the demand for a final good will increase the demand for labor used to produce that good, increasing the equilibrium wage. This approach can be used together with a negotiated union wage to prevent an excess supply of labor at the union wage.

A third approach—which may or may not increase wages—is to impose work rules that increase the amount of labor required to produce a given quantity of output. One example of featherbedding is a minimum crew size, which forces a firm to hire more workers than it needs to perform a particular task. For example, the typical unionized airline hires three workers to guide an airplane into the gate, while nonunion airlines use only two workers. In the past, railroad unions forced railroads to use firemen (whose job is to shovel coal) on diesel-powered engines, which don't use coal.

Featherbedding may or may not increase the demand for labor. Although featherbedding forces the firm to use more labor per unit of output, it also decreases the quantity of output. A firm suffering from featherbedding hires workers it doesn't need, so its production costs will be higher than it would be without featherbedding. Firms increase their prices to cover these extra production costs, and consumers respond by purchasing less output. Therefore, the direct effect of featherbedding (that is, the increase in the amount of labor required for a given quantity of output) will be at least partly offset by a decrease in output. The demand for labor is derived from the demand for the final good, so featherbedding may actually decrease the demand for labor, decreasing the wage and total employment.

A different approach to managing union employment comes from Volkswagen A.G., Europe's largest automaker. In 1993, Volkswagen got its labor unions to switch to a 4-day, 28-hour workweek, down from a 5-day, 36-hour workweek. If workers hadn't accepted the shorter workweek and lower pay, Volkswagen would have eliminated 30,000 of its 100,000 jobs in Germany. In other words, the switch to the shorter workweek preserved 30,000 union jobs in the automobile industry.[14] Some analysts suggest that shorter workweeks for union workers will become more common as European unions grapple with lower demand for their workers.

Do Labor Unions Increase Productivity?

We've seen that unions lead to higher wages and work rules that are designed to decrease labor productivity. In other words, there are some costs associated with labor unions. Could unions increase productivity?

Unions may increase productivity by facilitating communication between workers and managers. If a worker is unhappy with his or her job, one option is to quit. From the firm's perspective, this is costly because the firm loses an experienced worker and must train a new one. A dissatisfied worker who belongs to a union has a second option: The worker can use the union as an intermediary to discuss job issues with managers. This sort of communication can solve problems before they become so severe that the worker quits. There is evidence that firms whose workers are in unions have lower turnover rates, in part because they facilitate communication between workers and managers.[15] These lower turnover rates lead to lower training costs and a more experienced workforce.

Other Imperfections in the Labor Market

So far, our analysis of the labor market has been based on two key assumptions: First, there is perfect information in the labor market. Second, employers take the market wage as given. Let's see what happens when these assumptions are not satisfied.

Imperfect Information and Efficiency Wages

What happens when workers have better information than their employers? Workers differ in their skill levels and the amount of effort they exert on the job. Employers cannot always distinguish between skillful and unskillful workers or between hard workers and lazy workers. In other words, there is asymmetric information in the labor market.

We know from our discussion of the market for used cars that asymmetric information causes high-quality and low-quality goods to be sold in a mixed market at a single price. Suppose there are 2 types of workers:

- Low-skill workers, whose marginal revenue product = $100 per day
- High-skill workers, whose marginal revenue product = $200 per day

The employer cannot distinguish between these two types of workers and offers a single wage, realizing that it will probably hire some workers of each type.

What is the appropriate wage? Suppose the opportunity cost of high-skill workers is $130 and a firm offers a wage of $110. Because the wage is less than the opportunity cost of high-skill workers, only low-skill workers will apply for jobs. The firm will lose money because the $110 wage exceeds the $100 marginal revenue product of the low-skill workers. To get some high-skill workers, the employer must pick a wage that exceeds the $130 opportunity cost of high-skill workers. As the firm increases its wage, it will attract more high-skill workers, and the average productivity of its workforce will increase. Depending on the responses of the two types of workers to the higher wage, a firm could make more profit by offering a higher wage. This is known as **paying efficiency wages:** The firm pays a higher wage to increase the average productivity of its workforce.

Paying efficiency wages: The practice of a firm paying a higher wage to increase the average productivity of its workforce.

Another reason for paying relatively high wages is to encourage employees to work hard. Firms realize that their employees can vary their work efforts, from working hard to hardly working (shirking). To encourage their employees to work hard, employers fire workers who are caught shirking. The penalty associated with being fired will be much greater if the firm pays a wage above the worker's opportunity cost. For example, suppose a worker could earn $80 per day in another job. If the firm pays its workers $100 per day, a worker who is fired—and then immediately gets a job with another firm— would take a pay cut of $20 per day. This is another example of **paying efficiency wages:** By increasing the wage, the firm increases the work effort of its employees and increases the average productivity of its workforce.

Economic Detective

Higher Wages at Ford Motor Company

In the early days of the automobile industry, the prevailing wage for autoworkers was $3 per day. The assembly-line jobs were repetitive and tedious, and the turnover rate of workers was very high. When Henry Ford decided to increase the daily wage for his workers from $3 to $5, most observers were baffled. They figured that Ford's labor costs would be almost twice as high as those of his rivals, so he would lose a lot of money and quickly go out of business. The wage hike appeared to be a great act of generosity but very bad business. You can imagine their surprise when Ford's profit doubled from $30 million to $60 million. How was this possible? How can higher wages lead to higher profits?

The key to solving this puzzle is the concept of efficiency wages. When Ford raised the wage, the average productivity of Ford workers increased by about 50%, a result of several changes in the workforce:[16]

- The pool of job applicants improved, so Ford could choose better workers.
- Fewer workers were fired for shirking.

People were baffled when Henry Ford increased the daily wage for his assembly workers from $3 to $5.

- Fewer workers quit voluntarily.
- The rate of absenteeism was cut in half.

In the words of Henry Ford, "There was no charity in any way involved.... The payment of five dollars a day for an eight-hour day was one of the finest cost cutting moves we ever made."

Monopsony Power

We've assumed that each employer is such a small part of the labor market that it takes the market wage as given. The labor-supply curve faced by the firm is horizontal at the market wage. Although this is true for many labor markets, in some markets there is a single employer. For example, if your city has a single hospital, there will be a single employer of surgical nurses. This is the case of **monopsony:** There is a single buyer of a particular input.

Monopsony: A market in which there is a single buyer of an input.

A monopsonist faces a positively sloped market supply curve of labor. If the monopsonist hires more workers, it must pay a higher wage to attract them away from other activities. In Figure 18.9, the firm can hire 7 workers at a wage of $10 (point *c*) and 8 workers at a wage of $12 (point *d*). The firm's **marginal labor cost** (also known as *marginal factor cost*) is defined as the increase in total labor cost from hiring one more worker. When the firm decides to hire 8 workers instead of 7, its total labor cost increases from $70 per hour ($10 per worker per hour × 7 workers) to $96 per hour ($12 per worker per hour × 8 workers), an increase of $26. Therefore, the firm's marginal labor cost for the 8th worker is $26 (shown by point *e* in Figure 18.9).

Marginal labor cost: The increase in total labor cost resulting from hiring one more worker. (Also known as marginal factor cost.)

As shown in Figure 18.9, the marginal labor cost exceeds the hourly wage. The reason is that when the firm increases the wage to hire one more worker, the firm must increase the wage for all of its workers. To hire the 8th worker, the firm pays $12 to the new worker but also pays an extra $2 for each of the 7 workers who were willing to work at the $10 wage. We compute the marginal labor cost as follows:

marginal labor cost = wage paid to new worker + (change in wage × quantity of original workers

$26 = $12 + ($2 × 7)

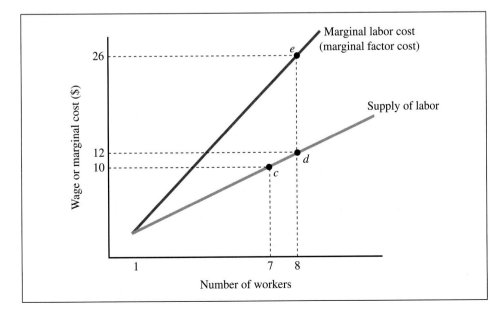

26 — *e*

12 — *d*
10 — *c*

Marginal labor cost
(marginal factor cost)

Supply of labor

Wage or marginal cost ($)

1   7   8

Number of workers

Figure 18.9

The Supply of Labor and Marginal Labor Cost for a Monopsonist

To hire more workers, the monopsonist must pay a higher wage, so the marginal labor cost exceeds the wage. To hire the 8th worker, the firm increases the wage from $10 to $12. The marginal labor cost for the 8th worker is $26, equal to $12 paid to the 8th worker plus $14 extra money paid to the 7 original workers, each of whom receives $2 more per hour.

In this case, the marginal labor cost is $26, including $12 for the new worker and $14 for the original workers.

Figure 18.10 shows how a monopsonist decides how many workers to hire. Using the marginal principle, the firm chooses the quantity of labor at which the marginal benefit of labor equals the marginal cost of labor. The marginal labor cost curve intersects the marginal revenue product curve (the marginal benefit curve) at point *m*, so the firm hires 36 workers. As shown by the supply curve, if the firm wants to hire 36 workers, it must pay a wage of $10 per hour (shown by point *w*).

How does the monopsony outcome compare to the perfectly competitive outcome? Any firm that hires workers—either a monopsonist or perfect competitor—will continue to hire more workers until the marginal cost equals the marginal benefit (the marginal revenue product). For a perfectly competitive firm, the marginal cost is simply the wage. For a monopsonist, the marginal cost is the marginal labor cost, which exceeds the wage because the monopsonist must increase its wage to hire more workers. The monopsonist will hire fewer workers because its higher marginal cost equals the marginal benefit at a smaller quantity of labor. A monopsonist will hire fewer workers than would be hired by a collection of perfectly competitive firms, each of which takes the market wage as given.

You may have noticed the similarity between a monopsonist and a monopolist. A monopolist (a single seller) uses its market power to increase the price of output, while a monopsonist (a single buyer) uses its market power to decrease the wage or other input prices. The monopolist produces an artificially small quantity of output, while the monopsonist hires an artificially small quantity of a particular input such as labor. Table 18.2 summarizes the key features of a monopolist and a monopsonist.

What is the role of a labor union in a labor market with a single buyer? Monopsony leads to an artificially low wage, and a union leads to an artificially high wage. A market with both a union and a monopsonist will have a wage somewhere between the two extremes, depending on the bargaining power of the two sides. It may be sensible to counteract market power on the demand side of the market (a monopsony) with market power on the supply side (a union).

Figure 18.10

The Hiring Decision of a Monopsonist

The monopsonist chooses point *m*, where the marginal benefit of labor (the marginal revenue product) equals the marginal labor cost. The supply curve indicates that to hire 36 workers, the monopsonist must pay a wage of $10 (point *w*).

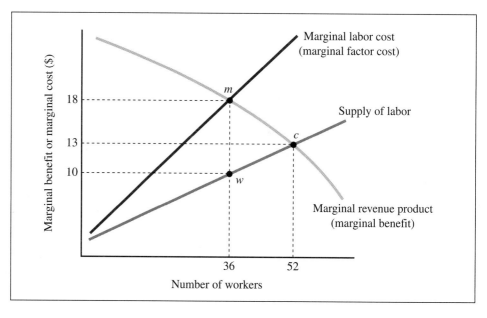

Table 18.2 Monopoly versus Monopsony

Monopoly	Monopsony
Single seller of output	Single buyer of input
High price of output	Low price of input
Small quantity of output	Small quantity of input

TEST Your Understanding

14. Explain how an increase in the wage can increase the average productivity of the firm's workforce.

15. Suppose a union's objective is to maximize total employment in a certain occupation, and it cannot affect the demand for labor. The firms in the market take the wage as given. What should the union do?

16. Suppose a union's objective is to maximize the total income of nurses (total money spent by firms on nurses). At the current wage, the price elasticity of demand for nurses is 1.5. Should the union increase or decrease the union wage? Explain.

17. Complete the statement with *high* or *low*. A monopolist sells its output at a relatively _____ price, while a monopsonist buys its inputs at a relatively _____ price.

Using the **TOOLS**

We've seen how to use supply and demand curves to explain differences in wages and to predict the effects of public policy on the equilibrium wage and employment. We've also seen the effects of unions and the rationale for paying a wage above the equilibrium wage. Here are some opportunities to do your own economic analysis.

APPLICATIONS

1. Market Effects of Immigration

In the initial equilibrium, the wage for farmworkers is $5 per hour. The elasticity of supply of farmworkers is 2.0, and the elasticity of demand for farmworkers is 1.0. Suppose that immigration increases the supply of farmworkers by 12%: The supply curve shifts to the right by 12%.

a. Predict the effect of immigration on the wage paid to farmworkers: By how much will the wage increase or decrease?

b. How will immigration affect the cost of producing food and the equilibrium price of food?

2. Effects of a Nurses' Union

Suppose that the nurses in the city of Florence form a union and that to work as a nurse, you must belong to the union. The nurses do not allow new nurses to join the union, so the supply of nurses decreases by 3% per year as old nurses retire. As shown in Figure 18.3, before the union is formed, the equilibrium wage is $15 and the equilibrium quantity is 16,000 hours per day.

a. Depict graphically the effect of forming the union on the nursing market.

b. If the price elasticity of demand for nursing is 1.5, by what percentage will the wage of nursing increase each year?

3. Demand for Newskids

Consider the market for newspaper delivery kids in Kidsville. Each newskid receives a piece rate of $2 per subscriber per month and has a fixed territory that initially has 100 subscribers. The price elasticity of demand for subscriptions is 2.0. Suppose the new city council of Kidsville passes a law that establishes a minimum piece rate of $3 per subscriber per month. As a result, the publisher increases the monthly price of a subscription by 20%. How will the new law affect the monthly income of the typical newskid?

4. Equilibrium with Efficiency Wages

Consider a labor market with asymmetric information: Each worker knows his or her marginal revenue product, but firms cannot distinguish between low-skill and high-skill workers. Each low-skill worker has an opportunity cost of $80 and a marginal revenue product of $100, and each high-skill worker has an opportunity cost of $130 and a marginal revenue product of $200. The workforce is divided equally between the two types of workers. Your job is to predict the equilibrium wage in the market given that each firm takes the price as given and earns zero economic profit. Try the following wages: (a) $90, (b) $100, (c) $140, (d) $150, (e) $170.

 Summary

We've seen how wages are determined in perfectly competitive labor markets and why wages differ from one occupation to another. We've also explored the effects of various market imperfections—public policies, unions, and imperfect information—on wages and employment. Here are the main points of the chapter:

1. The wage in a particular occupation will be relatively high if supply is small relative to demand. This will occur if (a) few people have the skills required for the occupation, (b) training costs are high, or (c) the job is dangerous or stressful.

2. College graduates earn more than high-school graduates because a college education provides new skills and allows people to reveal their skills to employers.

3. There are trade-offs with a minimum wage or a union wage: Some workers earn higher income, but others lose their jobs.

4. Occupational licensing increases the wage of the licensed occupation and increases the price of the good produced by that occupation.

5. A firm that increases its wage may increase the average productivity of its workers and increase its profit.

 Key Terms

Problems and Discussion Questions

1. You are an economic consultant to a city that just imposed a payroll tax of $1 per hour of work. This payroll tax is paid by workers through a payroll deduction: For each hour of work, the employer deducts $1 and sends the money to the city government. The initial wage (before the tax) is $10, and total employment is 20,000 hours per day. Use a graph to show the effect of the tax on the equilibrium wage and employment.

2. We discussed the response of Lester, Sam, and Maureen to an increase in the wage. Which person's response is closest to your own? If your wage increased, would you work more hours, fewer hours, or about the same number of hours?

3. Critically appraise the following statement from Mr. Chuckles: "The law of supply says that an increase in price increases the quantity supplied. A decrease in the income tax rate will increase the worker's net wage, so each worker will work more hours. As a result, the revenue from the income tax will increase."

4. Consider two markets for carpenters: the city of Portland and the United States. Draw two supply curves for carpenters: one for the city of Portland and one for the United States. In which market would you expect a more elastic supply of carpenters?

5. The advocates of higher salaries for teachers point out that most teachers have college degrees and that teaching children is an important job.
   a. Why aren't teachers' salaries higher, given the importance of the job and the education required?
   b. Suppose a new law requires that teachers are paid the same hourly wage as college graduates who work in business. Predict the effects of this law on the market for teachers.

6. Comment on the following: "There is no substitute for an airline pilot: Someone has to fly the plane. Therefore, an increase in the wage of airline pilots will not change the number of pilots used by the airlines."

7. Suppose a new government program improves worker safety in coal mines. Use a graph to predict the effect of the program on the equilibrium wage for coal workers.

8. Under some occupational licensing laws, licensed members of an occupation write licensing exams. An example is the bar exam for licensing lawyers. How might this practice limit entry into an occupation?

9. One response to the gap in wages between men and women is a policy called comparable worth, under which the government specifies a minimum wage for some occupations, typically the occupations with a disproportionate number of women. Evaluate the merits of a such a policy. What are the trade-offs?

10. Web Exercise. Visit a part of the census Web site devoted to income statistics [*http://www.census.gov/ hhes/www/income00.html*] and download the report "Money Income in the United States." How do the average earnings of women with bachelor's degrees compare to those of female high-school dropouts and women with masters' degrees? Do the same comparisons for men.

11. Web Exercise. Visit the Web site of the U.S. Bureau of Labor Statistics [*http://www.bls.gov/*]. Do a keyword search of the site to get some information on the bureau's projections of employment in different occupations. Try the following: "occupational + employment + projections." Which occupations are expected to grow most rapidly in coming years? Which are expected to grow slowly?

Take It to the Net

We invite you to visit the O'Sullivan/Sheffrin page on the Prentice Hall Web site at: **http://www.prenhall.com/osullivan/** for additional World Wide Web exercises for this chapter.

Model Answers to Questions

Chapter-Opening Questions

1. When the wage increases, some people work more hours, others work fewer hours, and others work about the same number of hours.

2. As we saw in the section on wages for different occupations, the worker's income would increase by about 3.7%.

3. The gender gap results from differences in skills and productivity as well as occupational discrimination.

4. As shown in "A Closer Look: Foreign Sweatshops and Codes of Conduct," U.S. corporations have developed codes of conduct and hired firms to audit their foreign suppliers.

5. Henry Ford described the wage hike as "one of the finest cost cutting moves we ever made."

Test Your Understanding

1. If the marginal revenue product of the new player exceeds $3 million. If the player increased attendance and increased the revenue from ticket sales by $4 million, it would be sensible to hire the player.

2. Decrease, decrease, increase, increase.

3. As the wage decreases, labor will become less expensive relative to other inputs, so the firm will substitute labor for other inputs.

4. You will work 30 hours per week instead of 20 hours.

5. No. An increase in the wage will increase the number of workers because of changes in occupational choices and migration.

6. Decrease, increase.

7. Demand, supply.

8. Wages are higher in cities where police officers face a greater chance of being killed on the job.

9. Waiters in tipping countries will have lower wages than waiters in nontipping countries.

10. Working between midnight and 8:00 A.M. disrupts sleeping and eating patterns and a person's social life. Because of these undesirable consequences, we expect workers on the midnight to 8:00 A.M. shift to receive higher wages than workers on the day shift.

11. Imelda's statement could be incorrect for three reasons: (1) She may lose her job as a result of the higher minimum wage; (2) if she keeps her job, her employer may ask her to work fewer hours per week; (3) as a consumer, she will pay higher prices for the goods produced by minimum-wage workers, partly offsetting any increase in income she may receive.

12. There are opportunities to substitute machinery for workers, as shown by the switch to "smart" cash registers (the pictures on the buttons speed up money collection; beaming the information to the kitchen speeds up the process of filling orders and collecting money) and automated cooking machines (burgers on tracks). In addition, there is the output effect: The increase in cost will increase price, so restaurants will sell less food and thus need fewer workers.

13. Decreases, increases, increases.

14. The firm will attract better applicants, and workers are less likely to shirk.

15. Total employment is maximized at the intersection of supply and demand, so the union should do nothing, letting the market reach the equilibrium.

16. If demand is elastic, a decrease in price will increase total expenditures (total revenue, total income). Therefore, the union should decrease its wage.

17. High, low.

Using the Tools

1. Market Effects of Immigration. Immigration will shift the supply curve to the right, decreasing the equilibrium wage. We can use the price-change formula for an increase in supply (explained in Chapter 5) to predict the change in the equilibrium wage (the price of labor):

   a. The wage will decrease from $5.00 to $4.80 per hour.

   b. The cost of producing food will decrease, so the price of food will decrease.

2. Effects of a Nurses' Union

   a. The union causes movement upward along the market demand curve as the number of nurses decreases by 3% per year.

   b. The quantity of labor decreases by 3% per year. To compute the resulting change in price, we can use the formula for price elasticity of demand. To be consistent with an elasticity of 1.5, a 3% decrease in quantity generates a 2% increase in the wage.

3. Demand for Newskids. The elasticity of demand is 2.0, so a 20% increase in price will decrease the quantity demanded by 40%: A price elasticity of 2.0 means the percentage change in quantity is 2 times the percentage change in price. In other words, the

number of subscribers per newskid will decrease from 100 to 60. The income of the typical newskid will decrease from $200 ($2 per subscriber × 100 subscribers) to $180 ($3 per subscriber × 60 subscribers). This is the output effect in action.

4. Equilibrium with Efficiency Wages

   a. Wage = $90. Each firm will get all low-skill workers, each with marginal revenue product (MRP) = $100. Each firm will make a profit, so this is not an equilibrium. Competition among the firms will bid up the wage.

   b. Wage = $100. Each firm will get all low-skill workers, each with MRP = $100. Each firm will make zero economic profit, so this is an equilibrium wage.

   c. Wage = $140. Each firm will get half low-skill workers and half high-skill workers, so the average MRP = $150. Each firm will make a profit, so this is not an equilibrium. Competition among the firms will bid up the wage.

   d. Wage = $150. Each firm will get half low-skill workers and half high-skill workers, so the average MRP = $150. Each firm will make zero economic profit, so this is an equilibrium.

   e. Wage = $170. Each firm will get half low-skill workers and half high-skill workers, so the average MRP = $150. Each firm will lose money, so this is not an equilibrium.

Notes

1. W. Michael Fox and Beverly J. Fox, "What's Happening to Americans' Income?" *The Southwest Economy*, Federal Reserve Bank of Dallas, Issue 2, 1995, pp. 3–6; U.S. Bureau of the Census, Current Population Reports, *Money Income in the United States: 1999* (Washington, DC: U.S. Government Printing Office, 2000).

2. Mark Killingsworth, *Labor Supply* (New York: Cambridge University Press, 1983).

3. Alan B. Krueger, "Economic Scene: Work Visas Are Allowing Washington to Sidestep Immigration Reform," *New York Times*, May 25, 2000, p. C2; Alex Pulaski and Jim Barnett, "High-tech Employers Push for More Visas," *The Oregonian*, September 5, 2000, p. A1; Doreen Hemlock and Joan Fleischer Tamen, "Expanded Visa Program Brings Global Opportunity to South Florida," *Sun-Sentinel*, October 17, 2000.

4. Craig Olson, "An Analysis of Wage Differentials Received by Workers on Dangerous Jobs," *Journal of Human Resources*, vol. 16, Spring 1981, pp. 167–185.

5. Suzanne Bianchi and Daphne Spain, "Women, Work, and Family in America," *Population Bulletin*, vol. 51, no. 3, 1998, pp. 2–48.

6. U.S. Department of Labor, *Employment and Earnings* (Washington, DC: U.S. Government Printing Office, 1996).

7. William Darity and Patrick Mason, "Evidence on Discrimination in Employment: Codes of Color, Codes of Gender," *Journal of Economic Perspectives*, vol. 12, no. 2, 1998, pp. 63–90.

8. James Heckman, "Detecting Discrimination," *Journal of Economic Perspectives*, vol. 12, no. 2, 1998, pp. 101–116.

9. Werner Hirsch, *Law and Economics: An Introductory Analysis*, 2nd ed. (San Diego, CA: Academic Press, 1988), pp. 347–350.

10. "Stamping Out the Sweatshops: Dress Code," *The Economist*, April 19, 1997.

11. "Sweatshop Wars," *The Economist*, February 27, 1999.

12. Lawrence J. McQuillan, "Pharmacists' Proposal Will Raise Costs of Medicine," *The Margin*, Spring 1993, p. 52.

13. Richard B. Freeman and James Medoff, *What Do Unions Do?* (New York: Basic Books, 1985).

14. Ferdinand Protzman, "VW Plan for 4-Day Workweek Is Adopted," *New York Times*, November 26, 1993, p. D11; Tyler Marshall, "VW, Unions, OK 20% Reduction in Work Week," *Los Angeles Times*, November 26, 1993, p. A1: "Worldwire," *Wall Street Journal*, July 8, 1994, p. A5.

15. Freeman and Medoff, *What Do Unions Do?*

16. J. R. Lee, "So-Called Profit Sharing System in the Ford Plant," *Annals of the American Academy of Political and Social Science*, May 1915, pp. 297–310; David Halberstam, *The Reckoning* (New York: William Morrow, 1986), pp. 91–92; Daniel M. G. Graff and Lawrence H. Summers, "Did Henry Ford Pay Efficiency Wages?" *Journal of Labor Economics*, vol. 5, 1987, pp. 557–586.

Economic Challenges: Poverty, Aging, and Health Care

Ethena Jones just graduated with an honors degree in computer engineering and is pleased with the high salary she will earn at her new job. But she wonders about her classmates from high school who did not go to college, especially the ones living in poverty. She also wonders whether her older brother, who recently lost his job, will be able to afford health insurance. She is concerned about her parents, who are near retirement age. Is the Social Security trust fund about to run out of money, and how might that affect her parents?

n this chapter, we discuss three economic challenges that confront the United States and other developed countries. Poverty is a persistent and vexing problem, and the growing frustration with traditional welfare policies—involving assistance for all poor families—led to a new welfare system that requires work in exchange for time-limited assistance. A second economic challenge is dealing with an aging population. In the next century, the proportion of the population over 65 years of age will increase sharply, requiring changes in the way we support the elderly population. A third economic challenge is dealing with the rising costs of health care. As health-care costs increase, it becomes more difficult to support the elderly and the poor—both large consumers of health care—and more difficult for all of us to maintain the same level of health care.

We explore the policy choices we will face as we try to deal with these issues in the twenty-first century. We first look at the possible causes of poverty and the policy options available to reduce poverty. We then turn to the problems generated by the aging of the population and the high costs of providing adequate health care. As you read this chapter, you will see that the fundamental problem in economics—scarcity of resources—is still with us. Here are some of the practical questions that we answer in this chapter.

1. Is poverty more prevalent among senior citizens or children?

2. Why is homelessness more prevalent in some cities?

3. What are the trade-offs—the advantages and disadvantages—of privatizing Social Security?

4. Why does the cost of health care continue to rise?

Poverty and Public Policy

In every society, some people do not earn enough income to provide what most of us consider a reasonable amount of food, clothing, housing, medical care, and other goods. In this part of the chapter, we explain the causes of poverty and discuss antipoverty policies.

Who Are the Poor?

Household: A group of related family members and unrelated individuals who live in the same housing unit.

Poverty budget: The minimum amount the government estimates that a family needs to avoid being in poverty; equal to 3 times the minimum food budget.

A **household** is a group of related family members and unrelated persons who live in the same housing unit. According to the U.S. government, a household is considered poor if its total income is less than the amount required to satisfy its minimum needs. The government computes a household's minimum needs or the **poverty budget** by estimating a minimum food budget and multiplying the minimum food budget by three. For example, in 1999, the poverty budget was $13,290 for a three-person household and $17,029 for a four-person household. A household whose income is less than the official poverty budget is considered poor.

Figure 19.1 shows the poverty rates for various groups. The poverty rate equals the percentage of people in a particular group who live in households below the official poverty line. In 1999, the overall poverty rate in the U.S. was 11.8%, and poverty rates differ sharply by groups:

- Race. The poverty rates for blacks and Hispanics are over twice as high as the rate for whites. The poverty rate for Asian-Americans is 14%.

- Family type. The poverty rate for female-headed households is about six times the rate for two-parent households.

- Age. One of the recent successes in the battle against poverty was the decrease in poverty among the elderly. The poverty rate for the elderly dropped from 35% in

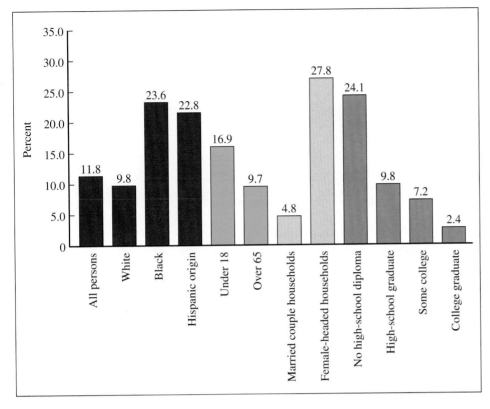

Figure 19.1

Poverty Rates for Different Population Groups
Poverty rates are highest among racial minorities, children, and people with low educational attainment.

Source: U.S. Bureau of the Census, Current Population Reports, Series P60-201, *Poverty in the United States, 1999* (Washington, DC: U.S. Government Printing Office, 1998).

1959 to 9.7% in 1999, largely as a result of increased Social Security benefits. In contrast, the poverty rate for children is almost 17%.

- **Education.** The poverty rate of high-school dropouts is over twice the poverty rate for high-school graduates and over 8 times the poverty rate of college graduates.

What Causes Poverty?

To put it simply, poverty results from the failure of the adults in a household to earn enough money to provide for the household's basic needs. Some adults are unable to work because of health problems, disabilities, or age. Others have limited work options because they are responsible for raising small children. A common perception is that most poor adults don't work, but this is incorrect. More than half of poor households have someone who works at least part-time, and one in five poor households has a full-time, year-round worker.[1] For the working poor, the problem is low wages and part-time employment, not the lack of a job. For example, a four-person household with one full-time worker will be below the poverty line if the worker's wage is less than $8.20 per hour, well above the minimum wage.

There are many reasons for poverty. It is difficult to disentangle the factors that cause poverty, and economists have not reached a consensus about which of these factors is the most important.

- **Inadequate education.** As shown in Figure 19.1, the poverty rate for high-school dropouts is about ten times the poverty rate for college graduates. Workers who do not complete high school lack many of the basic skills needed in the workplace. Therefore, they are less likely to be employed, and if they are employed, they earn low wages.

The poverty rate for children is about twice the poverty rate for senior citizens.

- **Racial segregation.** In most cities in the United States, racial minorities—especially blacks—are concentrated in the central cities, far from jobs in suburban areas. Many poor households don't own cars, and mass-transit systems are ill-equipped for commuting from the central city to the suburbs. A recent study shows that young black adults are much worse off in segregated cities: They earn less income, have lower high-school graduation rates, are more likely to be idle (neither working nor attending school), and are more likely to become single mothers.[2] The more segregated the city, the more prevalent are these adverse outcomes.

- **Weak economy.** Because the poor are usually less productive than other workers, they are the last hired and the first fired. They are the last hired when the economy grows rapidly and are the first to lose their jobs when the economy slows down.

- **Racial and gender discrimination in the labor market.** Although white workers earn more than minority workers and men earn more than women, most of the differences in wages are explained by differences in hours worked, education, and work experience. Part of the difference results from racial and gender discrimination: Whites are paid more than equally productive blacks; men are paid more than equally productive women. The size of the discrimination penalty has been shrinking over time, and there is some disagreement about the actual size of the penalty.

- **Single parenthood.** As shown in Figure 19.1, the poverty rate among female-headed households is about six times the poverty rate for two-parent families.

How have recent changes in production technology affected the wages of the least educated and least productive workers? Recent advances in technology have decreased the demand for these workers for two reasons: First, the new technology allowed firms to replace many low-skilled workers with "smart machines." Second, the least educated workers do not have the skills required to work in firms that produce and use the new technology. As a result, the demand for low-skilled workers has fallen, resulting in lower wages. As an illustration, the wage for a job that requires the use of a computer is about 19% higher than the wage for a similar job that does not require a computer.[3]

Anti-poverty Programs

As we saw in Chapter 3, the federal government and the states spend billions of dollars on programs designed to reduce poverty. Spending on anti-poverty programs accounts for about 14% of the federal budget, 32% of state budgets, and 5% of local-government budgets. This money is spent on job-training programs, cash assistance, and transfers of goods and services such as food stamps and medical care.

In August 1996, President Clinton signed into law the Personal Responsibility and Work Opportunity Reconciliation Act of 1996, a comprehensive welfare-reform plan. The plan abolished the traditional anti-poverty program for poor families (Aid to Families with Dependent Children, or AFDC) and thus eliminated the entitlement of poor families to receive cash assistance. The federal government now provides block grants to the states, and the states are responsible for designing and implementing programs to move most poor adults from welfare dependence to employment. The new program, called Temporary Assistance to Needy Families (TANF), has the following restrictions:

- After a maximum of 24 months of assistance (consecutive or nonconsecutive), a recipient must participate in work activities, defined as employment, on-the-job training, work experience, community service, vocational training, or child-care services for individuals providing community service. Single parents must participate at least 30 hours per week, and two-parent families must participate at least 35 hours per week. There are exceptions to this rule for the parents of very young children.

- After a total of 60 months of cash assistance (consecutive or nonconsecutive), assistance is stopped. States can allow exceptions to this rule, with the restriction that no more than 20% of the state's recipients exceed the 60-month limit.

The states are responsible for implementing welfare reform. Florida's reform law—known as Work and Gain Economic Self-Sufficiency (WAGES)—provides an example of one state's response to the new welfare law. The program gives temporary assistance to poor families with children and provides parents with work opportunities and support services. This is a work-first program: When a person applies for assistance, he or she is immediately referred for employment. Unless exempted, each recipient must participate in work activities to the full extent of the federal guidelines. For a family of three, the maximum cash assistance is $303 per month, which is less than one-third of the poverty budget for a family of three. Cash assistance is limited to 24 consecutive months in any 60-month period, and no recipient will receive payments for more than 48 months.

How will welfare reform affect the markets for low-skilled labor? The switch from a traditional welfare system to a program requiring work in exchange for time-limited assistance will increase the number of low-skilled people in the labor market. As shown in Figure 19.2, an increase in the number of low-skilled workers shifts the labor supply curve to the right: At each wage, more hours of labor are supplied. In this example, the wage drops from $7.00 to $6.50 per hour, and the quantity of labor increases. The actual effects of welfare reform on wages and employment will be determined by the elasticity of supply of low-skilled labor and the elasticity of demand for low-skilled labor. A recent study estimates that the wages for the least educated and lowest-skilled workers (high-school dropouts and the least productive high-school graduates) could drop by about 6%.[4] In general, low-skilled women will suffer the largest losses in earnings and wages because they are the workers who will face the most additional competition as many former welfare recipients join the workforce.

A Progress Report on Welfare Reform

Welfare reform was partly responsible for some dramatic changes in the number of welfare recipients. Between 1994 and 2000, the number of families on welfare dropped from 5 million to 2.2 million.[5] About three-fifths of the adults who left the welfare rolls were employed, resulting in a substantial increase in the employment rate of single mothers. Because welfare reform was implemented while the economy was growing, some of this

Figure 19.2

The Effects of Welfare Reform on the Market for Low-Skilled Labor

The welfare-reform program requires welfare recipients to join the workforce. The resulting increase in supply of low-skilled workers will decrease the equilibrium wages for low-skilled workers.

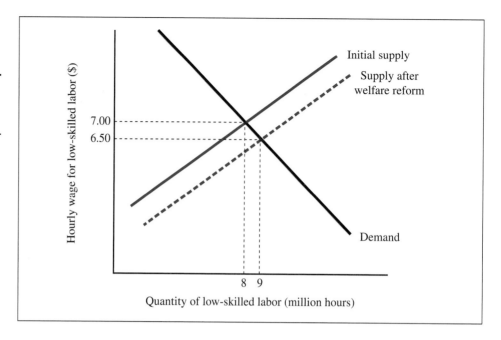

good news concerning welfare caseloads and employment rates is attributable to economic growth.

Although welfare reform reduced welfare caseloads, so far it has had mixed effects on poverty rates. About two-fifths of former welfare recipients are not working, and must get along with less income. Among former recipients who are working, the average wage is only $7.00 per hour, a wage that is not high enough to lift a single-earner family above the poverty line. Although the poverty rate for children has decreased, the incomes of the poorest fifth of the nation's population have continued to fall. In 1999, about 700,000 families were significantly worse off in 1999 than their counterparts in 1995.

Looking to the future, three questions remain. First, how will an economic slowdown—recession—affect caseloads and poverty rates? Second, will former welfare recipients acquire human capital on their new jobs, allowing them to earn higher wages? If so, the early gains in employment will translate into larger income gains for the former recipients. Third, how will welfare reform affect family structure? One policy objective was to decrease the number of children in single-parent households. So far, teen pregnancy rates have dropped, but the incidence of single-parent families has not changed.

Economic Detective

Wages of College Graduates and High-School Dropouts

During the 1980s and 1990s, the supply of both college graduates and high-school dropouts increased, with a larger increase in the supply of college graduates. Given the larger increase in supply of college graduates, we would expect the wage of college graduates to decrease relative to the wage of high-school dropouts. Yet the relative wage of college graduates actually increased. Use a supply and demand diagram to solve this mystery.

Figure 19.3 shows how to solve this puzzle. In each market, the supply curve shifted to the right, with a larger shift in the market for college graduates. At the same time, the demand curve for college graduates shifted to the right, a result of technological change

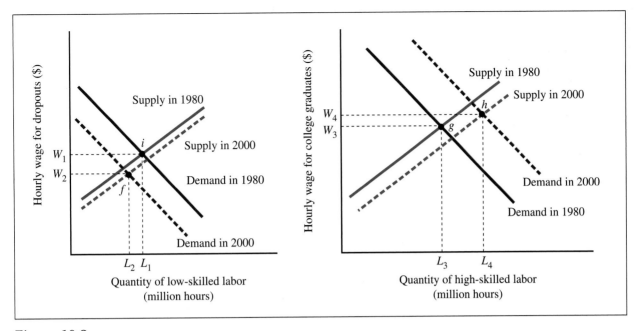

Figure 19.3

Changes in Equilibrium Wages for High-School Dropouts and College Graduates

Between 1980 and 2000, the supply of college graduates increased by more than the supply of high-school dropouts. Because the demand for low-skilled labor decreased, the wage for high-school dropouts decreased. The demand for high-skilled labor increased, more than offsetting the increase in supply of college graduates, so the wage of college graduates increased.

that caused employers to demand more workers with the skills required to produce and use new technology. The increase in demand was larger than the increase in supply, so the wage for college graduates increased. In the market for high-school dropouts, the demand curve for low-skilled labor decreased. The combination of increase in supply and decrease in demand resulted in lower wages for high-school dropouts. Because the college wage increased and the dropout wage decreased, the relative wage of college graduates increases.

TEST Your Understanding

1. Which of the following statements are true, and which are false?
   a. The poverty rate among the elderly exceeds the poverty rate among children.
   b. Most poor households have at least one part-time worker.
   c. A single parent can avoid poverty by getting a full-time job at the minimum wage.

2. How does the government determine the poverty budget for a three-person household?

3. Why is the poverty rate low when the economy is growing rapidly, and why does it increase when the economy slows down?

An extreme version of the problems experienced by the poor is homelessness. The McKinney Homeless Assistance Act of 1987 defines a homeless person as someone who sleeps (1) outside, (2) inside in places not intended for sleeping (e.g., the lobby of a public building), or (3) in housing shelters (places providing temporary housing). On a given night in the United States, the homeless population is between 250,000 and 350,000. About three-fourths of the homeless are single men, and 15% are children.[6]

Most homeless adults have suffered serious economic and social difficulties. About half are high-school dropouts, and about one in five has spent some time in a mental hospital. About one in three homeless people has spent some time as a patient in a chemical-dependency program. Over half of the homeless have spent time in jail (a short period for misdemeanor violations), and about one-quarter have spent time in prison (longer periods for felony violations). About one in five homeless people has attempted suicide.

What causes homelessness? From an economic perspective, a person will be homeless if his or her income is low enough relative to the price of housing that it is not sensible—or not even possible—to pur- chase housing services. The homeless rate varies considerably across metropolitan areas, the highest rates being in cities where low-quality housing is expensive, job growth is slow, welfare payments are low, and the percentage of the mentally ill in institutions is low.[7]

One factor in the growth of the homeless population in the last few decades was the loss of low-quality housing in large cities. Historically, many of the poor lived in boarding houses, rooming houses, and residential hotels (also known as single-room occupancy units, or SROs). This housing had small living quarters, shared bathrooms, and limited kitchen facilities, but it was affordable for most pensioners and day laborers. During the 1970s and 1980s, much of the SRO stock was eliminated, a result of urban renewal and conversion to other uses. Many of the hotels and large houses that were used for boarding or rooming houses have been renovated for higher-income households. Nationwide, over 1 million SRO units were lost during the 1970s and 1980s. The loss of SROs contributed to the homeless problem by decreasing the supply of low-quality housing and increasing its price.

The Aging of Society

In 1950, there were seven people aged 24 to 64 (prime working age) for every person 65 years and older. By 1990, that ratio had fallen to 4.8. Current projections indicate that by the year 2030, there will be only 2.8 people of working age for every person over retirement age. This dramatic change in the age distribution of our population will force us to reexamine many of our social programs.

These changes are not occurring only in the United States. Many countries around the world, both developed and developing countries, are facing an aging population in the future. Figure 19.4 presents projections of the **dependency ratio**, defined as the ratio of the population over 65 years of age to the population between 20 and 65, in Japan and the United States. As the diagram indicates, by the year 2050, the United States is projected to have a dependency ratio of 37%, while Japan is projected to have a much higher dependency ratio of 60.1%. This means that in the year 2050, Japan will have only 1.66 (1/0.601) people between the ages of 20 and 65 for every person over the age of 65.

Dependency ratio: The ratio of the population over 65 years of age to the population between 20 and 65.

The Social Security System

Social Security: A government program that provides retirement, survivor, and disability benefits.

As we saw earlier in this chapter, the poverty rate among the elderly is much lower than the poverty rate for other age groups. The reason for this low rate of poverty is the Social Security system. Started in 1935 during the depths of the Great Depression, the **Social Security** system provides retirement and health benefits to the elderly. It is one of our

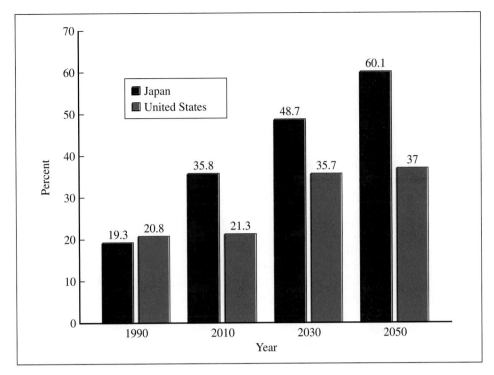

Figure 19.4
Dependency Ratios for Japan and the United States
The dependency ratio is the ratio of the population over 65 years to the population between 20 and 65 years.
Source: Congressional Budget Office.

most popular social programs and has widespread support throughout the entire political system.

The Social Security system is complex and has many different provisions. Here is a basic overview:

- Over 92% of the civilian workforce is included in the Social Security system today. (Not all employment is covered by Social Security, and there are minimum earning requirements.)

- Workers who are included in Social Security receive either retirement benefits at the age of 65 or reduced benefits at the age of 62.

- A recipient with a dependent wife, husband, or child receives 50% more than a recipient without dependents.

- If a worker dies, survivor benefits are provided to the family.

- Social Security also provides disability payments for workers who suffer from an illness that prevents them from working for a minimum of a year.

In addition to these retirement provisions, the other major part of the Social Security system is **Medicare**, health coverage for the elderly. Medicare consists of both hospital insurance and supplementary medical insurance for doctor services and other services outside the hospital. Medicare hospital benefits are provided automatically to workers and their married partners when they reach the age of 65. Supplementary medical insurance is voluntary and requires monthly payments, which are typically only about one-quarter of the cost of equivalent private insurance. Widows and widowers of deceased workers are also covered at the age of 65.

Medicare: A government program that provides health benefits to people over 65 years of age.

The Social Security system (except for supplementary medical insurance) is financed through flat payroll taxes on both employees and employers. Each contributes one-half the total tax. For all parts of the system except the hospital portion of Medicare, there is a yearly maximum amount (or "cap") beyond which a worker does not contribute in a given year.

The retirement benefits, survivor benefits, and disability benefits that Social Security pays are determined by an average of the wages the worker earned during employment. The Social Security system calculates a replacement rate for each worker, which is the fraction of their average wage they will receive. Replacement rates are higher for workers who earned lower wages. Therefore, the Social Security system redistributes income to retirees who had low wages and away from retirees who had higher wages. Despite the fact that the system is financed with a flat payroll tax, the system as a whole redistributes income toward low-wage workers. As a result, the system is viewed as a **social insurance** system, a program that takes care of those who have had bad luck, possess low skills, or experience misfortunes.

Social insurance: A system that compensates individuals for bad luck or low skills.

The Coming Financing Crisis

From nearly the beginning of the Social Security system, the payroll taxes paid by employees and employers in any given year paid for the benefits received by retirees in that same year. Thus, the payments that an employer and an employee made did not go into an account earmarked for that worker's retirement. Instead, these dollars were paid out immediately to current recipients. This type of financing mechanism is called a **pay-as-you-go** system.

Pay-as-you-go: A system that uses revenue collected this year to pay for benefits paid to recipients this year.

In the early days of the Social Security system, pay-as-you-go worked quite well. As long as the elderly population is small relative to the working population, it does not take a high level of payroll taxes to finance retirements. Throughout much of its history, retirees under Social Security received vastly more in benefits than they paid in taxes. In fact, the first recipient paid $22 in Social Security taxes, lived to the age of 99, and collected $20,000 in benefits.[8] The easy times for Social Security are behind us for two reasons:

- As we will see later in the chapter, medical costs have risen rapidly, and they are expected to continue rising. Rising medical costs increase the costs of Medicare.

- As the average age of the population increases, there will be fewer workers for each retiree.

Given rising medical costs and an aging population, it will be costly to continue providing the same level of payments to the recipients of Social Security and Medicare. How high must payroll taxes go to support the system at its current benefit levels? Projections far into the future are risky, but a typical estimate is that the combined employer-employee payroll tax rates, now 15.3%, may have to rise to about 26%.[9] Income taxes and other taxes come on top of these payroll taxes. Assuming that federal and state income taxes stay in the same range, this would mean the average worker could easily face total taxes between 50% and 60% of his or her income. While some European countries have tax rates this high, such rates would bring about a dramatic change in our fiscal system.

Challenge: Financing the Elderly

What are the options for dealing with the problem of supporting an aging population? There are three possible approaches.

1. Preserve Future Benefits But Invest More Today

If we increased our rate of investment today, we could increase the living standards of the next generation. With higher living standards, the next generation would be better able to bear the burden of financing Social Security and Medicare payments. We could view this as a generational compact or deal: Workers today will provide the next generation with higher living standards by consuming less and investing more, as long as the next generation provides Social Security and Medicare benefits to the members of the current generation when they retire.

Although this may seem like a reasonable bargain, higher living standards for future generations will not reduce the tax rates they face. As increased investment by today's generations raises real income over time, retirement benefits will rise because they are largely determined by wages near retirement. If current generations save more, they will receive larger retirement benefits. Total tax rates for the average worker in future generations could still range between 50% and 60%. Looking back, will future workers remember their bargain? Or will they just be dissatisfied with the high rates of taxation? Raising the standard of living for future generations does nothing to alleviate the redistribution between generations that will occur if the system is not changed.

2. Cut Benefits

A second possibility is to reduce benefits. Obviously, reducing benefits for current retirees or those nearing retirement would be perceived as unfair. However, it is possible to cut future benefits. For example, the retirement age is already scheduled to be increased in the twenty-first century, and further increases are possible. In addition, unlike private retirement plans, Social Security benefits are currently fully adjusted for inflation. Reducing the inflation adjustment could provide considerable long-run savings.

But we should not underestimate the degree of difficulty in even making these changes. Retirement ages, for example, have drifted down in recent years from an average age of 65 to 62. Workers anticipating an earlier retirement will not want to see benefits held off until a later age. Similarly, many elderly people worry that they will not have sufficient assets and that their only benefits will be from Social Security. If these benefits are not protected against inflation, will the elderly be forced into poverty?

3. Privatize the Entire System

A third—perhaps shocking—alternative would be to make the benefits received by any person depend directly on his or her own contribution. In other words, we could privatize the entire system. The government would require everyone to make at least a minimum contribution, but each contributor would be free to direct his or her funds among an approved set of alternatives. On retirement, the contributor could draw on his or her accumulated savings. Chile recently replaced its pay-as-you-go system with a fully funded privatized system.

Proponents of a privatized system point to several advantages. First, it would alleviate future workers from the burden of paying excessive taxes. Second, workers could invest their savings in the stock market. Historically the rate of return in the stock market has been high enough that money invested there would generate a more generous retirement plan than provided by the same amount of money put into the Social Security System. Third, total saving and investment in the economy are likely to increase as workers save for their own retirements rather than simply waiting to receive Social Security benefits as in the current system.

Nonetheless, there are some disadvantages to replacing our current system. First, there are transition problems. Consider a woman who is now 50 years old and anticipates retiring in 15 years. During her working career, she did not save very much because she knew that she would receive Social Security; so during all her working years, she paid taxes that financed the retirement of others. If we suddenly privatized the system, she would have only 15 years to save for her retirement, which is not sufficient time to set aside funds for her old age. Clearly, we would not think this was fair and would have to design some transition system that would supplement her savings. Still, she gets a raw deal: In the past, she paid for others to retire, and now she must pay for part of her own retirement as well. There is no way to escape this problem. During a transition, some groups in society will have to pay both for their own retirement and for the retirement of others.

Second, full privatization of the Social Security system would effectively end our current system of social insurance. Under the current system, if the breadwinner in the household dies, the family receives survivor benefits. Under full privatization, these benefits would not be available unless the government created a new program. Similarly, if a worker made a series of poor investments with his or her retirement funds and then died, would the widow or widower live in poverty?

As we enter the twenty-first century, the funding of Social Security and Medicare will be debated extensively. In 2001, President Bush appointed a commission to study the partial privatization of Social Security. The commission will confront all the issues we've raised, including the difficult issues associated with making the transition from the current system to an alternative system. As we have seen, some fundamental aspects of the nature of our society are at stake in this debate.

TEST Your Understanding

4. Because Social Security is financed by a flat payroll tax with a cap, it redistributes income from low-wage earners to high-wage earners. True or false? Explain.

5. Explain why the age distribution in a society matters for a pay-as-you-go system.

6. List two advantages and two disadvantages of privatizing the Social Security system.

Health Care

In recent years, the rising cost of health care for the poor and elderly has caused budgetary problems for the federal and state governments. At the same time, workers and businesses in the private sector find themselves struggling to afford health care. In the last part of the chapter, we look at our health-care system and the challenges we face in controlling costs and providing care.

Problems with Our Health-Care System

Despite the availability of the latest technology, many social scientists believe that our health system has serious difficulties. Over the last 40 years, real spending per person on medical care has risen at a rate of over 4% a year. Such rapid growth has meant that we are devoting an increasing fraction of our resources to health care. From 1960 to 1997, the share of total income devoted to health care rose from 6% to 13.6%. As shown by Figure 19.5, compared to other developed countries, the United States spends a much higher fraction of its total income on health care. The United Kingdom, for example, devotes 6.7% of its total income to health care, and Japan spends 7.6% of its total income.

In principle, there is no reason why such a high level of spending in the United States might not be worthwhile. But most observers believe that much of our spending is not worthwhile. In making spending decisions, we should be guided by the marginal principle.

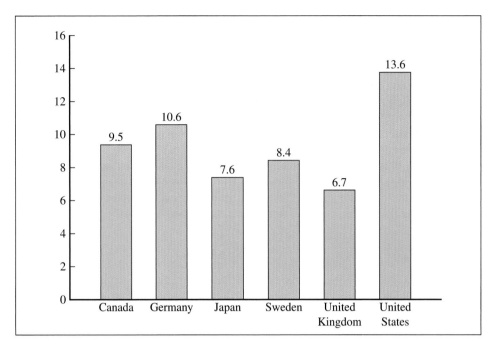

Figure 19.5
Health Expenditure as Percent of Total Income (Gross Domestic Product), 1999
The United States spends a relatively large fraction of total income on health care.

Source: OECD Health Data, 2000.

Marginal **PRINCIPLE**

Increase the level of an activity if its marginal benefit exceeds its marginal cost, but reduce the level if the marginal cost exceeds the marginal benefit. If possible, pick that level at which the marginal benefit equals the marginal cost.

In the health sector, we constantly violate the marginal principle: We make expenditures of little marginal value that have substantial marginal costs. For example, studies suggest that as many as one-fourth of common medical procedures for the elderly have costs that exceed the benefits.[10] The violation of the marginal principle is partly a result of the fact that physicians have traditionally been trained to heal the sick, not to make economic decisions. Another factor is the temptation to use new technology, regardless of its cost. Many patients and physicians choose high-cost treatments even when their advantage over lower-cost treatments is minimal.

Traditional health-care insurance does not provide physicians an incentive to control costs. Under a traditional insurance policy, insurance companies pay for any treatment. If doctors and hospitals are fully reimbursed for their expenses, they have little incentive to discourage patients from getting expensive care even if the marginal benefit of that care is extremely low. In recent years, many employers have required their employees to join health-maintenance organizations (HMOs), in which physicians are paid a fixed amount per patient regardless of the treatments that are actually provided. Under this type of system, doctors and hospitals have an incentive to contain costs. Because they are paid a fixed amount per patient, their profits increase as they reduce their costs. A health system in which HMOs and similar organizations compete for patients is commonly known as **managed competition**.

A second problem caused by the health-care insurance system is that many people are not insured. Insurance companies want to avoid providing insurance to people who have a high risk of large medical bills. If an insurance company is providing insurance to the employees of a large firm, it probably has a good idea of the total risk it faces because

Managed competition: A health system in which organizations such as HMOs compete for patients.

the employees of the large firm are likely to be a typical cross section of the labor force. But if it offers insurance policies to individuals, those at high risk (whom the insurance company cannot easily distinguish from those at low risk) will have the greatest incentives to purchase the policies. The insurance companies recognize this problem and charge high rates for individual policies or to small firms. Because of these high costs, many individuals and workers in small firms do not buy insurance.

In 2000, about 43 million people (about 15% of the population) were not covered by health insurance. Almost all the elderly are covered through Medicare, and many of the poor are covered under Medicaid. Most U.S. workers receive their health insurance through their employers. The uninsured are the people and their families who do not receive insurance through their employers, are unemployed or between jobs, or are poor but do not qualify for Medicaid in their state. People who do not have health insurance obtain care for emergencies but fail to receive routine, and less costly, preventive care.

Challenge: Reforming the System

It appears that there is little chance of an immediate, radical, sweeping reform of the health system. During 1993–1994, the Clinton administration tried to provide universal coverage, in part by requiring all firms to provide health insurance to their employees. This plan was soundly defeated because of its sheer complexity and the difficulties of developing policies to subsidize small firms so that they could provide insurance to their employees. However, as the costs of health care continue to grow and large numbers of people remain uninsured, there will be pressures for change. Let's look at some of the key issues that will be debated in the twenty-first century.

1. Work Toward Universal Coverage

The problem of so many uninsured people does not show any signs of improving. Although the defeat of the Clinton health plan probably means that universal coverage cannot be achieved by requiring employers to provide health insurance for all workers, there may be other solutions. Stanford health economist Victor Fuchs has suggested a voucher plan in which everyone would receive a health voucher to purchase insurance.[11] The difficulty with any voucher plan is that new taxes would be necessary to finance it. While it would be possible to raise rates on existing taxes to finance such a plan, most European countries that provide universal coverage have a value-added tax, essentially a national sales tax. Clearly, introducing a new tax or raising existing tax rates to finance a voucher plan would be very controversial and would require a broad political consensus that health reform is absolutely necessary.

Complex and expensive heart operations are commonplace today.

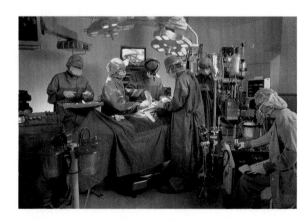

2. Reform Medicare

Some politicians and policymakers have suggested that managed competition needs to be introduced into Medicare to provide incentives to reduce costs. This would be a major departure from the current system because few of the elderly are currently enrolled in HMOs. Because Medicare expenses directly affect the federal budget, politicians are keenly aware of the need to reduce costs and have been discussing this option, despite resistance among the elderly, who want to ensure that the treatment they would receive from HMOs matches the quality of their current care.

3. Reform Insurance Markets

How can we ensure that everyone has access to some type of health insurance? What types of new laws or regulations are needed to address some of the problems in the market for insurance? Several states have experimented with plans to require insurance companies to provide broad coverage, that is, coverage to more firms and their workers. This approach has been difficult to implement because large firms that provide insurance to their own employees are, by federal law, exempt from state insurance laws.

Even with laws that require broad coverage, some economists believe subsidies would be required to entice many of the uninsured to purchase insurance. Many young and healthy people would rather take their chances and hope they stay healthy rather than pay for health insurance.

4. Manage Technological Change

How can we benefit from technological advance in medicine without bankrupting our society? Can the private market handle this problem? Or should the government play an active role in evaluating advances in medical technology? Fuchs proposed a small tax on health providers to fund a private institute devoted to assessing new medical technologies. Ideally, this institution would be able to uncover the technological advances for which marginal benefits truly exceed marginal costs.

TEST Your Understanding

7. Explain how to use the marginal principle to guide our choice of medical technology.

8. Why is the price of medical insurance for employees of a large firm lower than the price of medical insurance for an individual?

9. What is universal coverage? Why is it so difficult to achieve?

Using the **TOOLS**

In this chapter, we've explored some of the policy challenges associated with poverty, Social Security, and the health-care system. Here are some opportunities to do your own economic analysis.

APPLICATIONS

1. Welfare Reform and Wages of Low-Skilled Labor

Consider the market for low-skilled labor in a large metropolitan area. The initial wage is $6.00 per hour, and the initial quantity is 100 million hours per day. The elasticity of supply of labor for the market is 0.20, and the elasticity of demand is 1.0. Suppose welfare reform increases the supply of low-skilled labor in the city by 6%. Predict the effects of welfare reform on the equilibrium wage and equilibrium quantity of low-skilled labor. How does welfare reform affect the weekly pay of a low-skilled worker who worked 40 hours per week before the reform and continues to work 40 hours per week?

2. Chile's Transition to a Private Pension System

When Chile made the transition from a pay-as-you-go social security system to a private system, it had a very young population. Compared to the United States, the ratio of working-age people to retirees was three times as high. How did the age structure in Chile make it easier to move to a private system?

3. Evaluating Medical Technology

Suppose new technology enables patients of heart surgery to return to work one week earlier. The new technology is as safe as the old technology but very expensive. Hospitals and patients both want to use this new technology, and you must decide whether to allow Medicare to reimburse them. What information do you need before you make your recommendation?

Summary

We explored three policy issues that the United States and other countries will face in the twenty-first century. We will continue to grapple with poverty. At the same time, the aging of the population and the continued escalation of the cost of health care will pose new and difficult challenges. Here are the main points of the chapter.

1. The main causes of poverty are inadequate education, racial segregation, a weak economy, racial and gender discrimination in the labor market, and single parenthood.

2. Dramatic changes in the age distribution of the population—fewer workers per retiree—will force many countries to modify programs for the elderly.

In the United States, reform efforts have focused on the Social Security system, with proposals to cut benefits or privatize the system.

3. Compared to other developed countries, the United States spends a much larger fraction of its income on health care. The decisions to spend money on health care often violate the marginal principle.

4. About 15% of people in the United States are not covered by health insurance, and given the failure of recent proposals for universal coverage, there is no sign that the problem of the uninsured will be solved soon.

Key Terms

dependency ratio, 406
household, 400
managed competition, 411

Medicare, 407
pay-as-you-go, 408
poverty budget, 400

social insurance, 408
Social Security, 406

Problems and Discussion Questions

1. During the 1980s, the wages of older less-educated workers (those in their 40s) increased relative to the wages of young less-educated workers (those in their 20s). Explain why this could occur.

2. Suppose that the birth rate begins to fall. How would this affect a pay-as-you-go social security system?

3. Suppose state governments increased the funding for state colleges and universities, allowing the nationwide college enrollment to increase by 20%. Predict the effect of the increase in enrollment on the wage of college graduates relative to the wage of high-school graduates.

4. Explain why an HMO might encourage pregnant women to have regular appointments with their doctors.

5. What is a disadvantage of having employers provide health insurance?

6. Why might replacing a pay-as-you-go system with private pensions increase total savings?

7. **Web Exercise.** Visit the Web site of the U.S. Census bureau for the latest facts on poverty rates [*http://www.census.gov/hhes/www/poverty.html*]. Click on "Poverty in the United States" once and then again on the next page. Then click on "State Poverty Data" to check the poverty rate in your state. How does it compare to the national average?

8. **Web Exercise.** Visit the Web site of the Social Security Administration [*http://www.ssa.gov*] and access the on-line publications site [*http://www.ssa.gov/pubs*] to find publications that help you answer the following questions:

   a. What are the current tax rates for Social Security and Medicare?

   b. How much does your employer pay in Social Security and Medicare taxes?

   c. How is the money raised through these taxes used?

Take It to the Net

We invite you to visit the O'Sullivan/Sheffrin page on the Prentice Hall Web site at::
http://www.prenhall.com/osullivan/ for additional World Wide Web exercise for this chapter.

Model Answers to Questions

Chapter-Opening Questions

1. The poverty rate for children (19.9%) is higher than the poverty rate for senior citizens (10.5%).

2. The homeless rate is highest in cities where low-quality housing is expensive, job growth is slow, welfare payments are low, and the percentage of the mentally ill in institutions is low.

3. Privatizing Social Security may increase savings and investment in the economy. On the other hand, it would provide less protection for people who, because of bad luck or low skills, have low income.

4. Technological change has offered many opportunities for improving health care. However, society has not weighed the benefits from medical advances against their costs. The result has been continuing increases in costs.

Test Your Understanding

1. Statements (a) and (c) are false. Children have a higher poverty rate (a) and the minimum wage is not high enough to avoid poverty (c). Statement (b) is true.

2. The government estimates the food budget for the household and multiplies by 3.

3. Low-skilled workers are the last hired when the economy is growing and the first fired when the economy slows down.

4. False. The benefit structure redistributes income because the replacement rates are higher for lower-wage workers.

5. The age structure matters because the more workers per senior citizen, the lower the required tax rate.

6. Advantages: higher rates of return on investment and increased saving for society. Disadvantages: costs of making the transition and a weakening of the social-insurance aspects of the system.

7. The marginal principle tells us to adopt a new technology if its marginal benefit exceeds its marginal cost.

8. For a large firm, the average medical expense per employee will be close to the average expense for the entire U.S. labor force. If insurance is offered to individuals, people with the highest medical expenses have the greatest incentive to purchase the insurance.

9. Under universal coverage, all workers would be enrolled in medical insurance plans. The Clinton

plan for universal coverage was defeated because of the difficulty of developing policies to subsidize the insurance costs of small firms.

Using the Tools

1. **Welfare Reform and Wages of Low-Skilled Labor.** The supply curve shifts to the right by 6%. Use the formula for predicting price changes from changes in supply (Chapter 5): The percentage change in the price (the wage) is 5% = 6% / (0.20 + 1.0)$. The wage drops by 5%, from $6.00 to $5.70 per hour. Use the formula for the price elasticity of demand to predict the change in quantity of hours worked as we move downward along the market demand curve; the change in quantity is 5%. For a worker who initially worked 40 hours per week, welfare reform decreases weekly income from $240 to $228.

2. **Chile's Transition to a Private Pension System.** During any transition period from a pay-as-you-go system, it will be necessary to provide support for the retired and those near retirement. Managing this transition is easier if there is a young population because the necessary tax rate will be lower as more workers will be contributing.

3. **Evaluating Medical Technology.** You need to compare the marginal benefit of the new technology to its marginal cost. The marginal benefit is the value of returning people to work one week earlier. The marginal cost is the extra cost of this procedure over the original procedure. If there are no other considerations, the new technology should be used only if its marginal benefit exceeds its marginal cost.

Notes

1. U.S. Bureau of the Census, Current Population Reports, Series P60-201, *Poverty in the United States, 1997* (Washington, DC: U.S. Government Printing Office, 1998).

2. David M. Cutler and Edward L. Glaeser, "Are Ghettos Good or Bad?," *Quarterly Journal of Economics,* 1997, pp. 827–872.

3. Alan B. Kreuger, "How Computers Have Changed the Wage Structure: Evidence from Microdata, 1984–1989," *Quarterly Journal of Economics*, vol. 108, 1993, pp. 33–60.

4. Harry J. Holzer, "Employer Demand, AFDC Recipients, and Labor Market Policy," Institute for Research on Poverty Discussion Paper No. 1115-96, 1996.

5. Isabel Sawhill, "From Welfare to Work: Making Welfare a Was Station, Not a Way of Life," *Brookings Review*, Summer 2001, pp. 4–7.

6. Martha R. Burt, *Over the Edge: The Growth of Homelessness in the 1980s* (New York: Sage, 1992).

7. Marjorie Honig and Randall K. Filer, "Causes of Intercity Variation in Homelessness," *American Economic Review*, vol. 83, 1993, pp. 248–255.

8. "Your Stake in the Fight," *Consumer Reports*, September 1981, pp. 503–510.

9. For estimates of future tax rates, see Henry Aaron, Barry Bosworth, and Gary Burtless, *Can America Afford to Grow Old?* (Washington, DC: Brookings Institution, 1989).

10. For a discussion of inefficient spending in the health care system, see David Cutler, "Cutting Costs and Improving Health Care," in *The Problem That Won't Go Away*, edited by Henry Aaron (Washington, DC: Brookings Institution, 1996), pp. 250–265.

11. Victor Fuchs, "Economics, Values, and Health Reform," *American Economic Review*, March 1996, pp. 1–26.

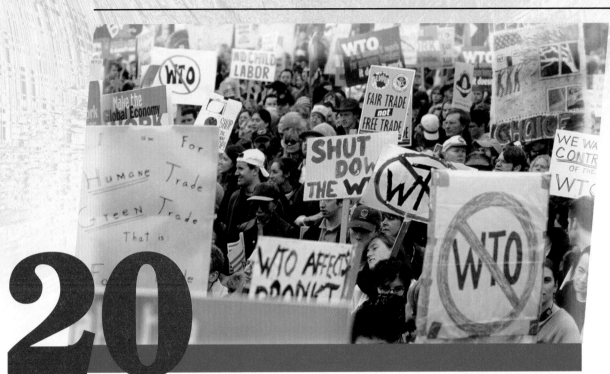

20

International Trade and Public Policy

In November 1999, large numbers of colorful protestors gathered in Seattle, Washington, at a meeting of world leaders, to express their indignation about recent developments in international trade, multinational corporations, and international organizations. Protestors carried signs denouncing the WTO, or World Trade Organization, a recently created and relatively obscure international agency.

The protest at times turned violent and protestors smashed windows in downtown Seattle. Protestors returned to their homes fondly remembering the "spirit of Seattle." The intensity of the protest took many observers by surprise. Since World War II, trade has grown steadily and the world has become more interdependent. Were the protestors just expressing discontent about modern life or were there fundamental problems with our system of international trade?

As the world economy grows, our policies toward international trade become ever more important. Many people view trade as a "zero-sum game." They believe that if one country gains from international trade, another must lose. Based on this belief, they advocate restricting trade with other countries. Indeed, the United States does restrict trade in many areas, for example, protecting jobs in apparel and steel. One lesson from this chapter is that free trade could, in principle, make everyone better off. The challenge for policymakers is to develop a set of principles that accomplish this goal—or come as close as possible to accomplishing it.

In this chapter, we discuss the rationale for international trade, and we explore the effects of policies that restrict trade. Here are some of the practical questions that we answer:

1. What are the trade-offs associated with free trade? Who wins? Who loses?
2. Why is a tariff (a tax on an imported good) superior to an import quota?
3. Why might a firm's export price be less than its domestic price? (The domestic price is the price in the domestic market.)
4. Do trade laws inhibit environmental protection?
5. Does trade increase income inequality?

Benefits from Specialization and Trade

If your nation produced everything it consumed, it would not be dependent on any other nation for its economic livelihood. If you were put in charge of your nation, would you pursue such a policy of national self-sufficiency? Although self-sufficiency may sound appealing, it would be better to specialize in some products and trade some of those products with other nations for products that your nation doesn't produce. You saw in Chapter 3 that specialization and exchange can make both parties better off. In this chapter, we use a simple example to explain the benefits of specialization and international trade between two nations.

Let's say there are two nations, each produces computer chips and shirts, and each nation consumes computer chips and shirts. Table 20.1 shows the daily output of the two goods for the two nations, Shirtland and Chipland. In a single day, Shirtland can produce a maximum of either 108 shirts or 36 computer chips, while Chipland can produce a maximum of either 120 shirts or 120 computer chips. The last two rows of the table show the opportunity costs of the two goods. Recall the principle of opportunity cost:

PRINCIPLE of Opportunity Cost

The opportunity cost of something is what you sacrifice to get it.

In Chipland, there is a one-for-one trade-off of shirts and chips: The opportunity cost of one shirt is one chip, and the opportunity cost of one chip is one shirt. In Shirtland, people can produce three times as many shirts as chips in a given amount of time: The opportunity cost of one chip is three shirts; that is, by producing one chip, we sacrifice three shirts; conversely, the opportunity cost of one shirt is one-third of a chip.

Production possibilities curve:
A curve showing the combinations of two goods that can be produced by an economy, assuming that all resources are fully employed.

Production Possibilities Curve

Let's start by seeing what happens if each nation is self-sufficient. Each nation can use its resources (labor, land, buildings, machinery, equipment) to produce its own shirts and its own chips. The **production possibilities curve** shows all the feasible combinations of

Table 20.1 Output and Opportunity Cost

	Shirtland	Chipland
Shirts produced per day	108	120
Chips produced per day	36	120
Opportunity cost of shirts	1/3 chip	1 chip
Opportunity cost of chips	3 shirts	1 shirt

the two goods, assuming that the nation's resources are fully employed. This curve, which we discussed in earlier chapters, provides a sort of menu of production options. To keep things simple, we assume that the curve is a straight line, indicating a constant trade-off between the two goods. As shown by Shirtland's production possibilities curve in Figure 20.1, the following combinations of chips and shirts are possible.

1. All shirts and no chips: point *r*. If Shirtland uses all its resources to produce shirts, it will produce 108 shirts per day.
2. All chips and no shirts: point *t*. If Shirtland uses all its resources to produce chips, it will produce 36 chips per day.
3. Equal division of resources: point *h*. Shirtland could divide its resources between shirts and chips to produce daily 54 shirts and 18 chips.

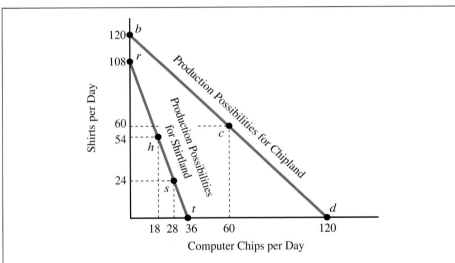

Figure 20.1
Production Possibilities Curve
The production possibilities curve shows the combinations of two goods that can be produced with a nation's resources. For Chipland, there is a one-for-one trade-off is between the two goods. For Shirtland, the trade-off is three shirts for every computer chip. In the absence of trade, Shirtland picks point *s* (28 chips and 24 shirts), and Chipland picks point *c* (60 chips and 60 shirts).

Shirtland Possibilites

Point	Shirts	Chips
r	108	0
h	54	18
s	24	28
t	0	36

Chipland Possibilities

Point	Shirts	Chips
b	120	0
c	60	60
d	0	120

All the other points on the line connecting points r and t are also feasible. One option is point s, with 28 chips and 24 shirts. The slope of the curve is the opportunity cost of computer chips: one chip per three shirts. Figure 20.1 also shows the production possibilities curve for Chipland. This nation can produce daily 120 shirts and no chips (point b), 120 chips and no shirts (point d), or any combination of chips and shirts between these two points. In Chipland, the trade-off is one shirt per computer chip: The opportunity cost of a chip is one shirt, so the slope of the production possibilities curve is 1.0.

Each nation could decide to be self-sufficient in chips and shirts. In other words, each nation could pick a point on its production possibilities curve and produce everything it wants to consume. For example, Shirtland could pick point s, producing daily 28 chips and 24 shirts, and Chipland could pick point c, producing daily 60 chips and 60 shirts. In the language of international trade, this is a case of **autarky**, or self-sufficiency (in Greek, *aut* means "self" and *arke* means "to suffice").

Autarky: A situation in which each country is self-sufficient, so there is no trade.

Comparative Advantage and the Terms of Trade

Would the two nations be better off if each nation specialized in the production of one good and traded with the other nation? To decide which nation should produce a particular good, we need to figure out which nation has a lower opportunity cost for that good. As you saw in Chapter 3, the nation with the lower opportunity cost has a **comparative advantage** in producing that good.

Comparative advantage: The ability of one nation to produce a particular good at an opportunity cost that is lower than the opportunity cost of another nation in producing the same good.

1. Chips produced in Chipland. The opportunity cost of one chip is one shirt in Chipland, and the opportunity cost of one chip is three shirts in Shirtland. Chipland has a comparative advantage in the production of chips. Because Chipland sacrifices fewer shirts to produce one chip, Chipland should produce chips.

2. Shirts produced in Shirtland. The opportunity cost of one shirt is one chip in Chipland, and the opportunity cost of one shirt is 1/3 of a chip in Shirtland. Shirtland has a comparative advantage in the production of shirts. Shirtland sacrifices fewer chips to produce one shirt, so Shirtland should produce shirts.

Trade will make it possible for people in each specialized nation to consume both goods. At what rate will the two nations exchange shirts and chips? To determine the **terms of trade**, let's look at how much Shirtland is willing to pay to get one chip and how much Chipland is willing to accept to give up one chip.

Terms of trade: The rate at which two goods will be exchanged.

1. To get one chip, Shirtland is willing to pay up to three shirts. That's how many shirts it would sacrifice if it produced its own chip: Shirtland's opportunity cost of one chip is three shirts. For example, if the nations agree to exchange two shirts per chip, Shirtland could rearrange its production, producing one less chip but three more shirts. After exchanging two of the newly produced shirts for one chip, Shirtland will have the same number of chips but one additional shirt.

2. To give up one chip, Chipland is willing to accept any amount greater than one shirt: Chipland's opportunity cost of one chip is one shirt. For example, if the nations agree to exchange two shirts per chip, Chipland could rearrange its production, producing one more chip and one less shirt. After it exchanges the newly produced chip for two shirts, Chipland will have the same number of chips but one additional shirt.

There is an opportunity for mutually beneficial trade because the willingness to pay—three shirts by Shirtland—exceeds the willingness to accept—one shirt by Chipland. It's possible the two countries will split the difference between the willingness to pay and the willingness to accept, exchanging two shirts per chip.

The Consumption Possibilities Curve

A nation that decides to specialize and trade will not be limited to the options shown by its own production possibilities curve. The **consumption possibilities curve** shows the combinations of two goods (computer chips and shirts in our example) that a nation can consume when it specializes in one good and trades with another nation.

Figure 20.2 shows the consumption possibilities curve for our two nations, assuming that they exchange two shirts per chip.

Consumption possibilities curve: A curve showing the combinations of two goods that can be consumed in a nation when that nation specializes in producing a particular good and trades with another nation.

- In panel A, Chipland will specialize in chips, the good for which it has a comparative advantage, so it produces 120 chips (point *d*). Given the terms of trade, Chipland can exchange 40 chips for 80 shirts, leading to point *x* on the consumption possibilities curve.

- In panel B, Shirtland specializes in shirts (point *r*) and can exchange 80 shirts for 40 chips, leading to point *y* on its consumption possibilities frontier.

How do the outcomes with specialization and trade compare to the autarky outcomes? Chipland moves from point *c* (autarky) to point *x*, so trade increases the consumption of each good by 20 units. Shirtland moves from point *s* to point *y*, so this nation consumes 12 additional chips and 4 additional shirts.

In Figure 20.2, each consumption possibilities curve lies above the nation's production possibilities curves, meaning that each nation has more options about how much to consume under specialization and trade. In most cases, a nation picks a point on the consumption possibilities curve that provides more of each good.

The Employment Effects of Free Trade

You've now seen that trade allows each nation to consume more of each good. But we haven't yet discussed the effects of trade on employment. Under free trade, each nation will begin to specialize in a single good, causing considerable changes in the country's employment in different industries. In Chipland, the chip industry doubles in size—output increases from 60 to 120 chips per day—while the shirt industry disappears.

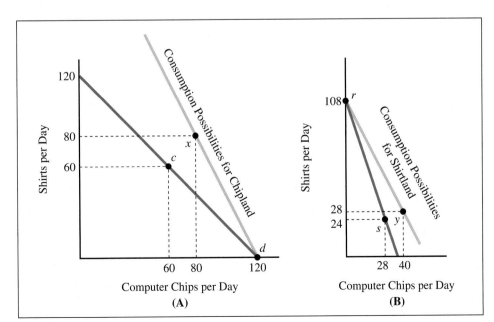

(A)

(B)

Figure 20.2
Consumption Possibilities Curve
The consumption possibilities curve shows the combinations of computer chips and shirts that can be consumed if each country specializes and trades. In panel A, Chipland produces 120 chips and trades 40 of these chips to Shirtland for 80 shirts. In panel B, Shirtland produces 108 shirts and trades 80 of these shirts to Chipland for 40 chips.

Workers and other resources will leave the shirt industry and move to the chip industry. In Shirtland, the flow is in the opposite direction: Workers and other resources move from the chip industry to the shirt industry.

Is free trade good for everyone? Switching from self-sufficiency to specialization and trade increases consumption in both nations, so on average, people in each nation will benefit from free trade. Some people will be harmed by free trade. In Chipland, people in the shirt industry will lose their jobs when the shirt industry disappears. Some workers can easily move into the expanding computer-chip industry; for these workers, free trade is likely to be beneficial. Other shirt workers will be unable to make the move to the chip industry; they will be forced to accept lower-paying jobs or face unemployment. Free trade is likely to make these displaced workers worse off.

There is a saying, "Where you stand on an issue depends on where you sit." In our example, a worker sitting at a sewing machine in Chipland is likely to oppose free trade because that worker is likely to lose his or her job. A worker sitting at a workstation in a computer-chip fabrication facility is likely to support free trade because the resulting increase in computer-chip exports will generate more employment opportunities in the industry.

TEST Your Understanding

1. Use Figure 20.1 to complete the following statements with numbers: If Chipland starts at point *c* and decides to produce 10 more chips, it will produce _____ shirts. If Shirtland produces only 10 chips, it will produce _____ shirts.

2. In nation H, the opportunity cost of tables is five chairs, while in nation B, the opportunity cost of tables is only one chair. Which country should produce tables, and which should produce chairs?

3. Nations H and B split the difference between the willingness to pay for tables and the willingness to accept. What are the terms of trade?

4. List the two bits of information you need to draw the consumption possibilities curve for a particular nation.

5. In Figure 20.2, suppose the nations agree to exchange one shirt for each chip. Will the consumption possibilities curve for Chipland still be above its production possibilities curve?

Protectionist Policies

Now that you know the basic rationale for specialization and trade, we can explore the effects of public policies that restrict trade. We will consider four common import-restriction policies: an outright ban on imports, an import quota, voluntary export restraints, and a tariff.

Import Ban

To show how an import ban affects the market, let's start with an unrestricted market—no import ban. Figure 20.3 shows the market for shirts in Chipland, a nation with a comparative advantage in computer chips, not shirts. The domestic supply curve shows the quantity of shirts supplied by firms in Chipland. Looking at point *m*, we see that Chipland firms will not supply any shirts unless the price is at least $17 per shirt. The total supply curve for shirts, which shows the quantity supplied by both domestic firms and foreign firms (in Shirtland), lies to the right of the domestic supply curve. At each

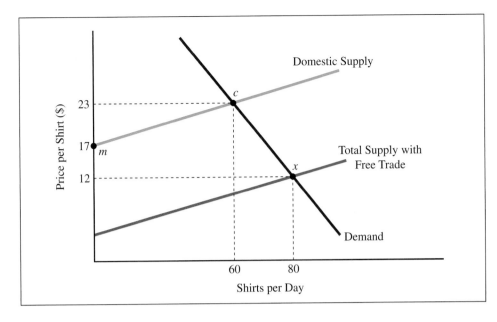

Figure 20.3
**Effects of an
Import Ban**
In the free-trade equilibrium,
demand intersects the total
supply curve at point x, with
a price of $12 and a quantity
of 80 shirts. If shirt imports
are banned, the equilibrium
is shown by the intersection
of the demand curve and the
domestic supply curve (point
c). The price increase to $23.

price, the total supply of shirts exceeds the domestic supply because foreign firms supply shirts too. Point x shows the free-trade equilibrium: The demand curve from domestic residents intersects the total supply curve at a price of $12 per shirt and a quantity of 80 shirts. Because this price is below the minimum price for domestic firms, domestic firms produce no shirts, and all the shirts in Chipland are imported from Shirtland.

What will happen if Chipland bans imported shirts? Foreign suppliers will disappear from the shirt market, so the total supply of shirts will be the domestic supply. In Figure 20.3, point c shows the equilibrium when Chipland bans imported shirts: The domestic demand curve intersects the domestic supply curve at a price of $23 per shirt and a quantity of 60 shirts. In other words, the decrease in supply resulting from the import ban increases the price and decreases the quantity of shirts.

Quotas and Voluntary Export Restraints

An alternative to an import ban is an **import quota**, defined as a limit on the amount of a good that can be imported. An import quota is a restrictive policy that falls between free trade and an import ban: Imports are decreased but not eliminated. Price falls between the price with free trade ($12 per shirt, as in our example) and the price with an import ban ($23 per shirt).

Figure 20.4 shows the effect of an import quota. Starting from the free-trade equilibrium at point x, an import quota will shift the total supply curve to the left: At each price there will be a smaller quantity of shirts because foreign suppliers cannot supply as many owing to the import limitation. The total supply curve when there is an import quota will lie between the domestic supply curve and the total supply curve under free trade. In the case of an import quota, the equilibrium occurs at point q, where the demand curve intersects the total supply curve, reflecting the import limitation. The $20 price per shirt with the import quota exceeds the $17 minimum price of domestic firms, so domestic firms supply 22 shirts (point e). Under a **voluntary export restraint [VER]**, an exporting nation voluntarily decreases its exports in an attempt to avoid more restrictive trade policies. A VER has the same effect as an import quota, which is illegal under the rules of the World Trade Organization (WTO), an organization with over 130 member nations that oversees the General Agreement on Tariffs and Trade and other international agreements. Although VERs are legal under WTO rules, they violate the spirit of

Import quota: A limit on the amount of a good that can be imported.

Voluntary export restraint [VER]: A scheme under which an exporting country voluntarily decreases its exports.

Figure 20.4

Market Effects of a Quota, a VER, or a Tariff

An import quota shifts the supply curve to the left. The market moves upward along the demand curve to point *q*, which is between point *x* (free trade) and *c* (an import ban). We can reach the same point with a tariff that shifts the total supply curve to the same position.

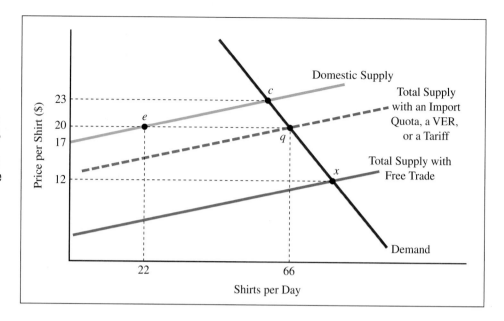

international trade agreements. Like a quota, a VER increases the price of the restricted good, allowing domestic firms to participate in the market.

A quota or a VER produces winners and losers. The winners include foreign and domestic shirt producers. In our example, foreign firms can sell shirts at a price of $20 instead of $12 each. In some cases, the government issues import licenses to some citizens, who can then buy shirts from foreign firms at a low price, such as $12, and sell the shirts at the higher domestic price, $20. In addition, the import restrictions allow domestic shirt firms to participate in the market, generating benefits for the firms and their workers. The losers are consumers, who pay a higher price for shirts.

Price Effects of Quotas and VERs

We know that consumers pay higher prices for goods that are subject to protectionist policies, but how much more? In the United States, voluntary export restraints for Japanese automobiles in effect in 1984 increased the price of a Japanese car by about $1,300 and increased the price of a domestic car by about $660.[1] In 1990, U.S. consumers incurred a total cost of $70 billion as a result of the nation's protectionist policies, about $270 per person per year.[2] The largest costs resulted from protectionist policies for apparel (about $84 per person) and textiles (about $13 per person).

Many European nations used VERs to limit their domestic market shares of Japanese automobiles. Figure 20.5 shows the cost of these policies in terms of their effects on the price of Japanese automobiles in several nations. For example, in France, the VERs increased the price of Japanese automobiles by 35%, compared to a 1% increase in price in Germany and a 55% higher price in Italy.

Tariffs

Tariff: A tax on an imported good.

An alternative to a quota or a VER is an import **tariff**, which is a tax on an imported good. We know from our earlier discussion of the market effects of taxes that a tax shifts the supply curve to the left and increases the equilibrium price. In Figure 20.4, suppose the tariff shifts the total supply curve, so it intersects the domestic demand curve at point *q*. In other words, we reach the same point we reached with the quota: Consumers pay the same $20 price per shirt, and domestic firms produce the same quantity: 22 shirts.

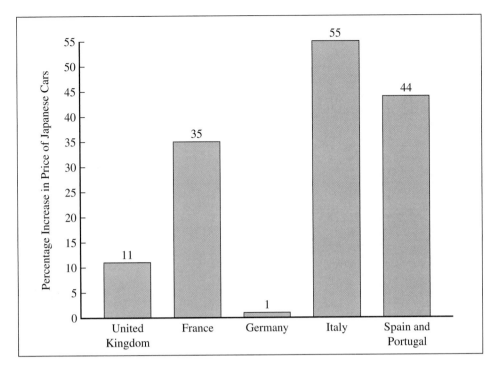

Figure 20.5

Price Effects of VERs for Japanese Cars
Many European nations use VERs to limit the number of Japanese cars imported. The VERs increase the price of Japanese cars.

Source: Alasdair Smith and Anthony J. Venables, "Cost of Voluntary Export Restraints in the European Car Market," Chapter 10 in *International Trade and Trade Policy*, edited by Ethanan Helpman and Asaaf Razin (Cambridge, MA: MIT Press, 1991).

There is one fundamental difference between a quota and a tariff. An import quota allows importers to buy shirts from foreign suppliers at a low price, say, $12 per shirt, and sell them for $20 each, the artificially high price. In other words, importers make money from the quota. Under a tariff, the government gets the money, collecting $8 per shirt from foreign suppliers. Citizens in Chipland will prefer the tariff to the quota because the government can use the revenue from the tariff to cut other taxes or expand public programs.

Responses to Protectionist Policies

A restriction on imports is likely to cause further restrictions on trade. For example, if Chipland bans shirt imports, the shirt industry in Shirtland may call for retaliation in the form of a ban on computer chips from Chipland. A trade war of this sort could escalate to the point at which the two nations return to self-sufficiency. If that happened, we could see the result by looking back at Figure 20.2: Chipland would move from point *x* to point *c*, and Shirtland would move from point *y* to point *s*. This sort of retaliatory response is common. Because it is, we know that the protection of one industry in a nation is likely to harm that nation's export industries. Chipland's shirt industry, if protected from imports, may grow, but at the expense of its computer-chip industry.

There are many examples of import restrictions that led to retaliatory policies that decreased trade substantially. Here are a few:

1. Smoot-Hawley tariff of 1930. When the United States increased its average tariff to 59%, its trading partners retaliated with higher tariffs. The trade war decreased international trade and deepened the worldwide depression of the 1930s.[3]
2. Chicken tariff of 1963. The European Economic Community (EEC, the predecessor of the European Union) imposed a large tariff on frozen chickens from the United States, cutting U.S. imports in half. The United States retaliated by increasing its tariffs on expensive brandies (from France), potato starch (from Holland), and light trucks (from Germany).[4]

3. Pasta tariff of 1985. The United States imposed tariffs on pasta from the EEC, and the EEC retaliated by increasing its tariffs on lemons and walnuts from the United States.[5]

The threat of retaliatory policies may persuade a nation to loosen its protectionist policies. In 1995, the United States announced that it would impose 100% tariffs on Japanese luxury cars (with total sales of $6 billion per year) if Japan didn't ease its restrictions on imported auto parts. Just hours before the tariffs were to take effect, the two nations reached an agreement that was expected to increase the sales of U.S. auto parts to Japanese firms by about $9 billion per year.[6]

Import restrictions also create an incentive to smuggle goods. The restrictions create a gap between the cost of purchasing the restricted goods abroad and the price of goods in the protected economy, so there is a profit to be made from smuggling.

Economic Detective

NAFTA and the Giant Sucking Sound

The North American Free Trade Agreement (NAFTA), which took effect in January 1994, will gradually phase out tariffs and other trade barriers between the United States, Canada, and Mexico. In the debates over the effects of NAFTA on trade between the United States and Mexico, economists predicted that NAFTA would increase both imports from Mexico and exports to Mexico. This is sensible because NAFTA decreases the tariffs and trade barriers of both nations. Because the pre-NAFTA tariffs between the United States and Mexico were low—about 4%—no one expected any dramatic changes in trade patterns. Instead, the expectation was for moderate growth in both imports and exports.

Table 20.2 provides some trade data for the United States and Mexico for the years surrounding the NAFTA agreement. Several observers, including two presidential candidates, used the figures for 1993 and 1995 to claim that NAFTA was responsible for turning the small $2 billion trade surplus in 1993 into the huge $16 billion trade deficit in 1995. One candidate suggested that NAFTA caused a "giant sucking sound" as jobs moved from the United States to Mexico.

Who is right? The economists who predicted that NAFTA would cause moderate growth in both imports and exports, or the presidential candidates?

The clues that we need to solve this puzzle are shown in the fourth column of Table 20.2. The exchange rate in 1994 was about the same as it was in 1993, so in the first year of NAFTA, imports and exports grew at nearly the same rate, about 22%, as predicted by economists. The following year was different: The exchange rate of the dollar for the peso rose from 3.11 to 5.33 pesos per dollar. An increase in the exchange rate—more

Table 20.2   Trade Data for the United States and Mexico

Year	U.S. Imports from Mexico (billions)	U.S. Exports to Mexico (billions)	Exchange Rate: Pesos per Dollar	U.S. Trade Surplus (+) or Deficit (−) with Mexico (billions)
1993	$40	$42	3.12	$+2
1994	$49	$51	3.11	$+2
1995	$62	$46	5.33	$−16

Source: U.S. Department of Commerce, *Statistical Abstract of the United States, 1996* (Washington, DC: U.S. Government Printing Office, 1996).

NAFTA helps promote the growth of foreign investment in Mexico.

pesos per dollar—will make U.S. goods more expensive for Mexican consumers, so U.S. exports to Mexico will drop. At the same time, Mexican goods will become less expensive for U.S. consumers, so U.S. imports from Mexico will rise. According to Table 20.2, that's exactly what happened: Imports increased by $13 billion, and exports dropped by $5 billion. This suggests that the U.S. trade deficit with Mexico was caused by the fall in the value of the peso, not by NAFTA.

TEST Your Understanding

6. Complete the following statement: If a country bans the importation of a particular good, the market equilibrium is shown by the intersection of the _____ curve and the _____ curve.

7. Complete the statement with *above* or *below*. The equilibrium price under an import quota is _____ the price that occurs with an import ban and _____ the price that occurs with free trade.

8. From the perspective of consumers, which is better: a tariff or a quota?

9. Under the quota system underlying Figure 20.4, what fraction of the shirt market is supplied by domestic firms?

Rationales for Protectionist Policies

What are the rationales for protectionist policies such as an import ban, an import quota, a voluntary restraint, or a tariff? We will discuss three possible motivations for policies that restrict trade:

1. To shield workers from foreign competition
2. To nurture infant industries until they mature
3. To help domestic firms establish monopolies in world markets

To Shield Workers from Foreign Competition

One of the most basic arguments for protectionism is that it protects workers in industries that would be hurt by trade. Suppose that relative to the United States, nations in the Far East have a comparative advantage in producing textiles. If the United States reduced existing tariffs for the textile industry, domestic manufacturers could not compete. They would have to close their factories and lay off workers. In an ideal world, the laid-off workers would take new jobs in other sectors of the economy. In practice, this is difficult. Many workers don't have the skills to work in other sectors, and obtaining these skills takes time. Moreover, the textile industry is heavily concentrated in the southeastern part of the United States. Politicians from that region will try to keep tariffs in place to prevent the temporary unemployment and changes in employment patterns that free trade would cause. The result of this protection is less efficient production, higher prices, and lower consumption for the United States. For a discussion of the trade-offs between job protection and consumer prices, read "A Closer Look: The Cost of Protecting Jobs."

To Nurture Infant Industries

Learning by doing: Knowledge gained during production, resulting in increases in productivity.

Infant industry: A new industry that is protected from foreign competitors.

During World War II, the United States built hundreds of boats, called Liberty Ships, for the Navy. As more and more of these ships were built, each required fewer hours to complete because workers learned from their experiences, acquiring knowledge during the production process. Engineers and economists call this phenomenon **learning by doing**. To learn a new game, such as Ping-Pong, you learn by doing. At first, you may find it difficult to play, but your skills improve as you go along.

Tariffs and other protectionist policies are often defended on the grounds that they protect new industries, or **infant industries**, that are in the early stages of learning by doing. A tariff shields a young industry from the competition of its more mature rivals.

A CLOSER LOOK   THE COST OF PROTECTING JOBS

What is the trade-off between protecting domestic jobs and higher prices for consumers? As shown in the table, protectionist policies for textiles and apparel imposed an annual cost of over $10 billion and saved 126,050 jobs—at a cost of $82,316 per job. To protect 300 jobs in the footwear industry, we spent over $1 million dollars per worker!

Industry Protected	Annual Cost (millions)	Jobs Protected	Cost per Job
Textiles and apparel	$10,376	126,050	$ 82,316
Maritime transport	$ 1,324	4,860	$ 272,427
Sugar	$ 986	1,990	$ 495,477
Footwear	$ 501	300	$1,670,000
Dairy	$ 152	160	$ 950,000

Source: Update of *The Economic Effects of Significant U.S. Import Restraints* (Washington, D.C., U.S. International Trade Commission, second update 1999).

After the infant industry grows up, the tariff can be eliminated because the industry is able to compete.

In practice, infant industries rarely become competitive with their foreign rivals. During the 1950s and 1960s, many Latin American countries used tariffs and other policies to protect their young manufacturing industries from foreign competition. Unfortunately, the domestic industries never became as efficient as foreign suppliers, and the Latin American countries that tried this policy suffered.

Another problem with protecting an infant industry is that once an industry is given tariff protection, it is difficult to take such protection away. For an interesting discussion of the merits of protecting an industry from "unfair" competition, read "A Closer Look: Protection for Candle Makers."

To Help Domestic Firms Establish Monopolies in World Markets

If the production of a particular good has very large-scale economies, the world market will support only a few firms. A nation might be tempted to adopt policies to capture the monopoly profits for itself. Suppose the commercial aircraft industry can support only one large firm; if two firms enter the industry, both will lose money. A nation that decides to get into this industry could agree to provide financial support to a domestic firm to guarantee that the firm will make a profit. With such a guarantee, the domestic firm will enter the industry. Knowing this, a foreign firm will be reluctant to enter, so the domestic firm will capture the monopoly profit.

One example of this is the Airbus, an airplane that is produced in Europe. Several European countries provided large subsidies for firms producing the Airbus. These subsidies allowed the Airbus firms to underprice some of their rivals in the United States, and at least one U.S. manufacturer of commercial airplanes was forced out of business. What could go wrong with these monopoly-creation policies? If both nations subsidize

A CLOSER LOOK   PROTECTION FOR CANDLE MAKERS

In response to the spread of protectionism, the French economist Frédéric Bastiat (1801–1851) wrote the following fictitious petition, in which French candle makers ask for protection from "unfair" competition:

> We are suffering from the intolerable competition of a foreign rival, placed, it would seem, in a condition so far superior to ours for the production of light, that he absolutely inundates our national market at a price fabulously reduced. The moment he shows himself, our trade leaves us— all of our customers apply to him; and a branch of native industry, having countless ramifications, is all at once rendered completely stagnant. This rival . . . is none other than the sun.
>
> What we pray for is, that it may please you to pass a law ordering the shutting up of all windows, sky-lights, dormerwindows, curtains, blinds, bull's eyes; in a word all openings, holes, chinks, clefts, and fissures, by or through which the light of the sun has been in use to enter houses, to the prejudice of the meritorious manufactures with which we . . . have accommodated our country—a country which, in gratitude, ought not to abandon us now.
>
> Does it not argue to the greatest inconsistency to check as you do the importation of coal, iron, cheese, and goods of foreign manufacture, merely because . . . their price approaches zero, while at the same time you freely admit, and without limitation, the light of the sun, whose price is during the whole day at zero?

Source: Frédéric Bastiat, *Economics Sophisms* (Edinburgh: Oliver & Boyd, 1873), pp. 49–53.

their domestic firms, both firms will enter the market and lose money. The taxpayers in both countries will then have to pay for the subsidies. And there is the possibility a nation may pick the wrong industry to subsidize. Together, the British and French subsidized an airplane known as the Concorde to provide supersonic travel between Europe and the United States. Although the Concorde captured the market, the market was not worth capturing. The Concorde lost money because it was very costly to develop, and people are not willing to pay a very large premium for supersonic travel.

TEST Your Understanding

10. Comment on the following statement: If we eliminated our textile tariffs, the dislocated workers could easily switch to other jobs.

11. Explain the infant-industry argument.

12. List the two problems associated with subsidizing an industry in the hope of establishing a worldwide monopoly.

Recent Policy Debates and Trade Agreements

We're now ready to discuss three recent policy debates concerning international trade:

1. Are foreign producers dumping their products?
2. Do trade laws inhibit environmental protection?
3. Does trade cause income inequality?

We also discuss some recent trade agreements that have lowered trade barriers and increased international trade.

Are Foreign Producers Dumping Their Products?

Dumping: A situation in which the price a firm charges for a product in a foreign market is lower than either the price it charges for that product in its home market or the product's production cost.

While tariff rates have been reduced in recent years, a number of trade controversies remain. One of these is the rules for dumping. A firm is **dumping** when the price it charges in a foreign market is either lower than the price it charges in its home market or lower than its production cost. Dumping is illegal under international trade agreements; hundreds of cases of alleged dumping are presented to WTO authorities each year. Here are some recent cases in which the WTO concluded that dumping had occurred: Hong Kong VCRs sold in Europe; Chinese bicycles sold in the United States; Asian TV sets sold in Europe; steel from Brazil, India, Japan, and Spain sold in the United States; U.S. beef sold in Mexico; and Chinese computer disks sold in Japan and the United States. Under the current provisions of the WTO, a nation can impose antidumping duties on products that are being dumped.

Why would a firm dump—charge a low price in the foreign market? The first reason is price discrimination. If a firm has a monopoly in its home market but faces strong competition in a foreign market, the firm will naturally charge a higher price in the home market. The foreign price looks low, but only because we compare it to a very high monopoly price in the home market. The firm uses its monopoly power to discriminate against consumers in its home market, so the problem is in the home market, not the foreign market.

To illustrate how international price discrimination works, let's look at the case of Korean VCRs.[7] In the 1980s there were only three firms, all Korean, selling VCRs in Korea, but there were dozens of firms selling VCRs in Europe. The lack of competition in Korea generated very high prices for Korean consumers: They paid much more than European consumers for identical Korean VCRs. Korean firms used their market power to discriminate against Korean consumers. When international trade authorities concluded that Korean firms were dumping VCRs in Europe, the Korean firms responded by cutting prices in their home market. They did not increase their prices in Europe—much to the dismay of European producers and the delight of European consumers.

The second reason for dumping is predatory pricing: cutting prices in an attempt to drive rival firms out of business. The predatory firm sets its price below its production cost. The price is low enough that both the predator and its prey (a firm in the foreign market) lose money. After the prey goes out of business, the predator increases its price to earn monopoly profit. This is also known as *predatory dumping*.

Although the rationale for antidumping laws is to prevent predatory dumping, it is difficult to determine whether low prices are the result of predatory pricing or price discrimination. Many economists are skeptical about how frequently predatory pricing actually occurs; they suspect that many nations use their antidumping laws as protectionist policies in disguise. Because WTO rules limit tariffs and quotas, some nations may be tempted to substitute antidumping duties for these protectionist policies.

Until the 1990s, antidumping cases were brought almost exclusively by Australia, New Zealand, Europe, Canada, and the United States. However, starting in the 1990s, the developing countries began to emulate the developed countries and now bring approximately one-half of the cases. Professor Thomas Prusa of Rutgers University has studied antidumping and found that it is a potent weapon for domestic industries. If a case is settled or a tariff is imposed, imports typically fall by 50 to 70% over the first three years of protection. Even if a country loses a claim, imports still fall by 15 to 20%.[8]

Do Trade Laws Inhibit Environmental Protection?

In recent trade negotiations, a new player—environmental groups—appeared on the scene. Starting in the early 1990s, environmentalists began to question whether policies that liberalized trade could harm the environment. The issue that attracted their attention was the killing of dolphins by tuna fishers.

Anyone who catches tuna with a large net will also catch the dolphins that swim with the tuna, and most of the captured dolphins will die. In 1972, the United States outlawed the use of tuna nets by U.S. ships. A short time later, ships from other nations, including Mexico, began netting tuna and killing dolphins. The United States responded with a boycott of Mexican tuna caught with nets, and the Mexican government complained to an international trade authority that the tuna boycott was an unfair trade barrier. The trade authority agreed with Mexico and forced the United States to remove the boycott.

Under current WTO rules, a country can adopt any environmental standard it chooses, as long as it does not discriminate against foreign producers. For example, the United States can limit the exhaust emissions of all cars that operate in the United States. As long as emissions rules apply equally to all cars, domestic and imports, the rules are legal according to the WTO. An international panel upheld U.S. fuel efficiency rules for automobiles on this principle.[9]

The tuna boycott was a violation of WTO rules because killing dolphins does not harm the U.S. environment directly. For the same reason, the United States could not ban imported goods that are produced in factories that generate air or water pollution in other countries. It is easy to understand why WTO rules do not allow countries to restrict trade on the basis of the methods that are used to produce goods and services. Countries differ in the value they place on the environment. For example, a poor nation may be willing to tolerate more pollution if it means attaining a higher standard of living.

If trade restrictions cannot be used to protect the dolphins and deal with other global environmental problems, what else can we do? International agreements have been used for a variety of different environmental goals, from limiting the harvest of whales to eliminating the chemicals that deplete the ozone layer. These agreements are difficult to reach, and some nations will be tempted to use trade restrictions to pursue environmental goals. If they do, they will encounter resistance because WTO rules mean that a nation can pursue its environmental goals only within its own borders.

Trade disputes about environmental issues are part of a larger phenomenon of trade issues intersecting with national regulations. At one time, most trade disputes were simply matters of protecting domestic industries from foreign competition. Agriculture, textile, and steel were frequently beneficiaries of protection in many different countries throughout the world. But in recent years, there has been a new breed of trade disputes that revolve around social issues and the role of government regulation.

As an example, the European Union and the United States became embroiled in a trade dispute over hormone-treated beef. After the European Union banned imports of hormone-treated beef, the United States and Canada successfully challenged this ban with the WTO because they argued that there was no scientific evidence that suggested any adverse health impacts from hormone-treated beef. The European Union refused to rescind the ban and, as a consequence, the United States and Canada were permitted to impose tariffs on a range of European products.

The European Union ban on hormone-treated beef was intended to protect European farmers from imports but also reflected the nervousness of European citizens about technology. After all, Europe banned all hormone-treated beef, not just imports. Shouldn't a country have a right to pursue this policy, even if it is not based on the best science of the day? While the costs of the policy are straightforward in terms of higher beef prices, the benefits, in terms of potential safety and peace of mind, are much more difficult to assess. Similar issues will arise as genetically modified crops become more commonplace. As a world trading community, we will have to decide at what point we allow national policy concerns to override principles of free trade.

Does Trade Cause Inequality?

Inequality in wages has been growing in the United States since 1973. Wages of skilled workers have risen faster than the wages of unskilled workers. World trade has also boomed since 1973. Could there be a connection between increased world trade and income inequality?

Trade theory suggests a link between increased trade and increased wage inequality. Here is how they might be linked: Suppose the United States produces two types of goods: one using skilled labor (say, airplanes) and one using unskilled labor (say, textiles). The United States is likely to have a comparative advantage in products that use skilled labor; developing countries are likely to have a comparative advantage in products that use unskilled labor. An increase in world trade will increase both exports and imports. An increase in U.S. exports means that we'll produce more goods requiring skilled labor, so the domestic demand for skilled labor will increase, pulling up the wage of skilled labor in the United States. At the same time, an increase in U.S. imports means that we'll import more goods produced by unskilled labor, so the domestic demand for unskilled labor will decrease, pulling down the wage of unskilled labor in the United States. As a result, the gap between the wages of the two types of workers will increase.

Economists have tried to determine how much trade has contributed to growing wage inequality. As usual, there are other factors that make such a determination difficult. It is difficult, for example, to distinguish between the effects of trade and the effects of technical progress. Technical change, such as the rapid introduction and use of computers, will also tend to increase the demand for skilled workers and decrease the demand for unskilled workers. Economists have noted, however, that the exports of goods using skilled labor and the imports of goods using unskilled labor have both increased, just as the theory predicts. At least some of the increased wage inequality is caused by international trade.

One response to this undesirable side effect of trade is to use trade restrictions to protect industries that use unskilled workers. Another approach is to ease the transition to an economy with a larger fraction of skilled jobs. In the long run, workers will move to industries that use skilled workers, so they will eventually earn higher wages. The government could facilitate this change by providing assistance for education and training.

Recent Trade Agreements

In the last few decades, there has been considerable progress in lowering the barriers to international trade. Here are some examples of international trade agreements:

1. North American Free Trade Agreement (NAFTA). Took effect in 1994 and is being implemented over the following 15 years. The agreement will eventually eliminate all tariffs and other trade barriers among Canada, Mexico, and the United States. NAFTA may soon be extended to other nations in the Western Hemisphere.

2. World Trade Organization (WTO). Has more than 130 member nations and oversees the General Agreement on Tariffs and Trade and other international trade agreements. There have been eight rounds of tariff negotiations, lowering tariffs among the member nations. For example, between 1930 and 1995, the average tariff in the United States has dropped from about 59% to about 5%. The last full set of negotiations, the so-called Uruguay Round, completed in 1994, decreased tariffs by about one-third their prior levels. WTO promotes trade in other ways: It has eliminated many import quotas, reduced agricultural subsidies, and outlawed restrictions on international trade in services such as banking, insurance, and accounting.

3. European Union (EU). Designed to remove all trade barriers within Europe and create a single market. Fifteen nations have joined.

4. Asian Pacific Economic Cooperation (APEC). In 1994, the leaders of 18 Asian nations signed a nonbinding agreement to reduce trade barriers among their nations.

These agreements have reduced trade barriers and increased international trade. For example, the Uruguay Round was expected to increase the volume of world trade by at least 9% and perhaps as much as 24%.[10]

TEST Your Understanding

13. What is dumping?

14. What restrictions do WTO rules place on a nation's environmental policies?

15. Consider a nation having a comparative advantage in the production of goods using unskilled labor. What types of workers will benefit from increased trade, and what types of workers will lose?

Using the TOOLS

In this chapter, we've discussed the trade-offs associated with protectionist policies and have used supply and demand curves to show the market effects of protectionist policies. Here are some opportunities to do your own economic analysis.

1. ECONOMIC EXPERIMENT: Protectionist Policies
Recall the market equilibrium experiment from Chapter 4. We can modify the experiment to show the effects of protectionist policies on equilibrium prices and quantities. On the supply side of the market, there are domestic apple producers and foreign apple produc-

ers; the domestic producers have higher unit costs. After several trading periods without any government intervention, you can change the rules as follows:

a. Apple imports are banned: Foreign producers cannot participate in the market.

b. There is a tariff (a tax on imports) of $5 per bushel.

APPLICATIONS

2. Incentives for Smuggling

If a country bans imports, smugglers may try to penetrate its markets. Suppose Chipland bans shirt imports, causing some importers to bribe customs officials, who "look the other way" as smugglers bring shirts into Chipland. Your job is to combat shirt smuggling. Use the information in Figure 20.3 in this chapter to answer the following questions:

a. Suppose importers can sell their shirts on the world market at a price of $12 per shirt. How much is an importer willing to pay to get customs officials to look the other way?

b. What sort of change in trade policy would make your job easier?

3. Trade in Genetically Modified Crops

Suppose the residents of a country become fearful of using genetically modified crops in their food supply. Consider the following two possible scenarios:

a. Aware of consumer sentiment, the largest supermarket chains in the country adopt a policy that they will not purchase food products that use genetically modified crops.

b. The government, aware of voter sentiment during an election year, bans the import of the food products that use genetically modified crops.

In both cases, no genetically modified crops enter the country. Do either of these cases run afoul of WTO policies?

4. Ban on Shoe Imports

Consider a country that initially consumes 100 pairs of shoes per hour, all of which are imported. The price of shoes is $40 per pair before a ban on importing them. Depict graphically the market effects of a ban on shoe imports.

Summary

In this chapter, we discussed the benefits of specialization and trade, and we explored the trade-offs associated with protectionist policies. There is a basic conflict between consumers, who prefer free trade because free trade decreases prices, and workers in the protected industries, who want to keep their jobs. Here are the main points of the chapter:

1. If one country has a comparative advantage vis-à-vis another country in producing a particular good (a lower opportunity cost), specialization and trade will benefit both countries.

2. An import ban or an import quota increases the prices of the restricted good and shifts resources from a domestic export industry into the protected domestic industries.

3. Because the victims of protectionist policies often retaliate, the protection of a domestic industry may harm an exporting industry.

4. A tariff (a tax on imports) generates revenue for the government, while an import quota—a limit on imports—generates revenue for foreigners or importers.

5. In principle, the laws against dumping are designed to prevent predatory pricing. In practice, it is difficult to prove predatory pricing, and the laws are often used to shield a domestic industry from competition.

6. Under WTO rules, each country may pursue its environmental goals only within its own borders.

7. International trade has contributed to the widening gap between the wages of low-skilled and high-skilled labor.

Key Terms

autarky, 420
comparative advantage, 420
consumption possibilities curve, 421
dumping, 430

import quota, 423
infant industry, 428
learning by doing, 428
production possibilities curve, 418

tariff, 424
terms of trade, 420
voluntary export restraint [VER], 423

Problems and Discussion Questions

1. In one minute, Country B can produce either 1,000 TVs and no computers or 500 computers and no TVs. Similarly, in one minute, country C can produce either 2,400 TVs or 600 computers.

    a. Compute the opportunity costs of TVs and computers for each country. Which country has a comparative advantage in producing TVs? In producing computers?

    b. Draw the production possibilities curves for the two countries.

2. In country U, the opportunity cost of a computer is 10 pairs of shoes. In Country C, the opportunity cost of a computer is 100 pairs of shoes.

    a. Suppose the two countries split the difference between the willingness to pay for computers and the willingness to accept computers. Compute the terms of trade, that is, the rate at which the two countries will exchange computers and shoes.

    b. Suppose the two countries exchange one computer for the number of shoes dictated by the terms of trade you computed in part (a). Compute the net benefit from trade for each country.

3. In Figure 20.2, suppose the two countries trade 35 computer chips for 70 shirts. For each country, compute the amounts of chips and shirts consumed.

4. Consider two countries, Tableland and Chairland, each capable of producing tables and chairs.

    Chairland can produce the following combinations of chairs and tables:

    • All chairs and no tables: 36 chairs per day

    • All tables and no chairs: 18 tables per day

    Tableland can produce the following combinations of chairs and tables:

    • All chairs and no tables: 40 chairs per day

    • All tables and no chairs: 40 tables per day

    In each country, there is a fixed trade-off of tables for chairs.

    a. Draw the two production possibilities curves, with chairs on the vertical axis and tables on the horizontal axis.

    b. Suppose that each country is initially self-sufficient and each country divides its resources equally between the two goods. How much does each country produce and consume?

    c. Which country has a comparative advantage in tables? Which has a comparative advantage in chairs?

    d. If the two countries split the difference between the buyer's willingness to pay for chairs and the seller's willingness to accept, in terms of chairs per table, what are the terms of trade?

    e. Draw the consumption possibilities curves.

    f. Suppose each country specializes in the good for which it has a comparative advantage, and they exchange 14 tables for some quantity of chairs. Compute the consumption bundles—bundles means the consumption of tables and chairs—for each country.

5. The current approach to restricting automobile imports is to use voluntary export restraints. Evaluate the wisdom of this approach and propose an alternative policy.

6. Evaluate this comment: "If a country bans imports, smuggling is inevitable. We should welcome smuggling because it improves consumer welfare."

7. The European Union is committed to eliminating most of the trade barriers among its 15 member nations. What types of people will benefit? Which types will lose?

8. What is the cost to consumers for each motor-vehicle job protected by import restrictions? In your opinion, is protecting these jobs worthwhile at this cost? If not, how much should we as a society be willing to pay for each job that is protected?

9. Suppose the president of a nation proposes to switch from a system of import quotas to a system

of tariffs, with the idea that the switch would not affect the quantity of goods imported. Who will be in favor of the switch? Who will oppose it? Would you expect the proponents and the opponents to have the same political influence on the president?

10. Suppose residents of one nation are very fearful of biotechnology and they pass a law prohibiting the sale of all genetically altered foods in their country. Another nation, which produces these foods, claims that this law is an unfair trade barrier. In your view, should the first nation be allowed to prevent these imports, even if there is no scientific basis for their claim?

11. **Web Exercise.** Go to the Web site for the World Trade Organization [*http://www.wto.org*] and explore some of the ongoing trade disputes. Pick one or two of these disputes and find additional background information, such as newspaper stories, on the Web. Use this information to understand the nature of the controversy.

12. **Web Exercise.** Go to the Web site for the U.S. Trade Representative [*http://www.ustr.gov*], which is an office within the executive branch of the government. From the Web site, what are some of the key trade issues for the U.S. government today?

Take It to the Net

We invite you to visit the O'Sullivan/Sheffrin page on the Prentice Hall Web site at: **http://www.prenhall.com/osullivan/** for additional World Wide Web exercises for this chapter.

Model Answers to Questions

Chapter-Opening Questions

1. The winners are the domestic nation's consumers, who pay lower prices, and the domestic nation's workers in export industries. The losers are people in the domestic nation who lose their jobs as imports replace domestically produced goods.

2. A tariff generates revenue for the government; a quota generates profits for importers.

3. First, if a firm has a monopoly in its home market but faces strong competition in a foreign market, the firm will naturally charge a higher price in the home market (price discrimination). Second, a firm may be engaging in predatory pricing, the practice of cutting prices in an attempt to drive rivals out of business.

4. Under current WTO rules, a country cannot adopt any environmental standard that discriminates against foreign producers. For example, the United States cannot impose an import ban on goods that are produced in polluting factories in other nations. This rule means that global environmental issues must be resolved with international agreements, not trade restrictions.

5. Although trade increases income inequality, it is unclear just how much of the recent increase in inequality can be attributed to the expansion of trade.

Test Your Understanding

1. 50, 78 (108 − 30).

2. Nation B should produce tables, and nation H should produce chairs.

3. Three chairs per table: Nation H is willing to pay five chairs, and nation B is willing to accept one chair.

4. We need to know the maximum output of the good for which the nation has a comparative advantage and the terms of trade.

5. No. The consumption curve will be the same as the production curve.

6. Demand, domestic supply.

7. Below, above.

8. If a quota and a tariff led to the same price for a good, consumers would be indifferent between them. However, as citizens, they should prefer the tariff which provides revenue to the government, allowing the government to either increase expenditure or reduce taxation.

9. Domestic firms supply 22 units, which is one-third of the total quantity (66).

10. This is false. Some workers do not have the skills to work in other sectors, and it takes time to obtain new skills.

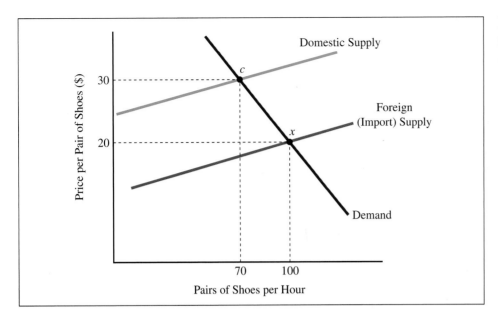

Figure 20.A

Ban on Shoe Imports

---

11. It takes some time for a new industry to learn by doing, so it may be sensible to protect a young industry when it is vulnerable to competition from foreign firms.

12. If two nations subsidize firms in the same industry, each nation could lose money. In addition, a nation might pick the wrong industry to subsidize.

13. A foreign firm is dumping when it sells a product in another country at a price below the price it charges in its own market. It is difficult to determine whether dumping is occurring, and many countries used dumping laws as a disguised form of protectionism.

14. A nation's environmental laws must not discriminate against imported goods. The laws must apply equally to imports and domestic goods.

15. The wage of unskilled labor will increase; the wage of skilled labor will decrease.

Using the Tools

2. Incentives for Smuggling

   a. Importers are willing to pay a bribe up to $11 per shirt (the difference between the equilibrium price with the import ban and the world price).

   b. If the import ban were replaced by a tariff of $11 per shirt, the smuggling problem might diminish, although there would still be an incentive to smuggle shirts to avoid the tariff.

3. Trade in Genetically Modified Crops. The WTO cannot prevent the large supermarket chains from not purchasing food that contains genetically modified crops. In the absence of scientific evidence, the government, however, could not ban the crops without violating WTO rules.

4. Ban on Shoe Imports. In Figure 20.A we move from point x (price = $20 per pair; quantity = 100 pairs) to point c (price = $30 per pair; quantity = 70 pairs).

Notes

1. *A Review of Recent Developments in the U.S. Automobile Industry Including an Assessment of the Japanese Voluntary Restraint Agreements* (Washington, DC: U.S. International Trade Commission, February 1985).

2. Gary C. Hufbauer, Diane T. Berliner, and Kimberly A. Elliot, *Measuring the Cost of Protectionism in the United States* (Washington, DC: Institute for International Economics, 1994).

3. Charles Kindleberger, *The World in Depression, 1929-1939* (London: Allen Lane, 1973).

4. John A. C. Conybeare, *Trade Wars* (New York: Columbia University Press, 1987).

5. Conybeare, *Trade Wars*.

6. Helene Cooper and Valerie Reitman, "Averting a Trade War, U.S. and Japan Reach Agreement on Autos," *Wall Street Journal*, June 29, 1995, p. 1.

7. Taeho Bark, "The Korean Consumer Electronics Industry: Reaction to Antidumping Actions," Chapter 7 in *Antidumping: How It Works and Who Gets Hurt*, edited by J. Michael Finger (Ann Arbor, MI: University of Michigan Press, 1993).

8. Virgina Postrel, "Curb Demonstrates Faults of Courting Special Interests," *New York Times*, June 14, 2001, p. C1.

9. "GATT Panel Supports U.S.," *New York Times*, October 1, 1994, p. A49.

10. Norman S. Fieleke, "The Uruguay Round of Trade Negotiation: An Overview," *New England Economic Review*, May/June 1995.

Glossary

Absolute advantage: The ability of one person or nation to produce a particular good at a lower absolute cost than that of another person or nation.

Accelerator theory: The theory of investment that says current investment spending depends positively on the expected future growth of real GDP.

Acid rain: Precipitation with an acidic combination of sulfur dioxides and nitrogen oxides.

Adverse-selection problem: The uninformed side of the market must choose from an undesirable or adverse selection of goods.

Aggregate demand: The relationship between the level of prices and the quantity of real GDP demanded.

Aggregate production function: Shows how much output is produced from capital and labor.

Aggregate supply: The relationship between the level of prices and the quantity of output supplied.

Anticipated inflation: Inflation that is expected.

Appreciation: An increase in the value of a currency.

Asian Pacific Economic Cooperation (APEC) organization: An organization of 18 Asian nations that attempts to reduce trade barriers between their nations.

Assets: The uses of the funds of a bank, including loans and reserves.

Asymmetric information: One side of the market—either buyers or sellers—has better information about the good than the other.

Autarky: A situation in which each country is self-sufficient, so there is no trade.

Automatic stabilizers: Taxes and transfer payments that stabilize GDP without requiring policymakers to take explicit action.

Autonomous consumption: The part of consumption that does not depend on income.

Average-cost pricing policy: A regulatory policy under which the government picks the point on the demand curve at which price equals average cost.

Average fixed cost (AFC): Fixed cost divided by the quantity produced.

Balanced budget: The situation in which total expenditures equals total revenues.

Balance of payments deficit: Under a fixed exchange rate system, a situation in which the supply of a country's currency exceeds the demand for the currency at the current exchange rate.

Balance of payments surplus: Under a fixed exchange rate system, a situation in which the demand for a country's currency exceeds the supply of the currency at the current exchange rate.

Balance sheet: An account for a bank that shows the sources of its funds (liabilities) as well as the uses for the funds (assets).

Barter: Trading goods directly for other goods.

Benefit-tax approach: The idea that a person's tax liability should depend on his or her benefits from government programs.

Board of Governors of the Federal Reserve: The seven-person governing body of the Federal Reserve system in Washington, DC.

Bond: A promise or IOU to pay money in the future in exchange for money now.

Budget deficit: The difference between a government's spending and its revenues from taxation.

Budget line: The line connecting all the combinations of two goods that exhaust a consumer's budget.

Budget set: A set of points that includes all the combinations of two goods that a consumer can afford, given the consumer's income and the prices of the two goods.

Business cycles: Another name for economic fluctuations.

Capital: See *physical capital*; see *human capital*.

Capital account: The value of a country's sales less purchases of assets. A sale of a domestic asset is a surplus item on the capital account, while a purchase of a foreign asset is a deficit item on the capital account.

Capital deepening: Increases in the stock of capital per worker.

Carbon tax: A tax based on a fuel's carbon content.

Cartel: A group of firms that coordinate their pricing decisions, often by charging the same price.

Central bank: A banker's bank; an official bank that controls the supply of money in a country.

Centrally planned economy: An economy in which a government bureaucracy decides how much of each good to produce, how to produce the goods, and how to allocate the products among consumers.

Ceteris paribus: Latin meaning "other things being equal."

Chain index: A method for calculating changes in prices that uses data from neighboring years.

Change in demand: A change in the amount of a good demanded resulting from a change in something other than the price of the good; represented graphically by a shift of a demand curve.

Change in quantity demanded: A change in the amount of a good demanded resulting from a change in the price of the good; represented graphically by a movement along a demand curve.

Change in quantity supplied: A change in the amount of a good supplied resulting from a change in the price of the good; represented graphically by a movement along a supply curve.

Change in supply: A change in the amount of a good supplied resulting from a change in something other than the price of the good; represented graphically by a shift of the supply curve.

Classical aggregate supply curve: A vertical aggregate supply curve. It reflects the idea that in the long run, output is determined solely by the factors of production.

Classical economics: A school of thought that provides insights into the economy when it operates at or near full employment.

Closed economy: An economy without international trade.

Command-and-control policy: A pollution-control policy under which the government commands each firm to produce no more than a certain volume of pollution and controls the firm's production process by forcing the firm to use a particular pollution-control technology.

Community rating: In a given community or metropolitan area, every firm pays the same price for medical insurance.

Comparative advantage: The ability of one person or nation to produce a good at an opportunity cost that is lower than the opportunity cost of another person or nation.

Complements: Two goods for which an increase in the price of one good decreases the demand for the other good.

Concentration ratio: A measure of the degree of concentration in a market; the four-firm concentration ratio is the percentage of output produced by the four largest firms.

Constant-cost industry: An industry in which the average cost of production is constant, so the long-run supply curve is horizontal.

Consumer Price Index (CPI): A price index that measures the cost of a fixed basket of goods chosen to represent the consumption pattern of individuals.

Consumer surplus: The difference between the maximum amount a consumer is willing to pay for a product and the price the consumer pays for the product.

Consumption expenditures: Purchases of newly produced goods and services by households.

Consumption function: The relationship between the level of income and consumption spending.

Consumption possibilities curve: A curve showing the combinations of two goods that can be consumed when a nation specializes in a particular good and trades with another nation.

Consumption taxation: A system of taxation which is based on the consuption, not the income, of individuals.

Contestable market: A market in which the costs of entering and leaving are very low, so the firms in the market are constantly threatened by the entry of new firms.

Contractionary policies: Government policy actions that lead to decreases in output.

Convergence: The process by which poorer countries "catch up" with richer countries in terms of real GDP per capita.

Cost-of-living adjustments: Automatic increases in wages or other payments that are tied to a price index.

Countercyclical: Moving in the opposite direction of real GDP.

Craft union: A labor organization that includes workers from a particular occupation, for example, plumbers, bakers, or electricians.

Creative destruction: The process by which competition for monopoly profits leads to technological progress.

Cross elasticity of demand: A measure of the responsiveness of the quantity demanded to changes in the price of a related good; computed by dividing the percentage change in the quantity demanded of one good (X) by the percentage change in the price of another good (Y).

Crowding in: The increase of investment (or other component of GDP) in the long run caused by a decrease in government spending.

Crowding out: The reduction in investment (or other component of GDP) in the long run caused by an increase in government spending.

Current account: The sum of net exports (exports minus imports) plus income received from investments abroad plus net transfers from abroad.

Cyclical unemployment: The component of unemployment that accompanies fluctuations in real GDP.

Deadweight loss from monopoly: A measure of the inefficiency from monopoly; equal to the difference between the consumer surplus loss from monopoly pricing and the monopoly profit.

Deadweight loss from taxation: The difference between the total burden of a tax and the amount of revenue collected by the government; also known as excess burden.

Deficit: The excess of total expenditures over total revenues.

Demand curve: See *individual demand curve*; see *market demand curve*.

Demand schedule: A table of numbers that shows the relationship between price and quantity demanded by a consumer, ceteris paribus (other things being equal).

Dependency ratio: The ratio of the population over 65 years of age to the population between 20 and 65.

Depreciation: The wear and tear of capital as it is used in production.

Depression: The common name for a severe recession.

Devaluation: A decrease in the exchange rate to which a currency is pegged in a fixed rate system.

Diminishing returns: As one input increases while the other inputs are held fixed, output increases but at a decreasing rate.

Discount rate: The interest rate at which banks can borrow from the Fed.

Discouraged workers: Workers who left the labor force because they could not find jobs.

Diseconomies of scale: A situation in which an increase in the quantity produced increases the long-run average cost of production.

Disposable personal income: The income that flows back to households, taking into account transfers and taxes.

Dominant strategy: An action that is the best choice under all circumstances.

Double coincidence of wants: The problem in a system of barter that one person may not have what the other desires.

Dumping: A situation in which the price a firm charges in a foreign market is lower than either the price it charges in its home market or the production cost.

Duopolists' dilemma: A situation in which both firms would be better off if they both chose a high price but each chooses a low price.

Durable goods: Goods that last for a long period of time, such as household appliances.

Econometric models: Mathematical computer-based models that economists build to capture the actual dynamics of the economy.

Economic cost: Explicit costs plus implicit costs.

Economic fluctuations: Movements of GDP above or below normal trends.

Economic growth: Sustained increases in the real production of an economy over a period of time.

Economic profit: Total revenue minus the total economic cost.

Economics: The study of the choices made by people who are faced with scarcity.

Economies of scale: A situation in which an increase in the quantity produced decreases the long-run average cost of production.

Elastic demand: The price elasticity is greater than one.

Employed: People who have jobs.

Entrepreneur: A person who has an idea for a business and coordinates the production and sale of goods and services, taking risks in the process.

Entrepreneurship: Effort used to coordinate the production and sale of goods and services.

Equilibrium output: The level of GDP at which the demand for output equals the amount that is produced.

Euro: The common currency in Europe.

European Union (EU): An organization of European nations that has reduced trade barriers within Europe.

Excess burden of a tax: Another name for deadweight loss from taxation.

Excess reserves: Any additional reserves that a bank holds above required reserves.

Exchange rate: The rate at which currencies trade for one another in the market.

Expansionary policies: Government policy actions that lead to increases in output.

Expectations of inflation: The beliefs held by the public about the likely path of inflation for the future.

Expectations Phillips curve: The relationship that describes the links between inflation and unemployment, taking into account expectations of inflation.

Expected real interest rate: The nominal interest rate minus the expected inflation rate.

Experience rating: Each firm pays a different price for medical insurance, depending on the past medical bills of the firm's employees.

Explicit costs: The firm's actual cash payments for its inputs.

Export: A good produced in the home country (for example, the United States) and sold in another country.

External benefit: Another term for spillover benefit.

External cost: Another term for spillover cost.

Factors of production: Labor and capital used to produce goods and services.

Federal funds market: The market in which banks borrow and lend reserves to and from one another.

Federal Open Market Committee (FOMC): The group that decides on monetary policy; it consists of the 7 members of the Board of Governors plus 5 of 12 regional bank presidents on a rotating basis.

Federal Reserve Banks: One of 12 regional banks that are an official part of the Federal Reserve System.

Financial intermediaries: Organizations that receive funds from savers and channel them to investors.

Financial liberalization: The opening of financial markets to participants from foreign countries.

Fiscal year: The calendar on which the federal government conducts its business, which runs from October 1 to September 30.

Fixed costs: Costs that do not change as the level of activity changes.

Fixed exchange rates: A system in which governments peg exchange rates.

Flexible exchange rates: A currency system in which exchange rates are determined by free markets.

Foreign exchange market: A market in which people exchange one currency for another.

Foreign exchange market intervention: The purchase or sale of currencies by governments to influence the market exchange rate.

Franchise or licensing scheme: A policy under which the government picks a single firm to sell a particular good.

Free-rider problem: Each person will try to get the benefit of a public good without paying for it, trying to get a free ride at the expense of others who do pay.

Frictional unemployment: The part of unemployment associated with the normal workings of the economy, such as searching for jobs.

Full employment: The level of employment that occurs when the unemployment rate is at the natural rate.

Full-employment or potential output: The level of output that results when the labor market is in equilibrium.

Game tree: A graphical representation of the consequences of different strategies.

General Agreement on Tariffs and Trade (GATT): An international agreement that has lowered trade barriers between the United States and other nations.

Generational accounting: Methods that assign the tax burden of debt and other programs to different generations.

Government debt: The total of all past deficits.

Government expenditure: Spending on goods and services plus transfer payments.

Government purchases: Purchases of newly produced goods and services by all levels of government.

Grim trigger: A strategy under which a firm responds to underpricing by choosing a price so low that each firm makes zero economic profit.

Gross domestic product (GDP): The total market value of all the final goods and services produced within an economy in a given year.

GDP deflator: An index that measures how the price of goods included in GDP changes over time.

Gross investment: Actual investment purchases.

Gross national product (GNP): GDP plus net income earned abroad.

Growth accounting: A method to determine the contribution to economic growth from increased capital, labor, and technological progress.

Growth rate: The percentage rate of change of a variable.

Growth version of the quantity equation: An equation that links the growth rates of money, velocity, prices, and real output.

Guaranteed price matching: A scheme under which a firm guarantees that it will match a lower price by a competitor; also known as a meet-the-competition policy.

Horizontal Equity: The idea that people in similar economic circumstances should pay similar amounts in taxes.

Household: A group of related family members and unrelated individuals who live in the same housing unit.

Human capital: The knowledge and skills acquired by a worker through education and experience and used to produce goods and services.

Hyperinflation: An inflation rate exceeding 50% per month.

Implicit costs: The opportunity cost of nonpurchased inputs.

Imports: A good produced in a foreign country and purchased by residents of the home country (for example, the United States).

Import quota: A limit on the amount of a good that can be imported.

Income effect for price change: The change in consumption resulting from an increase in the consumer's real income.

Income effect for wage change: An increase in the wage rate raises a worker's real income, increasing the demand for leisure.

Income elasticity of demand: A measure of the responsiveness of the quantity demanded to changes in consumer income; computed by dividing the percentage change in the quantity demanded by the percentage change in income.

Increasing-cost industry: An industry in which the average cost of production increases as the industry grows, so the long-run supply curve is positively sloped.

Indifference curve: A curve showing the set of combinations of goods that generate the same level of utility or satisfaction.

Indirect taxes: Sales and excise taxes.

Individual demand curve: A curve that shows the relationship between price and quantity demanded by an individual consumer, ceteris paribus (everything else held fixed).

Individual supply curve: A curve that shows the relationship between price and quantity supplied by an individual firm, ceteris paribus (everything else held fixed).

Indivisible input: An input that cannot be scaled down to produce a small quantity of output.

Industrial union: A labor organization that includes all types of workers from a single industry, for example, steelworkers or autoworkers.

Inelastic demand: The price elasticity is less than one.

Infant industry: A new industry that is protected from foreign competitors.

Inferior good: A good for which an increase in income decreases demand.

Inflation rate: The percentage rate of change of the price level in the economy.

Input-substitution effect: The change in the quantity of labor demanded resulting from a change in the relative cost of labor.

Insecure monopoly: A monopoly faced with the possibility that a second firm will enter the market.

Inside lags: Lags in implementing policy.

Intermediate good: Goods used in the production process that are not final goods or services.

International monetary fund: An organization that works closely with national governments to promote financial policies that facilitate world trade.

Invisible hand: The term that economists use to describe how the price system can efficiently coordinate economic activity without central government intervention.

Keynesian aggregate supply curve: A relatively flat horizontal supply curve. It reflects the idea that prices do not change very much in the short run and that firms adjust production to meet demand.

Keynesian economics: A school of economic thought that provides insights into the economy when it operates away from full employment.

Keynesian fiscal policy: The use of taxes and government spending to affect the level of GDP in the short run.

Kinked demand model: A model under which firms in an oligopoly match price reductions by other firms but do not match price increases.

Kyoto Agreement: An agreement among industrial nations to reduce carbon dioxide emissions.

Labor: Human effort, including both physical and mental effort, used to produce goods and services.

Labor force: The employed plus the unemployed.

Labor-force participation rate: The fraction of the population over 16 years of age that is in the labor force.

Labor productivity: Output produced per hour of work.

Labor union: An organized group of workers; the objectives of the organization are to increase job security, improve working conditions, and increase wages and benefits.

Laffer curve: A relationship between tax rates and tax revenues that illustrates that high tax rates may not always lead to high tax revenues if high tax rates discourage economic activity.

Law of demand: The lower the price, the larger the quantity demanded, ceteris paribus (other things being equal).

Law of diminishing marginal utility: As the consumption of a particular good increases, marginal utility decreases.

Law of one price: The theory that goods easily tradeable across countries, should sell at the same price, expressed in a common currency.

Law of supply: The higher the price, the larger the quantity supplied, ceteris paribus (other things being equal).

Learning by doing: Knowledge gained during production that increases productivity.

Learning effect: The increase in a person's wage resulting from the learning of skills required for certain occupations.

Lender of last resort: A central bank is the lender of last resort, the last place, all others having failed, from which banks in emergency situations can obtain loans.

Liabilities: The sources of funds for a bank, including deposits of a financial intermediary.

Limit pricing: A scheme under which a monopolist accepts a price below the normal monopoly price to deter other firms from entering the market.

Liquid: Easily convertible to money on short notice.

Liquidity demand for money: The demand for money that represents the needs and desires individuals or firms can fill on short notice without incurring excessive costs.

Liquidity trap: A situation in which interest rates are so low, they can no longer fall.

Long run: A period of time long enough that a firm can change all the factors of production, meaning that a firm can modify its existing production facility or build a new one.

Long-run average cost (LAC): Long-run total cost divided by the quantity of output produced.

Long-run demand curve for labor: A curve showing the relationship between the wage and the quantity of labor demanded over the long run, when the number of firms in the market can change and firms already in the market can modify their production facilities.

Long-run neutrality of money: An increase in the supply of money has no effect on real interest rates, investment, or output in the long run.

Long-run market supply: A curve showing the relationship between the market price and quantity supplied by all firms in the long run.

Long-run total cost: The total cost of production in the long run when a firm is perfectly flexible in its choice of all inputs and can choose a production facility of any size.

M1: The sum of currency in the hands of the public plus demand deposits plus other checkable deposits.

M2: M1 plus other assets, including deposits in savings and loans and money market mutual funds.

Macroeconomics: The branch of economics that looks at a nation's economy as a whole.

Managed competition: A health system in which organizations such as HMOs compete for patients.

Marginal benefit: The extra benefit resulting from a small increase in some activity.

Marginal cost: The additional cost resulting from a small increase in some activity.

Marginal labor cost (marginal factor cost): The increase in total labor cost resulting from hiring one more worker.

Marginal product of labor: The change in output from one additional worker.

Marginal propensity to consume (MPC): The fraction of additional income that is spent.

Marginal propensity to import: The fraction of additional income that is spent on imports.

Marginal propensity to save (MPS): The fraction of additional income that is saved.

Marginal rate of substitution (MRS): The rate at which a consumer is willing to substitute one good for another.

Marginal revenue product of labor (MRP): The extra revenue generated from one more unit of labor; equal to price of output times the marginal product of labor.

Marginal utility: The change in utility from one additional unit of the good.

Market: An arrangement that allows buyers and sellers to exchange things. A buyer exchanges money for a product, while a seller exchanges a product for money.

Market demand curve: A curve showing the relationship between price and quantity demanded by all consumers together, ceteris paribus (other things being equal).

Market equilibrium: A situation in which the quantity of a product demanded equals the quantity supplied, so there is no pressure to change the price.

Market supply curve: A curve showing the relationship between price and quantity supplied by all producers together, ceteris paribus (other things being equal).

Market supply curve for labor: A curve showing the relationship between the wage and the quantity of labor supplied.

Marketable pollution permits: A system under which the government picks a target pollution level for a particular area, issues just enough pollution permits to meet the pollution target, and allows firms to buy and sell the permits.

Median-voter rule: A rule suggesting that the choices made by government will reflect the preferences of the median voter.

Medicare: A government program that provides health benefits to those over 65 years of age.

Medium of exchange: The property of money that exchanges are made through the use of money.

Menu costs: Costs of inflation that arise from actually changing prices.

Merger: A process in which two or more firms combine their operations.

Microeconomics: The study of the choices made by consumers, firms, and government, and how these decisions affect the market for a particular good or service.

Minimum efficient scale: The output at which the long-run average cost curve becomes horizontal.

Mixed economy: A market-based economic system under which government plays an important role, including the regulation of markets, where most economic decisions are made.

Monetarists: Economists who emphasize the role of money in determining nominal income and inflation.

Monetary policy: The range of actions taken by the Federal Reserve to influence the level of GDP or the rate of inflation.

Monetizing the deficit: Purchases by a central bank of newly issued government bonds.

Money: Anything that is regularly used in exchange.

Money illusion: Confusion of real and nominal magnitudes.

Money multiplier: An initial deposit leads to a multiple expansion of deposits. In the simplified case increase in deposits = (initial deposit) × (1/reserve ratio).

Monopolistic competition: A market served by dozens of firms selling slightly different products.

Monopoly: A market in which a single firm serves the entire market.

Monopsony: A market in which there is a single buyer of an input.

Moral hazard problem: Insurance encourages risky behavior.

Multilateral real exchange rate: An index of the real exchange rate with a country's trading partners.

Multinational corporation: An organization that produces and sells goods and services throughout the world.

Multiplier: The ratio of changes in output to changes in spending. It measures the degree to which changes in spending are "multiplied" into changes in output.

Multiplier-accelerator model: A model in which a downturn in real GDP leads to a sharp fall in investment, which triggers further reductions in GDP through the multiplier.

National income: Net national product less indirect taxes.

Natural monopoly: A market in which the entry of a second firm would make price less than average cost, so a single firm serves the entire market.

Natural rate of unemployment: The level of unemployment at which there is no cyclical unemployment.

Natural resources: Things created by acts of nature and used to produce goods and services.

Negative relationship: A relationship in which an increase in the value of one variable decreases the value of the other variable.

Neoclassical theory of investment: A theory of investment that says both real interest rates and taxes are important determinants of investment.

Net exports: Exports minus imports.

Net international investment position: Domestic holdings of foreign assets minus foreign holdings of domestic assets.

Net investment: Gross investment minus depreciation.

Net national product (NNP): GNP less depreciation.

Net worth: The difference between assets and liabilities.

New growth theory: Modern theories of growth that try to explain the origins of technological progress.

Nominal GDP: The value of GDP in current dollars.

Nominal interest rates: Interest rates quoted in the market.

Nominal value: The face value of a sum of money.

Nondurable goods: Goods that last for short periods of time, such as food.

Normal good: A good for which an increase in income increases demand.

Normative economics: Analysis that answers the question, What ought to be?

North American Free Trade Agreement (NAFTA): An international agreement that lowers barriers to trade between the United States, Mexico, and Canada (signed in 1994).

Okun's law: A relationship between changes in real GDP and the unemployment rate.

Oligopoly: A market served by a few firms.

Open economy: An economy with international trade.

Open market purchases: The Fed's purchase of government bonds, which increases the money supply.

Open market sales: The Fed's sales of government bonds to the public, which decreases the money supply.

Opportunity cost: What you sacrifice to get something.

Output effect: The change in the quantity of labor demanded resulting from a change in the quantity of output.

Outside lags: The time it takes for policies to work.

Patent: The exclusive right to sell a particular good for some period of time.

Pay-as-you-go: A system that uses revenue collected this year to pay for benefits to recipients this year.

Paying efficiency wages: The firm's practice of paying wages to increase the average productivity of its workers.

Peak: The time at which a recession begins.

Perfectly competitive market: A market with a very large number of firms, each of which produces the same standardized product and takes the market price as given.

Perfectly elastic demand: The price elasticity of demand is infinite.

Perfectly elastic supply: The price elasticity of supply is infinite.

Perfectly inelastic demand: The price elasticity of demand is zero.

Perfectly inelastic supply: The price elasticity of supply is zero.

Permanent income: An estimate of a household's long-run average level of income.

Personal disposable income: Personal income after taxes.

Personal income: Income (including transfer payments) received by households.

Physical capital: Objects made by human beings and used to produce goods and services.

Political business cycle: The effects on the economy of using monetary or fiscal policy to stimulate the economy before an election to improve reelection prospects.

Pollution tax: A tax or charge equal to the spillover cost per unit of waste.

Positive economics: Analysis that answers the question, What is or what will be?

Positive relationship: A relationship in which an increase in the value of one variable increases the value of the other variable.

Poverty budget: The minimum amount the government estimates that a family needs to avoid being in poverty; equal to three times the minimum food budget.

Predatory pricing: A pricing scheme under which a firm decreases its price to drive a rival out of business, and increases the price when the other firm disappears.

Price ceiling: A maximum price; transactions above the maximum price are outlawed.

Price change formula: A formula that shows the percentage change in equilibrium price resulting from a change in demand or supply, given the values for the price elasticity of demand and the price elasticity of supply.

Price discrimination: The process under which a firm divides consumers into two or more groups and picks a different price for each group.

Price elasticity of demand: A measure of the responsiveness of the quantity demanded to changes in price; computed by dividing the percentage change in quantity demanded by the percentage change in price.

Price elasticity of supply: A measure of the responsiveness of the quantity supplied to changes in price; computed by dividing the percentage change in quantity supplied by the percentage change in price.

Price fixing: An arrangement in which two firms coordinate their pricing decisions.

Price floor: A minimum price; transactions below the minimum price are outlawed.

Price leadership: An implicit agreement under which firms in a market choose a price leader, observe that firm's price, and match it.

Price level: An average of all the prices in the economy as measured by a price index.

Price-support program: A policy under which the government specifies a minimum price above the equilibrium price.

Principle: A simple truth that most people understand and accept.

Private good: A good that is consumed by a single person or household.

Private investment expenditures: Purchases of newly produced goods and services by firms.

Privatizing: The process of selling state firms to individuals.

Procyclical: Moving in same direction as real GDP.

Producer surplus: The difference between the market price of a product and the minimum amount a producer is willing to accept for that product; alternatively, the difference between the market price and the marginal cost of production.

Product differentiation: A strategy of distinguishing one product from other similar products.

Production possibilities curve: A curve showing the combinations of two goods that can be produced by an economy, assuming that all resources are fully employed.

Protectionist policies: Rules that restrict the free flow of goods between nations, including tariffs (taxes on imports), quotas (limits on total imports), voluntary export restraints (agreements between governments to limit exports), and nontariff trade barriers (subtle practices that hinder trade).

Public choice economics: A field of economics that explores how governments actually operate.

Public good: A good that is available for everyone to consume, regardless of who pays and who doesn't.

Purchasing Power Parity: A theory of exchange rates, stating that the exchange rate between two currencies is determined by the price levels in the two countries.

Q-theory of investment: The theory of investment that links investment spending to stock prices.

Quantity demanded: The amount of a good a consumer is willing to buy.

Quantity equation: The equation that links money, velocity, prices and real output. In symbols, we have $M \times V = P \times y$.

Quantity supplied: The amount of a good a firm is willing to sell.

Rational expectations: The economic theory that analyzes how people form expectations in such a manner that, on average, they forecast the future correctly.

Real business cycle theory: The economic theory that emphasizes how shocks to technology can cause fluctuations in economic activity.

Real exchange rate: The market exchange rate adjusted for prices.

Real GDP: A measure of GDP that controls for changes in prices.

Real GDP per capita: Gross domestic product per person adjusted for changes in prices. It is the usual measure of living standards across time and between countries.

Real interest rate: The nominal interest rate minus the inflation rate.

Real value: The value of a sum of money in terms of the quantity of goods the money can buy.

Real wage: The wage paid to workers adjusted for changes in prices.

Real wages: Nominal or dollar wages adjusted for changes in purchasing power.

Recession: Six consecutive months of negative economic growth.

Rent control: A policy under which the government specifies a maximum rent that is below the equilibrium rent.

Rent seeking: The process under which a firm spends money to persuade the government to erect barriers to entry and pick the firm as the monopolist.

Required reserves: The fraction of banks' deposits that banks are legally required to hold in their vaults or as deposits at the Fed.

Reserve ratio: The ratio of reserves to deposits.

Reserves: The fraction of banks' deposits set aside in either vault cash or as deposits at the Federal Reserve.

Revaluation: An increase in the exchange rate in a fixed exchange system.

Ricardian equivalence: The proposition that it does not matter whether government expenditure is financed by taxes or by debt.

Saving: Total income minus consumption.

Savings Function: The relationship between the level of income and the level of savings.

Scarcity: A situation in which resources are limited and can be used in different ways, so we must sacrifice one thing for another.

Services: Reflect work done in which people play a prominent role in delivery, ranging from haircutting to health care.

Shoe-leather costs: Costs of inflation that arise from trying to reduce holdings of cash.

Short run: A period of time over which one or more factors of production is fixed; in most cases, a period of time over which a firm cannot modify an existing facility or build a new one.

Short-run average total cost (SATC): Short-run total cost divided by the quantity of output, equal to AFC plus AVC.

Short-run average variable cost (SAVC): Variable cost divided by the quantity produced.

Short-run demand curve for labor: A curve showing the relationship between the wage and the quantity of labor demanded in the short run, the period when the firm cannot change its production facility.

Short run in macroeconomics: The period of time that prices do not change very much.

Short-run marginal cost (SMC): The change in total cost resulting from producing one more unit of the good in the short run.

Short-run market supply curve: A curve showing the relationship between price and the quantity of output supplied by all firms in the short run.

Short-run production function: Shows how much output is produced from varying amounts of labor, holding the capital stock constant.

Short-run supply curve for a firm: A curve showing the relationship between the price of a product and the quantity of output supplied by a firm in the short run.

Shut-down price: The price at which the firm is indifferent between operating and shutting down.

Signaling effect: The increase in a person's wage resulting from the signal of productivity provided by completing college.

Slope: The change in the variable on the vertical axis resulting from a one-unit increase in the variable on the horizontal axis.

Social insurance: A system that compensates individuals for bad luck, low skills, or misfortunes.

Social Security: A government program that provides retirement, survivor, and disability benefits.

Speculative demand for money: The demand for money that reflects holding money over short periods is less risky than holding stocks or bonds.

Spillover: A cost or benefit experienced by people who are external to the decision about how much of a good to produce or consume.

Stabilization policy: Policy actions taken to bring the economy closer to full employment or potential output.

Stock of capital: The total of all the machines, equipment, and buildings in the entire economy.

Store of value: The property of money that it preserves value until it is used in an exchange.

Structural unemployment: The part of unemployment that results from the mismatch of skills and jobs.

Substitutes: Two goods related in such a way that an increase in the price of one good increases the demand for the other good.

Substitution effect for price changes: The change in consumption resulting from a change in the price of one good relative to the price of other goods.

Substitution effect for wage changes: An increase in the wage rate increases the opportunity cost of leisure and leads workers to demand less leisure and supply more labor.

Sunk cost: The cost a firm has already paid—or has agreed to pay some time in the future.

Supply curve: See *individual supply curve*; see *market supply curve*.

Supply schedule: A table of numbers that shows the relationship between price and quantity supplied, ceteris paribus (other things being equal).

Supply shocks: External events that shift the aggregate supply curve.

Supply-siders: Economists who emphasize the role of taxation for influencing economic activity.

Surplus: The excess of total revenues over total expenditures.

Tariff: A tax on an imported good.

Taxi medallion: A license to operate a taxi.

Technological progress: An increase in output without increasing inputs.

Terms of trade: The rate at which two goods will be exchanged.

Thin market: A market in which some high-quality goods are sold, but fewer than would be sold in a market with perfect information.

Tit-for-tat: A strategy under which the one firm in a duopoly starts out with the cartel price and then chooses whatever price the other firm chose in the preceding period.

Total burden of a tax: The loss in consumer surplus resulting from a tax (assuming a constant-cost industry).

Total product curve: A curve showing the relationship between the number of workers and the quantity of output produced.

Total revenue: The money the firm gets by selling its product; equal to the price times the quantity sold.

Total surplus of a market: The sum of the net benefits experienced by consumers and producers; equal to the sum of consumer surplus and producer surplus.

Total utility: The utility (measured in utils) from whatever quantity of the product the consumer gets.

Total variable cost (TVC): Cost that varies as the firm changes the quantity produced.

Trade deficit: The excess of imports over exports.

Trade surplus: The excess of exports over imports.

Transactions demand for money: The demand for money based on the desire to facilitate transactions.

Transfer payments: Payments to individuals from governments that do not correspond to the production of goods and services.

Transition: The process of shifting from a centrally planned economy toward a mixed economic system, with markets playing a greater role in the economy.

Trough: The time at which output stops falling in a recession.

Trust: An arrangement under which the owners of several companies transfer their decision-making powers to a small group of trustees, who then make decisions for all the firms in the trust.

Tying: A business practice under which a consumer of one product is required to purchase another product.

Unanticipated inflation: Inflation that is not expected.

Underemployed: Workers who hold a part-time job but prefer to work full time or hold jobs that are far below their capabilities.

Unemployed: People who are looking for work but do not have jobs.

Unemployment insurance: Payments received from the government upon becoming unemployed.

Unemployment rate: The fraction of the labor force that is unemployed.

Unitary elasticity: The price elasticity is equal to one.

Unit of account: The property of money that prices are quoted in terms of money.

Usury laws: Laws that do not allow interest rates to exceed specified ceilings.

Util: One unit of utility.

Utility: The satisfaction or pleasure the consumer experiences when he or she consumes a good, measured as the number of utils.

Utility-maximizing rule: Pick the affordable combination of consumer goods that makes the marginal utility per dollar spent on one good equal to that of a second good.

Value added: The sum of all the income (wages, interest, profits, rent) generated by an organization.

Variable: A measure of something that can take on different values.

Variable costs: Costs that vary as the quantity produced changes.

Velocity of money: Nominal GDP divided by the money supply. It is also the rate at which money turns over during the year.

Vertical equity: The idea that people with more income or wealth should pay higher taxes.

Voluntary export restraint (VER): A scheme under which an exporting country voluntarily decreases its exports.

Wage-price spiral: Changes in wages and prices causing more changes in wages and prices.

Wealth effect: The increase in spending that occurs because the real value of money increases when the price level falls.

World Trade Organization (WTO): An organization that oversees GATT and other international trade agreements.

Worldwide sourcing: The practice of buying components for a product from nations throughout the world.

Photo Credits

Chapter 1: Page 1, Scour Inc.; page 11 (left), Michael Newman/PhotoEdit; page 11 (right), © Catherine Karnow/CORBIS.

Chapter 2: Page 23 (left and right), Photofest; page 27, © Danny Lehman/CORBIS; page 31 (left), © Peter Turnley/CORBIS; page 31 (right), Klehr & Churchill/Getty Images, Inc.; page 35, Mark Richards/PhotoEdit.

Chapter 3: Page 41, AP/Wide World Photos; page 42, Ronnie Kaufman/Corbis/Stock Market; page 47, Y. Forestier/Corbis/Sygma; page 50, Photofest; page 57, Corbis/SABA Press Photos, Inc.

Chapter 4: Page 63, Michael Newman/PhotoEdit; page 80, Glen Allison/Getty Images, Inc./PhotoDisc, Inc.; page 85 (top), Tom Bross/Studio 20/Stock Boston; page 85 (bottom), Jow Towers/Corbis/Stock Market.

Chapter 5: Page 95, Jonathan Novrok/PhotoEdit; page 100, IPA/Chapman Parry/The Image Works; page 104, Les Stone/Corbis/Sygma.

Chapter 6: Page 119, David Young-Wolf/PhotoEdit; page 122, RB Studio 96/Corbis/Stock Market.

Chapter 7: Page 145, The Image Works; page 152, © Jonathan Blair/CORBIS.

Chapter 8: Page 163, Michael Newman/PhotoEdit; page 175, Billy E. Barnes/PhotoEdit; page 176, Marilyn Kazmers-SharkSong/Dembinksy Photo Associates; page 177, California Department of Water Resources.

Chapter 9: Page 187, Spencer Grant/PhotoEdit; page 194, Michael Newman/PhotoEdit; page 197, CORBIS; page 201, David Young-Wolff/PhotoEdit.

Chapter 10: Page 213, Barry Schwartz; page 215, Weizenbach/Corbis/Stock Market; page 224, R. Valladares/Getty Images Inc.; page 228, Photo Researchers, Inc.

Chapter 11: Page 235, Crutchfield; page 240, Ralf-Finn Hestoft/Corbis/SABA Press Photos, Inc.

Chapter 12: Page 251, Getty Images, Inc.; page 258, Beaura Katherine Ringrose; page 264, Billy E. Barnes/PhotoEdit.

Chapter 13: Page 277, Michael Newman/PhotoEdit; page 281, Reuters NewMedia Inc./CORBIS; page 284, Beaura Katherine Ringrose; page 286, David Young-Wolff/PhotoEdit.

Chapter 14: Page 293, Getty Images, Inc.; page 298, Michael Newman/PhotoEdit; page 299, © Michael S. Yamashita.CORBIS.

Chapter 15: Page 311, Michael Newman/PhotoEdit; page 318, Robert Rathe/Stock Boston; page 319, Bryan Yablonsky/Duomo Photography Incorporated; page 321, Spencer Grant/PhotoEdit.

Chapter 16: Page 329, Kauko Helavuo/Getty Images, Inc.; page 338, © Tony Arruza/CORBIS.

Chapter 17: Page 349 (left), Phil Borden/PhotoEdit; page 349 (right), © Michael Busselle/PhotoEdit; page 355, Mike Greenlar/The Image Works; page 358, Malcolm Fife/Getty Images, Inc./PhotoDisc, Inc.; page 363, Alan Oddie/PhotoEdit.

Chapter 18: Page 371, David Young-Wolff/PhotoEdit; page 380, Jon Riley/ Getty Images, Inc.; page 385, © Catherine Karnow/CORBIS; page 390, Ford Motor Company.

Chapter 19: Page 399, © David Leeson/The Image Works; page 402 (left), Tom McCarthy/PhotoEdit; page 402 (right), Paul Conklin/PhotoEdit; page 412, Pete Saloutos/Corbis/Stock Market.

Chapter 20: Page 417, Steven Rubin/The Image Works; page 427, Amy C. Etra/PhotoEdit.

Answers to Odd-Numbered Problems and Discussion Questions

Chapter 1

1. Buying a used car: It is difficult to determine the quality of the car.
   Providing health insurance: It is difficult to determine whether the customer will have large or small medical expenses.
3. The number of lectures attended, the hours of sleep the night before the exam.
5. Move along, shift.

Appendix to Chapter 1

1. a. See Figure S.1.
   b. The slope is $5.
   c. The monthly bill will increase by $15.
3. 10%, –2%, 6%.
5. The number of burglaries will decrease by 4.

Chapter 2

1. The statement ignores the opportunity cost of the time spent in college.
3. The marginal cost is the cost of equipping and paying one more officer. The officer would presumably decrease crime, and the marginal benefit is determined by the reduction in crime resulting from the additional officer. If you can measure the marginal cost and the marginal ben-

efit, you should continue to hire officers until the marginal benefit equals the marginal cost.
5. In the long run, the firm can modify its production facility or build a new one.
7. Eventually, we expect output to increase at a decreasing rate because more and more workers share the espresso machine.
9. Salaries increased faster than the price of consumer goods.

Chapter 3

1. Brenda could specialize in bread. Instead of producing one shirt for herself, Brenda could use the time it would take to produce one shirt to produce two loaves of bread. If she then trades one loaf of bread for one shirt, she will have one loaf of bread left over. She gets the same number of shirts and one extra loaf of bread. Sam could specialize in shirts. Instead of producing one loaf of bread for himself, Sam could use the time it would take to produce a loaf of bread to produce two shirts. If he trades one shirt for one loaf of bread, he will have the same amount of bread but one extra shirt.
3. Professor A has a comparative advantage in the graduate course: He is twice as productive as Professor B in that course (90/45), but only 1.5 times as productive in the undergraduate course (90/60). Looking at this another way, the total performance (score in the undergraduate course plus the score in the graduate course) is 150 when Professor A teaches the graduate course and Professor B teaches the undergraduate course (90 in G plus 60 in U), compared to only 135 when Professor A teaches the undergraduate course and Professor B teaches the graduate course.
5. Mexican goods are now less costly and therefore more attractive. An American who wants to buy a good that costs 5 pesos must spend $0.25 to get the pesos to pay for the good (5 pesos times the price of $0.05 per peso), compared to $0.50 before (5 pesos times the price of $0.10 per peso). From the perspective of a Mexican consumer, American goods are now more costly and therefore less attractive. A Mexican who wants to buy a good that costs $1 must spend 20 pesos to get the dollar to pay for the good ($1 divided by the price of $0.05 per peso), compared to only 10 pesos before ($1 divided by the price of $0.10 per peso).

Chapter 4

1. a. *w*, $150,200 per day.
   b. demand, increase.
   c. supply, decrease.

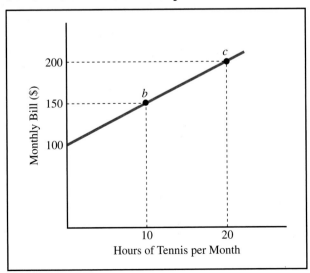

Figure S.1 **Relationship Between Hours of Tennis and the Monthly Tennis Club Bill**

3. a. The cost of producing computers will decrease, so the production of computers will be more profitable, so firms will supply more of them. The supply curve will shift to the right, decreasing the equilibrium price.

   b. The tax increases the production cost, shifting the supply curve to the left and increasing the equilibrium price.

5. Education at private and public schools are substitutes, so the tuition hike will shift the demand for private education to the right, increasing the equilibrium price and quantity.

7. If price and quantity both increase, we know from Table 4.1 that demand has increased. We shift the demand curve to the right, increasing the price and quantity.

9. How many people switch to automobile travel as a result of the higher cost of air travel? How does the shift to automobile travel affect the number of injuries and deaths on the highways? Does the airport security system reduce the number of injuries and deaths related to air travel? If so, how many lives are saved and how many injuries are avoided?

11. The supply curve for shirts shifts to the left, increasing the equilibrium price and decreasing the equilibrium quantity.

Chapter 5

1. The price elasticity is 1.30 = the percentage change in quantity (13%) divided by the percentage change in price (10%). Demand is elastic.

3. Each brand has many substitute goods (all the other brands), so the demand for a specific brand will be more elastic than the demand for running shoes in general.

5. Inelastic: An increase in price increases total revenue, while a decrease in price decreases total revenue.

7. Use the elasticity formula: The 10% increase in the price of beer will decrease the quantity of beer consumed by 13%, decreasing the highway death rate by the same percentage. Therefore, the number of highway deaths will decrease by 13 (13% of 100).

9. Use the price-change formula: The predicted change in price is 1% = 4%/(1 + 3). In the graph, we shift the supply curve to the left, so the restrictions increase the price from $100,000 to $101,000 and decreases the equilibrium quantity.

Chapter 6

1. We assume that buyers and sellers have enough information to make informed choices and that there are no spillover benefits nor spillover costs. The assumption of informed choices is likely to be violated in the case of used cars: buyers don't know the quality of the car. The assumption of no spillover benefits is likely to be violated for national defense, space exploration, public radio, and education. The assumption of no spillover costs is likely to be violated for goods that generate pollution such as paper, transportation (auto and bus), and electricity.

3. a. A + B + C
   b. D + E + F
   c. A + B + C + D + E + F
   d. A + B + D
   e. F
   f. A + B + D + F
   g. A
   h. B + D + F
   i. A + B + D + F

5. The supply of clothing to an individual city is much more elastic than the supply of housing, so price controls would decrease the quantity of clothing supplied by a larger amount. In addition, everyone would have to wait in line to get clothing. In contrast, people who occupy rent-controlled apartments don't have to find a new apartment every week, so they avoid most of the queuing and search costs and provide political support for rent control.

7. In the market equilibrium, there are 100 taxis and the price of taxi service is $3, which is just high enough to cover the cost of providing taxi service. If the government issues more than 100 medallions, no one will use the extra medallions, and the medallion policy will have no effect on the market: The price of taxi service will be $3, and the price of a medallion will be zero.

9. For parts (a) and (b), as in the case of taxi medallions, the quantity restrictions will increase the equilibrium price and decrease the equilibrium quantity. For part (c), the import restrictions shift the market supply curve to the left, increasing the equilibrium price and decreasing the equilibrium quantity.

11. With only 3 gallons of waste per ton of cardboard, the pollution tax increases the production cost per ton by $6 (instead of $10), so the supply curve shifts by a smaller amount. Compared to the case with 5 gallons per ton, the 3-gallon case generates a lower equilibrium price and a larger equilibrium quantity.

Chapter 7

1. Betty will consume 6 muffins. If Betty chooses 6 muffins, the marginal benefit is 8 utils (from the muffin table). Given a budget of $60, she would have $48 left to spend on cookies, meaning that she could buy 48 cookies at $1 each. If she consumes 48 cookies, the marginal utility of cookies is 4 utils per cookie (from the cookie table). Given the prices ($2 per muffin and $1 per cookie), she sacrifices 2 cookies for each muffin, so the marginal cost of muffins is 8 utils (2 cookies per muffin times 4 utils per cookie). The marginal benefit of muffins equals the marginal cost, so the best she can do is 6 muffins and 48 cookies.

3. What is the marginal utility of a dollar spent on food? What is the marginal utility of CDs? Your current choice maximizes your utility if the marginal utility of CDs is ten times the marginal utility of food.

Appendix to Chapter 7

1. The vertical intercept of the budget line is 40 violets, and the horizontal intercept is 10 hats.

   a. The slope is the price of hats divided by the price of violets, or 4.0.

b. An indifference curve that intersects the budget line is not the highest (most northeasterly) possible indifference curve.

c. The second indifference curve should be tangent to the budget line.

d. marginal rate of substitution.

3. Carla's MRS is 2.0, which exceeds the price ration of 1/3. Therefore, she should pick an auto with more horsepower and less interior space.

Chapter 8

1. The average cost is $15 for 40 shirts, $9 for 100 shirts, $7 for 200 shirts, and $6 for 400 shirts.

3.

Labor	Output	Marginal Product
0	0	
1	5	5
2	11	6
3	15	4
4	18	3
5	19	1

5. There are no diminishing returns, so marginal cost is constant.

7. The $12,500 figure includes some of the fixed cost of production (design and tooling costs), so it is an average cost, not a marginal cost.

9. As shown in Figure 8.6, the average cost for the large generator is $4.60 (point b), compared to an average cost of $5.00 for the small generator (point c).

Chapter 9

1.

Tables per hour	Total cost	Marginal cost
3	120	—
4	155	35
5	200	45
6	270	70

3. If the firm continues to operate its facility, its total revenue will be $9,000 = $30 times 300 units of output. This is the benefit of operating the facility. The cost of operating the facility is the variable cost, which equals labor cost ($7,000 = the $100 wage times 700 workers). Total revenue exceeds variable cost, so it is sensible to continue operating the facility, even though it is losing money.

5. The manager is bluffing. His total revenue ($35,000) exceeds the *variable cost* ($30,000 for the farm workers). The $20,000 paid for seed and fertilizer was incurred months ago, and it is a sunk cost that will be ignored in the decision about whether to harvest the crop. Because his total revenue exceeds his variable cost, the farmer will harvest the crop even if the workers don't accept a wage cut.

7. We cannot draw a supply curve or complete the price elasticity of supply because we cannot be certain that the other variables that affect the supply of gasoline (the price of inputs, technology) did not change over this period.

9.

Number of firms	Industry output	Total cost for typical firm	Average cost per lamp
40	400	$300	$30
80	800	$360	$36
120	1,200	$420	$42

We have 3 points on the long-run supply curve: At a price of $30, the quantity is 400 lamps; at a price of $36, the quantity is 800 lamps; at a price of $42, the quantity is 1,200 lamps.

11. Because the industry uses such tiny amounts of the relevant inputs, the prices of these inputs won't change as the industry grows. Therefore, the average cost per haircut does not depend on the quantity of haircuts. The long-run supply curve is horizontal, for example, at a constant cost of $10 per haircut.

Chapter 10

1. To maximize profit, the restaurant will pick the quantity at which marginal revenue equals marginal cost. Using the marginal-revenue formula, we can compute the marginal revenue at each price and quantity:

Price	$10	$9	$8	$7
Quantity	30	40	50	60
Marginal revenue	$7	$5	$3	$1

Marginal revenue equals marginal cost at a price of $8 and a quantity of 50 meals.

3. On average, the payback per dollar spent on these lottery games is about 50¢. In other words, for every $100 spent by players, the state pays $50 in prizes. The commercial gambling games have much higher paybacks: The payback per dollar is 81¢ for horse racing and 89¢ for slot machines. The lottery games have lower paybacks because each state has a monopoly on lottery games: The state outlaws commercial lotteries. If the state allowed other organizations to offer lottery games, the competition between commercial and state lottery games would increase the payback from lottery games.

5. The artificial barrier to entry will generate higher prices and a smaller quantity demanded. If we eliminated the barriers, there would be more teams, and ticket prices would fall, increasing total attendance.

7. A decrease in demand shifts the demand curve to the left, and the new demand curve will intersect the negatively sloped long-run average-cost curve at a smaller quantity and a higher average cost (price). The loss of scale economies will cause the regulated price to rise.

9. Monopoly power increases prices in the game of Monopoly, consistent with the conclusions in this chapter.

11. The consumer advocate is assuming that the demand for the drug is perfectly inelastic, so an increase in price does not have any effect on the quantity demanded. This is unrealistic and is inconsistent with the law of demand.

Chapter 11

1. The following table shows price and average cost for different numbers of arcades. Price exceeds average cost for the first four arcades, so the equilibrium number of arcades is 4.

Number of arcades	1	2	3	4	5
Price	50¢	48¢	46¢	44¢	42¢
Average cost	34¢	37¢	40¢	43¢	46¢

3. There are two logical errors in the expert's statement. First, the entry of firms will decrease the market price, and the market will move downward along the market demand curve. Therefore, the total quantity of pizzas demanded will exceed 3,000 (the quantity associated with the monopoly price). Second, as shown in all the examples in this chapter, we expect the typical firm to operate along the negatively sloped portion of its average-cost curve, not the horizontal portion. In other words, we expect each firm to produce fewer than 1,000 pizzas per day. These two observations suggest that there will be more than three pizzerias. For example, if the decrease in price increases the quantity demanded to 4,000 and each store produces only 800 pizzas per day, there will be five pizzerias (4,000 divided by 800).

5. A firm that cuts three lawns will have a total cost of $30 ($18 in fixed cost + $12 in variable cost (3 lawns times $4 per lawn), or an average cost of $10 per lawn. In equilibrium, the price will be equal to average cost, which happens with a quantity of 60 lawns. Dividing the 60 lawns cut by 3 lawns per firm, there will be 20 firms in equilibrium.

7. The city must have issued a sufficiently large number of licenses that entry continued to the point where economic profit reached zero. In graphical terms, the demand curve facing the typical firm is tangent to the negatively sloped average-cost curve: Average cost equals price, so economic profit is zero and no one is willing to pay anything for a license.

Chapter 12

1. See Figure S.2. The profit per firm under the duopoly outcome is $500 (a profit of $5 per passenger times 100 passengers). The profit per firm under the cartel is $750 (a profit of $10 per passenger times 75 passengers). Each firm will pick the low price. The path of the game is X to Z to rectangle 4.

3. One reason for low prices at these sales is that there is no punishment for underpricing the other firm. Any prior arrangement for cartel pricing would evaporate when one firm knows that it will soon go out of business.

5. If both firms pick the high price, each will get a profit of $360. If both pick the low price, each will get a profit of

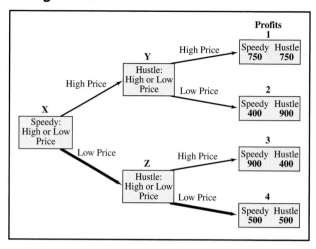

Figure S.2 Game Tree for Airporter Price-Fixing Game

$250. For each firm, picking the low price is the dominant strategy.

If firms pick prices each day, Bizarre weighs the benefit of undercutting ($140 on the day of undercutting) against the cost (the difference between the high-price profit ($360) and the low-price profit ($250) times the number of days remaining after the undercutting). On the first day, the cost is $220, which exceeds the benefit of $140. Assuming that Bizarre is not savvy enough to think about the end game (the last day), she will not undercut Weird.

7. The longer the time both firms will be in the market, the greater the opportunity for punishing a firm that undercuts, so the more likely price fixing will work. Longtime is more likely to have price fixing that keeps prices high.

Chapter 13

1. The marginal revenue for business travelers is MR = $300 − 2.0 × 120 = $60, which is less than the marginal cost, so the airline should increase the price for business travelers. The marginal revenue for tourists is MR = $300 − 1.0 × 80 = $240, which is greater than the marginal cost, so the airline should decrease the price for tourists.

3. This price-discrimination scheme is based on the notion that bargain hunters are early birds. The large discounts for early fabric purchases attract consumers who would otherwise not buy fabric at the regular price.

5. Car companies use price discrimination in their option pricing. They have higher markups on options that have relatively inelastic demand.

7. As shown in Table 13.2, the marginal benefit of advertising equals the change in quantity times the net revenue per unit. In contrast, the statement in the questions suggest that the marginal benefit is the increase in total revenue.

Chapter 14

1. Consumer surplus decreases by $700. For the 150 that are units sold at the higher price, consumers lose an amount equal to the change in price ($4) times the quantity con-

sumed (150), or $600. In addition, the price hike reduces the quantity consumed, and the loss of consumer surplus for the 151st through the 200th units is equal to the change in price ($4) times the change in quantity (50 units) times 1/2, or an additional $100. The total profit of the firms increases from $200 ($1 per unit times 200 units sold) to $750 ($5 per unit times 150 units). The increase in profit ($550) is less than the loss of consumer surplus ($700), so the net loss for society is $150.

3. Giving the gates to Gotcha will allow the airline to maintain its monopoly power and continue to charge higher prices than would occur if there was competition.

Chapter 16

1. a. No. Bertha is willing to pay the most ($100), but she is willing to pay less than the cost ($120).
   b. No. The cost per citizen will be $40, so Bertha is the only one who is willing to pay more than the cost per capita.
   c. Suppose each citizen pays $10 less than his or her willingness to pay: Bertha pays $90; Marian pays $20; Sam pays $10. This scheme raises $120 and benefits each citizen.

3. The free-rider problem disappears because if any person does not contribute, the public good won't be provided. This money-back guarantee makes it more likely that everyone will contribute and get 30¢ at the end of the experiment.

5. a. The benefit is $8,000 (80,000 citizens times $0.10 per person), which exceeds the cost of $5,000. Since the benefit exceeds the cost, the provision of the additional litter is socially efficient.
   b. No. The benefit to the rancher ($0.10) is less than the cost ($5,000).
   c. The citizens could contribute to a wolf-preservation fund to provide the rancher with enough money to offset the cost of a litter of wolves. For example, if each citizen contributed $0.07 (70% of his or her benefit), they could raise a total of $5,600. By paying this amount to the landowner who hosts the wolf litter, the rancher would be better off by $600, and each of the citizens would be better off by $0.03.

7. a. No. Part of the tax will be shifted backward onto input suppliers, including laborers who work in auto factories and dealerships.
   b. The price elasticity of demand for automobiles and the responsiveness of input suppliers to changes in input prices.

9. a. The median voter now has a desired budget of $6 billion, so each candidate will propose a budget very close to $6 billion.
   b. The answer will not change because the median voter is still the person with the $6 billion budget.

Chapter 17

1. See Figure S.3. The market equilibrium is shown by point *i*: The demand curve intersects the supply curve at 20 units per day. The pollution tax shifts the supply curve by such a

Figure S.3 **Pollution Tax Makes the Equilibrium Quantity of a Polluting Good Zero**

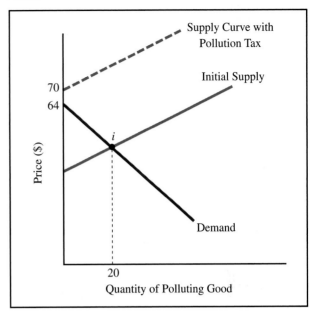

large amount that the supply curve lies entirely above the demand curve. For this to occur, the spillover cost from the pollutant must be very high, the cost of abatement must be very high, and the demand for good must be relatively low.

3. a. From Table 17.1, the production cost per ton with zero pollution is $116.
   b. The marginal cost associated with going from 1 gallon to 0 gallons is $30. For firms to make this choice, the marginal benefit of abatement (the tax savings) must be at least $30.

5. The supply curve will shift to the left as some of the cars are destroyed. The equilibrium price will increase, and the equilibrium quantity will decrease.

7. We could adjust other taxes to mitigate any undesirable effects on the poor. For example, we could decrease the sales tax rate or adjust the income tax rates.

Chapter 15

1. Suppose Groucho wants to join a social club to associate with people who are richer than he is, and he assumes that other people join clubs for the same reasons. A club will invite him to join only if he would increase the average income of the club. In other words, Groucho will be invited to join only groups in which most people are poorer than he is, clubs with an adverse selection of people. The same reasoning applies if Groucho wants to associate with people who are wittier than he is and he assumes that other people feel the same way. A club that asks him to join will have an average wit level that is less than his, so he will be forced to interact with dimwits.

3. Suppose you're willing to pay the average value of the two types of cameras ($60) for a 50% chance of getting a plum.

If you expect a greater than 50% chance of getting a plum, it will be wise to buy a used camera. Given the adverse-selection problem, your chance of getting a plum is likely to be less than 50%.

5. The detector eliminates the imperfect information problem, so the two types of used cars will be sold in separate markets, with one price for lemons ($2,000 in our example) and another price for plums ($4,000). There is no adverse selection because each buyer knows exactly what type of car he or she will get.

7. Like the lie detector, the genetic tests eliminate the adverse selection problem, this time for insurance companies. The insurance companies will charge higher prices to those who are likely to contract the diseases and lower prices to those who are not. This may strike many people as unfair.

9. If Ira doesn't have fire insurance, he will spend money on the prevention program because the benefit is the avoidance of an expected loss of $10,000 (a 10% chance of losing $100,000), which exceeds the $5,000 cost. If he has an insurance policy covering 80% of the loss, the benefit is the avoidance of an expected loss of $2,000 (a 10% chance of losing $80,000). The benefit is less than the $5,000 cost, so he won't spend money on the program. Ira will be indifferent with a coverage rate of 50%. In this case, the benefit is the avoidance of an expected loss of $5,000 (a 10% chance of losing $50,000), which is equal to the cost.

Chapter 18

1. The payroll tax shifts the supply curve to the left: At every price, a smaller quantity is supplied. The leftward shift of the supply curve increases the equilibrium wage to a wage above $10.

3. Some people will work fewer hours, so they will pay less in taxes: They pay a lower rate on fewer hours. Other people will work the same number of hours and pay less in taxes too: They pay a lower rate on the same number of hours. Even a person who works more hours could pay less in taxes: If the increase in hours is small relative to the decrease in the hourly tax rate, the tax bill (hours times the tax rate) will actually decrease. The only people who will pay more in taxes are the workers who increase their hours by an amount that is large relative to the decrease in the hourly rate.

5. a. The supply of teachers is large relative to demand, so wages are relatively low. This could result from the psychological rewards from teaching, the work hours, or the free summer time.

b. This is effectively a minimum wage for teachers, and it has the same effect as a minimum wage for any occupation: The increase in the wage will decrease the quantity demanded, so some teachers will lose their jobs.

7. Let's assume that the program is paid for by government, not coal companies. The program will increase the supply of coal workers, shifting the supply curve to the right. The equilibrium wage will decrease.

9. Like a minimum wage, a comparable-worth policy that increases wages in some occupations will decrease the quantity of labor demanded, so fewer workers will be hired. In addition, higher wages lead to higher production costs and output prices, so consumers will be harmed. An alternative policy is to break down the barriers that have discouraged women from choosing certain occupations.

Chapter 19

1. Perhaps the high-school education received 25 to 35 years ago by workers who are now in their 40s was superior to the education received 5 to 15 years ago by workers who are now in their 20s.

3. This policy will increase the supply of college graduates, increasing competition for jobs requiring a college education. As a result, we would expect lower wages for college graduates and a smaller gap between the wages of college graduates and high-school graduates (smaller than we would otherwise observe).

5. If health care is provided by the employer, there may be problems when workers change jobs.

Chapter 20

1. a. In Country B, the opportunity cost of 1 computer is 2 TVs, and the opportunity cost of 1 TV is 1/2 of a computer. In Country C, the opportunity cost of 1 computer is 4 TVs, and the opportunity cost of 1 TV is 1/4 of a computer. Country B has the comparative advantage of producing computers, and Country C the comparative advantage of producing TVs.

b. The production possibility curves are straight lines for both countries, the slope being the opportunity costs and the intercepts being the maximum level of production of each good.

3. Chipland produces 120 chips and exchanges them for 70 shirts, ending up with 85 chips and 70 shirts. Shirtland produces 108 shirts and exchanges 70 of them for 35 chips, ending up with 35 chips and 35 shirts.

5. If the VERs were replaced with a tariff, the government would collect revenue. Under VERs, the importers earn large profits.

7. Consumers will benefit because prices will decrease. As each nation shifts its production to the goods for which it has a comparative advantage, workers in expanding industries will benefit, while workers in other industries will lose. The challenge for policymakers is to facilitate this transition.

9. Taxpayers will favor the shift because they will earn revenue. The firms importing goods will lobby against this because they will lose the profits they earn from the quotas. Firms may be more effective in lobbying than taxpayers because the losses are concentrated among a few firms, but the benefits are spread widely across taxpayers.

Index

Price-change formula, 111–113
Price controls for natural monopoly, 229–230
Price discrimination, 278–281
    advertisers' dilemma, 284–287
    elasticity of demand and, 280
    trade-offs from advertising, 287
Price elasticity
    computing with midpoint formula, 101–102
    of demand, 96–103
    predicting price changes using, 111–113
    of supply, 96, 109–111
Price fixing, 255–257
    antitrust laws and, 263–264
    in cyberspace, 260
Price-fixing game, outcome of, 257
Price leadership, 264–265
Price matching, 259–262
    guaranteed, 259–260
Pricing, retaliation strategies and, 262–263
Principle, 24
Prisoners' dilemma, 258–259
Private goods, 331
    with spillover benefits, 331–332
Privatizing, 58
Producer surplus, supply curve and, 122–123
Product differentiation, 240
Production
    economies of scale in, 253
    in long run, 173–177
    marginal product and, 166–168
    in short run, 165–172
Production costs and size of industry in long run, 197–199
Production possibilities
    opportunity cost and, 25–26
    scarcity and, 2–5
Production possibilities curve, 3–5, 418–420
Production possibilities graph, 3
Productivity, impact of labor unions on, 389
Productivity changes in quantity supplied, 110
Product market, 45
Profit, economic, 188
Property crime, price elasticity, of demand in predicting, 106
Property tax, 55
Protectionist policies, 47–49
    import ban, 422–423
    import quota, 423
    rationales for, 427–430
    responses to, 425–426
    tariffs, 424–425
    voluntary export restraint, 423–424
Public choice, 340–344
Public goods, 331
    examples of, 331
    free-rider problem and, 332–333
Public policy
    aging of society and, 406–410
    global warming and, 359–362
    health care and, 410–413

labor markets and, 383–387
poverty and, 400–406
role of economic analysis in, 7

Q

Quantity, government intervention in restricting, 128–130
Quantity demanded, 65
    predicting changes in, 103
Quantity supplied, 68–69
    productivity changes in, 110
Quicken, 296
Quota, 48

R

Race, poverty and, 400
Racial discrimination, 382
    poverty and, 402
    in wages, 382
Racial segregation, poverty and, 402
Reality principle, 36–37
Real value, 36
Real world, entry in, 239
Regulation, pollution tax versus, 350–354
Relationship, using graphs to show, 14–19
Rental housing as example of increasing-cost industry, 201
Rent control, 127
Rent seeking
    theory of, 343
    using resources to get monopoly power, 223
Repeated pricing and retaliation for underpricing, 262–266
Replication, 173–174
Resources, rent seeking using, to get monopoly power, 223
Restaurants, senior discounts in, 279–280
Retaliation strategies, 262–263
Revenue
    marginal, 190
    predicting changes in total, 104–106
    total, 188
Reynolds International Pen Corporation, 270
RJR Nabisco, 252
Robinson-Patman Act (1936), 294, 295, 300

S

Sales taxes, 55
Satellite radio as natural monopoly, 228
SBC/Ameritec, 252
Scale economies in wind power, 177
Scarcity, 2
    production possibilities and, 2–5
Scott Graphics, Inc., 299
Second firm
    effect of, 238
    entrance of, and natural monopoly, 226–228
Self-interest, 8
Self-interest theory of government, 343
Sellers

firms as, 46
households as, 45–46
knowledgeable, 313–314
Senior, Nassau, 7
Senior discounts in restaurants, 279–280
Sherman Anti-Trust Act (1890), 263, 294
Short run
    diminishing returns in, 33
    labor demand by individual firm in, 372–374
    long-run decisions versus, 165
    market demand in, 374–375
    production and cost in, 165–172
Short-run average cost curves, 170–171
Short-run average total cost, 170
Short-run average variable cost, 170
Short-run cost, long-run cost versus, 180–181
Short-run demand curve for labor, 374
Short-run equilibrium in monopolistic competition, 241–242
Short-run marginal cost, 168–170
Short-run output decision, 188–192
Short-run supply curve of firm, 195–196
Short-run total cost, 168–170
Short-run versus long-run demand, 376
Shut-down decision, 192–194
Shut-down price, 193
    prices below, 195
Signaling effect, 383
Single parenthood, poverty and, 402
Slope of a curve, 16
    moving along versus shifting, 16–17
Smith, Adam, 6, 42, 126, 254
Smoot-Hawley tariff (1930), 49, 425
"Social Accountability 8000," 385
Social insurance, 408
Social Security, 406–408
    financial crisis and, 408
Song-Beverly Consumer Warranty Act (California), 317
Sony Corporation, 258
Sony Music, 252
Spatial differentiation in monopolistic competition, 243–244
Special-interest groups in manipulating government, 343
Specialization, 43–44
    economic benefits from, 418–422
Spillover benefits, 330–332
Spillover costs, 134
Spillover principle, 33–35
    environment and, 350
    public goods and, 330
    supply and demand and, 134
Spillovers, market inefficiency and, 133–137
Standard Oil Trust, 295
Staples, 297–299
State government. See also Government
    revenue sources of, 55
Steel beam pricing, 264
Substitutes, 73
    elasticity and, 98–99

SINGLE PC LICENSE AGREEMENT AND LIMITED WARRANTY

READ THIS LICENSE CAREFULLY BEFORE OPENING THIS PACKAGE. BY OPENING THIS PACKAGE, YOU ARE AGREEING TO THE TERMS AND CONDITIONS OF THIS LICENSE. IF YOU DO NOT AGREE, DO NOT OPEN THE PACKAGE. PROMPTLY RETURN THE UNOPENED PACKAGE AND ALL ACCOMPANYING ITEMS TO THE PLACE YOU OBTAINED THEM [[FOR A FULL REFUND OF ANY SUMS YOU HAVE PAID FOR THE SOFTWARE]]. ***THESE TERMS APPLY TO ALL LICENSED SOFTWARE ON THE DISK EXCEPT THAT THE TERMS FOR USE OF ANY SHAREWARE OR FREEWARE ON THE DISKETTES ARE AS SET FORTH IN THE ELECTRONIC LICENSE LOCATED ON THE DISK:***

1. GRANT OF LICENSE and OWNERSHIP: The enclosed computer programs <<and data>> ("Software") are licensed, not sold, to you by Prentice-Hall, Inc. ("We" or the "Company") and in consideration [[of your payment of the license fee, which is part of the price you paid]] [[of your purchase or adoption of the accompanying Company textbooks and/or other materials,]] and your agreement to these terms. We reserve any rights not granted to you. You own only the disk(s) but we and/or our licensors own the Software itself. This license allows you to use and display your copy of the Software on a single computer (i.e., with a single CPU) at a single location for academic use only, so long as you comply with the terms of this Agreement. You may make one copy for back up, or transfer your copy to another CPU, provided that the Software is usable on only one computer.

2. RESTRICTIONS: You may not transfer or distribute the Software or documentation to anyone else. Except for backup, you may not copy the documentation or the Software. You may not network the Software or otherwise use it on more than one computer or computer terminal at the same time. You may not reverse engineer, disassemble, decompile, modify, adapt, translate, or create derivative works based on the Software or the Documentation. You may be held legally responsible for any copying or copyright infringement which is caused by your failure to abide by the terms of these restrictions.

3. TERMINATION: This license is effective until terminated. This license will terminate automatically without notice from the Company if you fail to comply with any provisions or limitations of this license. Upon termination, you shall destroy the Documentation and all copies of the Software. All provisions of this Agreement as to limitation and disclaimer of warranties, limitation of liability, remedies or damages, and our ownership rights shall survive termination.

4. LIMITED WARRANTY AND DISCLAIMER OF WARRANTY: Company warrants that for a period of 60 days from the date you purchase this SOFTWARE (or purchase or adopt the accompanying textbook), the Software, when properly installed and used in accordance with the Documentation, will operate in substantial conformity with the description of the Software set forth in the Documentation, and that for a period of 30 days the disk(s) on which the Software is delivered shall be free from defects in materials and workmanship under normal use. The Company does not warrant that the Software will meet your requirements or that the operation of the Software will be uninterrupted or error-free. Your only remedy and the Company's only obligation under these limited warranties is, at the Company's option, return of the disk for a refund of any amounts paid for it by you or replacement of the disk. THIS LIMITED WARRANTY IS THE ONLY WARRANTY PROVIDED BY THE COMPANY AND ITS LICENSORS, AND THE COMPANY AND ITS LICENSORS DISCLAIM ALL OTHER WARRANTIES, EXPRESS OR IMPLIED, INCLUDING WITHOUT LIMITATION, THE IMPLIED WARRANTIES OF MERCHANTABILITY AND FITNESS FOR A PARTICULAR PURPOSE. THE COMPANY DOES NOT WARRANT, GUARANTEE OR MAKE ANY REPRESENTATION REGARDING THE ACCURACY, RELIABILITY, CURRENTNESS, USE, OR RESULTS OF USE, OF THE SOFTWARE.

5. LIMITATION OF REMEDIES AND DAMAGES: IN NO EVENT, SHALL THE COMPANY OR ITS EMPLOYEES, AGENTS, LICENSORS, OR CONTRACTORS BE LIABLE FOR ANY INCIDENTAL, INDIRECT, SPECIAL, OR CONSEQUENTIAL DAMAGES ARISING OUT OF OR IN CONNECTION WITH THIS LICENSE OR THE SOFTWARE, INCLUDING FOR LOSS OF USE, LOSS OF DATA, LOSS OF INCOME OR PROFIT, OR OTHER LOSSES, SUSTAINED AS A RESULT OF INJURY TO ANY PERSON, OR LOSS OF OR DAMAGE TO PROPERTY, OR CLAIMS OF THIRD PARTIES, EVEN IF THE COMPANY OR AN AUTHORIZED REPRESENTATIVE OF THE COMPANY HAS BEEN ADVISED OF THE POSSIBILITY OF SUCH DAMAGES. IN NO EVENT SHALL THE LIABILITY OF THE COMPANY FOR DAMAGES WITH RESPECT TO THE SOFTWARE EXCEED THE AMOUNTS ACTUALLY PAID BY YOU, IF ANY, FOR THE SOFTWARE OR THE ACCOMPANYING TEXTBOOK. BECAUSE SOME JURISDICTIONS DO NOT ALLOW THE LIMITATION OF LIABILITY IN CERTAIN CIRCUMSTANCES, THE ABOVE LIMITATIONS MAY NOT ALWAYS APPLY TO YOU.

6. GENERAL: THIS AGREEMENT SHALL BE CONSTRUED IN ACCORDANCE WITH THE LAWS OF THE UNITED STATES OF AMERICA AND THE STATE OF NEW YORK, APPLICABLE TO CONTRACTS MADE IN NEW YORK, AND SHALL BENEFIT THE COMPANY, ITS AFFILIATES AND ASSIGNEES. HIS AGREEMENT IS THE COMPLETE AND EXCLUSIVE STATEMENT OF THE AGREEMENT BETWEEN YOU AND THE COMPANY AND SUPERSEDES ALL PROPOSALS OR PRIOR AGREEMENTS, ORAL, OR WRITTEN, AND ANY OTHER COMMUNICATIONS BETWEEN YOU AND THE COMPANY OR ANY REPRESENTATIVE OF THE COMPANY RELATING TO THE SUBJECT MATTER OF THIS AGREEMENT. If you are a U.S. Government user, this Software is licensed with "restricted rights" as set forth in subparagraphs (a)-(d) of the Commercial Computer-Restricted Rights clause at FAR 52.227-19 or in subparagraphs (c)(1)(ii) of the Rights in Technical Data and Computer Software clause at DFARS 252.227-7013, and similar clauses, as applicable.

Should you have any questions concerning this agreement or if you wish to contact the Company for any reason, please contact in writing: Prentice Hall Inc., Higher Education Division, Business Publishing Technology Group, One Lake Street, Upper Saddle River, NJ 07458.